# Understanding
# FoxPro™ 2.0

## George T. Chou

BANTAM BOOKS
TORONTO • NEW YORK • LONDON • SYDNEY • AUCKLAND

*Dedicated to my wife, Jane-Wen*
*and our children, Doris, Tina, and Tom*

# Preface

Welcome to a new horizon in database management: the powerful FoxPro 2.0 database program developed by Fox Software. Just over a decade ago, the power of database management could be enjoyed only by users of large, expensive computer systems. However, the introduction of microcomputer software has drastically changed the way data is organized and manipulated. Because of its sound design and superior performance, FoxPro 2.0 has been widely recognized as one of the best database management software programs for microcomputers.

This is a book about understanding FoxPro 2.0. It illustrates how to use the software to develop your own database management system. With this system you will be able to effectively manage your data to provide comprehensive information when you need it.

FoxPro 2.0 makes it possible to process data in two ways: through interactive processing or batch command processing. Interactive processing enables you to perform all data management functions by choosing the appropriate options from the menu interface or by interactively issuing appropriate FoxPro commands. In the batch command mode, data is manipulated and information is extracted by executing a program that is written in the FoxPro command language. The emphasis of this book is on interactive processing.

## How To Use This Book

A primary function of this book is to demonstrate with a large set of examples how to use the software to develop a database system. For purposes of clarity, the examples have been kept simple and concise to make it easier to understand the underlying principles. And, in order to maintain continuity among the examples, the same databases are used throughout the book to illustrate as many different functions as possible.

To get the most from this setup, it is strongly recommended that you duplicate the examples as you read along in the book. Then, once you fully understand the principles from studying and working with the examples, you can set out to develop your own database system.

# Who Should Use This Book

If you own FoxPro 2.0, this is the book for you. But make no mistake—it is not intended to be a user's reference manual. It goes beyond that. Where a user's manual describes the functions of all the tools, this book actually demonstrates how to design and build a database system with the tools.

If you are a beginning user, you will find this book especially beneficial. In addition to learning how to use the software, you will learn the principles behind designing a versatile relational database system. Incorporating the easy-to-follow examples, you can begin developing a simple database after reading the first few chapters.

If you have used earlier versions of FoxPro and FoxBase, you'll no doubt notice that FoxPro 2.0 represents a significant improvement over its predecessors. A rich new set of tools and commands have been added to the program, which you will learn about by studying the examples presented in this book.

Finally, if you are a dBASE user and are planning to expand your productivity by switching to FoxPro 2.0, this book will illustrate how to use the powerful RQBE (Relational Query By Example) to extract information from your databases. In addition, you will learn how to use the versatile Screen Builder and Report Writer to design and develop data entry screens and custom reports.

# How This Book Is Organized

*Understanding FoxPro 2.0* is logically divided into three sections. The first section, comprised of the first three chapters, builds the foundation for understanding the principles of database management and the FoxPro 2.0 software. Chapters 4 through 7, the second section, present the basic operations for creating and maintaining a relational database. The final section of the book, Chapters 8 through 13, deals with advanced topics.

Chapter 1, "Introduction to Databases," defines the basic concept of database management. It presents commonly used data models and how they can be used to help you properly organize your data. This chapter will also teach you the principles behind the sound design of a relational database system.

Chapter 2, "An Overview of FoxPro," gives a brief introduction to the design philosophy of the software. In addition, it discusses FoxPro 2.0's powerful and user-friendly menu interface. This chapter also presents an overview of the major components of the program.

Chapter 3, "Getting Started," outlines the steps involved in setting up the program so that you can begin to design and develop your database management system. It details the procedures for using the keyboard and mouse, setting the screen colors, selecting the printers, and so forth. Working with FoxPro's window environment is also discussed in this chapter.

Chapter 4, "Creating Databases," opens the discussion of the procedures and menu options necessary for performing basic database management functions. It explains in detail the steps for creating a database. You will also learn how to define the structure of a database and enter data into it.

Chapter 5, "Displaying Data," explains how to display the data structure and contents of a database on the screen or output it to a printer. And, along with learning how to display all the data in a database, you will also discover how to define the conditions for displaying selected subset of the data.

Chapter 6, "Sorting and Indexing Data," deals with ordering data records in a database. This chapter compares and contrasts the Sort and Index operations so that you know the strengths and weaknesses of these two processes, enabling you to make the proper choice between the two for your applications.

Chapter 7, "Editing Data," covers how to modify the contents of a database. You will learn to change the data structure of an existing database and the contents of its data records. You also will learn how to modify the data records in both Browse and Change modes.

Chapter 8, "Linking Databases," discusses the procedures for linking two or more databases so that you can extract more comprehensive information from them. This chapter also illustrates how to join data records from more than one database.

Chapter 9, "Querying Data," explains how to efficiently extract useful information from databases. In addition to an explanation of the Locate and Seek operations, it shows how to use the powerful Relational Query By Example (RQBE) technique for finding the information you need.

Chapter 10, "Using Memory Variables and Built-in Functions," shows you how to create memory variables for storing individual data elements and summary statistics that you can pass to custom reports. You also will learn about the power of built-in functions.

Chapter 11, "Producing Reports and Mailing Labels," teaches you how to use FoxPro's versatile Report Writer and Label Designer to design and create custom reports and mailing labels.

Chapter 12, "Using Custom Data Screens," illustrates the steps required for designing and creating customized screens for viewing data and for data entry.

Detailed instructions for using FoxPro's Screen Designer for these purposes is also included in this chapter.

Chapter 13, "Putting It All Together," is the final chapter of the book. It is at this stage that you learn how to integrate all of the components of a database system by using FoxPro's Menu Builder to design and create a custom menu system for performing all data management functions.

I wish to thank my editor, Ron Petrusha who was instrumental in helping me shape the manuscript. Ron is one of the most knowledgeable and enthusiastic editors I have worked with. I am indebted to him for the many good ideas that he contributed to this book. I also wish to thank the Bantam Doubleday Dell Publishing Group, Inc. for giving me the opportunity to write this book. The warm relationship between the authors and the publisher, Mr. Kenzi Sugihara, has made this writing project very enjoyable. Finally, I am grateful for the support and encouragement my wife and children have given me in completing this book.

# Contents

## 3   Getting Started   67

## 4   Creating Databases   97

## 8   Linking Databases   273

## 11  Producing Reports and Mailing Labels  409

# 13 Putting It All Together 535

# 1

# Introduction to Databases

## An Overview

This is a book about understanding FoxPro 2.0, a very powerful database management system software. Its primary purpose is to show you how to use the software to develop your own database management system. With it, you will be able to effectively manage your data so that it provides the information you want when you want it. But before you can design and develop such a system, you need to be familiar with some of the basic concepts and terms of database management systems in general. These are the subjects covered in this chapter.

In simple terms, a database is a collection of interrelated data elements that are arranged and organized in a logical manner. These data elements, when combined in this way, make it possible to access useful information efficiently. However, the type of accessible information and how quickly you can retrieve it from your database is closely related to how you store and organize data elements.

A variety of data models are available for organizing data elements, but because FoxPro 2.0 uses the relational model, this chapter discusses only the concepts and structure of that model. As you will see later, the backbone of this structure is the logical relationship between data elements. Understanding how to define and structure these relations within your database is vital to the effectiveness and power of your system. Through the examples in this chapter, you will learn how to design a database with the correct structure that produces the desired information in the least amount of time and with the least amount of effort.

# What Is a Data Element?

A data element is a basic unit of information within a database management system. It usually consists of a set of characters that are in the form of alphabetic letters (A–Z, a–z), numeric digits (1–9), or text symbols (hyphens, commas, colons, semicolons, etc.). For example, an employee's last name, say Smith, consisting of a number of alphabetic letters, makes up a data element in a database system. The first name of that employee, say John, makes up another data element. A collection of these data elements makes up various components of a database. Thus, an employee's first and last names make up a database component. In turn, each of these data components can be given a special name, such as data field, data record, or data file. You will learn more about these terms later in this chapter.

# What Is a Database?

As already noted, a database is a collection of data elements that are organized in a logical manner and structure. Its actual structure depends on the data model in which you choose to organize those elements; its size is determined by the number of data elements. The relationship between these elements influences the complexity of a database.

A simple database usually has a small number of data elements that can be organized in a very simple structure. For example, a collection of the names and phone numbers of your friends could represent a small yet complete database in which you could organize the data elements in a structure that stores the last name, first name, area code, and phone number as separate items.

On the other hand, a company's sales database that contains a large number of data elements would be organized in a more complex structure. A database such as this would contain all the data elements about its customers, inventory, invoices, and sales transactions. Then, data elements that are associated only with customers would be stored in one group, and within that group, data belonging to any single customer would be stored in separate data elements; typically items such as the name, address, and phone number of the selected customer. Data elements associated just with merchandise would be stored in the inventory group; each time a transaction was made, the items about the sale and the invoice would be stored in yet other groups of data elements. Once these data elements are organized and stored in a logical manner, you can easily and quickly collect the appropriate data elements from these groups to generate inventory lists or reports.

# What Is a Database Management System?

A database management system (DBMS) offers a systematic approach for managing data elements so that information can be extracted and distributed with a minimum amount of effort. Besides providing information, a correctly designed and structured database management system permits you to efficiently manage data elements. In such a system you can easily add data elements to your database, modify and change any data elements you already have, or delete data elements you no longer need. The system also is fast—to allow you to quickly find selected elements, and once information is located, to quickly display or present results in an appropriate format.

Although we are talking about a system that is so complicated it requires a computer to handle, a database management system does not have to be complex. Neither must it be computerized. A database management system can be a manual system, and a card file that is used to manage information associated with all of your friends is a good example of this. The file, made up of a number of index cards each with a certain number of data elements on it, is a database.

To continue this example, let's say that in this manual database each card lists the name and address of one of your personal friends, and that these cards are arranged in a certain order—alphabetically by last name. As you add a new name, you add a new card in last name alphabetic order in the same way that you find data about an existing friend by searching for his or her last name in the card file. You also can update information or remove a card from your database when you no longer want to maintain data about a particular friend. And, if you need to produce a list of friends who live in the same city, you can sort these cards by city name and then copy the accompanying first and last names to a piece of paper. These are all examples of essential data management functions that you would expect a well-designed database management system to provide.

This book, of course, focuses on computerized database management using FoxPro 2.0. But even though you will be performing all data management functions on a computer, the same principles used in a manual system apply. If you have a good understanding of how to manage a manual system, you have a good foundation for learning the basic functions of a computerized database management system.

# Information vs. Data

In database management systems, data elements are ingredients of an information system. These data elements by themselves usually do not provide any meaningful and useful information. It is necessary to link those data elements that are associated with a certain subject in order to make some sense out of it. Therefore, data and information are different things by nature.

The primary purpose of a database management system is to organize data elements so that you can obtain desired information by retrieving all associated data elements. For example, you can save a friend's address in various components that separately hold his or her street address, the city and state, and the zip code. The information about his or her mailing address can be obtained only by retrieving the appropriate data elements from the correct database. The last name of an employee, as another example, is a data element that is made up of several alphabetic characters. All of the last names of the employees in a firm in turn represent a subset of that firm's personnel database. A listing of these last names provides useful information in the form of an employee roster.

# How to Organize Data

How to organize data elements is a major consideration in a database management system. The efficiency and usefulness of your database management system is significantly affected by the structure used to store and maintain data elements in the database. If your database is properly structured so that all the data elements are logically organized, you can maintain and manage your data with the least amount of effort.

Because useful information usually requires linking various appropriate data elements in the database, defining the relations among these elements plays a very significant role in determining the efficiency of a database management system. Therefore, before you learn how to design a database management system, you need to learn how to relate all of the data elements in your database.

## DATA RELATIONS

We stated earlier that a data element is the basic unit of a database. It describes a single property of a data entity. A data entity is any distinctive object—either a tangible property, such as a person, a table, or a chair; or an intangible object, such as a branch office or a sales region.

When we view the organization of a database, data entities form the building blocks that bring the structure together. For example, to design a database system that manages the activities and functions of a sales organization, you need to include data entities such as salesmen and saleswomen, sales offices, sales regions, and customer accounts.

Each of these data entities has a number of properties. A salesperson has a set of properties comprised of his or her first and last names, birthdate, salary, home

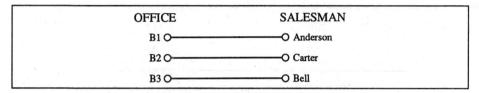

| OFFICE | SALESMAN |
|--------|----------|
| B1 O————————————O | Anderson |
| B2 O————————————O | Carter |
| B3 O————————————O | Bell |

**Figure 1.1  One-to-One Relations**

address, etc. A sales office has another set of properties that specifies its address and phone number. Typical database designs allow you to view the links among data entities in one of three basic ways: one-to-one relations, one-to-many relations, and many-to-many relations.

## One-to-One Relations

Of these three relations, the one-to-one is the simplest link between any two data entities. To describe such a relationship, we must assume the following set of rules in office assignment in this organization of salespeople: Only one salesperson can be assigned to each sales office and each sales office can have only one salesperson.

As an example, let's assume that you have three branch offices: B1, B2, and B3; and to fill these offices you have exactly three salespeople—Anderson, Bell, and Carter. In such a data structure you now have two data entities: sales staff and office. These two data entities are linked in a one-to-one relation as shown in Figure 1.1.

From Figure 1.1 you can see that each sales office has only one salesperson and that each salesperson belongs to only one sales office; i.e., B1 has only one saleswoman (Anderson), who in turn, belongs only to that one office.

## One-to-Many Relations

Of course, the one-to-one relation is no doubt too simple to reflect the actual links between sales staff and office entities in a real world. It is more likely that this organization would have a larger number of sales personnel and that each office would probably have more than one salesperson. Therefore, the one-to-one relation would not be adequate to describe all the links between the two data entities. A more realistic example relating the sales staff and branch office entities is shown in Figure 1.2.

As you can see, each sales office has more than one salesperson. Yet, each salesperson belongs only to one sales office. Note that sales office B1 has four salespeople: Anderson, Davidson, Gilbert, and Jones, each of whom belongs to only one sales office—B1.

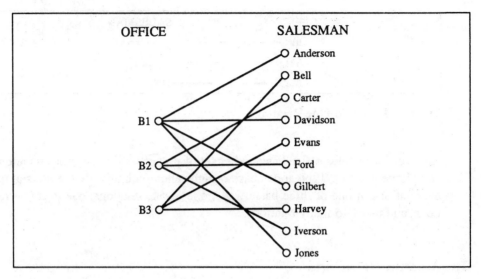

**Figure 1.2  One-to-Many Relations**

Of course, by switching the order of the two entities, you can call the relation in Figure 1.2 a many-to-one relation. Therefore, one-to-many relations and many-to-one relations are the same in a database design.

## Many-to-Many Relations

A many-to-many relation is the most complex for linking two data entities in a database design. Each object in one data entity is linked to several objects in another entity, and vice versa. To show you how these many-to-many relations look, let's assume that you have ten salesmen and saleswomen (as in Figure 1.2), each of whom will be assigned to service one or more of the six sales regions. These sales regions are designated as R1, R2, R3, R4, R5, and R6. Figure 1.3 shows how you can link the sales staff and sales regions in many-to-many relations.

In Figure 1.3 you can see that a salesperson can have more than one sales region assigned to him or her, and that each sales region is served by more than one salesperson. For example, saleswoman Harvey has three sales regions (R4, R5, and R6) and sales region R4 is served by two salespeople (Evans and Harvey). Of course, you also can see that not every salesperson has more than one sales region; some have only one sales region assigned to them.

Therefore, a data structure that can accommodate many-to-many relations is always able to handle one-to-many, many-to-one, and one-to-one relations as well. But, the reverse may not be true. That is, if your database design can handle only one-to-one relations, it may not be sufficient to manage one-to-many and many-to-many relations. As a result, you must understand the nature of your data elements

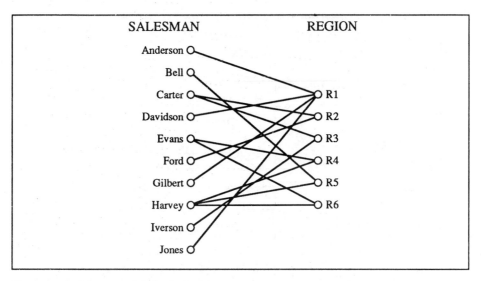

**Figure 1.3  Many-to-Many Relations**

and anticipate how they are to be used before you can design a sound database structure to accommodate the data and their relations.

# Data Models

A number of data models have been developed to manage databases that assume these relations. The three most common are the hierarchical, network, and relational data models. Although in this book we will focus mainly on the relational data model, a brief description of the others may help you to understand the relational model's simplicity and power. In addition, your knowledge of these models will help you design a better relational database.

## HIERARCHICAL DATA MODEL

A hierarchical data model views the relations among data entities as a tree structure with multiple levels of branches. If you were to use a hierarchical data model to view the relations among the three data entities (Office, Salesman, and Region) in our earlier example, it would look like that in Figure 1.4.

As you can see from this figure, the model assumes three levels, a main trunk and two sub-levels of branches. The first level describes Office, and each of its trunks represents an object of the entity and leads to a different number of sub-branches. In turn, each of these sub-branches represents an object in the next data entity, Salesman. As the model continues, each member of the sales staff

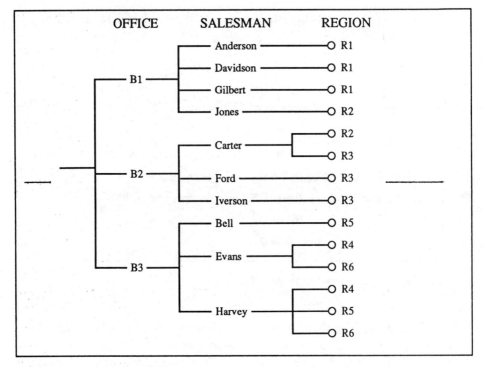

**Figure 1.4  A Hierarchical Data Model**

sub-branches in turn leads to yet another level of sub-branches—in this case, the third level of branches, which reflects the objects in Region.

When you look at the hierarchical model in Figure 1.4, you can see that all the data elements are organized in a very logical way; i.e., each object of a data entity is logically related to one or more objects in another data entity. You can determine the objects in each data entity and all the relations among them. But study the model a bit further and you will notice that the hierarchical model allows only one-to-one and one-to-many or many-to-one relations. To include many-to-many relations, they must be restructured with duplicated one-to-many relations.

As you saw in our earlier example (Figure 1.3), many-to-many relations exist among the objects in the sales staff and region data entities. That is, a salesperson can have more than one sales region and a sales region can be assigned to more than one salesperson. For example, Evans has two sales regions, R4 and R6, and each of these regions is assigned to more than one salesperson. Region 4 is assigned to two, Evans and Harvey, and so on.

But return to the hierarchical model in Figure 1.4 and you can see that these many-to-many relations must be structured in repeated one-to-many relations. Note in the tree structure that one branch can lead to several sub-branches, but all sub-branches always lead to only one branch in a higher level. In order to conform to this type of tree structure, you must repeat some objects in the sub-branches to describe many-to-many relations in terms of several one-to-many relations.

Also in Figure 1.4, notice that some objects in Region appear as multiple sub-branches in order to describe their relationship to the objects in Salesman, such as R4 of Region that appears twice as a sub-branch. Each is related to an object in Salesman—one to Evans and the other to Harvey. It is to accommodate this type of repetition that a different data model was developed. It is called a network model.

## NETWORK DATA MODEL

A network data model can be viewed as a modified version of the hierarchical model. It too organizes data elements in a tree structure just like the hierarchical model. Unlike a hierarchical model, however, a network model allows you to define many-to-many relations in a tree structure without repeating any object in a data entity. Look at Figure 1.5 to view the relations among the same three data entities in a network model.

Notice that the data model looks very similar to the one in Figure 1.4; they both use a tree structure to relate the objects in the three data entities. Because there is only a one-to-many relationship between the office and sales staff entities, the hierarchical and network models describe these relations in the same manner. But the way in which the network model describes the many-to-many relations between the sales staff and region entities looks quite different from that described by the hierarchical model.

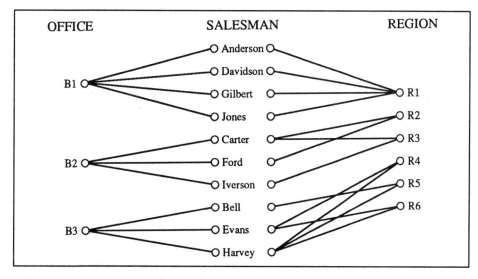

**Figure 1.5  A Network Data Model**

The important difference is that in the network model each object of the region entity always appears as only one sub-branch. And, a sub-branch in the region entity may come from more than one branch at a higher level. For example, the branch describing Evans leads to two sub-branches relating to regions R4 and R6. The sub-branch describing region R4 comes from two branches relating to Evans and Harvey. The branch describing Harvey relates to regions R4, R5, and R6, as represented by three sub-branches in the model.

In both of these models, data elements are organized in a logical way so that you can relate all of your data elements by providing the necessary links. If you were looking for a particular piece of information in your database, you would be able to trace through the appropriate links to retrieve its data elements. In order for you do that, however, the system must have built-in, rather detailed links in the form of pointers, each of which points from one object to another. In addition, in order to speed up the searching process, it is often necessary to arrange the data elements in a certain order. This ordering function is accomplished through operations such as sorting and indexing, but because FoxPro 2.0 does not use either one of these models to organize data elements, we will not go beyond this discussion to cover operational details about these two models.

## RELATIONAL DATA MODEL

A relational data model is the most popular one that you can use to organize and manage data elements. Most database management software for microcomputers is designed for handling data structures organized according to this model. FoxPro 2.0, FoxBase, Paradox, RBase, and the family of dBASE software products all choose relational data models for structuring their data elements. One of the reasons for the popularity of this model is that it is simple to understand and set up. It can accommodate one-to-one, one-to-many, and many-to-many relations in its structure. When a database structure is correctly set up, you can easily manage your data elements. Finding the desired information from the database becomes very quick once you have built in all the links and relations among the data objects.

## Data Tables

In a relational data model, all of your data elements and the relations among data objects are organized in data tables. You use a data table to hold data elements that are associated with data objects. Similarly, all the relations among these data objects also are saved as data elements in data tables. As a result, a database in a relational data model contains a set of data tables.

In order to get a better idea of how to organize data elements with a relational data model and store them in data tables, let's continue with the three data entities we discussed in the last two models—Salesman, Office, and Region. Each has a

```
Table: Salesman

Salesman ID    Last Name   First Name   Hire Date   Salary

S0             Anderson    Doris        07/01/86    2,800
S1             Bell        George       10/12/88    2,400
S2             Carter      Jack         05/14/87    2,550
S3             Davidson    Edward       06/04/90    1,500
S4             Evans       Henry        03/08/88    2,000
S5             Ford        Ida          11/22/87    2,600
S6             Gilbert     Fred         04/15/87    2,300
S7             Harvey      Candy        12/01/89    2,450
S8             Iverson     Albert       10/25/88    2,200
S9             Jones       Betty        09/26/89    2,500
```

**Figure 1.6  A Data Table in a Relational Model**

number of objects, which in turn have a set of properties. Data elements are then used to describe these properties.

If you look at Salesman, it contains a number of objects, each representing a salesperson—Anderson, Bell, Carter, and so on. Each data object or salesperson has a set of properties that includes his or her identification number, last name, first name, salary, and hire date. The data element used to describe a property consists of a set of characters in the form of alphabetic letters, numeric digits, and symbols. For example, the data elements describing Anderson's first name include a string of alphabetic characters spelling "Doris." A set of numeric digits and symbols—"07/01/86"—specifies her employment date as a data element. All the data elements in Salesman can be organized in a table that looks like the one in Figure 1.6.

### Components of a Data Table

In this figure all the data elements describing the properties of all the objects (salespeople) of the Salesman data entity are stored in a table. You can assign a name—Salesman, in this case—to the table for identification purposes and as a convenient way to refer to it. The table itself is divided into a number of rows and columns; each of the columns also can be named and used to save data elements describing a particular property of the data objects; the rows are used to store data elements associated with a given object—in this case, a salesperson. Rows are identified by the sequence number given as they are added to the table; you do not have to assign a name to each row in the table.

In the Salesman table, for example, store all of the data elements describing all the last names of the sales staff in the column labeled "Last Name." Monthly

```
Table: Office

Office ID Address              City         State Zip    Phone #

B1          100 Park Avenue     New York      NY    10016 800-123-5555
B2          200 Lake Drive      Chicago       IL    60607 800-234-5555
B3          500 Century Blvd.   Los Angeles   CA    94005 800-456-5555


Table: Region

Region ID   Region             Manager

R1          Northeast          Alice F. Gibson
R2          Southeast          Bob L. Major
R3          Northcentral       John K. Freed
R4          Southcentral       Cathy M. Wilson
R5          Northwest          Chris C. Hall
R6          Southwest          Helen T. Taylor
```

**Figure 1.7  The Office and Region Tables**

salaries are stored in the Salary column. Each row in the Salesman table holds data elements describing all the properties (ID #, Last Name, First Name, Hire Date, Salary) for a given salesperson.

Using a similar structure, you can organize all of the data elements associated with the sales office and sales region in two separate tables named Office and Region, respectively, as shown in Figure 1.7.

In this figure you can see that the Office and Region tables follow the same format as that of the Salesman table. They are both divided into a number of rows and columns, where each row holds the data elements belonging to an object of the data entity, and each column stores data elements associated with a property of that object.

In the Office table, data elements describing the properties of the offices—identification number, addresses, and phone numbers—are stored in the columns. Each row of the table holds data elements associated with a given office. Similarly, in the Region table, properties of the region are stored in the columns. The column named Manager, for example, saves data elements specifying the names of regional managers.

In a relational data model a database usually contains more than one of such data tables, and you should be aware that such data tables are often called database files by relational database software products such as FoxPro 2.0. Each row of the table is called a data record and contains a number of data fields, each of which corresponds to a column in the data table. Therefore, data elements in a relational database are organized in database files (tables). Each database file contains a number of records (rows) and each record (row) has a number of fields (columns).

Using these relational database terms, you can describe the database consisting of Salesman, Office, and Region in the following way:

| | |
|---|---|
| Table Name: | Salesman |
| Number of Records: | 10 |
| Data Fields: | Salesman ID |
| | Last Name |
| | First Name |
| | Hire Date |
| | Salary |

| | |
|---|---|
| Table Name: | Office ID |
| Number of Records: | 3 |
| Data Fields: | ID # |
| | Address |
| | City |
| | State |
| | Zip |
| | Phone # |

| | |
|---|---|
| Table Name: | Region ID |
| Number of Records: | 6 |
| Data Fields: | ID # |
| | Region |
| | Manager |

As stated earlier in this chapter, a relational data model not only saves all the data elements describing a data entity in a data table; data tables also are used to hold data elements describing relations among these data entities. Although you will learn more about how to set up and use this type of data table, Figure 1.8 shows you an example of such a relational table, named Assignment.

If you compare the structure of the Assignment table with that of the Salesman, Office, and Region tables, you will have no trouble noticing their similarities. They all are organized in rows and columns. But there is a significant difference between the Assignment table and the Salesman table. Recall that a row in the Salesman table describes the properties of a given salesperson. But unlike the Salesman table, a row in the Assignment table specifies the *link* between a sales region and a salesperson. For example, the first row in that table contains two data elements,

```
Table: Assignment

Region ID   Salesman ID

R1          S0
R1          S3
R1          S6
R1          S9
R2          S2
R2          S5
R3          S2
R3          S8
R4          S4
R4          S7
R5          S1
R5          S7
R6          S4
R6          S7
```

**Figure 1.8  A Relation Table**

R1 and S1, which are saved in the columns named Region ID and Salesman ID, respectively. The data elements in the first row relate the sales region R1 (Northeast in the Region table) to saleswoman S1 (Anderson in the Salesman table).

These relational tables play a very significant role in determining the usefulness and power of a relational database. When they are properly structured, you are able to handle any type of relationship that exists among your data entities. You will learn more about these relational data tables later in this chapter.

# Designing a Relational Database

The usefulness and power of a database depends greatly on how you set up its data tables to describe data entities and their relations. A correctly structured database gives you rapid and easy access to all the desired information by retrieving the related data elements in the database. But, if you fail to define your database structure correctly, you will find that managing your data becomes very difficult, if not impossible. Therefore, it is always helpful to invest some time in planning how to set up your data tables and establish the links that will be necessary for relating the data elements for later use.

When designing a database, begin by studying the nature of your business and thinking about what type of data elements make up the organization. Looking ahead at the types of information you will need will help you to determine the relevant data elements that you want stored in your database. To elaborate on our example, consider that it might, at some point, be necessary to produce a compensation report about the salaries of the sales personnel assigned to a given sales region. For that, you'll need data elements describing their salaries and the sales regions to which they are assigned. To produce invoices, on the other hand, you must have data elements describing each sales transaction; the invoice number; the name and address of the customer to whom you sold the merchandise; the description, price, and quantity of the merchandise, etc.

Once you have decided which data elements you need, the next step is to organize them in a logical manner. To do that, try to group those elements that are associated with an entity in one data table. You would include all the data elements describing the properties of a salesperson in the Salesman table, for example. Each property is, in turn, described by one data element in a data field.

After setting up all the necessary data tables for holding the data elements associated with all of your data entities, then set up the relation table to provide the links among the data elements in various data tables. The number of relational data tables is determined by how complex the relations are among your data tables. Usually you do not need to set up any relation tables to handle one-to-one and one-to-many relations; they are necessary only for taking care of many-to-many relations. In the forthcoming section you will learn how to structure these types of relations in your database.

## PROPERTIES OF A RELATIONAL DATABASE

Designing a database can be a complex process, especially if it has a large number of data tables that include multiple sets of many-to-many relations. But many useful databases have a small number of simple data tables with few relational data tables to handle their links. If you can understand the underlying principles behind a simple relational database, understanding a more complex one will come with experience.

Regardless of the complexity and size of a relational database, it must have a set of properties. Implementing these properties is essential if you want to avoid redundant data elements and correctly link your data elements. These essential properties can be summarized as follows:

- All data elements must be organized in data tables.
- Data elements in a single table must have a one-to-one relationship.
- There cannot be duplicate rows in a data table.
- There cannot be duplicate columns in a data table.
- Only one data element can be saved in each data cell.

## Organizing Data in Tables

The first essential property of a relational database is that data elements associated with a unique data entity must be organized in table form, as seen in earlier examples. A data table is the basic unit of a relational database. Each table may contain any number of rows (records) and columns (fields). The number and order of the columns are not important. Neither is the number of rows.

## No Duplicate Rows

In a properly structured relational data table you must not have two or more rows with identical data elements. Duplicate rows not only are wasteful of valuable storage space, but they slow down processing by making the table unduly large. More important, duplicate rows cause erroneous results (inaccurate row counts) when you include them in summary statistics. Say you have data elements associated with the same salesperson appearing in more than one row in the Salesman table. You would not get the correct total when you count the number of rows in that table. Neither would you get the real total salary for all the sales personnel in the firm when you add up all the salaries in that table.

## Using Single-Value Data Cells

The intersection between a row and column in a data table is often called a data cell. Another essential property of a relational database is that only one data element can be stored in a data cell. As an example, let's add the column Phone No to the Salesman table (see Figure 1.9). In that table, the data cell between a row and a column can only hold a single value representing the phone number.

```
Table: Salesman

Salesman ID   Last Name   First Name   Phone No   Hire Date   Salary

S0            Anderson    Doris        123-4567   07/01/86    2,800
S1            Bell        George       234-3456   10/12/88    2,400
S2            Carter      Jack         456-9023   05/14/87    2,550
S3            Davidson    Edward       234-5645   06/04/90    1,500
S4            Evans       Henry        635-2345   03/08/88    2,000
S5            Ford        Ida          345-2345   11/22/87    2,600
S6            Gilbert     Fred         234-4576   04/15/87    2,300
S7            Harvey      Candy        555-2323   12/01/89    2,450
S8            Iverson     Albert       123-3333   10/25/88    2,200
S9            Jones       Betty        342-4567   09/26/89    2,500
```

**Figure 1.9  Adding Phone No Column to the Salesman Table**

```
Table: Salesman

Salesman ID  Last Name  First Name  Phone #1   Phone #2   Hire Date  Salary

S0           Anderson   Doris       123-4567   987-6543   07/01/86   2,800
S1           Bell       George      234-3456              10/12/88   2,400
S2           Carter     Jack        456-9023              05/14/87   2,550
S3           Davidson   Edward      234-5645              06/04/90   1,500
S4           Evans      Henry       635-2345              03/08/88   2,000
S5           Ford       Ida         345-2345              11/22/87   2,600
S6           Gilbert    Fred        234-4576              04/15/87   2,300
S7           Harvey     Candy       555-2323              12/01/89   2,450
S8           Iverson    Albert      123-3333              10/25/88   2,200
S9           Jones      Betty       342-4567              09/26/89   2,500
```

**Figure 1.10  Adding Another Column to the Salesman Table**

But, suppose the person has more than one phone number. Perhaps saleswoman Anderson has two telephone numbers: 123-4567 and 987-6543. Now you have a problem. Because you cannot save both of them in the cell between the first row and the column labeled Phone No, you must save them in two different cells. There are different solutions to this problem. One is to add another column to accommodate a second phone number. Such a table looks like the one in Figure 1.10.

Look at this revised Salesman table and you will notice an undesirable feature in the new column. It has many blank cells, and unless most of the sales staff have two phone numbers, this will be the case. And these blank cells have two major problems associated with them. Because each cell occupies a certain amount of storage space on the disk, blank cells are wasteful. In addition, to find the salesperson with a particular phone number you now have to search two columns. As a result, it will take longer to get the information.

Another solution is to use two rows for storing information about Doris Anderson. Repeat all of the data elements belonging to Anderson, except for her first phone number in the new row. Then enter the second phone number in the second row. The revised table looks like that in Figure 1.11.

The revised Salesman table in Figure 1.11 shows that Anderson is assigned two different identification numbers, S0 and S1. This is necessary because each row must have a unique identification number if it is to be used in a master table that can be linked to another table, as we will see later in this chapter. But, by assigning Anderson two different identification numbers, essentially you are treating her as two different salespeople. It is confusing. Furthermore, using two rows to hold data elements belonging the same salesperson can cause other types of problems, such as if you have to determine how many salespeople you have by tallying the rows in the table. Obviously, you will get an erroneous head count.

```
Table: Salesman (Revised)

Salesman ID    Last Name   First Name   Phone No   Hire Date   Salary

S0             Anderson    Doris        123-4567   07/01/86    2,800
S1             Anderson    Doris        987-6543   07/01/86    2,800
S2             Bell        George       234-3456   10/12/88    2,400
S3             Carter      Jack         456-9023   05/14/87    2,550
S4             Davidson    Edward       234-5645   06/04/90    1,500
S5             Evans       Henry        635-2345   03/08/88    2,000
S6             Ford        Ida          345-2345   11/22/87    2,600
S7             Gilbert     Fred         234-4576   04/15/87    2,300
S8             Harvey      Candy        555-2323   12/01/89    2,450
S9             Iverson     Albert       123-3333   10/25/88    2,200
S10            Jones       Betty        342-4567   09/26/89    2,500
```

**Figure 1.11  Adding Another Row to the Salesman Table**

As you can see, these two solutions in turn introduced new problems. But, do not despair. There is a solution to all these problems. It involves separating the phone numbers from the Salesman table and saving them to another table. As an example, we split the original Salesman table into two tables: Salesman and Phone as shown in Figure 1.12. You then link them together when you need to know the phone numbers of anyone on the sales staff.

After splitting the Salesman table, treat the first as a master table and the second as a table to be linked with the master table as needed. All data elements associated with saleswoman Anderson, except for her phone numbers, are found on the master Salesman table. To locate her phone numbers, first find her identification number (S0) in the master table and then go to the Phone table to retrieve all the phone numbers associated with that identification number. But, if you want to retrieve *every* data element that is associated with a particular salesperson, you can link the two tables by using the identification number as a linking key, an operation we will discuss later in this chapter.

## OTHER DESIRABLE CHARACTERISTICS

We have mentioned some basic requirements that must be followed when designing a good relational database. They can be summarized as follows:

- Plan your data needs well and in advance.
- Anticipate information needs and store only relevant data.
- Group data elements logically in columns.
- Use tables to store all data elements and relations.

- Never allow duplicate rows in any table.
- Place only a single data value in a cell.
- Avoid blank cells if at all possible.

In addition to these requirements, there are other desirable characteristics you may want to build into your database. These are:

- Make database structure flexible to accommodate changes.
- Keep redundant data to a minimum.
- Keep tables logically indexed.
- Keep data tables as simple as possible.

```
Table: Salesman

Salesman ID    Last Name    First Name    Hire Date    Salary

S0             Anderson     Doris         07/01/86     2,800
S1             Bell         George        10/12/88     2,400
S2             Carter       Jack          05/14/87     2,550
S3             Davidson     Edward        06/04/90     1,500
S4             Evans        Henry         03/08/88     2,000
S5             Ford         Ida           11/22/87     2,600
S6             Gilbert      Fred          04/15/87     2,300
S7             Harvey       Candy         12/01/89     2,450
S8             Iverson      Albert        10/25/88     2,200
S9             Jones        Betty         09/26/89     2,500


Table: Phone:

Salesman ID    Phone No

S0             123-4567
S0             987-6543
S1             234-3456
S2             456-9023
S3             234-5645
S4             635-2345
S5             345-2345
S6             234-4576
S7             555-2323
S8             123-3333
S9             342-4567
```

**Figure 1.12   Splitting the Salesman Table into Two Tables**

## Making Data Structures Flexible

In structuring data tables you should try to include all columns that are associated with a data entity in the same table. These columns should be logically divided to anticipate future needs. Such a structure should be sufficient for all future applications, as well. That is, all the information about every data entity should be available from the data table. If your data tables are flexible enough to accommodate all the data manipulation and query needs, you will not need to restructure them each time you require a new report or a different kind of information. Restructuring data tables not only takes time, it often necessitates changing many related objects.

Therefore, if initially you decide to save the names of your customers in your data table, for example, you should consider at the same time how to structure the table to make it workable for other uses later. Should you save the first and last names as one data element in a single column? Or, should you save the first name and last name in two separate columns? How about middle initials? Should they be stored in a separate column or as part of the first name? Answers to these questions depend on how the data elements are to be used in your applications. If you plan to search the data records by using last names, you may want to save the last names in a separate column. If you need to produce a form letter in which you will address your customers by their first names, you must store all the first names in an independent column, too. If you do not take all potential applications into consideration, it will be much more difficult and time-consuming to extract information from your tables.

## Avoiding Redundant Data

A good relational database design does not have any single data element appearing more than once anywhere in the database. As you may recall, in Figure 1.10 we added the Phone #2 column in order to accommodate Anderson's second phone number. This, as also mentioned, is highly undesirable if you are to conserve valuable storage space and make searching and updating your records as efficient as possible. Therefore, try to avoid, at any cost, redundant data in your database.

The exceptions to this rule are those data elements that are to be used as linking keys. In order to link two data tables together, the rows must share the same identification number; therefore, this type of data duplication is necessary. Look at Figure 1.12. Notice that Salesman ID appears in both tables. These numbers are to be used as the linking keys when you need to join the tables together. They are necessary for relating the data elements in both tables.

## Indexing Data Logically

Indexing is an operation that you can use to order data records in a predetermined sequence. When you add data records to your data tables, they are usually stored in the order in which they are entered. This order may not be the one you desire when you later search for a record. To speed up your search, it is often desirable to arrange your tables in an order *other* than entry order. Say you would like to find a salesperson by his or her first name, but that the names were entered last name first. Naturally the search process would be quicker if those records could now be arranged in first name order. Therefore, if you know ahead of time that you might at some later date like to search your data records in other than entry order, it is very beneficial to index that data according to specific data values.

FoxPro makes it very easy to index your records by using one or more of your columns as key fields. You can arrange your database in ascending or descending order. You can even use a compound index key that consists of a combination of key values. We will discuss the details of the indexing operation in a later chapter. For now, all you have to keep in mind is the concept of indexing.

## Keeping Data Tables Simple

In most database management applications you need a set of data tables to hold all of your data elements. Ideally, try to keep these tables simple by having a small number of columns. The fewer the columns in the table, the quicker you can retrieve necessary information from them. It is also easier to maintain data in a small table than a large one.

The number of columns you have in a data table should be determined by the nature of your data elements. As we said earlier, try to group related columns that are associated with a data entity in the same table. However, good relational database design does not require that you store all the data elements of a data entity in the same table. In some cases, when there is a very large set of columns necessary to describe the properties of a data entity, you can place them in more than one table. This is especially applicable when some of these data elements are likely to be used later as a group. But, you *do* need to maintain a proper balance between the number of data tables and the size of these tables. However, the number of rows has a far greater impact on processing time than the number of columns in sequential operations.

## RELATING DATA

As we have said several times in this chapter, relations among data elements are the backbone of a relational database. They are the links to the data elements. Once you learn how to link tables together, you will have the freedom to structure very flexible data tables. For example, if the number of columns in a table becomes unduly large, you can split them into more than one table. Then, when you need to associate the data elements scattered in these tables, you can join them again to provide the necessary information. In addition, if there are many-to-many relations among your data elements, you can create the relation table to join them.

How you structure your data table to accommodate relations depends on what type of relations exist among your data elements. As mentioned earlier, there are basically three types of relations: one-to-one, one-to-many (or many-to-one), and many-to-many. Each type of relation requires a different structure to accommodate it.

## Handling One-to-One Relations

The simplest form of relation is the one-to-one. This type of relation associates one object with one other unique object. A data object may consist of one or more data elements. For example, you can assume that each salesperson has only one hire date. Therefore, a salesperson's last name has a one-to-one relation to his or her hire date. If you allow a salesperson to be assigned to one and only one sales office, then there would be a one-to-one relation between a salesperson and the office to which he or she belongs.

When you have one-to-one relations among data objects, you can include them in the same table. Recall that in Figure 1.1 we assumed the following one-to-one relations among the three salespeople, Anderson, Bell, and Carter, and the three sales offices B1, B2, B3. Anderson is assigned to office B1 (New York), Bell to B3 (Los Angeles), and Carter to B2 (Chicago). To accommodate these three one-to-one relations, you can store data elements about these salespeople and offices in the same table, as shown in Figure 1.13. (In order to fit the table on this page, we've eliminated the Salesman ID, the Office ID, and the phone numbers of the offices.)

Notice in Figure 1.13 that each row contains data elements not only about a salesperson, but also about his or her sales office. This is possible only if there are one-to-one relations among the three salespeople and their sales offices. If you have different types of relationships among these data objects, then you would need to structure the table differently.

## Handling One-to-Many Relations

When there are one-to-many relationships among data objects, you cannot store all the associated data elements in the same table if you are to avoid duplicate data. If you assign more than one salesperson to a given office, obviously you would have to repeat the data elements about the office more than once in the table. For example, if you assign four salespeople—Anderson, Davidson, Gilbert and

```
Table: Salesman (including data for sales offices)

Last      First   Hire      Salary Address              City         ST Zip
Name      Name    Date

Anderson  Doris   07/01/86  2,800  100 Park Avenue      New York     NY 10016
Bell      George  10/12/88  2,400  200 Lake Drive       Chicago      IL 60607
Carter    Jack    05/14/87  2,550  500 Century Blvd.    Los Angeles  CA 94005
```

**Figure 1.13  Handling One-to-One Relations in the Same Table**

Jones—to the same New York office (B1), the Salesman table would look like that in Figure 1.14.

As you look at this table, notice that redundant data appears in the second through fourth rows. Since the first four salespeople belong to the same New York office, data elements about that office appear in four different rows. If each office is occupied by several salespeople, the problem of redundant data becomes more severe. And, if we try to accommodate all the one-to-many relations as shown earlier in Figure 1.2, the amount of repeated data becomes very significant, as you can see in Figure 1.15.

These repeated data elements waste storage and endanger the accuracy of information in the database and should be avoided.

One way to eliminate these redundancies is to structure the table so that data elements about a given office appear in only one row in the database. In the new structure, save all the data elements associated with the sales offices in one table and leave those data elements about sales personnel in another table. To provide the link between these two tables, add a column in the Salesman table to hold the office identification number for the associated sales office. In Figure 1.16 you can see how these two tables are structured.

```
Table: Salesman (including data for sales offices)

Last      First   Hire      Salary Address              City         ST Zip
Name      Name    Date

Anderson  Doris   07/01/86  2,800  100 Park Avenue      New York     NY 10016
Davidson  Edward  06/04/90  1,500  100 Park Avenue      New York     NY 10016
Gilbert   Fred    04/15/87  2,300  100 Park Avenue      New York     NY 10016
Jones     Betty   09/26/89  2,500  100 Park Avenue      New York     NY 10016
Bell      George  10/12/88  2,400  200 Lake Drive       Chicago      IL 60607
Carter    Jack    05/14/87  2,550  500 Century Blvd.    Los Angeles  CA 94005
```

**Figure 1.14  Handling One-to-Many Relations in One Table**

```
Table: Salesman (including data for sales offices)

Last    First  Hire     Salary Address        City       ST Zip
Name    Name   Date

Anderson Doris   07/01/86 2,800  100 Park Avenue  New York   NY 10016
Davidson Edward  06/04/90 1,500  100 Park Avenue  New York   NY 10016
Gilbert  Fred    04/15/87 2,300  100 Park Avenue  New York   NY 10016
Jones    Betty   09/26/89 2,500  100 Park Avenue  New York   NY 10016
Bell     George  10/12/88 2,400  200 Lake Drive   Chicago    IL 60607
Evans    Henry   03/08/88 2,000  200 Lake Drive   Chicago    IL 60607
Harvey   Candy   12/01/89 2,450  200 Lake Drive   Chicago    IL 60607
Carter   Jack    05/14/87 2,550  500 Century Blvd. Los Angeles CA 94005
Ford     Ida     11/22/87 2,600  500 Century Blvd. Los Angeles CA 94005
Iverson  Albert  10/25/88 2,200  500 Century Blvd. Los Angeles CA 94005
```

**Figure 1.15  All One-to-Many Relations in the Salesman Table**

Notice that the Office ID column appears in both the Salesman and Office tables. It provides the link between these two tables. Then, to get information about a given office that belongs to a salesperson, first go to the Salesman table to find the

```
Table: Salesman (after adding the Office_ID column)

Salesman ID    Last Name   First Name   Hire Date   Salary   Office ID

S0             Anderson    Doris        07/01/86    2,800    B1
S1             Bell        George       10/12/88    2,400    B3
S2             Carter      Jack         05/14/87    2,550    B2
S3             Davidson    Edward       06/04/90    1,500    B1
S4             Evans       Henry        03/08/88    2,000    B3
S5             Ford        Ida          11/22/87    2,600    B2
S6             Gilbert     Fred         04/15/87    2,300    B3
S7             Harvey      Candy        12/01/89    2,450    B3
S8             Iverson     Albert       10/25/88    2,200    B2
S9             Jones       Betty        09/26/89    2,500    B1


Table: Office


Office ID Address           City         State Zip     Phone #


B1        100 Park Avenue   New York     NY    10016 800-123-5555
B2        200 Lake Drive    Chicago      IL    60607 800-234-5555
B3        500 Century Blvd. Los Angeles  CA    94005 800-456-5555
```

**Figure 1.16  Relating Office to Salesman**

salesperson either by his or her last name or identification number. After finding the row for that person, retrieve the office number from the Office ID column. Using the office number, then go to the Office table to find the information about a particular office. All these tasks can be done by linking the data elements in the two tables. In this example, the Salesman table is considered the master table and the Office table is referred to as the linkup table.

### Linking Keys

As stated above, the Office ID column serves as a linking key for joining the two tables. In the Salesman table, this column is called a foreign key because it provides a link to those data elements stored in another data table.

As we said before, a good relational database suggests that all the rows in a data table should be indexed according to specific values in one or more columns. The Salesman ID column can be used for such a purpose. Since each salesperson number is unique, it provides a quick and precise reference to a particular row relating to a given salesperson. Such a column can be called a primary key in a master table. Similarly, the Office ID column in the Office table is considered a primary key. It provides unique identification and reference for those rows in that table.

In summary, each data table should have a primary key. In order to link to another data table to handle one-to-many relations, you also must have a foreign key column that relates to the linking table. Of course, you can have more than one foreign key if you are to link one master table to several linking tables.

## Handling Many-to-Many Relations

Earlier examples proved that if only one-to-one relations exist among data objects, you can use a single data table to organize data elements. When you have one-to-many or many-to-many relations, however, you need to use at least two tables to accommodate the relations in order to avoid redundant data. But, if you have many-to-many relations among data objects, you must define and create one or more relation tables to handle these relations.

A relation table looks exactly like a regular data table. It is, in fact, a data table. As such, it contains a number of rows and columns. But an important difference between the two kinds of tables is that in a relation data table you save the data elements that specify the link between two objects. Each row of the table associates one primary key of one table with another primary key of the other table. The relation table may not have a a primary key column.

Examples of many-to-many relations are apparent among the data elements in the original Salesman and Region tables in Figure 1.3. For quick reference, these relations are repeated in Figure 1.17. Contents of the original Salesman and Region tables are shown in Figure 1.18.

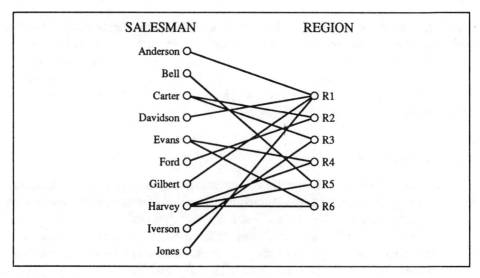

**Figure 1.17  Relations Between Salesman and Region**

In Figure 1.17 notice that saleswoman Harvey has three sales regions (R4, R5, and R6) assigned to her while each of these three regions in turn belongs to other salespeople. That is, sales regions R4 and R6 are assigned to Evans as well. Region R5 is assigned to Bell in addition to Harvey. If you were to structure all of these relations in a single table having data elements about the sales staff and their sales regions, it might look in part like that in Figure 1.19.

There is a lot of redundant data in the table in this figure. The redundant data are necessary to relate data associating salespersons Harvey, Evans, and Bell to the regions R4 (Southcentral), R5 (Northwest), and R6 (Southwest). The complete table showing all the relations among the salespeople and their assigned sales regions has even more redundant data. You can see that the table is not properly structured to conform to the requirements of a relational database.

To eliminate redundant data in the table, you must store the data elements for the sales staff and the sales regions in separate tables, as shown in Figure 1.18. In each of these tables data elements associated with each object appear only once. That is, data about a salesperson is saved in one and only one row in the Salesman table; and each of the sales regions occupies a single row in the Region table. But, in order to relate the objects in these two tables, you have to build a relation table that specifies the link between them. In the relation table, all you have to do is show the relations between the sales staff and the sales regions. In the table, each association between a salesperson and his or her sales region(s) is saved as one row. The Assignment table in Figure 1.20 is such a relation table.

Here you can see that the first four rows show the association between region R1 and the four salespeople assigned to it. The Assignment table has two columns,

```
Table: Salesman

Salesman ID    Last Name   First Name   Hire Date   Salary

S0             Anderson    Doris        07/01/86    2,800
S1             Bell        George       10/12/88    2,400
S2             Carter      Jack         05/14/87    2,550
S3             Davidson    Edward       06/04/90    1,500
S4             Evans       Henry        03/08/88    2,000
S5             Ford        Ida          11/22/87    2,600
S6             Gilbert     Fred         04/15/87    2,300
S7             Harvey      Candy        12/01/89    2,450
S8             Iverson     Albert       10/25/88    2,200
S9             Jones       Betty        09/26/89    2,500


Table: Region

Region ID    Region           Manager

R1           Northeast        Alice F. Gibson
R2           Southeast        Bob L. Major
R3           Northcentral     John K. Freed
R4           Southcentral     Cathy M. Wilson
R5           Northwest        Chris C. Hall
R6           Southwest        Helen T. Taylor
```

**Figure 1.18  The Original Salesman and Region Tables**

each of which can be linked to a data table. Thus, you can use the Salesman ID
column to link to the Salesman table, or use the Region ID to link to the Region
table.

```
Table: Salesman (including data elements for sales regions)

Last    First   Hire    Salary  Region        Manager
Name    Name    Date

Harvey  Candy   12/01/89 2,450  Southcentral  Cathy M. Wilson
Harvey  Candy   12/01/89 2,450  Northwest     Chris C. Hall
Harvey  Candy   12/01/89 2,450  Southwest     Helen T. Taylor
Evans   Henry   03/08/88 2,000  Southcentral  Cathy M. Wilson
Evans   Henry   03/08/88 2,000  Northwest     Chris C. Hall
Bell    George  10/12/88 2,400  Southwest     Helen T. Taylor
```

**Figure 1.19  Relating Salesman and Sales Region in a Data Table**

```
Table: Assignment

Region ID  Salesman ID

R1         S0
R1         S3
R1         S6
R1         S9
R2         S2
R2         S5
R3         S2
R3         S8
R4         S4
R4         S7
R5         S1
R5         S7
R6         S4
R6         S7
```

**Figure 1.20   The Relation Table Associating Sales Staff and Regions**

# Chapter Summary

In this chapter you learned the fundamentals of a database management system and database design. We discussed the basic ingredients and units of a database and the relations among them. Three data models for organizing data elements were introduced, with the focus placed on the relational data model. You also learned the desirable characteristics that your relational database should have. The knowledge you have acquired in this chapter will serve as the foundation on which to build as you design and develop your own database system. In the next chapter you will get an overview of FoxPro 2.0.

# 2

# An Overview
# of FoxPro

## An Overview

FoxPro 2.0 is one of the most user-friendly, yet powerful software programs that you can use for designing and developing relational database management systems (RDBMS). The comprehensive menu system is the center of the FoxPro user interface, and by selecting appropriate options from it you can perform virtually all of your data management functions. This chapter provides an overview of this system as well as other major components of the FoxPro user interface.

## What Is FoxPro 2.0?

FoxPro 2.0 is computer software that is used to design and develop relational database management systems. Because of its sound design and superior performance, it has been widely recognized as one of the best database management software programs in the industry. FoxPro 2.0 runs on all IBM PCs and compatible machines. It also can run on a single-user, stand-alone machine or a multiple-user local area network (LAN).

FoxPro 2.0 represents a significant improvement over the early versions of FoxPro and FoxBase+. If you have developed your database files with these programs, you should be able to use them in FoxPro 2.0 without any changes. In addition, all database files created in dBASE III Plus and dBASE IV are compatible with those used in FoxPro 2.0.

FoxPro 2.0 assumes a relational data model in which you organize all data elements in data tables. To link elements in these data tables you create relation tables and then store all the data and relation tables on disk as database files.

In FoxPro 2.0 you can process data in one of two ways: through interactive or batch processing. When you use the interactive processing mode, you perform all data management functions by choosing the appropriate options from the menu interface; or you can perform these functions by issuing the appropriate FoxPro commands.

If you choose the batch command processing mode, you manipulate data elements and extract information from them by executing a program that is written in the FoxPro command language. The program consists of a set of FoxPro commands and functions for performing the data management functions. There are two ways to use the batch processing method: either execute a program that you have written or execute the program generated by FoxPro. For example, to produce a customized report, you may write and execute a program to design and print the report. Alternatively, you may use the Report Writer provided by FoxPro to lay out the report. A program file is then automatically generated by FoxPro so that you can produce the report.

# The FoxPro User Interface

Thanks to its powerful and easy-to-use interface, FoxPro 2.0 is one of the most user-friendly database management software programs available. Even an end user without any programming knowledge can perform most data management functions with the user interface.

The heart of the user interface is the versatile and logically organized menu system. By choosing the appropriate options from the menu you can instruct FoxPro to carry out any operations that are required for managing your database. Once you have selected a given menu option, it returns a set of options—windows, dialog boxes, check boxes, push buttons, radio buttons, etc.—that you use to give further instructions to FoxPro.

## THE MENU SYSTEM: MENU BAR AND MENU PADS

The FoxPro menu system consists of four basic components: a menu bar, menu pads, menu popups, and menu options (see Figure 2.1).

The menu bar is usually the first thing that you see when you enter FoxPro. Each item displayed is called a menu pad. The actual number of menu pads that is available varies depending on precisely what you are using FoxPro to do. For example, a Browse menu pad will be displayed only after you have selected an existing database file and have opened a Browse window for it. Similarly, when you are designing a report, the Report menu pad will be added to the menu bar.

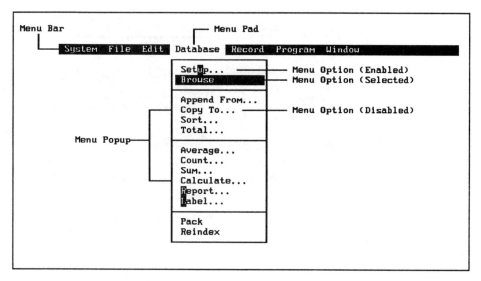

**Figure 2.1  The FoxPro Menu System**

Each menu pad contains a set of options for performing certain related data management functions. The Database menu pad contains the set of options used to manipulate data in the current database file, for instance.

You can select a menu pad either by clicking on it with your mouse, by holding down the Alt key and pressing the highlighted letter in the menu pad's name (for example, the D in Database), or by holding down the Alt key, moving the cursor to the menu pad, and pressing Enter. When you select a menu pad, a menu popup opens. This is a rectangular box that shows all the available options.

Depending on the current status of the database file, not all of the options may be selectable. The options that can be selected are displayed differently from the disabled options. An enabled option is indicated by the highlighting of one of its key letters. When the letter "u" of the Setup option on the Database menu pad is highlighted, it is selectable. Other options such as Append From, Copy To, etc., are disabled, because no database file is in use. If you are using a color monitor, disabled options are displayed with dimmed labels or in a different color.

You can select an item from a menu popup in much the same way you would select an option on the menu pad: either click on it with your mouse, press the highlighted letter (called the hotkey) on your keyboard, or cursor to the item with the up and down arrow keys and press Enter.

Once you have selected an option, FoxPro usually will present you with an array of interface objects that either carry out your selection or allow you to define more precisely just what you would like FoxPro to do.

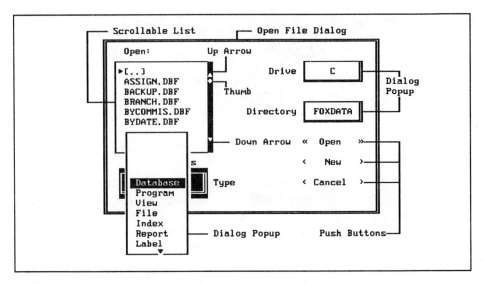

**Figure 2.2  The Open File Dialog**

## DIALOGS

FoxPro most commonly uses dialog boxes to get additional information for the menu option chosen. When you choose a menu option that is followed by an ellipsis (. . .), FoxPro responds with a dialog. So, when you select the Open . . . option from the File menu popup, you will be presented with the dialog box shown in Figure 2.2.

Here you can see that the File Open dialog asks you to provide FoxPro information on the current disk drive, the file directory, and the type of file you would like to open. You supply this information by using a number of objects provided by FoxPro and included in the dialog—popups, scrollable lists, push buttons, radio buttons, check boxes, and text boxes.

## Dialog Popups

Note in Figure 2.2 that the Open File dialog has three dialog popups: Drive, Directory, and Type. The Drive popup is for choosing the disk drive, the Directory popup is for identifying the file directory, and the Type popup is for selecting the type of file you want to open. Like a menu popup, a dialog popup, once selected, presents a list of data objects from which to choose. Select the Type dialog and a list of file types will be displayed. The size of a dialog box depends on the number of data objects in the list. If there are more objects than can be shown in the box, a small triangle is displayed at the bottom of the dialog box. Look at the Type dialog box to see such a triangle indicating there are items hidden from view in the dialog box. You can access these hidden items by scrolling downward either with the cursor keys or the mouse, or by clicking on the triangle.

Unlike a menu popup, the contents of the dialog popup's frame, when it is not selected, represents the current setting. For example, in Figure 2.2, FoxPro will use drive C: as its currently logged drive and Foxdata as the current directory. These can be changed, of course, by using the popup dialog to make another selection.

## List Boxes

In addition to popups, you often will find a list box within a dialog box. A list box allows you to select a data object from among a number of alternatives. In Figure 2.2, for example, the rectangular window beneath the Open label is a list box; it displays available files and you use it to select the file you would like to open.

When there are more items than can be shown in the list box at a single time, FoxPro displays a scrollable list box. This is very similar to a list box, except that a scroll bar with a set of control buttons is present on the right side of the box. The up and down arrows can be used to scroll upward or downward, while the diamond shaped object (called a thumb button) roughly indicates the position of the items displayed in the total list. In addition, the thumb button can be used to rapidly move from one part of the list to another.

## Push Buttons

There is also a set of push buttons in a dialog box. These buttons, also called text buttons, are used to carry out certain operations. To create a new file, for example, you would select the New text button. They are enclosed in brackets (e.g., < New >, < Cancel >) or in double brackets or chevrons (e.g., << Open >>). The default button is enclosed with chevrons (e.g., <<Open>>). Like selectable menu options, enabled buttons are often highlighted with a key letter in their names.

## Check Boxes

Another common object in dialogs is a check box. Check boxes are used to turn particular dialog box options on or off. In the Setup dialog, note that three different check boxes are provided: Set Fields, Filter, and Format (see Figure 2.3).

The Set Fields check box allows you to limit and select the data fields that FoxPro will display, while the Filter check box is used to limit and define eligible records. The Format check box is used similarly to identify the name of the format file you are going to use to view your data. Select a check box option either by clicking on it or by highlighting it and pressing the Spacebar. FoxPro then indicates that the option is in effect by displaying an X in the check box. In Figure 2.3, for example, the Filter check box contains an X; this indicates that a filter condition is in effect.

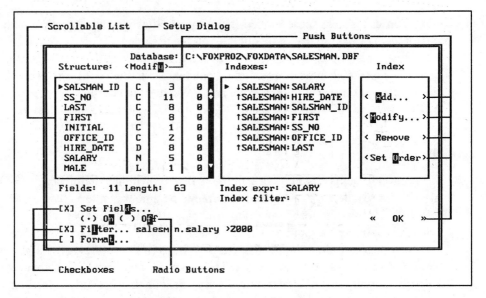

**Figure 2.3   The Setup Dialog**

On the other hand, the Format check box is not checked, which indicates that this option has not been selected.

Notice that the labels next to these check boxes also contain ellipses. This indicates that selecting the option will lead to another dialog box—for example, one that allows you to define the filter condition. So, check boxes with ellipses serve a dual purpose. On the one hand, they indicate whether an option is turned off or on; on the other, selecting the check box leads to another dialog box that allows you to define the precise meaning of the option or condition.

## Radio Buttons

Closely related to check boxes are radio buttons. Radio buttons also indicate whether an option is turned on or off; FoxPro indicates this by placing a dot within the parentheses to the left of the button. However, unlike check boxes, radio buttons occur in groups, one for each mutually exclusive option. Therefore, one of them must be turned on at all times. In Figure 2.3, for example, Set Fields can be either on or off. If you were to select the Off radio button, the On button would automatically be turned off.

## Nested Dialogs

When FoxPro requires additional information it presents a dialog. This is true when you choose some of the push buttons as well as when you select any object that

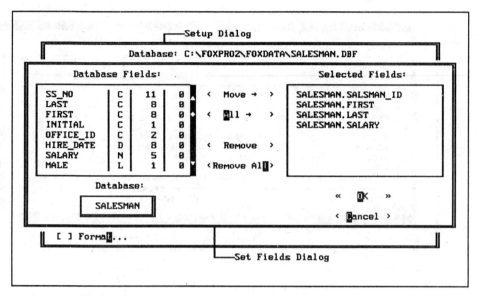

**Figure 2.4  The Set Fields Dialog**

displays ellipses (. . .). Watch this happen when you choose the Set Fields check box from the Setup dialog.

You can see in Figure 2.4 that the Set Fields dialog is nested within the Setup dialog. Be aware that it is actually possible to have dialogs nested several levels deep.

## Warning Dialogs

FoxPro sometimes uses a dialog box to display warning and confirmation messages so that you have a chance to cancel your action if you so desire. If you decide to delete a file, for instance, FoxPro will ask you to confirm your action in a dialog box (see Figure 2.5).

## ALERTS

FoxPro also displays a warning or informs you of an error by returning Alert messages, which are different from warning dialogs. In a dialog, you are normally given the option to continue or cancel the current process, while an Alert usually informs you of an unexpected condition causing the action to be aborted. So, if you try to use a nonexisting database file, an Alert of "File does not exist" will be returned (see Figure 2.6).

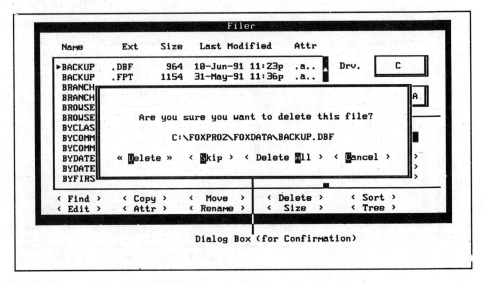

**Figure 2.5  A Confirmation Dialog**

## WINDOWS

A window is another object that you can use to communicate with FoxPro. It is a
screen area reserved for displaying a particular kind of information, and there are
a number of windows that you can use to perform different data management
operations. You can select the database files that you plan to process in the View

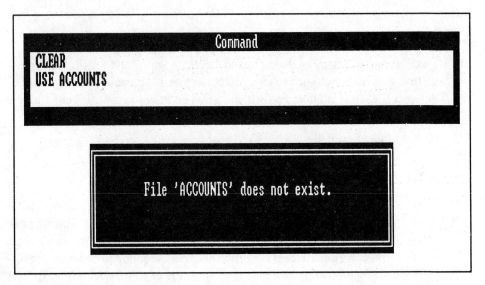

**Figure 2.6  An Alert Message**

window, design a custom report by laying out the report form in a Report Design window, or view the contents of your database files in Browse windows.

You can float (move) most windows around the screen; change their size from a full-screen display to a minimum size of one line high, 16 characters wide; or simultaneously open multiple, overlapping windows on the same screen. Then you can close the windows you have finished using, or make a window invisible by temporarily hiding it. Alternatively, you can reduce windows to their minimum size and dock them somewhere on the screen (without closing them) for later use.

There are many different types of windows that you can use in FoxPro for performing various data management functions. Each of these windows has its own set of characteristics and interface objects. In the forthcoming sections, we will examine these windows individually and in detail.

## The View Window

The View window permits you to open the databases you will be using in individual work areas. It also can be used to establish the relations among different database files. Or you can perform a number of operations on an opened file by choosing one of the text buttons provided (see Figure 2.7).

You can see that the View window, like any window, is identified by a title bar showing its name (i.e., View). Figure 2.7 also shows that two database files, SALESMAN and OFFICE, are open in work areas A and B. The currently selected database file (e.g., SALESMAN) is highlighted in the work area. These two files are also shown linked together in the relation box on the right of the window.

Objects such as push buttons and scrollable list boxes also exist in a window. To the left of the View window is a set of text buttons that enable you to perform designated operations, such as the <Browse> text button that, when chosen, allows you to view the contents of the currently selected database file.

The View window, like all windows, also has a Close control located on the upper left-hand corner of the window. Once you have closed a window you can no longer view its contents.

## Browse Windows

As noted above, a Browse window is used to display the contents of a database file. The Browse window in Figure 2.8, in addition to its title bar and Close control, contains many other types of controls that assist in displaying data. They include a Zoom control, Scroll controls, a Size control, and a Window Splitter (see Figure 2.8).

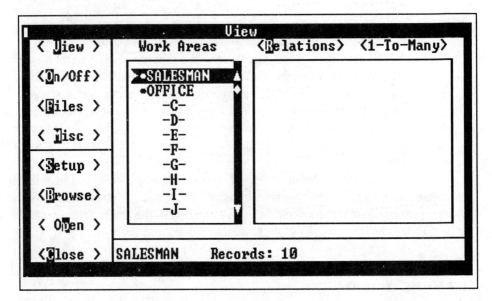

**Figure 2.7  The View Window**

## Zoom Control

The Zoom control, shown in the upper right-hand corner of the window, enables you to switch between a full-screen and a window display. When you switch to the full-screen display, the other objects that were previously on your screen are still there, but are hidden behind the zoomed window.

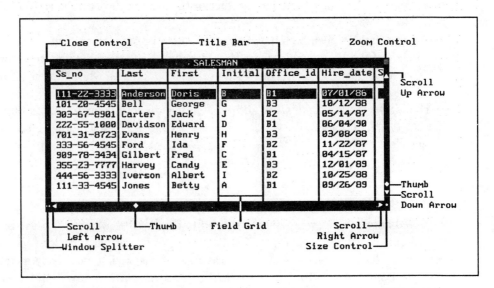

**Figure 2.8  The Browse Windows**

## Size Control

In the lower right-hand corner of the Browse window is the Size control, used to resize the window.

## Scroll Control

Two sets of controls enable you to scroll window contents: Use the Up and Down arrows to scroll vertically to reveal hidden data fields, and the Left and Right arrows to scroll horizontally to reveal hidden items in the window. Or you can use the Thumb control on the right edge of the window to scroll up and down in the window more quickly and the Thumb control on the bottom of the window to scroll left and right in the window.

## Window Splitter

The Window Splitter, shown in the lower left-hand corner of the window, is a special control provided by the Browse window. Unlike most windows, the Browse window permits you to view the contents of a database file in one of two modes. In Browse mode, data fields are shown as vertical columns, while data records are displayed as rows. In Change mode, each data field occupies its own row, and each data record is shown as a block. You also can use the Window Splitter to display a database file in both modes simultaneously in the same window (see Figure 2.9).

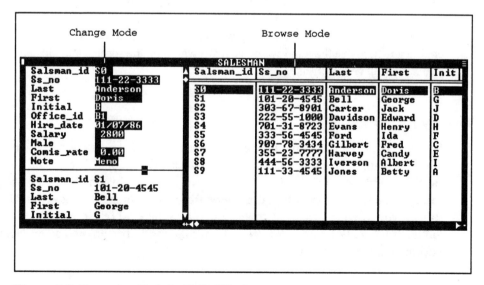

**Figure 2.9  Browsing Data in Split Windows**

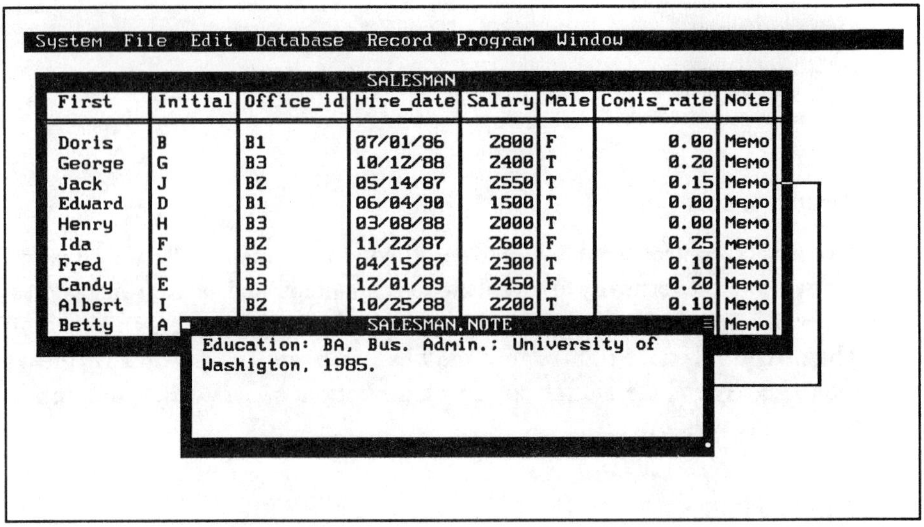

**Figure 2.10  The Memo Window**

## The Memo Window

FoxPro 2.0 allows you to save a block of text in a special type of data field called a memo field. Data stored in a memo field cannot be displayed with the other fields of a record in the Browse window. Instead, it only can be shown in a Memo window (see Figure 2.10).

This figure shows that a Memo window is used to display the contents of the memo field NOTE for a given data record. In addition to viewing the contents of the memo field, you also can modify the text shown in the Memo window.

You'll also find the Close, Zoom, and Size controls in a Memo window, which enable you to resize the window, place it anywhere on the screen, and close it when you have finished using it.

## The RQBE Window

One of the most significant enhancements of FoxPro 2.0 over the early versions of the program is the implementation of the powerful Relational Query By Example (RQBE). With the RQBE builder you can create a query by which you are able to search and extract meaningful information from one or more database files. Using RQBE, you provide FoxPro with an example of the kind of information you are looking for, and FoxPro takes over and finds the most efficient way to extract the information without the user's intervention.

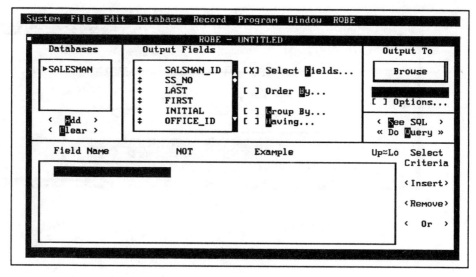

**Figure 2.11  The RQBE Window**

FoxPro uses a separate Relational Query By Example window, shown in Figure 2.11, that displays all the information and the options that are required to carry out the query operation.

Note in Figure 2.11 that the RQBE window includes list boxes for defining the files used and their output data fields, plus a popup for selecting the output destination. It also includes a number of check boxes and push buttons for defining the query settings. At the bottom of the window is an area for defining the selection criteria for the query.

## The Screen Design Window

FoxPro provides a number of standard form-based windows in which you can view and modify the contents of a database file. You can, for instance, display a file's contents in a Browse window for viewing and editing purposes. In addition, you can use the Browse window to enter data elements into a new data record.

While the standard forms provided by FoxPro are sufficient for many data entry operations, FoxPro also offers the Screen Builder, a tool that allows you to design customized, enhanced entry forms that include a variety of interface objects such as push buttons, check boxes, and radio buttons. Graphics features such as lines and boxes also can be drawn to further accentuate data entry forms.

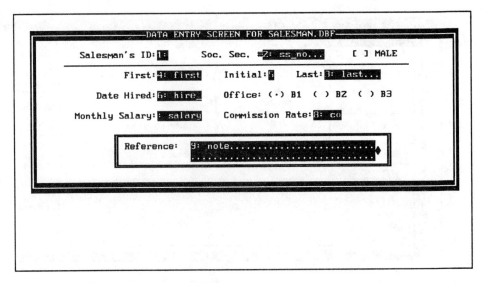

**Figure 2.12  The Screen Design Window**

When you use the Screen Builder to design a customized entry screen, FoxPro opens the Screen Design window shown in Figure 2.12. Here you lay out all the data fields and interface objects on the screen in the format you choose. These objects can include field labels, check boxes, radio buttons, lines, and boxes.

Figure 2.12 shows a data form design for the SALESMAN database file that was introduced in Chapter 1. This form can be used to view and enter data about the sales staff. In the design layout you can see that all the data fields are placed in various parts of the screen. A check box is used to indicate whether the salesperson is male or female. Radio buttons are used to identify the branch offices. A box is used to enclose the text stored in the NOTE memo field.

## The Report Layout Window

The Report Layout window is provided by the Report Writer for designing custom reports. It is here that you lay out all the objects related to the report in the form of your choice. The report form is divided into a number of bands used for defining the report title, page heading, record details, footers, and summary statistics (see Figure 2.13).

The design shown in this figure is of a columnar report. It shows the report title and all the column headings in the Title and PgHead bands respectively. In addition, all the data fields are placed in their designated positions in the Detail band. A column total is shown in the Summary band.

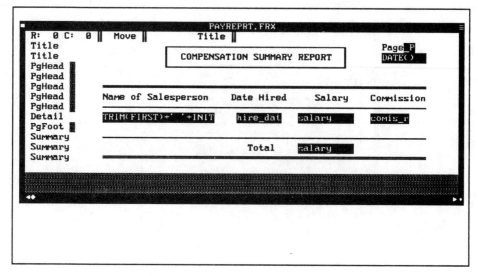

**Figure 2.13  The Report Layout Window**

## The Label Layout Window

FoxPro 2.0's Label Designer is used to produce mailing labels of different sizes and formats by extracting data elements from database files. You lay out a mailing label form in the Label Layout window where you specify the size of the mailing label, the placement of the data fields and text, and the height and width of the labels, along with the size of the margins and spaces between the labels.

Figure 2.14 shows the layout of a sample label design in the Label Layout window. All the data fields used to create a mailing label are specified in the middle of the window. Other layout settings for determining the relative positions of the mailing labels are also found here.

## The Menu Design Window

An attractive feature of the FoxPro user interface is its menu system. All the menu options are logically organized on the System menu bar as menu pads. By choosing the appropriate menu options you can perform the designated data management operations without any programming knowledge.

The power of the menu interface extends beyond the System menu, however. FoxPro also allows you to design and create a customized menu system tailored to your database applications, instead of using only those options included in the System menu pads. This is done in the Menu Design window (see Figure 2.15).

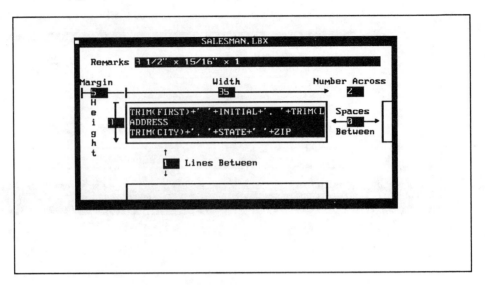

**Figure 2.14  The Label Layout Window**

This figure shows six menu pads (e.g., System, ViewData, EditData, Report, Label, and Window) specified in the Menu Design window. Within each menu pad, you specify as a submenu the menu options belonging to that pad.

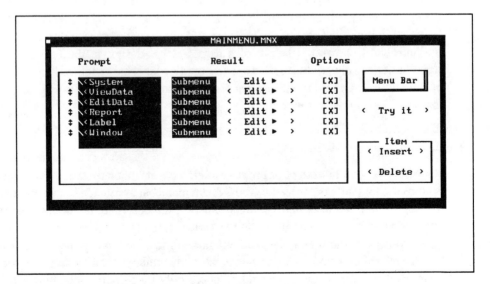

**Figure 2.15  The Menu Design Window**

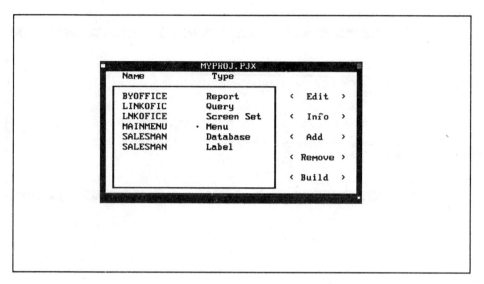

**Figure 2.16  The Project Window**

## Project Windows

The Project window is the interface provided by the FoxPro Project Manager. If you are a software developer, you can use the Project Manager to create a FoxPro application. After you have created all the components of a database management system, the next step is to organize them into a project; the components of the system are specified in the Project window.

Figure 2.16 shows a sample project that includes six components for managing the data elements related to each salesperson. In addition to identifying the database file, the project specifies the query, the custom menu, the report and label forms, and the data entry screen.

## The Command Window

The Command window displays and executes the FoxPro commands that are issued either by a user or by FoxPro itself. When you perform data management functions interactively by issuing FoxPro commands, you enter those commands in the Command window. As a matter of fact, even when you choose a menu option to carry out a data management operation, FoxPro usually translates that choice into an equivalent FoxPro command. As a result, the command is displayed in the Command window as if you had entered the command directly (see Figure 2.17).

The Command window of Figure 2.17 shows a list of FoxPro commands that were used to carry out certain management functions. They could have been

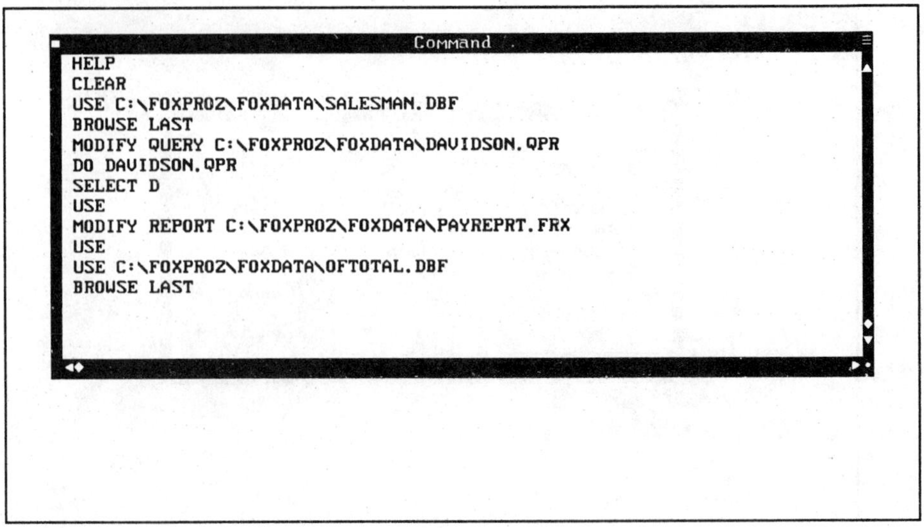

```
                          Command
  HELP
  CLEAR
  USE C:\FOXPRO2\FOXDATA\SALESMAN.DBF
  BROWSE LAST
  MODIFY QUERY C:\FOXPRO2\FOXDATA\DAVIDSON.QPR
  DO DAVIDSON.QPR
  SELECT D
  USE
  MODIFY REPORT C:\FOXPRO2\FOXDATA\PAYREPRT.FRX
  USE
  USE C:\FOXPRO2\FOXDATA\OFTOTAL.DBF
  BROWSE LAST
```

**Figure 2.17  The Command Window**

entered by a user or issued by FoxPro after you selected the corresponding menu options.

## Text Editing Windows

A program is a collection of commands grouped together in a single file that will perform one or more database management functions. This program file can be created and edited in a number of ways and with a wide range of text editors, including the text editor offered by FoxPro 2.0. When you select the editor, FoxPro opens a Text Editing window like the one shown in Figure 2.18.

You can see that the Text Editing window shows a listing of the program named GENMENU.PRG. You can make any modifications you want to the program listing in this window.

## Help Windows

FoxPro provides a comprehensive help facility that you can access at any time by simply pressing the F1 function key. Usually, help is context-sensitive—that is, the contents of the Help window that FoxPro opens in response to your request for help are related to how you are using FoxPro at that particular time.

If FoxPro cannot determine what you are doing or cannot find any information related to where you are in the FoxPro program, it displays the topics-level Help window shown in Figure 2.19. You can then scan the list of topics and select one

```
                              GENMENU. PRG
*
* Description:
* This program generates menu code which was designed in the
* FoxPro 2.0 MENU BUILDER.
*
* Notes:
* In this program, for clarity/readability reasons, we use variable
* names that are longer than 10 characters.  Note, however, that only
* the first 10 characters are significant.
*
* Modification History:
* December 13, 1990      JAC      Program Created
*
PARAMETER m.projdbf, m.recno

IF SET("TALK") = "ON"
    SET TALK OFF
    m.talkstate = "ON"
ELSE
    m.talkstate = "OFF"
```

**Figure 2.18  The Text Editing Window**

in which you are interested. Otherwise, FoxPro opens a details-level Help window that provides you with information about the task that you are currently performing. For example, if you press the Help (F1) key while using the Calculator, FoxPro will open a Help window that displays information about the operation of the Calculator desktop accessory.

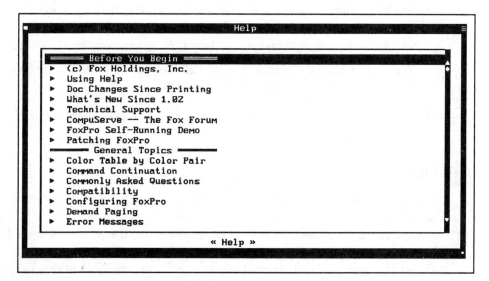

**Figure 2.19  The Help Window**

# The Major Components of FoxPro

The most important component of any relational database management system is, of course, its data and the associated tables for organizing the relations among data elements. And FoxPro naturally offers the capability to create and maintain database files and a number of different kinds of index files.

This potentially valuable data is meaningless, however, without tools that will allow you to insure its integrity and to extract the information you desire. Consequently, FoxPro offers more than the capability to create and maintain files; as a comprehensive environment for relational database management, it provides all the tools you need to create, maintain, and extract your data. Besides its file system, these tools, some of which we've already discussed, form the components of the system and include:

- Relational Query By Example (RQBE), a powerful tool for extracting information quickly and efficiently.

- The Screen Builder, a tool that creates customized data entry forms. It facilitates data entry and modification and can be used to insure the integrity and accuracy of your data.

- The Report Writer, a flexible tool that allows you to format output in the way you desire.

- The Label Designer, a tool that handles labels of virtually all sizes easily and elegantly.

- The Menu Builder, which allows you to replace FoxPro's menu system with a customized one that is tailored to a particular application. This allows users who have little or no knowledge of how FoxPro works to use the program.

- The Project Manager, a tool that links all these diverse components into an integrated database management system.

In the following section, we will survey these components in greater detail.

## THE FILE SYSTEM

Data and relational tables make up one major component of a relational database. Data elements are organized in tables by data fields and records. These tables are saved on disk as database files in FoxPro. In addition to data elements, these files also contain information about the structure of the data tables.

Index files also play an important role in a database management system. They provide information for arranging the data in database files. There are two types of index files that you can use in FoxPro: standard and compound.

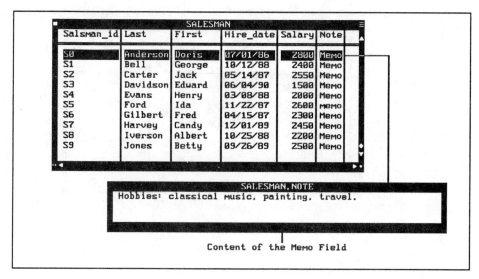

**Figure 2.20  A Sample Database File**

Each type of disk file is given a unique file extension. FoxPro database files are assigned .DBF as theirs. If you need to store large blocks of text in a data table, you can save them in memo fields, which FoxPro saves to a separate disk file with .FPT as the file extension. If you decided to create a database file in FoxPro to store the data table named SALESMAN in Chapter 1, it would contain six data fields and ten records (see Figure 2.20).

The database file named SALESMAN.DBF contains all its data elements in a data table. In addition, it contains information about the database structure (see Figure 2.21). The data structure contains a memo field named NOTE that is used for storing a block of text describing a salesperson's specifics such as hobbies, educational background, etc. Contents of this memo field are saved in the memo file named SALESMAN.FPT.

## THE RQBE BUILDER

As described earlier, the RQBE Builder allows you to create a data query for finding the information you want. This tool opens an RQBE window in which you specify all the conditions and select the options and settings that are required by the query operation. An RQBE window is shown in Figure 2.22.

In this window you select the database files from which the query will extract information. You can see in Figure 2.22 that the query uses two database files: SALESMAN.DBF and OFFICE.DBF. At the lower portion of the window are the conditions for linking the database files and for defining the selection criteria for the query. The first condition is used to link the two database files by using the

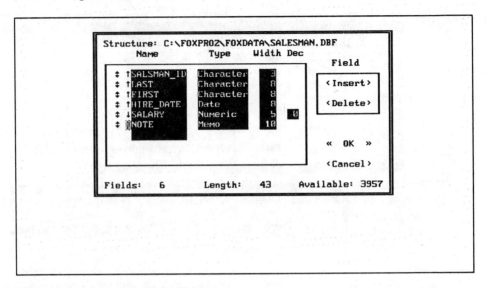

**Figure 2.21  A Sample Data Structure**

common data field, OFFICE_ID. The second condition specifies the selection criteria indicating that only those salespeople earning a salary of more than $2,000 will be chosen. When you carry out the query, it returns from the selected database file the data elements that satisfy the selection conditions.

Other settings in the RQBE window are for specifying and organizing the results returned from the query. They are used to identify the data fields to be returned by

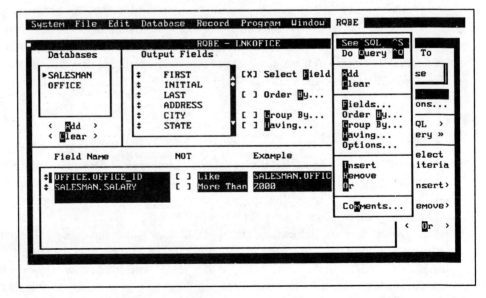

**Figure 2.22  The RQBE Builder**

the query and how they should be arranged and grouped. You can also direct the query results to a number of destinations, including on screen, saved to a database file, or sent to a report.

## THE SCREEN BUILDER

When you create a database file, FoxPro provides two modes that you can use to enter data elements into the data table, as well as view and edit the contents of your database files. These two modes are Browse and Change.

In Figure 2.23 you can see that the data fields in SALESMAN.DBF are shown as columns in Browse mode while each data record is displayed as one row. Conversely, in Change mode, each data record is shown as a group of rows, each of which shows the contents of a data field. By default, the sequence of the data fields is determined by the order in which they are saved in the data structure.

Although Browse mode and Change mode are sufficient for many data entry operations, from time to time you probably will feel the need for a customized form for data entry or browsing. It may be that you simply find the arrangement of the data entry window to be unattractive and would like some alternative to it. Or perhaps the organization of the window in Browse mode is not conductive to rapid data entry. Or possibly, in browsing records, you would like to highlight certain information so that it readily stands out.

In the past, designing a custom screen required a knowledge of programming. But even more importantly, it was a cumbersome process. The programmer first used a text editor to write some code, then used the database management system

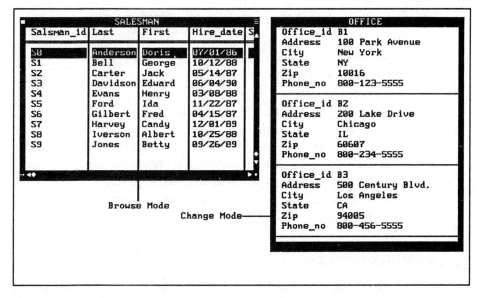

**Figure 2.23  Browse and Change Modes**

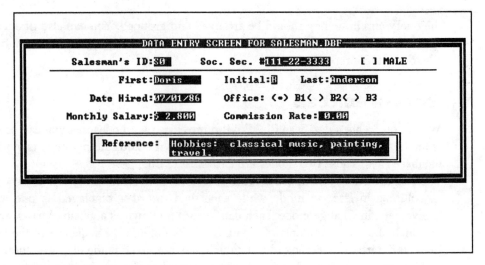

**Figure 2.24  A Custom Data Entry Form**

to inspect the results. This process was repeated any number of times, until the screen finally conformed to the programmer's original intention.

FoxPro 2.0, however, provides a tool, known as the Screen Builder, that allows you to create your own customized data entry and browsing forms. In contrast to the techniques used in the past, the Screen Builder offers a number of advantages:

- You do not have to know programming to design attractive, functional screens. The Screen Builder is easy to use.

- You can design your screen visually, by placing, moving, and sizing objects on the screen. Designing a screen is no longer a two-step process.

The Screen Builder permits you to determine the data entry order of individual fields, include calculated fields, and incorporate a number of graphics objects (like lines and boxes) and interface objects (push buttons, check boxes, radio buttons) into your forms. The Screen Builder is very flexible.

Figure 2.24 shows a custom screen created with the Screen Builder. Notice that the data fields are organized in the order of the user's choice. A check box identifies whether the salesperson is male or female, a radio button specifies the office to which the salesperson belongs, and a double-line box displays the contents of a memo field. Figure 2.25 shows the same screen in the process of being created with the Screen Builder.

## THE REPORT WRITER

FoxPro's Report Writer is one of the most versatile report generators provided by a database management system. It allows you to produce professional reports with

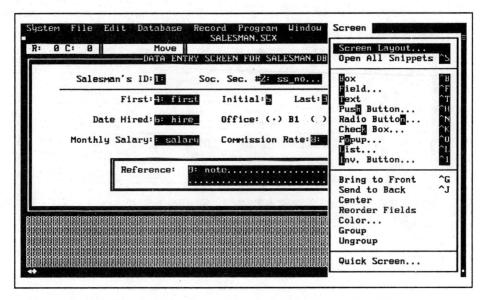

**Figure 2.25  Designing a Data Entry Form with the Screen Builder**

very little effort. You can choose either a columnar or a form report format. In a columnar report, values appear in columns; each row corresponds to a data record. Summary statistics (like totals) are shown at the bottom of the report (see Figure 2.26).

In a form format, text can be mixed with the contents of data fields in a free form. This is an efficient way to produce computer form letters in which you move information from your database files into precomposed text.

| COMPENSATION SUMMARY REPORT | | | Page 1<br>08/08/91 |
|---|---|---|---|

| Name of Salesperson | Date Hired | Salary | Commission |
|---|---|---|---|
| Doris B. Anderson | 07/01/86 | $2,800 | 0.00 |
| Edward D. Davidson | 06/04/90 | $1,500 | 0.00 |
| Betty A. Jones | 09/26/89 | $2,500 | 0.00 |
| Jack J. Carter | 05/14/87 | $2,550 | 0.15 |
| Ida F. Ford | 11/22/87 | $2,600 | 0.25 |
| Albert I. Iverson | 10/25/88 | $2,200 | 0.10 |
| George G. Bell | 10/12/88 | $2,400 | 0.20 |
| Henry H. Evans | 03/08/88 | $2,000 | 0.00 |
| Fred C. Gilbert | 04/15/87 | $2,300 | 0.10 |
| Candy E. Harvey | 12/01/89 | $2,450 | 0.20 |
| | Total | $23,300 | |

**Figure 2.26  A Sample Columnar Report**

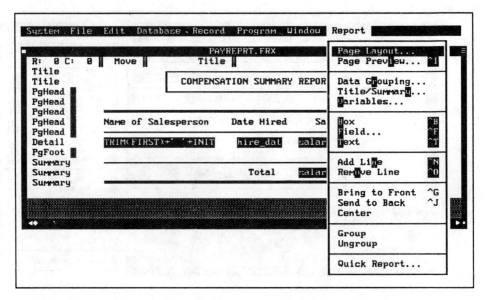

**Figure 2.27  Designing a Columnar Report with the Report Writer**

A report in either format can be designed by using the Report Layout window provided by the Report Writer. In the report layout, you specify the data fields in the Detail band. The necessary field labels are added to the PgHead band, and the report title is added to the Title band. Data is grouped and summary statistics are generated in the Summary band.

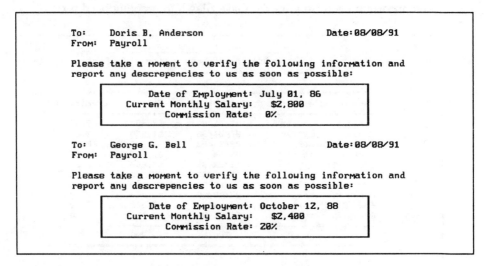

**Figure 2.28  A Sample Form Report**

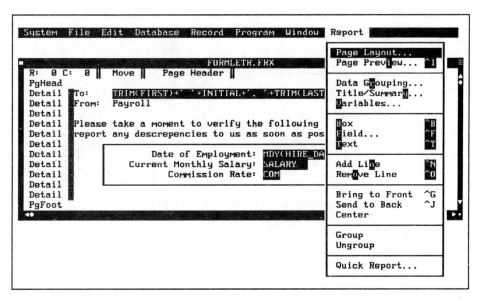

**Figure 2.29  Layout of a Form Report**

Figure 2.27 shows the report layout used to produce the report shown in Figure 2.26. In the figure you can see some of the basic components of a report layout, including report title, column heading, data fields, and summary statistics.

Figure 2.28 shows an example of a form letter that was produced by using the Report Writer in a form format. In the form letter the names of salespeople Doris B. Anderson, George B. Bell, etc., are taken from the SALESMAN.DBF database file and inserted into a block of text. The form letter also extracts data from other data fields such as HIRE_DATE and SALARY. To produce these form letters, you simply place the text and data fields in the location desired in the Report Layout (see Figure 2.29).

## THE LABEL DESIGNER

The Label Designer is provided by FoxPro for the design and production of mailing labels of various sizes and formats. You can define the number of labels across, their height (in number of lines), and the number of spaces between labels (see Figure 2.30).

Figure 2.30 shows mailing labels with a height of three lines and a width of 35 characters. Vertically, there is one line between two labels. Horizontally, there are two labels across.

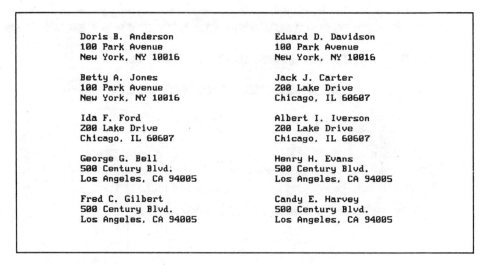

**Figure 2.30  Examples of Mailing Labels**

These labels are produced by using the design specified in the Label Design screen shown in Figure 2.31. In this figure you can see that the size of the mailing labels and the spacing settings are specified in the Label Designer screen, along with the data fields that make up the text for the labels.

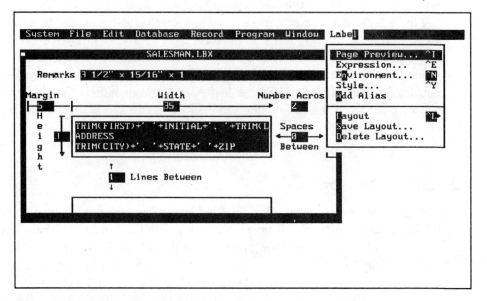

**Figure 2.31  Designing Mailing Labels**

## THE MENU BUILDER

The Menu Builder gives you the capability to design and create a menu system that is tailored to your applications. You can include some of the options from the System menu and create additional menu options for performing specific data manipulation operations. Your menu system will have the same appearance as the System menu, complete with menu pads, popups, and options.

The Menu Builder comes with a Menu Design window in which you lay out the menu structure. Besides the Menu Design window, the Menu option on the System menu provides additional options for creating a customized menu system. You begin by defining the menu pads to be included in the custom menu bar that will replace the FoxPro System menu. For each menu pad defined you then define its associated options as a submenu.

Figure 2.32 shows a custom menu that has six menu pads, each of which performs a certain function. For example, in the Report menu pad you can include options for producing certain types of reports. Similarly, you can choose to include in your menu pad any of the system options that are normally found in the FoxPro menu pad (e.g., Help, Filer, Calculator, Calendar/Diary, etc.). As a result, it will show only those options when you invoke your menu system (see Figure 2.33).

In this figure, you can see the six menu pads on the custom menu bar as defined in the Menu Builder. When you select the System menu pad, five menu options are displayed in its menu popup.

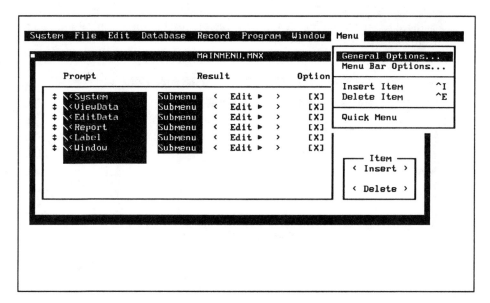

**Figure 2.32  Creating a Menu System with the Menu Builder**

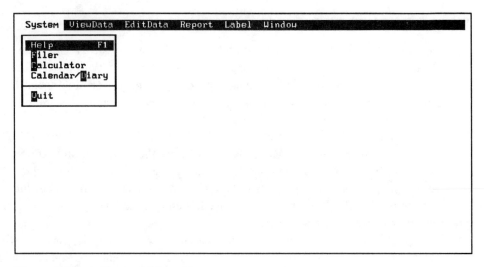

**Figure 2.33   A Custom Menu Bar**

## THE PROJECT BUILDER

To develop an integrated data management system, you use the tools provided by FoxPro to design and develop various components of the system: create the necessary database files for organizing data elements, design the screens for the data entry and data display operations, and create custom reports and label forms. To facilitate information searches, you create the necessary data queries. In

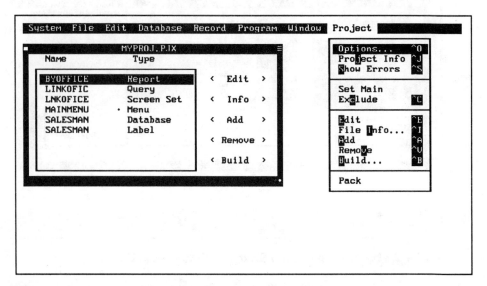

**Figure 2.34   Defining a Project with the Project Builder**

addition, you create a custom menu for carrying out the data management functions with these components.

Finally, you integrate all the components into a project with the Project Builder. If you are a software developer, you can use the Project Builder to create a database application for the end user; with the application, the end user can access all the database components through the custom menu system without using the general user interface provided by FoxPro. In the Project Builder you identify the name and type of management components to be included in the Project window. Then choose the appropriate options from which to build your project in the Project menu pad (see Figure 2.34).

## THE DESK ACCESSORIES

In addition to providing the tools for managing your databases, FoxPro gives you a set of handy desk accessories. These accessories, which include a Filer, a Calculator, a Calendar/Diary, and tables of ASCII and special characters, are accessed by choosing from the options in the FoxPro System menu pad. The desk accessories also include a screen capture utility and a simple puzzle game.

### The Filer

The Filer is a utility tool that helps you to manage your disk files efficiently. With the Filer you are able to perform all file manipulation operations by choosing the appropriate text buttons (see Figure 2.35).

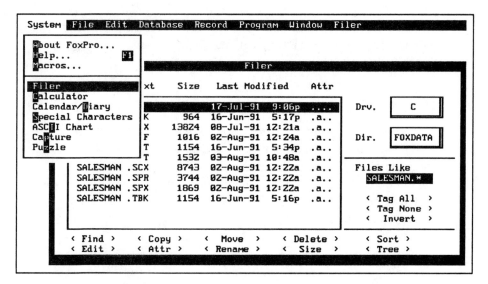

**Figure 2.35  The Filer**

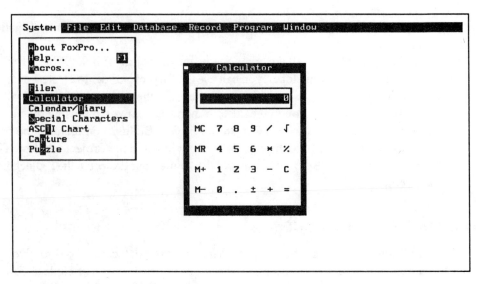

**Figure 2.36  The Calculator Desk Accessory**

In the Filer you can rename, copy, and delete an existing file; create a file directory; and move files between directories. You can sort files by their attributes, examine your file structure in a given directory in a disk drive by displaying the structure in a tree diagram, and perform some directory and file operations.

## The Calculator

When you choose the Calculator option from the System menu popup, a simple calculator appears on the screen (see Figure 2.36). You can invoke this handy tool while you are in most FoxPro operations. Once you are done using it, just close it and return to other operations.

## The Calendar/Diary

The Calendar/Diary option, which you invoke by choosing it from the System menu popup, allows you to view the calendar and enter appointments for a given date in the diary.

In Figure 2.37 you can see that some events and appointments have been entered into the diary for July 4, 1991. Use the text buttons to display a different month or year on the calendar.

## Special Characters

When designing data screens and reports you may want to use a special character in the layout. You can import such characters from the Special Characters desk

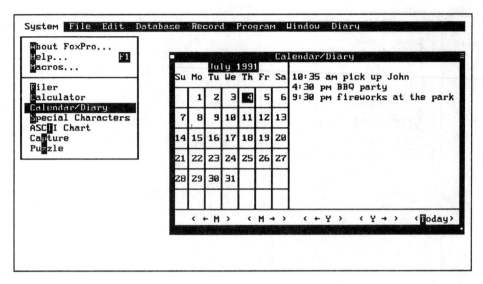

**Figure 2.37  The Calendar/Diary Desk Accessory**

accessory, which features a set of graphic symbols, mathematical and statistical notations, and special characters for foreign punctuations (see Figure 2.38).

## ASCII Chart

There are a variety of forms in which a computer can code and store characters—including letters, numbers, and special symbols—in its memory and on storage media. ASCII (American Standard Code for Information Interchange) is one of

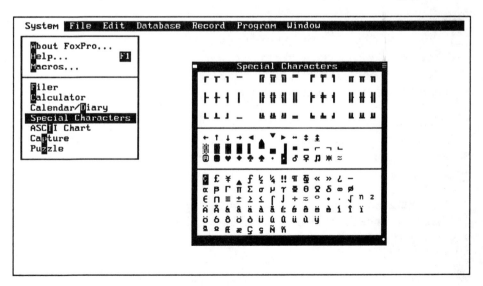

**Figure 2.38  The Special Characters Desk Accessory**

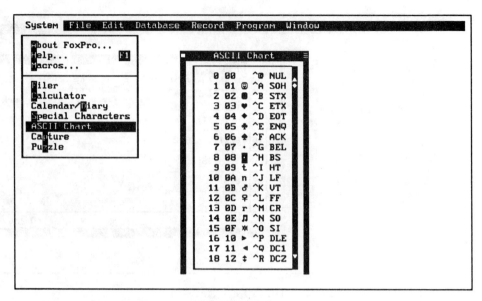

**Figure 2.39  The ASCII Chart Desk Accessory**

the most popular codes used. ASCII assigns a unique numeric code to each letter, number, and symbol. The numeric codes determine the order of the characters when you need to sort them into either ascending or descending order. To view these ASCII characters in numeric order, choose the ASCII Chart option from the System menu popup (see Figure 2.39).

## The Screen Capture Utility

While using FoxPro's design tools to create screens, reports, or labels, there may be times when you would like to incorporate the contents of one window into your design window. The Screen Capture utility allows you to share information between windows in this way. To use it to capture information from one window and then copy it to another window, choose the Capture option from the System menu popup.

## The Puzzle

The Puzzle is a simple game that you can play while you are in FoxPro. The object is to rearrange the numbers in an orderly fashion after you have shuffled them. It has little to do with any data management functions.

## FOXPRO FILES

FoxPro follows the DOS file-handling convention of identifying a file by a name and a file extension. The first part is a symbolic name that describes the object; the file extension identifies the file type. For example, the filename SALESMAN.DBF indicates that it is a database (.DBF) file containing data about sales personnel.

Some files containing information about the same data object are saved in different forms with different file extensions. For example, the layout of a data form created in the Screen Builder is saved in a file with .SCX extension. Before it generates the data form, the screen layout is translated into a set of FoxPro commands as a program and saved in a file with an .SPR extension. Furthermore, the compiled version of the program, which contains instructions coded in a machine language that can be understood by the computer, is saved in another file with an .SPX extension.

The types of FoxPro files can be summarized as follows:

| File Type (Extension) | Description/Contents |
| --- | --- |
| Database Files | |
|     Database (.DBF) | Data structure and table |
|     Database Backup (.BAK) | Backup of .DBF and others |
|     Memo (.FPT) | Contents of memo fields |
|     Memo Backup (TBK) | Backup of .FPT |
| Index Files | |
|     Standard Index (.IDX) | Standard indexes |
|     Compound Index (.CDX) | Compound indexes |
| RQBE Files | |
|     Generated Query (.QPR) | SQL commands of the query |
|     Compiled Query (.QPX) | Compiled version of .QPR |
| View Files | |
|     View (.VUE) | Open .DBF files and relations |
| Label Files | |
|     Label (.LBX) | Layout of labels |
|     Label Memo (.LBT) | Memo of the .LBX |
| Report Files | |
|     Report (.FRX) | Layout of report |
|     Report Memo (.FRT) | Memo of the .FRX |

*(continued)*

| *File Type (Extension)* | *Description/Contents* |
|---|---|
| **Screen Files** | |
| Screen (.SCX) | Screen layout of data form |
| Screen Memo (.SCT) | Memo of the .SCX |
| Generated Program (.SPR) | Command file about the .SCX |
| Compiled Program (.SPX) | Compiled version of .SPR |
| **Menu Files** | |
| Menu (.MNX) | Layout of menu structure |
| Menu Memo (.MNT) | Memo of the .MNX |
| Generated Program (.MPR) | Command file about the .MNX |
| Compiled Program (.MPX) | Compiled version of .MPR |
| **Project Files** | |
| Project (.PJX) | Listing of project components |
| Project Memo  (.PJT) | Memo of the .PJX |
| **Generated Applications** | |
| Generated Application (.APP) | Application program |
| Executable Program (.EXE) | Stand-alone executable program |
| **Memory Variable Files** | |
| Memory Variable Save (.MEM) | Memory variables |
| **FoxPro Command Files** | |
| Program (.PRG) | FoxPro commands |
| Compiled Program (.FXP) | Compiled version of .PRG |
| **Text Files** | |
| Text (.TXT) | Textual information |
| **Macro Files** | |
| Macro (.FKY) | — |
| **Window Files** | |
| Window (.WIN) | — |
| **Working Files** | |
| Temporary (.TMP) | — |
| **FoxPro System Files** | |
| Executable (.EXE) | — |
| Overlay (.OVL) | — |

# System Capacities

There are two versions of FoxPro from which to choose: the base and the extended versions. The maximum number of files that can be saved on your disk is limited by the amount of disk storage you have on your hard disk. But, the number of objects that you can access in FoxPro depends on the program version you have installed and the amount of computer memory you have on your system. The system capabilities for the objects to be discussed in this book can be summarized as follows:

|  | FoxPro Base | FoxPro Extended |
|---|---|---|
| Database files on disk | unlimited | unlimited |
| Database files open at one time | 25 | 25 |
| Data records per database file | 1 billion | 1 billion |
| Data fields per data record | 255 | 255 |
| Characters per data record | 4,000 | 4,000 |
| Characters per data field | 254 | 254 |
| Characters per standard index key (.IDX) | 100 | 100 |
| Characters per compound index key (.CDX) | 254 | 254 |
| Memory variables | 3,600 | 65,000 |

# Chapter Summary

This chapter presented the basic design philosophy and major components of FoxPro 2.0. In addition to the powerful user interface, you were introduced to the RQBE Builder, Screen Builder, Label Designer, Report Writer, Menu Builder, and Project Builder.

This chapter also discussed the comprehensive FoxPro menu system and its set of tools for working with the menu system. These tools include dialogs, alerts, popups, scrollable lists, push buttons, radio buttons, and various kind of windows. In the forthcoming chapters you will use these tools to effectively design, develop, and manage your relational databases.

# 3

# Getting Started

## An Overview

You are now ready to begin using FoxPro. But before you can design and develop your database management system, you first must install the program on your disk. This chapter outlines the steps involved in this process. You will learn how to navigate the FoxPro interface and its tools to carry out data manipulation operations.

## Installing FoxPro

The installation process involves setting up the necessary file directories and copying the program files from the distribution diskettes into these directories. This process is simple and automatic—FoxPro even checks to make sure that you have enough disk space.

The amount of disk space you need depends on the version of FoxPro you are installing. If you are installing the base version of FoxPro 2.0, you need about 6 megabytes (Mb). An additional 6 megabytes is necessary if you are installing the extended version of the program. In addition, the amount of required disk space may vary depending on the optional files you would like to include. If you have insufficient disk space, FoxPro warns you so that you can cancel the installation process.

To begin the installation, first put the distribution diskette in drive A (or B) and type INSTALL at the A> prompt:

```
A>INSTALL
```

Next follow the instructions to continue. By default, all the FoxPro program files will be installed and saved in the FOXPRO2 directory. You are then asked to indicate the version of FoxPro (base version vs. extended version) you intend to install. Once the basic files have been installed, you are directed to select the type of monitor you are using, followed by a question as to whether or not you plan to install supplemental files. These supplemental files include sample database application files and files for the tutorial examples. You can choose to install some or all of these files during this process. (If you have enough disk space, install all of these files.) Finally, you are notified when the installation process is completed.

# Getting Ready

Before starting to work with FoxPro it is highly recommended that you create a special subdirectory for saving all the disk files that you will create for your database. You can assign a name of your choice to that directory or name it FOXDATA. Create this subdirectory within the FOXPRO2 directory that was set up during the installation process. (If you already know how to do this, skip the next section and create the FOXDATA directory.)

## CREATING THE DATA DIRECTORY

If you have installed FoxPro in disk drive C, you should now be at the prompt that reads either C> or C:\>. If the latter appears, it indicates that you are at the home or root directory indicated by \. At this point you can continue on to the next step. If C> appears, issue the $P$G command at the prompt:

```
C>PROMPT $G$P
```

To execute the command, press the Enter key at the prompt. As a result, the prompt will become C:\> indicating that you are now at the home or root (\) directory. At this point, change your directory to the FOXPRO2 directory by issuing the CD (change directory) command at the prompt:

```
C:\>CD FOXPRO2
```

In return, you will be in the FOXPRO2 directory as indicated by the C:\FOXPRO2> prompt. To create the FOXDATA subdirectory in the FOXPRO2 directory, issue the MD (make directory) command at the prompt:

```
C:\FOXPRO2>MD FOXDATA
```

Now you have created the FOXDATA subdirectory below the FOXPRO2 directory. To verify its existence, issue the DIR *. command at the prompt (see Figure 3.1).

```
C>PROMPT $P$G

C:\>CD FOXPRO2

C:\FOXPRO2>MD FOXDATA

C:\FOXPRO2>DIR *.

 Volume in drive C has no label
 Directory of  C:\FOXPRO2

 .             <DIR>       8-12-91  11:06p
 ..            <DIR>       8-12-91  11:06p
 FOXDATA       <DIR>       8-12-91  11:15a
 COMMFUNC      <DIR>       8-12-91  11:10p
 GOODIES       <DIR>       8-12-91  11:11p
 SAMPLE        <DIR>       8-12-91  11:11p
 TUTORIAL      <DIR>       8-12-91  11:14p
         7 File(s)   1968128 bytes free

C:\FOXPRO2>
```

**Figure 3.1  Creating the FOXDATA Subdirectory**

## FILE ORGANIZATION

During the installation process, a number of subdirectories were created in the FOXPRO2 directory. In each of these subdirectories are disk files or more subdirectories. After you have created your own FOXDATA subdirectory in the FOXPRO2 directory, the file structure looks like the one shown in Figure 3.2.

## INSTALLING THE MOUSE

To take advantage of FoxPro's powerful user interface, it is recommended that you use a mouse. DOS does not automatically offer mouse support, however. This means that, without special software known as a device driver, your computer will not even be able to recognize that you have a mouse. Therefore, depending on the type of mouse and mouse device driver that you have, you must activate your mouse either when you turn on your computer or before you start the FoxPro program.

If you are using the Microsoft mouse with the driver program named MOUSE.COM, issue the command MOUSE in the directory where the driver is located. After the mouse driver is installed, you will be notified accordingly. For example, Figure 3.3 shows how to activate the mouse in the root directory of the C Drive. If the mouse driver program is located in another directory, switch to that directory to activate the mouse before returning to the FOXPRO2 directory.

If you are using the Microsoft mouse with a device driver named MOUSE.SYS, the device driver must be loaded by DOS in the process of booting up your

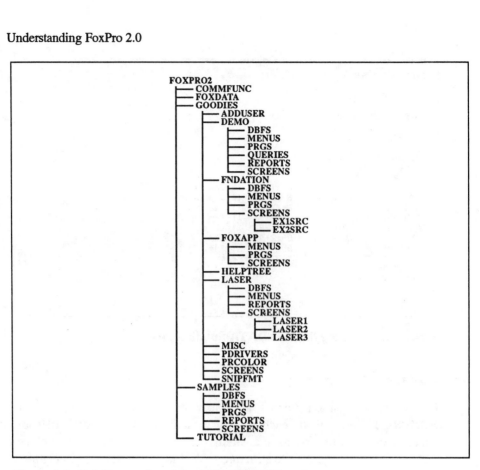

```
FOXPRO2
├── COMMFUNC
├── FOXDATA
├── GOODIES
│        ├── ADDUSER
│        ├── DEMO
│        │      ├── DBFS
│        │      ├── MENUS
│        │      ├── PRGS
│        │      ├── QUERIES
│        │      ├── REPORTS
│        │      └── SCREENS
│        ├── FNDATION
│        │      ├── DBFS
│        │      ├── MENUS
│        │      ├── PRGS
│        │      └── SCREENS
│        │             ├── EX1SRC
│        │             └── EX2SRC
│        ├── FOXAPP
│        │      ├── MENUS
│        │      ├── PRGS
│        │      └── SCREENS
│        ├── HELPTREE
│        ├── LASER
│        │      ├── DBFS
│        │      ├── MENUS
│        │      ├── REPORTS
│        │      └── SCREENS
│        │             ├── LASER1
│        │             ├── LASER2
│        │             └── LASER3
│        ├── MISC
│        ├── PDRIVERS
│        ├── PRCOLOR
│        ├── SCREENS
│        └── SNIPFMT
├── SAMPLES
│        ├── DBFS
│        ├── MENUS
│        ├── PRGS
│        ├── REPORTS
│        └── SCREENS
└── TUTORIAL
```

**Figure 3.2  Subdirectories of the FOXPRO2 Directory**

```
C:\>MOUSE
Microsoft (R) Mouse Driver  Version 6.14
Copyright (C) Microsoft Corp 1983-1988.  All rights reserved.
Existing Mouse driver enabled

C:\>
```

**Figure 3.3  Activating the Mouse**

computer. To do this, you must use a text editor (like EDIT, which comes with DOS 5.0, or FoxPro's own program editor) to modify your CONFIG.SYS file, which is located in the root directory of the hard disk from which DOS boots (usually C:). After you run the text editor and load the CONFIG.SYS file, insert the following line in the file:

```
DEVICE=C:\MOUSE.SYS
```

If the mouse device driver is not located in the root directory of drive C, substitute the exact path of the directory in which it resides. When you save the file and exit the word processor, you must then reboot for your change to take effect.

If you have trouble activating your mouse, or if you are using some other type of mouse, consult its user's manual.

# Starting FoxPro

The command used to invoke FoxPro depends on the version of the program you have installed. If you are using the single-user version of FoxPro, issue the FOXPRO command at the C:\FOXPRO2> prompt:

```
C:\FOXPRO2>FOXPRO
```

If you are using the extended, single-user version of FoxPro, issue the FOXPROX command at the prompt instead:

```
C:\FOXPRO2>FOXPROX
```

Users of the LAN (Local Area Network) version of FoxPro should issue FOXPROL and FOXPROLX commands for the regular and extended version respectively.

Shortly after executing the appropriate command you will see the first FoxPro screen indicating that you are in the program (Figure 3.4). This screen displays the FoxPro logo, along with the System menu bar and the Command window.

Now you are able to begin using FoxPro to design and develop your data management system. Before you actually can create the necessary database files, however, you need to learn the basics about working with the FoxPro user interface.

## MOUSE BASICS

The mouse is a pointer device used for selecting objects to perform data manipulation operations in FoxPro. Although there are many different brands of mice, they all have two buttons: the left and right buttons. Most mouse techniques involve four basic actions, namely, pointing, clicking, double clicking, and dragging.

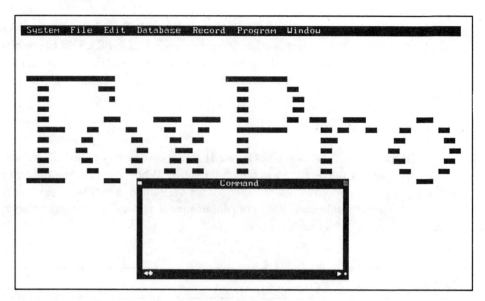

**Figure 3.4  The FoxPro Initial Screen**

## Pointing

When the mouse is active on the screen, a mouse cursor (or mouse pointer) in the shape of a small block is visible. As you move the mouse, the cursor moves in the same direction and the same relative distance. Therefore, you can point your mouse cursor at any location on the screen simply by moving your mouse, and this is the action that you use to point to an object that you are selecting or activating. As an exercise of this action, point your mouse cursor at the System menu pad (see Figure 3.5).

## Clicking

The clicking action involves pressing the mouse button once quickly and then releasing it. In FoxPro, normally you click only on the left button; rarely is the right button used. The clicking action usually follows pointing, so you would click the mouse button after you have pointed the mouse cursor at the selected object. This combined point and click action allows you to select an object without using the keyboard. So, to continue the exercise begun above, after pointing your mouse cursor at the System menu pad, select it by clicking your mouse button. As a result, the System menu popup appears (see Figure 3.6).

In Figure 3.6 you can see the list of options shown in the System menu popup. At this point you can use the point and click technique to select a menu option. To

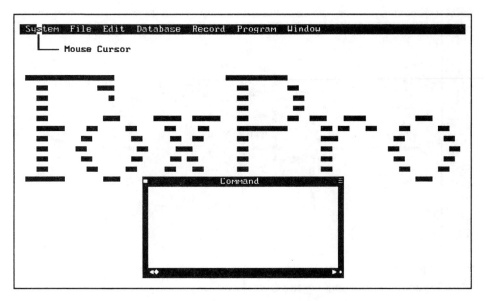

**Figure 3.5  Pointing Mouse Cursor at the System Menu Pad**

bring up the Calculator, for example, point and click the Calculator option, and the Calculator is displayed on the screen (see Figure 3.7).

Use the same point and click action to enter the number and operators (+, - , *, /, =, etc.) to the Calculator. After you are finished, close the Calculator by pointing and clicking on its Close control in the upper left-hand corner.

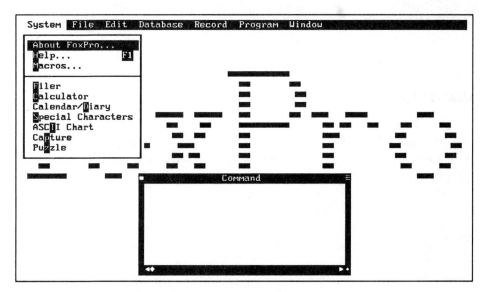

**Figure 3.6  Invoking the System Popup**

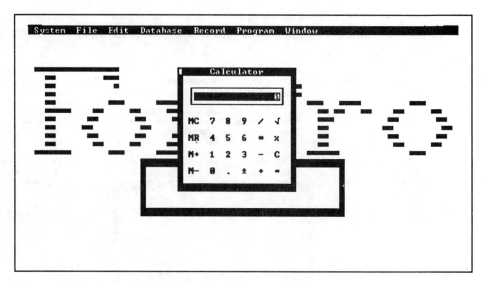

**Figure 3.7  Bringing Up the Calculator**

## Dragging

Dragging involves holding down the mouse button (again, in most cases, the left button) and simultaneously moving the mouse in the direction and distance desired. First point the mouse cursor at the location from which you want to move an object. Then drag the mouse to move and resize a window. If you want to move the Command window to a different location, for instance, first point the mouse cursor at the title bar (where the word Command appears) and then drag the mouse. As you drag the mouse, the window moves with it to a location of your choice.

## Double Clicking

Double clicking is the action of pressing the mouse button twice in rapid succession and then releasing it. In some cases, double clicking can serve as a shortcut to the point and click action. For example, you can select an object from a scrollable list in two ways: either point and click on an object to select it, and then point and click on a push button to confirm the selection; or, point the mouse cursor at the object and then double click the mouse button.

Try this exercise: Select a database file from the file directory; point and click the File menu pad. When the File menu popup appears, use the point and click action to select the Open option. As a result, the File Open dialog appears.

In Figure 3.8 you can see that a set of file directories is shown in brackets in a scrollable list. The Drive popup shows the current disk drive (C) and the current

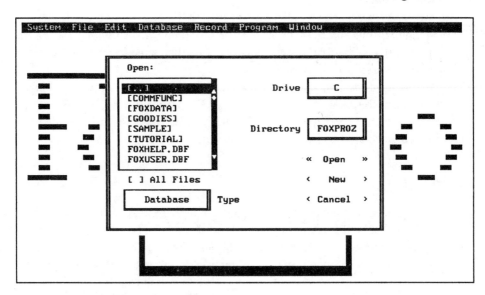

**Figure 3.8   The File Open Dialog**

directory (FOXPRO2) as indicated in the Directory popup. To open a file in one of the directories listed, select the directory by pointing and clicking on the one you want and then selecting the Open push button; or double click on the directory name in a single step. As an exercise, try double clicking on the TUTORIAL directory. Once you do, TUTORIAL will become the current directory, and all database files in it will be shown in a list box (see Figure 3.9).

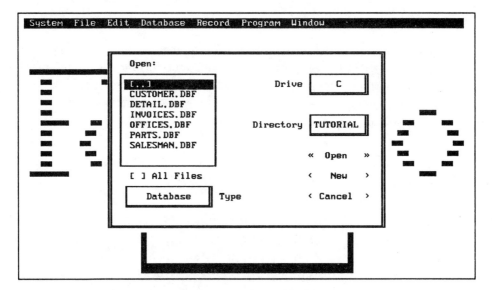

**Figure 3.9   Database Files in the Tutorial Subdirectory**

Notice in this figure that there are no scroll controls provided for the list box. This is because the list is short enough to be displayed in its entirety in the box; you do not need to scroll the list.

Now, if you would like to open a database file in the list, just double click on the name of the database file. To open the CUSTOMER database file, for instance, double click on the filename CUSTOMER.DBF. FoxPro will open the database file in a work area and return you to the initial screen.

## KEYBOARD BASICS

Although it is recommended that you have a mouse, the keyboard remains an important tool for using FoxPro. All of the operations that can be performed with a mouse can also be performed with the keyboard, although the latter may often be more cumbersome. However, for many data entry functions, you can use *only* the keyboard.

On the keyboard, in addition to the keys that you normally find, there is a set of keys specially designed for computer use. These keys, called function keys, are Esc, Alt, Ctrl, Shift, and Enter. Many of them are also used in conjunction with other keys.

There is another set of cursor keys, which include Home, End, PgUp (Page Up), PgDn (Page Down), and four arrow keys that are used for moving the cursor on the screen. These keys come in handy when you are editing data in a data table. They allow you to position your cursor at a specific location on the screen and edit the selected data items. Other useful editing keys are Ins (insert) and Del (delete).

### Function Keys

There are ten function keys on a standard computer keyboard and they are labeled F1 through F10 (some keyboards may have more than ten, although these extra keys are generally not functional). Function keys are programmed by FoxPro to perform certain predefined operations while you are in the program:

| Function Key | Function |
|---|---|
| F1 | Help |
| F2 | SET |
| F3 | LIST |
| F4 | DIR |
| F5 | DISPLAY STRUCTURE |
| F6 | DISPLAY STATUS |
| F7 | DISPLAY MEMORY |
| F8 | DISPLAY |
| F9 | APPEND F10 |
| F10 | Activate/Deactivate System menu bar |

Thus, if you press the F1 key when in FoxPro, the Help screen will appear. Depending on where you are in the program, it displays help messages pertinent to the current operation. Similarly, if you press F10, you activate or deactivate the menu bar. Other function keys are used for issuing FoxPro commands. Pressing F4, for example, is equivalent to issuing the DIR command in the Command window, and as a result, it displays the list of database files in the current directory.

## The Esc Key

The Esc key is usually used to exit from the current operation and return to your previous location. For example: If, after you have finished using the Calculator, you press the Esc key, you will exit from the Calculator and return to the System menu. You also can use Esc to abort the current operation. Say you are viewing your data in the Browse window and you want to abort the operation: Simply press the Esc key. Be aware, however, that if you do this, you interrupt the current operation and the actions you have already taken will be cancelled and results voided. So, if you were editing data in a data field in the Browse window before you pressed the Esc key, all the changes you made would not be recorded or saved.

## The Enter Key

The Enter key, which is also called the Return key, is similar to a carriage return on a normal typewriter. It signifies that you are at the end of a string of characters that you have entered. For example, when you are entering a data element to a data field, you press the Enter key to complete the field and move on to the next field.

In FoxPro, the Enter key is often used to accept or to confirm an action. To use it in this way, select an object from the menu, position the cursor at the object and then press the Enter key to accept it.

## Cursor Keys

Besides the mouse cursor (or mouse pointer), FoxPro maintains a second cursor in the form of a blinking dash. This is the keyboard cursor. It shows the location at which input from the keyboard will be placed.

The position of the keyboard cursor can be changed by using any of a number of cursor keys. These include the four arrow keys—the left arrow, right arrow, up arrow, and down arrow. When you press one of these keys, the cursor moves in the designated direction. But the distance you move depends on the operation on which you are working. For example, when editing data, pressing the left or right arrow keys moves you one character to the left or right respectively; pressing the up and down arrows moves you up or down one line. But there are exceptions to these rules. When a menu popup is displayed, for example, you still move up and down by pressing the up and down arrows, but if you press the left and right arrows at this time, the current menu popup is closed and the menu popup of the menu pad to the left or right of the current one is opened.

To move more than one line or one character at a time, use the PgUp, PgDn, Home, and End keys. By pressing the PgUp and PgDn keys you move respectively to the top and bottom of a data block, which may occupy the whole screen or only a section of the window. By pressing the Home and End keys you move to the beginning and end of a block that can be a data record or a data field, etc. Again, these keys are used to move the cursor to a different location depending on the mode you are in. For example, if you are viewing data in Browse mode, you would move to the top of the screen by pressing the PgUp key. You would jump from the beginning to the end of a data field by pressing the End key. Likewise, when you press the Home key you would jump from the end to the beginning of the data field.

## The Tab Key

The Tab key is used to move around objects in FoxPro. Each time you press the key, the cursor cycles from one object to another. Depending on where you are in a FoxPro session, the type of objects that you can cycle with the Tab key varies. In some cases, you can use the Tab key to cycle among the push buttons for performing certain operations. In others, you may move among the items in a table or list. In most cases, you can point to an object with the Tab key in the same way that you would with a mouse. The object of the current cursor is highlighted; to select the highlighted object, just press the Enter key.

## The Ctrl Key

The Ctrl (Control) key is always used in combination with one or more other keys for carrying out various operations. To show the current window on the whole screen with the zoom up action, press the F10 function key while holding down the Ctrl key. Such a key combination is represented in writing either as Ctrl+F10 or ^F10 (the upper arrow [^] symbol denotes the Ctrl key). If the Command window appears on the screen and the cursor appears somewhere within it, use the Ctrl+F10 to switch the window to a full-screen display. Press Ctrl+F10 again and the Command window returns to its original form.

## The Alt Key

Like the Ctrl key, the Alt key is always used together with one or more other keys. These key combinations are usually used to select a menu pad from the System menu bar by holding down the Alt key and pressing the highlighted letter in the menu pad name. As an exercise, press the Alt+F key combination to bring up the

File menu popup and press the Alt+W key combination to select the Window menu pad from the System menu bar.

## The Shift Key

In addition to using the Shift key to switch between upper- and lowercase, you also can use it with one or more other keys to perform certain functions. For example, pressing the Shift and one of the arrow keys enables you to select a block of text when you are in the editing mode. And, in the same way that you use the Tab key to cycle through objects on the screen from top to bottom and left to right, pressing the Shift+Tab key combination cycles you through the objects in a reverse direction, from bottom to top and from right to left.

## SETTING SCREEN COLORS

During the installation process you were asked to specify whether your monitor is color or monochrome. Depending on your response, FoxPro automatically chooses a set of default screen colors whenever you bring up the program. This color set determines the colors to be used to display various FoxPro objects such as windows, dialogs, reports, etc. But you can substitute the default color set with your own set of colors in two ways: Either select from given sets of screen colors the one that best suits your taste, or choose individual colors for each selectable screen object. The second alternative is a tedious process, to be sure, but this method means you can customize the screen colors to your exact specifications. For example, in order to reproduce the screen figures in a black-and-white scheme for this book, a set of custom colors were chosen. As a result, you may note minor variations in some screens between what you see on the screen and what you see reproduced on paper.

To define your own screen colors, first select the Color menu option from the Window popup. If you are using the mouse, point and click on the Window menu pad on the menu bar. With the keyboard, press the Alt+W key combination to do the same thing. Then, when the Window menu popup appears, select the Color menu option with your mouse or keyboard (see Figure 3.10).

In response to the menu option selection, the Color Picker dialog shown in Figure 3.11 appears. The Color Picker dialog enables you either to load a predefined color set or to specify the color for each item in a FoxPro display object.

To select a predefined color set, choose the <Load...> push button, and a list of color sets is displayed in the Color Sets dialog (see Figure 3.12). Choose any one of the displayed sets by double clicking the mouse on your choice. If you are using the keyboard, first use either the up or down arrow key to highlight the color set you want and then press the Enter key to accept it. You can experiment with the color sets until you find one that best suits your taste.

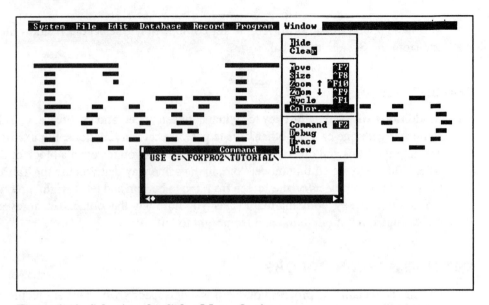

**Figure 3.10   Selecting the Color Menu Option**

If you decide not to use any of the predefined color sets, but rather to choose your own, first select the interface object whose color is to be defined from the popup that appears in the upper right-hand corner of the Color Picker dialog. Refer to Figure 3.11 and you can see that the currently selected object in the dialog popup is Windows. The center of the dialog displays a set of radio buttons, each of which

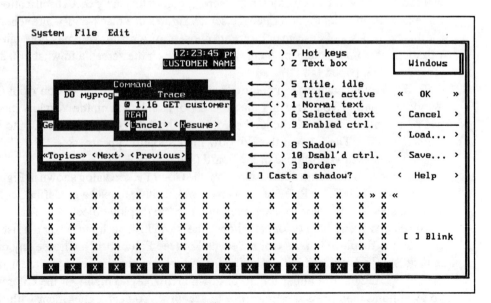

**Figure 3.11   The Color Picker Dialog**

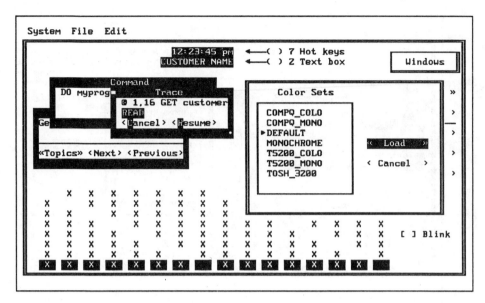

**Figure 3.12  Showing the Color Sets**

represents a particular element in a Windows interface object. The current item is indicated with a period in the radio button (e.g., Normal text in Figure 3.11). Use the mouse to point and click on any item whose color you want to define. If you are using the keyboard, use the Tab key to turn on the radio button and then press the Enter key to accept it.

Each item is displayed in one of the default colors, indicated by a color pattern in the color set shown at the bottom of the dialog. If you want to select a different color for any item, use the mouse to point and click on the color pattern of your choice; or use the arrow keys on the keyboard to select the color pattern after pressing the Spacebar once. After selecting the color, press the Enter key to accept your choice.

Once you have picked colors for all the items of an object, you can go on to select other objects (e.g., menu bar, menu popups, dialogs, dialog popups, etc.) from the dialog popup and define their colors. When you have finished defining the colors for all the objects, save the color set for later use by selecting the <Save...> push button. At this point, in the text box provided by the Color Sets dialog, you are asked to assign a name (up to ten characters long—e.g., MYCOLORS) to the color set you have just defined (see Figure 3.13). After the color set is named, select the <<Save>> push button to continue.

## SETTING UP PRINTERS

When you are in FoxPro, you can display your data and processed results on the screen or route them to a printer. But before using a printer you must tell FoxPro

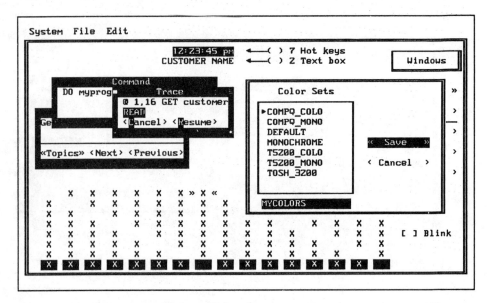

**Figure 3.13  Naming the Custom Color Set**

the kind of printer you intend to use, because each type of printer has its own operating characteristics that FoxPro has to know. Characteristics about specific printers are contained in a program file called a printer driver. A set of commonly used printer drivers was included at the time you installed the FoxPro program. It is from this set of printers that you activate the printer or printers that you are planning use. You can do this any time prior to using the printer. You also can set up one or more printers at a time and change them as often as you wish.

To set up printers, select the Printer Setup menu option from the File menu popup. When the Printer Setup dialog appears (see Figure 3.14), you'll see a popup from which to select the printer port and printing destination. In addition, there are options to turn on and off your printer and to set the left and right margins. At this point, ignore these settings and concentrate on setting up the printer(s) you need. You will learn how to use the other settings in later chapters.

To set up a printer driver, select the Printer Driver Setup check box by pointing and clicking your mouse on the check box. If you are using the keyboard, use the Tab key to highlight the check box and then press Enter to select it. As a result, it displays the Printer Driver Setups dialog (see Figure 3.15).

If you have not previously set up a printer driver, the selected printer driver list will be empty. If there are printer drivers that have been set up earlier, they will be displayed in the dialog. In either case, choose the <New> push button to add a new printer driver to the list of printers you intend to use later. Then the Printers dialog will be displayed (see Figure 3.16).

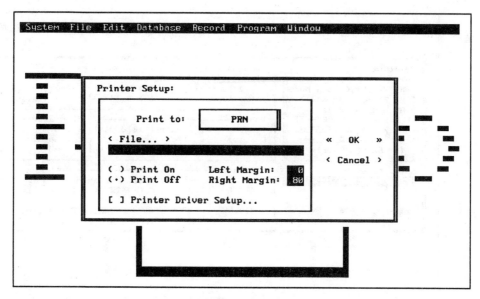

**Figure 3.14  The Printer Setup Dialog**

In the Printers dialog you will find the names of available printers shown in the scrollable list. To the right of the list is a set of radio buttons provided for specifying information about the printer, the printing options, etc. If you intend to use an HP LaserJet II printer, for example, you would select it from the scrollable list. If the printer you need is not visible on the list, scroll down or up using the arrow keys

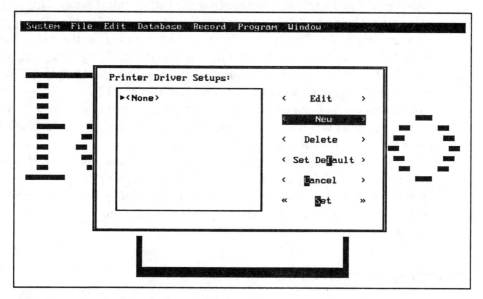

**Figure 3.15  The Printer Driver Setups**

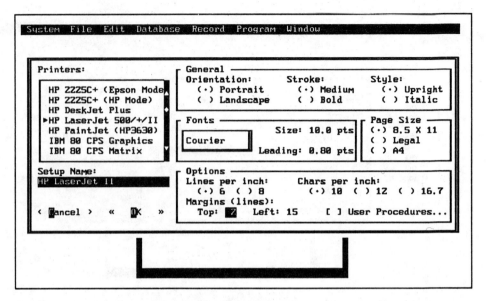

**Figure 3.16  Specifying Printer Characteristics**

to move the list. When the printer you want appears, point and click your mouse on it and then press the Enter key to accept it. If you are using the keyboard, first use the Tab key to highlight the first entry in the printer list and then use the up or down arrow keys to select the printer you need. Finally, press Enter to accept the selected printer.

After selecting the printer you need from the list, you must assign a name (e.g., HP LaserJet II in Figure 3.16) to the printer in the Setup Name text box that appears below the printer list. Finally, specify other printer settings in the dialog before selecting the <<OK>> push button to exit from the Printers dialog. When you return to the Printer Driver Setups you will see that the printer you have specified has been added to the selected printer driver list (see Figure 3.17).

To set up more than one printer driver, simply repeat the same process. You also can edit the printer driver list by choosing the <Edit> button, or remove a selected printer from the list by selecting the <Delete> push button.

Once you have finalized the printer list, set the one that you intend to use for your next printing job by pointing and double clicking on the printer of your choice. If you are using the keyboard, use the Tab key to first highlight the printer and then press the Enter key to accept it. Then select the <Set Default> push button to exit from the dialog.

## WORKING WITH WINDOWS

Because FoxPro offers a character-based windowing interface, windows play a very important role in FoxPro. Among other things, FoxPro opens a window to

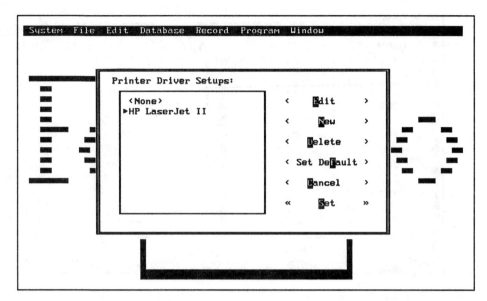

**Figure 3.17  The Selected Printer Driver**

allow you to browse or edit data. And windows are also used when you define data entry forms and reports. FoxPro windows are movable; that is, by clicking and dragging on a window's title bar, you can position it anywhere on the screen. FoxPro windows are also sizable; they can be maximized to take up the full screen (thus hiding other windows behind them) or sized both horizontally and vertically. This is particularly important because FoxPro allows you to have multiple windows open and displayed on the screen simultaneously. Then, to avoid a cluttered screen, you can reduce the size of your windows and position them in the way that you find most convenient. And, once you have finished using a window, you can clear it off the screen by closing it. It is important to note that, although you can have multiple windows open on the screen simultaneously, only one window may be active at a time.

## Opening Windows

There are a number of ways to bring up a window, and a common one is to select one or more menu options. For example, if you want to view the contents of an existing database file, you could open the Browse window by selecting the Browse menu option from the Database menu popup after you have opened the database file in a work area. Or you could first bring up the View window by choosing the View menu option from the Window menu popup, and, when it appears, open the database file in a work area and then select the <Browse> push button.

As an exercise, open the Browse window to display the contents of a sample database file named CUSTOMER in the Tutorial subdirectory. To do that, choose

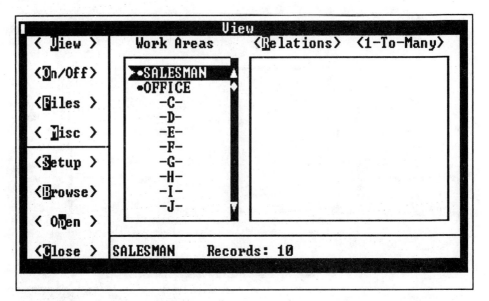

**Figure 3.18  The View Window**

the View menu option from the Window menu popup after you have selected the Window menu pad from the menu bar. In response to the menu selection you will see the View window appear on the screen (see Figure 3.18).

In the View window, select a work area in which to open your database file. If you want to open the CUSTOMER database file in work area A, for instance, double click your mouse on the work area. If you are using the keyboard, press the Enter key as work area A is highlighted. Next you are asked to select the database file to be opened in that work area. Since we already selected the Tutorial subdirectory (see Figure 3.9), a list of database files in that subdirectory is displayed in the Select Database dialog. At this point, select the CUSTOMER.DBF file from the database list by double clicking your mouse on that file, or use the Tab and down arrow keys to highlight the database file and then press Enter to open the file (see Figure 3.19).

When you return to the View window, the CUSTOMER database file you have selected will be open in work area A. To view the contents of that file, select the <Browse> push button by clicking your mouse once on that button. On the keyboard, use the Tab key to highlight the push button and press Enter to accept it. As a result, you will see the contents of the CUSTOMER database file displayed in a Browse window in Browse mode, which is a columnar format (see Figure 3.20). If your screen shows the database file in Change mode (in which data fields are displayed in rows), you can switch to Browse mode by selecting the Browse option from the Browse menu popup. Do not be concerned if the location and size of your window on the screen differ from that shown in Figure 3.20. You will be able to relocate and resize it later.

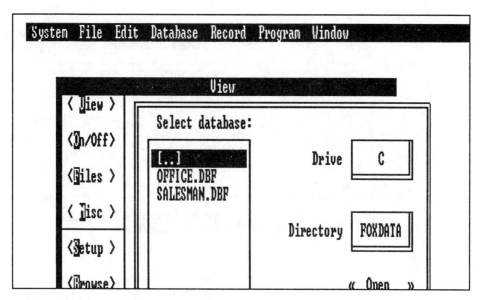

**Figure 3.19  Selecting a Database File**

## Moving Windows

Because FoxPro allows you to have several windows displayed on the screen at one time, some may be hidden and overlapped by others. You can reveal the hidden windows by moving them around on the screen with your mouse or by using the keyboard.

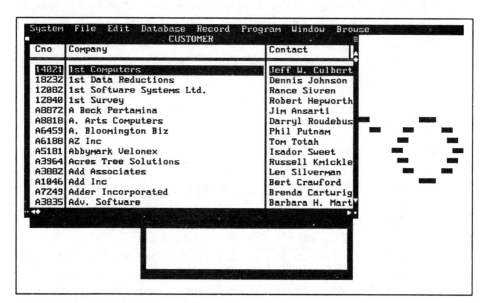

**Figure 3.20  Viewing Data in the Browse Window**

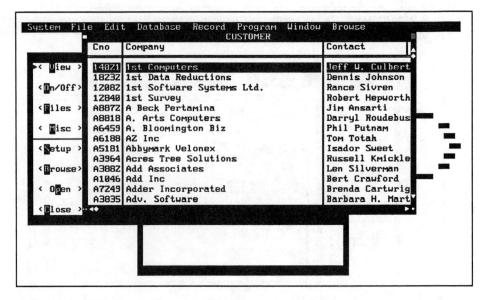

**Figure 3.21  Moving the Browse Window**

To move a window with the mouse, point it on the title bar of the window and then drag it to a new location. To move the CUSTOMER window to the right, for example, point the mouse on the title bar (where the database filename CUSTOM appears) and then drag it to the right.

If you are using the keyboard, select the Move option from the Window menu. Then, instead of selecting the menu option, just press the Ctrl+F7 key combination. As a result, the border of the window begins to blink. Now move the window in the desired direction by using the cursor keys; in this case, the right arrow key. When you are done, press the Enter key to accept the new window location (see Figure 3.21).

## Sizing Windows

The size of a window also can be changed either with the mouse or the keyboard. You can make the window shorter, longer, narrower, wider, smaller, or larger. Experiment making the CUSTOMER Browse window shorter and longer by pointing the mouse on the Size control (at the lower right-hand corner of the window) and then dragging it up and down, respectively. To make the window narrower and wider, drag the mouse to the left and right accordingly. The window becomes smaller (shorter and narrower at the same time) when you drag the mouse to the upper left, and larger (longer and wider) when you drag the mouse to the lower right.

To make these size changes using the keyboard, select the Size option from the Window menu popup or press the Ctrl+F8 key combination and wait for the

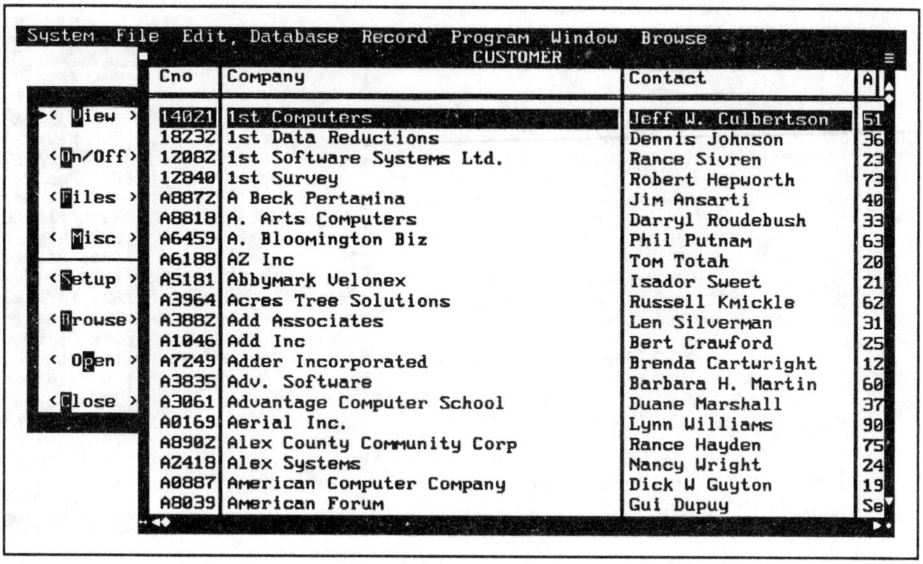

```
 System  File  Edit  Database  Record  Program  Window  Browse
                                    CUSTOMER
        Cno   Company                        Contact              A
 <  View  > 14021 1st Computers              Jeff W. Culbertson   51
          18232 1st Data Reductions          Dennis Johnson       36
 <On/Off> 12082 1st Software Systems Ltd.    Rance Sivren         23
          12840 1st Survey                   Robert Hepworth      73
 <Files > A8872 A Beck Pertamina             Jim Ansarti          40
          A8818 A. Arts Computers            Darryl Roudebush     33
 < Misc  > A6459 A. Bloomington Biz          Phil Putnam          63
          A6188 AZ Inc                       Tom Totah            20
 <Setup > A5181 Abbymark Velonex             Isador Sweet         21
          A3964 Acres Tree Solutions         Russell Kmickle      62
 <Browse> A3882 Add Associates               Len Silverman        31
          A1046 Add Inc                      Bert Crawford        25
 < Open  > A7249 Adder Incorporated          Brenda Carturight    12
          A3835 Adv. Software                Barbara H. Martin    60
 <Close > A3061 Advantage Computer School    Duane Marshall       37
          A0169 Aerial Inc.                  Lynn Williams        90
          A8902 Alex County Community Corp   Rance Hayden         75
          A2418 Alex Systems                 Nancy Wright         24
          A0887 American Computer Company    Dick W Guyton        19
          A8039 American Forum               Gui Dupuy            Se
```

**Figure 3.22  Resizing the Browse Window**

window border to begin to blink. Then press the up and left arrow keys to make the window shorter and narrower, and the down and right arrows to make the window longer and wider (see Figure 3.22).

## Maximizing Windows

You can enlarge the window to its maximum size thereby displaying the window contents on the whole screen. So, if you want to use the full screen to display the contents of the CUSTOMER database file, click your mouse on the Zoom control at the upper right-hand corner of the window; or, on the keyboard, choose the Zoom up-arrow option from the Window popup or press the Ctrl+F10 key combination. As a result, the Browse window fills the whole screen (see Figure 3.23).

To return the maximized window to its original size, click the mouse on the Zoom control again or, on the keyboard, select the Zoom up-arrow option from the Window menu popup or press the Ctrl-F10 key combination again.

## Minimizing Windows

The opposite—minimizing windows—also can be achieved, usually in order to free up screen space to show other objects without closing the minimized windows. When a window is minimized it is displayed in a small block that is one line high and 18 characters long.

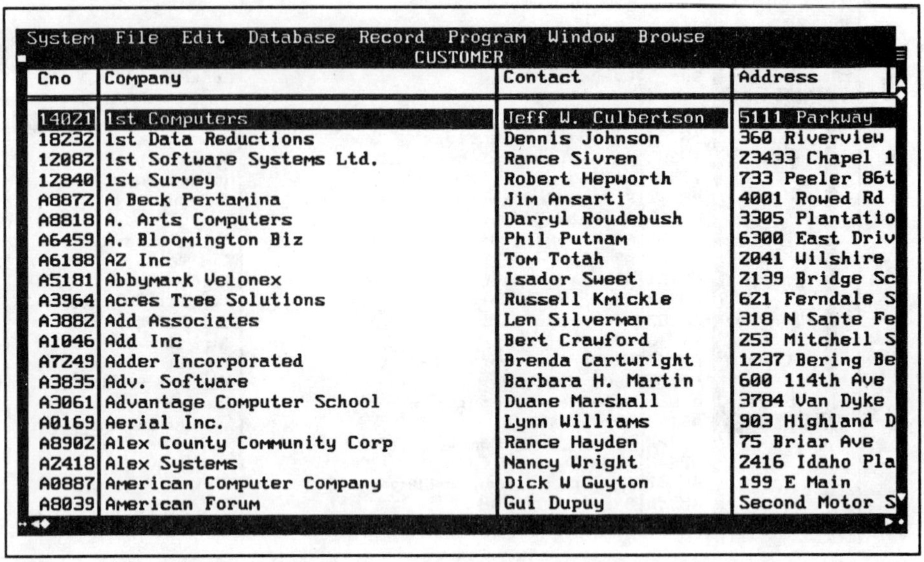

**Figure 3.23  Maximizing the Browse Window**

To minimize a window, point the mouse on the title bar of the window you would like to shrink and double click on it. To continue with our sample, minimize the CUSTOMER browse window by double clicking your mouse on its title bar. If you are using the keyboard, select the Zoom down-arrow option from the Window menu popup or press the Ctrl+F9 key combination. You'll see the CUSTOMER Browse window displayed as the small block just described (see Figure 3.24).

To return the minimized window to its original size, double click the mouse on the window; or, on the keyboard, select the Zoom down-arrow option from the Window menu popup or press the Ctrl+F9 key combination.

## Stacking Windows

There will probably be times when you are working with several windows on the screen at the same time and you will want to minimize and stack them somewhere on the screen to free up screen space. To do that, first minimize the windows and then rearrange them in a stack. Use the procedure described previously to minimize the CUSTOMER Browse window and the View window. After they are minimized, move them around so that they form a stack on the screen (see Figure 3.25).

In Figure 3.25 you can see that the CUSTOMER and View windows have been minimized and stacked in the lower left-hand corner of the screen so that the Command window is revealed.

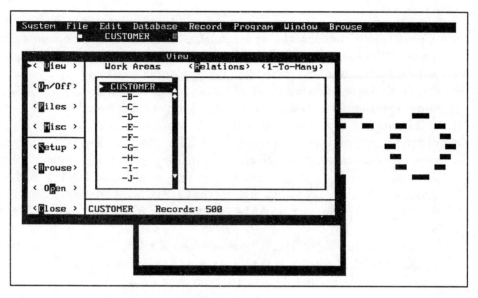

**Figure 3.24 Minimizing the Browse Window**

## Activating Windows

When you have several windows open on the screen at the same time, only one window may be active. The active window is indicated by the appearance of its title and its Close and Zoom controls. The title of the active window is always

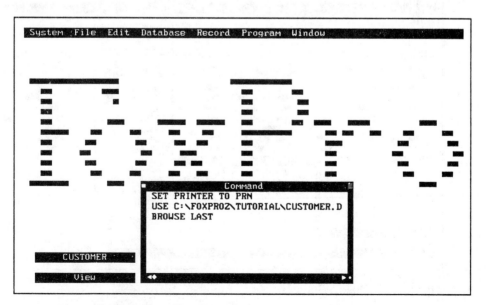

**Figure 3.25 Stacking Minimized Windows**

highlighted, and its Close and Zoom controls are always visible. In contrast, the titles of inactive windows are not highlighted and their window controls are not visible. If the windows overlap, the active one is always displayed in the foreground and the inactive windows are hidden in the background. In Figure 3.25 you can see that the Command window is active because its Close and Zoom controls appear on the upper left-hand and upper right-hand corners of the window.

It is simple to activate a window if its title bar or its border is visible—just click on the bar or the border. Otherwise, move the window that's in the foreground to reveal the hidden one. Alternatively, you can bring up the Window menu popup to select the window you want. For example, while the CUSTOMER and View windows are inactive, you will find that the CUSTOMER window is displayed at the bottom of the window popup when you select the Window menu pad (see Figure 3.26).

To activate the CUSTOMER Browse window, select it from the menu popup. Activate the View window in the same manner. Once this is done, you can return them to their original size if they have been minimized.

## Closing Windows

After you have finished using a window you can erase it from the screen by closing it. Either click the mouse on the Close control that appears in the upper left-hand corner of the screen; or, if you are using the keyboard, press the Esc key.

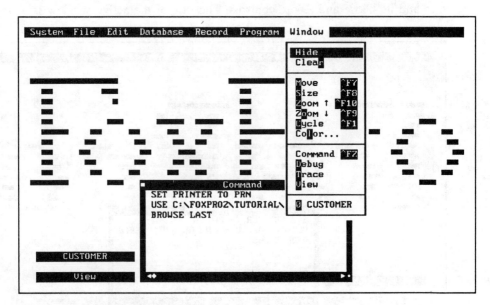

**Figure 3.26  Open Windows**

# Getting Help

If you need help while you are in FoxPro, press the F1 function key. Most help is context-sensitive, meaning that the help messages returned by FoxPro are related to the subject you are working with when you press the function key. Thus, if you press F1 while you are viewing a database's contents in a Browse window, a help message regarding the process of browsing appears (see Figure 3.27). Use the scroll controls to reveal the portion of the message that is hidden from view when it is too long to be displayed in the window.

The Help window contains four push buttons—<<Topics>>, <Next>, <Previous>, and <Look Up>. Use the default button, <<Topics>>, to select another subject that you need help with by using the mouse or pressing the Enter key. <Next> moves you to the next help subject in the list, and <Previous> returns you to the previous help subject.

The <Look Up> push button displays a help message about a topic invoked by the highlighting of a keyword or phrase. For example, if you would like to find information about Popup, you would highlight the word "topic" on the screen and then choose the <Look Up> push button. You can highlight the keyword of the topic by using the mouse or the keyboard. If you are using a mouse, point on the beginning of the keyword and then drag it to the end of the word. With the keyboard, move the cursor to the beginning of the keyword and then press the right arrow key so that it passes over the word while you are holding the Shift key. As an

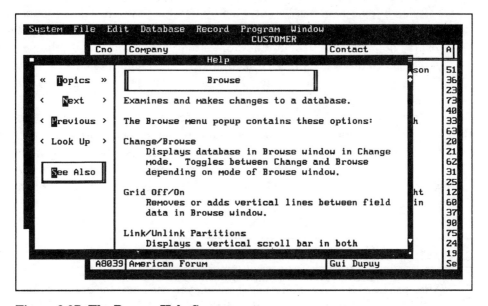

**Figure 3.27  The Browse Help Screen**

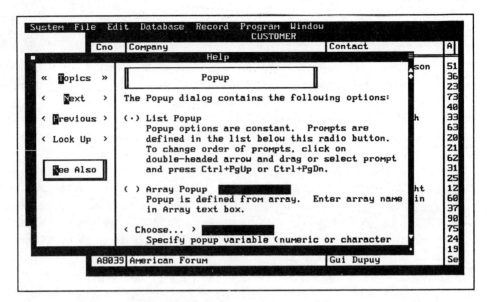

**Figure 3.28  The Popup Help Message**

exercise, highlight the word "popup" in the Help window (in the second line of the Browse help message in Figure 3.27) with the mouse or keyboard and then select the <Look Up> push button. A help message about Popup appears in another Help window (see Figure 3.28).

Related topic help can be accessed by invoking the See Also popup. Thus, while you are in the Popup Help window, you can select the See Also popup to display help messages about other topics that are related to the help messages you are currently viewing. To select the See Also popup, click your mouse on the popup or use the Tab key to first highlight it and then accept it by pressing the Enter key.

Note in Figure 3.29 that, among other topics, it lists Browse, where you were before bringing up the Popup Help window. If you select the Browse option from the popup at this point, you will return to the previous Browse Help window.

Once you have finished reading the help messages you selected, exit the Help window either by pressing the Esc key or by pointing and clicking your mouse on the Close control.

## Exiting FoxPro

After you have completed a FoxPro session, you can leave the program and return to DOS only by choosing the Quit option from the File menu popup. *Do not exit*

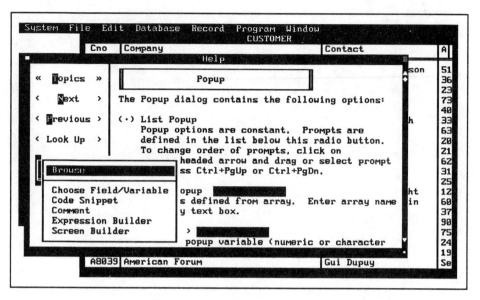

**Figure 3.29  Displaying Messages About Related Topics**

*the program by turning off or rebooting (pressing Ctrl+Alt+Del key combination) the computer. Failure to exit the program properly will damage your database files and you risk losing valuable data.*

# Chapter Summary

This chapter prepared you to make efficient use of the tools provided by FoxPro for designing and developing a database management system. You learned how to customize screen colors and to set up printers correctly. You also became familiar with the basic techniques for using either the mouse or keyboard to work with the FoxPro menu system and the Windows interface. In the next chapter you will begin using these techniques to create your database files.

# 4

# Creating Databases

## An Overview

You are now ready to begin to develop a relational database, and this chapter will show you the correct procedures for setting up data tables to hold your data elements.

Defining the structure of a data table is the first step. The structuring procedure involves identifying and specifying all of the attributes of the data fields that you would like to include in the data table. The differences in the character of your data elements require that you set up different data fields to accommodate these various types of data.

The first part of this chapter describes the types of data fields and how to define them when structuring a database. Once a table structure is properly defined, data can be entered; the procedure for entering data into data tables is covered in the latter part of the chapter. All of these procedures are explained and illustrated in detail by incorporating some of the data tables introduced in Chapter 1. You are advised to take a hands-on approach, following these steps as you read.

## Defining the Data Structure

As defined in Chapter 1, a data table is the basic unit of a relational database. It is where all of the data elements associated with a data entity in a data table are stored. You may recall from Chapter 1 that data columns are also called data fields. They form the segments of the data structure that accommodate those data elements describing the properties of the data entity.

## IDENTIFYING DATA FIELDS

The first step in structuring your data table is to identify its data fields. Each data field is chosen to describe a unique property of the data entry associated with the table. For example, the Salesman table introduced in Chapter 1 has the following columns:

Identification Number
Last Name
First Name
Hire Date
Monthly Salary

Each of these columns describes a property about each salesperson and will therefore be structured as a data field in the Salesman table. And, as just noted, because the types of data elements to be saved in the table are different, the data fields must be set up with different attributes. For instance, the first three data fields are set up to accommodate strings of alphabetic and numeric characters only. A different format must be used to hold the hire dates. The salary data field can hold only numeric values, so it has to be set up in yet another way. In addition to these types of data fields, there are other kinds of data fields—logical and memo fields—that are necessary for many data structures. In order to demonstrate how they are set up, let's add the following two data fields to the Salesman table:

Commission status—called COMMISSION
Reference note—called NOTE

The commission status column reveals whether or not a salesperson is compensated with commission; the reference note field holds information such as the hobbies and educational background (or any other pertinent data) about each salesperson.

## DEFINING DATA FIELD ATTRIBUTES

Once you have identified the necessary data fields for your table you can define the attributes for each of these fields. The attributes of a data field are: the name of the field, the type of data to be stored in the field, and the size or width of the data field.

A field name is used to refer to the columns as a whole.The field's data type determines how the data field can be used, as well as the format in which the data is stored in the database. For example, the data elements in the LAST and FIRST name character fields will probably be used only as textual information for identifying a salesperson, while values in the salary field will most likely be used for computations and to provide summary statistics; dates will be used for still other purposes. Finally, the size or width of a field determines the number of characters or numbers that can be stored to it.

## Naming a Data Field

The rules governing the naming of a data field may vary among different database software, but we are only concerned with the conventions prescribed by FoxPro 2.0. Its rules state that a field name can be no more than 10 characters long. It can be made up of a combination of alphabetic letters, numeric digits, and underscores (_), but it must begin with a letter; blank spaces *cannot* be included in a field name, nor can most symbols such as commas, periods, dollar signs, colons, semi-colons, and question marks.

You should always try to create names that help to define the nature of the data elements, and make them as descriptive as possible. Obviously, due to the width limit, you may need to abbreviate them; and, if the name includes more than one word, separate them with underscores for clarity (e.g. AREA_CODE, ACCT_NAME, etc.).

If your database has more than one data table, assign unique field names to them. For example, use SALESMAN_ID in the Salesman table and OFFICE_ID in the Office table. Avoid using just ID or ID_NO to represent the identification number fields for both the Salesman and Office tables. And, although it is not against FoxPro 2.0 rules for naming fields, it is just good practice not to duplicate field names in the same database in order to avoid confusing yourself.

When alphabetic letters are included in a field name, case is ignored. All alphabetic characters are automatically converted by FoxPro 2.0 to uppercase. Here are some examples of acceptable field names, some of which you've seen used already in this book:

SALSMAN_ID
ACCOUTNAME
ACCT_NAME
HIRE_DATE
ADDRESS_1
ADDRESS_2
BIRTHDATE
AREA_CODE
PHONE_NO
UNIT_COST

## Specifying Field Type

As already stated, different types of data elements are saved in different formats in data fields. A salesperson's monthly salary takes the form of a number, like 2500, while a date value is normally expressed as 07/04/91. You must tell the program what type of data elements you intend to store in each field, and there are seven different types of data fields from which you can choose to hold your data elements. They are:

| | |
|---|---|
| C | Character Fields |
| N | Numeric Fields |
| D | Date Fields |
| L | Logical Fields |
| M | Memo Fields |
| F | Float Fields |
| P | Picture Fields |

Of these seven data fields, you probably will be concerned with only the first five, the most common ones. The float data field is designed for saving scientific data when very large or very small values are involved. You can do without this type of data field in most business-related applications, as most numbers you would encounter can be accommodated by the regular numeric data fields. Picture fields are reserved for holding graphic images which can only be generated outside of FoxPro 2.0 (coverage of these fields is beyond the scope of this book).

### Character Fields

A character data field is used to hold a string of characters consisting of a combination of alphabetic letters; numeric digits; and symbols, which include most of the punctuation marks and symbols that you would find on a regular computer keyboard. Any foreign alphabet and graphic symbols for drawing boxes and borders can also be included.

A maximum of 254 characters can be stored in a character field. Examples of character strings are sales staff identification numbers, addresses of customers, first and last names of individuals, telephone numbers, etc. The string in a character field is used primarily for holding textual information; it cannot be used for calculation.

### Numeric Fields

Numeric fields hold numbers in data tables. Numbers can take the form of integers or values with decimal points. Any values used in business applications can be stored in these fields; negative values are expressed with leading minus signs.

Although it is necessary to display monetary values with dollar signs and grouped by commas (e.g., $123,4456.78) in your reports, dollar signs or commas cannot be included in a numeric field. They must be added to the screen display or reports as needed.

The maximum width of a numeric field is 20, including a place for the plus or minus sign and for the decimal point. You can specify the desired number of places after the decimal point, in order to include, for example, the values of 123.45 or -123.45, which occupies six and seven places respectively in a numeric field with two places after the decimal point. Data elements stored in numeric fields can be used in formulas for calculations and for providing summary statistics.

### Date Fields

Date fields are used to save calendar dates. Each date is always stored in a field with a length of 8 characters in the form of YYYYMMDD, where MM/DD/YYYY are formats representing month, day and year respectively. The default format for entering dates is mm/dd/yy. But you also can display dates in formats such as DD-MM-YY, YY.MM.DD, or MM/DD/YYYY.

In addition to representing calendar dates, dates can be used in calculations. You can compute, for example, the number of days between any two dates by taking the difference of the two dates (e.g., DATE1 – DATE2). You will learn more about this capability later.

### Logical Fields

A logical field is a special kind of data field for saving answers to a true/false (yes/no) type of question. It occupies only a one-character width in the form of T (true) or F (false). Say you want to store the answer to the question, "Is (a given salesperson) compensated with commission?" A logical field would be used to save T (for yes) or F (for no). You also can use this type of field to hold answers regarding whether an employee is male or female, an account is invoiced or not, etc. Logical fields play a very significant role in a data structure. When properly defined, they provide a useful means for efficiently categorizing data elements.

### Memo Fields

Memo fields are set up to hold text information. They can hold character strings composed of the same elements as defined for character fields. Generally, character strings stored in memo fields are used for reference purposes. A memo field occupies a 10-character width in a table structure, but the actual contents of the memo field are saved in a separate file instead of in the data table where the field is defined.

Note that although FoxPro 2.0 allows you to find a substring in a memo field, its primary purpose is not for query operations. Character fields are better candidates for those operations because searching a large memo field can be a very slow process and the number of ways in which you can manipulate a memo field is very limited.

## Creating a Data Table

With the basic components of a data structure in mind, let's create a data table. We'll call it SALESMAN and it will consist of the following data fields with the following attributes:

| Field Name | Field Type | Field Width | |
| --- | --- | --- | --- |
| SALSMAN_ID | Character | 3 | |
| LAST | Character | 8 | |
| FIRST | Character | 8 | |
| HIRE_DATE | Date | 8 | |
| SALARY | Numeric | 5 | 0 (decimal places) |
| COMMISSION | Logical | 1 | |
| NOTE | Memo | 10 | |

Table names used in this book have, until now, been spelled with initial capitalization only, e.g., Salesman, Office, Region, etc. These are ordinary descriptive names assigned to a proper object. From this point on, however, in order to follow the naming convention adopted by FoxPro 2.0, all uppercase letters will be used for the names of actual data tables and their data fields.

Notice above that the first data field is named SALSMAN_ID instead of SALESMAN_ID in order to stay within the 10-character width limitation; abbreviation is necessary here. The fields LAST and FIRST refer to the sales staff's first and last names. For now, we are ignoring middle initials. They will be added to the database structure later. As an example of readability in naming conventions, note the underscore (_) used to separate the two words in the HIRE_DATE field. Of course, it could have been called HIREDATE as well. And recall from the beginning of the chapter that COMMISSION is the logical field that identifies the commission status of each saleperson, and NOTE stores reference information about the sales staff.

The procedure for setting up a data structure with these data fields involves the following steps:

Opening a new database file
Defining the structure
Assigning a name to the table
Saving the structure

## OPENING A NEW DATABASE FILE

To set up a new database file, begin by selecting the File option from the menu pad. (Refer to Chapter 3 if you need to refresh your memory regarding the steps used to select an option from the menu pad with a mouse or the keyboard. You may also want to review the procedures to open a window, enter text in a dialog box, and select and use the control buttons. Knowledge of these procedures is necessary for setting up a new data table.) After selecting the menu option, a menu popup is displayed. From that, select the Open option and then specify the type of file you would like to open (see Figure 4.1).

In this instance, because the default is a database file, you need not select a file type; simply press the Enter key to accept the default. If you are using a mouse, point its cursor on the OK button and then click once to accept the default file type.

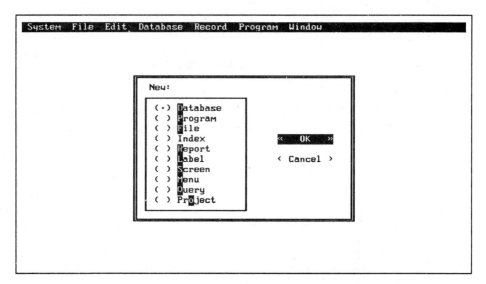

**Figure 4.1  Setting up a New Database File**

(If you decide not to create a new database, return to the previous step by choosing the Cancel option. If you are using a mouse, just point its cursor on the <Cancel> button and click once. On the keyboard, press the Esc key.)

## SPECIFYING FIELD ATTRIBUTES

Once you have accepted the default option, a dialog box showing a data structure definition form appears, as shown in Figure 4.2. This form provides the space in which to enter the attributes for all the data fields you intend to include in the table.

The screen also shows the name of the structure. Note that currently it is labeled "Untitled" in the upper left-hand corner. You will be asked later to assign a name to the table.

At the bottom of the form FoxPro displays some statistics on the database you are now defining. There are also two push buttons <<OK>> and <Cancel>. <<OK>> lets you accept the structure after you have completed defining it. You can always quit this step and exit the procedure by using the <Cancel> push button or by pressing the Esc key on your keyboard.

Once in this form, you can specify your data fields. Begin by typing in the name of the first data field, followed by the field type, and the appropriate width. To continue with the creation of the SALESMAN table, enter SALSMAN_ID as the first field name; then press the Enter key. The cursor moves to the column for defining field type. Here the default field type "Character" is shown. To accept this, press the Tab or the right arrow key, which moves the cursor to the Width

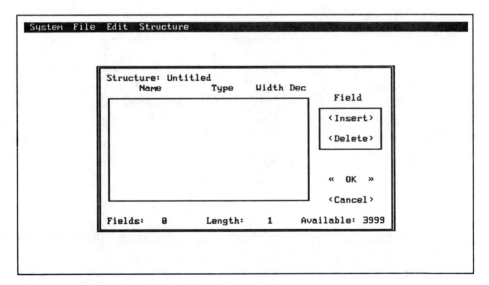

**Figure 4.2  Data Structure Definition Form**

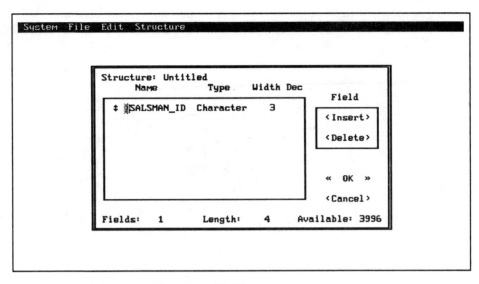

**Figure 4.3 Defining the First Data Field**

column. The default width of 10 appears for the width field. To change it, just type in the desired width. In this case, enter 3 and then press the Enter key. You have now finished defining the first data field. It should look like Figure 4.3.

In general, when determining the width of a character field, you should plan ahead by anticipating the maximum number of characters you might need for your data elements in that field. FoxPro 2.0 then uses that fixed number of characters that you define in the structure to hold your character strings. That is, regardless of the number of characters a string may actually have, the field will always occupy a fixed number of characters. Unused spaces become blank spaces in the data table, while extra characters become truncated. You should keep the field width as small as possible in order to conserve disk space and reduce processing time. Do not worry about setting it too small now, however, as it can be changed later.

If you make mistakes in entering the field names and field widths, use the left and right arrow keys to move around in the row and make the necessary corrections. Pressing the Tab key moves you one column to the right; the Shift+Tab key moves you one column to the left. With a mouse, point and click the cursor on the spot at which you would like to make a correction and then type in the changes.

Now define the second (LAST) and third (FIRST) fields. Because they are all character fields you can follow the procedure you used to define the SALS-MAN_ID field. To specify the HIRE_DATE field, however, you must choose a date field instead of the default character field. To do that, either press D or select Date from the Field Type Picker dialog box (see Figure 4.4).

The width of a date field is always set to 8 characters. Just press the Enter key to accept the date type and move on to the next field.

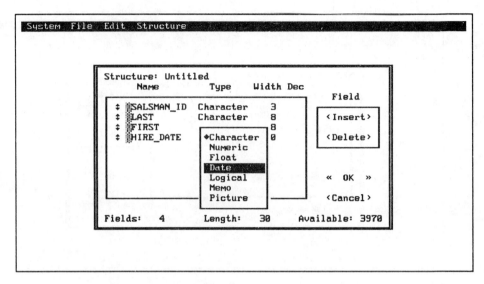

**Figure 4.4  Selecting a Date Field Type**

To define COMMISSION, enter L to specify a logical field. Remember that the width of a logical field is always set to 1 by FoxPro.

When you define the numeric SALARY field, specify the field width as 5 with 0 decimal places. By specifying the number of decimal places as 0, you are indicating that the salary values are to be treated as integers. Otherwise, you would set Dec to 2 to accommodate the dollar and cents format for most monetary values.

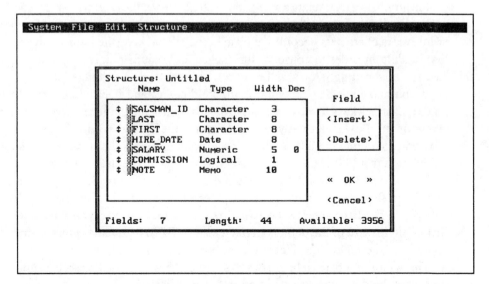

**Figure 4.5  Data Structure for SALESMAN Table**

The NOTE memo field is automatically set to a width of 10. Press the Enter key to accept it. This completes the definition process for the structure of the SALES-MAN table (see Figure 4.5).

If, when you are defining fields, you find you have skipped one by mistake, you can insert a new column at the cursor position. First position the cursor in the field *below* where you want to insert the field. Then choose the <Insert> push button. In response to the button selection, a new space will open up for defining the new field. Similarly, you can delete a field at the current cursor position by choosing the <Delete> push button.

## SAVING A DATA STRUCTURE

To save the structure you have just defined, select the OK response to continue by pointing your mouse cursor on the OK button and clicking it once; or press the Tab key to move your cursor to the OK button and press Enter to accept it.

Now you are required to assign a name to the database file. The next screen will ask you in the lower left-hand corner of the dialog box for the database name. Type in the table name SALESMAN (see Figure 4.6).

The dialog box also shows you the disk drive (C) and the directory (FOXDATA) to which to save your table. The default disk drive and directory are shown in the Drive and Directory popup controls in the upper right-hand corner. (Setting up the default drive and directory were covered in Chapter 3.)

To change to a different disk drive, open a Drive Picker dialog box and select the drive you want. With a mouse, point its cursor on the Drive popup control and

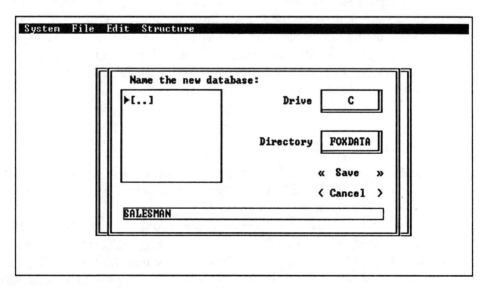

**Figure 4.6  Naming the Database File**

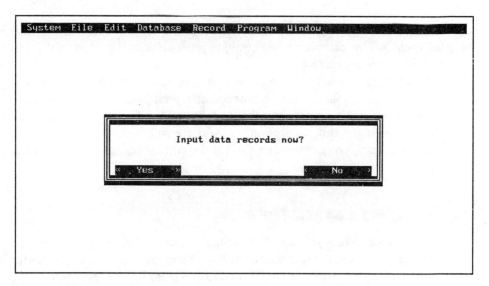

**Figure 4.7  Request for Data Input**

hold down the mouse button and drag it to the desired disk drive; then release the button. From the keyboard, press the Tab key until the Drive popup control is highlighted, then press the Enter key to open the Drive Picker box. Finally, use the cursor key to select the desired disk drive. Use the same procedure to select a different directory from the Directory popup control.

Assuming for now that you intend to save the SALESMAN table to the default disk drive and directory, choose the Save button. Of course you can go back to the previous step by pressing the Esc key from the keyboard, or by choosing the <Cancel> button with your mouse. After selecting Save, a data table named SALESMAN with the structure you have specified is saved to the disk. You are then asked in a dialog box whether or not you intend to begin entering data values in the table (see Figure 4.7).

## ENTERING DATA VALUES

If you decide to enter data to the SALESMAN data table at this point, select Yes as the response to the prompt, "Input data records now?" A default data entry form is displayed (see Figure 4.8).

Data can now be entered into the table, one record at a time. Begin by typing the data value (S0) in the first data field, SALSMAN_ID. Next type Anderson in the LAST field, Doris in the FIRST field. Enter a numeric value (2800) in the SALARY field. (Don't forget: Do not include a dollar sign or commas in the salary figure. If you make a mistake, use the left or right arrow key to move within a data

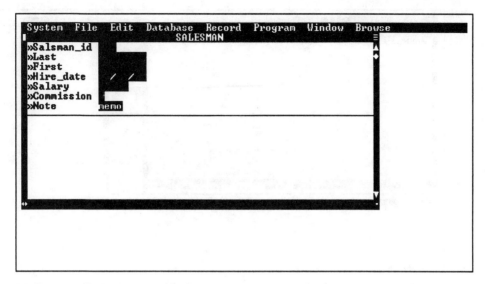

**Figure 4.8 Default Data Entry Form**

field, or use the up or down arrow key to move between data fields to make the corrections. With a mouse, point to the particular position and click to make any changes.)

When you come to the COMMISSION logical field, you'll see the default value of F in the field. To accept the default, enter F; otherwise, type in T (see Figure 4.9). You *must enter either F or T* in this field or the value will not be displayed later in the table. You cannot just press the Enter key to accept the default F value.

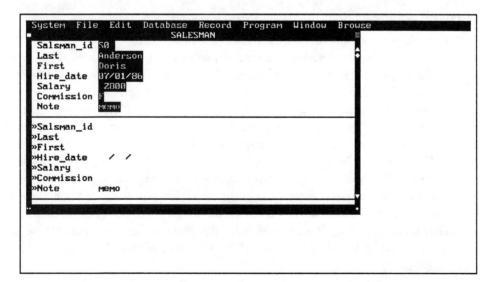

**Figure 4.9 Entering Data to Character, Date, and Numeric Fields**

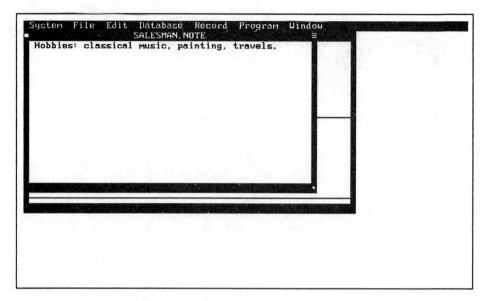

**Figure 4.10  Entering Text to a Memo Field**

The procedure for entering text in a memo field differs slightly from that for other fields. When you move the cursor to the memo field, the field will show "memo," indicating the type of data field. To enter text in that field, you must use a text editor. To open the text editor with a mouse, point its cursor on the memo field and click the button twice. On the keyboard, press the Ctrl+Home key combination while the cursor is resting on the memo field. As a result, a text box is opened. The top of the box shows the name of the data table and the memo field with a period separating them (SALESMAN.NOTE). At this point, type in the text that you want to save to the memo field (see Figure 4.10).

Once you have entered all the text you want, close the box with the mouse by clicking the Close box control button. On the keyboard, press the Ctrl+W key combination. Once the text box is closed, you are returned to the data entry form. At this point, notice that the memo field displays "Memo" (instead of "memo" as before) in the field. This change indicates that there is something stored in that field; "memo" shows the memo field is empty.

Now you can clearly see that the actual text in the memo field is not shown with the rest of the field values. To view its entire contents again, reopen the text editor. Stay in the text editor to enter the next data record by repeating the same procedure. The contents of the memo fields for the ten records in the SALESMAN table are shown in Figure 4.11. It is recommended that you enter the contents of these fields in your SALESMAN table as shown, as they will be used for exercises in later chapters.

```
Salesman   Contents of the NOTE data field

Anderson   Hobbies: classical music, painting, travels.
Bell       Hobbies: fishing, hunting, country music.
Carter     Education: BA, Bus. Admin.; University of Washington, 1985.
Davidson   Citizenship: Canadian.
Evans      Education: BA, Marketing; UCLA, 1986.
Ford       Hobbies: classical music, sailing, travel.
Gilbert    Hobbies: classical music, opera, foreign travel.
Harvey     Hobbies: ballet, classical music, travel.
Iverson    Hobbies: hunting, fishing, sailing.
Jones      Education: BA, Social Studies; University of Oregon, 1987.
```

**Figure 4.11  Contents of Memo Fields**

## Entering Data in Change Mode

The default data form provides space in which to enter data for a new record. This is Change mode. In this mode, the number of records that you can view at a single time on the same screen depends on the number of data fields there are per record and the size of the open window. As discussed in Chapter 3, the window can be enlarged to show the maximum number of records at a time. In our example, you can fit three records per screen (see Figure 4.12).

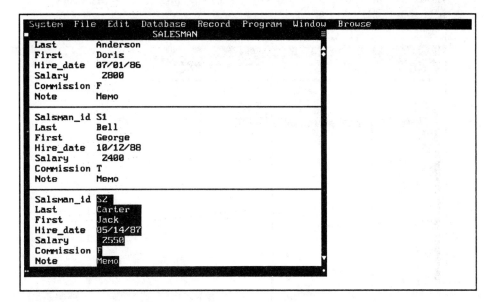

**Figure 4.12  Entering Data in Change Mode**

Press the Enter key after entering data in the last field of the third record. The form will scroll up, providing space to enter values for the next record.

In Change mode each data field is shown as a line in the data entry form. All the data fields for a record are grouped and separated from the next record by a horizontal line. When you are in Change mode, it is usually possible to see the complete contents of the record being entered unless the fields are too long or too numerous to fit on the same screen. But you can view only a limited number of records at any one time on the screen.

## Entering Data in Browse Mode

To be able to see more records on the screen, switch to Browse mode by choosing the Browse option from the Browse menu pad. In response to this menu option selection, the records in the SALESMAN table will be displayed in a Browse window. If the window is too small to show all the data fields, widen it by choosing the Zoom operation. To do this, point the mouse cursor on the Zoom control button in the upper right-hand corner of the window; on the keyboard, press the Ctrl+F10 key combination to use the whole screen for Browse mode. In Browse mode each record is displayed as a row; data fields are displayed as columns in table form (see Figure 4.13).

Continue entering the rest of the data records to the table. As in Change mode, use the arrow keys to move within a field or between records. To move between fields, use the Tab or Shift-Tab keys. The same procedure applies for entering text to memo fields.

| System  File  Edit  Database  Record  Program  Window  Browse | | | | | | | |
|---|---|---|---|---|---|---|---|
| SALESMAN | | | | | | | |
| Salsman_id | Last | First | Hire_date | Salary | Commission | Note | |
| S0 | Anderson | Doris | 07/01/86 | 2800 | F | Memo | |
| S1 | Bell | George | 10/12/88 | 2400 | T | Memo | |
| S2 | Carter | Jack | 05/14/87 | 2550 | F | Memo | |
| | | | / / | | | MEMO | |

**Figure 4.13  Entering Data in Browse Mode**

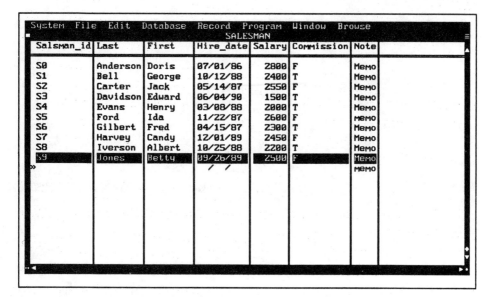

**Figure 4.14  Records of the SALESMAN Table**

## SAVING DATA RECORDS

After you have entered all ten records to the SALESMAN table (Figure 4.14), save the records by exiting from the data entry operation. With a mouse, close the Browse window by clicking on the Close control button. If you are using a keyboard, press the Ctrl+End key combination to terminate the data entry operation.

# Using FoxPro Commands

So far we have set up a data structure for the SALESMAN table and filled it with ten data records. We accomplished these tasks by using the FoxPro 2.0 menu interface. The initial step of setting up the data structure was done by choosing the File option from the menu pad. After that, you chose the appropriate menu option, control buttons, etc., to complete the task.

The setup procedure to create a new data table or database file can also be initiated by entering a FoxPro command in the Command window. Practice this option now by going to the Command window.

If you cleared the screen and closed the Command window before you created the SALESMAN table, bring it back by pressing the Ctrl+F2 key combination or by choosing the Command option from the popup box under the Window menu pad.

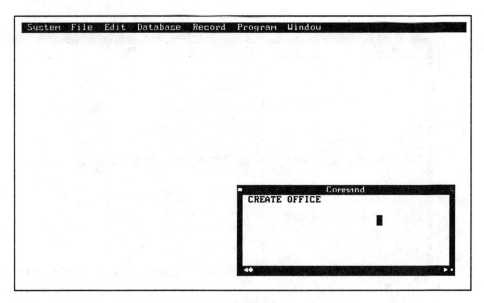

**Figure 4.15  Creating the OFFICE Database File**

In response to the key combination or menu option selected, the Command window will reappear. Its actual location on the screen will be the same as when you closed it, as will its size.

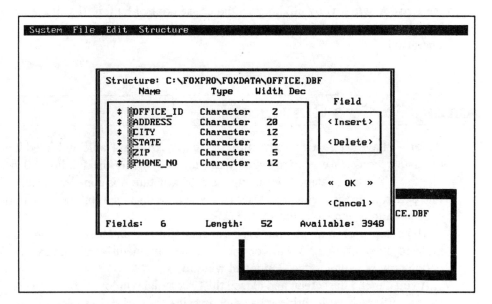

**Figure 4.16  Data Structure of the OFFICE Database File**

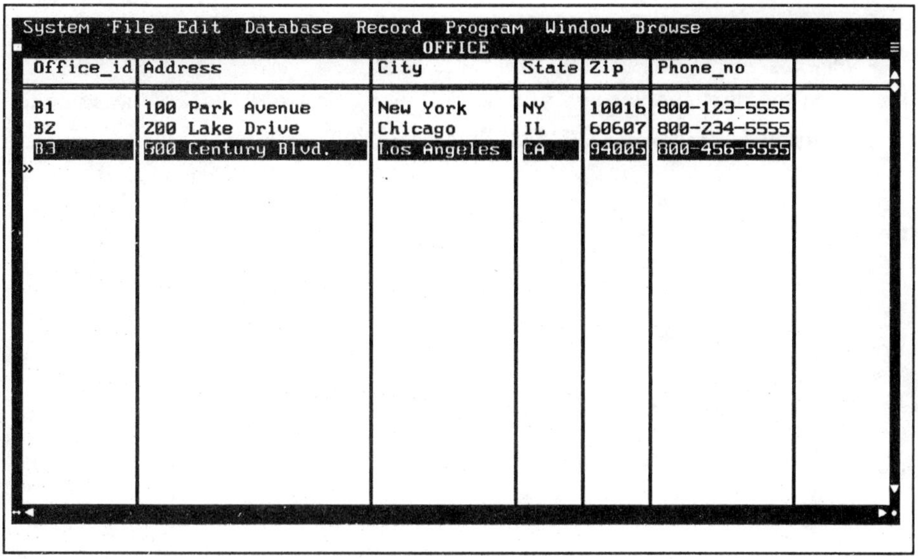

```
System  File  Edit  Database  Record  Program  Window  Browse
                              OFFICE
 Office_id Address                City       State Zip   Phone_no

   B1      100 Park Avenue        New York    NY   10016 800-123-5555
   B2      200 Lake Drive         Chicago     IL   60607 800-234-5555
   B3      500 Century Blvd.      Los Angeles CA   94005 800-456-5555
```

**Figure 4.17   Records in the OFFICE Database File**

Now let's create another data table called OFFICE by using a FoxPro command. This table will hold data elements regarding the sales offices discussed in Chapter 1. The command for creating a new database file is CREATE, followed by the name of the database file:

```
CREATE <database filename>
```

The brackets are used to describe the object to be created; do not enter them in the command. To create the OFFICE database file, type CREATE OFFICE in the Command window (see Figure 4.15).

In response to the command, a new data structure definition form is displayed as before. From this point on, follow the same steps used for creating the SALES-MAN table. The OFFICE database file contains six character fields for describing the properties of the sales office entity (see Figure 4.16).

After defining and saving the data structure OFFICE, enter the three records in the database file (see Figure 4.17).

# Chapter Summary

This chapter detailed the procedure for creating a new database file, including the setup of a proper data structure and the insertion of all the necessary records. The SALESMAN table was used as an example to show all the steps for creating the database file with the FoxPro menu interface. Finally, the FoxPro command that enables you to do the same thing was described.

In the next chapter you will learn how to view and display the contents of the database files that were created in this chapter.

# 5

# Displaying Data

## An Overview

In Chapter 4 you learned how to create a database file, which involved first defining its data structure and then filling the data table with the necessary records. The first part of this chapter will show you how to display the data structure of an existing database file. You will then learn how to display the contents of all the data fields in every record of a database file.

Then, because in many applications you will want to look at only a selective set of the data records in a table, this chapter will explain how to filter out unwanted records. You will also learn how to select only designated data fields without displaying all the data fields in a database file.

In addition, this chapter will demonstrate how all the data display functions can be executed easily by using the FoxPro menu interface, followed by a discussion on how to display data using the appropriate FoxPro commands.

## Displaying File Directories

We explained in Chapter 2 that all of your data files are saved and organized in various file directories on your disk. For example, the FoxPro program stores all of its files in the FOXPRO directory (C:\FOXPRO). Further, we recommended that all database files and other related disk files be saved in a subdirectory named FOXDATA under the FOXPRO directory (C:\FOXPRO\FOXDATA). As an example, we saved all the database files that we created in Chapter 4 in that subdirectory.

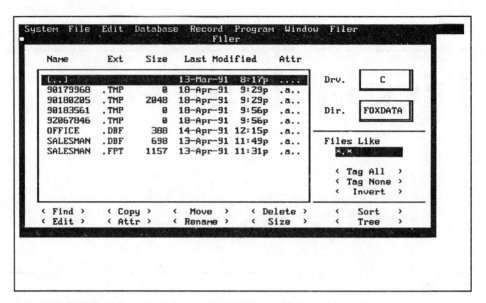

**Figure 5.1  Displaying the File Directory**

## USING THE FILER

To view all of your disk files in that subdirectory, choose the Filer option from the System menu pad. In response, the Filer displays all the files in the current subdirectory of the default disk drive (see Figure 5.1).

In this figure you can see that the default disk drive is C and the current subdirectory is FOXDATA (under the FOXPRO directory). The list shows the names and extensions of all the disk files in that subdirectory, together with their sizes (in bytes), and the date and time the files were last changed. Other information on the screen relates to other types of file management functions that we will discuss elsewhere.

This screen is very useful when you need to know what data files you have created. From the directory list in Figure 5.1 you can see that two database files (SALESMAN.DBF and OFFICE.DBF) have been created. In addition, it is apparent that the SALESMAN database file contains one or more memo fields because the contents of the memo fields are saved in the SALESMAN.FPT file.

To switch to a different disk drive, use the Drv popup control. Similarly, you can change your subdirectories by using the Dir popup control, or by double clicking your mouse on the directory on the file list.

To exit from the Filer, close the Filer box by pressing the Esc key on the keyboard; with a mouse, exit by clicking on the Close control button.

## Using Foxpro Commands

You can also invoke the Filer by issuing the FILER command in the Command window. In response, the Filer window of Figure 5.1 appears. (Recall that if the Command window is hidden, you can display it by pressing the Ctrl-F2 key combination.)

As an alternative to using the Filer to list the disk files in the current subdirectory of the default disk drive, you can also list them by issuing the appropriate FoxPro command. To list all the database files, issue the DIR command. As a result, information about the database files will be displayed on the screen (see Figure 5.2).

Notice that the DIR command displays only database files (files with a .DBF file extension) and ignores other types of disk files. After viewing the database file list, you can clear the screen by issuing the CLEAR command.

To list every disk file in the current subdirectory, issue the DIR *.* command. The asterisks are called wildcard parameters and indicate that everything is to be included. Thus, *.* means that you want to view all files regardless of their names and types (see Figure 5.3).

Notice that the DIR *.* command produces only a list of filenames with their file extensions. If you would like to look only at a specific type of file, issue the

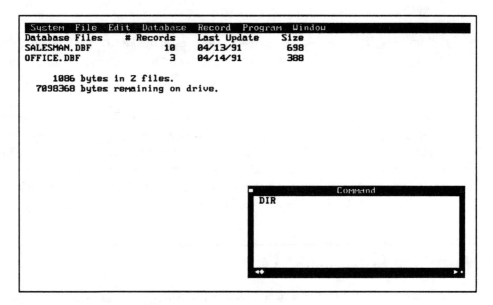

**Figure 5.2  Using the DIR Command**

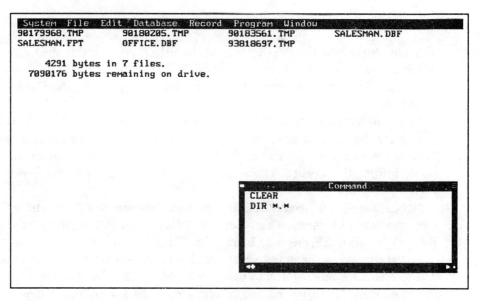

**Figure 5.3   Listing All the Disk Files**

DIR command and specify a file extension. For example, to view only memo files, issue the following command:

```
DIR *.FPT
```

Similarly, if you would like to list all the files named SALESMAN, regardless of their file extension, issue the following command:

```
DIR SALESMAN.*
```

When you issue the DIR command along with a file specification, the resulting file list does not contain any information about the size of the files. Neither does it show the time and date you changed the files. To view detailed information about these files, you must issue a DOS command in the FoxPro Command window. All DOS commands must begin with the keyword RUN. To issue the DOS DIR (for directory) command, enter RUN DIR in the FoxPro Command window (see Figure 5.4).

# Viewing Database Files

As discussed, when you create a database file, you begin by defining its structure and then fill it with your data records. You save the data structure with its records in the database file you name. To view the structure of that, or of any existing

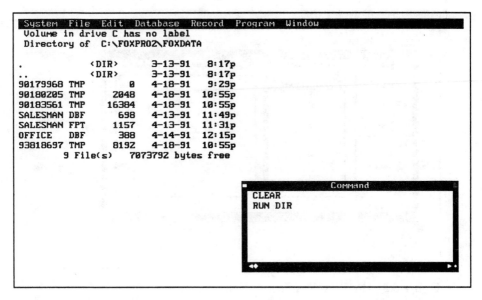

```
 System   File   Edit   Database   Record   Program   Window
 Volume in drive C has no label
 Directory of  C:\FOXPRO2\FOXDATA

 .             <DIR>       3-13-91    8:17p
 ..            <DIR>       3-13-91    8:17p
 90179968 TMP       0      4-18-91    9:29p
 90180205 TMP    2048      4-18-91   10:55p
 90183561 TMP   16384      4-18-91   10:55p
 SALESMAN DBF     698      4-13-91   11:49p
 SALESMAN FPT    1157      4-13-91   11:31p
 OFFICE   DBF     388      4-14-91   12:15p
 93818697 TMP    8192      4-18-91   10:55p
         9 File(s)    7073792 bytes free

                                    ┌────────────────Command────────────┐
                                    │ CLEAR                              │
                                    │ RUN DIR                            │
                                    │                                    │
                                    │                                    │
                                    │                                    │
                                    │                                    │
                                    └────────────────────────────────────┘
```

**Figure 5.4  Issuing a DOS Directory Command**

database file, or manipulate your data in any way, you must first open it in a work area.

A work area is a temporary working space reserved for storing data in an open database file. It is identified either with a letter or a number. There are 25 different work areas (A through J and 11 through 16, or 1 through 25) from which you can choose to hold your database files. It is possible to open up to 25 database files at one time. Furthermore, you can switch from one database to another while you are working.

## INVOKING THE VIEW WINDOW

There a number of ways to open a database file in a work area. One way is to choose the View menu option from the Window menu popup, after which a View window appears on the screen (see Figure 5.5).

The View window can serve as a general control center for handling your database files. Among other functions, it enables you to open database files in work areas A through J and to link your files together. On the left-hand side of the window, there are eight push buttons: <View>, <On/Off>, <Files>, <Misc>, <Setup>, <Browse>, <Open>, and <Close>. These push buttons are for invoking various panels. Although you will learn in detail later how to use these panels, we will briefly discuss these push buttons here.

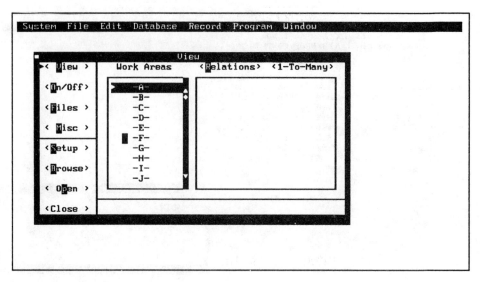

**Figure 5.5   The View Window**

## The <View> Push Button

The <View> push button returns you to the View window after you have selected another push button. For example, if you pushed the <On/Off> button, and then want to return to the View window, use the <View> button.

## The <Setup> Push Button

The Setup panel is used for viewing and modifying an existing data structure. You can invoke the panel by selecting the <Setup> push button. But before you can bring up the Setup panel, you must open a database in a work area. If no database file is open, FoxPro displays the Open File dialog asking you to open a database file. (We will continue with the Setup panel after you have learned to open a database file in a work area in the next section.)

## The <Browse> Push Button

The Browse panel, which is invoked by selecting the <Browse> push button, lets you view the records in a database file. Like the Setup panel, you need to open a database file before using the Browse panel. Again, if you have not opened a database file in a work area, FoxPro will display the Open File dialog, indicating that you must select a database file before initiating the Browse operation. You will learn how to use the Browse panel in viewing your data records later in this chapter.

## The <Open> Push Button

There are a number of ways to open a database file in a work area. One is to select the <Open> push button. Other procedures for opening a database file involve using the FoxPro menu interface and FoxPro commands, both of which are covered in the next section.

## The <Close> Push Button

The <Close> push button provides the means for removing an open database file from a work area. The button is active only when there is at least one open database file in the work areas. Closing a database file is very important for some database file manipulations. For example, you can make a duplicate copy of a database file only if you have first closed the file.

## OPENING DATABASE FILES

Opening a database file in a work area can be done in a variety of ways. One is to select the <Open> push button from the View window by clicking on it with your mouse or by pressing the letter "p" on your keyboard. Alternatively, you can simply move the highlight to a work area that does not have an open file and press <Enter>. Then select the database file to be opened in the indicated work area regardless of where the cursor is (see Figure 5.6).

As you can see in this figure, selecting the Open option leads to the Open File dialog that shows the list of database files available for opening. At this point, select the one you would like to open. With a mouse, double click on the database file; with the keyboard, use the up and down arrow keys to highlight the file and then press Enter to open it. The name of the database file opened is then displayed in the indicated work area (see Figure 5.7).

You can see that the name of the database file that was opened in the highlighted work area also appears at the bottom of the dialog box, together with its number of records.

You can open more than one database file in the work areas. For example, you also can open OFFICE.DBF in work area B after opening SALESMAN.DBF in work area A.

Another method for opening a database file is to double click the mouse button on an unused work area. Use this method to open OFFICE.DBF in work area

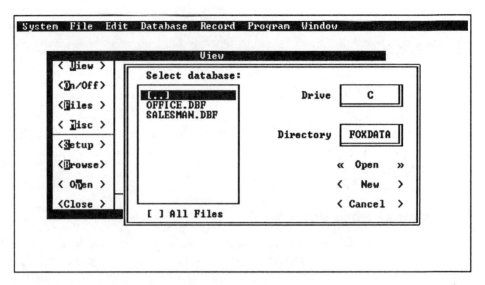

**Figure 5.6  Selecting the Database File to Be Opened**

B—point and double click the mouse on the letter B in the work area; or, if you are using the keyboard, use the down arrow to highlight work area B and then press Enter to invoke the File Open dialog. In either case, when the File Open dialog appears, select OFFICE.DBF and open it. As a result, there are two database files open in work areas A and B (see Figure 5.8).

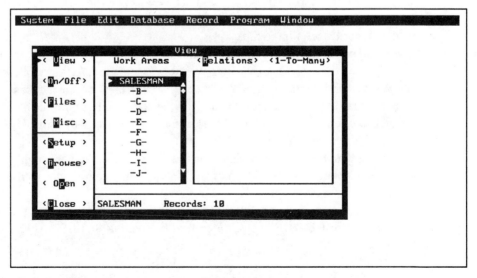

**Figure 5.7  Displaying an Opened Database File in a Work Area**

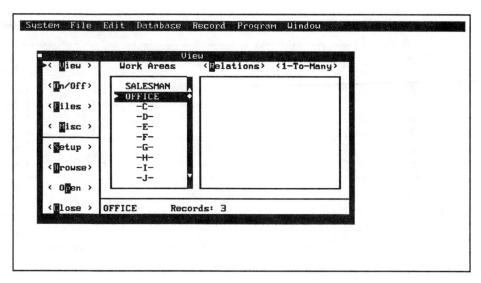

**Figure 5.8  Opening Two Database Files in Different Work Areas**

## CLOSING DATABASE FILES

A database file remains open until you close it, and you should get into the habit of closing files once you have finished using them. Open files are more susceptible to the accidental loss of data as a result of power failure, for example, where the contents of a database can be damaged when the power goes down. In addition, there are some operations (such as file copying and deletion) that cannot be carried out on an open file.

To close a database, select the <Close> push button by pressing the letter "C" or by clicking the mouse on the push button. As an exercise, close OFFICE.DBF. First highlight the database file in work area B and then select the <Close> push button. In response to selecting the push button, OFFICE.DBF is removed from work area B. Now only SALESMAN.DBF remains open in work area A in the View window.

## DISPLAYING DATABASE STRUCTURES

Once a database file is open in a work area, you can view its structure and contents by selecting the appropriate push buttons.

To display the structure of an existing database file, all you have to do is open it in a work area and then select the <Setup> push button. So to display the structure of SALESMAN, select the <Setup> push button while the database file is open in work area A by pressing the letter "S" or by clicking on the push button when the

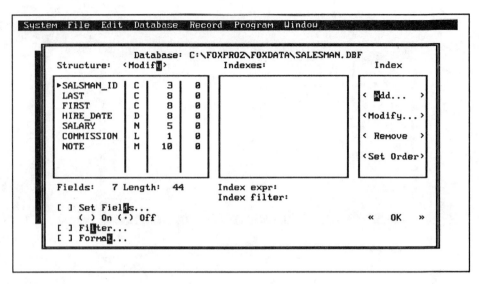

**Figure 5.9  Displaying a Data Structure in the Setup Dialog**

database file is highlighted. In response, the data structure associated with the open database file is displayed in the Setup dialog (see Figure 5.9).

You can see in this figure that all the data fields defined in the open database file, SALESMAN.DBF, are displayed in a list, along with their type, width, and number of decimal places. There are other items displayed in the Setup dialog, but they will be discussed later; you do not have to be concerned with them at this point.

After viewing the structure, you can exit from the Setup dialog and return to the View window by clicking the <<OK>> push button or by pressing the Esc key.

## VIEWING DATA RECORDS

You may recall from Chapter 4 that when you were entering data into a database file, you could choose one of two views: Record view or Browse view. From the View window, you can also choose one of two display modes for showing the data records in an existing database: Change or Browse. When data is displayed in Record view, it is in Change mode, so called because it is the usual mode for making changes to data records. Otherwise, it is in Browse mode.

### Using Browse Mode

Browse mode displays data records in table form, using one row per record and one column for each data field. To bring up Browse view, select the <Browse> push button in the View window when a database is open in a work area. Try

```
 System   File   Edit   Database   Record   Program   Window   Browse
┌─────────────────────────────── SALESMAN ───────────────────────────────┐
│ Salsman_id│ Last    │ First   │ Hire_date│ Salary│ Commission │ Note│   │
│───────────┼─────────┼─────────┼──────────┼───────┼────────────┼─────│   │
│ S0        │ Anderson│ Doris   │ 07/01/86 │ 2800  │ F          │ Memo│   │
│ S1        │ Bell    │ George  │ 10/12/88 │ 2400  │ T          │ Memo│   │
│ S2        │ Carter  │ Jack    │ 05/14/87 │ 2550  │ F          │ Memo│   │
│ S3        │ Davidson│ Edward  │ 06/04/90 │ 1500  │ T          │ Memo│   │
│ S4        │ Evans   │ Henry   │ 03/08/88 │ 2000  │ T          │ Memo│   │
│ S5        │ Ford    │ Ida     │ 11/22/87 │ 2600  │ F          │ Memo│   │
│ S6        │ Gilbert │ Fred    │ 04/15/87 │ 2300  │ T          │ Memo│   │
│ S7        │ Harvey  │ Candy   │ 12/01/89 │ 2450  │ F          │ Memo│   │
│ S8        │ Iverson │ Albert  │ 10/25/88 │ 2200  │ T          │ Memo│   │
│ S9        │ Jones   │ Betty   │ 09/26/89 │ 2500  │ F          │ Memo│   │
│           │         │         │          │       │            │     │   │
└─────────────────────────────────────────────────────────────────────────┘
```

**Figure 5.10  Displaying Data Records in Browse Mode**

clicking on the <Browse> push button or pressing the letter B while SALESMAN
is open in work area A. Watch as the records of the SALESMAN database are
displayed in Browse mode (see Figure 5.10).

The size and location of the Browse window are carried over from the
previous application. Because of this, your Browse window may look different
from that shown in Figure 5.10. If it is too small to display all the data fields in
the SALESMAN table, you can resize the window to display as much data as
the window allows. (The procedures for moving and sizing a window were
covered in Chapter 2. You may want to review them before proceeding to the
next section.)

One advantage to using Browse mode is that you can view many records on
one screen because each record occupies only one line. But if your data table
has a large number of data fields, you may not be able to view all of them on
the same screen without scrolling the data fields. In this case, you may want to
view your records in Change mode, which enables you to display more fields
on the same screen. Of course, you still can view only a limited number of
records per screen.

## Using Change Mode

To switch from Browse mode to Change mode, select the Change option from the
Browse menu popup. In response to the menu selection, FoxPro displays the data
records in Change mode. Again, you can adjust the window size to reveal as many
records as possible (see Figure 5.11).

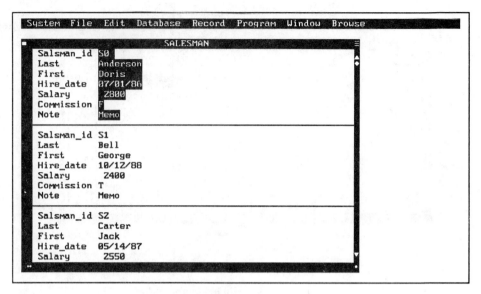

**Figure 5.11   Records in Change Mode**

Because you can see only a few records at a time in Change mode, you will have to scroll up and down to bring hidden records into view. Either click on the Scroll control or use the PgUp and PgDn keys to do so.

Now that you have seen how data records are displayed in Change mode, let's return to Browse mode, as there are many desirable features of this mode that you can use for displaying your data.

## Switching to Browse Mode

To switch from Change to Browse mode, select the Browse option from the Browse menu popup and you will be returned to Browse mode. Remember though, if you changed the window while you were in Change mode, the size and location of the Browse window will now reflect those alterations.

### Sizing Browse Columns

In Figure 5.10 you saw that data fields are displayed in columns in the Browse window. The default width of the column is determined by the length of the field name or the field width specified in the structure, whichever is greater. For example, even though the SALSMAN_ID field is defined as three characters long in the database structure, the field occupies ten spaces in the Browse window because that is the length of its field name. On the other hand, the LAST field occupies an eight-character wide column—the size of the field in the database structure—even though the field name itself has only four letters.

Because of this, you may want to adjust the width of a column so that you can display its data more suitably. Then, if some columns in the Browse window appear to be too crowded, you can widen them so that the data fields appear in a more pleasing format. Or, if you want to display more data fields on the same screen in the Browse window, you can narrow some of the columns.

You can size a column either by using the mouse or by choosing a menu option with the keyboard. It is important to remember that changing the size of a Browse column does not affect the actual field width in the data structure.

To resize a Browse column with a mouse, first position the mouse cursor on the vertical grid line to the right of the column. Then hold down the mouse button and drag it to the right to widen the column, or to the left to narrow the column. You can go back and forth until you have achieved the desired column width. As an exercise, place the mouse cursor on the right-hand grid line of the LAST column and drag it to the right several spaces.

To resize a column with the keyboard, first position the cursor on the column you would like to size. Then choose the Size Field option from the Browse menu popup. Press the right or left arrow keys to widen or narrow the column. Finally, press Enter to establish the new column width. As a demonstration of this method, widen the FIRST column. First position the cursor anywhere in that column (regardless of the row or character position). Then choose the Size Field option from the Browse menu popup. In response, the FIRST column is highlighted. Next press the right arrow key several times to widen the column until you have achieved the desired width (see Figure 5.12).

When you look at the Browse window in Figure 5.12, notice that widening these two columns did not change the window size. Sometimes, as result of this, other data fields may become hidden after you have widened columns. To view the hidden data fields, you can widen the Browse window if there is sufficient space on the screen to do so. Otherwise, you will have to scroll the data fields to view those hidden fields.

### Scrolling Data Fields and Records

In Browse view, you can scroll to the left or right to reveal any data fields that are hidden from the Browse window. Similarly, if you have more records than can be displayed on the same screen in the Browse window, you can also scroll up and down the window to reveal hidden records.

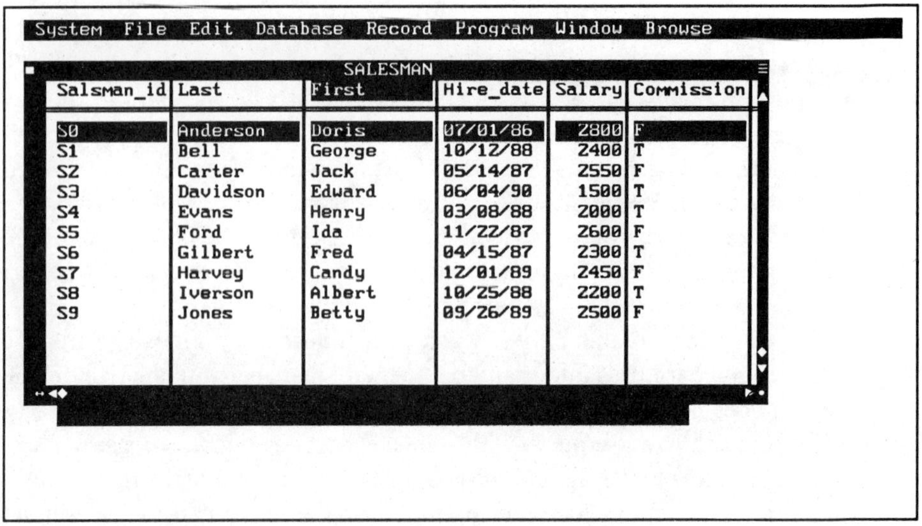

**Figure 5.12  Widening the LAST and FIRST Columns**

If you are using a mouse, click on the left or right arrows in the horizontal scroll bar at the bottom of the window. This allows you to scroll left and right along the data fields. Or point your mouse cursor at the thumb button in the scroll bar and drag it to the left or right to reveal the hidden data fields.

To scroll data records up and down, use the vertical scroll bar on the right of the window; on the keyboard, press the Tab or Shift+Tab key to move to the right or left one data field. After you have reached the last column shown in the window, FoxPro will reveal the hidden fields as you continue to press one of these keys. Similarly, by pressing the up and down arrow keys, you move up and down one record at a time in the window. FoxPro reveals the hidden records after you have moved beyond the top or bottom of the Browse window.

## Hiding Data Fields

Browse view displays all of the data fields defined in the database structure, but if you would like to view only selected data fields, you can choose one of two options: Either select only those data fields to be included in Browse view (you will learn how to do this later in the chapter); or hide those fields you don't want to see from Browse view.

The procedure to hide a data field is the same for narrowing a Browse column. By shrinking a column to its minimum width, you hide its contents. As a test, try shrinking some of the data columns in Browse view. To redisplay the reduced column, widen the column again to the desired width.

## Removing Column Grids

By default, Browse mode uses a vertical grid to divide the columns for showing your data fields. But you can remove the grid lines by choosing the Grid Off option from the Browse menu popup. To replace the grids, simply choose the Grid On option from the Browse menu popup.

## Moving Data Fields

In its default layout, Browse view displays all the data fields in the order in which they are defined in the database structure. But you can rearrange them in whatever order you choose by moving the data fields around in the Browse window.

Moving a data field with a mouse is very simple. All you have to do is first place your mouse cursor on the name of the field you would like to move. Then hold down the left button and drag to the field's new position. For example, if you would like to move the FIRST field to the left of the LAST field, position your mouse cursor on the column label, e.g., FIRST. Then hold down the left mouse button and drag it to the left until FIRST appears to the left of LAST.

You can also move a field by using the keyboard. To do so, first place your cursor anywhere in the field to be moved by using the Tab or Shift-Tab keys and then choose the Move Field option from the Browse menu popup. Next use the left or right arrow keys to move to the left or right in the window. As a test, try moving the HIRE_DATE field to the right of the SALARY field by first placing your cursor in the Hire_date column and then choosing the Move Field option from the Browse menu popup. In response to the menu choice, the column is highlighted. Now, press the right arrow key until the HIRE_DATE field appears to the right of the SALARY field (see Figure 5.13). Finally, press Enter to complete the operation.

## Partitioning the Browse Window

In those situations when you have a data table with a large number of data fields, you may want to view certain fields in sections in Browse view. You can do this by partitioning the Browse window into two sections, each of which shows a group of data fields. Or you may want to view data records in Record and Browse views simultaneously on the same screen. This requires splitting the window into two parts.

You can partition a Browse window by using either the mouse or the keyboard. With the mouse, first position the mouse cursor on the Window Splitter button, which appears at the bottom left-hand corner of the window. Then, hold down the mouse button and drag it to the right. As a result, the Browse window splits into two sections (see Figure 5.14).

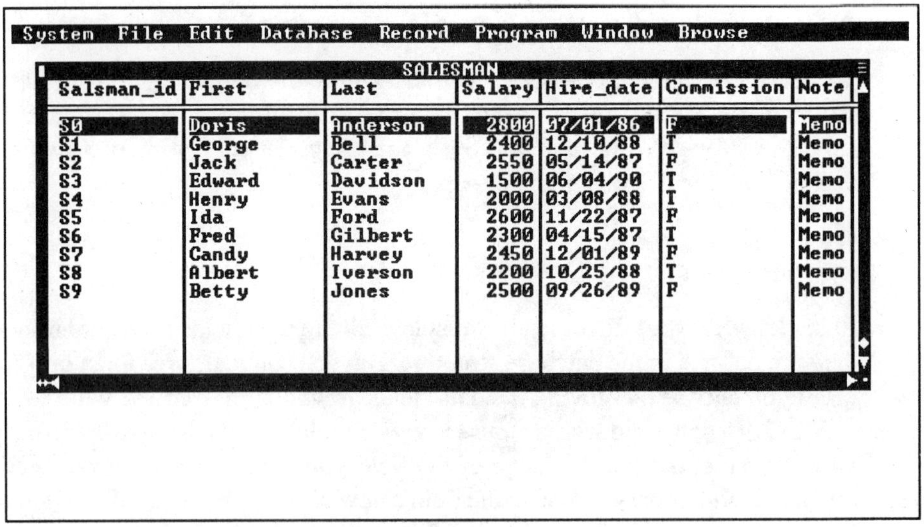

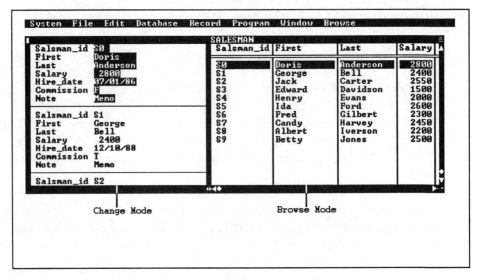

**Figure 5.13  Moving the FIRST and HIRE_DATE Data Fields**

When you split the Browse window into two sections, each section may be in a different view. In Figure 5.14 you can see that the left section is in Change mode while the right section is in Browse mode. You can move from one section to another by moving your mouse cursor or by pressing the Ctrl+H key combination. With one section of the split window, you can switch from Browse mode to Change mode or vice versa by selecting the appropriate option on the Browse menu popup.

**Figure 5.14  Partitioning the Browse Window**

You can partition the Browse window or change the size of the partitions with the keyboard by first selecting the Resize Partitions option from the Browse menu popup. In response to the menu selection, the Window Splitter button blinks. At this point, press the left or right arrows to resize the partitions. When you have finished, press the Enter key to accept the new partitions.

When you split a Browse window into two sections, the data records displayed in the partitions can be linked or unlinked depending on the last window settings you have saved. (Note: When you first invoke FoxPro, records are linked together by default.) In linked partitions, any movement from one record to another in one partition also occurs in the other partitions.

The same record is always highlighted in both partitions, and the highlighted record, along with assorted records surrounding it, is always displayed in both partitions. If you move the highlight to a record that is displayed in one partition but not in the other, FoxPro will immediately update the records being displayed in the second partition to include the highlighted record and the records immediately around it. On the other hand, when two partitions are unlinked, it is still true that the same record is always highlighed in both partitions. But if there are more database records than can fit in a window, requiring that the records in the partition be scrolled, the same highlighted record is not necessarily displayed in both partitions. Unlinking partitions allows you to scroll one partition while maintaining a stationary display of the records in the second partition. It is important to note that unlinking does not allow you to highlight a different record in each partition. In Figure 5.15, for example, the highlighted record in the Change mode partition is the same as that highlighted in the Browse mode partition. In

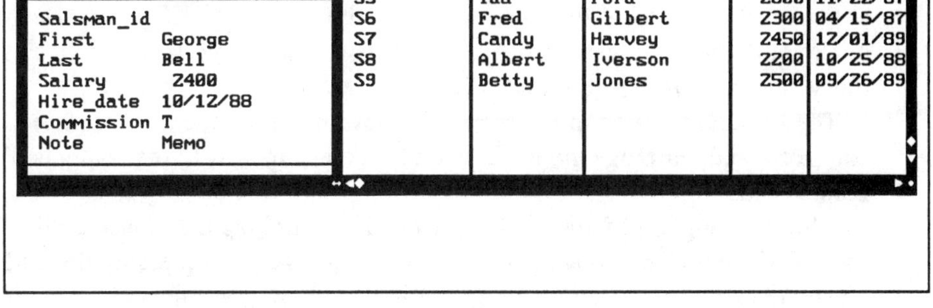

**Figure 5.15  Linked Records in Partitions**

addition, a comparable set of records are displayed in the two partitions. As you move around the records in one partition, the corresponding records in the other partition will be highlighted. If you would like to hold records stationary in one partition while you move around the records in the other partition, you can unlink them. All you have to do is choose Unlink Partitions from the Browse menu popup. As a result, when you move around the records in one partition, the records in the other partition will remain stationary once you have moved beyond the current screen of records being displayed.

## Viewing Memo Fields

(To prepare for the next exercise, close the left partition and display the records in Browse view.)

In our previous examples, the contents of the memo fields are hidden in both Change and Browse modes. Instead, only the word "Memo" appears in the memo field, indicating that there is text stored in that field. This is because a memo field is a variable-length field and requires special handling. All other FoxPro field types—character, numeric, float, date, and logical—are fixed-length fields. The length of these fields is declared in advance, at the time that the database structure is defined. All data stored to a particular field will have the same length. In contrast, memo fields, which are intended to store free-form textual information, are not assigned a fixed length at the time the file is created, and the actual length of a memo field depends on the amount of text that has been stored to that memo field for a particular record. The advantage of a memo field is that vastly different amounts of information can be stored to each record of a database without wasting disk storage space. The disadvantage is that FoxPro stores memo fields in a separate file apart from the database (.DBF) file itself.

To view the memo field contents, bring up the Memo window by pressing the Ctrl+Home (or Ctrl+PgUp key combination) after placing your cursor on the memo field you would like to view. If you are using a mouse, double click on the memo field.

To view the contents of the NOTE memo field for salesman Bell, place the cursor at the word "Memo" of the first record and then press Ctrl-Home. Alternatively, click your mouse on that word. The contents of that memo field are displayed in the Memo window (see Figure 5.16).

The size and location of the Memo window are set by the last application. You can resize and rearrange the window on the screen to best fit the contents of your memo fields.

After viewing the Memo window, close it by clicking the mouse on the Close control at the upper left-hand corner of the window, or by pressing the Ctrl+End key combination.

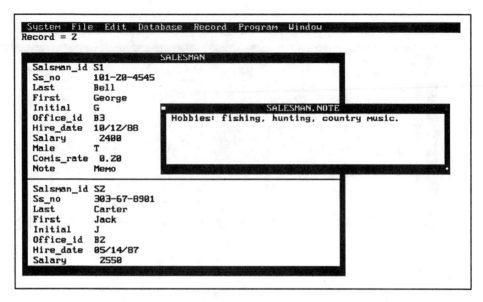

**Figure 5.16  Contents of a Memo Field**

## Viewing Multiple Database Files

As mentioned, you can open database files in up to 25 work areas at a time in FoxPro. While the files are open, you can view any of them in either Change or Browse mode. As a result, you are able to view multiple files on the same screen simultaneously with overlapping Browse windows. If the contents of your database files are small, you can size and arrange the windows so that you can view them all on the same screen.

If you would like to view more than one database file at a time, all you have to do is to open, one at a time, those you want in work areas using the View window. Once the files are open in their respective work areas you can then select the <Browse> push button to display them in sequence.

To view the SALESMAN and OFFICE databases, open SALESMAN.DBF in work area A and OFFICE.DBF in work area B. Because you already opened the SALESMAN database in a previous exercise and displayed its records in Browse mode, all you have to do now is bring up the View window. To do that, click anywhere on the View window to bring it up to the foreground, if it is partially visible in the background. Otherwise, move the Browse window in the foreground to reveal the View window before clicking on it. Or choose the View option from the Window menu popup to bring the View window to the foreground. Once the View window appears, you can open the OFFICE database in work area B (see Figure 5.17).

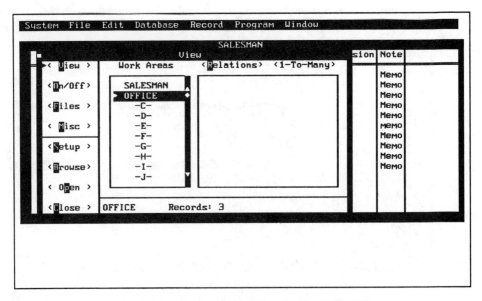

**Figure 5.17   Opening Multiple Database Files in the View Window**

You can display the records of the OFFICE database file in the Browse window by selecting the <Browse> push button when the OFFICE database is highlighted. The records of the database file will then be displayed in a Browse window on top of the one showing the records from the SALESMAN database file (see Figure 5.18).

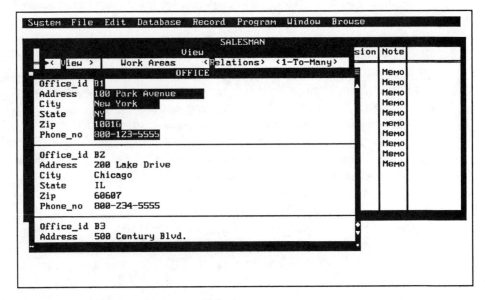

**Figure 5.18   The Second Browse Window**

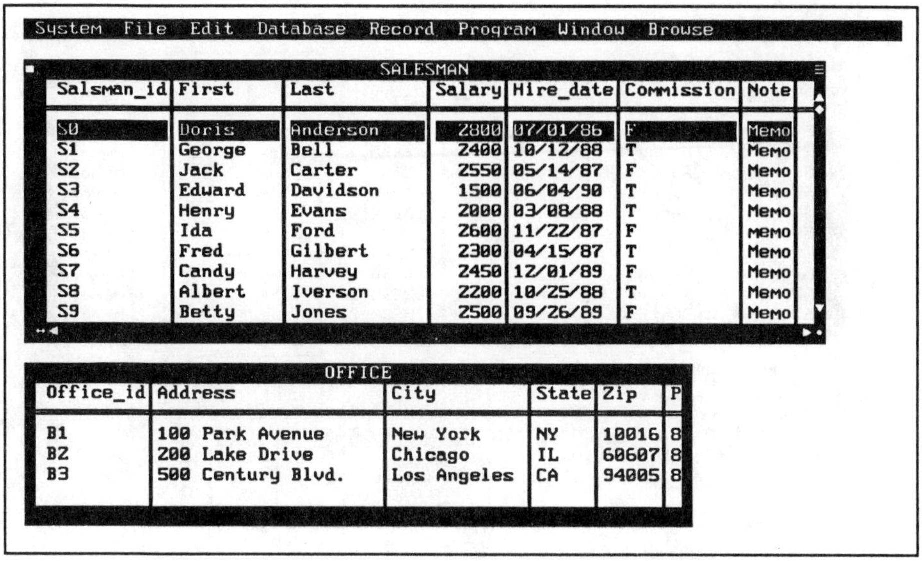

```
 System  File  Edit  Database  Record  Program  Window  Browse
■                              SALESMAN                              ≡
  Salsman_id│First     │Last      │Salary│Hire_date│Commission│Note
  S0          Doris      Anderson   2800  07/01/86  F           Memo
  S1          George     Bell       2400  10/12/88  T           Memo
  S2          Jack       Carter     2550  05/14/87  F           Memo
  S3          Edward     Davidson   1500  06/04/90  T           Memo
  S4          Henry      Evans      2000  03/08/88  T           Memo
  S5          Ida        Ford       2600  11/22/87  F           Memo
  S6          Fred       Gilbert    2300  04/15/87  T           Memo
  S7          Candy      Harvey     2450  12/01/89  F           Memo
  S8          Albert     Iverson    2200  10/25/88  T           Memo
  S9          Betty      Jones      2500  09/26/89  F           Memo
··◄                                                              ►·
                              OFFICE
  Office_id│Address          │City        │State│Zip   │P
  B1         100 Park Avenue   New York     NY    10016  8
  B2         200 Lake Drive    Chicago      IL    60607  8
  B3         500 Century Blvd. Los Angeles  CA    94005  8
```

**Figure 5.19  SALESMAN.DBF and OFFICE.DBF in Browse Windows**

You can see in this figure that the records of the OFFICE database file are displayed in Change mode while the records of the SALESMAN database file are shown in Browse mode.

Of course, you can switch from Change mode to Browse mode and vice versa by using the procedure you learned earlier. While you are in the OFFICE Browse window, you would choose the Browse option from the Browse menu popup to make the switch. You can also clean up the screen by removing the View window from the screen. To do that, close the View window by first bringing the window to the foreground and then clicking on the Close box with the mouse; or press the Esc key. You could also choose the Hide option from the Browse menu popup to close the View window. Later, you can resize the Browse windows so that you can view records in the SALESMAN and OFFICE database files on the same screen (see Figure 5.19).

## Switching Between Browse Windows

When database files are displayed in more than one Browse window on the screen, you can switch from one to the other by using either the mouse or the keyboard. The current active window is indicated by a highlighted record and by the presence of the Close control at the upper left-hand corner of the window. In addition, the active window is shown in the foreground if the Browse windows overlap.

If you are using a mouse, click it anywhere within the Browse window that you would like to be active. With the keyboard, switch from one Browse window to

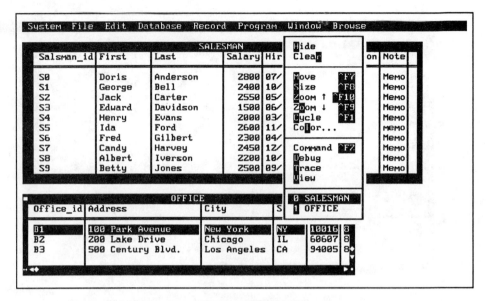

**Figure 5.20  Switching Between Browse Windows**

another by selecting the Cycle option available on the Window menu popup or by pressing the Ctrl+F1 key combination. In response to the menu selection, the other Browse window will become the active one. If you have more than two Browse windows open when you select the Cycle option, it will bring the active window to the foreground.

When database files are displayed in Browse windows, their names are shown at the bottom of the Window menu popup (see Figure 5.20). Because of this, you can designate the database file that you would like to display in the active Browse window by selecting it from the Window menu popup accordingly. Thus, while the OFFICE database file is displayed in the active window, you can choose the SALESMAN database file from the Window menu popup to make it the active window. This option is very useful when you are displaying a number of database files in multiple Browse windows. It allows you to go to a specific database file directly without cycling through other Browse windows.

## VIEWING SELECTIVE FIELDS

When you view the contents of a database file in Browse or Change mode, all of the records and data fields in the database file are displayed. If you would like to view only selective data fields or records, you have to let the program know before invoking the Browse window.

Earlier in this chapter you learned how to hide Browse columns and show only those data fields that you want to see. But you can do this only in Browse view; in

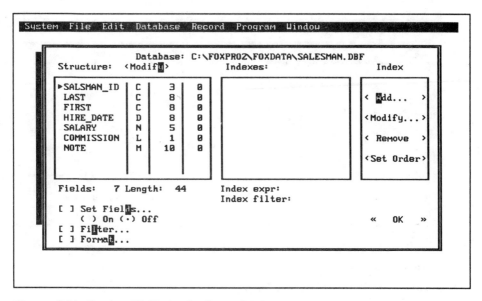

```
 System  File  Edit  Database  Record  Program  Window

        ┌──────────────────────────────────────────────────────────┐
        │            Database:  C:\FOXPRO2\FOXDATA\SALESMAN.DBF      │
        │   Structure:  <Modify>            Indexes:        Index    │
        │  ┌────────────────────┐  ┌──────────────┐  ┌─────────────┐ │
        │  │▶SALSMAN_ID  C │ 3 │ 0│  │              │  │ < Add...   >│ │
        │  │ LAST        C │ 8 │ 0│  │              │  │             │ │
        │  │ FIRST       C │ 8 │ 0│  │              │  │<Modify... > │ │
        │  │ HIRE_DATE   D │ 8 │ 0│  │              │  │             │ │
        │  │ SALARY      N │ 5 │ 0│  │              │  │ < Remove  > │ │
        │  │ COMMISSION  L │ 1 │ 0│  │              │  │             │ │
        │  │ NOTE        M │10 │ 0│  │              │  │<Set Order>  │ │
        │  │                    │  │              │  │             │ │
        │  └────────────────────┘  └──────────────┘  └─────────────┘ │
        │   Fields:   7 Length:  44     Index expr:                  │
        │                               Index filter:                │
        │   [ ] Set Fields...                                        │
        │        ( ) On (·) Off                        «   OK   »    │
        │   [ ] Filter...                                            │
        │   [ ] Format...                                            │
        └──────────────────────────────────────────────────────────┘
```

**Figure 5.21  Setting Fields in the Setup Dialog**

Change mode, FoxPro shows *all* the existing data fields. Therefore, if you want to display only selective data fields in either mode, you must specify those data fields.

To select the data fields to be displayed in the Browse window, use the Setup dialog, which is available by choosing the Setup push button in the View window. Let's say that you want to display only the LAST, FIRST, and SALARY fields of the SALESMAN database file. First, bring up the Setup panel; then return to the View window and close the OFFICE database so that only the SALESMAN database remains open in work area A. In addition, select the SALESMAN database as the current database. In the View window, select the <Setup> push button to bring up the Setup dialog (see Figure 5.21).

The Setup dialog, in addition to showing the structure of the database file, has many controls, including three check boxes that are located at the bottom left side of the dialog. These check boxes allow you to select the data fields, records, and the display format that you will use to view your data. Under the Set Fields check box, there are two radio buttons indicating whether the check box is set to On or Off.

### Picking Data Fields

To pick the data fields that you would like to display, check the Set Fields box by clicking your mouse on the check box or by pressing the letter "d." Now the Field Picker dialog appears (see Figure 5.22).

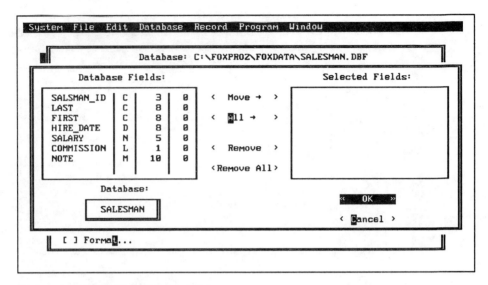

**Figure 5.22  The Field Picker Dialog**

There is a set of four push buttons in this dialog—<Move>, <All>, <Remove>, and <Remove All>—which are for selecting or deselecting one or all of the data fields in the database file. The <<OK>> button lets you exit from the dialog with the selected data fields, and <Cancel> enables you to exit from the dialog without completing the field selection.

To include all the data fields in the display, select the <All> push button either by clicking the mouse on the button or by pressing the letter "A." To deselect all the data fields, press the letter "1" or click the mouse on the <Remove All> push button. Notice that the <Remove All> button becomes active only when at least one field has been selected.

An easy way to select an individual data field for display is to double click your mouse on the field you want to pick. With a keyboard, first highlight the field name by pressing the Tab key continuously until the first field name is highlighted and then use the down arrow key to select the field you want to pick. Press the Enter key to select it, and the field name is moved to the list of selected fields on the screen. To select another data field, use the up or down arrow keys to highlight another data field and press the Enter key.

Now you can use the mouse or keyboard to select the FIRST, LAST, and SALARY fields in that order. The selected data fields are then displayed in the right-hand side list (see Figure 5.23).

If you make a mistake, just double click your mouse on the field you would like to deselect. On the keyboard, you must first highlight the field in the Selected Fields list (with Tab and arrow keys) and then press the Enter key.

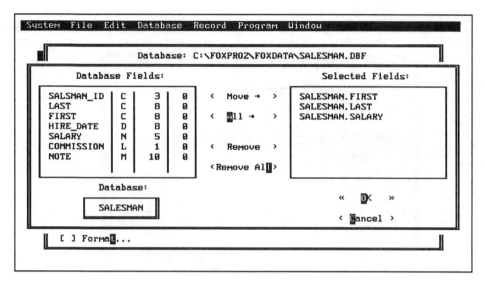

**Figure 5.23  Showing Selected Fields**

After you select all the data fields—but before you display the data—you must exit from the Field Picker dialog by selecting the <<OK>> push button. FoxPro then returns you to the Setup dialog (see Figure 5.24).

Notice in this figure that the Set Fields box has been checked and the On radio button has been turned on. In addition, although the structure list box displays all the field names, those fields that you have *not* selected appear grayed. Now you

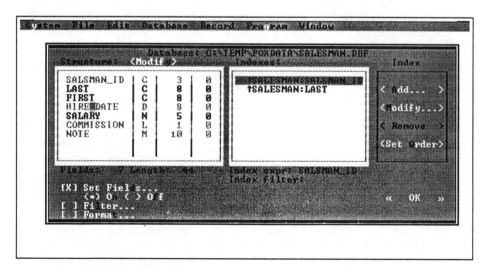

**Figure 5.24  Checking the Set Fields Box**

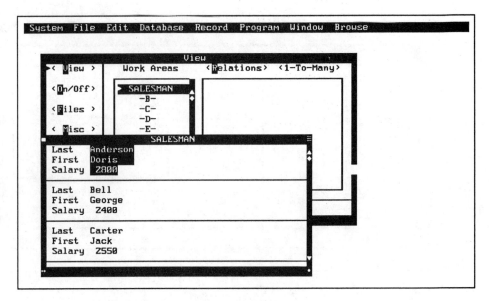

**Figure 5.25  Displaying Selected Data Fields**

can bring up the Browse window to display the selected data fields. To do that, select the <<OK>> push button from Setup dialog. This returns you to the View window, at which point you choose the <Browse> push button to bring up the Browse window (see Figure 5.25).

The Browse window of Figure 5.25 shows the contents of the selected data fields in Change mode. You can, if you prefer, switch to Browse mode. Be aware that the order of the data fields follows that of the data structure, regardless of the sequence in which the data fields were picked. To rearrange the order, move the data fields around using the procedure you learned earlier.

### Resetting Data Fields

After examining the data in the selected fields, you can change the list of selected fields by returning to the Setup dialog from the View window and invoking the Field Picker dialog to revise the selected fields list. After you have made the necessary change(s) bring up the Browse window again to display the data. Note, however, that when you return to the Browse window, the original set of selected data fields will remain on the screen. To update the screen for showing the revised list of selected data fields, select the Change option from the Record menu popup.

Similarly, if you would like to redisplay all the data fields in the database file, you must return to the Setup dialog to deselect the data fields that you picked earlier. You can do this either by deselecting all the data fields in the Field Picker dialog or by unchecking the Set Fields Off radio button. But remember that when you return to the Browse window, you must select the Change option from the Record menu popup to update the screen.

## VIEWING SELECTIVE RECORDS

Now, because you have learned how to pick the data fields you would like to browse, we'll show you how to select and view only a subset of the records in a database file. This procedure is very similar to that for picking fields. It requires that you bring up the Setup dialog so that you can define the filter conditions that will be used to screen out the unwanted records and select only those you want.

### Using Filter Conditions

Filter conditions are written in the form of expressions made up of the following: the names of your data fields, any logical operators and mathematical functions, and the filtering values for the data fields. Examples of such expressions are:

```
SALARY >= 2500
SALARY >= 2000 AND SALARY <= 2500
SALARY > 2500 OR SALARY < 2000
FIRST = 'Jack' OR FIRST = 'John'
HIRE_DATE > {01/01/88}
HIRE_DATE > {01/01/88) OR SALARY >2600
COMMISSION = .T.
BETWEEN (SALARY,2000,2400)
```

The first expression, SALARY >= 2500, for example, specifies the name of the data field SALARY, the logical operator (>= indicating greater than or equal to), and the filter value (2500). The expression means that you would like to select only those records whose values in the SALARY field satisfy the filter condition (greater than or equal to $2,500). The next two expressions include the logical operators AND and OR. They are used to define the relationship between two conditions (such as SALARY >=2000 and SALARY <=2500).

You can also define your expressions with character, date, and logical fields, but remember to enclose the filter string in quotation marks for the character field, such as FIRST = 'Jack'; and use the curly brackets to define the data value for the filter condition, such as HIRE_DATE > {01/01/88}. For logical fields, use either .T. or .F. as a filter value in the expression, such as COMMISSION = .T.

In addition to field names, logical operators, and filter values, you also can use mathematical functions in an expression. The last expression, BETWEEN(SALARY, 2000, 2400), is an example. BETWEEN is a function that evaluates the value in the SALARY field to determine whether it lies between the two limits (2000 and

2400). If you specify the filter condition with this expression, it will select those salaries between $2,000 and $2,400 inclusively.

There is a large set of functions that you can use to define your expressions, and we will discuss them in more detail in later chapters. For now, all you need to be concerned with are the more simple expressions.

### Defining Filter Conditions

To specify filter conditions for viewing selective records, first bring up the Setup dialog from the View window. Let's assume that you have SALESMAN.DBF open in the work area in the View window and that you have selected the <Setup> push button so that the Setup dialog appears. Now select the Filter check box at the bottom of the screen with the mouse. Alternatively, you can press the letter "l" (a copy of the Setup dialog was shown earlier in Figure 5.21). After selecting the Filter check box, the Expression Builder appears (see Figure 5.26).

The Expression Builder is a special dialog that allows you to define an expression—a formula that, when evaluated, generates of new value with a data type of character, numeric, logical, or date. The Expression Builder contains a number of popups and list boxes that make it extremely easy for you to build expressions. This ease of use is enhanced by the <Verify> push button, which instructs FoxPro to check the expression that you have created to make sure that it is valid and to report any errors to you.

On the top of the Expression Builder four menu popups are visible: Math, String, Logical, and Date. Open these menu popups by using the procedure for selecting a menu option from the menu popup—click your mouse on the popup or press the

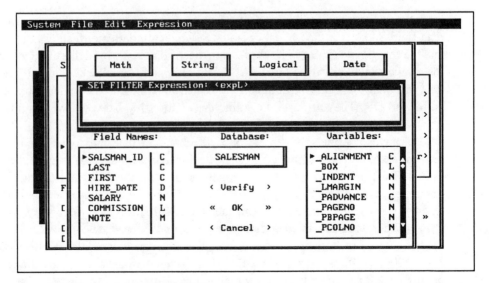

**Figure 5.26  The Expression Builder**

Ctrl key plus the first letter of the popup name (Ctrl-M, Ctrl-S, Ctrl-L, and Ctrl-D); or press the Tab key to cycle through the choices.

The Math menu popup lists the mathematical functions and operators that are available for inclusion in your expression. Likewise, all the functions and operators for string manipulation appear in the String menu popup, and all the logical functions and operators are in the Logical popup. And if you intend to use a function for manipulating your date fields in an expression, open the Date menu popup. To familiarize yourself with these popups, open each of them and take a look at their contents. You will learn to use some of them in later exercises.

### Entering Filter Expressions

In the center of the Expression Builder is a small Expression window in which you specify your filter expression. The easiest way to enter an expression is to type it in on the keyboard. For example, if you want to view only those records whose values in the SALARY field are at least $2,500, type in the appropriate filter expression (see Figure 5.27).

After you have completed defining the filter expression, select the <Verify> push button to check its validity. If the expression is invalid, FoxPro will display an alert dialog that attempts to diagnose the problem. Clicking anywhere on the screen or pressing any key will clear the dialog and allow you to correct the expression. If you decide at any time that you do not want to correct it, you can exit the dialog by selecting the <Cancel> push button. Otherwise, if the expression is valid, choose the <<OK>> push button to exit from the Filter Builder and return to the View

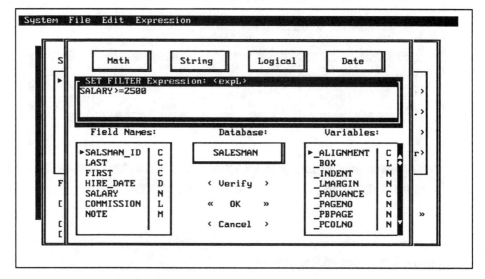

**Figure 5.27  Entering a Filter Expression**

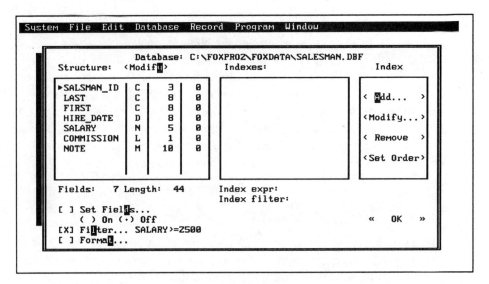

**Figure 5.28  Filter Expression in the View Window**

window. At this point, the filter expression you entered appears next to the Filter check box in the View window (see Figure 5.28).

Now you can proceed to display the records in the Browse window by returning to the View window and selecting the <Browse> push button. The new Browse window will display only those records that satisfy the conditions specified in the filter expression (see Figure 5.29).

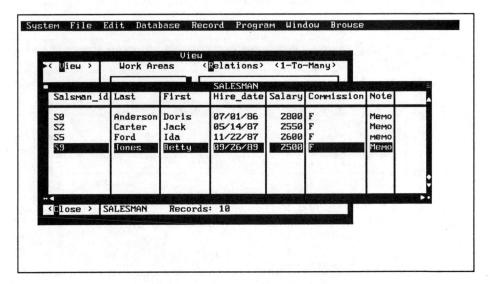

**Figure 5.29  Selected Records**

**Modifying Existing Filter Expressions**

After displaying the selected records, you may decide you want to look at a different set of records, a procedure easily accomplished by revising the filter expression. To do so, return to the Expression Builder and change the current filter expression by modifying it. Or, if you would like to write an entirely new expression, just press the Del key to erase the existing expression. So, to replace the current expression with the new expression, HIRE_DATE > {01/01/88} OR SALARY > 2600, type it in after erasing the existing one.

Another way to define a filter expression is to build it with the components selected from the field list and options from the menu popups. To build a new expression in this way, follow these steps:

1. First select the HIRE_DATE field from the field list (use the Tab and arrow keys to highlight it; then press the Enter key). The name of the selected field will be added to the expression.

2. Choose the > operator from the Logical menu popup.

3. Type in the filter value {01/01/88} for the HIRE_DATE date field from the keyboard.

4. Choose the OR operator from the Logical menu popup.

5. Select the SALARY field from the field list.

6. Select the > operator from the Logical menu popup.

7. Finally, type in the filter value of 2600 for the SALARY field.

Although blank spaces are not important in an expression, for clarity purposes you may want to insert blank spaces between components. Case is also not important in an expression. Field names, for example, can be in either lowercase or uppercase letters. However, logical operators such as AND and OR are usually expressed in uppercase letters for easy identification (see Figure 5.30). If the expression is too long to be displayed in the expression box, it will scroll and leave a part of the expression hidden from your view. (To access the hidden portion of an expression, simply use the up and down arrow keys.)

After verifying its validity, use the filter expression to display those records you want; in this case, the records belong to those salespeople who were hired after January 1, 1988, or whose salaries are greater than $2,600 (see Figure 5.31).

## PRINTING DATA

The procedures that you have learned so far allow you to display your data on the screen only. And although there is a Print menu option in the File menu popup, it

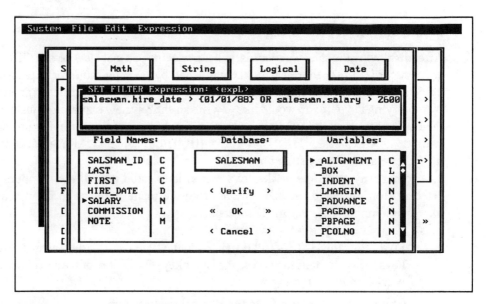

**Figure 5.30  Building a Filter Expression**

is used primarily for printing reports and labels. (You will learn these printing operations in later chapters.) But if you would like to route displayed data to a printer, you can do so with the appropriate FoxPro Commands described in the next section.

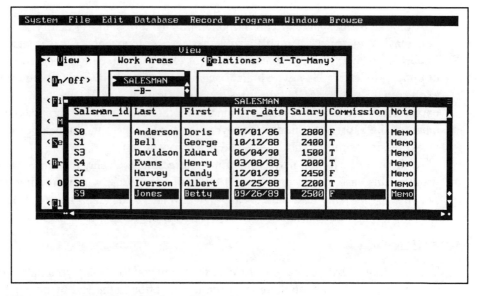

**Figure 5.31  New Set of Selected Records**

# Using Foxpro Commands

So far in this chapter we have used the menu interface for viewing data. But you can accomplish most of the same tasks by issuing the appropriate FoxPro commands. And, once you have mastered the FoxPro commands, you may find you prefer to use them as a short cut to the menu interface.

## OPENING A DATABASE FILE

The FoxPro command to open a database file in a work area has the following format:

```
USE <name of database file>
```

Use brackets to describe the object you need to enter. In this case, the object is the database file you would like to open in a work area. So to open SALES-MAN.DBF, issue the following command:

```
USE SALESMAN
```

You do not need to include the file extension. The USE command automatically assumes .DBF. And, if you do not specify the work area, A (or #1) is assigned by default.

You can open more than one database file in different work areas, but to do that you must select the work area for the database file before you issue the USE command, as in this example:

```
SELECT A
USE SALESMAN
SELECT B
USE OFFICE
```

These four commands open SALESMAN.DBF in work area A and OFFICE.DBF in work area B.

## CLOSING DATABASE FILES

After you have finished using your database files, close them by using the following command:

```
CLOSE DATABASES
```

This command closes all the open database files in all the work areas. However, if you need to close an individual database file, you must use the menu option as described earlier in this chapter. For now though, let's close all the open database files before proceeding to the next exercises.

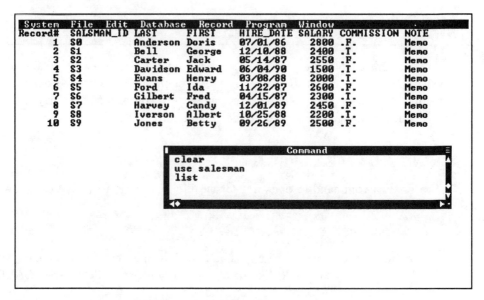

**Figure 5.32  Listing Every Record in SALESMAN.DBF**

## LISTING DATA RECORDS

When you want to put a list of all the records in the current database file, use the LIST command. It lists all of the records on the screen, one line for each record with the field names shown on top as labels (see Figure 5.32).

You can see that all of the records in that database file are displayed and that the list includes their record numbers. But if you would like to omit the column of record numbers, simply add the keyword "OFF" in the LIST command so that it reads LIST OFF (see Figure 5.33).

### Listing Selected Fields

To list only those data fields you want to view, add the FIELDS keyword in the LIST command. Following the keyword, specify the names of these data fields. Then, if you would like to view the FIRST, LAST, SALARY, and HIRE_DATE data fields, the command would read:

```
LIST FIELDS FIRST, LAST, SALARY, HIRE_DATE
```

As a result, these fields will be listed in the order they are specified, with all the records in the database file (see Figure 5.34).

```
System  File  Edit  Database  Record  Program  Window
SALSMAN_ID LAST       FIRST     HIRE_DATE SALARY COMMISSION NOTE
S0           Anderson Doris      07/01/86  2800  .F.        Memo
S1           Bell     George     10/12/88  2400  .T.        Memo
S2           Carter   Jack       05/14/87  2550  .F.        Memo
S3           Davidson Edward     06/04/90  1500  .T.        Memo
S4           Evans    Henry      03/08/88  2000  .T.        Memo
S5           Ford     Ida        11/22/87  2600  .F.        Memo
S6           Gibert   Fred       04/15/87  2300  .T.        Memo
S7           Harvey   Candy      12/01/89  2450  .F.        Memo
S8           Iverson  Albert     10/25/88  2200  .T.        Memo
S9           Jones    Betty      09/26/89  2500  .F.        Memo



                                           Command
         CLEAR
         USE SALESMAN
         LIST OFF
```

**Figure 5.33  Omitting Record Numbers in Record List**

As a short cut, you can omit FIELDS in the LIST command for displaying records of selective data fields. The command would then read:

```
LIST FIRST, LAST, SALARY, HIRE_DATE
```

```
System  File  Edit  Database  Record  Program  Window
Record#  FIRST    LAST     SALARY HIRE_DATE
      1  Doris    Anderson 2800   07/01/86
      2  George   Bell     2400   10/12/88
      3  Jack     Carter   2550   05/14/87
      4  Edward   Davidson 1500   06/04/90
      5  Henry    Evans    2000   03/08/88
      6  Ida      Ford     2600   11/22/87
      7  Fred     Gilbert  2300   04/15/87
      8  Candy    Harvey   2450   12/01/89
      9  Albert   Iverson  2200   10/25/88
     10  Betty    Jones    2500   09/26/89



                                           Command
         CLEAR
         LIST FIELDS FIRST, LAST, SALARY, HIRE_DATE
```

**Figure 5.34  Listing Selective Data Fields**

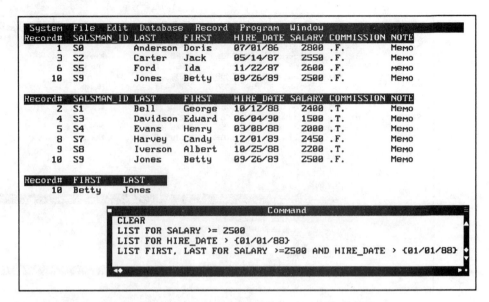

**Figure 5.35  Adding the FOR Clause to the LIST Command**

## Listing Selected Records

If you would like to display only a subset of the records in the current database file, add a FOR clause in LIST command to qualify the records. The format of such a LIST command is:

```
LIST [FIELDS] [<field names>] FOR <conditions>
```

The qualifying conditions are the same as the filter conditions you saw earlier. The objects in the square brackets ([ ]) are optional. Examples of these commands and their results are shown in Figure 5.35.

In this figure you can see that different sets of records are listed in response to the filter conditions specified in the LIST commands. The first set shows those salaries that are greater than or equal to $2,500. Those records having hire dates after January 1, 1988, are listed in the second set. The third command specifying the joint conditions resulted in only one record, the salesperson whose salary is $2,500 and was hired on September 26, 1989.

## LISTING MEMO FIELDS

When you display data records with the LIST command, the contents of the memo fields will not be listed. This is because memo fields are organized and stored differently than the other types of data fields. To show the contents of the memo

```
 System  File  Edit  Database  Record  Program  Window
Record#  MLINE(NOTE,1)
      1  Hobbies: classical music, painting, travel.
      2  Hobbies: fishing, hunting, country music.
      3  Education: BA, Bus. Admin.; University of
      4  Citizenship: Canadian.
      5  Education: BA, Marketing; UCLA, 1986.
      6
      7  Hobbies: classical music, opera, foreign travel.
      8  Hobbies: ballet, classical music, travel.
      9  Hobbies: hunting, fishing, sailing.
     10  Education: BA, Social Studies; University of

Record#  MLINE(NOTE,2)
      1
      2
      3  Washington, 1985.
      4
      5
      6                              ┌──────────── Command ────────────┐
      7                              │ CLEAR                           │
      8                              │ LIST MLINE(NOTE,1)              │
      9                              │ LIST MLINE(NOTE,2)              │
     10  Oregon, 1987.              └─────────────────────────────────┘
```

**Figure 5.36  Listing Contents of the NOTE Memo Field**

fields, you must include the MLINE function in your LIST command to show a specific line of the memo text. It has the following format:

```
MLINE(<memo field name>, <line #>)
```

For example, if you would like to list the first line of the NOTE memo field in SALESMAN.DBF, issue the following command:

```
LIST MLINE(NOTE,1)
```

Text in a memo field is divided into lines, each of which is set to a default width of 50 characters. If the text width is greater than the default width, it is pushed to the next line. Therefore, you may want to display the second line of the memo field as well (see Figure 5.36).

## Changing Memo Field Width

You can change the width of the memo field in the display by issuing the SET MEMOWIDTH command in the following format:

```
SET MEMOWIDTH TO <number of characters>
```

So, if you would like to set the memo width to 65 characters, issue the command SET MEMOWIDTH TO 65 accordingly (see Figure 5.37). Note in this figure that, after changing the memo field display width to 65, the contents of the NOTE memo

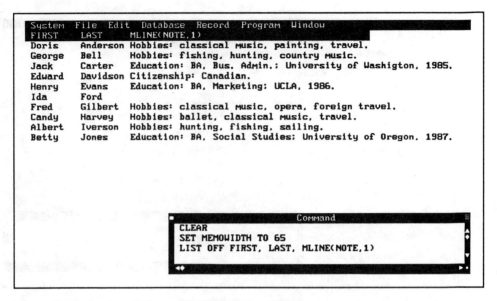

**Figure 5.37  Setting a Memo Field's Display Width**

field are displayed in full. The memo field contents are also listed. (Add the keyword OFF, if you don't want the record numbers to appear.)

## DISPLAYING DATA STRUCTURE

The command for showing the data structure of the current database file is:

```
DISPLAY STRUCTURE
```

Issue this command after selecting the database file and opening it in a work area with the USE command (see Figure 5.38).

### Using the Display Command

In addition to the LIST command, FoxPro provides another command for displaying data. In most cases, you can use DISPLAY in place of LIST in the command, as in the following:

| *LIST Command* | *DISPLAY Command* |
|---|---|
| LIST | DISPLAY ALL |
| LIST FIELDS ... | DISPLAY ALL FIELDS ... |
| LIST ... FOR | DISPLAY ... FOR |

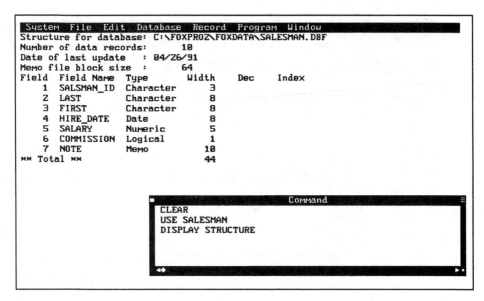

**Figure 5.38  Displaying Data Structure**

Examples of valid DISPLAY commands are:

```
USE SALESMAN
DISPLAY ALL
DISPLAY ALL FIELDS LAST, FIRST, SALARY, HIRE_DATE
DISPLAY ALL LAST, FIRST, SALARY, HIRE_DATE
DISPLAY FOR SALARY >= 2500
DISPLAY FOR SALARY >= 2500 AND HIRE_DATE >= {01/01/88}
DISPLAY ALL MLINE(NOTE,1)
DISPLAY ALL FIRST, LAST, MLINE(NOTE,1)
```

But there are a few differences. First, DISPLAY ALL, like LIST, shows all the records in the database file. However, in databases whose records will fill more than one screen, DISPLAY ALL pauses after displaying each screen full of data, while LIST does not. So when you use LIST to view a large number of records, they may scroll out of sight before you actually have a chance to examine them. Unlike LIST, which by default works with all the records of a database, the command DISPLAY alone shows only the contents of the current record. And to display a specific record, you must first go to that record before issuing the DISPLAY command. To go to the very first record in a database file, use the GO TOP command; to go to the very last record, use the GO BOTTOM command. To go to a specific record, specify the record number in the GOTO <record number> command (see Figure 5.39).

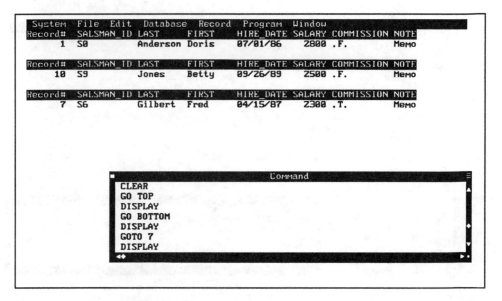

**Figure 5.39  Displaying a Specific Data Record**

Another difference is that you cannot include the keyword "OFF" in a DISPLAY to omit record numbers.

## SETTING FILTER CONDITIONS

When you use the FOR clause in the LIST and DISPLAY commands, you are qualifying the records before they are displayed. There is, however, another way to filter out unwanted records—use the SET FILTER command before issuing the LIST and DISPLAY command, in this format:

```
SET FILTER TO <filter conditions>
```

For example, to display only those records whose values in the SALARY field are greater than or equal to $2,500, use the following filtering command:

```
SET FILTER TO SALARY >= 2500
```

To remove the filter conditions, simply issue the SET FILTER TO command and leave out the filter conditions (see Figure 5.40).

Note that, after issuing the filter conditions, only records satisfying those conditions will be the subject of the subsequent LIST command. After removing

```
System  File  Edit  Database  Record  Program  Window
Record#  SALSMAN_ID LAST      FIRST    HIRE_DATE SALARY COMMISSION NOTE
      1  S0           Anderson  Doris   07/01/86   2800  .F.        Memo
      3  S2           Carter    Jack    05/14/87   2550  .F.        Memo
      6  S5           Ford      Ida     11/22/87   2600  .F.        memo
     10  S9           Jones     Betty   09/26/89   2500  .F.        Memo

Record#  SALSMAN_ID LAST      FIRST    HIRE_DATE SALARY COMMISSION NOTE
      1  S0           Anderson  Doris   07/01/86   2800  .F.        Memo
      2  S1           Bell      George  10/12/88   2400  .T.        Memo
      3  S2           Carter    Jack    05/14/87   2550  .F.        Memo
      4  S3           Davidson  Edward  06/04/90   1500  .T.        Memo
      5  S4           Evans     Henry   03/08/88   2000  .T.        Memo
      6  S5           Ford      Ida     11/22/87   2600  .F.        memo
      7  S6           Gilbert   Fred    04/15/87   2300  .T.        Memo
      8  S7           Harvey    Candy   12/01/89   2450  .F.        Memo
      9  S8           Iverson   Albert  10/25/88   2200  .T.        Memo
     10  S9           Jones     Betty   09/26/89   2500  .F.        Memo

                              ┌──────────── Command ────────────┐
                              │ SET FILTER TO SALARY >= 2500     │
                              │ LIST                             │
                              │ SET FILTER TO                    │
                              │ DISPLAY ALL                      │
                              └──────────────────────────────────┘
```

**Figure 5.40  Setting Filter Conditions**

the filter conditions with the SET FILTER TO command, all the records become available for the LIST command.

## DIRECTING DISPLAYED DATA TO PRINTERS

The LIST and DISPLAY commands are used to display the data structure and records of your database files on the screen. To then route the displayed data to your printer, either add the TO PRINT clause to your LIST or DISPLAY commands as in these examples:

```
USE SALESMAN
LIST TO PRINT
LIST LAST, FIRST TO PRINT
LIST LAST, FIRST, SALARY FOR SALARY >=2500 TO PRINT
DISPLAY ALL TO PRINT
DISPLAY FOR SALARY >= 2500 TO PRINT
DISPLAY ALL MLINE(NOTE,1) TO PRINT
DISPLAY ALL FIRST, LAST, MLINE(NOTE,1) TO PRINT
```

or print your data by issuing the SET PRINT ON command to activate your printer. Once the printer is activated, all the displayed data will be routed to the default printer. (They will be displayed on the screen as well.) After you have finished printing your data, remember to issue the SET PRINT OFF to deactivate the printer; otherwise, results of subsequent commands will be directed to your printer as well.

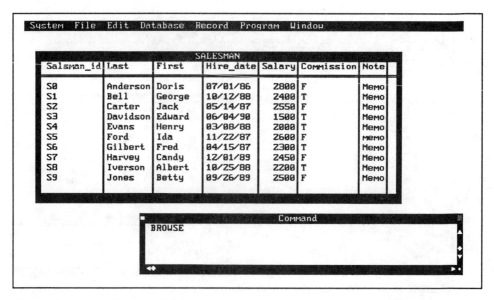

**Figure 5.41  Invoking the Browse Window with the BROWSE Command**

## BROWSING DATA

You can bring up the Browse window for displaying your data with the BROWSE command. Without adding any other keywords or filter conditions, the BROWSE command displays all the records and data fields in the current database file in the current Browse window. In Figure 5.41, for example, the Browse window displays all of the existing records. The location and size of the Browse window are carried over from the last exercise.

Like the DISPLAY and LIST commands, the BROWSE command allows you to view multiple records. However, it offers three major advantages over DISPLAY and LIST. First, since it presents its data in a window, it offers a more attractive, formatted display. Second, it allows you to scroll among the records in a database. Finally, BROWSE allows you to modify the contents of your database, whereas DISPLAY and LIST only show the contents of fields and records.

### Browsing Selected Data Fields

It is possible to display selected data fields and records with the BROWSE command by adding the keyword "FIELDS" and the data fields you would like to view. The command would read:

```
BROWSE FIELDS <field list>
```

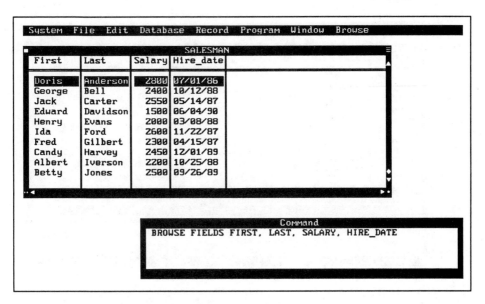

**Figure 5.42  Browsing Selective Data Fields**

For example, you can specify the data fields in SALESMAN.DBF that you would like to display in the Browse window by listing the fields in the BROWSE FIELDS command, as shown in Figure 5.42.

Notice that the order of the displayed data fields is determined by what was specified in the BROWSE command.

## Browsing Selected Records

As with the LIST and DISPLAY commands, you can also add filter conditions in the BROWSE command to select only those data records that you need. Just specify the filter conditions as an expression in a FOR clause, such as:

```
BROWSE [FIELDS <field list>] FOR <filter conditions>
```

Here are some examples:

```
BROWSE FOR COMMISSION = .T.
BROWSE FOR HIRE_DATE >= {01/01/88}
BROWSE FIELDS LAST, SALARY FOR SALARY >= 2500
BROWSE FIELDS LAST, SALARY FOR SALARY >= 2000 AND SALARY <= 3000
```

When the last BROWSE command is executed, it displays only those records that satisfied the filter conditions (see Figure 5.43).

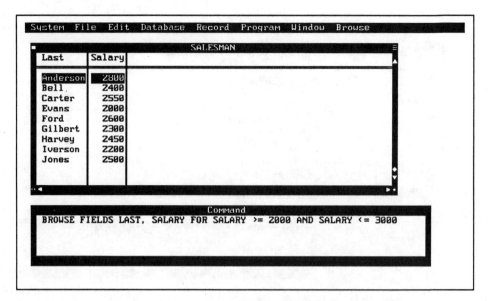

**Figure 5.43  Adding Filter Conditions to a BROWSE Command**

Of course, you can also issue the SET FILTER TO command to screen your records before issuing the BROWSE command to display selected records, in which case you would replace the final BROWSE FIELDS command with the following commands:

```
SET FILTER TO SALARY >=2000 AND SALARY <= 3000
BROWSE FIELDS LAST, SALARY
```

## DEFINING CUSTOM WINDOWS

As you have seen in all the examples, the size and location of the Browse window are retained from their previous use. You can use the mouse or the appropriate menu options to resize and move the window, or define the exact size and location of the window with a FoxPro command. The command for setting up a custom window is:

```
DEFINE WINDOW <custom window name> FROM <row,column> TO
            <row,column>
```

In this command, you must supply the name of the window that you are setting up. In addition, it is necessary to specify the screen locations for the upper left- and lower right-hand corners of the window. Each location is defined by a pair of numbers indicating the row number and the column number. When you display text on the screen, it is divided into 25 rows and 80 columns. Rows are numbered from 0 to 24, columns from 0 to 79. This is a sample command for setting up a custom window named Bwindow:

```
DEFINE WINDOW Bwindow FROM 3,10 TO 15,40
```

The window defined here has its upper left-hand corner at the intersection of the third row from the top, and tenth column from the left. The lower right-hand corner of the custom window is located at the fifteenth row from the top and fortieth column from the left. As a result, the size of the window is 13 rows high and 31 columns wide.

## Browsing Data in a Custom Window

After a custom window is defined, you use it in the BROWSE command in the following format:

```
BROWSE WINDOW <window name> ......
```

You can add the necessary keywords and filter conditions to the command as well (see Figure 5.44).

Pay particular attention to this figure, because there is an important difference between a custom window and a regular Browse window. A custom window cannot be resized or moved. Note that it does not have the Size control at the lower right-hand corner of the window. In order to change the custom window, you must redefine it with the DEFINE WINDOW command.

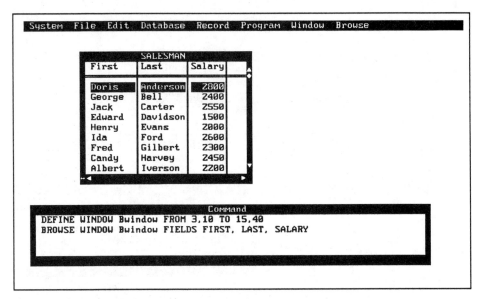

**Figure 5.44  Browsing Data in a Custom Defined Window**

To display data in a regular Browse window, just issue the BROWSE command with the WINDOW clause in it. You can resize and move the Browse window after it appears.

## Browsing Memo Fields in a Custom Window

The custom window you set up with the DEFINE WINDOW command can also be used to display contents of memo fields. Instead of using the default window carried over from the last application, just use the custom window that you defined. To do that, designate the custom window as your Memo window with the SET WINDOW OF MEMO TO command:

```
SET WINDOW OF MEMO TO <window name>
```

Here is an example:

```
DEFINE WINDOW Mwindow FROM 7,10 TO 9,60
SET WINDOW OF MEMO TO Mwindow
BROWSE
```

When the BROWSE command is executed, the records of the current database file are displayed in the normal Browse window, and the contents of the memo field are shown in the custom window (see Figure 5.45).

In this figure you can see that the contents of the NOTE memo field of the first record are displayed in the custom window. Remember, to view the memo field,

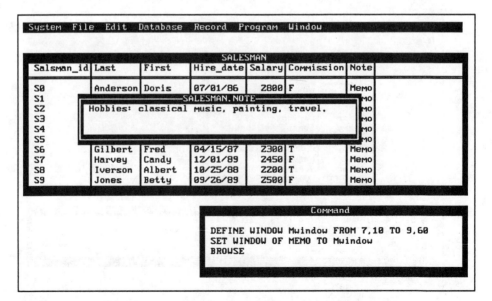

**Figure 5.45  Memo Fields Displayed in a Custom Memo Window**

click the mouse twice on the field, or press the Ctrl-PgUp key while the memo field is highlighted.

### Closing Custom Windows

After you have finished using the custom defined windows, you can close them by issuing the command:

```
CLEAR WINDOWS
```

This command clears the screen and closes all the custom windows that you set up with the DEFINE WINDOW command. It is a good practice to close any unused windows to conserve memory space.

## Browsing Multiple Database Files

Recall that we said it is possible to have more than one database file open in different work areas at a time. Likewise, you can view these database files in multiple Browse windows. First, open the database files in their respective work areas and then issue the BROWSE command to display their contents. Try using the following commands to open and browse the contents of the SALESMAN.DBF and OFFICE.DBF databases:

```
SELECT A
USE SALESMAN
BROWSE
SELECT B
USE OFFICE
BROWSE
```

After executing these commands, two Browse windows appear, each of which is used to display the contents of a database file. These windows overlap, the last one appearing on top of the first (see Figure 5.46).

The Browse window that includes the records of OFFICE.DBF appears on top of the SALESMAN.DBF Browse window because OFFICE.DBF was opened and browsed *after* you opened and browsed SALESMAN.DBF. Obviously then, the database that you browse last becomes the current active window. In order to switch to the hidden window, you must make the other database (in this case, SALESMAN.DBF) the current active one. There are two ways you can do this. One is to issue the SELECT command. In this instance, while OFFICE.DBF (in work area B) is active, issue the following command to make SALESMAN.DBF (in work area A) the active database:

```
SELECT A
```

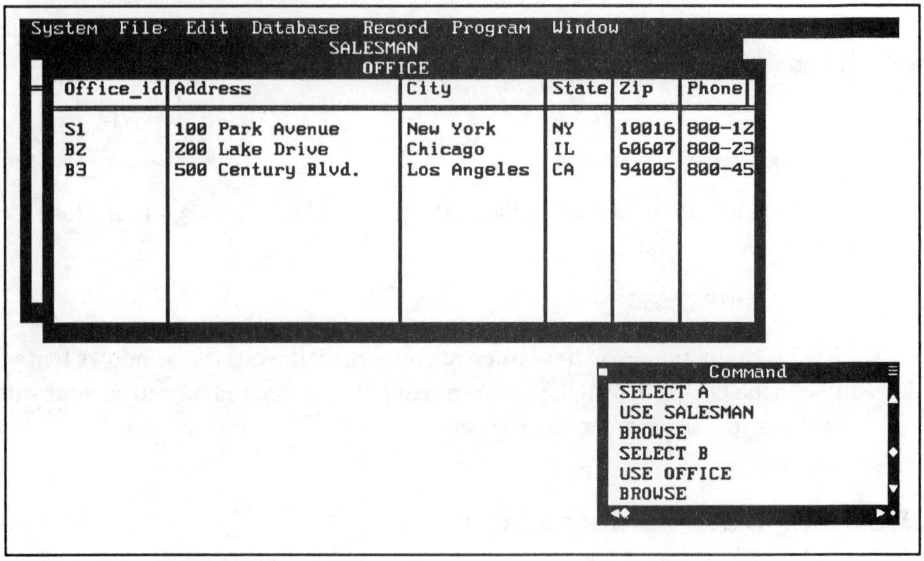

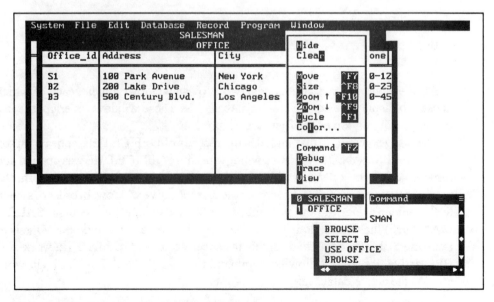

**Figure 5.46  Browsing Multiple Database Files in Browse Windows**

You can then switch to the Browse window for the SALESMAN database by reissuing the BROWSE command.

The second way to switch from one Browse window to another is to select the Browse window in the Window menu popup (see Figure 5.47). You can see that two Browse windows are visible in the Window menu popup. The number to the

**Figure 5.47  Selecting the Browse Window**

left of the database name indicates the order in which the window was opened. Select the database file you would like to view in the current Browse window by clicking your mouse on that file, or by entering the window number from the keyboard (e.g., 0 for SALESMAN.DBF, 1 for OFFICE.DBF).

### Abbreviating Command Keywords

Earlier in the chapter we introduced a list of keywords common in FoxPro commands: LIST, DISPLAY, FIELDS, STRUCTURE, SELECT, BROWSE, etc. As a shortcut, you can abbreviate all the longer keywords to only the first four letters. That is, replace DISPLAY with DISP, FIELDS with FIEL, STRUCTURE with STRU, SELECT with SELE, and BROWSE with BROW. Commands would then read:

```
SELE A
USE SALESMAN
DISP ALL
DISP STRU
BROW FIEL LAST, FIRST, SALARY
DEFI WIND Bwindow FROM 5,5 TO 20,20
BROW WIND Bwindow
```

# Chapter Summary

In this chapter you learned how to display the data structure and records of your database files. You were also made aware of the option to use either Browse or Change modes to view your data in a Browse window.

We showed that the Browse window provided by FoxPro is a very powerful tool for displaying data. In it you can display all or some of the records of your database files, and if necessary, you can partition it so that you can display various parts of a database file on the same screen. In addition, you can display multiple database files on several Browse windows simultaneously.

Furthermore, you can issue the LIST or DISPLAY commands to display data on the screen. Then, by adding the TO PRINT clause to the LIST or DISPLAY commands, you can direct the displayed data to your printer as well.

This chapter also clarified how data records are displayed—in the order that they were entered into the database file. Then you learned that you could rearrange these records into a specific order (e.g., in ascending or descending order) by sorting or indexing your database file. These operations—sorting and indexing—are the subject of discussion in the next chapter.

# 6

# Sorting and Indexing Data

## An Overview

As discussed in Chapter 5, when data in a database file is displayed in either Change or Browse mode, its records are arranged in the same order in which they were entered into the database file. This arrangement will not be desirable for all applications, such as when you want to display the records according to the values in specific data fields. Sorting and indexing are the two methods that enable you to reorder your data records.

There are advantages and disadvantages to both of these methods. Depending on your objectives, you will decide on one over the other for different applications. In the beginning of this chapter, we will explore the strengths and weaknesses of both methods. Later, you will learn how to apply these two methods.

## Ordering Data Records

As seen in earlier examples, a relational database stores and organizes its data elements in table form. Data records are entered into the table after its data structure has been set up. The order in which the records are added to the table determines the order in which they will be displayed in the Browse window, unless other steps are taken to alter their order.

In Figure 6.1, for example, all of the records are displayed in the order they were entered. Although no sorting operation has been performed on the table, you can see that the records in SALESMAN.DBF appear to be in the order of salesperson identification number and last name. It is not unusual to arrange data records in such a manner before entering them into a table when you first set up the table. For example, initially we entered the records for each of the ten salespeople by

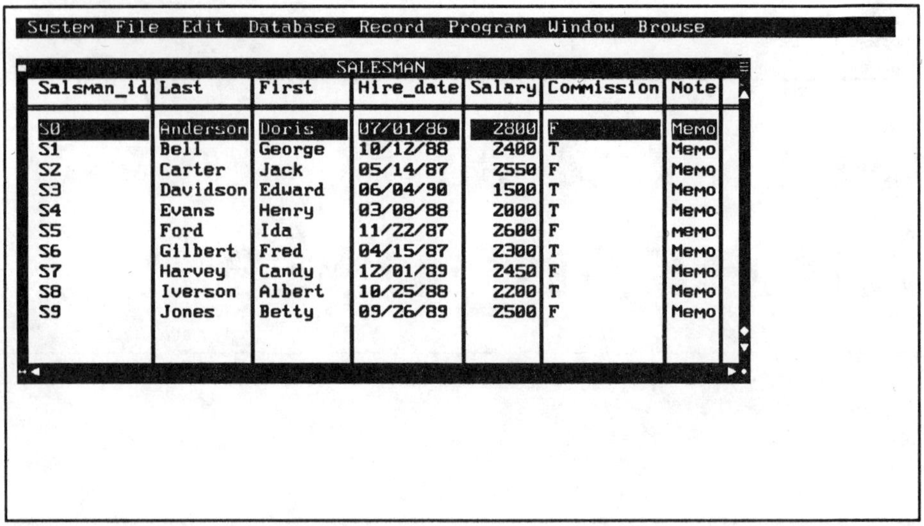


| Salsman_id | Last | First | Hire_date | Salary | Commission | Note |
|---|---|---|---|---|---|---|
| S0 | Anderson | Doris | 07/01/86 | 2800 | F | Memo |
| S1 | Bell | George | 10/12/88 | 2400 | T | Memo |
| S2 | Carter | Jack | 05/14/87 | 2550 | F | Memo |
| S3 | Davidson | Edward | 06/04/90 | 1500 | T | Memo |
| S4 | Evans | Henry | 03/08/88 | 2000 | T | Memo |
| S5 | Ford | Ida | 11/22/87 | 2600 | F | Memo |
| S6 | Gilbert | Fred | 04/15/87 | 2300 | T | Memo |
| S7 | Harvey | Candy | 12/01/89 | 2450 | F | Memo |
| S8 | Iverson | Albert | 10/25/88 | 2200 | T | Memo |
| S9 | Jones | Betty | 09/26/89 | 2500 | F | Memo |

**Figure 6.1 Data Records in Original Order**

assigning a sequential identification number (from S0 to S9). We also arranged the data records alphabetically by last name. But from this point on, all data records that you enter into the table will appear as they occur and no longer will follow the original order. So if a new salesperson named Charles Gilmore is hired and you enter his data into the table as the eleventh record, with S10 as his identification number, the records in SALESMAN.DBF will no longer be alphabetical by last name.

In addition, in some applications you will no doubt want to display your records in an order that is determined by the values in only some of the data fields. You may want, for example, to arrange the records in chronological order by the values in the HIRE_DATE field. Or you might want to produce a roster showing the sales staff's names, but ordered according to their salaries. Obviously, you need to be able to order your records according to a set of predetermined criteria, and both sorting and indexing allow you to do this.

## SORTING VS. INDEXING

Sorting involves physically rearranging records in a database file according to a predetermined order, and you can use one or more data fields to define the sort order. The values in these fields determine the order of the records.

Sorted records are saved in a separate database file with a different name. Then, if you need to view the sorted records, you select the sorted file. Let's continue with our example and sort the SALESMAN database according to the hiring dates in the HIRE_DATE field and then save the sorted records in a new file named BYDATE.DBF. In this case, the HIRE_DATE field is used to set the sort order. The records in the original SALESMAN.DBF will remain unchanged, while the records in BYDATE.DBF will be ordered by the dates in the HIRE_DATE field.

The indexing method arranges records according to the values in one or more fields, which is called an index key. But be aware that the indexing operation does not actually *rearrange* the records in a database file. Instead, it creates a separate index file whose records are arranged based on the values of the index key. Each time you need to view the records in a database file in a particular order, the index file is used. You can create a number of index files, each of which is set up according to an index key, and you can later use the existing index files to display your records in a number of different ways.

One advantage to using the sorting method is that sorted records are created and stored in separate files which you can access at any time to show the ordered records. You don't have to re-create the files as long as the contents of the original database remain unchanged. If you do modify the contents of the original database file, however, the sorted file is not updated automatically. You must re-sort the records and replace the sorted file with the new set of sorted records. This process can require great amounts of time when working with large databases. It can also lead to enormous confusion if you forget to re-sort a modified database file.

In addition, because sorting results in the creation of other files, valuable disk space is taken up for the storage of the sorted files. And this is an especially important point to remember if the database file has a large number of records and numerous data fields.

The indexing operation, on the other hand, rearranges the records by using the information in the index files each time that you need to order the records. The index file contains only the information necessary for arranging the data records in the database file; it is used for ordering the actual records. It is easier to keep an index file updated each time you modify the contents of the database file because whenever you modify your records in a database file in FoxPro, the corresponding index files are updated automatically as long as the index files remain open. It is possible, however, to corrupt the contents of an index file if you fail to open it before making changes to its associated database file. To avoid such a risk, use a structural index file that automatically opens when you open its database file. You will learn about this later.

Moreover, in an indexing operation, the original index file occupies a small amount of disk space because the index file usually contains only the values of the index key and is relatively small.

Finally, because sorting is much slower than indexing, indexing is a more desirable approach for ordering data records in most applications. An exception is when you have a relatively small database file and you do not expect to make any changes to its contents.

## SORTING DATA RECORDS

You can use either the menu interface or FoxPro commands with the sorting method. First we'll discuss the procedure for sorting records with the menu interface.

The first step in sorting data records in a database file is to open the database file in a work area. Do this in the View window by opening a database file in any one of the 25 work areas. Or, choose the Open option from the File menu popup, followed by selecting the database file to be opened from the File Open dialog. When you open a database file this way, the file is always opened in the default work area—A (#1). If you subsequently open another database file by using the same Open menu option, the current open file will be closed automatically and the new database file will be opened in work area A. This method is very useful when all you need to work on is one database file.

As an exercise, open SALESMAN.DBF in work area A by choosing the Open option from the File menu popup. After selecting the Open menu option, open the SALESMAN.DBF file from the File Open dialog (see Figure 6.2). In addition to the three push buttons (<Open>, <New>, and <Cancel>) and the Drive and Directory popups, there is a Type popup shown in the bottom left of the dialog box. This indicates the types of files that you can open. In this case, we want it to read "Database." If it does not, simply open the popup and select the correct type.

Once you have opened the SALESMAN.DBF database file, the File Open dialog disappears. To proceed to sort the data records in the database, choose the Sort option from the Database menu popup; now the Sort dialog appears. Specify in the

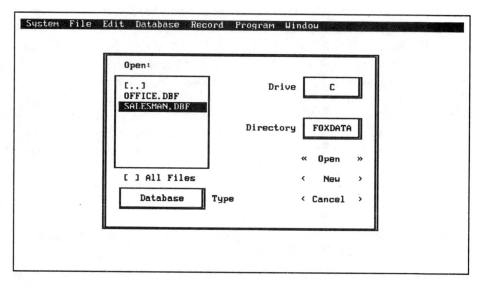

**Figure 6.2  Opening a Database File in the File Open Dialog**

dialog how you would like to sort the records, and identify the file to which you would like to save the sorted records. This dialog is also where you define the filter conditions for selecting the data records that you would like to save to the output file, as well as the list of data fields to be included in the sorted file (see Figure 6.3).

The name of the database file being used (e.g., SALESMAN) appears in the lower left-hand corner of the dialog. Next to it in the Input box are three check boxes (Scope..., For..., and While...), which are used to specify the filter conditions for selecting the data records that you would like to sort. Above these check boxes is the list of data fields in the database file. One or more of these fields can be used to define the sort order.

The <Move> and <Remove> push buttons are provided so that you can move the data fields from the Database Fields list into the Sort Order list that appears to the right of the push buttons. Use one of the two radio buttons (Ascending or Descending) to specify how you would like the sorting operation to be carried out. The Ignore Case check box gives you the option to ignore case when sorting character strings. These radio buttons and the check box appear in the center of the dialog box above the Field Options box.

Finally, the Output box at the bottom center of the dialog box is where you specify the name of the output file for the sorted records in the <Save As...> dialog. Next to it, in the Fields check box, is where you select the data fields to be included in the output file.

The usual <<OK>> and <<Cancel>> push buttons are in the lower right-hand corner of the dialog box.

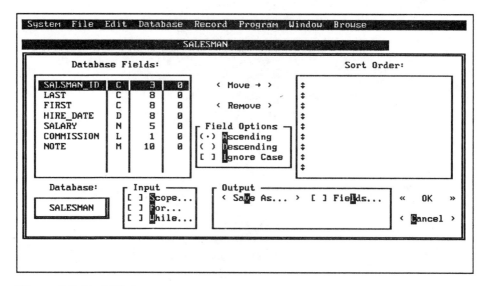

**Figure 6.3  Sort Dialog**

## Defining Sort Order

Before you sort data records, you must specify the sort order. This involves selecting the data fields whose values will be used to determine the order in which the records are to be sorted.

You can use most types of data fields as sort fields, but you cannot sort on a memo field. Each of the sortable fields can have its values arranged either in ascending or descending order. Therefore, you can arrange the character strings in a character field alphabetically from A to Z (ascending) or from Z to A (descending). Similarly, you can sort a numeric field from smallest to largest, or from largest to smallest. You also can arrange dates chronologically from earliest date to most recent date (ascending) or from most recent date to earliest date (descending). But when you sort a logical field, the records are grouped into those having .T. (True) values and .F. (False) values.

### Sorting Character Fields

When sorting character strings, remember that case is important. Uppercase and lowercase letters are treated differently, and the order follows that of the ASCII (American Standard Code for Information Interchange) code in which uppercase and lowercase letters are assigned different codes. Although you can find a copy of the complete ASCII table showing all of the characters in their predefined order in Appendix A of this book, a brief definition is necessary here: In ascending order, the set of capital letters A–Z appears *before* the lowercase letters a–z; digits 0–9 appear before letters; and blank spaces appear before letters and digits. For example:

| Ascending Order | Descending Order |
| --- | --- |
| 100 MAIN STREET | Peterson |
| 100 Main Avenue | PETER |
| 1000 MAIN STREET | monkeys |
| DAVID | Monkey |
| DAVIDSON | Jackie |
| David | Jack |
| Davidson | JOHN |
| JOHN | Davidson |
| Jack | David |
| Jackie | DAVIDSON |
| Monkey | DAVID |
| monkeys | 1000 MAIN STREET |
| PETER | 100 Main Avenue |
| Peterson | 100 MAIN STREET |

As an exercise, let's sort the SALESMAN.DBF records into ascending order by using the contents of the FIRST data field. First define the sort order in the Sort dialog by selecting the data field whose values you intend to sort by. Then choose the sort order by turning on the radio button for either ascending or descending. To turn on a radio button, either click your mouse button once on the name of the radio button or press the letter "A" or "D" to turn on the Ascending or Descending radio button. In our exercise, because we want to sort the FIRST data field in ascending order, turn on Ascending (indicated with a dot inside the parentheses).

For this procedure you must decide whether case is important in sorting the character strings selected. If you do not want to differentiate between upper- and lowercase letters in the sorting operation, select the Ignore Case check box. Do this by clicking the mouse button on the box or by pressing the letter "I" and then Enter on the keyboard. Our exercise requires that this box be checked because the first names are composed of upper- and lowercase letters.

After the field options are defined, select the data field from the Field list and move it to the Sort Order list by double clicking your mouse on the field name. With the keyboard, position the cursor on the data field and then press Enter. If you make a mistake, you can remove the selected data fields using exactly the same procedure. With that in mind, move the FIRST data field into the Sort Order box (see Figure 6.4). The Sort Order box now has the FIRST field listed. The up arrow that appears in front of the field name indicates an ascending sort order.

You are now ready to specify the name of the database file for holding the sorted records. Do this either with the mouse or by pressing the letter "v" to select the

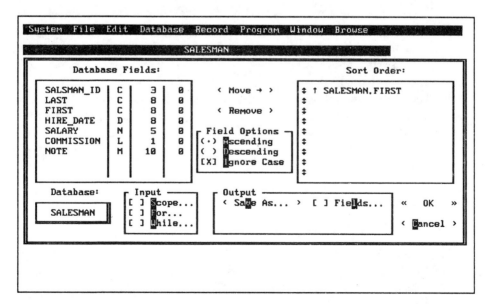

**Figure 6.4  Defining a Sort Order**

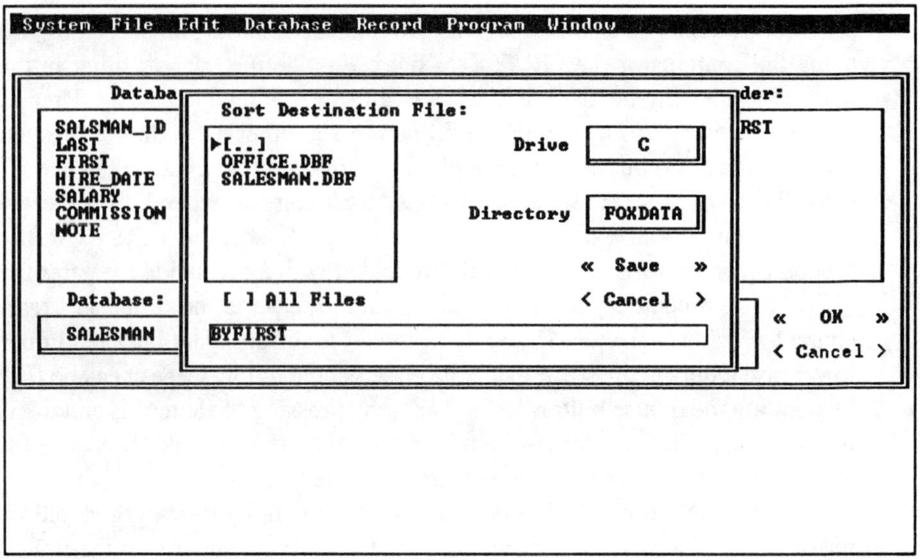

**Figure 6.5  Naming the Sorted Output File**

<Save As...> push button. Then enter the name of the output file (BYFIRST) accordingly in the Filename dialog (see Figure 6.5).

After you have specified the output filename and selected the <<Save>> push button, FoxPro returns you to the Sort dialog. At this point, the output filename appears at the bottom of the Output box (see Figure 6.6).

If you are using a mouse, you can enter the output filename directly into the Output box in the Sort dialog without going through the Filename dialog. Double click on the location where the name of the output file should appear (in the dialog box, below the <Save As...> push button). When the cursor appears, enter the filename with the keyboard.

The sorting operation is now defined. It is time to begin the actual sorting operation itself: Just select the <<OK>> push button. Watch as the records in the SALESMAN.DBF file are sorted in ascending order according to the contents of the FIRST field. When the sorting operation is finished, the message "10 records sorted" appears.

**Viewing the Sorted Records**

After the records in SALESMAN.DBF are sorted, the output file named BY-FIRST.DBF contains the sorted records. To view them you must open the output file. Remember: The records in SALESMAN.DBF remain unchanged.

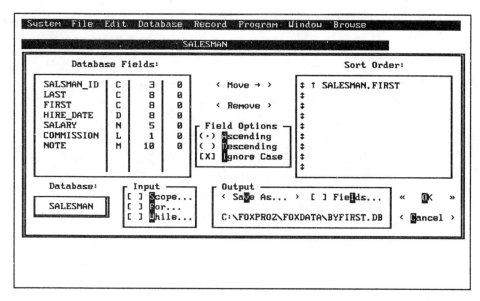

**Figure 6.6  Name of Sorted Output File Displayed**

To view *only* the sorted records, open just the BYFIRST.DBF in work area A. You can, however, open both the original and sorted files in the View window and then verify their contents in the Browse windows (see Figure 6.7).

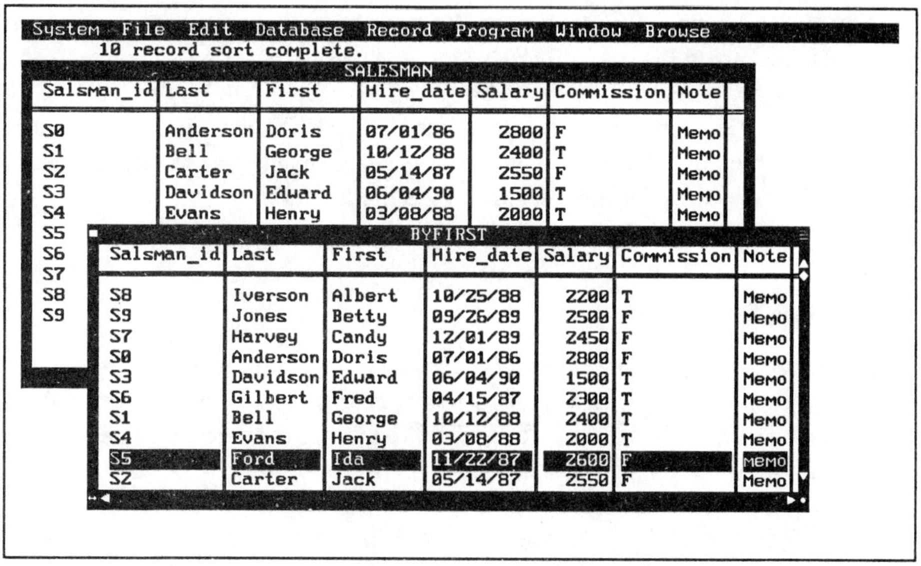

**Figure 6.7  Comparing the Original and Sorted Databases**

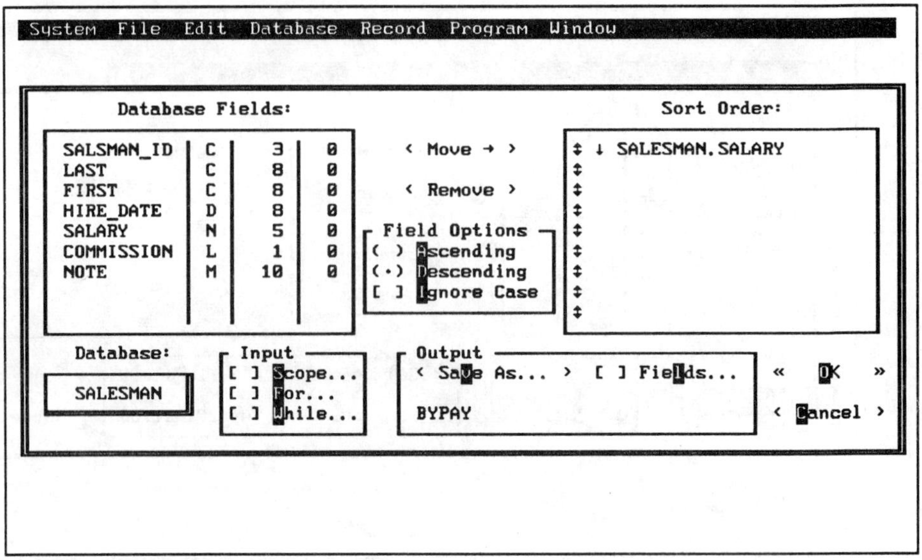

**Figure 6.8  Sorting the SALARY Numerical Field**

### Sorting Numerical Fields

To use the sorting operation to rank records according to the values in a numerical data field, choose either ascending order (numbers arranged from the smallest to the largest values), or descending order for the reverse. Utilizing the sorting operation in this way enables you to produce, for example, a roster of sales personnel from the SALESMAN.DBF database ranked by salary in descending order based on the values in the SALARY data field (see Figure 6.8).

When you view the sorted records in the BYPAY.DBF output file, you can see that the records are arranged in this way. As a result, you can quickly tell which salesperson earns the highest salary (see Figure 6.9).

### Sorting Date Fields

Records also can be arranged by the date values in a date field; in ascending order they are listed from earliest to most recent date, and in descending order from most recent date to earliest. Say that you want to arrange the records in the SALESMAN database in ascending order by the date values in the HIRE_DATE field. To do that, turn on the Ascending radio button in the Field Options box. After that, select HIRE_DATE as the sort field and move it to the Set Order box. Finally, enter BYDATE as the name of the output file (see Figure 6.10). As a result, the sorted records in the output file named BYDATE, are arranged from the earliest to the most recent (see Figure 6.11).

```
System  File  Edit  Database  Record  Program  Window  Browse
                           SALESMAN
 Salsman_id Last      First    Hire_date Salary Commission Note

 S0        Anderson  Doris    07/01/86   2800  F          Memo
 S1        Bell      George   10/12/88   2400  T          Memo
 S2        Carter    Jack     05/14/87   2550  F          Memo
 S3        Davidson  Edward   06/04/90   1500  T          Memo
 S4        Evans     Henry    03/08/88   2000  T          Memo
 S5        Ford      Ida      11/22/87   2600  F          Memo
 S6        Gilbert   Fred     04/15/87   2300  T          Memo
 S7                                  BYPAY
 S8        Salsman_id Last      First    Hire_date Salary Commission Note
 S9
           S0        Anderson  Doris    07/01/86   2800  F          Memo
           S5        Ford      Ida      11/22/87   2600  F          Memo
           S2        Carter    Jack     05/14/87   2550  F          Memo
           S9        Jones     Betty    09/26/89   2500  F          Memo
           S7        Harvey    Candy    12/01/89   2450  F          Memo
           S1        Bell      George   10/12/88   2400  T          Memo
           S6        Gilbert   Fred     04/15/87   2300  T          Memo
           S8        Iverson   Albert   10/25/88   2200  T          Memo
           S4        Evans     Henry    03/08/88   2000  T          Memo
           S3        Davidson  Edward   06/04/90   1500  T          Memo
```

**Figure 6.9   Sorted SALARY Numerical Field**

## Sorting Logical Fields

Values in a logical field are expressed in the form of either .T. or .F. and hence, you can sort your records into these two groups—one with values of .T. (true), the other with values of .F. (false). When you are using a logical field as the sorting key, the

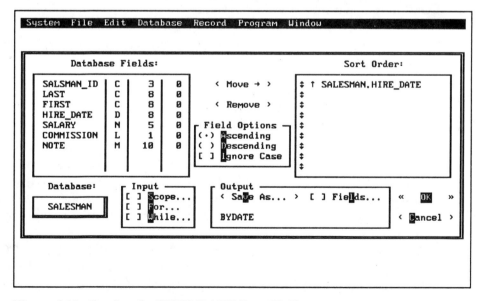

**Figure 6.10   Sorting the HIRE_DATE Date Field**

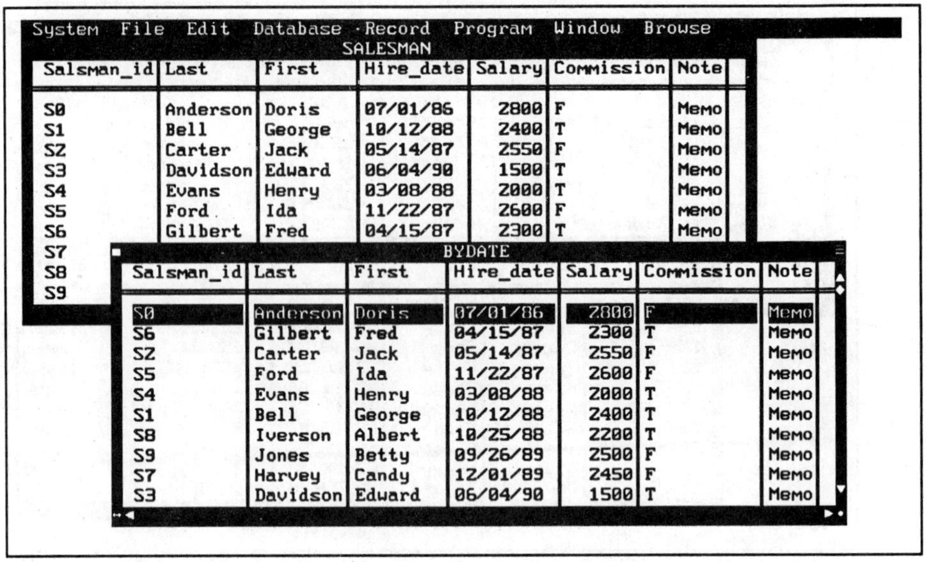

**Figure 6.11  Viewing the Sorted HIRE_DATE Date Field**

group of records having .F. values always appears first in the sorted database. Subsequently, records with logical values of .T. appear second. The choice of ascending or descending order is irrelevant here.

As an exercise, let's sort the records in the SALESMAN database according to the logical values in the COMMISSION field and save them to the BY-COMMIS.DBF output file (see Figure 6.12).

When you view the BYCOMMIS.DBF output file, note that all of the records with the value .F. in the COMMISSION field appear first. The others appear in the second group of sorted records (see Figure 6.13).

### Sorting Multiple Fields

When you define a sort order, it is possible to include more than one data field as the sorting key. In such a situation, the records will be sorted in sequence. For example, if you select two data fields as the sort order, the records initially will be arranged according to the values in the sorting field you specified first. Those records having the same value in the first sorting field will then be arranged by the values in the second sorting field.

As an exercise, let's sort the records in SALESMAN.DBF by using the COMMISSION and SALARY fields. Choose descending order for the SALARY sorting field and save the sorted records to the output file COMISPAY (see Figure 6.14).

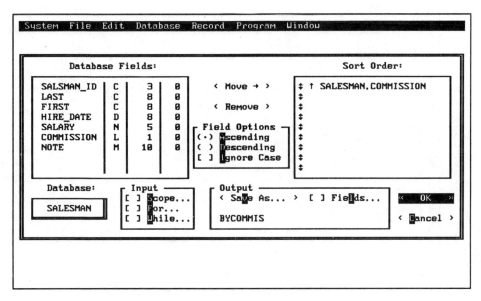

```
 System  File  Edit  Database  Record  Program  Window

        Database Fields:                                    Sort Order:

    SALSMAN_ID  C   3   0       < Move → >         ↕ ↑  SALESMAN.COMMISSION
    LAST        C   8   0                          ↕
    FIRST       C   8   0       < Remove >         ↕
    HIRE_DATE   D   8   0      ┌ Field Options ┐   ↕
    SALARY      N   5   0       (·) Ascending      ↕
    COMMISSION  L   1   0       ( ) Descending     ↕
    NOTE        M  10   0       [ ] Ignore Case    ↕
                                                   ↕
                                                   ↕

        Database:      ┌ Input ─────┐   ┌ Output ──────────────────────
                        [ ] Scope...    < Save As... >  [ ] Fields...     « OK »
        SALESMAN        [ ] For...
                        [ ] While...    BYCOMMIS                        < Cancel >
```

**Figure 6.12    Sorting the COMMISSION Logical Field**

When the sorting operation begins, it first arranges the records in SALES-MAN.DBF into two groups according to the values in the COMMISSION logical field. Those records in the group with an .F. value in the logical field are then sorted

```
 System  File  Edit  Database  Record  Program  Window  Browse
                                SALESMAN
   Salsman_id│Last    │First   │Hire_date│Salary│Commission│Note

   S0          Anderson Doris    07/01/86   2800  F           Memo
   S1          Bell     George   10/12/88   2400  T           Memo
   S2          Carter   Jack     05/14/87   2550  F           Memo
   S3          Davidson Edward   06/04/90   1500  T           Memo
   S4          Evans    Henry    03/08/88   2000  T           Memo
   S5          Ford     Ida      11/22/87   2600  F           Memo
   S6          Gilbert  Fred     04/15/87   2300  T           Memo
   S7 ┌                        BYCOMMIS                              ≡┐
   S8 │ Salsman_id│Last    │First   │Hire_date│Salary│Commission│Note│
   S9 │                                                               ◆
      │  S0         Anderson Doris    07/01/86   2800  F           Memo│
      │  S2         Carter   Jack     05/14/87   2550  F           Memo│
      │  S5         Ford     Ida      11/22/87   2600  F           Memo│
      │  S7         Harvey   Candy    12/01/89   2450  F           Memo│
      │  S9         Jones    Betty    09/26/89   2500  F           Memo│
      │  S1         Bell     George   10/12/88   2400  T           Memo│
      │  S3         Davidson Edward   06/04/90   1500  T           Memo│
      │  S4         Evans    Henry    03/08/88   2000  T           Memo│
      │  S6         Gilbert  Fred     04/15/87   2300  T           Memo│
      │  S8         Iverson  Albert   10/25/88   2200  T           Memo│▼
      └◄                                                             ►┘
```

**Figure 6.13    Viewing the Sorted COMMISSION Logical Field**

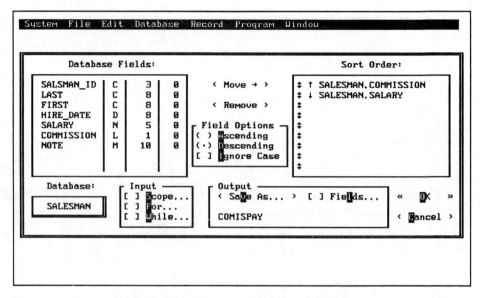

**Figure 6.14   Sorting COMMISSION and SALARY Fields**

into descending order based on their values in the SALARY field. As a result, the
largest salary for the salesperson not earning any commission appears on the top
of the first group. Likewise, the salesperson who earns a commission and has the
highest salary is shown at the beginning of the second group (see Figure 6.15).

```
System  File  Edit  Database  Record  Program  Window  Browse
                                SALESMAN
 Salsman_id│Last     │First    │Hire_date│Salary│Commission│Note│

 S0        │Anderson │Doris    │07/01/86 │2800  │F         │Memo│
 S1        │Bell     │George   │10/12/88 │2400  │T         │Memo│
 S2        │Carter   │Jack     │05/14/87 │2550  │F         │Memo│
 S3        │Davidson │Edward   │06/04/90 │1500  │T         │Memo│
 S4        │Evans    │Henry    │03/08/88 │2000  │T         │Memo│
 S5        │Ford     │Ida      │11/22/87 │2600  │F         │Memo│
 S6        │Gilbert  │Fred     │04/15/87 │2300  │T         │Memo│
 S7 ┌─────────────────────────COMISPAY──────────────────────────
 S8 │Salsman_id│Last     │First    │Hire_date│Salary│Commission│Note│
 S9 │
    │ S0        │Anderson │Doris    │07/01/86 │2800  │F         │Memo│
    │ S5        │Ford     │Ida      │11/22/87 │2600  │F         │memo│
    │ S2        │Carter   │Jack     │05/14/87 │2550  │F         │Memo│
    │ S9        │Jones    │Betty    │09/26/89 │2500  │F         │Memo│
    │ S7        │Harvey   │Candy    │12/01/89 │2450  │F         │Memo│
    │ S1        │Bell     │George   │10/12/88 │2400  │T         │Memo│
    │ S6        │Gilbert  │Fred     │04/15/87 │2300  │T         │Memo│
    │ S8        │Iverson  │Albert   │10/25/88 │2200  │T         │Memo│
    │ S4        │Evans    │Henry    │03/08/88 │2000  │T         │Memo│
    │ S3        │Davidson │Edward   │06/04/90 │1500  │T         │Memo│
```

**Figure 6.15   Viewing the Records Sorted by COMMISSION and SALARY**

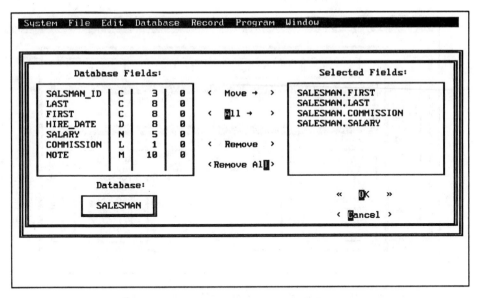

**Figure 6.16   Selecting Data Fields for the Output File**

## Saving Selected Data Fields

In the preceding examples the sorted output file that we saved contained every data field in the original database file, by default. But it is possible to save only selected data fields by choosing the Fields check box in the Sort dialog when you define the contents of the output file.

As an exercise, use the same sort order as shown in the previous example and sort on the COMMISSION field in ascending order and the SALARY field in descending order. Then, instead of saving all of the data fields in the output file, save only the FIRST, LAST, COMMISSION, and SALARY data fields. To select these fields for the output file, choose the Fields check box; the Field Picker dialog appears. Now choose the data fields you would like to include in the Sort Destination File (see Figure 6.16). The procedure for selecting data fields is identical to the one defined earlier. After selecting your output data fields, select the <<OK>> push button to continue.

## Saving Selected Records

Following a sorting operation, the sorted output file normally contains all of the data records in the original database file. But if this is not what you want, you can save a subset of these records to the output file by defining the appropriate filter conditions in the Sort dialog.

First select the FOR check box in the Sort dialog either by clicking your mouse button on the check box or by pressing the "F" key. As a result, FoxPro presents

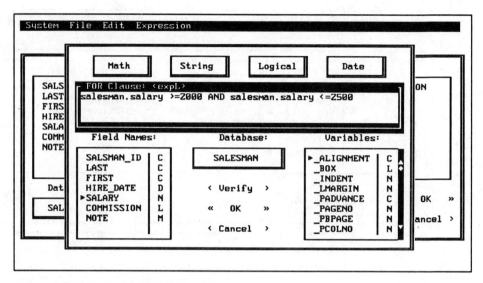

**Figure 6.17  Defining Filter Conditions**

you with the Expression Builder where you enter the filter condition, which determines the records that are subject to the sorting operation. (This Expression Builder is identical to that covered in Chapter 5.) So, if you want to save only the records for those salespeople whose salaries are between $2,000 and $2,500, you would enter the filter conditions accordingly (see Figure 6.17).

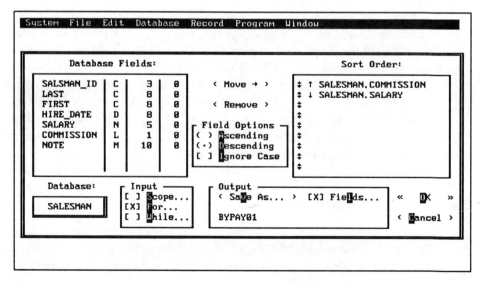

**Figure 6.18  Showing the For and Fields Boxes Checked**

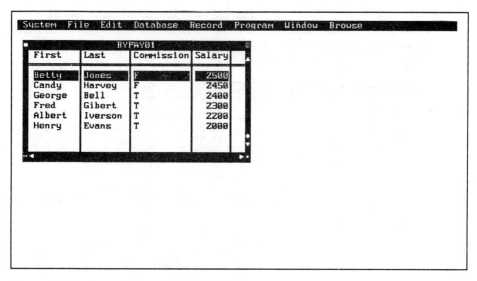

**Figure 6.19   Sorted Records in BYPAY01.DBF**

After building the filter expression, check its validity by selecting the <Verify> push button. If the expression is valid, you then can exit from the Expression Builder by choosing the <<OK>> push button.

When you return to the Sort dialog, you can see that the For check box has been selected, together with the Fields box you marked earlier (see Figure 6.18).

Now you are ready to sort your records by choosing the <<OK>> push button from the Sort dialog. The records to be saved in the output file, BYPAY01.DBF, contain only those data fields you selected earlier along with those records that satisfy the filter conditions (see Figure 6.19).

You can see that the output file contains only the four data fields that you selected: FIRST, LAST, COMMISSION, and SALARY. Concomitantly, the output file contains only those records whose values in the SALARY field range from $2,000 to $2,500.

## SORTING WITH FOXPRO COMMANDS

We said earlier that you also can perform the Sort operation by issuing the appropriate FoxPro commands. The command for sorting a database file uses the following format:

```
SORT TO <output filename> ON <field list>
```

The field list can contain one or more sort fields. If you intend to sort on several data fields, you must separate them with commas. Thus, to sort the

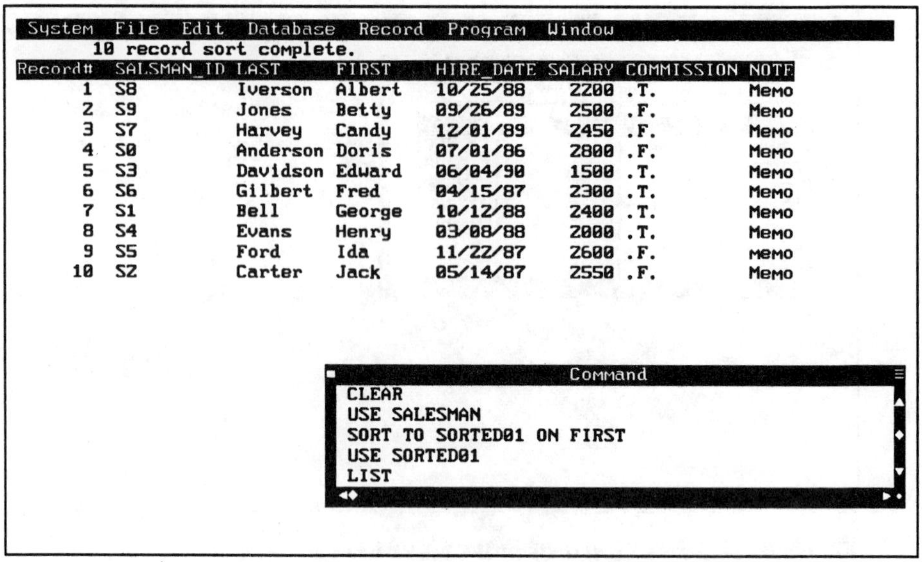

```
 System  File  Edit  Database  Record  Program  Window
      10 record sort complete.
Record#   SALSMAN_ID LAST      FIRST     HIRE_DATE SALARY COMMISSION NOTE
       1  S8         Iverson   Albert    10/25/88    2200 .T.        Memo
       2  S9         Jones     Betty     09/26/89    2500 .F.        Memo
       3  S7         Harvey    Candy     12/01/89    2450 .F.        Memo
       4  S0         Anderson  Doris     07/01/86    2800 .F.        Memo
       5  S3         Davidson  Edward    06/04/90    1500 .T.        Memo
       6  S6         Gilbert   Fred      04/15/87    2300 .T.        Memo
       7  S1         Bell      George    10/12/88    2400 .T.        Memo
       8  S4         Evans     Henry     03/08/88    2000 .T.        Memo
       9  S5         Ford      Ida       11/22/87    2600 .F.        memo
      10  S2         Carter    Jack      05/14/87    2550 .F.        Memo



                                           Command
          CLEAR
          USE SALESMAN
          SORT TO SORTED01 ON FIRST
          USE SORTED01
          LIST
```

**Figure 6.20   Sorting on the FIRST Data Field**

records in the SALESMAN database by first name, issue the following SORT command:

```
SORT TO SORTED01 ON FIRST
```

In this command, you sort on the FIRST data field and save the sorted records to SORTED01.DBF. After the sort is complete, you can view the contents of the output file by issuing the LIST and USE commands (see Figure 6.20).

## Specifying Sort Order

The FoxPro SORT command sorts records in ascending order by default. You can reverse that order simply by including /D (for descending) at the end of the sort field name. Then if you decide to arrange the records in descending order by the values in the FIRST field, issue the following command:

```
SORT TO SORTED02 ON FIRST /D
```

Alternatively, you can spell out the sort order (DESCENDING or ASCENDING) following the sort field:

```
SORT TO SORTED02 ON FIRST DESCENDING
```

Of course, you can abbreviate the word DESCENDING to DESC:

```
SORT TO SORTED02 ON FIRST DESC
```

```
System  File  Edit  Database  Record  Program  Window
        10 record sort complete.
Record#  SALSMAN_ID LAST      FIRST     HIRE_DATE SALARY COMMISSION NOTE
      1  S2         Carter    Jack      05/14/87   2550  .F.        Memo
      2  S5         Ford      Ida       11/22/87   2600  .F.        memo
      3  S4         Evans     Henry     03/08/88   2000  .T.        Memo
      4  S1         Bell      George    10/12/88   2400  .T.        Memo
      5  S6         Gilbert   Fred      04/15/87   2300  .T.        Memo
      6  S3         Davidson  Edward    06/04/90   1500  .T.        Memo
      7  S0         Anderson  Doris     07/01/86   2800  .F.        Memo
      8  S7         Harvey    Candy     12/01/89   2450  .F.        Memo
      9  S9         Jones     Betty     09/26/89   2500  .F.        Memo
     10  S8         Iverson   Albert    10/25/88   2200  .T.        Memo


                                           Command
                        CLEAR
                        USE SALESMAN
                        SORT TO SORTED02 ON FIRST /D
                        USE SORTED02
                        LIST
```

**Figure 6.21    Sorting the FIRST Field in Descending Order**

Regardless of which method you choose, the records in the database will be arranged by first name in the FIRST field in descending order, from Z to A (see Figure 6.21).

## Sorting Multiple Fields

It is possible to sort more than one data field at a time in a database with the SORT command as well. Just list the sort fields following the keyword ON in the command. But remember to separate the sort fields with commas. And, if you intend to sort the data field in descending order, specify the sort order in the field list as well. For example:

```
SORT TO SORTED03 ON COMMISSION, SALARY /D
```

This command will result in records that are arranged first in ascending order based on the values in the COMMISSION field; then, for each commission group, the records will appear in descending order according to SALARY (see Figure 6.22).

## Saving Selected Data Fields and Records

In a SORT command, you can specify the data fields that you would like to save to the sorted output file by adding the FIELDS clause:

```
SORT TO <output filename> ON <field list>
    FIELDS <output field list>
```

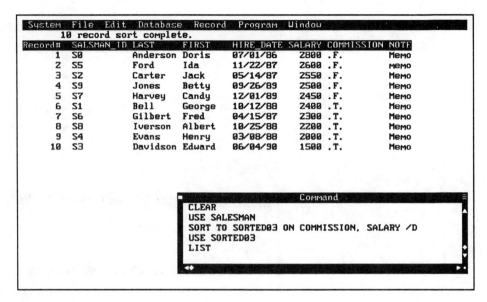

**Figure 6.22   Sorting Multiple Data Fields**

Similarly, you can define a filter condition for screening the data records that you would like to sort. Filter conditions are specified with a FOR clause:

```
SORT TO <output filename> ON <field list>
     [FIELDS <output field list>]
     FOR <filter conditions>
```

Here is an example:

```
SORT TO SORTED04 ON COMMISSION, SALARY/D
        FIELDS FIRST, LAST, COMMISSION, SALARY /D
        FOR SALARY >= 2000 AND SALARY <= 2500
```

The resulting output file contains only those records that satisfied the filter conditions and has only the four data fields specified in the FIELDS clause, as shown in Figure 6.23.

The SORT command in the example above is a long one. Look again at Figure 6.23 and you can see that it is too long to be fully displayed in the Command window. When you enter this command, continue typing even when you reach the end of the display line. The maximum length of a command line is 255 characters. Then you can scroll left and right to view the command line in its entirety.

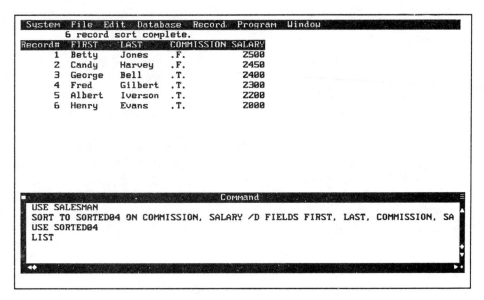

**Figure 6.23    Saving Selected Data Fields and Records**

## INDEXING DATA

Unlike sorting, indexing does not create another database for saving sorted records. Instead it creates an index that contains information that tells where the actual records are located in the original database file.

An index in a database is comparable to the subject index located at the end of this book. An index arranges alphabetically all the keywords describing the subjects covered in the book. Following each subject keyword are the page numbers indicating where in the book the subject is mentioned, and these page numbers represent a set of pointers that you use to refer to the subjects. A subject index can be used in a variety of ways.

The most common way to read the material in a book is to go through it page by page from beginning to end, but it is not the only way. For instance, although it is not recommended, you could read this book by choosing from the subjects that are listed alphabetically in the index, going down the subject list and finding the page numbers associated with particular subjects. You would then read just the sections of text related to those subjects, jumping from one section to another in the book. In a sense, then, you would be using the subject index to arrange the subjects you would like to read in the order in which you would like to read them.

Another way to use a subject index is to seek out only the subject that you would like to read and ignore the rest. In this case, you would be using the subject index as a quick way to locate one specific topic in a book.

In a database index each record can be treated like a subject in a book, and, like reading a book from beginning to end, you can view your data records in the order in which they were entered; or you can read them in a different order based on the values in a certain data field. Say you want to view the records in the SALESMAN database in descending order based on the values in the SALARY field. In this case, you would create an index that contains the actual locations of the records that are arranged by salary values.

Although the content of a database index is very similar to that of a subject index of a book, one difference is that it does not contain the actual subjects. Instead it holds only the reference information to help you find the actual subjects in the database. And while the subject index of a book lists reference page numbers, an index created for a database file contains pointer information about the actual data records in the database file.

## Index Keys

A database index can be created by using one or more data fields as an index key. The values in the index key determine how the data records are to be arranged. For example, you can use the SALARY field in the SALESMAN database as an index key for creating an index file; therefore, the index will contain pointers indicating the locations of the records that are arranged by the values in that field.

If you use more than one data field as an index key, the data records are arranged according to the *combined* values of the data fields. So, if you create an index using the FIRST and LAST data fields in the index key expressed as

```
FIRST+LAST
```

the combined value of this expression will be used to arrange your data records.

You can create as many as 25 indexes for the same database file, and each index will be defined with an index key which may contain one or more data fields. Once these indexes are created and saved in one or more index files, they can be used later to arrange your data records. Remember, however, that when you change the contents of a database file, you must open and update its associated index files as well. Otherwise, you will get erroneous results because you used an outdated index file for ordering the records.

## FoxPro Index Files

In FoxPro 2.0, there are two kinds of index files: the standard index file using the .IDX file extension and a compound index file with the .CDX file extension.

The .IDX standard index file has been around since the early versions of FoxPro and FoxBase+. It contains only one index, and that index is made up of only one index key that, in turn, may consist of one or more data fields.

The compound index file, on the other hand, is an enhanced feature of FoxPro 2.0 and it can contain multiple indexes, each of which may be made up of one or more data fields. Each index in a compound index file is called an index tag. If your index tag contains only one data field, FoxPro, by default, automatically names the index tag after the data field. But if the index tag is made up of multiple data fields, you need to provide a name for the tag.

When working with a compound index file, only one index tag at a time is used, and that one tag is called the master index. Obviously then, when an index file contains multiple tags, you must designate one index tag as the master index. The other tags remain open in the background. If you rearrange your records in a different order later, you must designate another index tag as the master index.

### Saving Index Files in a Compact Format

In FoxPro 2.0, all compound index (.CDX) files are saved in a compact format; standard index (.IDX) files can be saved either in a compact or regular format. In the compact format, the size of index files is reduced to approximately one-sixth, and this size reduction results in a much shorter processing time. Therefore, if you want to speed up indexing time, save your index files in a compact format (assuming that you are using standard indexes). There is one exception, however. Early versions of FoxPro accept only standard format, so if you want to export your standard indexes from 2.0 to these earlier versions, you may need to save your .IDX files in standard format.

### Saving Compound Index Files in a Structural Format

Compound index files can also be saved in a structural format, and there are many advantages for doing so. First, using an existing compound index in a structural format is automatic; that is, when you open a database file in a work area, it automatically opens its associated compound index file. You do not have to remember to open the index file yourself. As a result, you are able to use any index tags in the index file as long as the database file remains open.

This is not the case when you save an index file in a normal format where you must open your index file *after* you have opened your database file. If you do not, the index file will not be updated after you have made changes to the database, causing the database to be corrupted because you used an outdated index file for the index operation.

Another advantage to maintaining index tags in a structural compound index file is that the process is simple and systematic. Whenever you modify the contents of the database file, all the associated index tags in the index file are automatically updated. You do not have to rebuild the index tags to reflect the changes in the database file. But, if your compound index file is not saved in a structural format, you must remember to update the standard index file after you have made changes to the contents of the database file.

Because of these advantages, a structural compound index file is the preferable method for indexing data, and you should try to use structural compound index files for most of your index operations. One more thing: There is a unique reference between the database file and its associated structural compound index file—they share the same filename, but with different file extensions. So, if you create a structural compound index file for the SALESMAN.DBF file, the index file is automatically named SALESMAN.CDX. In addition, FoxPro 2.0 saves all structural compound index files in a compact format, thereby improving processing speed.

## Creating a Structural Compound Index File

In the next exercise, we create a structural compound index file to hold a set of index tags, which is used to arrange data records in the SALESMAN database.

First, open your database file in a work area. Once it is open, bring up the Setup dialog. When the dialog appears, define the index tags that will become the components of the compound index file that you are creating.

For example, if you intend to use indexes to arrange the records in SALES-MAN.DBF, you must create a compound index file to hold all the index tags that you will create. Later you will choose one as the master index for ordering your records.

For this exercise, we'll display records in the SALESMAN database according to the values in the SALARY and HIRE_DATE fields, respectively. First, set up two index tags and save them to an index file. The first index tag is made up of the SALARY field and the second uses HIRE_DATE as the index key.

Once these tags have been set up, choose the appropriate one for arranging your records; that is, designate the first one as the master index if you want your records arranged according to salary values. Choose the second if you want your records arranged according to the values in the HIRE_DATE field.

To create your new compound index file, use the View option from the Window menu popup to open the SALESMAN database and bring up the Setup dialog (see Figure 6.24).

In the middle of the Setup dialog is a space for displaying your index tags. Four push buttons are shown on the right-hand side of the dialog—<Add...>, <Modify...>, <Remove>, and <Set Order>— and their functions are:

| | |
|---|---|
| <Add...> | Adds and opens a new index file |
| <Modify...> | Modifies existing index tags |
| <Remove> | Closes an open index file |
| <Set Order> | Designates the master index |

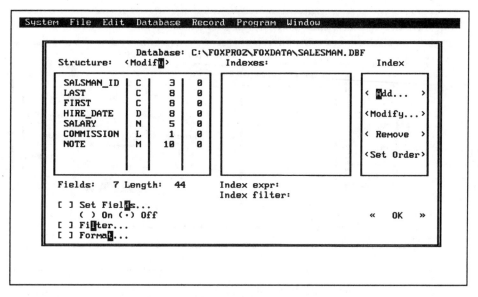

**Figure 6.24    Defining Index Tags in the Setup Dialog**

### Creating an Index Tag

The first time you create an index file, set up a new index tag by choosing the <Add...> push button from the Setup dialog. This brings up the Open Index File dialog (see Figure 6.25). At this point, choose the <New> push button to add a new index tag to the index file. The Index On dialog box appears (see Figure 6.26). Now you can define the new index tag.

To construct the index tag, choose from the names and types of data fields on the left-hand side of the dialog. Then specify index order by selecting either the Ascending or Descending radio button in the middle of the dialog.

Below the radio buttons is a Unique check box. Select it if you want to exclude duplicate values from the index tag. Select the <For...> push button to define the filter condition for selecting the data records to be affected by the index operation. The name of the index tag that you are creating will be displayed in the dialog at the bottom of the Options box.

The <Move> push button enables you to select a data field from the field list and move it to the Index On list for defining an index tag. Choose the <Remove> push button to reverse the field selection.

At the bottom center of the Index On dialog is an Output box where you choose the type of index file by turning on either the IDX or CDX radio button. If you are creating a standard index (.IDX) file, check the Compact box to specify the index file format; if you are creating a compound index, check the Structure box instead. Finally, the name of the index file is displayed below the <Save As...> push button.

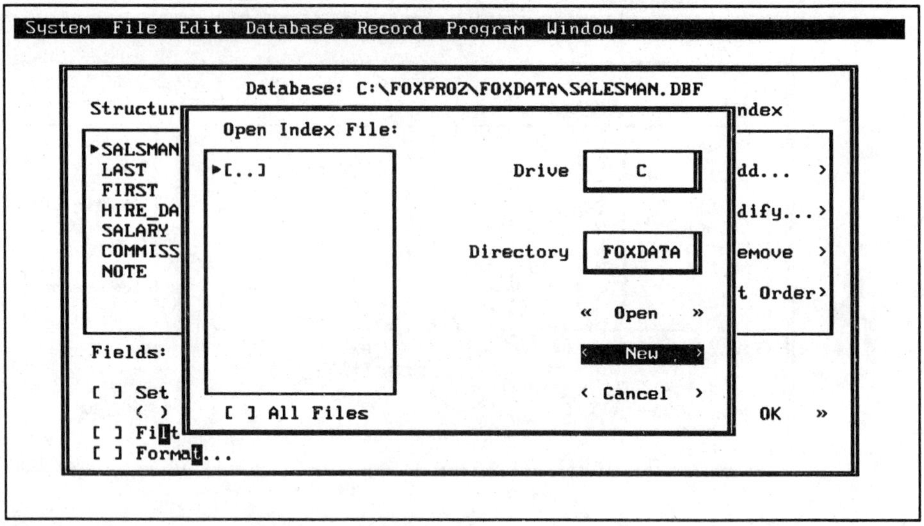

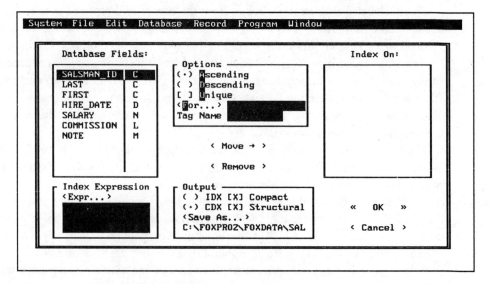

**Figure 6.25  The Open Index File Dialog**

Now create the first index tag for the SALESMAN.DBF file. This will consist only of the SALARY data field, sorted in descending order. First select the SALARY data field to be included in the index tag by double clicking your mouse on that field. Or, on the keyboard, use the Tab and arrow keys to highlight the data field and then press the Enter key. Then turn on the Descending button either by clicking your mouse on the button or by pressing the letter "D." As a result, the data field selected appears in the Index On list (see Figure 6.27).

**Figure 6.26  The Index On Dialog**

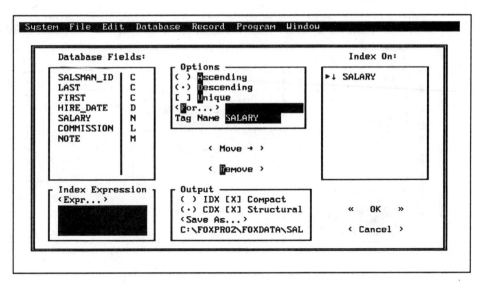

**Figure 6.27    Creating an Index Tag with the SALARY Field**

Notice that the index tag you just created was named SALARY automatically. (We mentioned earlier that an index tag made up of a single data field is named after that data field automatically. You must name the index tag yourself when it is composed of more than one data field.) Next look at the <Save As...> push button at the bottom center of the Index On dialog; below it is the name of the index file. Because you are allowed only one structural compound index file for each database file, the name of the index file will automatically be set to that of the database file—in our example, C:\FOXPRO\FOXDATA\SALESMAN.CDX. Unfortunately, you may not always be able to see the filename with its full directory path on the screen due to the limited space.

At this point, you either can exit from the Index On dialog or create another index tag. If you would like to create another index tag, repeat the same process. Try creating another index tag by selecting HIRE_DATE as the index key (see Figure 6.28).

### Defining Index Tags

As just mentioned above, an index tag can be defined with a single data field or with more than one data field. If you intend to sort your records according to the combined character strings in the FIRST and LAST fields, for example, you would define the index tag as:

```
FIRST+LAST
```

Specify the tag with an index expression by selecting the <Expr...> push button at the lower left-hand corner of the Index On dialog with the mouse or keyboard.

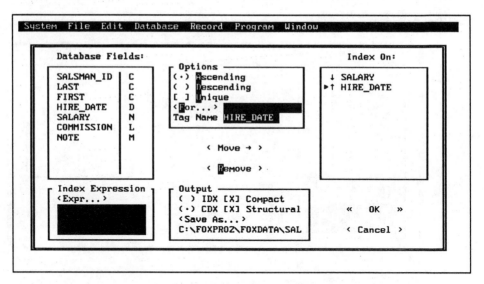

**Figure 6.28   Creating an Index Tag with the HIRE_DATE Field**

This causes the Index Expression Builder dialog box to appear; it has the same format as the Expression Builder that you were introduced to earlier. Build the index expression with the data fields (FIRST, LAST) and the necessary mathematical operator (e.g., +) as shown in Figure 6.29.

Verify the expression and then return to the Index On dialog by choosing the <<OK>> push button. When you return to the dialog, you can see that the index expression appears in the Index Expression box (see Figure 6.30).

Also note that the name of the index tag has not changed since the last index tag was created; it still reads HIRE_DATE. Therefore, you must assign a different name to the tag you are creating by modifying the index tag name that is currently shown in the Options box. With a mouse, point and click at the beginning of the current index tag name. When the blinking cursor appears, type in the name—let's call it FULLNAME—for the new index tag. If you don't have a mouse, first highlight the current tag name with the Tab and cursor key and then type in the new index tag name. After that, select the <Move> push button to move the index expression into the Index On list (see Figure 6.31).

Like a field name, the name of an index tag can have as many as 10 characters. It must begin with a letter or an underscore, but may consist of any combination of letters, digits, or underscores.

## Saving Index Tags to a Compound Index File

To save the index tags you have created to a structural compound index file, first verify the type and format of the index file. Make sure that the CDX radio button

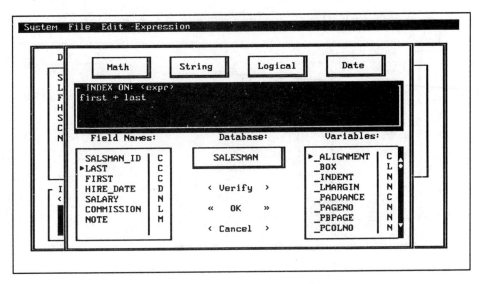

**Figure 6.29   Defining the Expression for an Index Tag**

has been turned on (indicated with a dot) and then verify that the Structural check box has been selected.

Now you can proceed to create the index file and exit from the Index On dialog by selecting the <<OK>> push button. FoxPro then creates all the index tags in the file. As each index tag is created, the following message appears:

```
10 records indexed
```

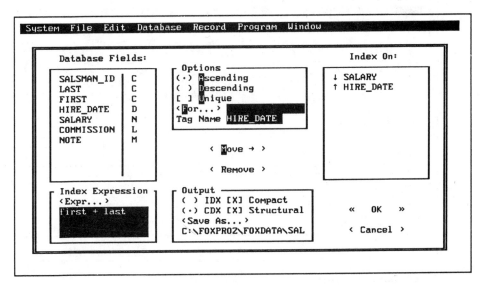

**Figure 6.30   Accepting the Index Expression**

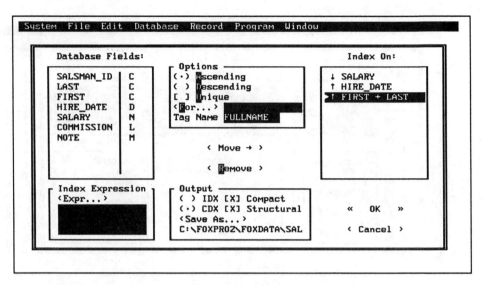

**Figure 6.31   Creating an Index Tag with an Index Expression**

Of course, the number of indexed records is determined by the number of records in any given file. Afterwards, you will return to the Setup dialog (see Figure 6.32).

All the index tags that were created are now visible in the Indexes list box in this figure. Each index tag name is preceded by the name of the compound index file. Notice that there is a dot to the left of the index tag most recently created (SALESMAN:FULLNAME). The dot indicates that that index tag is the current

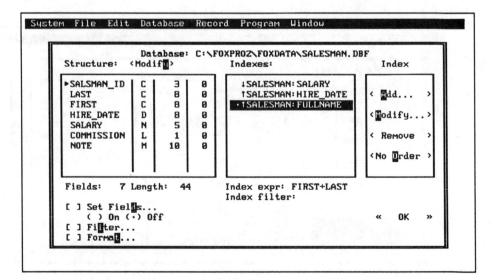

**Figure 6.32   Returning to the Setup Dialog**

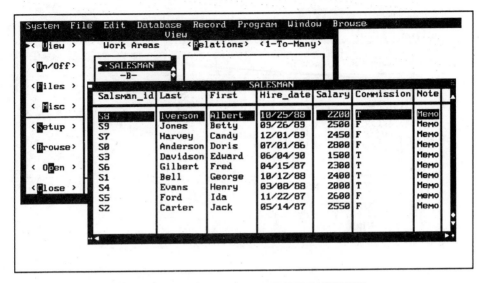

**Figure 6.33   Viewing Indexed Records in SALESMAN.DBF**

master index, and that the records in the database file are now being arranged according to the values of that tag.

At this point, if you want to view the ordered records, leave the Setup dialog by choosing the <<OK>> push button. Display the records in the SALESMAN database now and you can see that they are arranged in alphabetical order by the character strings in the FIRST and LAST data fields, i.e., alphabetically arranged by first name (see Figure 6.33). Because there are no duplicate first names, the index tag of FIRST+LAST yielded the same results as an index tag using only the FIRST data field.

If there had been more than one record sharing the same first name, their associated last names would have been alphabetized accordingly. Thus, if you had John Smith, John Albertson, and John Nelson in the database file, they would have been arranged as follows:

| | |
|---|---|
| Albertson | John |
| Nelson | John |
| Smith | John |

### Designating the Master Index

Although you can *save* multiple index tags in a compound index file, you can *use* only one of them at a time to arrange your data records. The one in use is called the master index.

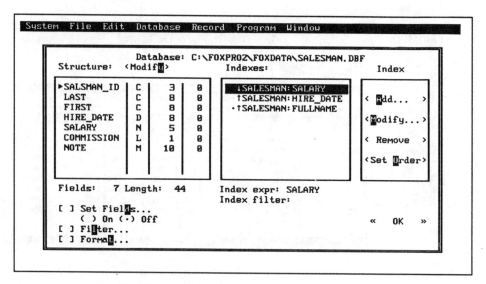

**Figure 6.34   Designating a Master Index**

You can designate any one of the index tags as the master index by using the Set Order operation. Recall that when you returned to the Setup dialog after you had created the index tags, it automatically designated the last index tag as the master index, which was indicated with a dot.

To designate a different index tag as the master index, return to the Setup dialog and select any other index tag as the master index by using the mouse or the keyboard. With a mouse, first click on the index tag that you want to select. With the keyboard, use the arrow keys to move the cursor to the index tag you want to select. It is then highlighted and its associated index expression is displayed below the Indexes list box. Next select <Set Order> to designate this index tag as the master index.

As an exercise, designate the SALARY index tag as the master index. Click your mouse on that tag in the Indexes box. Watch as it is highlighted and the index expression (in this case, the SALARY data field) is displayed below the Indexes box (see Figure 6.34). Finally, select the <Set Order> push button to designate the selected index tag as the master index. A dot now appears to the left of the SALARY index tag (see Figure 6.35).

Figure 6.35 also shows the confirmation message for the selection of your new master index:

```
Master index: C:\FOXPRO\FOXDATA\SALESMAN.CDX   Tag: SALARY
```

After you have designated your new master index, select the <<OK>> push button to exit from the Setup dialog and then display the records as they are arranged by the master index (see Figure 6.36). Notice that all of the records in SALESMAN now are ordered according to the values in the current master index, SALARY.

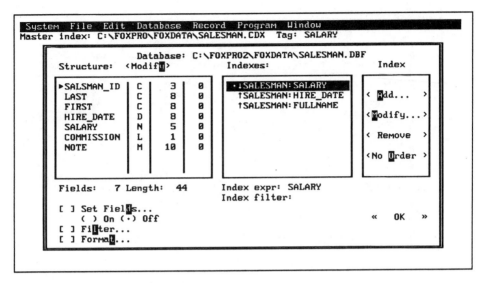

**Figure 6.35    Designating SALARY as the Master Index**

## Modifying Index Files

After creating a structural compound index file, you can modify its contents to accommodate your new indexing needs. Add a new index tag to the index file when you need to arrange your records in a different order or remove existing index tags that you no longer need. You also can change the index expression that makes up an existing index tag.

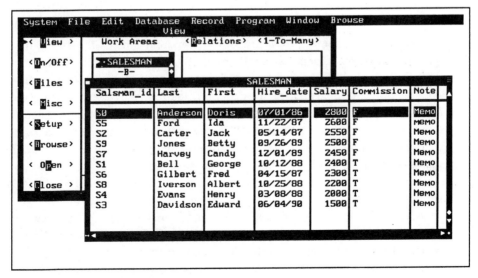

**Figure 6.36    Records Indexed by a New Master Index**

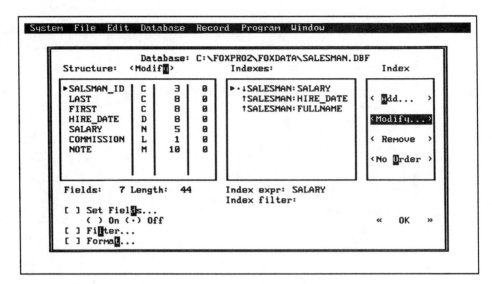

**Figure 6.37   Modifying a Structural Compound Index File**

There are a number of ways to enter Edit mode in order to alter the contents of an existing structural compound index file. The simplest is to choose the <Modify...> push button from the Setup dialog. Follow this procedure to change the contents of SALESMAN.CDX (see Figure 6.37). FoxPro opens the Index On dialog which enables you to see all of the index fields and expressions that you used to define the existing index tags.

### Adding New Index Tags

To add a new index tag to a structural compound index file, follow the same procedure that you learned earlier: Using the SALSMAN_ID data field as the index key, first highlight the data field and then press the Enter key. If you are using a mouse, simply double click on the data field, then use the radio button to select the sort order (choose ascending for this example). Note that the data field selected now is displayed in the Index On list for the new index tag (see Figure 6.38).

If the index tag that you would like to add requires an index expression, define that expression in the Index Expression dialog using the same procedure described earlier. That is, select the <Expr...> push button to bring up the Index Expression Builder.

After defining the new index tag, either exit from the Index On dialog or continue to modify other index tags. If you select the <<OK>> push button, you will be returned to the Setup dialog after the new index tag is added to the index file.

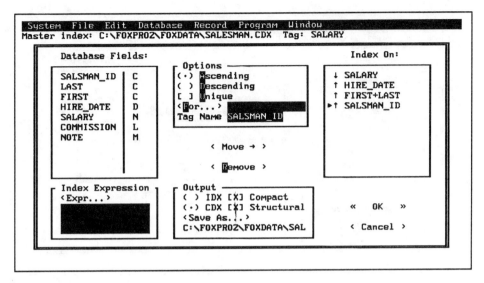

**Figure 6.38   Adding a New Index Tag**

Otherwise, you may stay in the Index On dialog so that you can make other changes to the index tags. After you have made all the changes that you want, exit the Index dialog by choosing the <<OK>> push button. At that point, the contents of the index file will be updated.

Do that now: Select the <<OK>> push button to create the new index tag. Watch as the following message is displayed:

```
10 records indexed
```

indicating that the new index tag has been created and added to the index file.

## Removing Existing Index Tags

The procedure to remove an existing tag from the index file is very simple. Return to the Index On dialog by selecting the <Modify...> push button from the Setup dialog. Once there, remove any existing index tag either with the mouse or keyboard.

If you are using a mouse, double click on an existing index tag to remove it from the index file. To remove the index tag SALSMAN_ID, for example, double click on the index key SALSMAN_ID in the Index On box. You are then prompted for confirmation (see Figure 6.39). If you choose Yes, the index tag named SALS-MAN_ID will be eliminated. But because we do not want to remove it from the index file, answer No to abort the action.

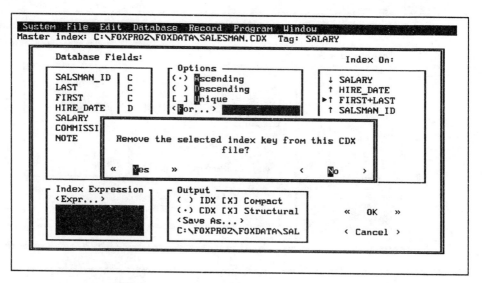

**Figure 6.39   Removing an Existing Index Tag**

If you are using the keyboard, remove an existing tag by first highlighting the index tag and then pressing the Enter key or the letter "R" (for the <Remove> push button). You are prompted for confirmation as above. Answer either Yes or No to continue.

At this point, you can choose to return to the Setup dialog or remain in the Index On dialog. For our purposes, stay in the Index On dialog for the next exercise.

### Modifying Existing Index Tags

In addition to adding a new tag or removing an existing tag, you can also modify an existing index tag. This involves first removing the index tag that you intend to modify and then redefining it with another index key. There are two ways to accomplish this. For this exercise, let's assume that you are going to modify the index tag, FULLNAME, by replacing its current index expression, FIRST+LAST, with a new expression that includes only the FIRST data field. The first method is to use the procedure that you have just learned—remove the FULLNAME index tag and then add a new index tag by choosing the FIRST data field as an index key. This method is adequate for this example because it is easy to redefine the index expression for the new index tag after you have removed the old one.

But, if would like to create a new index by editing the existing index expression, there is an easier way. Like the first method, this one requires that you first remove the index tag you would like to modify. But, after removing the index tag, edit the index expression from the removed tag and use it to create a new index tag. In this case, first remove the FULLNAME index tag from the index file by double clicking

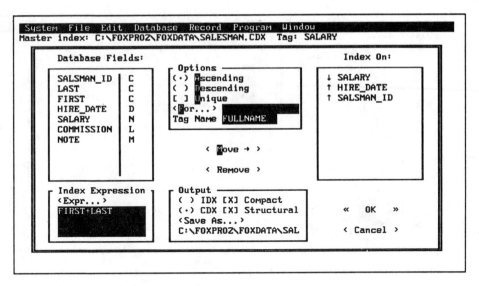

**Figure 6.40   Modifying an Index Expression**

your mouse on the index key (FIRST+LAST) in the Index On box. On the keyboard, highlight the index key and press Enter. Then answer Yes to the confirmation prompt.

As a result, the index key associated with the FULLNAME index tag is removed from the Index On box, and the index expression remains in the Index Expression box in the lower left-hand corner of the Index On dialog (see Figure 6.40).

Now choose the <Expr...> push button to bring up the Index Expression Builder where you edit the expression from the removed index tag. Change the index expression from FIRST+LAST to FIRST and then return to the Index On dialog and change the name of the tag from FULLNAME to FIRST (see Figure 6.41).

Finally, choose the <<OK>> push button to exit from the Index On dialog. When you return to the Setup dialog, all the index tags are updated accordingly (see Figure 6.42).

## Creating Standard Index Files

In general, it is recommended that you use structural compound index files; standard .IDX and nonstructural compound .CDX index files should be reserved for special occasions, e.g., if you intend to use different sets of indexes for different applications. Then you may want to save these indexes in several .IDX and nonstructural compound index files, instead of in a structural compound index file. In such a case, open those indexes only when you need them and do not keep all your indexes open all the time. And remember to update your indexes before using them.

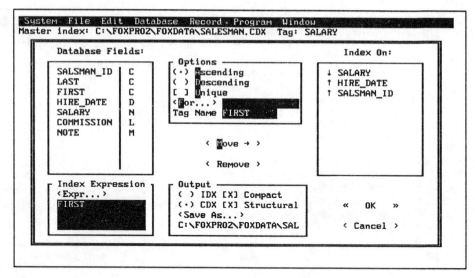

**Figure 6.41   Editing the Tag Name**

Remember, unlike compound index files that may contain multiple indexes, a standard index file can have only one index, and that index is expressed as a key consisting of one or more data fields. Because you can create only one structural compound index file for a database file, this index file is always named after its associated database file. But because you may create several standard .IDX index

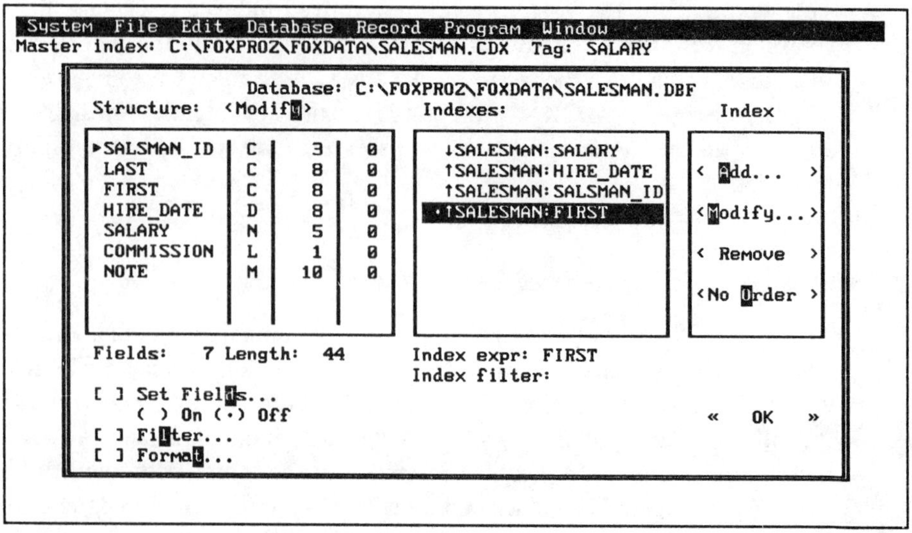

**Figure 6.42   Updating All the Index Tags**

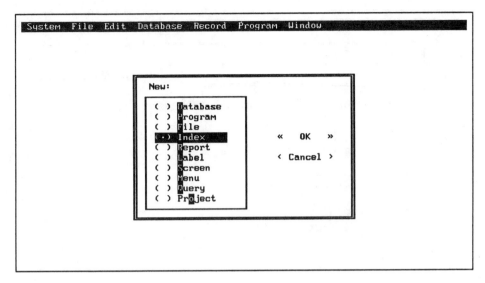

**Figure 6.43   Creating a New Index File**

files and nonstructural compound index files for the same database file, unique names must be assigned to each index file.

Although there a number of ways to create a new standard index file, a simple one is to select the New option from the File menu popup after you have opened its associated database file in a work area. When the File New dialog appears, select Index as the type of file to be created. With a mouse, click on the Index radio button to turn it on. If you are using the keyboard, highlight the Index radio button with the Tab key and then press the spacebar to turn it on (see Figure 6.43).

Next select the <<OK>> push button to bring up the Index On dialog, and when it appears, begin defining the new index file. First, select the type of index file (.IDX or .CDX) you want to create. Then assign a name to the index file, and before saving it, define its associated index key.

To create a sample .IDX index file named BYLAST by using the LAST data field as its index key, first turn on the IDX radio button. To conserve disk space, save the index file in compact format (FoxPro 2.0's default format). If you do not want this feature, remove the checkmark from the Compact check box.

After selecting the index type, assign a name to the index file by typing in the filename (e.g., BYLAST) in the dialog box below the <Save As...> push button. Alternatively, bring up the Index File Name dialog by choosing the <Save As...> push button and then enter your filename.

Now you are ready to define the index key for the file that you are creating. Follow the same procedure that you learned earlier in this chapter for this step. As an exercise, select the LAST data field and move it to the Index On box to define the index key (see Figure 6.44).

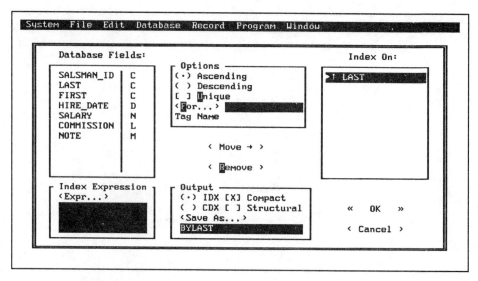

**Figure 6.44   Defining the New .IDX Index File**

After defining the index file, select the <<OK>> push button to exit from the Index On dialog. Consequently, the .IDX index file is created and saved to disk. At the same time, the index file is opened and added to the active indexes. You can verify this by bringing up the Setup dialog.

Look at Figure 6.45 to see the BYLAST.IDX index file displayed in the Indexes box. Be aware that a standard .IDX index file is displayed differently from an index tag of a compound index file. Whereas an .IDX file is listed by its filename, an index tag is displayed in two parts: the name of the .CDX file and the name of the index tag.

## Removing Active .IDX Index Files

To remove a standard .IDX index file from the current indexes, simply select the <Remove> push button in the Setup dialog while the index file is highlighted. Highlight the index file to be removed either with the mouse or by using the Tab key.

Another way to remove a standard .IDX index file from the current indexes is to close its associated database file and then reopen it. When you close a database file, all of the .IDX files that are currently open will be closed automatically. When you reopen the database file, only the index tags in the structural compound index file will be opened.

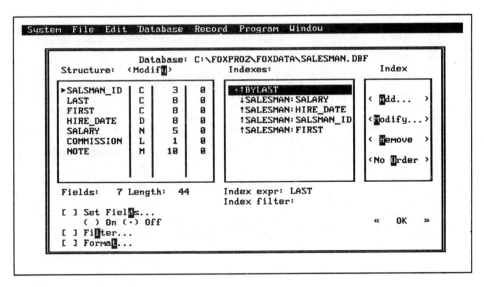

**Figure 6.45   Adding .IDX Index File to Current Indexes**

## Creating Nonstructural Compound Index Files

In addition to standard .IDX index files, you can also create nonstructural compound index files. A nonstructural compound index file is very similar to a structural compound index file; it too stores multiple indexes as index tags. But there are minor differences between them. First, while the name of a structural compound index file is always the same as that of its associated database file, a unique name can be assigned to a nonstructural compound index file. Second, when you open a database file in a work area, its associated structural compound index file is automatically opened; this is not true for nonstructural compound index files. They must be added to the currently open indexes if they are to maintain their index tags.

To create a nonstructural compound index file, follow the same procedure used for creating a standard .IDX index file. The only difference is that when you define the index file, choose .CDX as your output file and do not select the Structural check box in the Index On dialog.

## Deleting Index Files

Any index file that you have created may be erased from your disk. The procedure for doing this is the same as for deleting any disk file. Choose the Filer option from the System menu popup. From there choose the <Delete> push button after you

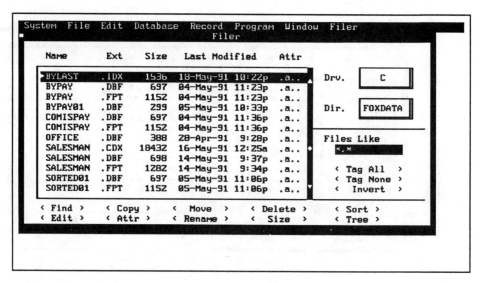

**Figure 6.46   Tagging an Index File to Be Deleted**

have tagged the files you intend to delete. Remember though, before you can delete a disk file, it must be closed. Therefore, to delete an index file, close it first; otherwise, the Filer will not allow you to tag that file.

As an exercise, delete the BYLAST.IDX index file. First tag the index file with your mouse or the keyboard. Click the mouse on the BYLAST.IDX file to tag it; or on the keyboard, use the up or down arrow keys to highlight the index file and then press the spacebar to tag it. The tagged file is indicated by a small triangle in front of the filename (see Figure 6.46).

Once you have tagged the file earmarked for deletion, choose the <Delete> push button either by clicking your mouse on that button or by pressing the Ctrl+D key combination. You are then prompted to confirm your action (see Figure 6.47).

At this point, select the <Delete> push button to confirm the deletion and the tagged file is permanently removed from your disk.

## INDEXING WITH FOXPRO COMMANDS

Index operations also can be performed by issuing the appropriate FoxPro commands. These commands enable you to create any type of index file (including standard .IDX files and structural and nonstructural compound .CDX index files). You can use a command to add an index tag to the index file of a compound index file; likewise, you can remove any existing index tag from a compound index file or designate an existing index tag as the master index.

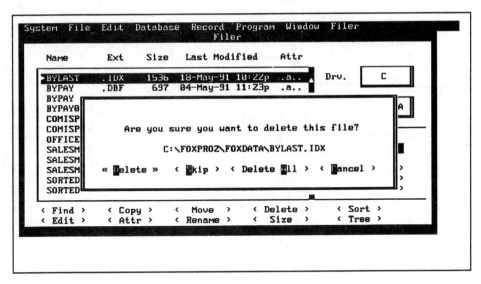

**Figure 6.47   Confirmation for Deleting Files**

## Creating Structural Compound Index Files

To create a structural compound index file with a FoxPro command, you must first issue the USE command to open the database file whose records you want to order. Then issue the INDEX ON command in the following format:

```
INDEX ON <expression> TAG <index tag name>
        [DESCENDING]
        [UNIQUE]
```

In this command you define the expression that serves as the index key and specify the index tag name. If you are using a single data field as your index key, name the index tag after that data field. Otherwise, assign a unique name to any index tag that represents an expression consisting of more than one data field.

Like a field name, the name of an index tag can be any combination of letters, digits, or underscores up to 10 characters long; and it must begin with a letter or an underscore.

Use the DESCENDING (or just DESC) keyword to change the default (ascending) order for arranging your records. To ignore duplicate values in the index key, add the UNIQUE keyword to the INDEX ON command.

Although the INDEX ON command defines an index tag, it creates its associated structural compound index file if the index tag is the first tag you are creating for the file. Here is an example:

```
USE OFFICE
INDEX ON OFFICE_ID TAG OFFICE_ID
```

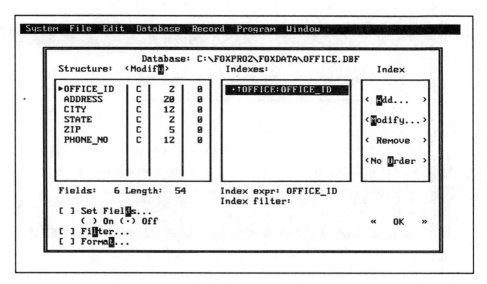

**Figure 6.48   Verifying the OFFICE.CDX Index File**

The INDEX ON command sets up the index tag, OFFICE_ID, by using the OFFICE_ID field as an index key. Because this is the first index tag you have defined, FoxPro creates a structural compound index file to hold the index tag. The index file will be named after its associated database file (i.e., OFFICE.CDX).

### Displaying Index Status

After creating the structural compound index file, you can verify its existence in a variety of ways. Either use the procedure that you learned earlier in this chapter by bringing up the Setup dialog (see Figure 6.48), or issue the following command:

```
DISPLAY STATUS
```

This command directs FoxPro to display information about the status of your current database, and it may take several screens to display all the information. On the first screen, among other items, FoxPro will list all of the database files that are currently open, along with their associated structural compound index files (see Figure 6.49).

Figure 6.49 shows OFFICE.DBF as currently open in work area #1. The index tag, OFFICE_ID, (which uses OFFICE_ID as the index key) is also shown, along with the name of its structural compound index file, OFFICE.CDX.

Information about other items is displayed on subsequent screens, but because they are related to subjects we will discuss in later chapters, skip them at this point by pressing the Esc key.

```
          3 records indexed
                                    ┌──────────────────────────────────┐
Processor is INTEL 80386            │ Press any key to continue ...    │
Currently Selected Database:        └──────────────────────────────────┘
Select area:  1, Database in Use: C:\FOXPRO2\FOXDATA\OFFICE.DBF     Alias: OFFICE
  Structural CDX file:    C:\FOXPRO2\FOXDATA\OFFICE.CDX
    Master Index tag:    OFFICE_ID   Key: OFFICE_ID

File search path:
Default disk drive: C:
Print file/device:  PRN:
Work area =   1
Margin    =   0
Decimals  =   2
Memowidth =  50
Typeahead =  20
Blocksize =  64
No EMS

Date format: American
Macro Hot Key = SHIFT+F10
```

**Figure 6.49   Displaying Database Status**

## Adding Index Tags

Once you have created a structural compound index file, use the INDEX ON command to add more index tags to the file. For example, the following three commands will add three different index tags to the OFFICE.CDX index file:

```
INDEX ON ZIP TAG ZIP DESCENDING UNIQUE
INDEX ON CITY TAG CITY UNIQUE
INDEX ON CITY+STATE TAG LOCATION
```

As an exercise, enter these commands to add the three index tags to the index file. Next issue the DISPLAY STATUS command to verify them (see Figure 6.50). This figure lists all of the new index tags. Notice that the most recently created index tag, LOCATION, has been designated as the master index.

## Designating the Master Index

If you have more than one index tag in a structural compound index file, any one of them can be designated as the master index by using the SET ORDER command:

```
SET ORDER TO <index tag name>
```

To designate the index tag ZIP as the master index, issue the following command:

```
SET ORDER TO ZIP
```

FoxPro then displays the following message to confirm the identity of the master index:

```
Processor is INTEL 80386                  ┌─────────────────────────────────┐
Currently Selected Database:              │ Press any key to continue ...   │
Select area: 1, Database in Use: C:\FOXPROZ\FOXDATA\OFFICE.DBF    Alias: OFFICE
  Structural CDX file:    C:\FOXPROZ\FOXDATA\OFFICE.CDX
          Index tag:     OFFICE_ID   Key: OFFICE_ID
          Index tag:     ZIP   Key: ZIP Unique (Descending)
          Index tag:     CITY   Key: CITY Unique
     Master Index tag:   LOCATION   Key: CITY+STATE

File search path:
Default disk drive: C:
Print file/device:   PRN:
Work area =    1
Margin    =    0
Decimals  =    2
Memowidth = 50
Typeahead = 20
```

**Figure 6.50   Added Index Tags**

```
Master index: C:\FOXPRO\FOXDATA\OFFICE.CDX   Tag: ZIP
```

If you issue the DISPLAY STATUS command again, the ZIP index tag will be labeled as the Master Index.

## Removing an Index Tag

When you no longer need it, remove an existing index tag from a structural compound index file with the command:

```
DELETE TAG <index tag name>
```

For example, issue the following command to remove the index tag LOCATION from the OFFICE.CDX index file:

```
DELETE TAG LOCATION
```

## Modifying Index Tags

DELETE and INDEX ON are the commands to invoke if you want to modify an existing index tag in a compound index file. Issue the DELETE command to remove the index tag earmarked for modification and then use the INDEX ON command to create another one. Note: There is no command that enables you to edit the definition of an existing index tag.

## Creating Standard Index Files

The FoxPro command to create a standard .IDX index file is INDEX ON used in the following format:

```
INDEX ON <index key> TO <name of .IDX file>
         [COMPACT]
         [DESCENDING]
         [UNIQUE]
```

Here is an example:

```
USE OFFICE
INDEX ON STATE TO BYSTATE COMPACT DESCENDING
```

This command will create a standard .IDX index file named BYSTATE that uses the STATE data field as its index key for arranging the data records in descending order. The file is to be saved in a compact format.

## Creating Nonstructural Compound Index Files

The command to create a nonstructural compound index file, while similar to that for creating a structural one, requires that you assign a name to it in the INDEX ON command:

```
INDEX ON <expression> TAG <index tag name>
         OF <name of .CDX file>
         [DESCENDING]
         [UNIQUE]
```

The following command will set up an index tag named BYPHONE and create the OFPHONE.CDX compound index file and save it in a compact format:

```
USE OFFICE
INDEX ON PHONE_NO TAG BYPHONE OF OFPHONE
```

After executing the INDEX ON command, you may issue the DISPLAY STATUS command to verify the index file's existence. The DISPLAY STATUS command will display the nonstructural compound index file along with the structural compound index file (see Figure 6.51).

Figure 6.51 shows that the nonstructural compound index file just created (OFPHONE.CDX) is listed below the structural compound index file (OFFICE.CDX). At this point, you can choose any index tag in either index file as the

```
Processor is INTEL 80386                    ┌──────────────────────────────┐
Currently Selected Database:               │ Press any key to continue ... │
Select area:  1, Database in Use: C:\FOXPRO2\FOXDATA\OFFICE.DBF    Alias: OFFICE
 Structural CDX file:    C:\FOXPRO2\FOXDATA\OFFICE.CDX
          Index tag:     OFFICE_ID   Key: OFFICE_ID
          Index tag:     ZIP    Key: ZIP Unique (Descending)
          Index tag:     CITY   Key: CITY Unique
          Index tag:     LOCATION   Key: CITY+STATE
            CDX file:    C:\FOXPRO2\FOXDATA\OFPHONE.CDX
  Master Index tag:      BYPHONE    Key: PHONE_NO

File search path:
Default disk drive: C:
Print file/device:  PRN:
Work area =   1
```

**Figure 6.51   Verifying a Nonstructural Compound Index File**

master index. But, if you no longer need the nonstructural index file, you can remove it by first closing the OFFICE.DBF and then reopening it with these commands:

```
USE
USE OFFICE
```

The first command closes the database file that is currently open in default work area #1. When you reopen the OFFICE database with the USE OFFICE command, only the structural compound index file will be reopened. Consequently, any previously opened standard .IDX and nonstructural compound .CDX index files will not be opened.

## Deleting Index Files

To permanently remove any index files from your disk, invoke this command:

```
ERASE <filename>
```

It deletes any type of index file, but you must specify the filename with its file extension. For example:

```
ERASE XYZ.IDX
ERASE ABC.CDX
```

The ERASE command allows you to remove those standard .IDX and nonstructural compound .CDX index files that you no longer need in order to conserve storage space. Remember that you must close these index files before you can erase them.

Although it is not recommended, it is also possible to erase a structural compound index file. If you do, you will be warned about the absence of the index file when you try to open its associated database file:

```
        Structural CDX file not found
<Ignore>                        <<  Cancel  >>
```

When this happens, choose the <Ignore> push button to continue.

# Chapter Summary

This chapter detailed the two methods for ordering records in a database file—sorting and indexing. In discussing the strengths and weaknesses of both methods you learned that sorting causes the creation of duplicate files, which take up valuable disk space. Therefore, it is faster to order records with the indexing operation, and unless you need to work repeatedly with sorted records, you should choose the indexing operation.

You also learned how to create different types of index files, but it was made clear that you should always try to use a structural compound index file for your indexing operations because of its power and ease of use. With a structural index file, whenever you open a database file, all the index tags in that file will be opened and updated automatically. As a result, the task of using and maintaining your indexes with a structural index file is simple and automatic.

Indexing plays a very important role in manipulating data in a database. Besides speeding up the process of data query, it allows you to build the links for joining different database files together. Indexing also allows you to group data elements so that you can produce summary reports. Furthermore, by arranging your data records with the indexing operation, you are able to systematically edit your data in the database. In the next chapter you will learn how to modify the contents of your database files.

# 7

# Editing Data

## An Overview

In preceding chapters, you learned how to create database files and order their records. This chapter explains how to make changes to database files and includes modifying the database structure and editing the contents of its data records.

Modifying a database structure enables you to add new data fields to and remove existing data fields from an existing database file, as well as change the attributes of existing data fields. In addition to showing you how to modify data structures, this chapter will also discuss potential problems. Then you will learn how to add new records to and permanently remove existing records from your database files; finally, you'll learn how to edit the contents of those records.

Modifying the structure of a database file and its data records can be done either with the menu interface or the appropriate FoxPro commands, and both methods will be detailed in this chapter.

## Copying Database Files

Although the primary focus of this chapter is on modifying the structure and contents of existing database files, it is important to address the process of copying database files because modifications become permanent once they are carried out, and you may want to make a copy of your original files to use for reference and as backup files. This practice gives you the opportunity to return to the original contents of a database file at any time, a necessary option if you discover that you have made mistakes in your changes or simply decide to discard all the changes that you made and start over.

There are two ways to make a copy of an existing database file from the menu popup. One is to use the System's Filer utility to copy an existing database file to a new database file. The other is to select the Copy To option.

## USING THE SYSTEM'S FILER

To make a copy of an existing database file using the System's Filer utility, select Filer from the System menu popup. When the Filer window appears, it contains all of the disk files in the current directory. At this point, tag the database file that you would like to copy with either the mouse or the keyboard. Note, however, that you can tag only those files that are *not* currently open in any work area. Therefore, you must close any open file that you would like to copy before selecting the Filer option. After you have tagged the file, select the <Copy> push button and assign a name to the duplicate file.

As an exercise, make a copy of SALESMAN.DBF. First tag that file by clicking the mouse button on SALESMAN.DBF or by moving the cursor to that file and pressing the spacebar. A tagged file is indicated with a triangle tag symbol in front of the filename (see Figure 7.1).

If you try to tag a file whose name appears in light grey in the File list, there will be no response because that file is currently open in a work area. If this is the case, exit the Filer and close the file. Then you can return to the Filer and continue.

If you tag the wrong file, just move to a different file and tag it. Or you can select the <Tag None> push button to remove the current tag and then tag the one you want.

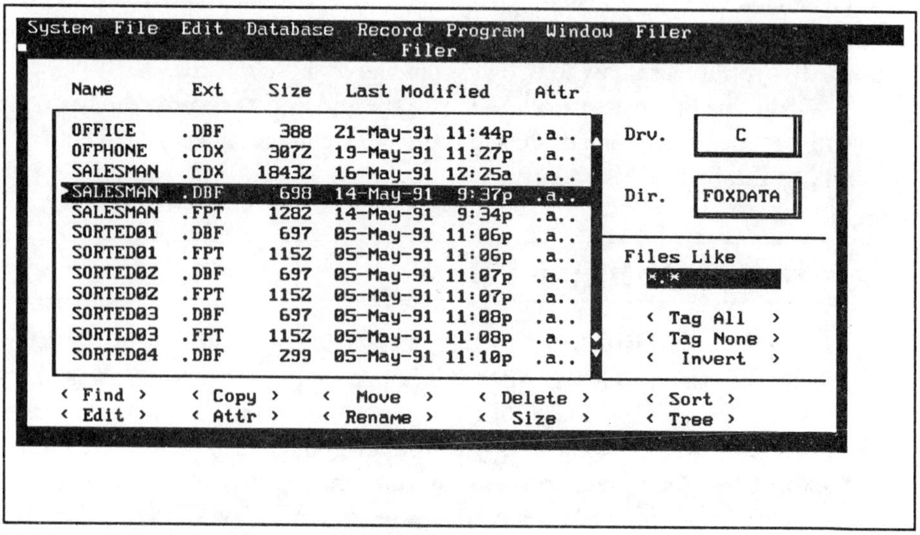

**Figure 7.1  Tagging a Database File**

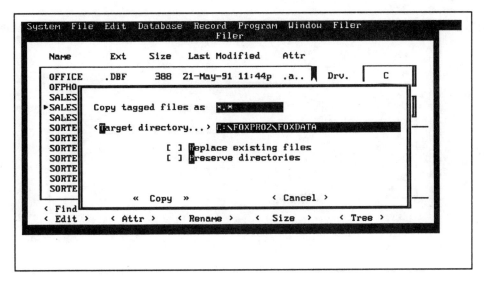

**Figure 7.2  Target Directory**

Once the file is tagged, create the duplicate file by clicking your mouse on the <Copy> push button or by pressing the Ctrl+C key combination. The Copy dialog appears, showing the directory and filename to which you would like to save your duplicate copy (see Figure 7.2). To save the duplicate file to a directory that is different from that shown in the dialog, change it accordingly.

In Figure 7.2, you can see that the default setting of the Copy tagged files as text box is *.*. This allows you to copy an entire set of tagged files at one time. You will learn how to use this feature in later exercises, but here, because you are copying only the SALESMAN.DBF file, replace the *.* with the name of your duplicate file (e.g., OLDFILE.DBF).

Two check boxes are provided in the Copy dialog: Replace existing files and Preserve directories. If you check Replace existing files, any files with the same name as the duplicate in the target directory will be overwritten. Otherwise, you will be warned about the existence of a file with the same name before the file is overwritten. If you check the Preserve directories box, the current directory structure will be copied to the target directory. For this exercise, however, you do not need to check either box because you will be saving the duplicate file in the current directory with a different filename (see Figure 7.3).

After naming your output file and specifying the target directory, select the default <Copy> push button to create the duplicate file. You will return to the Filer window and see the duplicate file (OLDFILE.DBF) listed in the window (see Figure 7.4).

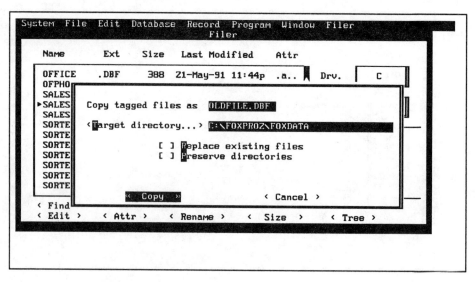

**Figure 7.3  Naming the Duplicated Database File**

## Copying Associated Files

When you make a copy of an existing database that contains memo fields, you may not be able to use the duplicate database file unless you also have copied its associated memo file. For example, if you attempt to open OLDFILE.DBF at this point, the following error message would result:

```
MEMO file is missing/invalid.
```

```
 System  File  Edit  Database  Record  Program  Window  Filer

                              Filer

      Name       Ext    Size   Last Modified     Attr

      BYDATE    .FPT    1152   04-May-91 10:40p   .a..        Drv.      C
      BYPAY     .DBF     697   04-May-91 11:23p   .a..
      BYPAY     .FPT    1152   04-May-91 11:23p   .a..
      BYPAY01   .DBF     299   05-May-91 10:33p   .a..        Dir.   FOXDATA
      COMISPAY  .DBF     697   04-May-91 11:36p   .a..
      COMISPAY  .FPT    1152   04-May-91 11:36p   .a..
      OFFICE    .CDX    9216   21-May-91 11:39p   .a..        Files Like
      OFFICE    .DBF     388   21-May-91 11:44p   .a..         *.*
      OFPHONE   .CDX    3072   19-May-91 11:27p   .a..
      OLDFILE   .DBF     698   14-May-91  9:37p   .a..       < Tag All  >
      SALESMAN  .CDX   18432   16-May-91 12:25a   .a..       < Tag None >
     >SALESMAN  .DBF     698   14-May-91  9:37p   .a..       <  Invert  >

    < Find >     < Copy >    < Move  >    < Delete >    < Sort >
    < Edit >     < Attr >    < Rename >   < Size  >     < Tree >
```

**Figure 7.4  Duplicated Database File**

The reason for this is that the contents of the memo fields are saved in the SALESMAN.FPT memo file. Therefore, to use the SALESMAN.DBF database file, you also must create the OLDFILE.FPT memo file by making a copy of SALESMAN.FPT.

Similarly, if the database file you are copying has a structural compound index file, you will want to duplicate its .CDX file as well. Otherwise, you must re-create the structural compound index file.

## Copying Multiple Files

There is a shortcut that enables you to copy all the files that are associated with a database file: Collectively tag all the files that you need to copy and then copy them as a group. The wildcard character (*) is used to select all the files sharing the same filename as OFFICE. For example, to make a copy of all the files that are associated with OFFICE.DBF, specify OFFICE.* in the text box in the Filer window (see Figure 7.5).

Then the Filer displays only those files that are associated with OFFICE.DBF. At this point, choose the <Tag All> push button to tag all these files (see Figure 7.6). You also can tag multiple files by pressing the Shift key while clicking the mouse on the filename. This method is very useful when you have different filenames that you need to tag as a group.

After tagging your files, choose the <Copy> push button. When the Copy dialog appears, enter the names for the target files (e.g., BRANCH.*) in the Copy tagged files as text box (see Figure 7.7).

| System | File | Edit | Database | Record | Program | Window | Filer |
|--------|------|------|----------|--------|---------|--------|-------|

```
                              Filer

   Name       Ext    Size    Last Modified    Attr

   BYPAY     .DBF     697   04-May-91 11:23p   .a..      Drv.     C
   BYPAY     .FPT    1152   04-May-91 11:23p   .a..
   BYPAY01   .DBF     299   05-May-91 10:33p   .a..
   COMISPAY  .DBF     697   04-May-91 11:36p   .a..      Dir.  FOXDATA
   COMISPAY  .FPT    1152   04-May-91 11:36p   .a..
   OFFICE    .CDX    9216   21-May-91 11:39p   .a..
   OFFICE    .DBF     388   21-May-91 11:44p   .a..      Files Like
   OFPHONE   .CDX    3072   19-May-91 11:27p   .a..        OFFICE.*
   OLDFILE   .DBF     698   14-May-91  9:37p   .a..
 ▶ OLDFILE   .FPT    1282   14-May-91  9:34p   .a..       < Tag All  >
   SALESMAN  .CDX   18432   16-May-91 12:25a   .a..       < Tag None >
   SALESMAN  .DBF     698   14-May-91  9:37p   .a..       <  Invert  >

   < Find >    < Copy >    <  Move  >    < Delete >    < Sort >
   < Edit >    < Attr >    < Rename >    <  Size  >    < Tree >
```

**Figure 7.5  Displaying Files Associated with OFFICE.DBF**

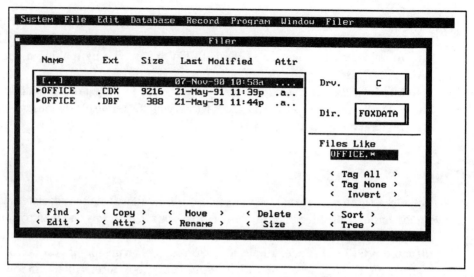

**Figure 7.6  Tagging Files Associated with OFFICE.DBF**

After the target files are named, select the <Copy> push button to create the duplicate files and exit the Copy dialog. When you return to the Filer, you can change the Files Like text box to BRANCH.* to view the files you have just created (see Figure 7.8).

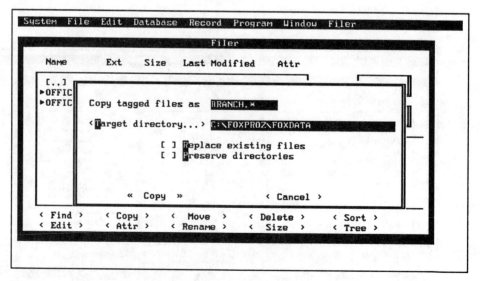

**Figure 7.7  Naming Target Files**

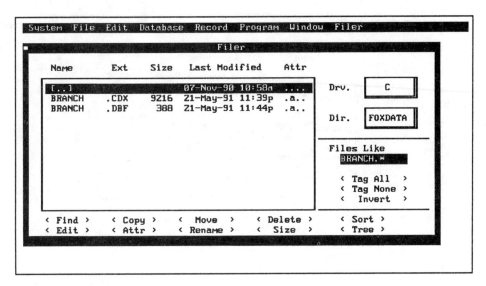

**Figure 7.8  Listing the Duplicated Files**

## USING THE COPY TO MENU OPTION

Instead of using the Filer, a copy of an existing database file also can be made by choosing the Copy To option from the Database menu popup. This option allows you to create a copy of the current database file. It creates a new structure and then copies all the data records from the existing database file to the new structure. If the database file contains memo fields, it copies the memo fields to a memo file as well. Note that it does not copy the associated structural compound index file.

As an exercise, use the Copy To option to make a copy of SALESMAN.DBF and its associated .FPT memo file. Then name the duplicate files TEST.DBF and TEST.FPT respectively. To do that, open the SALESMAN.DBF in the current work area and then choose the Copy To option from the Database menu popup. When the Copy To dialog appears, enter the name of the duplicate file either by selecting the <Save As...> push button to bring up the screen for entering your filename or by entering the filename at the text box below the <Save As...> push button (see Figure 7.9).

It is not necessary to specify the file extension when you enter the filename. When "Database" is shown in the TYPE: box on the screen, the file that you are creating will have .DBF as its file extension. Its associated memo file with the same root filename also will be created. It is important to remember that the Copy To option will not duplicate the structural compound index file belonging to the database file you have just copied. You must use the Filer to duplicate it if you want to copy its .CDX index file.

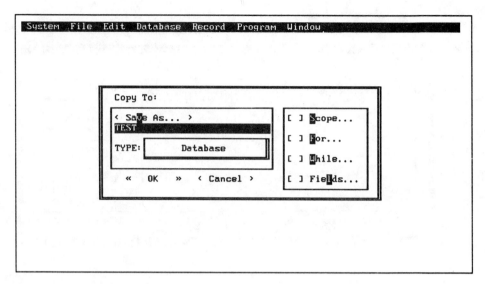

**Figure 7.9    Naming the Duplicate Database File**

## Copying Selected Data Fields and Records

In the preceding example, the Copy To option was invoked to make a copy of an existing database file that has the same data structure and includes all the data records of the original database file. This same option allows you to copy selected data records to your target file by specifying a filter condition to identify the designated records that you want to save; this is also possible for data fields.

As an exercise, assume that you want to copy records for members of the sales staff in SALESMAN.DBF whose salaries are greater than $2,500 to a file named HIGHPAY.DBF. In addition, you want to include only the LAST and SALARY fields in the target file. To do that, first open the SALESMAN database in the current work and then select the Copy To option from the Database menu popup. This brings up the Copy To dialog.

When the Copy To dialog appears, check the FOR box to bring up the FOR Clause Expression Builder. In this Expression Builder specify the filter condition for selecting the records that fit the parameters given above—in this case, SALARY > 2500 (see Figure 7.10). After defining the filter condition, select the <<OK>> push button to exit from the Expression Builder dialog.

To choose the data fields to be included in your target file, check the Field box when you return to the Copy To dialog and, when the Fields Picker dialog appears, select the data fields that you want to copy. For this exercise, select LAST and SALARY and move them to the Selected Fields list as shown in Figure 7.11.

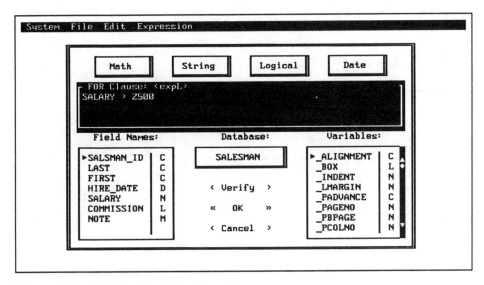

**Figure 7.10  Defining the Filter Condition**

After you have defined the field list, exit from the Field Picker dialog by selecting the <<OK>> push button. When you return to the Copy To dialog, type in the name of the target file (e.g., HIGHPAY). It is not necessary to include the file extension—FoxPro assumes it is a database file. Note at this point that the For and Fields boxes have been checked (see Figure 7.12).

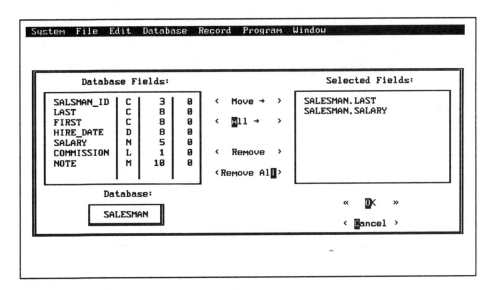

**Figure 7.11   Selecting Data Fields to Copy**

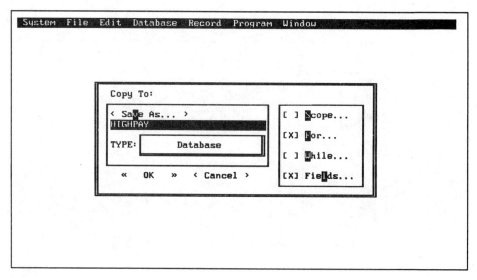

**Figure 7.12   Saving the HIGHPAY.DBF**

The final step in the creation of the duplicate file HIGHPAY.DBF is simply to select the <<OK>> push button. Now you can open and view the contents of the duplicate file in the usual way. Do that now and compare your screen with Figure 7.13 to see that the file contains three data records and two fields from the SALESMAN database.

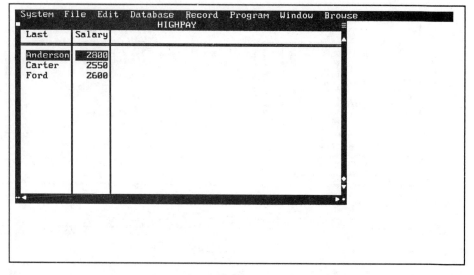

**Figure 7.13   Contents of HIGHPAY.DBF**

# Renaming Database Files

There may be occasions when you want to change the filename of a database. This involves using the Filer and choosing the Rename operation to assign a new name to an existing database file. Just remember to rename its associated memo and index files, as well.

You may want to try this procedure using the duplicate file named TEST.DBF that you created in an earlier exercise. Because SALESMAN.DBF has its associated memo file named SALESMAN.FPT, the Copy To operation also created a corresponding TEST.FPT memo file. To rename the TEST.DBF file to BACKUP.DBF, you must also rename the TEST.FPT to BACKUP.FPT. If this is not done, you will not be able to open the BACKUP.DBF without its associated memo file. So, to rename TEST.DBF and its associated TEST.FPT memo file, bring up the Filer dialog by selecting the Filer option from the System menu popup. (Make sure that the files you want to rename are not open.) When the Filer dialog appears, select the files you would like to rename by specifying TEST.* in the Files Like text box. When the files that you have specified appear, select the <Tag All> push button to tag them.

Next choose the <Rename> push button by pressing the Ctrl+R key combination or by clicking the mouse on the button. When the Rename dialog appears, you are asked to assign a name to each of the files that you tagged—in this exercise, TEST.DBF and TEST.FPT. After you have renamed the two tagged files, you can verify the operation by listing Files Like BACKUP.* in the Filer.

In Figure 7.14 you can see that TEST.DBF and TEST.FPT have been renamed as BACKUP.DBF and BACK.FPT respectively. Also notice that the Rename operation did not alter the sizes of the renamed files, nor did it change the time and date when the files were last modified.

# Deleting Database Files

The System's Filer also can be used to permanently remove any files that you no longer need. First tag the files that you want deleted and then choose the <Delete> push button. It's also a good idea to delete all the memo and index files that are associated with the database files that you are deleting. Again, remember that you must close the database files before you can delete them; you cannot delete any database file that is open in any of the work areas.

The procedure for deleting a set of files is very similar to that for renaming files. After you have tagged your files, choose the <Delete> push button by pressing Ctrl+D or clicking your mouse on the button. A prompt appears asking you to confirm your decision to delete the tagged files. Try this process with

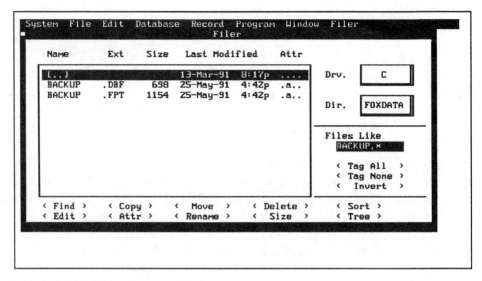

**Figure 7.14  Listing Renamed Files**

BACKUP.DBF and BACKUP.FPT. Once you have tagged the two files in the Filer dialog and chosen <Delete>, you can respond to the confirmation prompt by choosing either the <Delete> push button to delete the files you have tagged in successive steps, or by selecting the <Delete All> push button to delete all the files you have tagged at one time (see Figure 7.15).

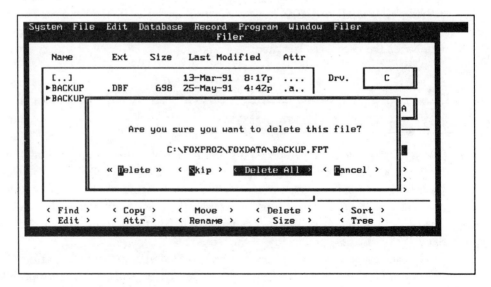

**Figure 7.15  Confirming File Deletion**

It is important to note that the deletion of a file is permanent. Once you have deleted a file, it cannot be recovered by FoxPro. (It may, however, be possible to recover files through the use of special utilities such as UNDELETE in DOS 5.0 or The Norton Utilities.) Nevertheless, always be careful when deleting files.

# Modifying the Database Structure

When you create a database file, every effort should be made to ensure that its data structure is correctly set up. It should include the correct data fields with the properly defined attributes enabling you to use the structure to organize your data elements efficiently for most, if not all, data management applications.

Sometimes, however, because of unforeseen changes in data requirements, you will need to modify your database structure at a later date to accommodate these changes, which may require the addition of new data fields or the deletion of others. Or you may need to change the attributes of some data fields to satisfy the new data requirements.

FoxPro accommodates the inevitability of changes to a database structure, and its procedure for modifying a data structure is simple. The Setup dialog is brought up after you have opened the database file in a work area. From the Setup dialog, you select the <Modify> push button to change the database structure.

During modification of a database structure, you can edit all the attributes of your existing data fields. Although you should be careful in making changes, do not worry about making mistakes in the process. You will be given the opportunity to cancel any changes that you make to the structure and will be asked if you want the modifications to be made permanent after you have finished the editing process. And in some cases, as a safety feature, you are able to return a structure to its original form.

To modify the structure of the SALESMAN database, invoke the Setup dialog after opening the database file in a work area by choosing the <Setup> push button from the View window. Alternatively, select the Setup option from the Database menu popup. In response to your selection, FoxPro displays the Setup dialog—the same Setup dialog used in an exercise in Chapter 6. There it was used to create the index tags for your structural compound index file. Now it is invoked to modify the structure of the database file. Choose the <Modify> push button by pressing the letter "y" or by clicking your mouse on the button. In return, FoxPro displays the current structure of the database file (see Figure 7.16).

All the information about the existing data structure is visible in the Modify Structure dialog shown in Figure 7.16: the name of the database file, the type and width of each of its data fields, and the data fields that have been used as index

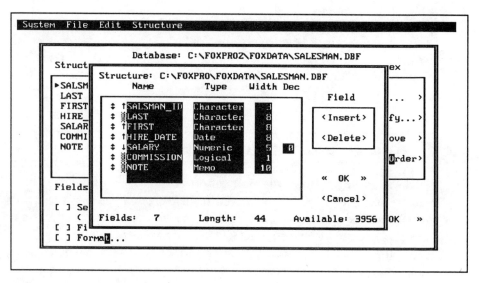

**Figure 7.16  Showing the Existing Data Structure**

keys (identified with either an up arrow for ascending order or a down arrow for descending order).

## ADDING NEW DATA FIELDS

There are three types of changes that you can make to a data structure. Of the three, two can be carried out by choosing the <Insert> and <Delete> push buttons in the Modify Structure dialog. Their use is fairly obvious: Select the <Insert> push button to insert a new data field at the cursor position; select the <Delete> push button to delete an existing data field in the same way.

For practice, choose the <Insert> push button to add the following three new data fields to the structure:

| Name | Type | Width |
|------|------|-------|
| SS_NO | Character | 11 |
| INITIAL | Character | 1 |
| MALE | Logical | 1 |

The data field SS_NO is used for storing social security numbers for the sales staff, INITIAL is for their middle initials, and the MALE logical field is used to code gender.

The order in which data fields appear in a structure is not an important factor in determining how you organize your data. You will learn in later chapters that you can display your data fields in whatever order you choose in the Browse window or in custom reports. Therefore, when you add new data fields to the structure, their order is really a matter of personal preference.

You do need to be aware, however, that you can insert data fields in the structure only one field at a time. Position your cursor where you would like to insert the data field. Then choose the <Insert> push button to open a row for the new data field. To insert the SS_NO field between the SALESMAN_ID and the LAST data fields, for instance, first place your cursor on the LAST field by pressing the Tab key until the symbol in front of the LAST field is highlighted. Or click your mouse immediately to the left of the LAST field name. Then select the <Insert> push button. As a result, a new field with the default name of NEWFIELD is displayed at the current cursor position (see Figure 7.17).

You can see that the new data field is set to a character field with a default width of 10 characters. At this point you can change the name and the other attributes of the field that you inserted. Just type your changes over the default values provided for the new data field. Use the left or right arrow key to move to the left or right one character. Press the Tab or the Shift-Tab key combination to move one column to the left or right. In this case, replace NEWFIELD with SS_NO and change its field width from 10 to 11 (see Figure 7.18).

Insert the INITIAL and MALE new fields in the structure in the same way. So that your screen looks like Figure 7.19, place the INITIAL character field between

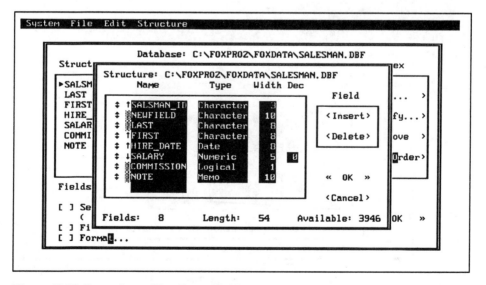

**Figure 7.17  Inserting a New Data Field**

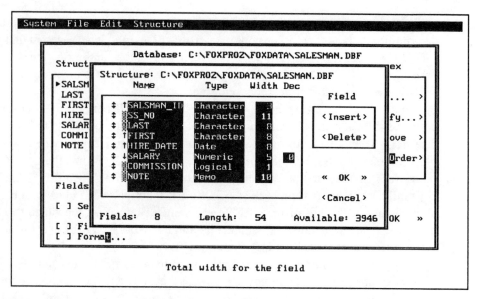

**Figure 7.18  Defining the Inserted Data Field**

the FIRST and HIRE_DATE fields and MALE above the COMMISSION field. The widths of these two new fields are set to 1; MALE is a logical data type.

If you make a mistake and insert the new fields in the wrong place you can, of course, delete them and reinsert them correctly.

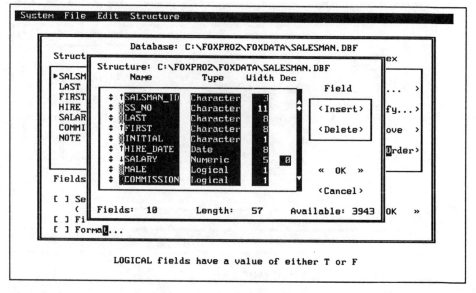

**Figure 7.19  Inserting the INITIAL and MALE New Fields**

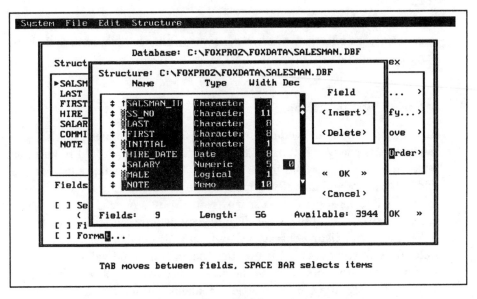

**Figure 7.20  Deleting an Existing Data Field**

## DELETING EXISTING DATA FIELDS

The procedure for removing an existing data field from the database structure is very simple. All you have to do is select the data field to be deleted and then choose the <Delete> push button. For example, to delete the COMMISSION field from the current structure, select that field either with your mouse or the keyboard. Then select the <Delete> push button and the COMMISSION field is removed from the structure (see Figure 7.20). If you made the mistake of deleting the wrong data field, choose the <Cancel> push button to exit from the Modify Structure dialog without making any changes and start over.

## REDEFINING EXISTING DATA FIELDS

The third type of change that you can make to a structure, is the redefinition of existing fields. This may include renaming your existing data fields, changing their field widths, and redefining their field types. Some of these operations can be carried out by editing field attributes; others require replacing the existing data fields with new data fields.

### Renaming Data Fields

You can rename any existing data field just by editing its current name in the structure. As long as the new field name follows the naming convention, FoxPro will modify the existing field names. You may want to try renaming some of the data fields as an exercise. Afterward, however, change them back to their original names so that you can follow the next set of exercises.

## Resetting Field Widths

You can also modify the width of existing character and numeric fields if your data requirements change. A longer last name, for example, would require that you widen the LAST data field in the structure. To do that, simply increase its field width. On the other hand, if you have set the field width too wide, you may want to shorten it to conserve storage space. (Note: You cannot change the widths of the date, memo, or logical fields because they are determined by FoxPro.)

Widening an existing character data field adds blank spaces at the end of that field for each record. This has no effect on existing field values, except that the field will take up more space in the screen display. But, if you shorten its field width, you may lose part of the field contents for some records—FoxPro will truncate the field by deleting the outermost right columns. Therefore, you must be careful not to shorten the field width when those fields contain character strings that are longer than what the new field width can accommodate.

Changing the width of a numeric field also allows you to store larger or smaller values in the redefined field. But again, you must not shorten the width of an existing field so that it becomes too small to accommodate existing values. If you do, some of the values will be lost. When you try to view these lost values, they will be displayed as a string of asterisks.

## Changing Field Types

Although you can rename an existing data field and reset its width by just editing its field name and field width in the database structure, it does not necessarily make sense to redefine its field type in the same way. Each type of data field is set up to hold a specific type of data element in a predetermined format. And although FoxPro will permit you to modify the database structure in this way, the result will frequently be a complete loss of the original data in that field. In cases where you intend to replace one field with another that has a completely different type of data (in other words, in cases where changing the field type is a shortcut for deleting an existing field and inserting a new one), this data loss is acceptable. In other cases, however, you may discover that you incorrectly defined the original field type, or that particular items of information can be handled more efficiently if their field type is changed. Let's assume, for example, that you've defined ZIP as a five-digit numeric field. You will probably find that it is far easier and more efficient to handle this data element if it were a character data type. In cases such as these, a precise understanding of how changing the field type affects the data contained in the field will allow you to choose the best method for modifying the database structure.

The following specific changes in the field type will result in either no loss of data or in a minimal loss of data:

- Character fields to memo fields. Character fields can be safely and accurately changed to memo fields without risking a loss of data.

- Character fields that contain numeric strings (0 through 9, -, and . only) can be successfully changed to numeric or float fields with a minimal loss of data. Any leading zeros, however, will be lost, and the numeric data will be right justified.

- Character fields that contain dates can be changed to date fields with no data loss.

- Character fields can be converted to logical fields if they contain Yes, Y, or T (which are converted to a logical true value), or if they contain No, N, or F (all of which are converted to a logical false).

- Numeric fields can be changed to float fields with no loss of data.

- Float fields can usually be changed to numeric fields with no data loss.

- Numeric or float fields can be changed to character fields with no loss of data. Leading zeros will not be added to the character string.

- Date fields can be successfully changed only to character fields.

- Logical fields can be changed only to character fields without losing data. A logical true will become the letter T, a logical false will become F.

In all other cases, when you do not want to discard the information in the field and simply changing the field type will not preserve the contents of the data field, the best method is to modify the database structure by adding a new field, then enter data into the new field, and finally delete any field that is no longer needed.

For example, to change the COMMISSION logical field to a numeric field named COMIS_RATE (for saving rates of commissions), you cannot just edit the attributes of the COMMISSION field. Instead, you must first delete the existing field and then insert a new data field. But because we deleted the COMMISSION logical field in the last exercise, just insert the COMIS_RATE as a new numeric field in its place. Set the width of the numeric field to 5 characters with 2 decimal places (see Figure 7.21).

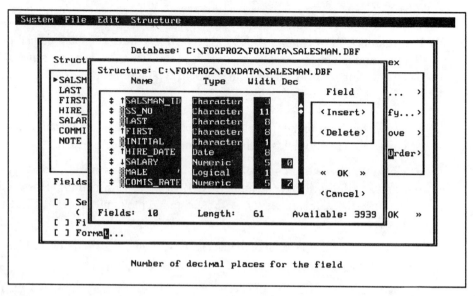

**Figure 7.21  Inserting the COMIS_RATE Data Field**

## SAVING MODIFIED DATA STRUCTURES

After you have made all your changes to the existing data structure of a current
database file, it is important to save the changes by choosing the <<OK>> push
button. Until you take that step, all the changes you have made up to this point are
temporary. (This means that you can still discard these changes by choosing the
<Cancel> push button to exit the Modify Structure dialog.) Once you select the
<<OK>> push button, you are prompted to confirm that you want to save these
changes permanently (see Figure 7.22).

Answer Yes to the prompt and all the changes are saved and you will be returned
to the Setup dialog. At this point, the Setup dialog will display the modified data
structure (see Figure 7.23).

## VIEWING RECORDS IN MODIFIED DATA STRUCTURES

After you have modified the structure of a database file, you can view the original
data records in the new structure. But to do that, first close the database file. If you
do not take this step, FoxPro may display the data records with the previous
database. After you reopen it, you can view the data records in the new structure
in the Browse window in either Browse or Change mode (see Figure 7.24).

The records of the revised SALESMAN database are displayed in Browse mode
in Figure 7.14. Notice that all the new data fields that you created are blank. These
fields will be filled with appropriate data elements later.

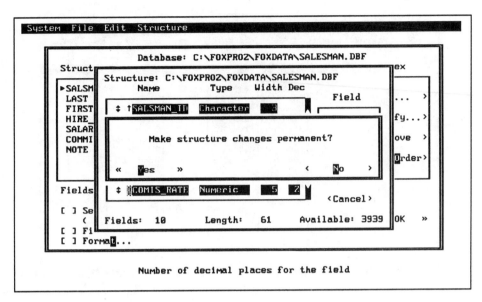

**Figure 7.22  Saving Structure Changes**

## CANCELLING STRUCTURAL CHANGES

FoxPro is a very forgiving program. It allows you to reverse many actions you have taken. For example, during the process of making changes to the data structure, you had several opportunities to abort the process by choosing the <Cancel> push button. Even after the changes were made permanent, the option was offered to

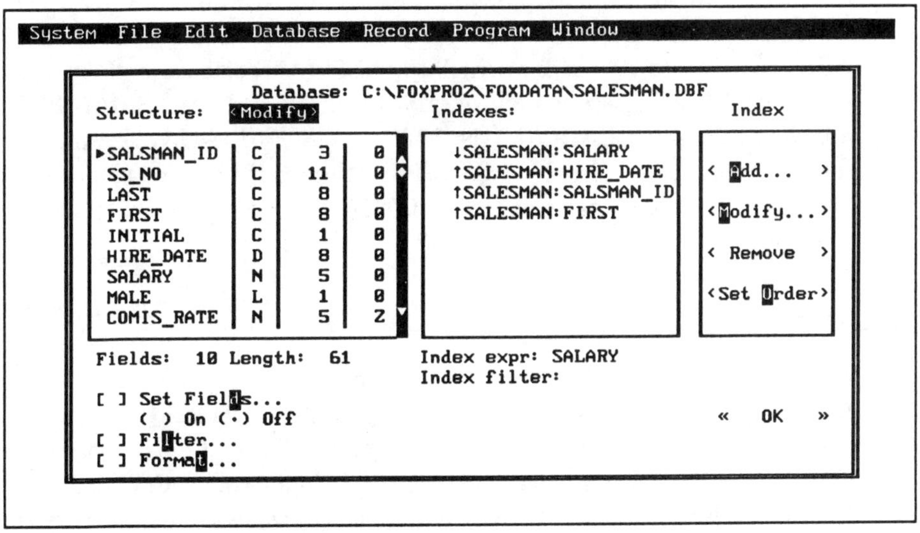

**Figure 7.23  Modified Data Structure**

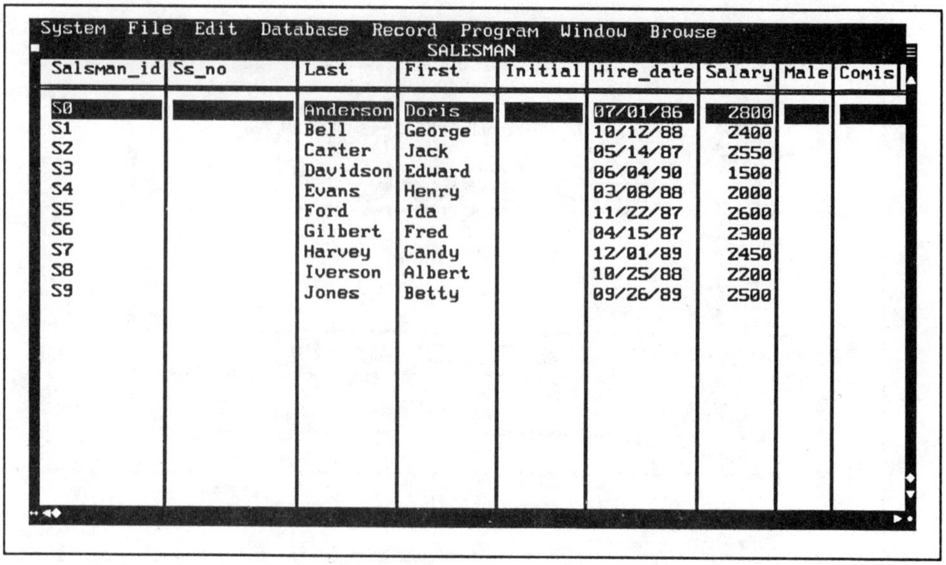

```
 System  File  Edit  Database  Record  Program  Window  Browse
                                  SALESMAN
 Salsman_id Ss_no      Last      First    Initial Hire_date Salary Male Comis
 S0                    Anderson  Doris            07/01/86   2800
 S1                    Bell      George           10/12/88   2400
 S2                    Carter    Jack             05/14/87   2550
 S3                    Davidson  Eduard           06/04/90   1500
 S4                    Evans     Henry            03/08/88   2000
 S5                    Ford      Ida              11/22/87   2600
 S6                    Gilbert   Fred             04/15/87   2300
 S7                    Harvey    Candy            12/01/89   2450
 S8                    Iverson   Albert           10/25/88   2200
 S9                    Jones     Betty            09/26/89   2500
```

**Figure 7.24  Viewing Records in the Modified Structure**

return your database file to its status before the last structural change. This is possible because FoxPro always saves a copy of the original database file in a backup file. The backup file is named after its original, but with .BAK as its extension. If the database file has an associated .FPT memo file, FoxPro creates a corresponding backup file with a .TBK file extension.

For example, after making your structural changes to SALESMAN.DBF, two new files were created: SALESMAN.BAK and SALESMAN.TBK. These two new files now store the original records in the database structure (see Figure 7.25).

Therefore, if you wanted to return the SALESMAN database to its original form, you would delete the current files SALESMAN.DBF and SALESMAN.FPT. Then you would rename SALESMAN.BAK to SALESMAN.DBF and SALES-MAN.TBK to SALESMAN.FPT. But to continue with our exercises, do not reverse the modifications made to SALESMAN.DBF and SALESMAN.FPT.

## REBUILDING INDEXES

When you modify a data structure, it is very important that you update all associated index files as well; and when you delete any existing data fields from a structure, you must also remove those indexes that used the deleted fields as index keys.

Using a structural compound index file to hold all your index tags means that this index upkeep is automatic. When you open a database file in a work area, its

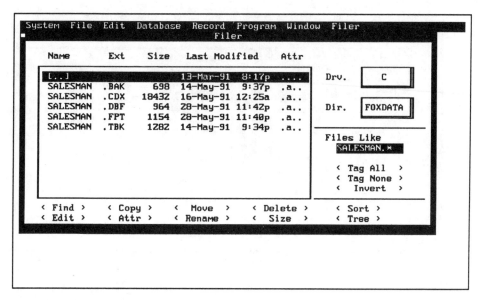

**Figure 7.25  Backup Files**

associated structural file also will be opened. After you have finished modifying the data structure, the index tags will be updated automatically to reflect the changes. All the index tags that referred to any of the deleted data fields will be removed from the structural compound index file as well. This is a major advantage of using a structural compound index to hold all your indexes.

If you have added new data fields to a database structure, you can build new index tags that include any of these new fields. To do that, just modify the contents of the structural compound index file, adding the new index tags. For example, because we added the SS_NO field to the SALESMAN database structure in the last exercise you may also want to add a new index tag, SS_NO, to its structural compound index file (see Figure 7.26).

If, however, you use other types of index files, you must modify them yourself to accommodate any changes that you make to the data structure. Those standard .IDX files that are no longer valid after the structural changes must be removed. Similarly, the contents of those nonstructural compound index files that contain index tags that use the deleted data fields must also be revised.

# Modifying Data Records

To accommodate changes in your data elements, you may find it necessary to modify the contents of your database records. This may involve editing the field

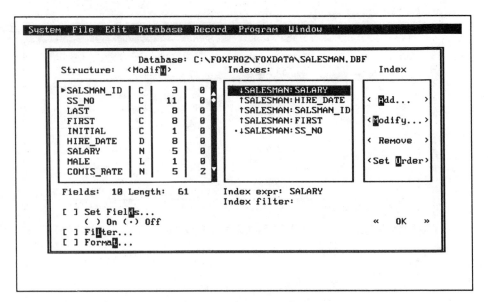

**Figure 7.26  Updating Indexes After Modifying Structure**

values of existing records, adding new records to the database, and/or deleting existing records from the database.

## EDITING RECORD CONTENTS

The contents of existing records in a database file can be edited while on display in the Browse window. Data values can be added to blank fields and alternate values can replace existing field values; these changes can be done either in Browse or Change mode.

### Editing Records in Change Mode

As an exercise of the editing process, let's assign values to the fields we added in the last exercise—SS_NO, INITIAL, MALE, and COMIS_RATE. First, display the records in the Browse window. Note that the new structure has more fields than can be shown on the same screen in Browse mode; therefore, let's switch to Change mode to complete the exercise. Just select the Change option from the Browse menu popup (see Figure 7.27).

This screen shows that currently, the fields that you created during the restructuring process are blank and ready to have appropriate values entered into them. It is important to remember that the order in which the records are displayed is determined by the master index that you designate. If you choose SALSMAN_ID as the master index, the data records are displayed according to the values in that

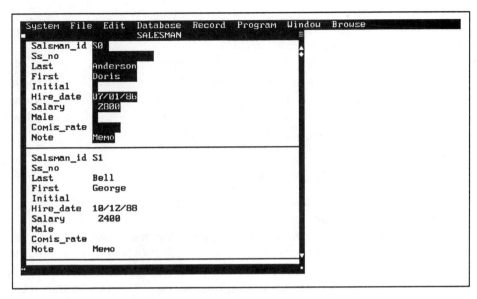

**Figure 7.27  Editing Data Records in Change Mode**

field; if you designate SALARY as the master index, the records would be arranged by those values. But for this exercise, keep SALSMAN_ID as the master index.

When you are ready to edit the field values, use your mouse to position the cursor on the field that you intend to change. On the keyboard, use the arrow keys to select the field earmarked for editing. With the cursor positioned on the correct data field, use the following keys for editing:

| Key | Function |
|---|---|
| Left arrow | Move one character to the left |
| Right arrow | Move one character to the right |
| Up arrow | Move to the beginning of the previous field |
| Down arrow | Move to the beginning of the next field |
| Shift+Tab | Move to the beginning of the previous field |
| Tab | Move to the beginning of the next field |
| Home | Move to the beginning of the current field |
| End | Move to the end of the current field |
| PgUp | Move up one record |
| PgDn | Move down one record |
| Esc | Abort editing |
| Ctrl+End | Save changes and exit |

After you have finished editing one record, move on to the next (as soon as you move the cursor beyond the last data field in the record you are editing, you will move to the next record). To skip the next record, press the PgDn key; to return to the preceding record, press the PgUp key.

If you make mistakes during the editing process, you either can reedit the changes, or abort all the changes made to that point by pressing the Esc key to exit from the Edit operation. If necessary, you can return to the data records to continue modifying the field values. But do not *close* the Browse window, because that step will render all the changes (mistakes included) permanent.

## Editing Records in Browse Mode

Although more data fields can be viewed at one time in Change mode, editing records in Browse mode gives you the advantage of viewing more records on the same screen at one time, thus making it easier to move between existing records. One way to make use of both modes (using SALESMAN as an example) is to edit the first record in the SALESMAN database in Change mode, and then switch to Browse mode by choosing the Browse option from the Browse menu popup.

While you are in Browse mode, use these keys to edit your records:

| *Key* | *Function* |
|---|---|
| Left arrow | Move one character to the left |
| Right arrow | Move one character to the right |
| Up arrow | Move one record up |
| Down arrow | Move one record down |
| Shift+Tab | Move to the beginning of the previous field |
| Tab | Move to the beginning of the next field |
| Home | Move to the beginning of the current field |
| End | Move the the end of the current field |
| PgUp | Move to the first record on the screen |
| PgDn | Move to the last record on the screen |
| Esc | Abort editing |
| Ctrl+End | Save changes and exit |

Other ways to manipulate the contents of a database for display are: Use the scroll control to display most of the data fields on the same screen; or, if you cannot display all the fields you want on the screen, rearrange them in the manner that best suits your editing needs. The procedure for rearranging displayed fields was discussed in Chapter 5.

So that you can continue with the exercises in this chapter, fill in the first five blank fields with the values as shown in Figure 7.28.

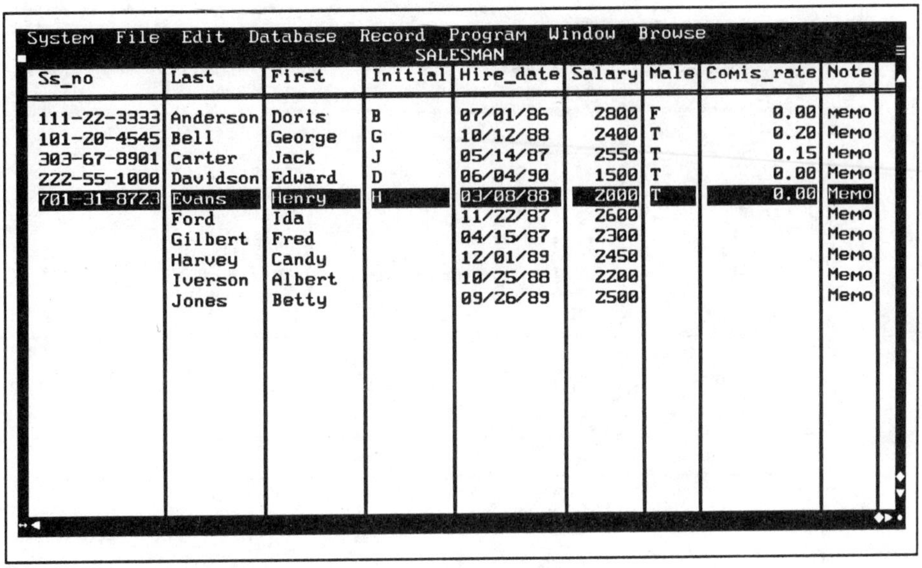

```
 System  File  Edit  Database  Record  Program  Window  Browse
                              SALESMAN
 Ss_no         Last      First    Initial Hire_date Salary Male Comis_rate Note

 111-22-3333 Anderson  Doris     B      07/01/86  2800 F       0.00 Memo
 101-20-4545 Bell      George    G      10/12/88  2400 T       0.20 Memo
 303-67-8901 Carter    Jack      J      05/14/87  2550 T       0.15 Memo
 222-55-1000 Davidson  Edward    D      06/04/90  1500 T       0.00 Memo
 701-31-8723 Evans     Henry     H      03/08/88  2000 T       0.00 Memo
             Ford      Ida              11/22/87  2600           Memo
             Gilbert   Fred             04/15/87  2300           Memo
             Harvey    Candy            12/01/89  2450           Memo
             Iverson   Albert           10/25/88  2200           Memo
             Jones     Betty            09/26/89  2500           Memo
```

**Figure 7.28  Revised Fields Values**

## Editing Selected Data Fields

When you have a database that has more data fields than can be displayed in the same Browse window, you have the option of displaying only those fields that you need to edit. This is achieved by selecting the data fields earmarked for editing in the Setup dialog *before* displaying them in the Browse window.

We'll use this procedure to finish adding values to the blank fields for the last five records. Therefore, instead of showing all the data fields, we'll display in Browse mode only those fields that are related to your editing needs. They are: SS_NO, INITIAL, MALE, and COMIS_RATE. Other fields—the SALS-MAN_ID, LAST, and FIRST fields—should be displayed to provide a reference point.

To select the data fields to be shown in Browse mode, check the Set Fields box after you have invoked the Setup dialog from the View window. Then select the fields you want in the Field Picker dialog. Figure 7.29 shows seven data fields selected.

When you return to the Setup dialog, note that the Set Fields box is checked and that the On radio button has been turned on (see Figure 7.30).

At this point, select the <<OK>> push button to exit the Setup dialog and return to the View window; then select the Browse option. You'll see that only those data fields that you selected are displayed, whether you are in Browse or Change mode.

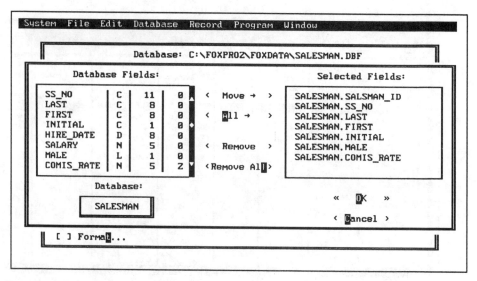

**Figure 7.29  Selecting Fields to Be Edited**

Now you can continue entering values in those blank fields for the last five records as illustrated in Figure 7.31.

If you want to display all the data fields after you have completed the editing operation, you must return to the Setup dialog and deselect the Set Fields check box.

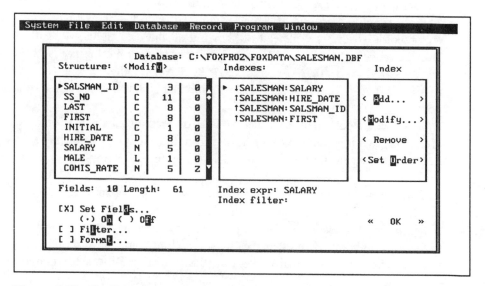

**Figure 7.30  Checking the Set Fields Box**

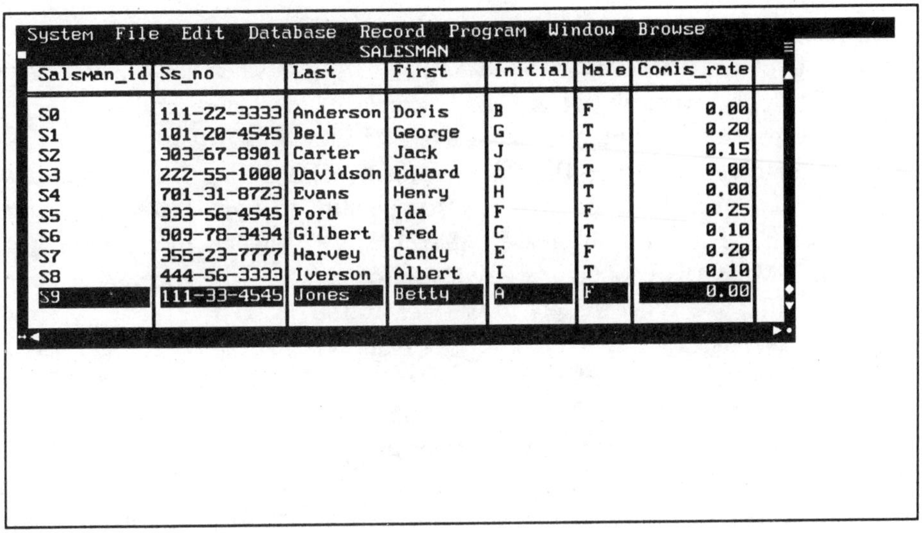

**Figure 7.31  Editing Selected Data Fields**

## Editing Selected Data Records

The previous exercise showed you how to use the Set Fields operation to display only those fields that you need for editing your data records. Similarly, you can display in the Browse window only a certain set of data records that you would like to edit. This is done by specifying a filter condition that screens the data records. Simply check the Filter box in the Setup dialog and then follow the procedure that you learned in Chapter 6 for creating a filter condition to display selected records.

## Saving Edited Data Records

Any changes made to a data field during the editing process are considered temporary until you decide to save them. So be aware that if you press the Esc key in the middle of editing a field, you will lose all the changes that you have made to the field so far. To save these changes, either exit the window view by selecting the Close control or by pressing the Ctrl+End key combination; or move the cursor to another field or another record in the Browse window.

## ADDING NEW DATA RECORDS

In addition to editing existing records, you also can add new records to a database file by selecting the Append option from the Record menu popup. This option is available after you have opened a database file in a work area, regardless of whether or not you are in the Browse window. In every case, when you select the Append option, a blank data entry form will be displayed in Change mode.

In order not to disturb the contents of SALESMAN.DBF, let's copy its records to a temporary database file (to be named SAMPLE.DBF) for the next set of exercises. To do that, use the Copy To operation that you learned earlier in this chapter. The resulting database, SAMPLE.DBF, will be an exact duplicate of SALESMAN.DBF. Remember, the Copy To operation will automatically copy the memo file, SALESMAN.FPT to the SAMPLE.TBK. But to create the structural compound index for SAMPLE.DBF you must copy SALESMAN.CDX to SAM-PLE.CDX using the system's Filer. Then you must add SAMPLE.CDX to the database's index files by using the Setup dialog (see Figure 7.32). This step is necessary if you intend to use the indexes to arrange the records in SAMPLE.DBF.

To add new records to the SAMPLE database, choose the Append option from the Record menu popup after you have opened the database file in a work area. In response to selecting this menu option, a standard data entry form for a new record will be displayed. Note that in order to show as many data fields as possible, FoxPro always displays the data entry form in Change mode. You can switch to Browse mode by selecting the Browse option from the Browse menu popup. But in this case, because the SAMPLE database has too many data fields to be shown on the same screen, it is better to use Change mode for entering your data values.

Enter data values in the new record by using the editing keys discussed earlier. You may enter as many new records as needed. You'll see that as soon as one record

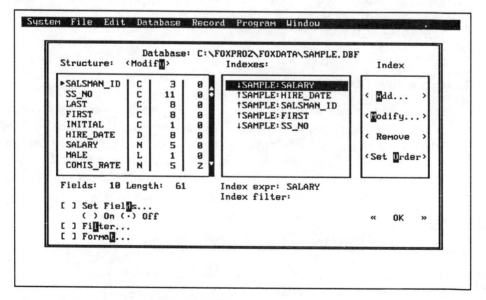

**Figure 7.32 Creating SAMPLE.DBF**

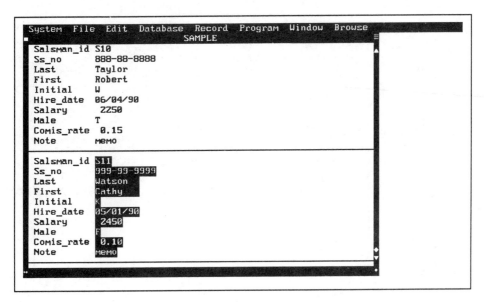

**Figure 7.33  Adding New Records**

begins to fill, the data entry form for the next new record will begin to show. As an exercise, add to the SAMPLE database the two new records that are shown in Figure 7.33. Leave their memo fields blank.

New records will always be appended to the end of the file. If, however, you view them in Browse mode, they appear in a different order because the order in which these records are displayed is determined by the master index that you designate. If you did not designate any index tag as the master index, the records would be displayed in the order in which they were entered. In this case, however, the records were entered in the order based on values in the SALSMAN_ID field as illustrated in Figure 7.34.

If you had chosen another index tag as the master index, they obviously would be displayed in that order. Say you selected SALARY as the master index in the Setup dialog. When you returned to Browse mode, the records would be ordered by their salary values as shown in Figure 7.35.

Notice in this figure that a line is open at the end of the table for appending another new record. You could continue adding new records to the file at this stage; otherwise, save the new records either by closing the Browse window or by pressing the Ctrl+End key combination.

## DELETING EXISTING DATA RECORDS

Any records that you no longer need can be deleted permanently from a database file by following a two-step process: mark the records to be deleted, and then

System File Edit Database Record Program Window Browse

SAMPLE

| Salsman_id | Ss_no | Last | First | Initial | Hire_date | Salary | Male | Comis |
|---|---|---|---|---|---|---|---|---|
| S0 | 111-22-3333 | Anderson | Doris | B | 07/01/86 | 2800 | F | |
| S1 | 101-20-4545 | Bell | George | G | 10/12/88 | 2400 | T | |
| S2 | 303-67-8901 | Carter | Jack | J | 05/14/87 | 2550 | T | |
| S3 | 222-55-1000 | Davidson | Edward | D | 06/04/90 | 1500 | T | |
| S4 | 701-31-8723 | Evans | Henry | H | 03/08/88 | 2000 | T | |
| S5 | 333-56-4545 | Ford | Ida | F | 11/22/87 | 2600 | F | |
| S6 | 909-78-3434 | Gilbert | Fred | C | 04/15/87 | 2300 | T | |
| S7 | 355-23-7777 | Harvey | Candy | E | 12/01/89 | 2450 | F | |
| S8 | 444-56-3333 | Iverson | Albert | I | 10/25/88 | 2200 | T | |
| S9 | 111-33-4545 | Jones | Betty | A | 09/26/89 | 2500 | F | |
| S10 | 888-88-8888 | Taylor | Robert | W | 06/04/90 | 2250 | T | |
| S11 | 999-99-9999 | Watson | Cathy | K | 05/01/90 | 2450 | F | |
| | | | | | / / | | F | |

**Figure 7.34 Appended Records**

perform the Pack operation that physically removes records marked for deletion. These procedures are detailed in the next sections. (Note: Until you pack the database file, any records marked for deletion can still be recalled. This is a safety

System File Edit Database Record Program Window Browse

SAMPLE

| Salsman_id | Ss_no | Last | First | Initial | Hire_date | Salary | Male | Comis |
|---|---|---|---|---|---|---|---|---|
| S0 | 111-22-3333 | Anderson | Doris | B | 07/01/86 | 2800 | F | |
| S5 | 333-56-4545 | Ford | Ida | F | 11/22/87 | 2600 | F | |
| S2 | 303-67-8901 | Carter | Jack | J | 05/14/87 | 2550 | T | |
| S9 | 111-33-4545 | Jones | Betty | A | 09/26/89 | 2500 | F | |
| S11 | 999-99-9999 | Watson | Cathy | K | 05/01/90 | 2450 | F | |
| S7 | 355-23-7777 | Harvey | Candy | E | 12/01/89 | 2450 | F | |
| S1 | 101-20-4545 | Bell | George | G | 10/12/88 | 2400 | T | |
| S6 | 909-78-3434 | Gilbert | Fred | C | 04/15/87 | 2300 | T | |
| S10 | 888-88-8888 | Taylor | Robert | W | 06/04/90 | 2250 | T | |
| S8 | 444-56-3333 | Iverson | Albert | I | 10/25/88 | 2200 | T | |
| S4 | 701-31-8723 | Evans | Henry | H | 03/08/88 | 2000 | T | |
| S3 | 222-55-1000 | Davidson | Edward | D | 06/04/90 | 1500 | T | |

**Figure 7.35 Ordering New Records by SALARY Master Index**

feature that guards against deleting the wrong data records by accident. Once the database file is packed, all the records that were marked for deletion will be permanently removed; you will not be able to recover them using FoxPro.)

## Marking Data Records for Deletion

There are a number of ways to mark records for deletion: one at a time, as a group, by defining the record Scope, or by specifying the appropriate filter condition.

To delete an individual record, just mark that record in either Browse or Change mode. Select the record using either the mouse or the keyboard and then choose the Delete option from the Record menu popup. Using the mouse, simply click on the column between the window frame and the record's first field. Try this on the fourth record (SALSMAN_ID = "S3"). Click the mouse in front of the "S3" field value; a dot is placed to the left of the record indicating that it is marked for deletion. If you click the mouse on the same location again, the deletion mark will be removed. If you are using the keyboard, choose the Delete option from the Record menu popup after highlighting the record (see Figure 7.36).

You are next asked to define the scope and filter condition to identify the records to be deleted. In this case, all you want to delete is the highlighted record, so simply choose the <Delete> push button to mark the record, as shown in Figure 7.37.

The highlighted record is then marked for deletion—indicated by a dot to the left of the record as seen in Figure 7.38.

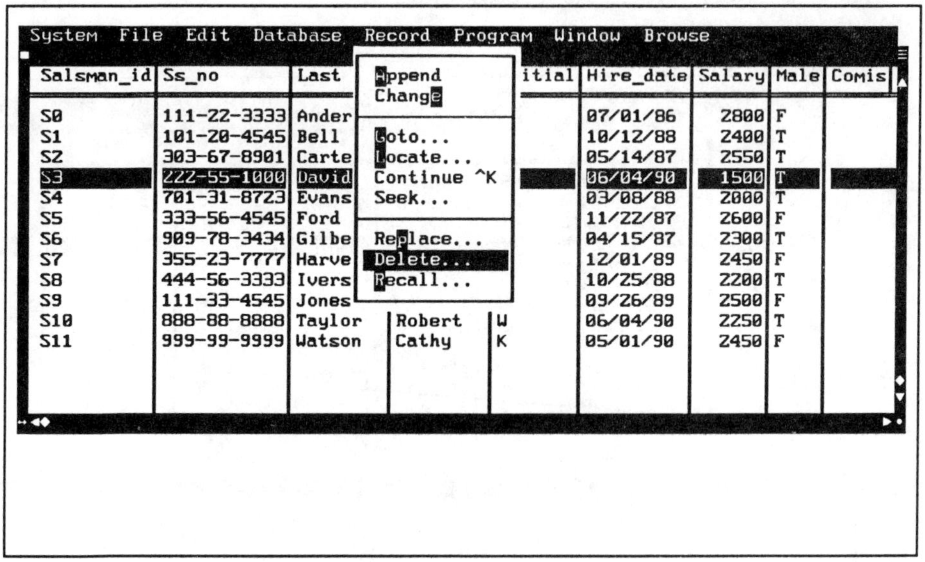

**Figure 7.36  Marking a Record for Deletion**

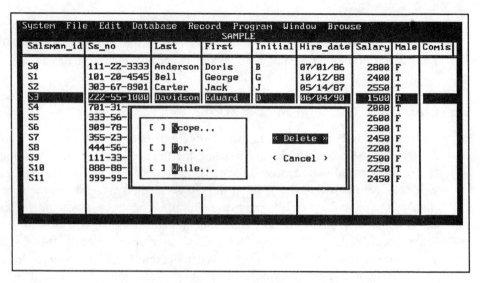

**Figure 7.37  Marking the Highlighted Record for Deletion**

## Marking a Group of Records for Deletion

You can delete more than one record at a time by defining either the record scope or the filter condition to select a group of records for deletion. The record scope specifies a section of records and includes one or more contiguous records. The filter condition screens the records for deletion.

```
 System  File  Edit  Database  Record  Program  Window  Browse
                                SAMPLE
 Salsman_id Ss_no        Last      First    Initial Hire_date Salary Male Comis

 S0         111-22-3333  Anderson  Doris    B       07/01/86  2800  F
 S1         101-20-4545  Bell      George   G       10/12/88  2400  T
 S2         303-67-8901  Carter    Jack     J       05/14/87  2550  T
 S3         222-55-1000  Davidson  Edward   D       06/04/90  1500  T
 S4         701-31-8723  Evans     Henry    H       03/08/88  2000  T
 S5         333-56-4545  Ford      Ida      F       11/22/87  2600  F
 S6         909-78-3434  Gilbert   Fred     C       04/15/87  2300  T
 S7         355-23-7777  Harvey    Candy    E       12/01/89  2450  F
 S8         444-56-3333  Iverson   Albert   I       10/25/88  2200  T
 S9         111-33-4545  Jones     Betty    A       09/26/89  2500  F
 S10        888-88-8888  Taylor    Robert   W       06/04/90  2250  T
 S11        999-99-9999  Watson    Cathy    K       05/01/90  2450  F
```

**Figure 7.38  Record Marked for Deletion**

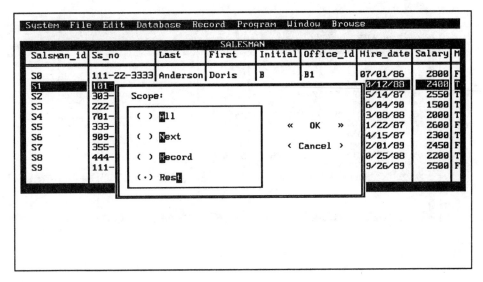

**Figure 7.39 The Scope Dialog**

## Defining the Record Scope

To delete a set of records, check the Scope box to select the range of contiguous records to delete. A Scope dialog appears that contains the following four radio buttons, as shown in Figure 7.39:

- ALL. Marks every record in the database for deletion. The result will be an empty database file that contains only the database structure.

- NEXT. Marks a block of consecutive records starting from the current cursor position. The default value of NEXT is 1, meaning that only the current record will be deleted. However, you can enter any number you choose.

- RECORD. Marks a specific record for deletion by prompting you to enter the record number in a text box. The text box will appear next to the radio button once the button is selected.

- REST. Marks for deletion all the records from the current record to the end of the file.

## Specifying Filter Conditions

To mark a set of records for deletion by specifying a filter condition—let's say all the records belonging to the male sales staff—check the For box after you select the Delete option from the Record menu popup; then use the Expression Builder to define the filter condition MALE = .T. As a result, all the male records are marked for deletion as illustrated in Figure 7.40.

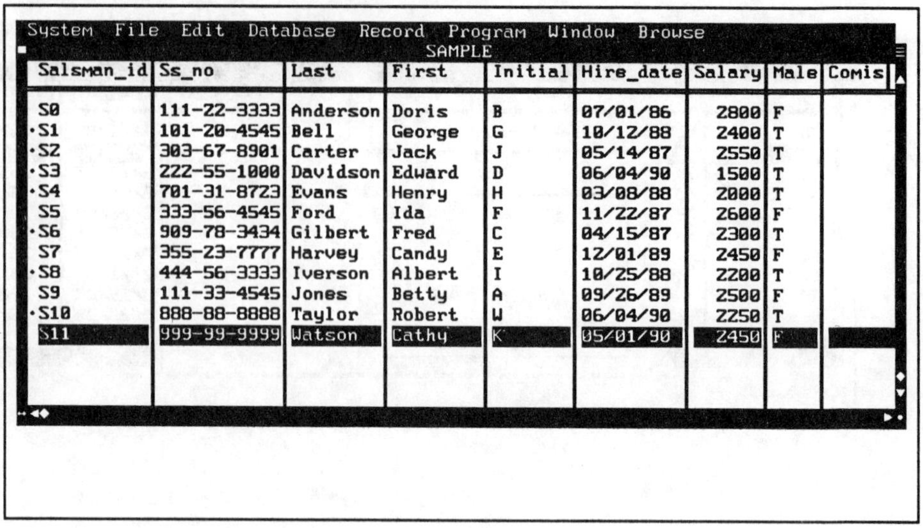

System File Edit Database Record Program Window Browse

SAMPLE

| | Salsman_id | Ss_no | Last | First | Initial | Hire_date | Salary | Male | Comis |
|---|---|---|---|---|---|---|---|---|---|
| | S0 | 111-22-3333 | Anderson | Doris | B | 07/01/86 | 2800 | F | |
| • | S1 | 101-20-4545 | Bell | George | G | 10/12/88 | 2400 | T | |
| • | S2 | 303-67-8901 | Carter | Jack | J | 05/14/87 | 2550 | T | |
| • | S3 | 222-55-1000 | Davidson | Edward | D | 06/04/90 | 1500 | T | |
| • | S4 | 701-31-8723 | Evans | Henry | H | 03/08/88 | 2000 | T | |
| | S5 | 333-56-4545 | Ford | Ida | F | 11/22/87 | 2600 | F | |
| • | S6 | 909-78-3434 | Gilbert | Fred | C | 04/15/87 | 2300 | T | |
| | S7 | 355-23-7777 | Harvey | Candy | E | 12/01/89 | 2450 | F | |
| • | S8 | 444-56-3333 | Iverson | Albert | I | 10/25/88 | 2200 | T | |
| | S9 | 111-33-4545 | Jones | Betty | A | 09/26/89 | 2500 | F | |
| • | S10 | 888-88-8888 | Taylor | Robert | W | 06/04/90 | 2250 | T | |
| | S11 | 999-99-9999 | Watson | Cathy | K | 05/01/90 | 2450 | F | |

**Figure 7.40 Male Records Marked for Deletion**

It is important to note that when using filter conditions to select records for deletion, in most cases you will want to set the Scope to All because the All scope subjects all the records in the database file to the filter conditions; otherwise, only the highlighted record will be subjected to the filter conditions. The FOR filter determines which records are deleted within the range of records defined by Scope.

## Recalling Marked Data Records

Once you have marked a record for deletion, the deletion tag remains attached to the records until you take one of two actions. One is to remove the marked record permanently from the database file; the other is to remove the deletion tag by recalling the marked records. Otherwise, the deletion marks (and the deleted records) will remain even after you close the database file.

The first way to recall a record marked for deletion is to select the Recall option from the Record menu popup and then define the record scope and filter condition. The second is to remove the deletion marks from records one by one while you view the records in the Browse window. For example, if you decide to recall some of the records that are marked for deletion in the SAMPLE database, select the Recall option from the Record popup. FoxPro then displays the Scope, For, and While check boxes from which you can choose to specify the record scope and filter conditions for selecting the records that you intend to recall (see Figure 7.41).

The process of defining the record scope and filter conditions for restoring records is identical to that used to select the records for deletion. Any marked records that satisfy the filter condition and are within the scope will be recalled.

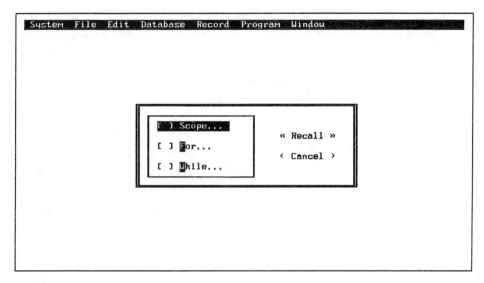

**Figure 7.41  Selecting Marked Records to Recall**

So, to recall some of the records that we marked for deletion above—let's say those belonging to male salespeople whose salaries are at least $2,400—specify the record scope and filter condition accordingly. That is, select the All radio button after checking the Scope box, then enter SALARY > 2400 as the filter condition after checking the For box. As a result, when you view the records in the SAMPLE database, you can see that some of the records that were marked for deletion have been recalled. Compare Figure 7.42 with Figure 7.40. The records for Bell and Carter have been recalled.

Recalling records one by one while they are displayed in the Browse window has the advantage of allowing you to review the records that you think you want to recall. To use this method, simply click your mouse on the deletion mark next to the record you intend to remove; repeat this process for each record that you are going to recall. Try this method by recalling the record belonging to Henry Evans (SALSMAN_ID = "S4"). Click your mouse on the deletion mark next to the record. Note that there are now only four records marked for deletion.

## Removing Marked Records

The Pack operation should be used only after you are sure that the records that you have selected are the ones that you want to delete from the database file. Select the Pack option from the Database menu popup and you will see the following prompt that requires you to confirm your action:

```
Pack C:\FOXPRO\FOXDATA\SAMPLE.DBF?
```

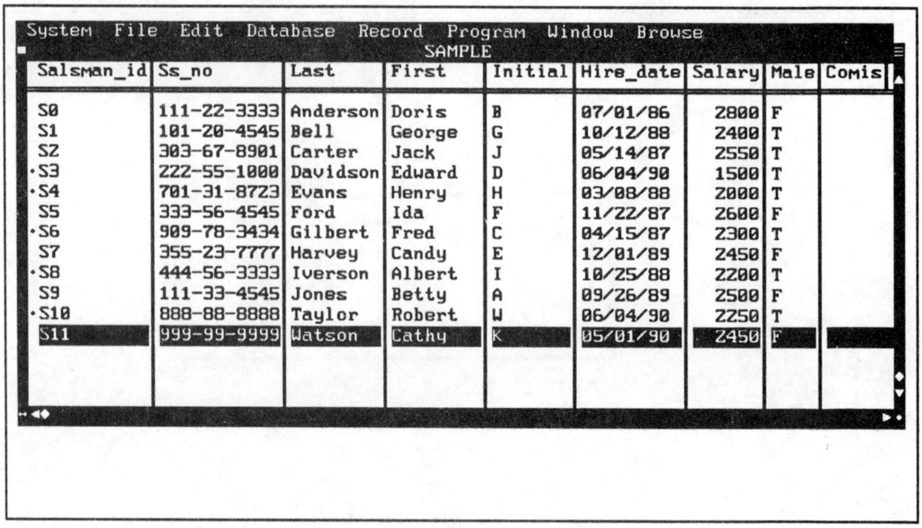

```
 System  File  Edit  Database  Record  Program  Window  Browse
                                 SAMPLE
 Salsman_id Ss_no       Last     First    Initial Hire_date Salary Male Comis

   S0       111-22-3333 Anderson Doris    B       07/01/86   2800  F
   S1       101-20-4545 Bell     George   G       10/12/88   2400  T
   S2       303-67-8901 Carter   Jack     J       05/14/87   2550  T
  ·S3       222-55-1000 Davidson Edward   D       06/04/90   1500  T
  ·S4       701-31-8723 Evans    Henry    H       03/08/88   2000  T
   S5       333-56-4545 Ford     Ida      F       11/22/87   2600  F
  ·S6       909-78-3434 Gilbert  Fred     C       04/15/87   2300  T
   S7       355-23-7777 Harvey   Candy    E       12/01/89   2450  F
  ·S8       444-56-3333 Iverson  Albert   I       10/25/88   2200  T
   S9       111-33-4545 Jones    Betty    A       09/26/89   2500  F
  ·S10      888-88-8888 Taylor   Robert   W       06/04/90   2250  T
   S11      999-99-9999 Watson   Cathy    K       05/01/90   2450  F
```

**Figure 7.42  Recalling Selected Records**

Answer Yes to the prompt and all the marked records will be permanently removed from the database file. Display the contents of SAMPLE.DBF now and you will see that only eight records remain (see Figure 7.43).

Remember, the Pack operation is permanent, so it is a good idea to make a backup copy of your database file before packing it. To repeat: Once the Pack operation is complete, there is no way to recover the deleted records.

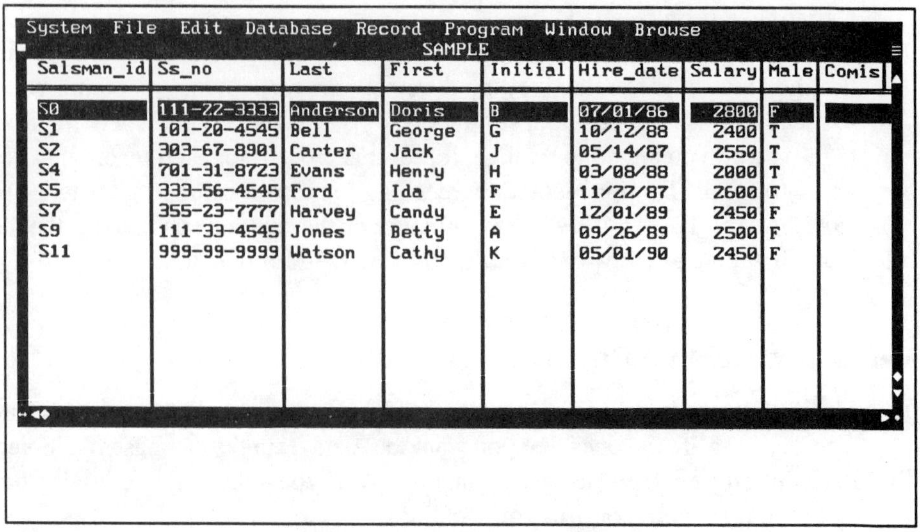

```
 System  File  Edit  Database  Record  Program  Window  Browse
                                 SAMPLE
 Salsman_id Ss_no       Last     First    Initial Hire_date Salary Male Comis

   S0       111-22-3333 Anderson Doris    B       07/01/86   2800  F
   S1       101-20-4545 Bell     George   G       10/12/88   2400  T
   S2       303-67-8901 Carter   Jack     J       05/14/87   2550  T
   S4       701-31-8723 Evans    Henry    H       03/08/88   2000  T
   S5       333-56-4545 Ford     Ida      F       11/22/87   2600  F
   S7       355-23-7777 Harvey   Candy    E       12/01/89   2450  F
   S9       111-33-4545 Jones    Betty    A       09/26/89   2500  F
   S11      999-99-9999 Watson   Cathy    K       05/01/90   2450  F
```

**Figure 7.43  Data Records Remaining After Pack Operation**

## REPLACING DATA FOR MULTIPLE RECORDS

There are a number of ways to replace individual field values in one or more data records. One is to edit the existing records individually with the procedure discussed earlier in this chapter so that they contain new values in the data fields. But another—easier—way to replace a set of values in a given field is to select the Replace option from the Record menu popup.

Let's say that as a result of a decision to award a 10 percent salary increase to those salespeople who were hired before December 31, 1988, you have to change the salaries for several members of the sales staff. There are two ways to do this. The first way—a tedious process—is to edit the value in the SALARY field for each salesperson who qualified for the increase. The better way is to systematically replace all the field values involved as a group. To do that, first choose the Replace option from the Record menu popup. When the Replace dialog appears, select from the field list the data field whose existing value you would like to replace with a new value. In the <With...> text box enter the new value in the form of an expression. Use the Scope, For, and While check boxes to specify the record scope and filter condition for selecting the records involved.

For this exercise, select SALARY as the data field whose values you would like to replace. Then enter the expression that will create the new value in the <With...> text box, in this case:

```
SALARY*1.10
```

which represents a 10 percent increase in the value of the existing SALARY field (see Figure 7.44). Note that clicking on <With...> leads to the Expression Builder where you are asked to verify the correctness of an expression.

If you were simply to select the <<Replace>> push button at this point to make the change, only a single record would be affected; this is because the Replace option by default only operates on the current record. But because you want to make changes to multiple records, the next step involves defining the record scope and filter condition for the data records whose values you are replacing. First, check the Scope box. Because you want to make changes to all the records in the database that meet a specific condition, select ALL for the record scope. Because you want to change the contents of the salary fields for only some of the records—namely, those showing the hire date as on or before December 31, 1988, enter HIRE_DATE <= {12/31/88} as the expression in the FOR Clause dialog after you check the FOR box in the Replace dialog (see Figure 7.45).

Selecting the <<OK>> push button will return you to the Replace dialog. To start the Replace operation, select the <<Replace>> push button; the values in the SALARY field for all the records that you selected will be replaced with the new values (see Figure 7.46).

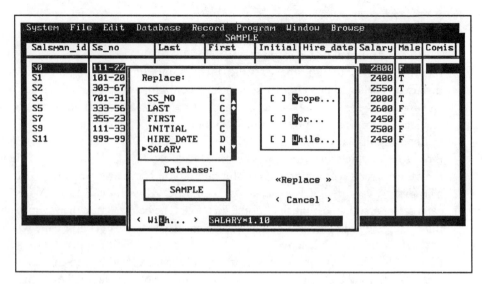

**Figure 7.44  Defining the Expression for Replacing a Value**

In this figure you can see that the salary values for the first five salespeople in the SAMPLE database have changed because they were hired before December 31, 1988, i.e., the salary for Anderson has changed from $2,800 to $3,080, an increase of $280 (10 percent of $2,800).

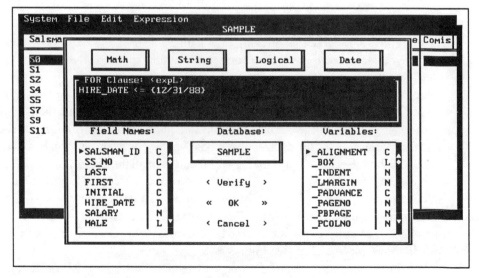

**Figure 7.45  Defining Filter Conditions for Replacing Records**

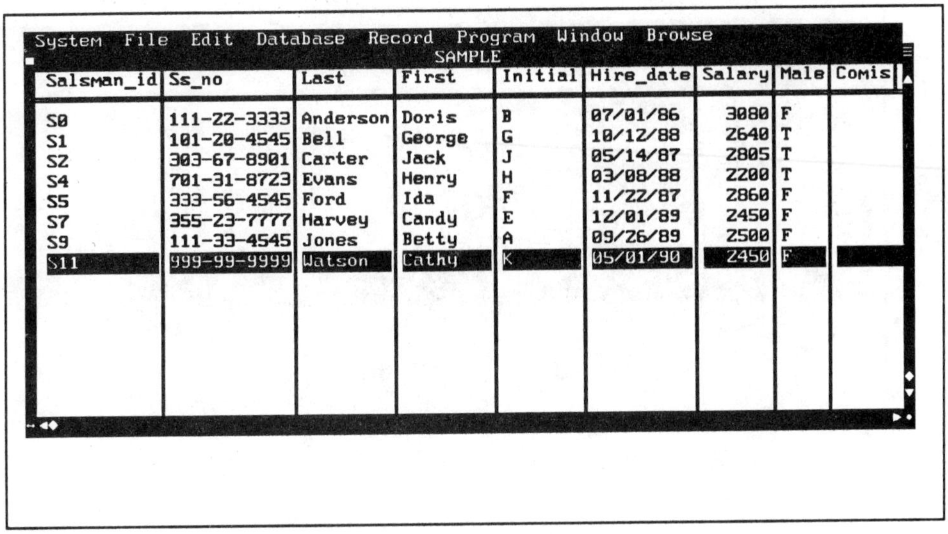

```
 System  File  Edit  Database  Record  Program  Window  Browse
                            SAMPLE
 Salsman_id Ss_no        Last      First     Initial Hire_date Salary Male Comis

 S0          111-22-3333 Anderson  Doris     B       07/01/86  3080   F
 S1          101-20-4545 Bell      George    G       10/12/88  2640   T
 S2          303-67-8901 Carter    Jack      J       05/14/87  2805   T
 S4          701-31-8723 Evans     Henry     H       03/08/88  2200   T
 S5          333-56-4545 Ford      Ida       F       11/22/87  2860   F
 S7          355-23-7777 Harvey    Candy     E       12/01/89  2450   F
 S9          111-33-4545 Jones     Betty     A       09/26/89  2500   F
 S11         999-99-9999 Watson    Cathy     K       05/01/90  2450   F
```

Figure 7.46  Replaced Field Values

## IDENTIFYING AND REMOVING DUPLICATED RECORDS

In a database file, there may be duplicate values in different records for the same data field. Some of these duplicate values are necessary and acceptable. Others may represent data entry errors. For example, while it is acceptable to have more than one record with the same state code in the STATE data field, the same social security number obviously should not appear in the SS_NO data field in more than one record. Such a duplicate field value means either that you have mistyped the social security number in a new record or that you have entered a duplicate record to the database file. In either case, you should correct the error.

Obviously, if a database file has a large number of records, it can be difficult to spot any duplicate records. One possible solution is to index the database on the data field in which you think the duplicate field values may occur. When this index is designated as the master index, all the records will be arranged by their values in this field. As a result, it is easier to notice any duplicate values in the index field. For example, if the SS_NO index is tag set as the master index, a new record entered with a duplicate value in the SS_NO field of the SALESMAN database will be displayed right below an existing record with the same social security number, making it easy to spot.

Once you have found the records with duplicate field values, you either can edit them or remove them from the file. If you choose to remove the records, use the procedures discussed earlier to mark and then delete them with the Pack operation.

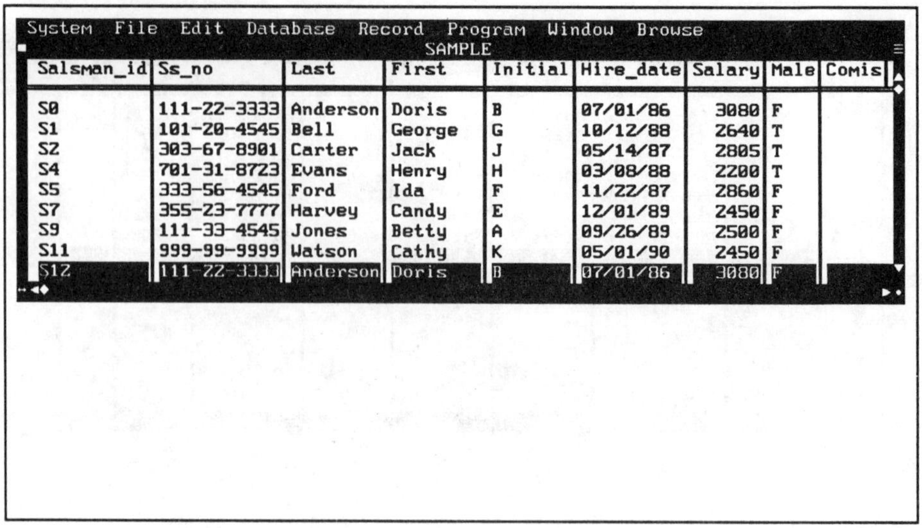

**Figure 7.47  Duplicate Records**

Another method for removing duplicate records is to copy the unique records in the database file to another database. To do that, again index the database on the data field that contains duplicate values. This time, however, select the Unique option. As a result, all the records with duplicate values in the index field will be ignored and only unique values in the indexed field will remain. Therefore, if you copy these records to a new file, the file will no longer contain any duplicate records. You can then replace the original database file with the file just created.

As an exercise, add a duplicate record to the SAMPLE file for Anderson, as shown in Figure 7.47. Notice that records S0 and S12 are identical except for their identification numbers—every record entered, regardless of its contents, receives a different identification number. To remove the duplicate record, index on one of the data fields where duplicate values occur. In this example, choose SS_NO as the key field. Because an index tag named SS_NO was set up earlier, you can modify the tag by choosing Unique as the indexing option (see Figure 7.48).

When you exit from the Index dialog, designate SS_NO as the master index. As a result, when you view the records in the SAMPLE database, the duplicate record (S12) is no longer there (see Figure 7.49).

In Figure 7.49, all the records are now arranged in descending order by social security number. As you can see, the duplicate record (S12) has been excluded from the Browse view. It is important to note, however, that this record is still physically present in the database file. The unique index that we generated governs our access to records in the physical database. Since we have created a unique index on the SS_NO field, all records with duplicate social security numbers are

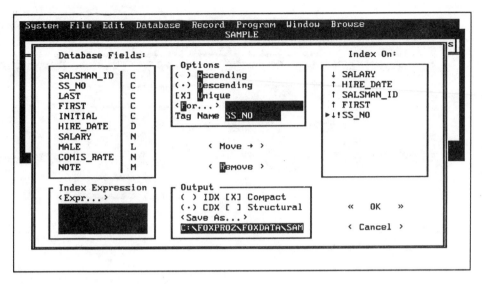

**Figure 7.48  Setting Unique Index Option**

hidden from view. To remove those duplicate records that are not shown in the Browse view, copy the records in the Browse view to a temporary file named TEMP.DBF by selecting the Copy To menu option (see Figure 7.50).

There are a number of ways to perform the next step, which involves replacing the records in the SAMPLE database with those in TEMP.DBF. You can use FoxPro's Filer, or you can first delete all the records in the SALESMAN database and then append records from TEMP.DBF.

```
 System  File  Edit  Database  Record  Program  Window  Browse
                              SAMPLE
 Salsman_id Ss_no      Last    First   Initial Hire_date Salary Male Comis
 S11        999-99-9999 Watson  Cathy   K       05/01/90  2450   F
 S4         701-31-8723 Evans   Henry   H       03/08/88  2200   T
 S7         355-23-7777 Harvey  Candy   E       12/01/89  2450   F
 S5         333-56-4545 Ford    Ida     F       11/22/87  2860   F
 S2         303-67-8901 Carter  Jack    J       05/14/87  2805   T
 S9         111-33-4545 Jones   Betty   A       09/26/89  2500   F
 S0         111-22-3333 Anderson Doris  B       07/01/86  3080   F
 S1         101-20-4545 Bell    George  G       10/12/88  2640   T
```

**Figure 7.49  Showing Unique Records**

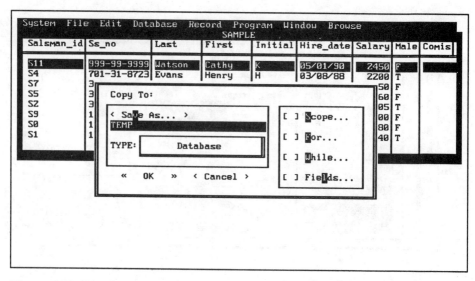

**Figure 7.50  Copying Unique Records to a Database File**

To empty the records in the SAMPLE database, choose the Delete option from the Record menu popup and set the record scope to All; this marks all the records in the database for deletion. You can then remove them by selecting the Pack option from the Database menu popup. Finally, select the Append From option from the Database menu popup. When the Append From dialog appears, specify TEMP.DBF as the source database file (see Figure 7.51). As a result, FoxPro adds all the records in the TEMP.DBF to the SAMPLE database.

```
 System  File  Edit  Database  Record  Program  Window




            Append From:

            <   From...   >
            TEMP                              [ ] Scope...

            TYPE:       Database              [ ] For...
                                             [ ] While...
              «   OK   »   < Cancel >         [ ] Fields...


```

**Figure 7.51  Appending Records from TEMP.DBF**

After the Append operation, the SAMPLE.DBF file contains all the original unique records. Unfortunately, deleting all the data records in the SAMPLE database also deletes its structural compound index file; therefore, these index tags must be re-created.

# Splitting Database Files

When you design a good relational database, it is wise to keep your database files simple. If a database file becomes too large and contains too many fields, you may want to split it into two or more database files. Then each file will contain a subset of the data fields in the original database. But to provide links among themselves, these database files should share a common data field.

The SALESMAN database contains ten fields describing the attributes of a company's sales staff. Some fields contain personal data, while others contain payroll information. Although the database file is not too large and would not be divided in a real situation, as an exercise, let's split it into two files: PERSONAL.DBF and PAYROLL.DBF. The former will hold the personal data while the latter will contain the payroll information. The two database files contain the following data fields:

| Database File | Data Fields |
|---------------|-------------|
| PERSONAL.DBF | SALSMAN_ID |
| | LAST |
| | FIRST |
| | INITIAL |
| | HIRE_DATE |
| | MALE |
| | NOTE |
| PAYROLL | SALSMAN_ID |
| | SS_NO |
| | SALARY |
| | COMIS_RATE |

The easiest way to split the file is to create the two database files by using the Copy To operation discussed earlier. So, to create PERSONAL.DBF, select the Copy To option from the Database menu popup after you have opened the SALESMAN database in the current work area. To select the fields to be included in PERSONAL.DBF, choose the Fields check box to bring up the Field Picker, as shown in Figure 7.52.

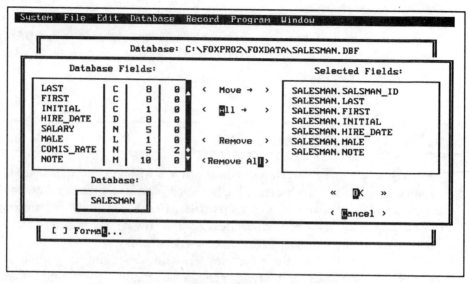

**Figure 7.52  Selecting Fields for PERSONAL.DBF**

After selecting the fields, create the PERSONAL database containing the selected fields by entering the name of the output file as PERSONAL in the Save As text box of the Copy To dialog. Follow the same procedure to create the PAYROLL database file. You can verify the contents of these two files in the Browse window (see Figure 7.53).

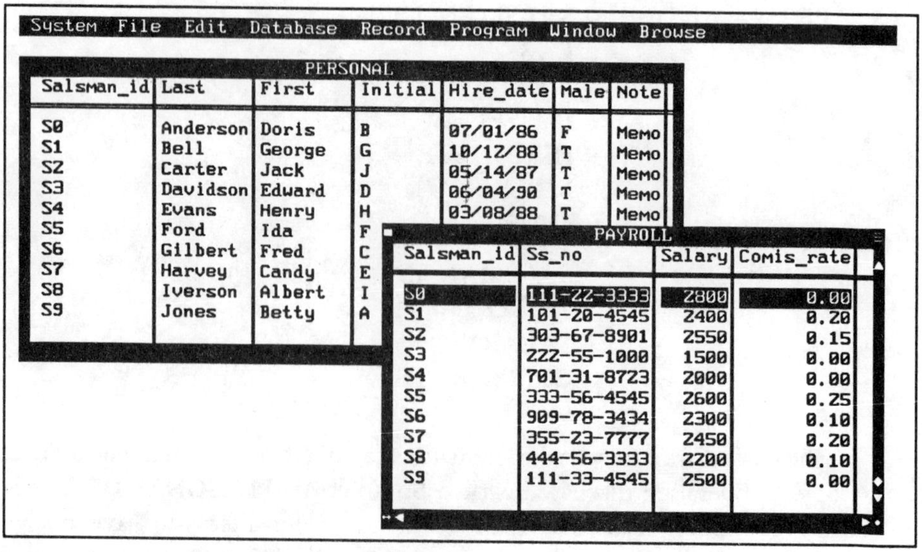

**Figure 7.53  Viewing Split Database Files**

# Using FoxPro Commands

In the preceding sections we used FoxPro's menu interface to modify the structure and contents of database files in a number of ways: We made duplicate copies of database files, and renamed or restructured them; in addition, we edited the contents of databases, including adding new records to and removing existing records from existing database files. Many of these same tasks can be done by issuing the appropriate FoxPro commands.

## COPYING DATABASE FILES

FoxPro offers a number of ways to copy database files with commands. One command for making duplicate copies of an existing database file follows this format:

```
COPY FILE <source filename> TO <target filename>
```

Note that the filenames must include their file extensions. To copy SALES-MAN.DBF to BACKUP.DBF, the command would read:

```
COPY FILE SALESMAN.DBF TO BACKUP.DBF
```

To copy the associated memo and compound index files, the commands would be:

```
COPY FILE SALESMAN.FPT TO BACKUP.FPT
COPY FILE SALESMAN.CDX TO BACKUP.CDX
```

No wildcard characters—* or ?—can be used with the COPY FILE command. Wildcards can, however, be used with a DOS COPY command. For example, to copy SALESMAN.DBF and its associated files to the target files named BACKUP (with different file extensions) you could issue the DOS COPY command in the format:

```
RUN COPY SALESMAN.* BACKUP.*
```

To verify the existence of the duplicate files, issue one of these commands:

```
DIR  BACKUP.*
RUN DIR BACKUP.*
```

The COPY FILE and RUN COPY commands make a duplicate copy of each source file. If the file is a database file with a .DBF extension, the database as a whole will be duplicated, including its database structure and all of its records; you cannot copy only selected data fields or selected records with these commands. To do that, you must use FoxPro's COPY TO command. Its format is:

```
COPY TO <.dbf filename>
        [FIELDS <field list>]
        [<scope>]
        [FOR <expression>]
```

The COPY TO command allows you to copy a certain portion of the currently selected database file. To include selected fields from the source file in the target database, add the FIELDS clause to the COPY TO command; to include selected records in the target database, specify the filter condition in a FOR clause; use the scope clause to define the scope for the records to be copied.

To create a duplicate copy of the SALESMAN database, for example, you would issue the following commands:

```
USE SALESMAN
COPY TO TEST
```

The COPY TO command creates a duplicate copy of the database file and its associated memo file. The files created here, TEST.DBF and TEST.FPT, have the same structure as the SALESMAN database and contain all of its records. Note, however, that the COPY TO command will not create a copy of its associated structural compound index file.

A command to copy only selected data fields to the target file using the FIELDS clause, as described above, would read:

```
COPY TO TEST FIELDS LAST, FIRST
```

And, to define a filter condition with a FOR clause for selecting data records, a sample command would read:

```
COPY TO TEST FOR MALE = .F. AND COMIS_RATE  0
COPY TO TEST FIELDS LAST, FIRST, COMIS_RATE FOR COMIS_RATE > 0
```

To specify a scope to select a range of records that you would like to copy, the command would read:

```
USE SALESMAN
GOTO 2
COPY TO TEST NEXT 5
```

In this example, the GOTO 2 command positions the cursor at the beginning of the second record. The NEXT 5 clause in the COPY TO command copies the next five records, beginning from the current record to the target file.

## RENAMING DATABASE FILES

The command for assigning a new filename to an existing database file follows this format:

```
RENAME <old filename> TO <new filename>
```

The RENAME command requires that you include the .DBF as its file extension, as in:

```
RENAME BACKUP.DBF TO TEST.DBF
```

This command can also be invoked to rename other types of files. The following commands rename the memo and compound index file that are associated with BACKUP.DBF to TEST.FPT and TEST.CDX:

```
RENAME BACKUP.FPT TO TEST.FPT
RENAME BACKUP.CDX TO TEST.CDX
```

You can use the DOS RENAME command to rename a group of files that share the same name. The following DOS RENAME command accomplishes the same tasks as multiple RENAME commands:

```
RUN RENAME TEST.* TEST1.*
```

## MODIFYING DATA STRUCTURES

The command to bring up an existing data structure so that it can be modified is MODIFY STRUCTURE. As shown in the example below, it redefines the SALES-MAN.DBF data structure:

```
USE SALESMAN
MODIFY STRUCTURE
```

The resulting data structure will be displayed as in Figure 7.54. It can then be edited with the procedures that you learned earlier.

## EDITING DATA RECORDS

The command to modify the contents of your records is EDIT. This command provides a great deal of flexibility. By using its FIELDS clause, you can choose to select only certain data fields to edit, edit only selected data records by specifying the appropriate filter condition, or define the scope of those records that you would

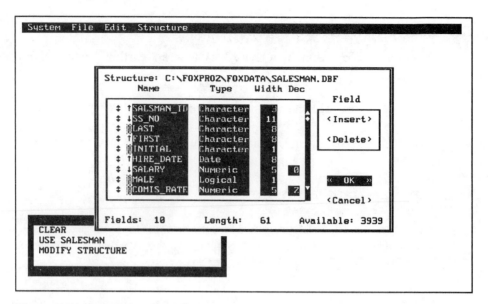

**Figure 7.54  Modifying Data Structure**

like to edit. In addition, you can limit the movement of the cursor to selected data fields with the FREEZE clause. The format of the EDIT command is:

```
EDIT [FIELDS <field list>]
     [<scope>]
     [FOR <expression>]
     [FREEZE <field>]
```

To edit the records in the SALESMAN database, for instance, issue the following commands:

```
USE SALESMAN
EDIT
```

If you do not include a clause that specifies individual records to be edited, all records are subjected to the Edit operation. As a result, in executing the EDIT command, FoxPro will display the first record of the SALESMAN database in an editing window in Change mode (see Figure 7.55).

At this point, you can edit the contents of the first record and then continue to the next. You can abort the Edit operation at any time by pressing the Esc key. To save the changes, either close the window or press the Ctrl+End key.

To position the cursor at a specific record before issuing the EDIT command, use the GOTO command. The sample commands below direct the operation to begin editing from record #5:

```
GOTO 5
EDIT
```

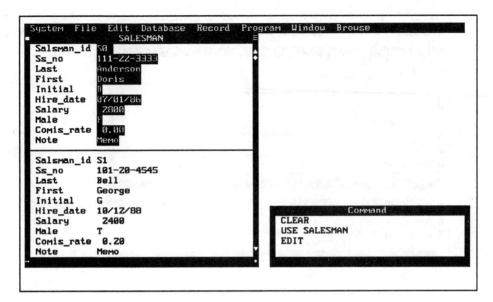

**Figure 7.55  Edit Window**

The same task can be accomplished by issuing the following command:

```
EDIT 5
```

This command begins the Edit operation at record number 5. FoxPro will display all subsequent records until the end of the file.

Alternatively, you can define filter conditions for any records that you would like to edit. The following command would be used to edit the records of those salespersons who were hired on or before December 31, 1988:

```
EDIT FOR HIRE_DATE <= {12/31/88}
```

Similarly, the next command lets you edit all the records belonging to male salespersons:

```
EDIT FOR MALE = .T.
```

You can display selected data fields to be edited by adding a FIELD clause, such as:

```
EDIT FIELDS FIRST, LAST, SALARY, COMIS_RATE
EDIT FIELDS LAST, SALARY FOR SALARY > 2000
```

As a result, you can move among the data fields specified in the EDIT command.

Some of the fields, however, such as LAST and FIRST, are displayed primarily for reference purposes and you probably would not want to edit them. Instead of

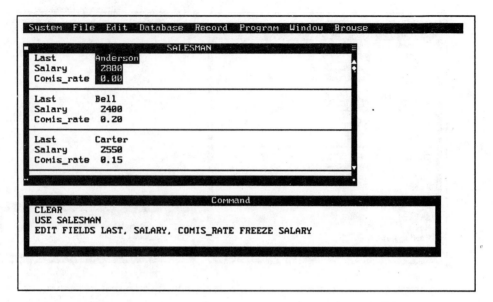

**Figure 7.56  Editing the Freeze Field**

moving around in reference fields such as these, you can freeze the cursor at a specific field during editing; to do this, use the FREEZE clause in this way:

```
EDIT FIELDS LAST, SALARY, COMIS_RATE FREEZE SALARY
```

In executing this command, FoxPro displays the contents of only the LAST, SALARY, and COMIS_RATE fields (see Figure 7.56). When the edit form appears, the cursor is positioned in the frozen field, and FoxPro will permit you to edit only the frozen field. You cannot move around within a record, and pressing the Enter key will not advance you to a new field or a new record. Instead, you can move from record to record by pressing the Page Up and Page Down keys in Change mode, and by pressing the up arrow and down arrow keys in Browse mode.

## ADDING NEW DATA RECORDS

If you need to add new records to the end of a database file, issue the APPEND command, which has the following format:

```
APPEND
```

To add new records to the TEST database, for instance, you would issue the following command:

```
USE TEST
APPEND
```

In return, FoxPro displays a data form for the new record that will be added to the end of the file. You can then enter the field values for the new record. After finishing entering data, you can continue adding more records.

## DELETING DATA RECORDS

You can mark any records for deletion by using the DELETE command in the following format:

```
DELETE [<scope>]
       [FOR <expression>]
```

Use the scope and filter condition to select the records that you would like to mark. For example:

```
USE TEST
DELETE NEXT 3
DELETE FOR MALE = .T.
DELETE FOR SALARY > 2000 AND HIRE_DATE > {01/01/89}
```

The NEXT 3 scope clause in the first DELETE command marks three records starting from the current record. The last two commands use the FOR clause to define the filter condition for selecting the records to be deleted.

To permanently remove the marked records from the database file, issue the following command:

```
PACK
```

If you decide to unmark records flagged for deletion, issue the RECALL command in the following format, but only *before* issuing the PACK command:

```
RECALL [<scope>]
       [FOR <expression>]
```

Here are some examples:

```
USE TEST
RECALL ALL
RECALL NEXT 5
RECALL FOR MALE =.T.
RECALL FOR SALARY > 2000 AND HIRE_DATE > {01/01/89}
```

Ordinarily, to delete all the records in a database, you must first mark them for deletion and then pack the database, as discussed earlier. There is a shortcut, however—the ZAP command. This command, used in the format shown, would enable you to delete all the records from TEST.DBF:

```
USE TEST
ZAP
```

This command results in a warning prompt asking you to confirm your action. It reads:

```
Zap C:\FOXPRO\FOXDATA\TEST.DBF?
```

If you answer Yes to the prompt, all the records in the database file will be permanently removed.

## DELETING DATABASE FILES

Although the DELETE and ZAP commands will permanently delete records from your database files, they will not remove the data structure. To delete the database file from the disk, you must issue the ERASE command. To permanently remove TEST.DBF from your disk, issue the following command:

```
ERASE TEST.DBF
```

You can use this command to delete other files that are associated with the erased database file, as well. For example:

```
ERASE TEST.FPT
ERASE TEST.CDX
```

But, before erasing these files, you must first close them. FoxPro will not allow you to erase any files that are in use. You also can choose to erase your files with the DOS DELETE or ERASE command in formats such as:

```
RUN DELETE TEST.DBF
RUN DELETE TEST.*
RUN ERASE TEST.DBF
RUN ERASE TEST.*
```

## BORROWING EXISTING DATA STRUCTURES

The COPY TO and ZAP commands enable you to borrow an existing data structure for a new database file. For example, the following commands will create a database file named TEST.DBF by borrowing the structure from SALES-MAN.DBF:

```
USE SALESMAN
COPY TO TEST
USE TEST
ZAP
```

Of course, you can borrow selected data fields from the existing database as well. Here is an example:

```
USE SALESMAN
COPY TO ROSTER FIELDS LAST, FIRST
USE ROSTER
ZAP
```

The resulting database file, ROSTER.DBF, will have a data structure containing only the LAST and FIRST fields.

# Chapter Summary

This chapter defined the procedures necessary to modify the contents of database files. You learned how to modify the data structure of an existing database file, to insert new fields in the existing data structure, and to remove existing data fields; you also learned how to redefine the attributes of existing fields.

This chapter also covered the editing processes that enable you to change the contents of your data records using either Browse or Change modes in the Browse window. You were introduced to the methods for adding new records to the file and deleting records that are no longer needed. It was pointed out that most of the procedures covered in this chapter can be carried out either by using the menu interface or by issuing the appropriate FoxPro commands.

You learned how to make duplicate copies of your database files before you begin modifying them. This important safety precaution means that you can revert to the original copies if you decide to cancel all the changes you make to the database.

Up to now you learned the procedures related to creating and maintaining your database files. In the next chapter you will begin to see how you can efficiently retrieve useful information from the database.

# 8

# Linking Databases

## An Overview

In showing you how to create and maintain data in your database files, the preceding chapters have all assumed that you are working with a single file at a time. Although it is perfectly acceptable to use FoxPro in this way, FoxPro is also a powerful relational database management system. As you may recall from our discussion of relational database concepts in Chapter 1, a relational database management system allows you to store related information in multiple files. Designing your database system in this way provides the most efficient storage for your data at the same time as it insures the integrity of your data.

It is through file linking that you can take advantage of FoxPro's power as a relational database management system. To manage or display related information from separate database files, FoxPro links data records in these files temporarily. Once their records are linked, their contents can be manipulated simultaneously. This ability to link different database files is vital to your success in managing relational databases. It enables you to efficiently organize data elements and to produce useful and complex reports.

This chapter will introduce you to FoxPro's relational database capabilities by demonstrating how to link data elements in different database files. Because some procedures for linking database files can be carried out only by using FoxPro commands, this chapter will show you how to link database files both through the FoxPro's menu interface and by issuing FoxPro commands.

# Joining Database Files

When organizing data elements in different database files, it is sometimes useful to combine the contents of these files in order to have all the necessary information available in a single file. For example, to produce invoices, information must be extracted from various database files. These files probably contain data elements in different fields relating to a customer's billing information, prices of the merchandise sold, etc. In this case, different database files can be joined and the combined data fields can be saved in a single database file. This combination of the data elements into the same database is horizontal joining—i.e., creating a new database file that combines data fields from two different database files.

Or when a database file gets too big, you may want to divide its records into separate files. You could, for example, divide the records in the SALESMAN database file into two separate files: MALE.DBF and FEMALE.DBF, and then store all the records for salesmen in MALE.DBF., and the records for saleswomen in FEMALE.DBF. When needed, the records in these two database files can be combined, a process that involves joining your database files vertically—i.e., merging records from multiple files into a single file.

When you join database files, the combined data fields and records are saved in another database file so that all the data elements you need can be found in a single database file. As a result, data manipulation operations are simplified because you work with one file. Then, if you need to extract information from the joined database files, you can perform the query operations on a single file. Similarly, you can design and produce reports by using one database file, and the process is much simpler than if you had to work with multiple database files.

Joining database files does have some drawbacks, however. First, the database file resulting from joining databases will not be updated automatically when the contents of the individual databases are changed. In such a case, the joining operation must be repeated in order to reflect the changes. A second drawback is that the joining operation creates another database file that uses valuable storage space.

## HORIZONTAL JOINING

To combine data fields from two database files, use the Join operation, which allows you to select data fields from two database files and then save them in a new database file. The resulting new file contains records with the values in the selected data fields that came from the two database files. Recall that you created PERSONAL.DBF and PAYROLL.DBF by splitting SALESMAN.DBF. As a result, PERSONAL.DBF contains seven fields containing personal information about the sales staff; PAYROLL.DBF has four fields with their payroll data (see Figure 8.1).

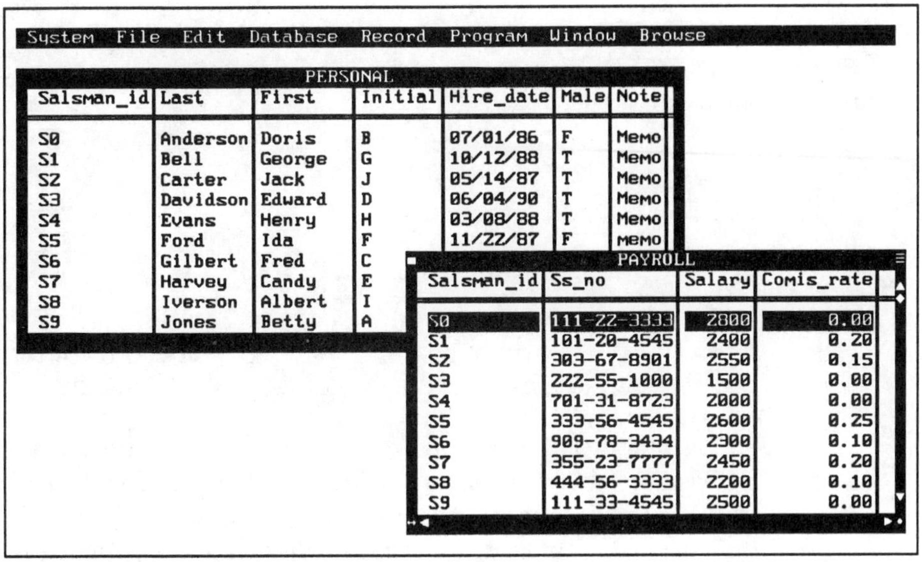

**Figure 8.1 Contents of PERSONAL and PAYROLL Databases**

As mentioned above, to create a new database file containing data fields selected from these two database files, you use the Join operation. FoxPro, however, does not provide a menu option for this operation, so you must invoke the FoxPro JOIN command in the following format:

```
JOIN WITH <alias of the file to be joined>
      TO <name of resulting file>
      FOR <joining and filter conditions>
      [FIELDS <field list>]
```

But before issuing the JOIN command, remember to open the database files that are to be joined in separate work areas. In addition, you must index the second file on a field that will be used to link it to the first file. For example, to join PERSONAL.DBF and PAYROLL.DBF, open them in work areas A and B respectively. Then index the PERSONAL database on the common field, SALSMAN_ID.

Having finished with these preliminaries, you can then issue the JOIN command. Its syntax requires that you first identify the alias of the database file you will join with the currently selected database. (An alias is the name of the work area in the form of A–J or 1–25.) Then you must name the database that you are creating to save the data fields selected from the joined files.

For two database files to be joined, they must share a common data field that provides the necessary link between these two files. The FOR clause specifies the link field and should also be the active index of the nonselected database. You also can include in the FOR clause any filter conditions for selecting your records. Finally, use the FIELDS clause to select the data fields that you want to include in the resulting database file.

```
SELECT A
USE PERSONAL
SET ORDER TO SALSMAN_ID
SELECT B
USE PAYROLL
SET ORDER TO SALSMAN_ID
JOIN WITH A TO COMBINED FOR SALSMAN_ID = A->SALSMAN_ID
     FIELDS SS_NO, SALSMAN_ID, FIRST, LAST, SALARY
```

These commands detail the sequence for the Join operation: first PERSONAL.DBF is opened in work area A, followed by the setting of the index tag, SALSMAN_ID, as the master index. (If the index tag is not set up, you may need to create the structural compound index file PERSONAL.CDX.) Then the second file, PAYROLL.DBF, is opened in work area B.

After the database files to be joined are opened, the JOIN command is issued. Because you are now in work area B, and the file (PERSONAL.DBF) that you would like to join is open in work area A, it is necessary to specify A as the file's alias in the JOIN command. In the FOR clause, the linking condition is identified as:

```
FOR SALSMAN_ID = A->SALSMAN_ID
```

The symbol A- is used to identify the alias in order for the file to be linked. You also could replace A- with the name of the database file and rewrite the linking conditions as:

```
FOR SALSMAN_ID = PERSONAL->SALSMAN_ID
```

The linking condition tells FoxPro to join the records from the two database files when the values in the common link field, SALSMAN_ID, are the same.

Finally, the data fields that you would like to include in the resulting SALARY file are specified in the FIELDS clause. If you do not specify anything in the FIELDS clause, all the data fields in both database fields will be included. After executing these commands, FoxPro creates the combined database that contains these fields whose values were copied from PERSONAL.DBF and PAYROLL.DBF files (see Figure 8.2).

You can see in Figure 8.2 that each record in the resulting SALARY database file contains data fields that are extracted from the PERSONAL and PAYROLL database files. For example, record #1 is extracted from the FIRST and LAST data fields of the PERSONAL database file. The SS_NO and SALARY fields came from the PAYROLL database file. This information was combined based on the

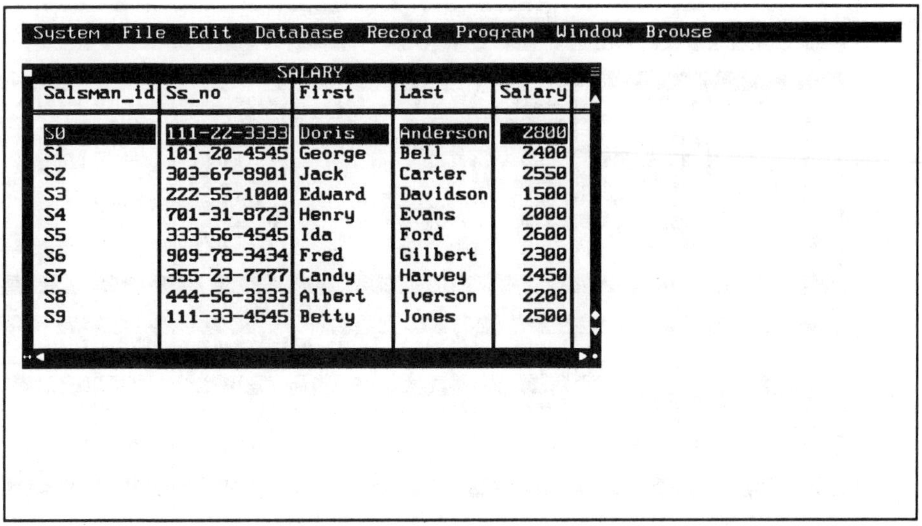

```
 System  File  Edit  Database  Record  Program  Window  Browse

■                        SALARY                              ≡
 Salsman_id Ss_no        First    Last      Salary  ▲

 S0         111-22-3333 Doris    Anderson   2800
 S1         101-20-4545 George   Bell       2400
 S2         303-67-8901 Jack     Carter     2550
 S3         222-55-1000 Edward   Davidson   1500
 S4         701-31-8723 Henry    Evans      2000
 S5         333-56-4545 Ida      Ford       2600
 S6         909-78-3434 Fred     Gilbert    2300
 S7         355-23-7777 Candy    Harvey     2450
 S8         444-56-3333 Albert   Iverson    2200
 S9         111-33-4545 Betty    Jones      2500      ◆
 ■◀                                          ▶◀
```

**Figure 8.2  Combined Database File**

link field, SALSMAN_ID, that is common to the two database files you have joined.

Because the values in the link field, SALSMAN_ID, are unique in the PERSONAL and PAYROLL database files, they are also unique in the resulting SALARY database file. That is, each record in the PERSONAL database is matched with one and only one record in the PAYROLL database.

If one or both of the database files to be joined have records with duplicate values in the link field, the resulting database file also will have records with the duplicate values in that field. For example, if the PERSONAL database contains more than one record with the same values in the SALSMAN_ID field, each of these records will be matched with every record in the PAYROLL database having the same value in the link field. If there are two records in PERSONAL.DBF and three records in PAYROLL.DBF with the same values in the link field, the resulting database will have six records with the same values in that field.

To include only selected records in the resulting file, add filter conditions in the FOR clause. For example, if you replace the current FOR clause with the following clause, the resulting SALARY database file will contain only those records whose values in the SALARY field are greater than $2,200:

```
FOR SALSMAN_ID = A->SALSMAN_ID AND SALARY > 2200
```

## VERTICAL JOINING

In the same way that data fields from two database files can be combined, data records can be merged from one database file to another file by using the Append

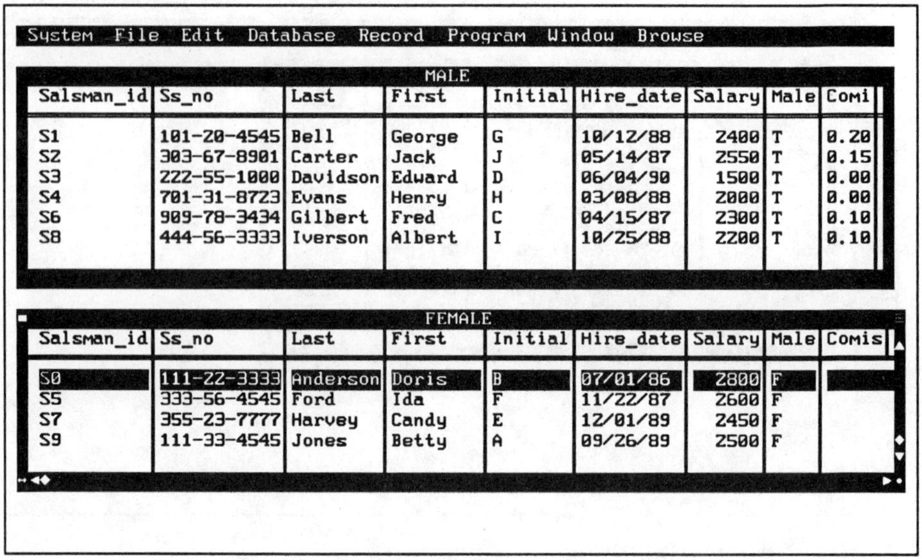


| Salsman_id | Ss_no | Last | First | Initial | Hire_date | Salary | Male | Comi |
|---|---|---|---|---|---|---|---|---|
| S1 | 101-20-4545 | Bell | George | G | 10/12/88 | 2400 | T | 0.20 |
| S2 | 303-67-8901 | Carter | Jack | J | 05/14/87 | 2550 | T | 0.15 |
| S3 | 222-55-1000 | Davidson | Edward | D | 06/04/90 | 1500 | T | 0.00 |
| S4 | 701-31-8723 | Evans | Henry | H | 03/08/88 | 2000 | T | 0.00 |
| S6 | 909-78-3434 | Gilbert | Fred | C | 04/15/87 | 2300 | T | 0.10 |
| S8 | 444-56-3333 | Iverson | Albert | I | 10/25/88 | 2200 | T | 0.10 |

| Salsman_id | Ss_no | Last | First | Initial | Hire_date | Salary | Male | Comis |
|---|---|---|---|---|---|---|---|---|
| S0 | 111-22-3333 | Anderson | Doris | B | 07/01/86 | 2800 | F | |
| S5 | 333-56-4545 | Ford | Ida | F | 11/22/87 | 2600 | F | |
| S7 | 355-23-7777 | Harvey | Candy | E | 12/01/89 | 2450 | F | |
| S9 | 111-33-4545 | Jones | Betty | A | 09/26/89 | 2500 | F | |

**Figure 8.3 MALE.DBF and FEMALE.DBF**

From operation. This involves opening in the current work area the file to which you would like to add records. Records are then appended from another database file to the first. The two database files may or may not have the same data structure—one may have more data fields than the other.

To illustrate the procedure for combining data records, create two sample database files by splitting SALESMAN.DBF into two databases: MALE.DBF and FEMALE.DBF. Choose the Copy To menu option from the Database menu popup or simply issue the following FoxPro commands:

```
USE SALESMAN
COPY TO MALE FOR MALE = .T.
COPY TO FEMALE FOR MALE = .F.
```

The resulting MALE file will contain six records belonging to the male sales staff, and FEMALE.DBF will have only four records for the female sales personnel (see Figure 8.3).

To add data records from FEMALE.DBF to MALE.DBF, first open MALE.DBF in the current work area. Then choose the Append From option from the Database menu popup. When the Append From dialog appears, specify the name of the database file (e.g., FEMALE.DBF) from which you want to get records (see Figure 8.4.).

To add all the records from FEMALE.DBF to MALE.DBF, select the <<OK>> push button. As a result, after executing the Append From operation, the MALE database file will also contain all the records from FEMALE.DBF. It is important to note that the operation did not *empty* the FEMALE database file; the records

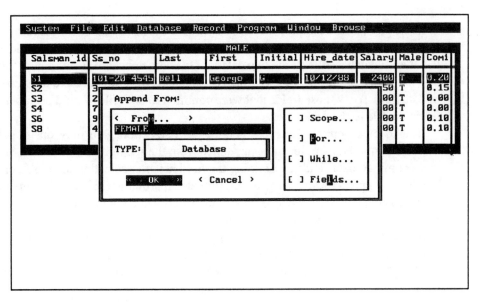

**Figure 8.4  Appending Records from FEMALE.DBF**

have only been copied to the MALE file. To verify this, display the contents of
MALE.DBF and FEMALE.DBF (see Figure 8.5).

Notice in Figure 8.5 that all of the records in FEMALE.DBF have been copied
and added to MALE.DBF. If the MALE file was not indexed, the records added
would appear at the end of the file when displayed in Browse mode.

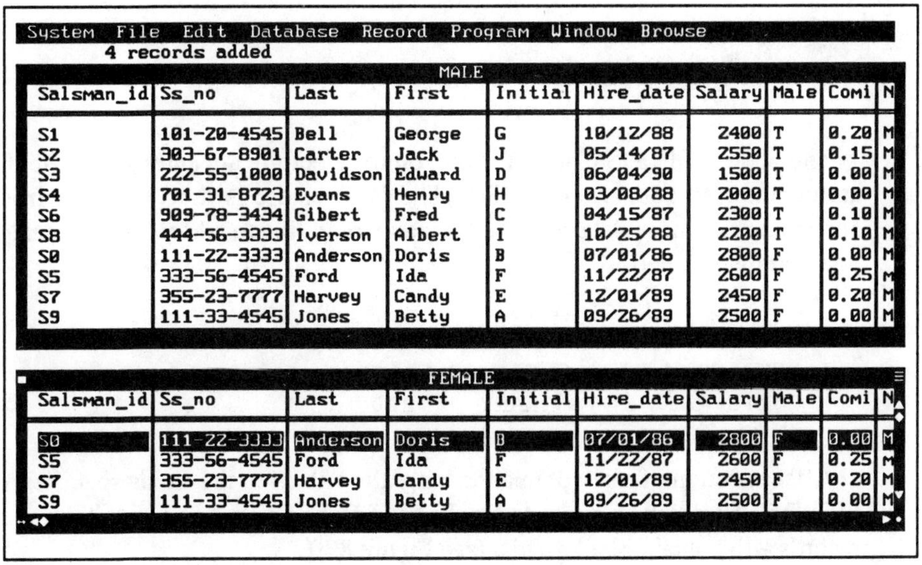

**Figure 8.5  Appended MALE.DBF**

In the preceding example, because the MALE file has an identical data structure to that of FEMALE.DBF, all of the field values in FEMALE.DBF can be added to the MALE database file. If the two database files did not share any common fields, no records would be added; and if the two database files did not have the same set of data fields, only those fields that were common to both files would be appended from one file to the other file.

Instead of accepting FoxPro's default field selection, you may opt to select certain common data fields to be appended from the second file to the first. Select these common data fields by defining the field list after selecting the Fields check box in the Append From dialog. Similarly, select particular records to be appended by specifying the necessary filter conditions after selecting the FOR check box or by defining the record scope in the same dialog.

As an alternative to selecting the Append From option from the Database menu popup, records in two database files can be combined by directly issuing the APPEND FROM command in the FoxPro Command window in the following format:

```
APPEND FROM <database filename>
    [FIELDS <field list>]
    [FOR <expression>]
```

In the APPEND FROM command the name of the database file from which you want to retrieve records must be supplied. Therefore, to add all the records from FEMALE.DBF to MALE.DBF, the command would read:

```
USE MALE
APPEND FROM FEMALE
```

The option FIELDS clause allows you to select the appending data fields that are common to both database files. The FOR clause is used to select from the appending file those data records that you would like to add to the appended file. For example:

```
USE MALE
APPEND FROM FEMALE FIELDS SALSMAN_ID, SS_NO, SALARY,
    COMIS_RATE FOR SALARY > 2200
```

After executing these commands, only the values in the fields specified in the FIELDS clause will be appended to the MALE.DBF file. As a result, the appended records will contain blank fields. (see Figure 8.6).

System  File  Edit  Database  Record  Program  Window  Browse

| Salsman_id | Ss_no | Last | First | Initial | Hire_date | Salary | Male | Comis |
|---|---|---|---|---|---|---|---|---|
| S1 | 101-20-4545 | Bell | George | G | 10/12/88 | 2400 | T | 0.20 |
| S2 | 303-67-8901 | Carter | Jack | J | 05/14/87 | 2550 | T | 0.15 |
| S3 | 222-55-1000 | Davidson | Edward | D | 06/04/90 | 1500 | T | 0.00 |
| S4 | 701-31-8723 | Evans | Henry | H | 03/08/88 | 2000 | T | 0.00 |
| S6 | 909-78-3434 | Gibert | Fred | C | 04/15/87 | 2300 | T | 0.10 |
| S8 | 444-56-3333 | Iverson | Albert | I | 10/25/88 | 2200 | T | 0.10 |
| S0 | 111-22-3333 | | | | / / | 2800 | | 0.00 |
| S5 | 333-56-4545 | | | | / / | 2600 | | 0.25 |
| S7 | 355-23-7777 | | | | / / | 2450 | | 0.20 |
| S9 | 111-33-4545 | | | | / / | 2500 | | 0.00 |

**Figure 8.6  Selected Appended Data Fields**

# Relating Database Files

Earlier, you learned how to combine data fields and records from two database files, and you created a new database file for holding the combined fields and records. This approach is appropriate if these records and fields are in a file whose contents are to be permanently saved and that you do not intend to update. But there are disadvantages associated with this approach. First, the resulting database file takes up valuable storage space. Second, every time you modify the original database files that have been used for the join, you will have to recombine their data fields and records to accommodate the changes. Third, the fact that the same data exists in two or more different database files can easily create a nightmarish situation in which the information contained in identical records is different and you have no way of knowing which version of your data is accurate.

Fortunately, there is another way to join database files. Instead of saving the results in a permanent file, you *temporarily* relate the data in database files so that you can manipulate them simultaneously. Afterwards, you simply release them from their work areas.

If the information you need for an application is scattered in more than one data table, a link field—a field whose value is common to two databases—must be incorporated to relate them. How these databases are linked depends on the exact relationship between the databases. If there are one-to-one and one-to-many relations (defined below) between two database files, they can be linked directly through a common link field. Otherwise, when many-to-many relations exist between two database files, they may need to be linked by using information in a third relation table.

## HANDLING ONE-TO-ONE RELATIONS

One-to-one relations exist when each record in a database file corresponds to one—and only one—record in another database file. As noted above, to link two database files with one-to-one relations, the two files must share a common field, called a link field, that provides the information for relating one file to another. You can, for instance, link the PERSONAL and PAYROLL files by using SALSMAN_ID as the link field. PERSONAL.DBF, to which you want to link another file, is called the parent. PAYROLL.DBF, the file that you want to link with the parent, is called a child. With a one-to-one relationship, however, the designation of the child and parent files is arbitrary, depending on which one is in control. The relationship between these two database files is depicted in Figure 8.7.

Parent: PERSONAL.DBF

| SALSMAN_ID | LAST | FIRST | INITIAL | HIRE_DATE | MALE | NOTE |
|---|---|---|---|---|---|---|
| S0 | Anderson | Doris | B | 07/01/86 | .F. | Memo |
| S1 | Bell | George | G | 10/12/88 | .T. | Memo |
| S2 | Carter | Jack | J | 05/14/87 | .T. | Memo |
| S3 | Davidson | Edward | D | 06/04/90 | .T. | Memo |
| S4 | Evans | Henry | H | 03/08/88 | .T. | Memo |
| S5 | Ford | Ida | F | 11/22/87 | .F. | Memo |
| S6 | Gilbert | Fred | C | 04/15/87 | .T. | Memo |
| S7 | Harvey | Candy | E | 12/01/89 | .F. | Memo |
| S8 | Iverson | Albert | I | 10/25/88 | .T. | Memo |
| S9 | Jones | Betty | A | 09/26/89 | .F. | Memo |

Child: PAYROLL.DBF

| SALSMAN_ID | SS_NO | SALARY | COMIS_RATE |
|---|---|---|---|
| S0 | 111-22-3333 | 2800 | 0.00 |
| S1 | 101-20-4545 | 2400 | 0.20 |
| S2 | 303-67-8901 | 2550 | 0.15 |
| S3 | 222-55-1000 | 1500 | 0.00 |
| S4 | 701-31-8723 | 2000 | 0.00 |
| S5 | 333-56-4545 | 2600 | 0.25 |
| S6 | 909-78-3434 | 2300 | 0.10 |
| S7 | 355-23-7777 | 2450 | 0.20 |
| S8 | 444-56-3333 | 2200 | 0.10 |
| S9 | 111-33-4545 | 2500 | 0.00 |

**Figure 8.7  One-to-One Relations Between PERSONAL.DBF and PAYROLL.DBF**

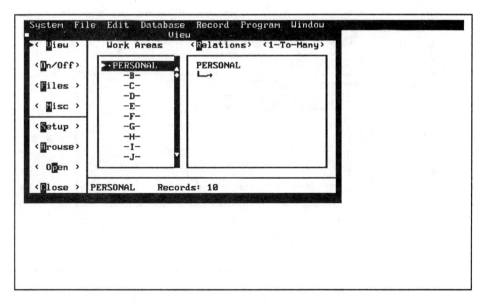

**Figure 8.8  Opening the Parent File in Work Area A**

As you can see in Figure 8.7, one-to-one relations exist between PER-SONAL.DBF and PAYROLL.DBF because each record in the parent can be uniquely linked to a record in the child. That is, you can relate each PER-SONAL.DBF record that has a unique value in the link field (SALSMAN_ID) to a unique record in the PAYROLL file.

After linking these two files, each record in the parent that has a unique value in the link field will be related to a child record having the same value in that field. Once the two files are linked, data elements in the two related records can be treated as if they are in the same record.

Before you try to link the database files though, you must index the child on the link field. In this case, it means that before you begin linking PERSONAL.DBF and PAYROLL.DBF, you must index the latter on the SALSMAN_ID field. If you have set up the index tag with the link field, designate that tag as the master index. The parent, however, need not be indexed on the link field—it can be indexed on any field in the database or on none at all.

The first step in linking is to bring up the View window. When it appears, open the parent in a work area. Then choose the Relations operation and link it to the child that is open in *another* work area. As an exercise of this procedure, link PERSONAL.DBF and PAYROLL.DBF. First use the View window to open PERSONAL.DBF as the parent in work area A. Then select the Relations text button, which causes the relation symbol (an arrow) to appear (see Figure 8.8).

Next open the child, PAYROLL.DBF, by clicking on work area B and selecting it in the Open File list box. At this point, FoxPro will ask you to select a link expression from among the child's available index files. (see Figure 8.9). (If

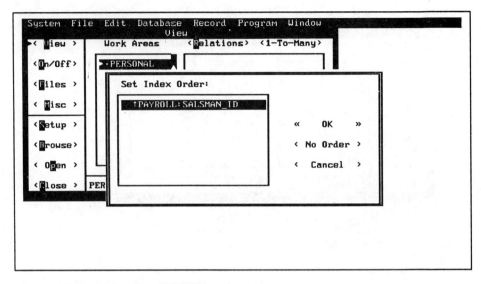

**Figure 8.9  Indexing the Child File**

FoxPro cannot find any index files for the child, the message "Database is not ordered" will appear, and FoxPro will not permit you to link the files.)

After selecting the index tag that will link the child to the parent database, choose the <<OK>> push button to define the relation. You are then asked to define the link field in the SET RELATION expression dialog. When the dialog appears, it shows the indexed field as the default link field (see Figure 8.10).

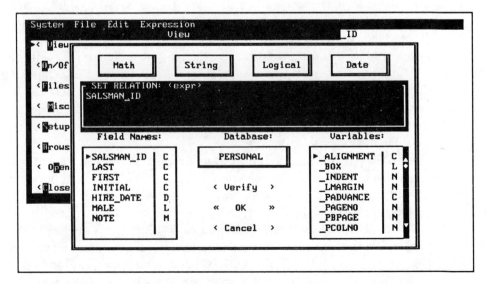

**Figure 8.10  Defining Relation Expression**

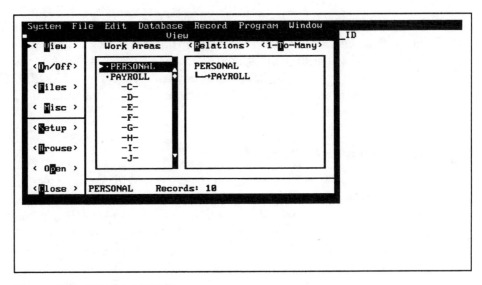

**Figure 8.11 The Linked Files**

After verifying its validity, accept the relation expression by choosing the <<OK>> push button. As you return to the View panel, note that SALES-MAN.DBF and PAYROLL.DBF are linked, as indicated by the arrow joining the two files (see Figure 8.11). This graphically identifies the PERSONAL database as the parent and the PAYROLL database as the child.

Database files also can be linked by issuing FoxPro commands directly in the Command window. The command invoked for this purpose is SET RELATION, which has following syntax:

```
SET RELATION TO <link field INTO <child>
```

Before you issue this command, however, the parent must be open in one work area, and the child in another. In addition, the child must be indexed on the link field.

When you specify the child in the SET RELATION TO command, use either its filename or its alias. A file alias is represented by the work area in the form of a letter (such as A–J) or a digit (1–25). For example, the following commands will establish the relationship between PERSONAL.DBF and PAYROLL.DBF:

```
SELECT A
USE PERSONAL
SELECT B
USE PAYROLL
SET ORDER TO SALSMAN_ID
SELECT A
SET RELATION TO SALSMAN_ID INTO B
```

The first two commands open the parent, PERSONAL.DBF, in work area A. Then the child, PAYROLL.DBF, is opened in work area B. Before issuing the SET RELATION command, the child is indexed on the link field, SALSMAN_ID. And, as noted above, the file to be linked may be identified in the SET RELATION command either by its filename or by its alias (e.g., B, denoting the work area where the file is being opened).

## Viewing Related Data Records

Once the database files are linked and you view a record in the parent, you are also able to view its related records in the child. Thus, as long as the PERSONAL and PAYROLL database files are linked, you can view the related records in both files simultaneously in separate Browse windows. To do this, use the View window to open separate Browse windows for the PERSONAL and PAYROLL databases and make the Browse window for PERSONAL.DBF the active window. Then when you place the cursor on a record in PERSONAL.DBF, its related record in PAYROLL.DBF automatically is displayed (see Figure 8.12).

Because there are one-to-one relations between PERSONAL.DBF and PAYROLL.DBF, each record in the parent shows only one record in the child. Notice in Figure 8.12 that when you highlight the S5 record in PERSONAL.DBF, PAYROLL.DBF shows its related record. If you highlight another record in the PERSONAL file, it will display its related record in PAYROLL.DBF.

It is important to note that you can move around only the records in the parent for the change to be reflected in the child; FoxPro will not allow you to move among

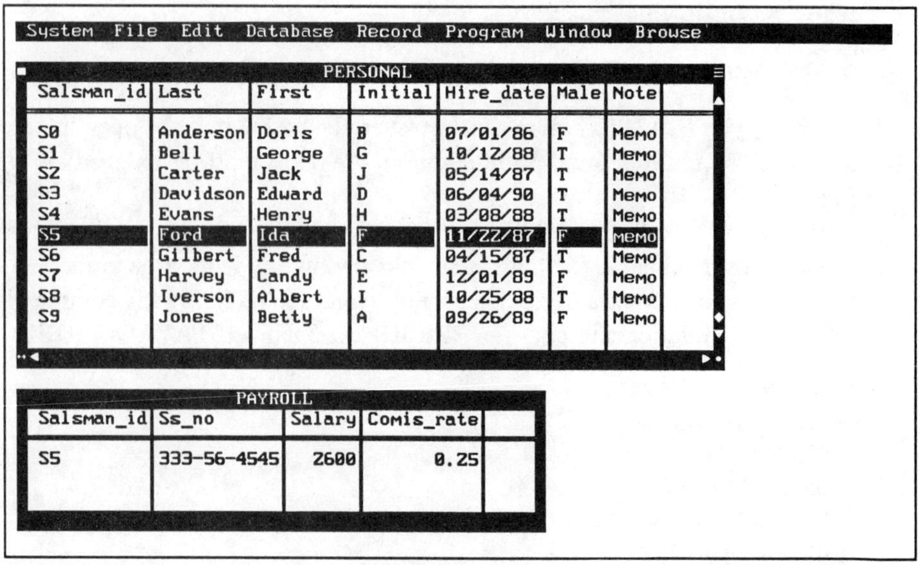

**Figure 8.12  Viewing Related Records**

the records in the child's Browse window. For example, when you display records from the PERSONAL and PAYROLL files in the Browse windows, you can only highlight different records in the PERSONAL file. When you position the cursor in PAYROLL.DBF, it remains on the record related to that record highlighted in PERSONAL.DBF. You cannot move to a different record in PAYROLL.DBF. To move around the records in PAYROLL.DBF, you must designate it as the parent when you link it to PERSONAL.DBF.

If you are using FoxPro commands, selected fields from the two database files that have been related may be displayed simultaneously. After relating PERSONAL.DBF and PAYROLL.DBF, for example, you can display records that belong to either database file. Here is an example:

```
SELECT A
USE PERSONAL
SELECT B
USE PAYROLL
SET ORDER TO SALSMAN_ID
SELECT A
SET RELATION TO SALSMAN_ID INTO B
LIST SALSMAN_ID, B->SS_NO, LAST, FIRST, B->SALARY-or BROWSE FIELD...
```

In the LIST command, some of the fields are taken from the parent (PERSONAL.DBF in work area A) while others are extracted from the child (PAYROLL.DBF in work area B). To identify a field, add the file alias in front of the field name if you are not in that work area. Use B->SS_NO to identify the SS_NO field in work area B (where PAYROLL.DBF is open).

## Saving Relations to View Files

When you join two database files in this manner, their relationship is temporary. It remains intact only as long as the two files remain linked in the View panel. When you close one or both of the related files, or exit from FoxPro, the link is destroyed. PERSONAL.DBF and PAYROLL.DBF will be cancelled if either of these two files is closed, for example. Therefore, in order to relate the two files for another application, their relationship must be set up again.

FoxPro does, however, make accommodations for cases in which you intend to use the same relation repeatedly—it allows you to save the relation to a view file. This prevents the necessity of re-creating the link. To save an established relation to a view file, select the Save as option from the File menu popup while the relation remains valid in the View panel. When the Save View dialog appears, enter the name of the view file in the filename text box (see Figure 8.13).

The view file you have created will be given a default file extension of .VUE. The information contained in the view file will be used later solely to re-establish

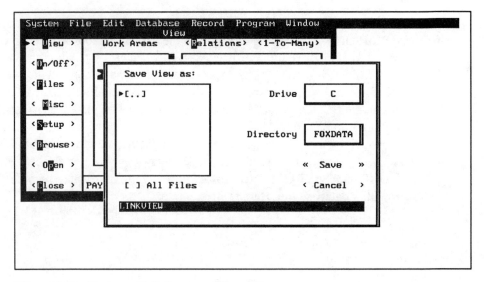

**Figure 8.13  Saving a Relation to a View File**

the relationship between the two database files; the view file does not contain any records belonging to any of the related database files.

Another way to save all relations to a view file is to issue the CREATE VIEW command in the following format:

```
CREATE VIEW <name of view file>
```

Then, while all the database files are being linked, you create the following command to save their relations:

```
CREATE VIEW LINKDBFS
```

The resulting view file, LINKDBFS.VUE, will contain all the information needed to re-create the relations between the two linked database files.

## Using Existing View Files

Once you have saved an established relation to a view file, the database files can be closed. The same relationship can be re-established later by opening the view file. In the last exercise, for instance, we saved the relationship between the PERSONAL and PAYROLL databases to the LINKVIEW.VUE view file. To re-establish that relationship now, choose the Open option from the File menu popup, and when the Open dialog appears, select View as the file type and then open the view file of your choice (see Figure 8.14).

When an existing view file is opened, the information in the file will be used to set up the relation that you have saved. The database files do not need to be opened

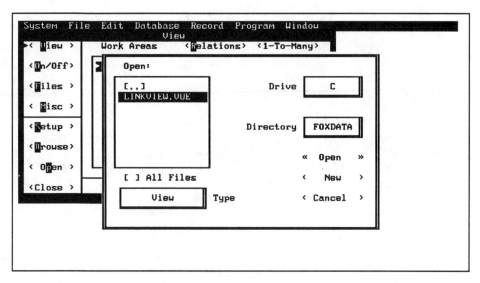

**Figure 8.14   Opening an Existing View File**

individually. Opening the view file also opens all the related database files in the appropriate work areas where they are linked with the relation previously established. The effect is the same as if you had reset the relationship between the database files all over again.

To re-establish relations that were previously saved in a view file by using a FoxPro command, issue the SET VIEW TO command:

```
SET VIEW TO <name of view file>
```

So, to re-establish the relation that we set up in LINKDBFS.VUE, issue the following command:

```
SET VIEW TO LINKDBFS
```

As a result, all the linked databases (PERSONAL.DBF and PAYROLL.DBF) will be opened in separate work areas and then linked with the information stored in the view file.

## HANDLING ONE-TO-MANY RELATIONS

A similar procedure is used to relate database files that have one-to-many relationships. In linking files that have a one-to-many relationship, however, it is critical that you properly designate the parent. Otherwise, related records in the child cannot be identified or displayed correctly. To demonstrate how to link two database files having one-to-many relations, we will use the OFFICE (created in

```
Parent: OFFICE.DBF

OFFICE_ID    ADDRESS            CITY          STATE    ZIP      PHONE_NO
B1           100 Park Avenue    New York      NY       10016    800-123-5555
B2           200 Lake Drive     Chicago       IL       60607    800-234-5555
B3           500 Century Blvd.  Los Angeles   CA       94005    800-456-5555


Child: SALESMAN.DBF

SALSMAN_ID   SS_NO         LAST       FIRST    INITIAL  OFFICE_ID  ...
S0           111-22-3333   Anderson   Doris    B        B1         ...
S1           101-20-4545   Bell       George   G        B3         ...
S2           303-67-8901   Carter     Jack     J        B2         ...
S3           222-55-1000   Davidson   Edward   D        B1         ...
S4           701-31-8723   Evans      Henry    H        B3         ...
S5           333-56-4545   Ford       Ida      F        B2         ...
S6           909-78-3434   Gilbert    Fred     C        B3         ...
S7           355-23-7777   Harvey     Candy    E        B3         ...
S8           444-56-3333   Iverson    Albert   I        B2         ...
S9           111-33-4545   Jones      Betty    A        B1         ...
```

**Figure 8.15   One-to-Many Relations Between OFFICE.DBF
and SALESMAN.DBF**

Chapter 4) and SALESMAN files. The relationship between the two database files
is depicted in Figure 8.15.

Note that each record in the parent (OFFICE.DBF) corresponds to one or more
records in the child (SALESMAN.DBF). For example, record B1 (in OFFICE_ID)
in the OFFICE file relates to records S0, S3, and S9 (in SALSMAN_ID) in
SALESMAN.DBF.

Before you link OFFICE.DBF and SALESMAN.DBF, you must insert a new
data field, OFFICE_ID, into SALESMAN.DBF's data structure. Then create a new
index tag, OFFICE_ID, and, in ascending order, modify each of the records by
adding the appropriate OFFICE_ID code. OFFICE_ID is a character field that is
two characters in length; it contains the code representing the office to which each
salesman is assigned. This new field will then serve as the link field for relating
the two database files. It is considered the primary field in the parent database
(OFFICE.DBF) and a "foreign field" in the child database (SALESMAN.DBF).

Use the View panel to establish the relationship between the OFFICE and
SALESMAN database files in a manner similar to that detailed previously: Open
OFFICE.DBF as the parent in work area A, and SALESMAN.DBF as the child in
work area B. Next, make the OFFICE_ID index tag the controlling index of the
SALESMAN database. Then link the two databases by using this common link
field. To do this, select the OFFICE database, then the Relations push button, and
click on the SALESMAN database. FoxPro will then open the Expression Builder
and select OFFICE_ID as the field to which to set the relation. After verifying the

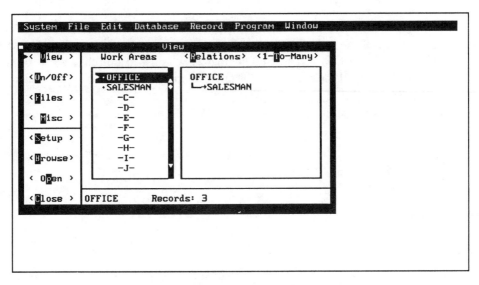

**Figure 8.16    Relating OFFICE.DBF and SALESMAN.DBF**

expression, selecting <<OK>> should cause the View window to appear as it does in Figure 8.16.

Once the two database files are linked, each record in the OFFICE file is automatically related to its corresponding records in the SALESMAN file. If you view their records in the Browse windows, you will see that for each record you choose in the parent, its corresponding records in the child are displayed (see Figure 8.17).

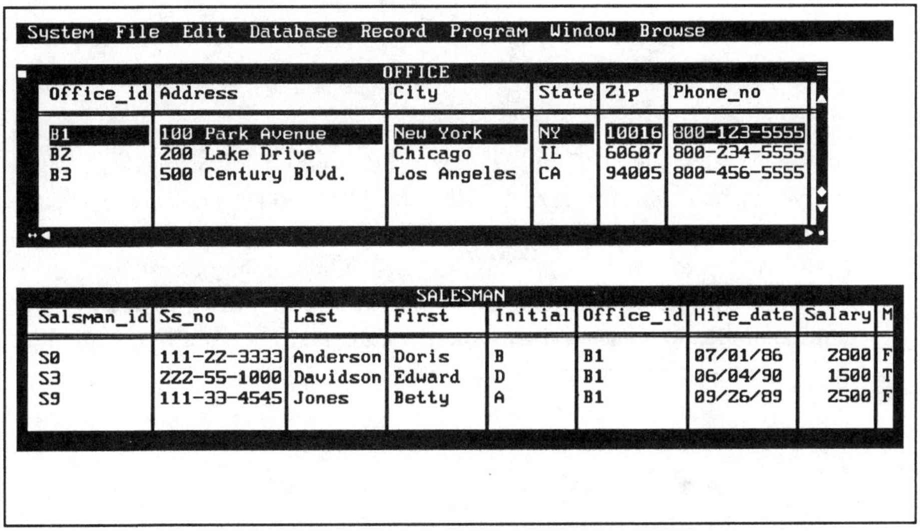

**Figure 8.17    One-to-Many Related Records**

To watch this happen, highlight the first record (B1) in OFFICE.DBF in one Browse window—all of its corresponding records (S0, S3, and S9) in SALES-MAN.DBF are displayed in another Browse window. Highlight another record in the parent, and all the records in the child relating to that record will be displayed accordingly.

The FoxPro commands to relate the OFFICE and SALESMAN database files are:

```
SELECT A
USE OFFICE
SELECT B
USE SALESMAN
SET ORDER TO OFFICE_ID
SELECT A
SET RELATION TO OFFICE_ID INTO B
```

While the two database files are linked, related records may be listed by invoking the LIST or DISPLAY commands. But, for each record in the OFFICE file that you list, only the first record from the SALESMAN file relating to the record in OFFICE.DBF will show—all of its related records will not be displayed. To confirm this, issue the following command after you have linked the two database files:

```
LIST OFFICE_ID, B->SALSMAN_ID, B->LAST
```

The result will be the following record list:

| Record# | OFFICE_ID | B.SALSMAN_ID | B.LAST |
|---|---|---|---|
| 1 | B1 | S0 | Anderson |
| 2 | B2 | S2 | Carter |
| 3 | B3 | S1 | Bell |

Although record B1 in OFFICE.DBF corresponds to three records (S0, S3, and S9) in SALESMAN.DBF, only the first (S0) record is displayed.

There is, however, a workaround that will allow you to show the multiple records that correspond to a single parent record when working with FoxPro's command-driven interface: Use the SET RELATION TO command to establish the one-to-many relationship by reversing the parent and child databases and by selecting a common index expression to order both databases. The FoxPro commands necessary to do this with our sample databases are as follows:

```
SELECT A
USE SALESMAN
SET ORDER TO OFFICE_ID
SELECT B
USE OFFICE
```

```
SET ORDER TO OFFICE_ID
SELECT A
SET RELATION TO OFFICE_ID INTO B
LIST OFF SALSMAN_ID, LAST, B->OFFICE_ID, B->ADDRESS, B->CITY
```

After you execute the LIST command, the following list of records from the two linked files is displayed:

```
SALSMAN_ID LAST      B.OFFICE_ID B.ADDRESS          B.CITY


S0         Anderson B1         100 Park Avenue     New York
S1         Bell     B1         100 Park Avenue     New York
S4         Evans    B1         100 Park Avenue     New York
S2         Carter   B2         200 Lake Drive      Chicago
S5         Ford     B2         200 Lake Drive      Chicago
S7         Harvey   B2         200 Lake Drive      Chicago
S3         Davidson B3         500 Century Blvd    Los Angeles
S6         Gilbert  B3         500 Century Blvd    Los Angeles
S8         Iverson  B3         500 Century Blvd    Los Angeles
S9         Jones    B3         500 Century Blvd    Los Angeles
```

Note that each record in SALESMAN.DBF is linked with a record from OFFICE.DBF. Records S0, S3, and S9 in SALESMAN.DBF are linked to the same B1 record from the OFFICE database file. As a result, the address and city for office B1 are displayed in three lines, linking to salespeople Anderson, Davidson, and Jones.

Also note that, because we have reversed the parent and child databases to mimic a one-to-many relationship, you can no longer directly view the one-to-many relationship in the Browse window. You may highlight only one record at a time in the parent file Browse window. Therefore, you can see only one record in the child Browse window that is related to the highlighted record in the parent (see Figure 8.18).

## HANDLING MANY-TO-MANY RELATIONS

Many-to-many relations are the most complex relationships that exist between any two data entities. You learned in Chapter 1 that one way to link two data entities is to use one or more relation tables. Many-to-many relations may exist, for example, between SALESMAN.DBF and REGION.DBF—one salesperson may be assigned to more than one sales region and one sales region may be assigned to several salespersons. To properly link these two database files, a relation table must be created, which, for this example, we will name ASSIGN.DBF. It contains information about how the salespeople are assigned to various sales regions.

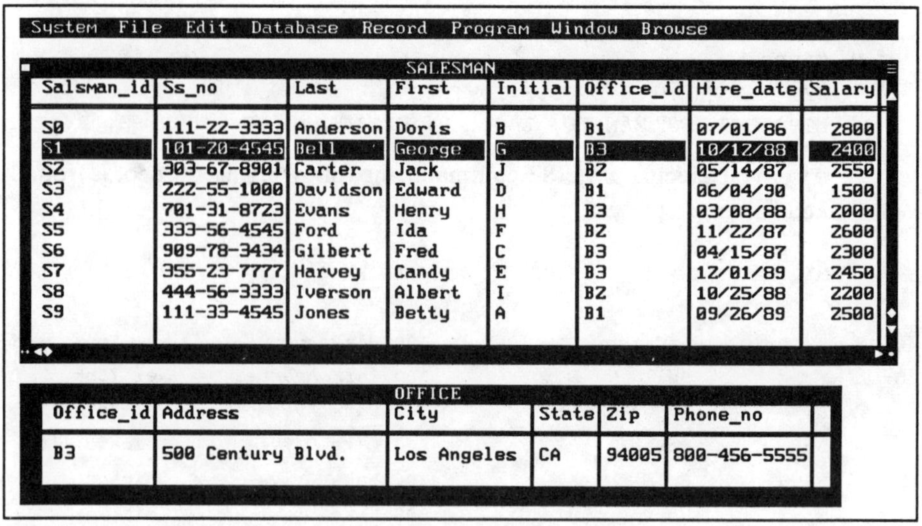

**Figure 8.18    Viewing Many-to-One Related Records**

But, before learning how to define many-to-many relationships, you must create the necessary sample database files. In addition to the existing SALESMAN database file, you need to create the REGION database file for holding data associated with the sales regions. The data structure of REGION.DBF is:

```
Field   Field Name   Type         Width     Dec

    1   REGION_ID    Character       2
    2   REGION       Character      12
    3   MANAGER      Character      15
```

After you have defined the database structure, you should also create a structural compound index with a tag for the REGION_ID field. This will allow the REGION database to be used as the child database when you link databases.

As an example, the database file might contain the following records:

```
Record#   REGION_ID REGION        MANAGER

1         R1        Northeast     Alice F. Gibson
2         R2        Southeast     Bob L. Major
3         R3        Northcentral  John K. Freed
4         R4        Southcentral  Cathy M. Wilson
5         R5        Northwest     Chris C. Hall
6         R6        Southwest     Helen T. Taylor
```

Each of these records holds data elements associated with a given sales region and contains the identification of each sales region and the name of the manager in charge of that region.

To relate the records in REGION.DBF to those in SALESMAN.DBF, a relation table, ASSIGN_DBF, also must be created with the following data structure:

```
Field   Field Name   Type        Width   Dec

  1     REGION_ID    Character      2
  2     SALSMAN_ID   Character      3
```

When you finish defining the database structure, you also should create a compound index with tags for the REGION_ID and SALSMAN_ID fields. Each record in the ASSIGN file relates a sales region to a salesperson. If you assign more than one salesperson to a sales region, use separate records to represent assigned sales regions in ASSIGN.DBF:

```
Record#   REGION_ID SALSMAN_ID

    1     R1          S0
    2     R1          S3
    3     R1          S6
    4     R1          S9
    5     R2          S2
    6     R2          S5
    7     R3          S2
    8     R3          S8
    9     R4          S4
   10     R4          S7
   11     R5          S1
   12     R5          S7
   13     R6          S4
   14     R6          S7
```

The ASSIGN.DBF relation table provides the necessary link between the REGION and SALESMAN database files and allows you to find many-to-many relations. Records in the REGION and SALESMAN databases now can be linked to provide more comprehensive information. You can find, for example, all the sales regions that have been assigned to a given salesperson or all those sales-people who are supervised by the same regional manager. Figure 8.19 shows how to relate the REGION and SALESMAN database files by using ASSIGN.DBF as their link.

Figure 8.19 also shows that a SALESMAN.DBF record may be related to more than one record in REGION.DBF, and vice versa. For example, record S2 of

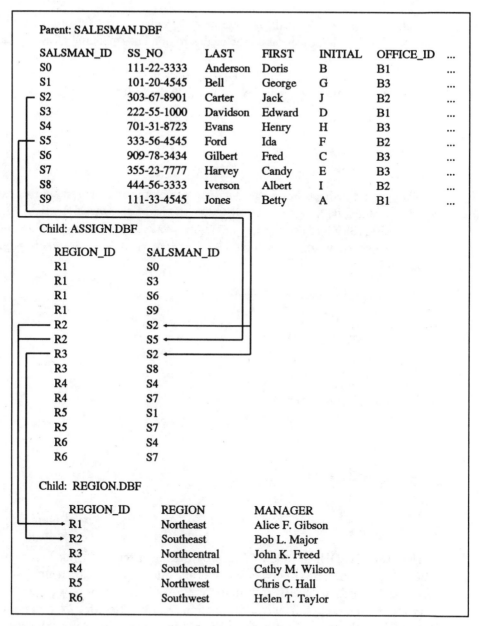

**Figure 8.19    Many-to-Many Relations between Salespeople and Sales Regions**

SALESMAN.DBF is related to records R2 and R3 in REGION.DBF. Likewise, record R2 in REGION.DBF is related to records S2 and S5 in SALESMAN.DBF.

To set up these many-to-many relationships between salespeople and sales regions, first bring up the View panel. Then open SALESMAN.DBF, ASSIGN.DBF, and REGION.DBF in three separate work areas. Designate

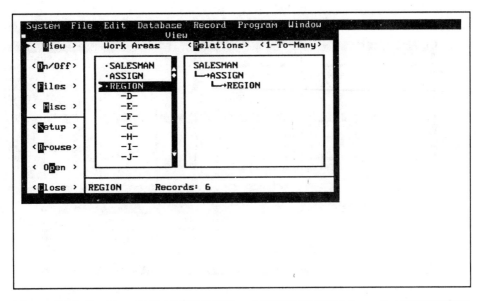

**Figure 8.20  Linking SALESMAN.DBF and REGION.DBF through ASSIGN.DBF**

SALESMAN.DBF as the parent of ASSIGN.DBF, and ASSIGN.DBF as the parent of REGION.DBF (see Figure 8.20).

The figure depicts the relations as a relation chain. SALSMAN_ID is used as the link field to relate SALESMAN.DBF and ASSIGN.DBF. ASSIGN.DBF and REGION.DBF are linked through the REGION_ID field.

Once these files are linked, the related records can be displayed in different Browse windows. When you move around the records in the parent, the related records in its children are displayed. Highlight record S4 in SALESMAN.DBF, for instance; its related records, R4 and R6, in ASSIGN.DBF are displayed (see Figure 8.21).

Notice, however, that only one record is displayed in the REGION Browse window when you would expect two to be displayed. There are direct one-to-many relations between SALESMAN.DBF and ASSIGN.DBF, and FoxPro is able to successfully handle these. But the REGION database is the child of the ASSIGN database. Between ASSIGN.DBF and REGION.DBF are many-to-one relations. FoxPro does not provide direct many-to-many relations between SALES-MAN.DBF and REGION.DBF. As a result, their relations have to be expressed indirectly through the set of one-to-many relations between SALESMAN.DBF and ASSIGN.DBF and the set of many-to-one relations between ASSIGN.DBF and REGION.DBF. FoxPro, however, is unable to graphically depict these latter many-to-one relationships.

To show the record in the REGION Browse window corresponding to the record in ASSIGN.DBF, that record must be highlighted in the ASSIGN Browse window.

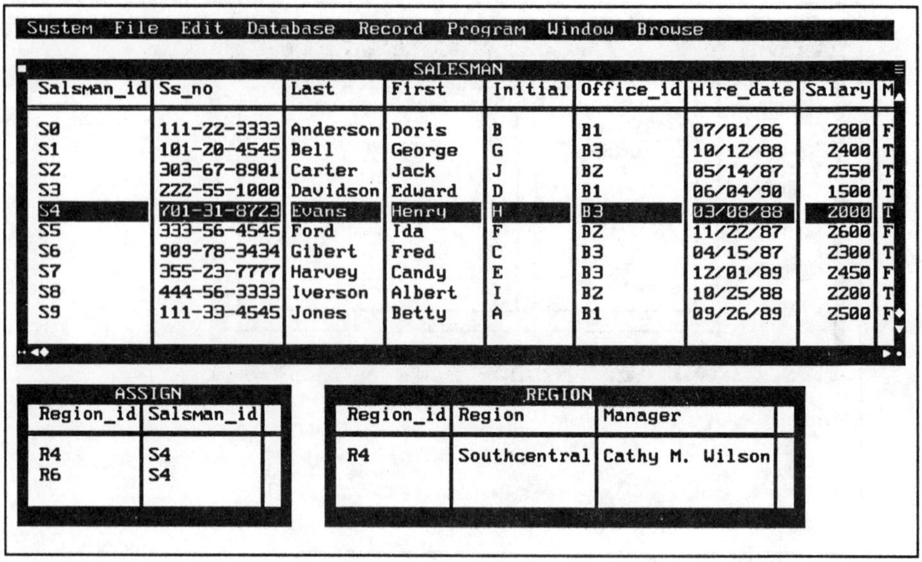

**Figure 8.21   Linked Many-to-Many Relations**

So, to see the information about region R6 in REGION.DBF, highlight R6 in the ASSIGN Browse window (see Figure 8.22).

In short, relating databases in this way—with ASSIGN as the child of SALESMAN, and REGION as the child of ASSIGN—allows you to focus on the regions

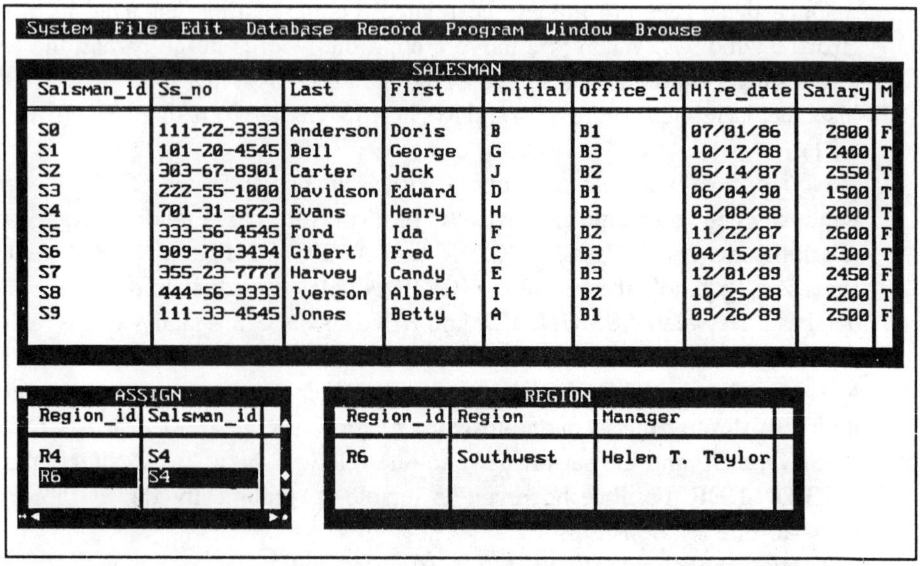

**Figure 8.22   Related Records between ASSIGN.DBF and REGIONS.DBF**

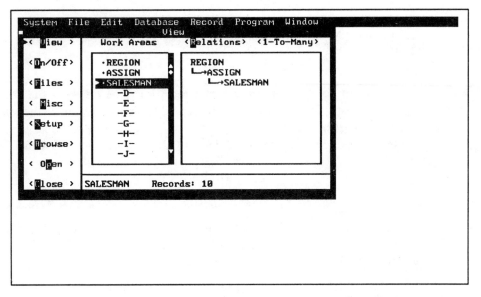

**Figure 8.23   Designating REGION.DBF as the Parent in the Relation Chain**

to which a given salesperson is assigned. But, to view information regarding all the salespeople assigned to a given region, choose REGION.DBF as the parent in the relation chain (see Figure 8.23) and designate the REGION_ID tag as the index controlling the ASSIGN database.

As a result, all the records related to a given sales region can be displayed in ASSIGN.DBF. When you highlight the R1 record in the REGION Browse window, for example, four records are displayed in the ASSIGN Browse window linking S0, S3, S6, and S9 in SALESMAN.DBF (see Figure 8.24).

To view detailed data for a specific record displayed in the ASSIGN Browse window, simply highlight that record. In return, all the fields about that record in SALESMAN.DBF will be displayed in the SALESMAN.DBF Browse window accordingly.

The three database files also can be linked by using FoxPro commands. Use the following commands to link the SALESMAN and REGION database files through the ASSIGN.DBF relation table:

```
SELECT A
USE SALESMAN
SELECT B
USE ASSIGN
SET ORDER TO SALSMAN_ID
SELECT C
USE REGION
SET ORDER TO REGION_ID
```

```
SELECT A
SET RELATION TO SALSMAN_ID INTO B
SELECT B
SET RELATION TO REGION_ID INTO C
```

After setting up the relations, their related records can be viewed in the Browse windows. Alternatively, issue the LIST command to display records in the related database files. If, for example, you want to know all the salespeople who are supervised by the manager named Alice F. Gibson, issue the following LIST command:

```
SELECT A
LIST LAST, C->MANAGER, C->REGION FOR C->MANAGER='Alice F. Gibson'
```

The LIST command displays all the records in the parent (SALESMAN.DBF in work area A) related to the records having values 'Alice F. Gibson' in the MANAGER field of the child (REGION.DBF in work area C).

```
Record#    LAST       C.REGION      C.MANAGER

     1    Anderson  Northeast    Alice F. Gibson
     4    Davidson  Northeast    Alice F. Gibson
     7    Gilbert   Northeast    Alice F. Gibson
    10    Jones     Northeast    Alice F. Gibson
```

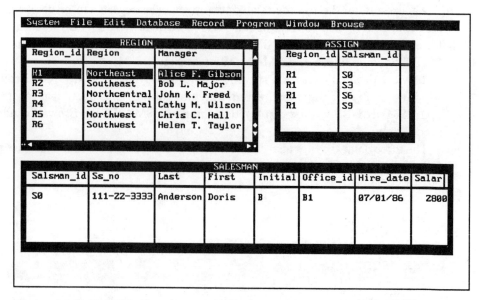

**Figure 8.24   Relating Records in REGION.DBF and SALESMAN.DBF**

Be aware, however, that the power of the LIST command is limited and results produced may be incomplete. To find all the managers for the sales regions assigned to salesperson Harvey, issue the following commands:

```
SELECT A
LIST LAST, C->MANAGER FOR LAST = 'Harvey'
```

When you execute this command, you will see only the name of one regional manager displayed, even though Harvey has been assigned to more than one sales region:

```
Record#  LAST     C.MANAGER

     8  Harvey   Cathy M. Wilson
```

Although Harvey has been assigned to regions R4, R5, and R6, only the manager of Region R4 is displayed as her regional manager. Managers for Regions R5 (Chris C. Hall) and R6 (Helen T. Taylor) are not displayed. Obviously, the LIST command is not always an appropriate command for extracting information from within multiple related database files. Instead, you would use the data query technique discussed in the next chapter to find the information you want from the related files.

# Chapter Summary

This chapter detailed the procedures for combining data fields and records from different database files; as a result, new database files can be created with these combined fields and records. You also learned how to temporarily relate records in these database files so that their data elements can be manipulated. This capability is the most powerful tool that you can use to manage relational databases. With it, you are able to efficiently access all data elements that are logically organized in different database files. In subsequent chapters you will learn how to use this tool to find information and produce reports from multiple database files.

# 9

# Querying Data

## An Overview

So far we have covered a variety of topics that relate to organizing and putting information *into* databases. But of real interest to most database users is how to find and get information *out* of databases. In this chapter you will learn different ways to do just that.

We will focus primarily on FoxPro's powerful Relational Query By Example (RQBE) techniques, which enable you to locate a set of records from one or more database files that provide the information you want. In addition, you will learn how to use the Locate and Seek operations to quickly extract records from a current database file for viewing and editing purposes.

## Locating Data Records

For each database file that you open, FoxPro maintains a **record pointer** that is responsible for keeping track of where you are in the file. The record pointer indicates the **current record** to FoxPro—this is the individual record with which FoxPro is actually working at any given time. When you open a database file, the record pointer is placed on the first record in the database. Then when you move to the next record in the database, for example, the record pointer is accordingly positioned on the second record. When you are using the FoxPro interface to interactively browse a database, for example, the current record is the record that is highlighted.

There are two ways of moving the record pointer from one record to another: sequentially, or directly. When FoxPro traverses a database file sequentially, it moves the record pointer from one record to the next, very much as you might move the cursor record by record through a database while searching for a particular record in the Browse window. To search a database sequentially, FoxPro provides the Locate operation.

In some cases, however, FoxPro can move the record pointer directly from the current record to another record that you identify. This ability to move from one record directly to the record that you specify requires that the database be indexed, and that you are seeking a value that corresponds to all or part of the index expression. FoxPro offers the Seek operation to allow you to move the record pointer directly from the current record to a noncontiguous record.

The Locate and Seek operations both are designed to allow you to pinpoint records in a database file. While the Seek operation tends to work much faster than the Locate operation, it also requires that the database be indexed. The Locate operation, although it can be significantly slower than seeking, can also be much more versatile.

## USING THE LOCATE OPERATION

To use the Locate operation in a current database file to find a record that meets certain criteria, first choose the Locate option from the Record menu popup while the database is open in the current work area. Then provide the selection criteria that will enable FoxPro to identify the record for which you are looking.

The Locate operation searches sequentially from the beginning (top) to the end (bottom) of a database file until it finds the first record that satisfies the criteria specified. When it finds a record, it places the record pointer on that spot, at which time it becomes the current record. If Locate fails to find any record satisfying the search criteria, it places its record pointer after the last record in the database file.

The Locate option may be selected as long as the database file through which you are searching is open in the current work area. Although it is not required, normally you would choose the option while the data records are displayed in the Browse window.

Once the Locate operation has found a record, it is available for examination or modification. As an exercise, use the Locate operation to point out Davidson's salary record in SALESMAN.DBF by opening the database in the current work area and then choosing the Locate option from the Record menu popup. FoxPro then displays the Locate dialog (see Figure 9.1), where the searching criteria is defined by checking the Scope and For boxes.

Note: If you are searching *all* the records in the database file, it is not necessary to check the Scope box because its default setting is All. Otherwise, check it and then select the records to be searched by turning on the appropriate radio button in the Scope dialog (see Figure 9.2). For a discussion of how each option affects the records you select, see Chapter 7.

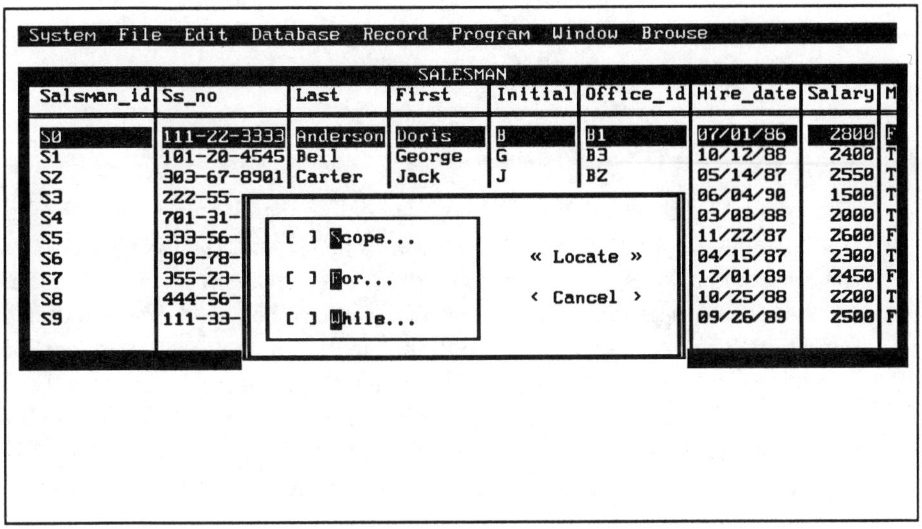

**Figure 9.1  The Locate Dialog**

Selecting the All radio button means that all the records in the current database will be subjected to the Locate operation; Next directs the Locate operation to act on a range of records beginning with the current record and continuing for the number of records specified in the text box next to the radio button. To select a specific record for the Locate operation, enter the record number in the box next to the Record radio button after selecting that button; select Rest to direct the Locate

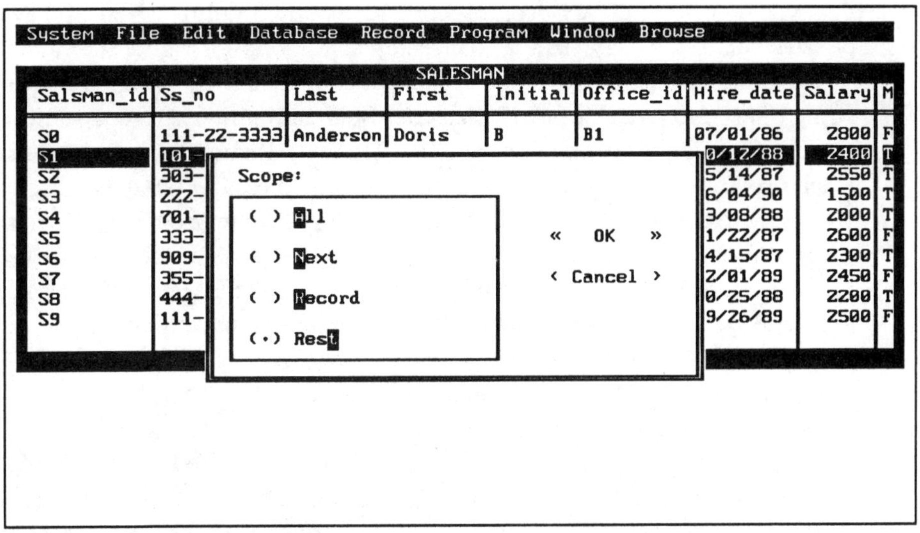

**Figure 9.2  The Scope Dialog**

operation to act on the range of records beginning with the current record and ending with the last record in the current data file.

## Defining Search Conditions

The For and While check boxes are used to define search conditions. Checking the For box enables you to define the expression that directs the Locate operation. All the records that satisfy the conditions defined in the expression will be searched by the Locate operation. Select the While check box to define another search condition. The Locate operation continues searching the records only as long the condition remains true. As soon as it encounters a record that fails to meet the While condition, the search is halted. If you select both the For and While check boxes, only those records that satisfy both the For and While conditions will be included for the Locate operation. Note that the While condition is valid only when the data scope is set to All.

The Expression Builder is used to specify both For and While conditions. To define a For condition, check the For box to bring up the Expression Builder. Then define the expression in the For Clause text box, describing the search conditions in the same way that you defined record filter conditions. Any type of data fields may be included in the expression, along with the necessary mathematical and logical operators.

## Searching for Character Strings

Records can be searched by comparing a search string with the contents of a database field. To find Davidson's record, for example, define LAST = 'Davidson' or salesman.last = 'Davidson' as the search condition (see Figure 9.3).

When the Locate operation is executed, it compares each string with the search string ('Davidson') in the LAST character field until it finds an acceptable match. Once it does, it displays a message (e.g., Record = 4) showing its record number. If the Browse window is open, it may overlay this message, but the record pointer will move to the record that FoxPro has located. If the Browse window is not open, the record found by the Locate operation will be highlighted when it is opened (see Figure 9.4). Note that the record with "Davidson" in the LAST field is highlighted in both Browse and Change modes. At this point, you may choose to view or edit its contents.

In this example, the Locate operation found the character string "Davidson" in record S3 when it compared the string with the search string 'Davidson'. This happens to be an exact match; that is, every character in the LAST field of record S3 matched those in the search string. But the Locate operation will accept a partial match as long as all the characters in the search string match, character by character, the string against which it is comparing. The string in the data field may contain

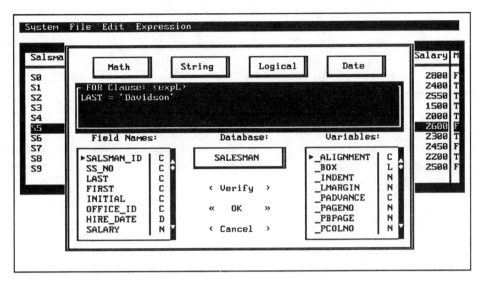

**Figure 9.3  Searching for a Specific Character String**

more and different characters beyond those contained in the search string. With these parameters then, it is possible to find 'Davidson' in the LAST field by using any one of following search conditions:

```
LAST = 'Davids'
LAST = 'David'
LAST = 'Dav'
LAST = 'D'
```

| System  File  Edit  Database  Record  Program  Window  Browse |
| --- |

Record = 4

SALESMAN

| Salsman_id | Ss_no | Last | First | Initial | Office_id | Hire_date | Salary | M |
| --- | --- | --- | --- | --- | --- | --- | --- | --- |
| S0 | 111-22-3333 | Anderson | Doris | B | B1 | 07/01/86 | 2800 | F |
| S1 | 101-20-4545 | Bell | George | G | B3 | 10/12/88 | 2400 | T |
| S2 | 303-67-8901 | Carter | Jack | J | B2 | 05/14/87 | 2550 | T |
| S3 | 222-55-1000 | Davidson | Edward | D | B1 | 06/04/90 | 1500 | T |
| S4 | 701-31-8723 | Evans | Henry | H | B3 | 03/08/88 | 2000 | T |
| S5 | 333-56-4545 | Ford | Ida | F | B2 | 11/22/87 | 2600 | F |
| S6 | 909-78-3434 | Gilbert | Fred | C | B1 | 04/15/87 | 2300 | T |
| S7 | 355-23-7777 | Harvey | Candy | E | B3 | 12/01/89 | 2450 | F |
| S8 | 444-56-3333 | Iverson | Albert | I | B2 | 10/25/88 | 2200 | T |
| S9 | 111-33-4545 | Jones | Betty | A | B1 | 09/26/89 | 2500 | F |

**Figure 9.4  Record with the Located String**

The above are acceptable because as soon as a string in the data field that is being searched matches, character by character, the search string, it is considered an acceptable match. This partial match requirement often makes the search process less restrictive; you do not have to remember the whole string in order to find it. Be aware, however, that if you use LAST = 'Dav' as the search string, you may find a character string such as 'Davis'; or a search string of 'D' may find the first character string beginning with 'D'.

One restriction on defining a search string in a data field is that the string must appear *after* the data field. Therefore, all of the following search conditions are unacceptable:

```
'Davidson' = LAST
'David' = LAST
'D' = LAST
```

### The Exact Setting

If an exact match is required, you must check SET EXACT in the On/Off panel after you have brought up the View panel. Normally, EXACT is set to OFF (see Figure 9.5).

So, to find the person whose first name is 'John', not 'Johnny', define the following search condition after setting SET EXACT on:

```
FIRST = 'John'
```

```
 System  File  Edit  Database  Record  Program  Window
┌──────────────────────────────────────────────────────┐
│                          View                          │
│  < View >    [ ] ALTERNATE      [X] FULLPATH           │
│              [ ] AUTOSAVE       [X] HEADINGS           │
│ ►<On/Off>    [X] BELL           [X] HELP               │
│              [ ] CARRY          [X] INTENSITY          │
│  <Files >    [X] CLEAR          [ ] NEAR               │
│              [ ] COMPATIBLE     [ ] PRINTER            │
│  < Misc >    [ ] CONFIRM        [X] RESOURCE           │
│              [X] DEBUG          [X] SAFETY             │
│              [ ] DELETED        [X] SHADOWS            │
│              [X] DEVELOPMENT    [X] SPACE              │
│              [ ] ECHO           [X] STICKY             │
│              [X] ESCAPE         [X] TALK               │
│              [ ] EXACT          [ ] UNIQUE             │
│           SET ... [ ON | OFF ]                         │
└──────────────────────────────────────────────────────┘
```

**Figure 9.5  The SET EXACT Check Box**

**Ignoring Case**

When search strings are specified, case is important. You will not find 'Davidson' if you type 'davidson' or 'DAVIDSON'. To ignore case, convert the strings in the data field either to all upper- or all lowercase letters by creating an expression that uses the UPPER( ) or LOWER( ) function. (A function tells FoxPro to return a predefined value. The object enclosed in the parentheses is called an argument. A function argument may be a data field or an expression. You will learn more about this in a later chapter.) UPPER(LAST), for instance, will return a string in which the contents of the LAST field have been converted to uppercase. Similarly, the function LOWER(LAST) will return a string that consists of the LAST field in lowercase letters only. Therefore, any one of the following expressions may be used as a search condition for finding a record in which the LAST field has been entered as 'Davidson', 'DAVIDSON', or 'davidson':

```
UPPER(LAST)  =  'DAVIDSON'
LOWER(LAST)  =  'davidson'
```

The UPPER(LAST) function in the first search condition returns a string in which all the letters in the LAST data field are converted to uppercase before it is compared with the search character string 'DAVIDSON'. As a result, case is ignored in the character string in the LAST data field. The second search condition works the same way by converting the character string to lowercase before it is compared with the character string 'davidson'.

Two additional points that relate to ignoring case when searching a database are worth noting. First, an expression, like UPPER(LAST), that converts the contents of a database field into a new string, does not actually modify the contents of the database field itself. Second, a frequent cause of error in searching a database occurs when the search string and the database field expression are in different cases. For example, if you are attempting to make the search case insensitive by using the UPPER function to convert the contents of a particular field, the search string must also be entirely in uppercase. As a result, the following search conditions will not succeed in locating the desired record:

```
UPPER(LAST)  =  "Davidson"
LOWER(LAST)  =  "DAVIDSON"
```

## Searching for Numeric Values

The Locate operation also can be used to find a numeric value in a current database file. To find a salesperson who has a monthly salary of $2,000 or less from SALESMAN.DBF, the search condition would be defined as SALARY <= 2000. Upon execution, the Locate operation finds in the SALARY field the first record having a salary that is less than or equal to $2,000 (see Figure 9.6).

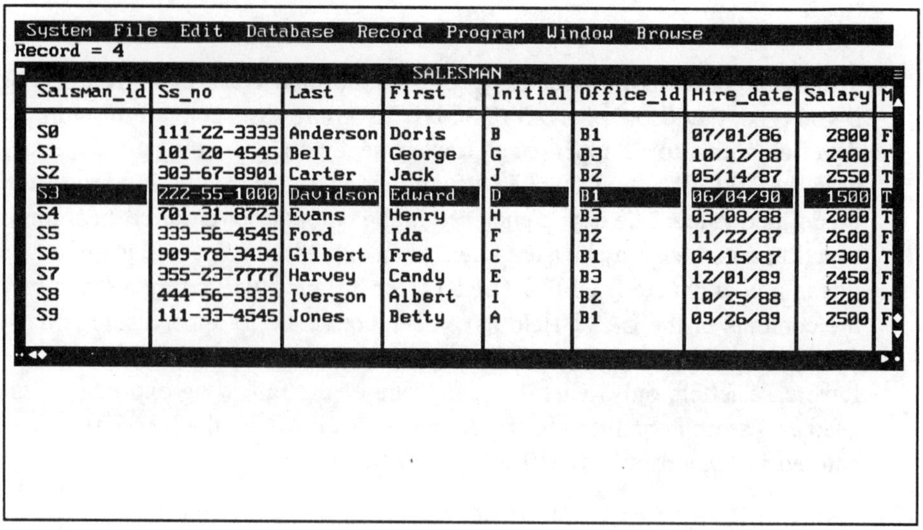

```
 System  File  Edit  Database  Record  Program  Window  Browse
 Record = 4
                            SALESMAN
 Salsman_id Ss_no       Last       First     Initial Office_id Hire_date Salary M
 S0         111-22-3333 Anderson   Doris     B       B1        07/01/86  2800  F
 S1         101-20-4545 Bell       George    G       B3        10/12/88  2400  T
 S2         303-67-8901 Carter     Jack      J       B2        05/14/87  2550  T
 S3         222-55-1000 Davidson   Edward    D       B1        06/04/90  1500  T
 S4         701-31-8723 Evans      Henry     H       B3        03/08/88  2000  T
 S5         333-56-4545 Ford       Ida       F       B2        11/22/87  2600  F
 S6         909-78-3434 Gilbert    Fred      C       B1        04/15/87  2300  T
 S7         355-23-7777 Harvey     Candy     E       B3        12/01/89  2450  F
 S8         444-56-3333 Iverson    Albert    I       B2        10/25/88  2200  T
 S9         111-33-4545 Jones      Betty     A       B1        09/26/89  2500  F
```

**Figure 9.6  Using Locate to Find a Numeric Value**

You can see that record S3 (the fourth record or Record=4) was found by the Locate operation. It is important to note that if there is more than one record in the SALARY field satisfying the search criteria, the record pointer will be placed at the *first* record that satisfies the search condition. The Locate operation does not return a set of records; it stops searching once the first record is found that satisfies the search criteria.

To find the *next* record that satisfies the search criteria, select the Continue option from the Record menu popup. As a result, the record pointer is positioned on the next record that satisfies the search criteria. If, as an exercise, you select the Continue option from the Record menu popup now, the next record (i.e., S4, SALARY <= 2000) is highlighted (see Figure 9.7).

## Searching for Dates

Extracting a specific date from a data field in a database file is similar to finding a character string or a numeric value. But, when you specify the search criterion for a date value, it must be enclosed in a pair of braces ({ }). So, to find the salesperson who was hired on November 22, 1987, define the search criterion as HIRE_DATE = {11/22/87}.

When the Locate operation is carried out with this search criterion, FoxPro moves the record pointer to the first record it finds with 11/22/87 as the value in the HIRE_DATE field; in our sample database, that record belongs to Ida Ford (see Figure 9.8).

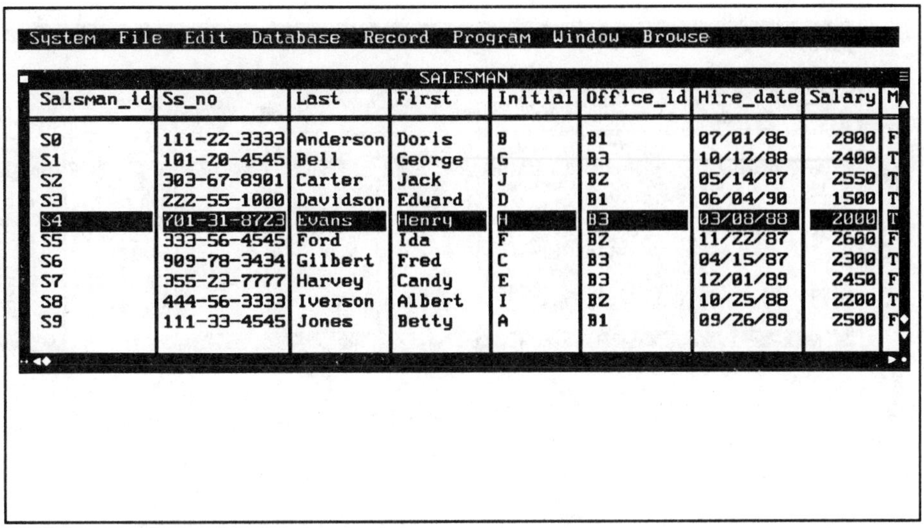

```
System  File  Edit  Database  Record  Program  Window  Browse
```

| Salsman_id | Ss_no | Last | First | Initial | Office_id | Hire_date | Salary | M |
|------------|-------|------|-------|---------|-----------|-----------|--------|---|
| S0 | 111-22-3333 | Anderson | Doris | B | B1 | 07/01/86 | 2800 | F |
| S1 | 101-20-4545 | Bell | George | G | B3 | 10/12/88 | 2400 | T |
| SZ | 303-67-8901 | Carter | Jack | J | BZ | 05/14/87 | 2550 | T |
| S3 | ZZZ-55-1000 | Davidson | Eduard | D | B1 | 06/04/90 | 1500 | T |
| S4 | 701-31-8723 | Evans | Henry | H | B3 | 03/08/88 | 2000 | T |
| S5 | 333-56-4545 | Ford | Ida | F | BZ | 11/22/87 | 2600 | F |
| S6 | 909-78-3434 | Gilbert | Fred | C | B3 | 04/15/87 | 2300 | T |
| S7 | 355-23-7777 | Harvey | Candy | E | B3 | 12/01/89 | 2450 | F |
| S8 | 444-56-3333 | Iverson | Albert | I | BZ | 10/25/88 | ZZ00 | T |
| S9 | 111-33-4545 | Jones | Betty | A | B1 | 09/26/89 | 2500 | F |

**Figure 9.7  Using the Continue Menu Option**

## Searching for Logical Values

If you want to locate the first record in a current database file with the value of either true (.T.) or false (.F.) in one of its logical fields, simply define the search criterion for the Locate operation by including periods around the logical value. To find the first record belonging to a male salesperson in SALESMAN.DBF,

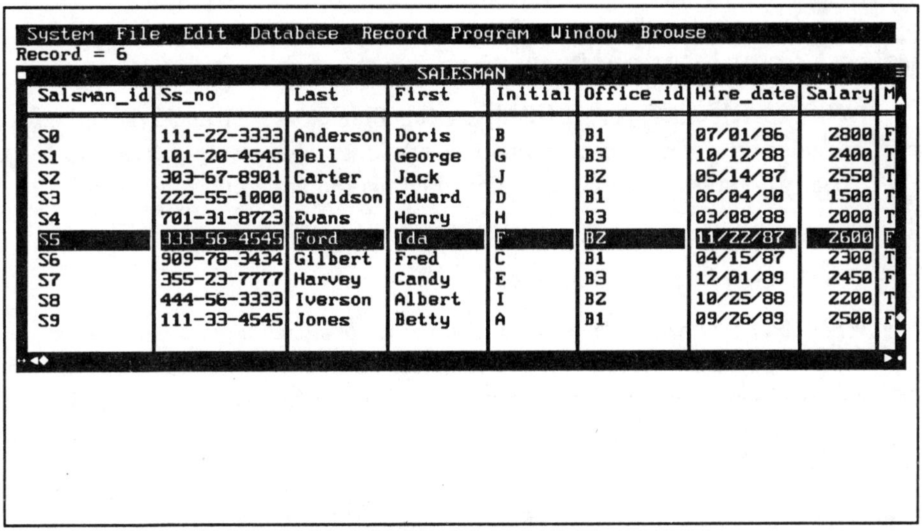

```
System  File  Edit  Database  Record  Program  Window  Browse
Record = 6
```

| Salsman_id | Ss_no | Last | First | Initial | Office_id | Hire_date | Salary | M |
|------------|-------|------|-------|---------|-----------|-----------|--------|---|
| S0 | 111-22-3333 | Anderson | Doris | B | B1 | 07/01/86 | 2800 | F |
| S1 | 101-20-4545 | Bell | George | G | B3 | 10/12/88 | 2400 | T |
| SZ | 303-67-8901 | Carter | Jack | J | BZ | 05/14/87 | 2550 | T |
| S3 | ZZZ-55-1000 | Davidson | Eduard | D | B1 | 06/04/90 | 1500 | T |
| S4 | 701-31-8723 | Evans | Henry | H | B3 | 03/08/88 | 2000 | T |
| S5 | 333-56-4545 | Ford | Ida | F | BZ | 11/22/87 | 2600 | F |
| S6 | 909-78-3434 | Gilbert | Fred | C | B1 | 04/15/87 | 2300 | T |
| S7 | 355-23-7777 | Harvey | Candy | E | B3 | 12/01/89 | 2450 | F |
| S8 | 444-56-3333 | Iverson | Albert | I | BZ | 10/25/88 | ZZ00 | T |
| S9 | 111-33-4545 | Jones | Betty | A | B1 | 09/26/89 | 2500 | F |

**Figure 9.8  Record with the Located Date**

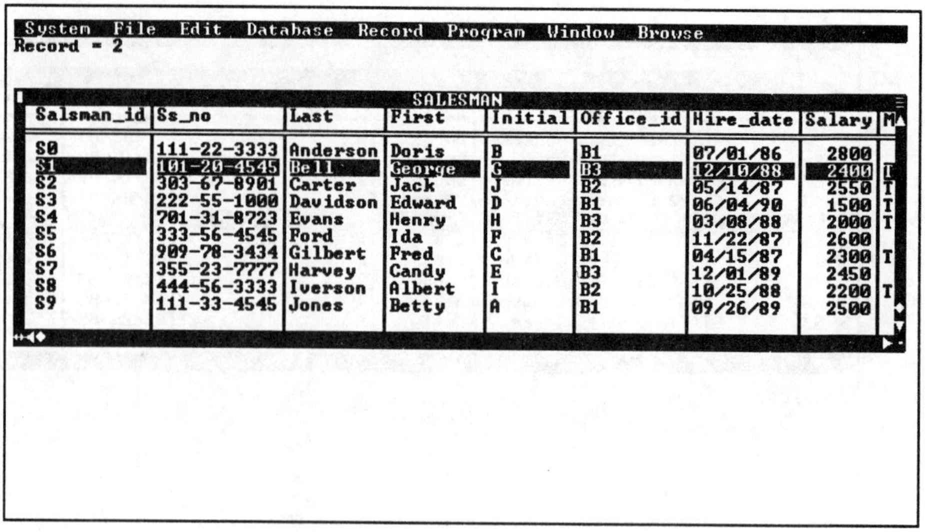

```
System  File  Edit  Database  Record  Program  Window  Browse
Record = 2
```

| Salsman_id | Ss_no | Last | First | Initial | Office_id | Hire_date | Salary | M |
|---|---|---|---|---|---|---|---|---|
| S0 | 111-22-3333 | Anderson | Doris | B | B1 | 07/01/86 | 2800 | |
| S1 | 101-20-4545 | Bell | George | G | B3 | 12/10/88 | 2400 | T |
| S2 | 303-67-8901 | Carter | Jack | J | B2 | 05/14/87 | 2550 | T |
| S3 | 222-55-1000 | Davidson | Edward | D | B1 | 06/04/90 | 1500 | T |
| S4 | 701-31-8723 | Evans | Henry | H | B3 | 03/08/88 | 2000 | T |
| S5 | 333-56-4545 | Ford | Ida | F | B2 | 11/22/87 | 2600 | |
| S6 | 909-78-3434 | Gilbert | Fred | C | B1 | 04/15/87 | 2300 | T |
| S7 | 355-23-7777 | Harvey | Candy | E | B3 | 12/01/89 | 2450 | |
| S8 | 444-56-3333 | Iverson | Albert | I | B2 | 10/25/88 | 2200 | T |
| S9 | 111-33-4545 | Jones | Betty | A | B1 | 09/26/89 | 2500 | |

**Figure 9.9  Using Locate to Find a Logical Value**

specify MALE = .T. as the search criterion for the Locate operation. Then execute Locate; it scans the values in the MALE logical field until it finds the first record having a true value; in our sample database, as Figure 9.9 shows, it is the record for George Bell.

If there is no record satisfying the search criteria, the record pointer is placed at the last record in the database file.

## Using Logical Connectors

When search criteria are defined, logical connectors such as AND and OR can be included to define more complex conditions. These connectors enable you to specify compound search conditions that may include multiple fields.

### AND as the Logical Connector

The AND connector is used to join two or more search conditions in search criteria. A record is then selected by the Locate operation only when it satisfies all the conditions in the criteria. Here are some examples of expressions incorporating AND:

```
MALE = .T. AND COMIS_RATE > 0.10
SALARY > 2500 AND HIRE_DATE >= {01/01/89}
MALE = .T. AND SALARY <= 2500 AND COMIS_RATE > 0.10
```

The first two expressions use AND to join two search conditions involving two different fields. As a result, the Locate operation will find the first record that satisfies both these conditions simultaneously. The first expression uses AND to join the MALE = .T. condition with the COMIS_RATE > 0.10 condition; FoxPro will search for those salespeople who are male *and* receive a commission of under 10 percent. Similarly, the second expression joins SALARY > 2500 and HIRE_DATE >= {01/01/89} with the AND logical connector; and FoxPro searches for the records of salespeople hired on or after January 1, 1989, and whose salaries exceed $2,500. AND may also be used to join more than two search conditions. The third expression joins three search conditions with two logical AND connectors. FoxPro will locate the first record for which all three conditions are true.

### OR as the Logical Connector

Using OR as the logical connector to define compound search conditions for the Locate operation results in a record that is selected as long as one of the two conditions is met. Here is an example:

```
MALE = .T. OR COMIS_RATE > 0.10
```

This expression uses OR to connect the MALE = .T. and COMIS_RATE > 0.10 conditions. As a result, a record will be selected when either the MALE = .T. or the COMIS_RATE > 0.10 condition is true. Of course, if both conditions are met in the same record, the record will be selected as well. As with AND, more than one OR connector may be included in an expression to build complex search conditions:

```
MALE = .T. OR COMIS_RATE > 0.10 OR HIRE_DATE >= {01/01/89}
```

In this case, a record will be selected as long as one of the three conditions in the expressions is true.

Furthermore, AND and OR may be combined in an expression to define search conditions. But, to avoid confusion, you may want to use parentheses to clearly define the conditions. For example:

```
(MALE =.T. OR SALARY < 2200) AND (MALE = .F. OR SALARY > 2800)
```

The parentheses are used to group the conditions and determine which is to be evaluated first. If there is more than one pair of parentheses in an expression, evaluation is from left to right. Therefore, when the above condition is evaluated, the expression contained in the first pair of parentheses, (MALE = .T. OR SALARY < 2200) will be evaluated before the expression, (MALE = .F. OR SALARY > 2800) in the second pair of parentheses.

The placement of parentheses is important, because conditions can have different meanings if you eliminate or rearrange them. If, for example, you eliminate all the parentheses in the preceding expression, the search condition will have a different meaning.

Nested parentheses also may be used to define search criteria, in which case, the expression in the inner parentheses is evaluated before the expression specified in the outside parentheses. Then, in the expression:

```
(MALE = .T. OR (SALARY >= 2000 AND SALARY <= 4000))
```

(SALARY >= 2000 AND SALARY <= 4000) will be evaluated first. The records that satisfy the condition defined by this expression will be evaluated with the MALE = .T. condition.

## Using LOCATE Commands

As an alternative to choosing the Locate option from the Record menu popup, a database file can be directed to search for records by invoking the LOCATE command. The search conditions then would be defined as an expression in the FOR clause:

```
LOCATE FOR <expression>
            [<record scope>]
```

The LOCATE command sequentially searches the current database file for the first record that satisfies the conditions specified in the FOR expression. The optional record scope can be added to identify the records that are subjected to the search. Here are examples of LOCATE commands:

```
USE SALESMAN
LOCATE FOR LAST = 'Davidson'
LOCATE FOR UPPER(FIRST) = 'DORIS'
LOCATE FOR MALE = .F. AND SALARY > 2500
LOCATE FOR HIRE_DATE > {01/01/89} OR COMIS_RATE > 0.20
```

## USING SEEK OPERATIONS

Because the Locate operation scans through the database file sequentially from top to bottom and examines each record in passing, the amount of time it takes to find a record depends largely on the number of records in the database file. If your database file has fewer than a thousand records, it may be acceptable to use the Locate operation to find your records. But the search process becomes unacceptably slow if the database file has a very large number of records. For such large files, the Seek operation is much faster; it works with an indexed database file whose records have been ordered, and therefore provides direct access to the first record meeting the search criteria.

To find records with the Seek operation, the database file must first be indexed on the key expression whose values you are searching for. Usually this is done by designating as the master index an existing index tag whose key field matches the

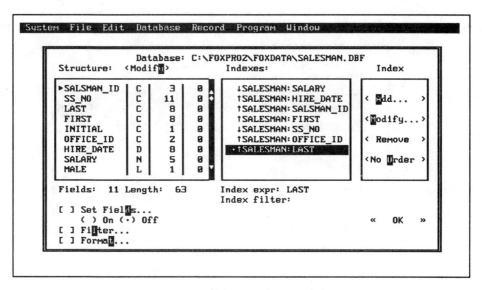

```
 System  File  Edit  Database  Record  Program  Window

            Database: C:\FOXPROZ\FOXDATA\SALESMAN.DBF
   Structure:  <Modify>           Indexes:              Index

  ▶SALSMAN_ID   C    3    0     ↓SALESMAN:SALARY
   SS_NO        C   11    0     ↑SALESMAN:HIRE_DATE    <  Add...  >
   LAST         C    8    0     ↑SALESMAN:SALSMAN_ID
   FIRST        C    8    0     ↑SALESMAN:FIRST       <Modify...>
   INITIAL      C    1    0     ↓SALESMAN:SS_NO
   OFFICE_ID    C    2    0     ↑SALESMAN:OFFICE_ID   <  Remove  >
   HIRE_DATE    D    8    0     ·↑SALESMAN:LAST
   SALARY       N    5    0                           <No Order >
   MALE         L    1    0

   Fields:  11 Length:   63     Index expr: LAST
                                Index filter:
   [ ] Set Fields...
       ( ) On (·) Off                              «   OK   »
   [ ] Filter...
   [ ] Format...
```

**Figure 9.10  Setting LAST Index Tag as Master Index**

expression for which you are searching. (It is also possible to create the appropriate index tag and make it the current master index, but this is done less frequently because it too is time-consuming.) All you need to do to find a record is to specify the value of the index tag. You do not have to specify the complete expression as the search criteria. To find a salesperson by his or her last name in the SALES-MAN.DBF database file, for example, set the LAST index tag as the master index in the Setup window (see Figure 9.10).

Once the database file is ordered appropriately, choose the Seek option from the Record menu popup to begin the record search. In response to the menu option selection, you are asked to specify the value you are seeking in the expression text box provided. If the value is a character string, enclose the string in a pair of single quote marks (see Figure 9.11).

Figure 9.11 displays the current index key in parentheses (e.g. Index = LAST). Remember: The value entered for the Seek operation must be of the same type as the index key. So, because the LAST index tag consists of the LAST field—a character type—only a character string may be entered as a seek value (e.g., 'Davidson'); if you enter an incorrect value type, FoxPro will display a message informing you that "Expression must be of type C," or whatever type is correct.

Once executed, the Seek operation searches the indexed file for the first occurrence of a record whose index key expression matches the expression you have specified. Unlike the Locate option, however, Seek uses the index file to search the database. This difference means that Seek has nearly direct and immediate access to the first record whose key meets the Seek expression. If you view the records in SALESMAN.DBF at this point, you would find that the record selected

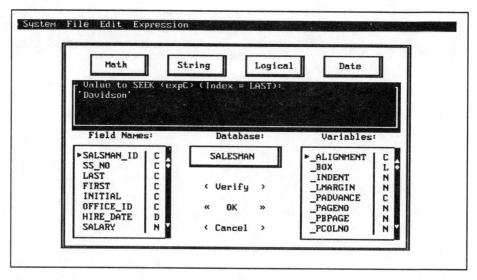

**Figure 9.11   Specifying the Value to Seek**

by the Seek operation is highlighted and belongs to salesperson Davidson (see Figure 9.12).

Like the Locate operation, the Seek operation accepts a partial match unless EXACT is set to ON. Thus, if you specify 'David' as the Seek value, it will find Davidson in the LAST data field in the file.

When the index key is not a character string, date, numeric, and logical values can also be located with the Seek operation. It is important to stress once again,

System   File   Edit   Database   Record   Program   Window   Browse

SALESMAN

| Salsman_id | Ss_no | Last | First | Initial | Office id | Hire_date | Salary | M |
|---|---|---|---|---|---|---|---|---|
| S0 | 111-22-3333 | Anderson | Doris | B | B1 | 07/01/86 | 2800 | |
| S1 | 101-20-4545 | Bell | George | G | B3 | 12/10/88 | 2400 | T |
| S2 | 303-67-8901 | Carter | Jack | J | B2 | 05/14/87 | 2550 | T |
| S3 | 222-55-1000 | Davidson | Edward | D | B1 | 06/04/90 | 1500 | T |
| S4 | 701-31-8723 | Evans | Henry | H | B3 | 03/08/88 | 2000 | T |
| S5 | 333-56-4545 | Ford | Ida | F | B2 | 11/22/87 | 2600 | |
| S6 | 909-78-3434 | Gilbert | Fred | C | B1 | 04/15/87 | 2300 | T |
| S7 | 355-23-7777 | Harvey | Candy | E | B3 | 12/01/89 | 2450 | |
| S8 | 444-56-3333 | Iverson | Albert | I | B2 | 10/25/88 | 2200 | T |
| S9 | 111-33-4545 | Jones | Betty | A | B1 | 09/26/89 | 2500 | |

**Figure 9.12   A Selected Record**

however, that the data type of the index key and the search expression must correspond. When searching for a date value, enclose it in braces (e.g., {01/01/89}; for numeric values, just specify the value as the Seek expression itself; when expressing a logical value, include the periods (e.g., .T. or .F.) in the Seek expression.

## Using SEEK Commands

The Seek operation, too, may be executed by issuing a FoxPro command in the following format:

```
SEEK <expression>
```

So to find and edit the record belonging to the salesperson who was hired on March 8, 1988, the following commands may be invoked:

```
USE SALESMAN
SET ORDER TO HIRE_DATE
SEEK {01/01/88}
EDIT
```

The SET ORDER command is issued to designate the existing index tag named HIRE_DATE as the master index. The index tag uses the HIRE_DATE data field as the index key. If you have not set up such an index tag, you can create one and add it to the compound index file, SALESMAN.CDX. Although it is not a good practice, you may create a standard HIREDATE.IDX index file, as shown below to order your records before carrying out the Seek operation.

```
USE SALESMAN
INDEX ON HIRE_DATE TO HIREDATE
SEEK {12/01/89}
EDIT
```

# Querying Data with RQBE

RQBE is a flexible tool that enables you to easily and efficiently isolate the information you would like to extract, and then determine how and where you would like it to appear. RQBE, by incorporating what Fox Software calls Rushmore Technology, executes most queries very quickly; this is particularly important if you are working with large databases.

In addition to its speed and flexibility, RQBE offers a number of other attractive features:

- *Ease of use*. Define selection criteria by providing an example of the kind of records you would like to include in the query.

- *Optimization.* We saw earlier that, in choosing between the Locate and Seek options to query databases, a decision had to be made, whether deliberate or not, about *how* the results of a query should be found. RQBE, however, relieves you of this responsibility. It examines your query and the data, and decides on the best available access path to the data.

- *Set Orientation.* In contrast to Seek and Locate that find one record at a time, RQBE returns *all* of the records that meet your selection criteria. These can then be manipulated as a set, rather than individually.

## CREATING RQBE QUERIES

The process of querying data with RQBE requires several steps. First, bring up the RQBE window and specify a number of query settings. These settings determine which database files to use, which fields to include in output from the query, how to organize that output, and where to send it. The next step involves defining the selection criteria for the query operation. This requires identifying the query field and specifying the query conditions. Finally, the query is saved and executed.

### The RQBE Window

The first step in creating a new query is to bring up the RQBE window. To do that, first open the database file you need in the current work area. Although you can open other database files later, FoxPro requires that at least one file be open before it allows you to access the RQBE window. To query data in the SALESMAN database file, for example, open it in work area A; then select the New option from the File menu popup, followed by selecting Query as the type of new file to create. As a result, the RQBE window appears (see Figure 9.13).

In the upper left-hand corner of Figure 9.13 you can see the database files that are available for the query operation. In this example, because SALESMAN.DBF is open in the current work area, it is shown in the Databases list box. Below that are two push buttons: <Add> and <Clear>. If you need to use more than one database file, use the <Add> push button to insert the others to the list box. To remove an existing database file from the list box, choose the <Clear> push button.

In the top center of the window are the selected output fields that will be included in the query results. By default, FoxPro includes all the data fields associated with the selected database files in the output field list. But you may change the output field list by selecting the Select Fields... check box that appears next to the Output Fields list box.

Below the Select Fields check box are three more check boxes: Order By..., Group By..., and Having.... Use one or more of these to order and organize your query results.

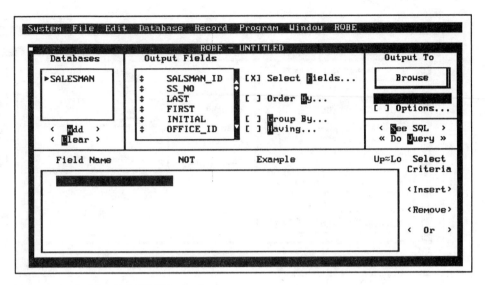

**Figure 9.13  The RQBE Window**

In the upper right-hand corner is an Output to popup that is used to specify where the results of your query will appear. By default, output is sent to a Browse window after FoxPro carries out the query operation. You may choose, however, to create a formatted report or labels that FoxPro will print, display, or write to a file; you also may store the results of the query either in a permanent or a temporary database file.

The lower portion of the RQBE window is used for defining the selection criteria for the query operation. Use one line to define each selection criterion in the text box provided; to build a compound selection criterion, use one or more of the three text buttons provided: <Insert>, <Remove> and <Or>.

Finally, the <Do Query> text button is provided for executing the query operation after all the query settings and selection criteria have been specified.

At this point, take note of the <See SQL> text button in the RQBE window. If you select this button, you will see that FoxPro has translated all the query instructions into a set of Structured Query Language (SQL) commands. This is an excellent way to learn about SQL commands, if they are of interest to you. If, however, you do not intend to familiarize yourself with the SQL language, this button may be ignored.

## Selecting Output Data Fields

After opening the RQBE window, the first step in defining a query is to identify the data fields that you would like to include for output. To include all the existing data fields of the selected database file, do nothing. By default, all of the existing

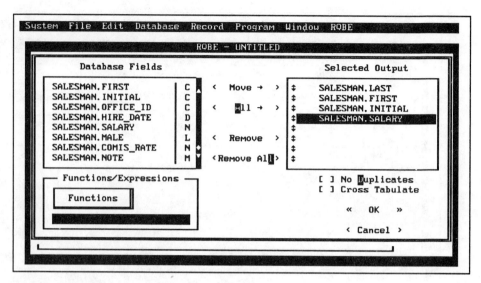

**Figure 9.14  Selecting Output Data Fields**

data fields of the open database file are selected automatically by FoxPro as output fields, and subsequently are shown in the Output Fields box.

But, to select only some of these data fields for output, click on the Select Fields... check box. The RQBE Select Fields dialog, which is used to select data fields, appears. Then, to maintain only the FIRST, INITIAL, LAST, and SALARY fields from the database file, remove the unwanted fields from the selected field list.

In Figure 9.14, only four fields remain after removing the unwanted fields from the Selected Output box. This list controls not only whether or not a field is included in the query, but also determines the order in which fields will appear in the final output.

If you would like to change the order of the selected data fields, there are two ways to do so. First, although this is somewhat cumbersome, you can remove all the data fields from the selected field list and then select them again in the order that you want. The second, preferable, method is to rearrange the order of the selected fields. This can be accomplished either with the mouse or the keyboard. With the keyboard, first position the cursor on the field you would like to move. Then press Ctrl-PgUp to move the record up one position and Ctrl-PgDn to move it down one position. (On some keyboards, you can press Ctrl-UpArrow and Ctrl-DownArrow, as well.) With the mouse, select the field you intend to move, position the mouse pointer on the double arrow immediately to the left of the field name and drag it to the desired position.

To position the LAST field between the INITIAL and SALARY fields in this example, move the LAST field down three lines. If you are using the mouse, point it on the double-headed arrow to the left of the LAST field and then drag it to its new position. With the keyboard, use the Tab and arrow keys to highlight the LAST field and then press the Ctrl-PgDn (or Ctrl-DownArrow) key combination to move it to its new position. To move the selected field list up, use the Ctrl-PgUp (or Ctrl-UpArrow) after you have highlighted the field you want to move.

The RQBE Select Fields dialog also provides the No Duplicates check box that makes it possible to eliminate duplicate records from query results. This option is very useful for removing redundant information from the database. If, for example, you have entered duplicate records for the same salesperson in the SALESMAN database, simply choose this option to discard the extraneous record. Another situation that can be solved by checking the No Duplicates check box is when you want to eliminate records containing the same values in the data fields selected by the query. For example, although no two records in the original database have the same values for all the data fields, some of the data fields share the same data values in some records. When you select these data fields for query output, the query produces duplicate records. In this case, the No Duplicates option can eliminate these records.

In our example, however, there are no records in the SALESMAN file with identical values to those in the data fields selected, so do not check the No Duplicates box.

After you have finished selecting the data fields in the order of your choice, select the <<OK>> push button to exit from the RQBE Select dialog. When you return to the RQBE window you will see that the selected data fields are displayed in the Output Fields box in the order specified (see Figure 9.15).

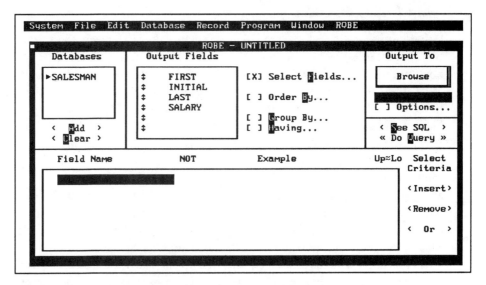

**Figure 9.15  Selected Output Fields**

## Identifying Output Destinations

After selecting the fields for which FoxPro will *return* information for each record that matches your selection criteria, you also can determine where FoxPro is to *send* the information about these records. You may choose to view the resulting records in a Browse window; or you can save them in a temporary or permanent database file. In addition, you can use the resulting records to produce reports and mailing labels.

There are four possible destinations—Browse, Report/Label, Table/DBF, Cursor—that you can choose from the Output To popup in the RQBE window to handle the query results. To view the resulting records in a Browse window, choose the Browse option as the output destination; a Browse window is, in any case, the default destination for all RQBE output. If you intend to use the query results in custom reports and mailing labels, choose the Report/Label option.

If you need to save the resulting records in a database file, choose either the Cursor or the Table/DBF option. If you choose Cursor as the destination, all the resulting records will be saved in a temporary database file that FoxPro will open automatically. Once you close this database, FoxPro will also erase it, effectively removing all its records in the process. But, if you intend to use the resulting records from the query operation later, they should be saved in a permanent database file with a name of your choice. To do that, choose the Table/DBF option as the output destination. In return, you will be asked to name the database file. By default, FoxPro will display the resulting records in a Browse window on the screen.

## Ordering Query Results

If the query operation returns more than one record, you can specify how you would like to order those records in the RQBE window by selecting the Order By... check box. In return, you are asked to select the order in which the resulting records are to be arranged. To arrange the resulting records in descending order by the values in the SALARY field, for example, move the salary field to the ordering criteria list box and select the Descending radio button (see Figure 9.16).

Multiple ordering criteria can be specified as well. If the Salesman database were much larger, for instance, there easily could be a number of salespeople with the same last names. In this case, we would want the records to be ordered by last name and, for those records with the same last name, by first name as well. To specify multiple ordering criteria in this way, first decide which fields will determine the order of the report; then choose them in the Selected Output list box and select the Move push button to move them to the Ordering Criteria list box.

As was the case in the Selected Output list box in the RQBE Select Fields dialog, the order in which field names appear in the Ordering Criteria list box determines

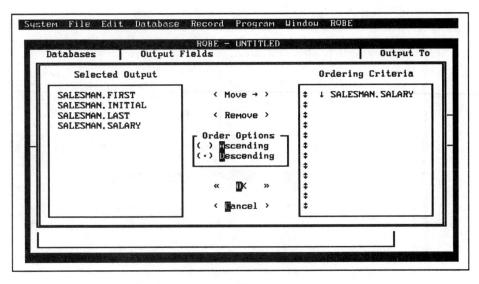

**Figure 9.16  Ordering Resulting Records**

their sequence returned by the query. This order can be changed by selecting a field name and either pressing CTRL-PgUp or CTRL-PgDn on the keyboard or clicking and dragging the adjacent double arrow with the mouse until the field is in the proper position.

If you do not specify order for the output records, FoxPro will return the records in the order in which they are stored in the database file or in the order determined by the master index active at the time the query executes. Of course, if you expect the query operation to return only one record, you do not have to select Order By... check box.

## Defining Selection Criteria

The most important step in creating a RQBE query is to define its selection criteria. The lower half of the RQBE window is provided for this. Its basic purpose is to allow you to create queries that are more English than "computerese." To specify selection criteria, select an item of information from your database (usually a field) and then provide an example of a value that would qualify that record for inclusion in the query.

To find the record belonging to salesperson Davidson, for example, you would specify the following selection criterion:

```
Field Name   Comparison Operator   Example (Criterion Value)
LAST         Exactly Like          Davidson
```

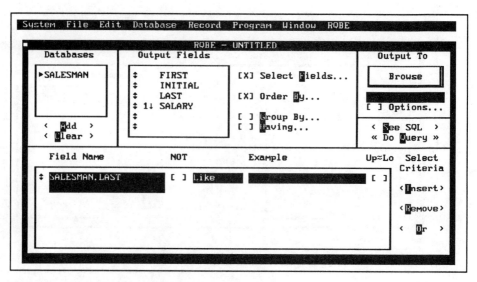

**Figure 9.17   Selecting the Query Data Field**

Then, to enter such a selection criterion, first choose the data field from the list of fields associated with the current database file. If you are using the mouse, click the button on the Field Name popup and select the field you want. With the keyboard, use the Tab key to open the Field Name popup and then select the field accordingly. Besides selecting a field, you also can create an expression by selecting <expression...> from the popup and using the Expression Builder. As an exercise, select the LAST data field from the Field Name popup (see Figure 9.17).

This figure shows that as soon as a field is entered into the Field Name text box, the default—Like—comparison operator appears. To use another comparison operator, select a different one from the comparison popup. FoxPro's RQBE window offers the following comparison operators:

- *Like.* A record will be selected if its field or expression matches the example. To select all salespeople whose last names begin with "D," for example, define the selection criterion as:

  ```
  Salesman.Last      Like      D
  ```

- *Exactly Like.* A record will be selected if its field or expression exactly matches the example, character for character.

- *More Than.* A record will be selected if its field or expression is greater than the example. If the field is a character string, this means that it follows the example in alphabetical order.

- *Less Than.* A record will be selected if its field or expression is less than the example. If the field is a character string, this means that it precedes the example in alphabetical order.

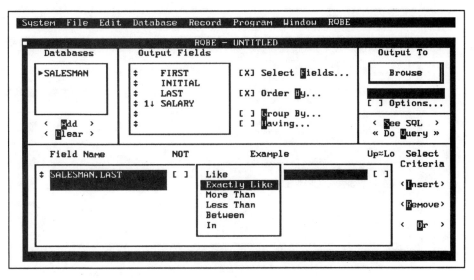

**Figure 9.18 Selecting Comparison Type**

- *Between.* A record will be selected if it falls between a range of values. To select all salespeople whose last names begin with the letters C, D, E, F, and G, for example, define the selection criterion as:

```
SALESMAN.LAST    BETWEEN    C,G
```

- *In.* A record will be selected if its field value is included in a list of example values. For example, to select salespeople whose last names begin with A, C, and G, define the selection criterion as:

```
SALESMAN.LAST    IN    A,C,G
```

(These options will be discussed in greater detail later in this chapter in the section, "More on Selection Criteria.") In this case, because you want to find the record belonging to salesperson Davidson, select Exactly Like as the comparison operator (see Figure 9.18).

Finally, enter the criterion value in the Example text box. If the criterion value is a string of characters (including spaces), just enter the character string (e.g., Davidson) without enclosing it in quotes (see Figure 9.19). If, however, the character string includes commas, it must be enclosed in quotes to avoid confusion because a comma is used to separate two characters strings when you choose the Between or In comparison operator in a selection criterion.

## EXECUTING RQBE QUERIES

After you have specified all the query settings and defined the selection criteria, you are ready to execute the query operation. To do that, select the <Do Query>

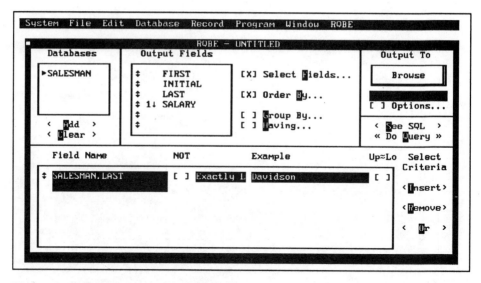

**Figure 9.19   Specifying Criterion Value**

push button. FoxPro then searches through the records in SALESMAN.DBF and finds the records that meet the selection criteria you have specified. They are then sent to the destination selected. Here, Browse was chosen as the destination for the query results, so FoxPro displays the selected records in a Browse window (see Figure 9.20).

If you want to return to the RQBE window to perform other operations after you have viewed the query results, close the Query Browse window by pressing the

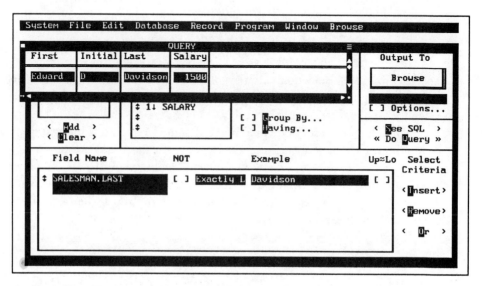

**Figure 9.20   Showing the Record Selected by the Query**

Esc key. If you are using a mouse, either click the button on the Close control or anywhere visible in the RQBE window. Once the window is closed, the results of the query are lost. In order to retrieve those same records, you must run the query again.

## SAVING THE CURRENT QUERY TO A FILE

To terminate the query operation, close the RQBE window. But, if you expect to repeat the current query at a later date, you should save all the query settings and selection criteria in a permanent query file by selecting the Save as... option from the File menu popup. In return, you will be asked to assign a name (e.g., DAVID-SON) to the query file (see Figure 9.21). Note that FoxPro automatically assigns a .QPR file extension to your query unless you explicitly specify some other file extension.

Notice in Figure 9.21 that the file list box shows a query file named UN-TITLED.QPR. FoxPro uses this query file to *temporarily* hold the settings and selection criteria for the current query. If you exit from RQBE without saving the query to a permanent file, the UNTITLED.QPR temporary file will be closed and all information about the query will be lost. Therefore, you must save the query to a permanent query file if you plan to repeat the same query at a later date. Once you have done this you can exit from the RQBE window by pressing the Esc key or by clicking the mouse on the Close control.

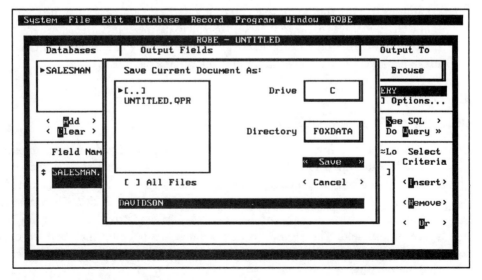

**Figure 9.21  Naming a Query File**

## REPEATING AN EXISTING QUERY

To repeat the query about salesperson Davidson, simply recall the DAVID-SON.QPR query file by selecting the Open... option from the File menu popup. When the Open file dialog appears, select Query in the Type popup and then open DAVIDSON.QPR accordingly. As a result, you will return to the RQBE window and the query settings and selection criteria previously saved will be intact. You can then carry out the query as if you had created it anew.

## MODIFYING EXISTING QUERIES

If you need to change the query settings and selection criteria for an existing query, bring it up in the RQBE window by opening its associated query file. When the RQBE window appears, make all the necessary changes to the query.

As an exercise, recall the DAVIDSON.QPR to explore ways of using different comparison operators in defining selection criteria.

## MORE ON SELECTION CRITERIA

Working interactively with FoxPro to query a database can be frustrating if you do not have a basic working knowledge of how FoxPro searches a database. Such factors as the EXACT setting or how FoxPro handles case are factors that must always be considered when searching a database. In contrast, a major strength of RQBE is that it allows you to select the records that interest you by specifying conditions that are more intuitive and easily understandable. But at the same time that RQBE attempts to make it easier for you to define selection criteria, its use of the comparison operators and pattern symbols that we will examine in this section make it a flexible and powerful tool for querying a database.

### Using the Like Comparison Operator

In one of the previous exercises Exactly Like was selected as the comparison operator with which to define the selection criteria. In that case, a record was selected if and only if the character string in the LAST field exactly matched the example character string "Davidson." Exactly Like requires that every character in the field string matches that of the example character string, including any blank spaces in the field. Therefore, it is obvious that this operator may be used only if you know precisely what the character string looks like; otherwise, FoxPro cannot find the records.

If you cannot recall exactly the makeup of a character string, the Like operator can be used to find a partial match. Thus, you can find Davidson in the LAST field if you use any one of the following examples:

```
Field Name        Operator   Example
SALESMAN.LAST     Like       David
```

or

```
SALESMAN.LAST     Like       Davids
```

or

```
SALESMAN.LAST     Like       Dav
```

FoxPro will select the records as long as the character string specified in the example matches the first set of characters in the query field. Similarly, if you specify "111-" as the example string for searching the values in the SS_NO data field, you would find all the social security numbers beginning with 111- (see Figure 9.22).

### Ignoring Case

Ordinarily, RQBE is sensitive to case when comparing example strings with character fields. So, in our original example, defining a selection criterion such as

```
SALESMAN.LAST        LIKE        DA
```

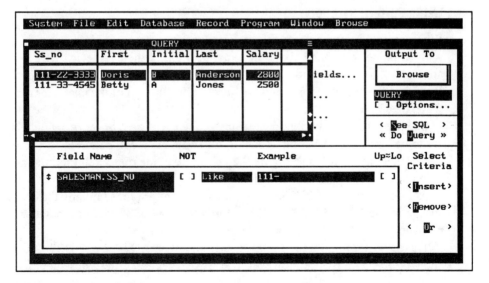

**Figure 9.22  Results from Using the Like Operator**

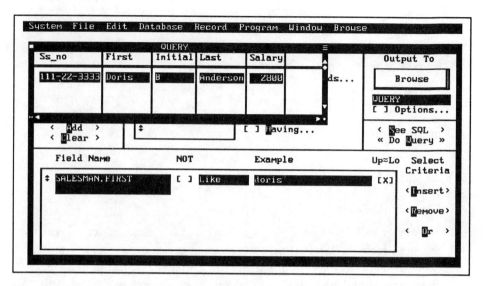

**Figure 9.23  Ignoring Case in Searching Character Strings**

would not have returned any records. If you do not remember whether a character string is in upper- or lowercase letters, select the Up=Lo check box to direct FoxPro to search the field strings while ignoring case. Then the salesperson whose first name is Doris can be found by using 'doris' as the example string in the selection criterion (see Figure 9.23).

### Using Pattern Symbols

When searching character strings it is often helpful to specify a certain pattern without being concerned about the exact position of the character string that you are looking for. For example, to find all the salespeople whose last names end with 'son', use the percent (%) symbol to describe the pattern of the character string as %son (see Figure 9.24).

Use the percent symbol to denote any sequence of zero or more characters that are to be ignored in the comparison. In this way, the %son pattern selects any last names that end with 'son'. Figure 9.24 shows that the query returned the records belonging to Anderson and Davidson.

As another example, if %333% is used as the pattern for searching the character strings in the SS_No field, all the records having "333" in their social security numbers would be returned (see Figure 9.25).

The query returned three social security numbers: 111-22-3333, 333-56-4545, and 444-56-3333. Notice, however, that if the selection criterion is specified as

    SALESMAN.SS_NO   Like   %333

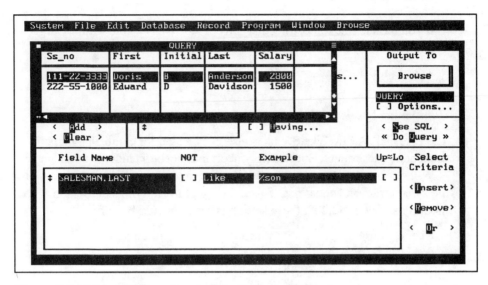

**Figure 9.24  Using Pattern Symbols in Selection Criteria**

FoxPro will return only two records—those belonging to Doris Anderson and Albert Iverson. Hence, the percent sign serves as a substitution or wild card symbol for any number of characters at one end of the string only. So, to search for a string located at the end of a field, the pattern should be specified as:

```
%<string>
```

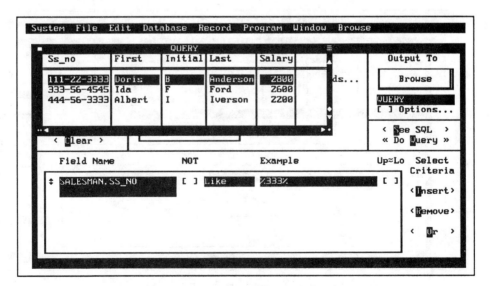

**Figure 9.25  Second Example Using Pattern Symbols**

If you want to find a substring that can be located anywhere within a larger string, you must specify the search pattern as

```
%<string>%
```

### Comparing Numeric Values

The Like and Exactly Like operators also can be used for comparing numeric values, dates, and logical values. But pattern symbols may not be included in the example value.

When comparing numeric values, the Like and Exactly Like operators produce the same effect as "equal to." This means that to find the salesperson who has a monthly salary of $2,200, the selection criterion would be defined as:

```
Field Name              Operator        Example
SALESMAN.SALARY         Like            2200
```

or

```
SALESMAN.SALARY         Exactly Like    2200
```

and both of these selection criteria would return the same records (see Figure 9.26).

### Comparing Dates

In a similar fashion, the Like and Exactly Like operators may be incorporated to compare dates in selection criteria, such as to find the records belonging to those

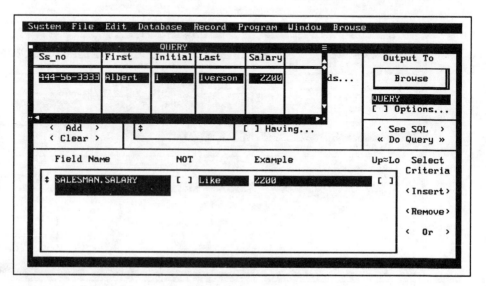

**Figure 9.26  Comparing Numeric Values**

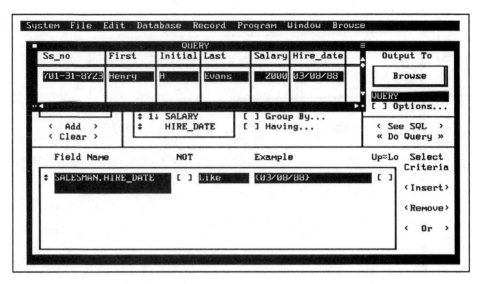

**Figure 9.27  Comparing Dates**

salespeople who were hired on a certain date (see Figure 9.27). Remember that the date value must be enclosed in braces in the selection criterion (e.g., {03/08/88}).

### Comparing Logical Values

When comparing logical values in selection criteria, periods must be included for defining the values. To find information about the female sales staff, for instance, define .F. as the example value in the selection criterion. You may use either the Like or Exactly Like operator for comparing the example value with that in the MALE logical data field (see Figure 9.28). This figure shows that the query returned all the records belonging to sales*women* in the Browse window.

## Using the NOT Operator

To reverse the result of a given comparison, select the NOT check box. In this case, to find information about all the male sales staff, define the selection criterion as:

```
Field Name          Operator          Example
SALESMAN.MALE       Like              .T.
```

Selecting the NOT check box reverses the comparison. In Figure 9.29, for example, you are searching for all records that do not have a false value in the MALE field—in other words, for all records belonging to males.

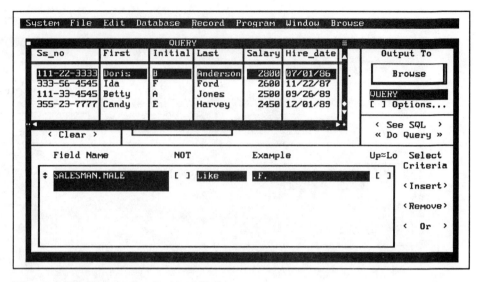

**Figure 9.28  Comparing Logical Values**

The NOT operator can be used with other data types as well. When combined with the pattern symbols and the various comparison operators provided by RQBE, it allows you to define some very precise and powerful queries.  For example, if you are interested in salary extremes—those employees at both the low end and the high end of the salary scale—you could combine the NOT operator and the

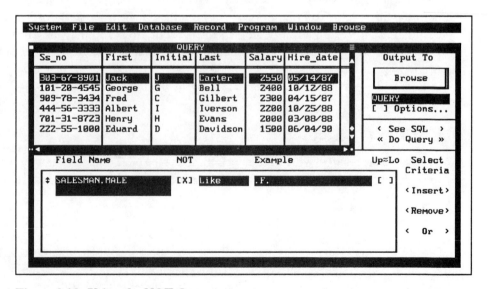

**Figure 9.29  Using the NOT Operator**

BETWEEN comparison operator (which we will discuss later in this section) to formulate your selection criteria as:

```
Field Name              NOT            Example
SALESMAN.SALARY          X    BETWEEN  2000,2500
```

## Using the More Than/Less Than Operator

When selecting records using numeric values it is often useful to set the maximum or the minimum value as the query criterion. Therefore, to find information about those salespeople who are making a certain minimum amount as their monthly salaries, use the More Than operator in the selection criterion for the query operation (See Figure 9.30).

The selection criterion in this figure instructs FoxPro to accept any records that have a value greater than $2,500 in the SALARY field. As a result, it returned three records. It is important to note that the More Than operator did not select the record belonging to Betty Jones whose salary is equal to $2,500. If you would like to include the minimum value, you could use the NOT and Less Than operators jointly in the selection criterion (see Figure 9.31). You can see in this figure that the record having 2500 in the SALARY field was chosen by the NOT Less Than selection criterion. (This selection criterion also could be expressed as SALESMAN.SALARY Greater Than 2499.)

More Than and Less Than can be used for evaluating character strings as well. For example, if you want to find all the last names that begin with C through Z you

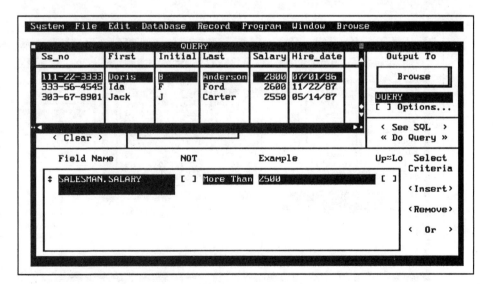

**Figure 9.30  Using the More Than Operator**

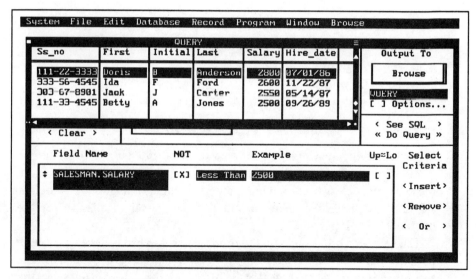

**Figure 9.31   Using the NOT Less Than Operator**

would define the selection criteria as shown in Figure 9.32. (Alternately, it could be defined as SALESMAN.LAST Greater Than B.)

Similarly, the More Than and Less Than operators may be used for comparing dates in selection criteria. When the More Than operator is used, FoxPro selects the dates that are one day or more after the example date. So, to find information about salespeople who were hired after March 7, 1988, define {03/07/88} as the example date in the selection criterion (see Figure 9.33).

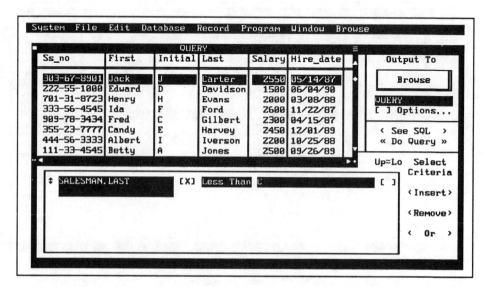

**Figure 9.32   Using NOT Less Than for Selecting Character Strings**

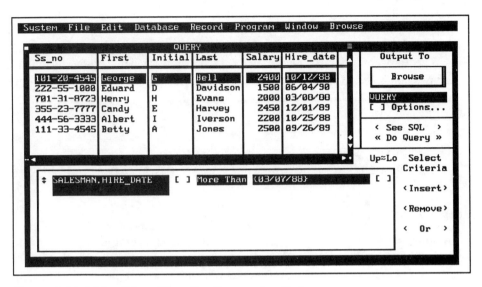

**Figure 9.33  Using More Than for Comparing Dates**

## Using the Between Operator

To retrieve records with field values that are within a given range, use the Between operator. When this operator is used, the lower and upper limits that cover the range must be specified. Therefore, to find the salary values that fall in the range $2,200-$2,600, identify in the selection criterion the lower and upper limits as two example values separated by a comma (see Figure 9.34).

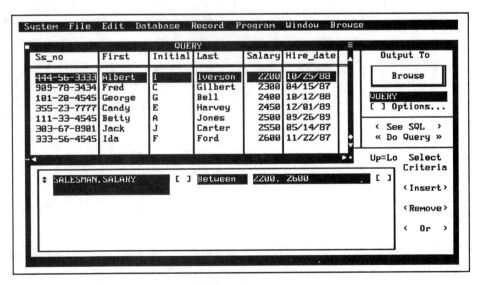

**Figure 9.34  Using the Between Operator**

Notice that the query returned all the salaries between $2,200 and $2,600 and included the two end values (e.g., 2200 and 2600).

The Between operator also may be incorporated when comparing character strings and dates. Here are examples of such selection criteria using the Between operator:

| Field Name | Operator | Example |
|---|---|---|
| SALESMAN.LAST | Between | C, G |
| SALESMAN.HIRE_DATE | Between | {01/01/88}, {12/31/88} |

## Using the In Operator

As discussed, when using the Like and Exactly Like operators, a *single* example value is specified in selection criteria; the Between operator requires that limits for a *range* of values be set. But, to find records with a *set* of individual values, the In operator is chosen. To find those salespeople whose first names are Doris, George, and Betty, for instance, specify those first names in the selection criterion as shown in Figure 9.35.

This operator is also used to locate dates and numerical values as detailed in these examples:

| Field Name | Operator | Example |
|---|---|---|
| SALESMAN.SALARY | In | 2200, 2500, 2550, 2400 |
| SALESMAN.HIRE_DATE | In | {05/14/87}, {09/26/89} |

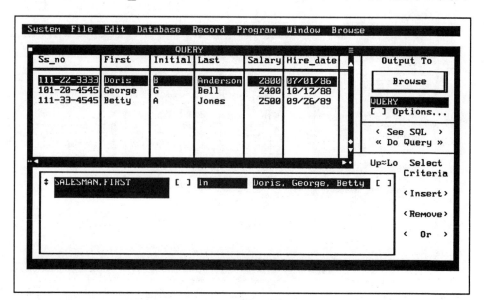

**Figure 9.35  Using the In Operator**

## Using Formulas in Selection Criteria

In addition to using data fields in selection criteria, a formula may be included to define conditions. To find those salespeople who have been with the company for more than three years (say, 1095 days), the criterion would read:

| Field Name | Operator | Example |
|---|---|---|
| {10/25/91} - SALESMAN.HIRE_DATE | More Than | 1095 |

In this criterion, the formula {10/25/91} - HIRE_DATE returns the number of days between the two dates specified. If the current date is October 25, 1991, the formula calculates and returns the number of days since the HIRE_DATE. As a result, the query returns all the hire dates that occurred more than 1095 days (three years) from the current date. To specify the formula, select the <expression...> text button from the Field Name popup (see Figure 9.36).

When the Expression Builder appears, enter the formula in the text box as the selection expression. Note: If you are querying from more than one database when entering a data field, it is best to include the name of the database as the prefix, such as salesman.hire_date. If you are querying from only one database, however, you do not have to include the prefix; there would be no question as to which database you are referring. When more than one database is involved in the query, the prefix identifies which is currently being used. This is especially important if an identical field name appears in more than one database.

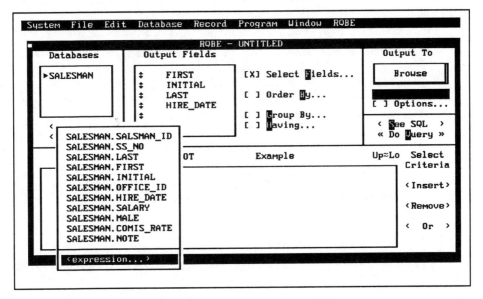

**Figure 9.36  Selecting Expression From Field Name Popup**

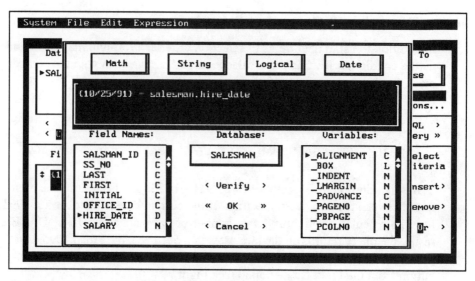

**Figure 9.37   Entering a Formula as Selection Criterion**

When you return to the RQBE window, finish defining the selection criterion by adding the comparison operator and the example value (see Figure 9.37). When executed, the query returns all the records belonging to salespeople who were hired more than three years ago (see Figure 9.38). This figure also shows that the records returned by the query include hire dates that occurred more than three years prior to the present date ({10/25/91}).

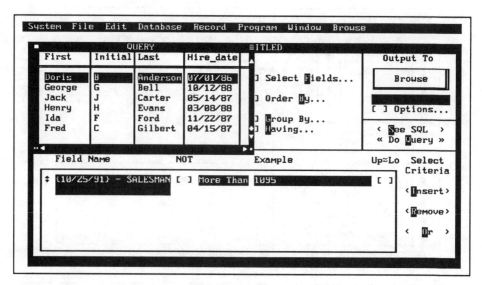

**Figure 9.38   Records Resulting from the Query**

## Using Functions in Selection Criteria

Any of FoxPro's many functions may be included in a formula that is part of a selection criterion. In previous chapters you became familiar with functions such as AVG( ), MAX( ), MIN( ), SUM ( ), and DATE( ) that returned summary statistics. As an exercise of how functions are used here, include DATE( ) in the selection criterion. When the function is executed, it returns the current system date. You do not have to specify an argument in the parentheses. The selection criterion should look like this:

```
Field Name                          Operator        Example

DATE() - SALESMAN.HIRE_DATE         More Than        1095
```

The DATE( ) function is used to replace the current date, in this case, {10/25/91}. When you carry out the query with this selection criterion it will always return the records of employees who have been employed for more than three years (assuming that the computer's system date is correct).

## Specifying Compound Selection Criteria

In all of the preceding examples we used a single selection criterion for selecting records. Each criterion had only one search condition involving one data field. Although many data query operations require only simple selection criteria, other data search tasks may need compound criteria, which in turn require more than one search condition involving multiple data fields in one or more database files.

### Defining Joint Search Conditions

Compound selection criteria instruct the query operation to find records that satisfy *all* the specified conditions simultaneously. If you want to find those female members of the sales staff who are earning a monthly salary of more than $2,500, for instance, specify the following conditions in the selection criteria for the query operations:

```
Field Name              Operator        Example

SALESMAN.MALE           Like            .F.
```

and

```
SALESMAN.SALARY         More Than        2500
```

To find the same information with a RQBE query, enter these two conditions jointly in the selection criteria (see Figure 9.39).

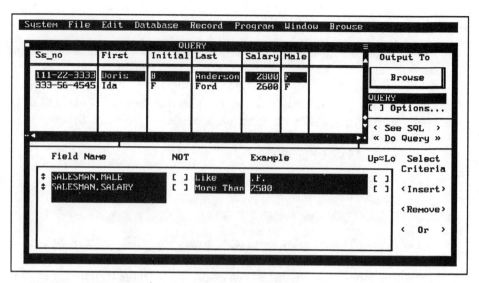

**Figure 9.39  Defining Joint Search Conditions**

This figure shows that these two search conditions were entered on two separate lines in the selection criteria text box. If you need more than two conditions, you may continue entering additional conditions on subsequent lines. The query operation will select only those records that satisfy all the joint conditions. The query in Figure 9.39 returned two records that met the conditions specified in the selection criteria, i.e., records belonging to those salespeople who are female and earn a monthly salary of more than $2,500.

## Using the OR Logical Connector

In the preceding example, records that met a set of multiple conditions simultaneously were retrieved. Sometimes, however, you may be interested in finding records that meet at least one of the conditions specified in the selection criteria. To do that, use the OR logical connector to link the conditions in the criteria. Then, you can find those salespeople who are either female or who earn a monthly salary or more than $2,500. In a case such as this, enter the two conditions that are connected by OR in the selection criteria (see Figure 9.40). The two conditions that occupied a separate line in the selection criteria box are linked by the OR connector.

You can either enter the OR line at the cursor position by selecting the <Or> push button; or move it up and down by using the mouse or keyboard. If you are using the mouse, click on the double-headed arrow to the left of the line containing OR and then drag it to its new position. With the keyboard, use the Tab and arrow

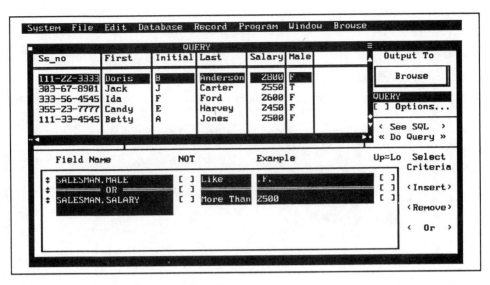

**Figure 9.40  Using the OR Logical Connector**

keys to highlight the line and then press the Ctrl-PgUp or Ctrl-PgDn key combinations to move it to its new position.

When two conditions are joined by OR, the query operation returns those records that meet any one or both of these conditions. You can see in Figure 9.41 that the query selected four records, each of which satisfied at least one of the two search conditions specified. As is true of the AND connector, if there are more than two conditions, continue inputting the additional conditions on subsequent lines. When you execute the query, FoxPro will return all records that meet any of these conditions.

For more complex selection criteria, define multiple joint search conditions (i.e., search conditions joined by an AND connector) that are then connected by one or more OR connectors as shown in Figure 9.41. In this example the selection criteria includes three search conditions. The query operation will select those records that satisfy either the first two joint conditions or the third condition. This query returned four records belonging to the salespeople who are either female and earn more than $2,500 per month, or who were hired prior to December 12, 1987.

In general, regardless of the number of conditions you specify, FoxPro will evaluate conditions linked by the AND connector before it evaluates conditions linked by OR.

## Using Multiple Database Files in RQBE Queries

One of the most powerful features of RQBE is its capability to join several database files so that you can locate information from more than one database file in the

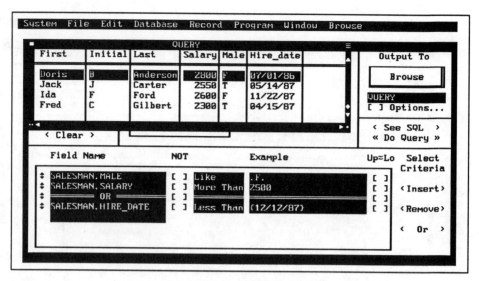

**Figure 9.41   An Example of Multiple Search Conditions**

same query. As a result, you are able to query data from any data field in the joined database files as if they were in the *same* database file.

In our sample database files, information about a fictional sales staff was stored in SALESMAN.DBF. Information about their sales offices was saved in another database file, OFFICE.DBF. The SALESMAN file includes OFFICE_ID as a foreign field, which can be used as a link to OFFICE.DBF. Because these two databases can be linked, you are able to extract information from them with a RQBE query. Therefore, by linking SALESMAN.DBF and OFFICE.DBF in a query, you can find out information about a salesperson (e.g., Davidson) and his sales office at the same time.

To create such a query, first open the first database file, SALESMAN.DBF, in current work area A. Then select the New option from the File menu popup and select Query as the file type to bring up the RQBE window. As the RQBE window appears, note that SALESMAN.DBF is selected as the database for the query operation. Now join it with the second database file, OFFICE.DBF, by selecting the <Add> text button. When the Database Selection dialog appears, open the OFFICE.DBF database file from the database popup (see Figure 9.42).

In return, you will be asked in the RQBE Join Condition dialog to specify the join condition for linking OFFICE.DBF to SALESMAN.DBF. The join condition involves identifying the linking field that is common to the two files. From the left popup, select the linking field (OFFICE_ID) from the database file (OFFICE.DBF) that is being added to the query. From the right popup, select the linking field (OFFICE_ID) from the database file (SALESMAN.DBF) that you are linking. In the dialog is a third popup. This middle popup is for selecting a comparison operator

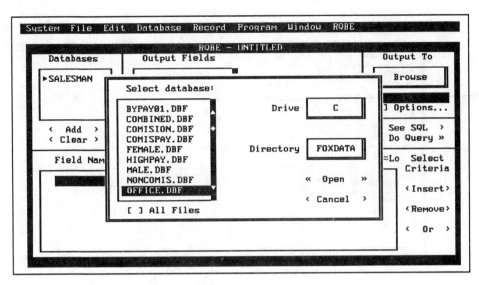

**Figure 9.42  Adding a Database File to the Query**

from FoxPro's choices of Like, Exactly Like, More Than, Less Than, Between, and In. Most join operations require either the Like or Exactly Like operator (see Figure 9.43).

After defining the join condition, return to the RQBE window by selecting the <<OK>> push button. Once you are back in the RQBE window, note that the join condition is displayed as a part of the selection criterion and is indicated by a

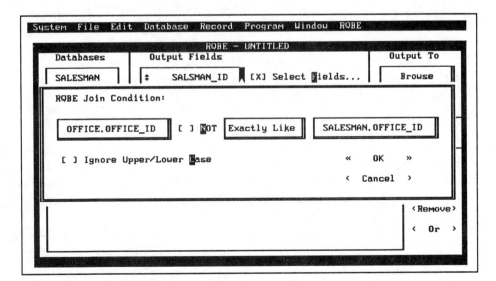

**Figure 9.43  Defining the Join Condition**

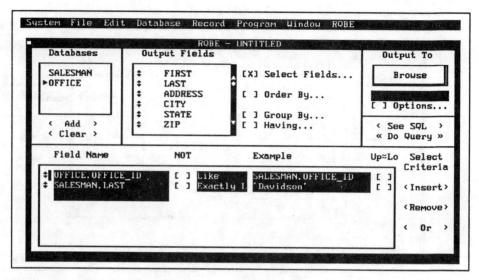

**Figure 9.44  The Join Condition in the Selection Criteria**

vertical bar to the left of the field name (see Figure 9.44). You now can add any search condition to the selection criterion. If, for example, you want to find out information about salesperson Davidson and his sales office, search the database by last name, looking for a match with "Davidson" as shown in Figure 9.44.

At this point, select the data fields from the joined database file for your output. To do that, select the Select Fields... check box. When you are in the Field Selection dialog, you may select any fields from the two database files. For example, you can select the FIRST and LAST fields from SALESMAN.DBF, and the AD-DRESS, CITY, STATE, ZIP, and PHONE_NO fields from OFFICE.DBF (see Figure 9.45).

After selecting the output destination (e.g., Browse), carry out the query operation by selecting the <Do Query> push button. As a result, the query returns the records from the joined database files that satisfy the selection criteria (see Figure 9.46).

This figure shows that the query returned data fields extracted from SALES-MAN.DBF and OFFICE.DBF. The FIRST and LAST fields are from SALES-MAN.DBF and the rest are from the OFFICE database file. The query first found the record with "Davidson" in the LAST field in the Salesman database, then it used the value in the linking field (e.g.,"B1") to find the associated record for the New York office in the OFFICE file.

As another exercise, join SALESMAN.DBF and OFFICE.DBF in the query to find all salespeople who are either in the New York or Chicago sales offices (see Figure 9.47).

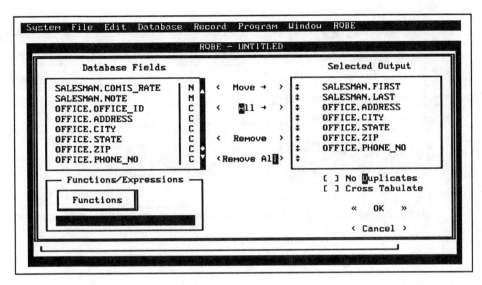

**Figure 9.45  Selecting Fields from Joined Database Files**

In Figure 9.47 two selection criteria are joined by the OR connector. As a result, the query returned all salespeople belonging to either the New York or Chicago sales offices. The first two fields were extracted from OFFICE.DBF; the rest were taken from the SALESMAN database file.

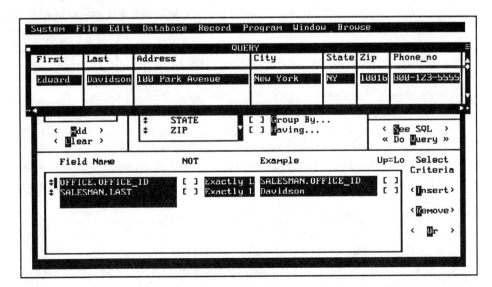

**Figure 9.46  Record Returned by the Query**

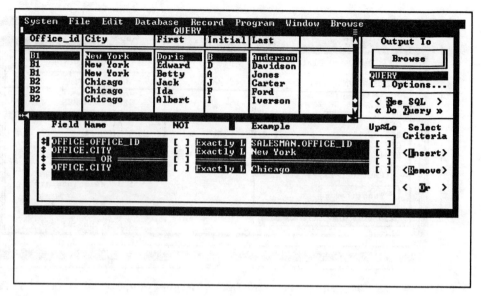

**Figure 9.47  Extracting Information from Joined Database Files**

## DISPLAYING CALCULATED DATA FIELDS

The output from a query operation usually consists of data fields existing in the database files used. But a query also can be instructed to calculate values that are based on the existing data fields and functions. To do that, incorporate a formula when defining an output field. Let's assume, for instance, that you want to examine the monthly withholding taxes deducted from the sales staff's pay, and that these taxes total 20 percent of their monthly salaries. The following formula would be used to define the output field:

```
SALESMAN.SALARY * 0.2
```

To enter this formula as an output field, select the Select Fields check box from the RQBE window. When FoxPro displays the RQBE Select Fields dialog, simply enter the formula in the Functions/Expressions text box. Then select the Move text button to move the formula to the Selected Output list box (see Figure 9.48).

After defining the output fields, add the necessary selection criteria to the query. When the query is executed, the value of the output field is calculated according to the formula (see Figure 9.49).

The calculated field is labeled automatically by FoxPro as Exp_6, indicating that it is the sixth field in the output and was the result of evaluating an expression (formula). You cannot specify a custom label for the output field in the query, so if you want to display the calculated field with a more descriptive label, you must

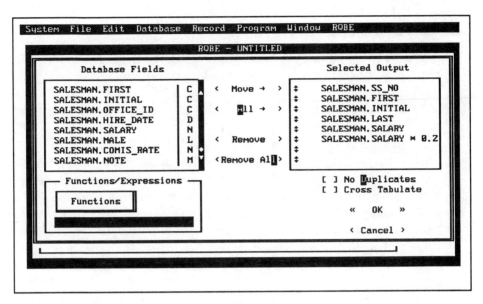

**Figure 9.48  Using a Calculated Output Field**

manipulate the output outside the query operation. One way to do this is to present the query results in a report in which custom labels can be assigned to all the data fields. (This topic is covered thoroughly in the next chapter.) Alternatively, you may save the query results in a database file and then rename the calculated fields in the data structure.

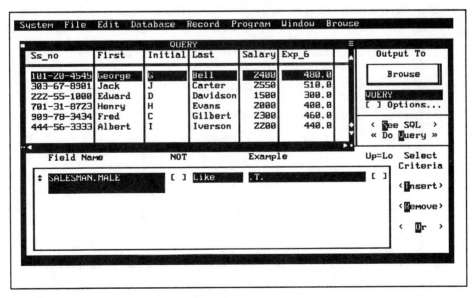

**Figure 9.49  Results of Using a Formula in an Output Field**

## DISPLAYING SUMMARY STATISTICS

Because FoxPro allows you to use functions in an expression and to define the result of that expression as an output field, you can produce summary statistics from the values of particular database fields. Thus, you can use the AVG(SALES-MAN.SALARY) function to calculate and display the average salary for all or some of the sales staff.

By allowing us to define a calculated field that will display a summary statistic, FoxPro substantially enhances our flexibility in generating queries of various kinds. All of the sample queries generated so far have been record-oriented; that is, they have returned a set of records that meet some selection criteria. In working with summary statistics, in contrast, we are no longer interested in the contents of individual records; indeed, all individual fields should be removed from the Selected Output list box in the RQBE Select Fields dialog because we are exclusively interested in generating a single figure that characterizes a set of records.

To generate such a summary query, define an output field with a function as an expression. Enter the function directly into the Functions/Expressions text box in the Select Fields dialog, which is accessed by selecting the Select Fields check box in the RQBE window. Alternatively, select the AVG( ) function from the Functions popup, followed by highlighting the numeric field (e.g., SALESMAN.SALARY) as the function argument (see Figure 9.50).

After highlighting the function argument, select it by pressing either the Enter key or by double clicking on the mouse. The function selected appears in the

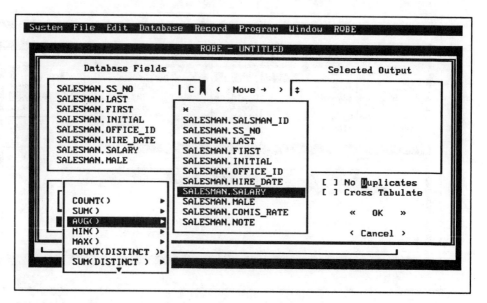

**Figure 9.50  Selecting a Function from Functions Popup**

Functions/Expressions text box. Then add it to the selected output field list by selecting the <Move> push button.

If there is the possibility of duplicate records in the database (i.e., records with identical values in every field), you should decide whether or not to exclude the duplicate values from the calculation of summary statistics. Do this by selecting the version of the appropriate function that contains DISTINCT as an argument. In this example, select AVG(DISTINCT). When the query operation is executed, it calculates the average salary from the selected records and displays it in a calculated field (see Figure 9.51).

Notice that the query returned only one record in the calculated field, Avg_salary. The calculated value (e.g., 2158.33) was computed from the values of all the records in the SALARY field belonging to the male sales staff.

Multiple output fields containing functions can be used to display several summary statistics. To find out the salary range for the male sales staff, for example, use MAX( ) and MIN( ) as the output fields to display the highest and lowest salary values. Use the COUNT( ) function to determine the number of records selected by the query; use SUM( ) to total the values in an existing or calculated field. Several kinds of summary statistics are shown in Figure 9.52. This figure shows that the query returned summary statistics that were calculated with the following functions in the output fields:

| *Output Field* | *Functions used in the Expression* |
| --- | --- |
| Cnt | COUNT(SALESMAN.SALARY) |
| Min_salary | MIN(SALESMAN.SALARY) |
| Max_salary | MAX(SALESMAN.SALARY) |
| Exp_4 | MAX(SALESMAN.SALARY) - MIN(SALESMAN.SALARY) |
| Sum_salary | SUM(SALESMAN.SALARY) |
| Avg_salary | AVG(SALESMAN.SALARY) |

The output field labeled as Exp_4 and representing the salary range was calculated by taking the difference between the maximum salary and the minimum salary. Note that the returned records belong only to male salespeople as a result of the selection criteria specified. If you later need to display the summary statistics for the female group, carry out a similar query by changing the selection criteria to SALESMAN.MALE Like .F. or by selecting the NOT check box.

## PRODUCING GROUP SUMMARY STATISTICS

It is possible to produce separate sets of summary statistics, each of which is calculated by using a specific group of records selected by the query. To do that, group the records in the database file according to a specified criterion. You can group the records in SALESMAN.DBF by the values in the MALE field and then

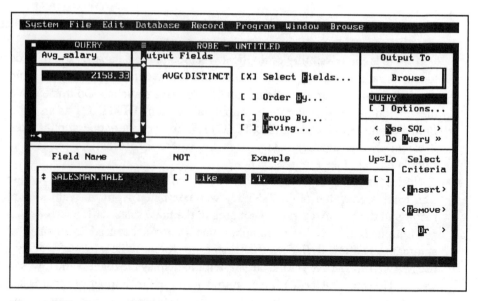

**Figure 9.51  Average Salary**

produce summary statistics for each of the two groups, for example. As a result, you are able to compare the summary statistics between the male and female groups.

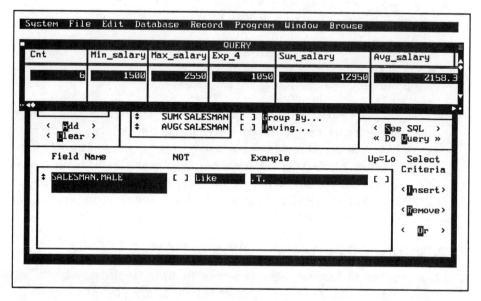

**Figure 9.52  Using Multiple Summary Functions**

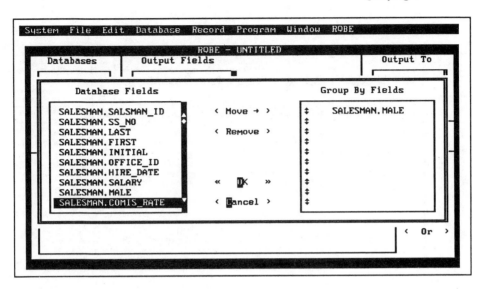

**Figure 9.53   Selecting Grouping Fields**

To divide records into groups for the query operation, select the Group By... check box in the RQBE window. When the Group By Fields picker appears, select the field whose values you want to use to group the records. For example, to divide the sales staff into male and female groups, choose the MALE data field (see Figure 9.53).

You must add the MALE data field to the selected output field list as identification for which set of summary statistics belongs to which group. In addition, because we are now interested in including all records for the two groups in our summary statistics, no selection criteria should be specified. When you execute the query, it will return separate summary statistics that were calculated from the records belonging to the groups of male and female salespeople (see Figure 9.54).

Records were grouped according to their distinct values in the field that was specified for the grouping operation. Because the MALE data field has only two distinct values (.T. and .F.), RQBE provides summary statistics for these two groups. As a result, Figure 9.54 shows that the query returned two records, each showing a set of summary statistics for a given group. The first record shows the number of female salespeople in the field labeled Cnt; the next three fields show their minimum, maximum, and average salaries. Concomitantly, the second record shows all the summary statistics for the male salespeople.

It is also possible to screen the results so as to display only those summary statistics that meet certain requirements. For example, in Figure 9.54 the query returned two average salaries: 2587.50 for the female group and 2158.33 for the

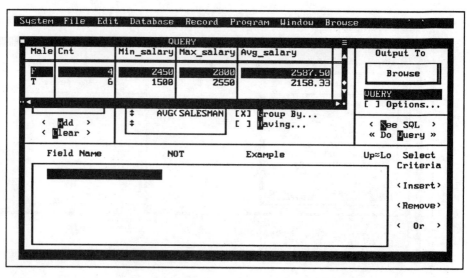

**Figure 9.54  Group Summary Statistics**

male group. You may want to display only the summary statistics for groups with an average salary that is greater than $2,500. To do this, choose the Having... check box to specify the screening conditions for the summary statistics.

In response to checking the Having... box, the Search for Groups Having... dialog box appears. Enter the following condition in the text box provided as shown in Figure 9.55.

| Fields | Operator | Example |
|---|---|---|
| AVG(SALESMAN.SALARY) | More Than | 2500 |

When this query is executed, it returns summary statistics for only those groups whose average salaries are greater than $2,500. As a result, only the summary statistics belonging to the female sales staff are displayed in the query results (see Figure 9.56).

## USING FOXPRO COMMANDS

If you prefer to use commands, you can create a new query by using the FoxPro CREATE QUERY command in the following format:

```
CREATE QUERY <name of the query file>
```

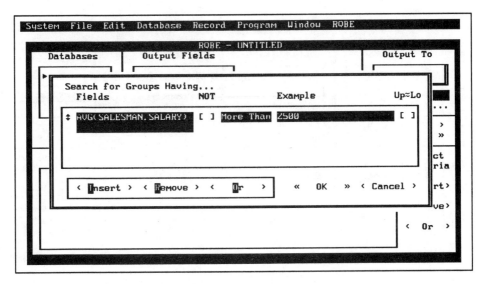

**Figure 9.55   Defining Group Having... Conditions**

After opening the SALESMAN database file in the current work area, issue the following commands to create a new query named SAMPLE.QPR:

```
USE SALESMAN
CREATE QUERY SAMPLE
```

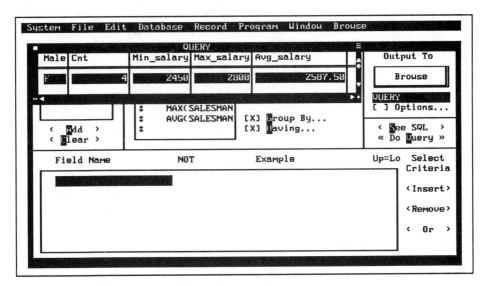

**Figure 9.56  Screened Group Summary Statistics**

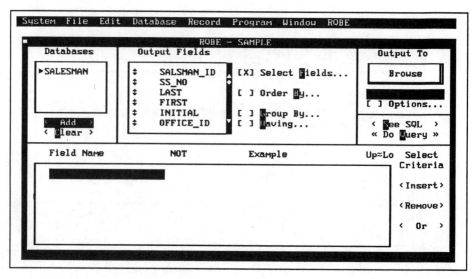

**Figure 9.57   Creating a New Query**

FoxPro opens the RQBE window in which the current database is selected for the query operation (see Figure 9.57). From this point on, continue to specify the query settings, define the query selection criteria, and then execute the query by selecting the <Do Query> push button. Save the query to a file with the procedure defined in the last section.

After saving the query to a query file, it can be recalled for the purpose of repeating the query or for inserting modifications. To do that, issue the MODIFY QUERY command:

```
MODIFY QUERY <name of the query file>
```

In order to recall the query that has been saved in the SAMPLE.QPR file, issue the following command:

```
MODIFY QUERY SAMPLE
```

After the command is executed, FoxPro displays the query in the RQBE window with all the existing settings and selection criteria intact. If necessary, modify the query settings and selection criteria; otherwise, just repeat the existing query.

## QUERYING MEMO FIELDS

Although memo fields provide an efficient means for saving large blocks of text in a database file, you cannot use them in RQBE query operations. Neither can you specify memo fields as a part of selection criteria. Therefore, if you need to find information in memo fields, the Locate operation must be used. So, to find those

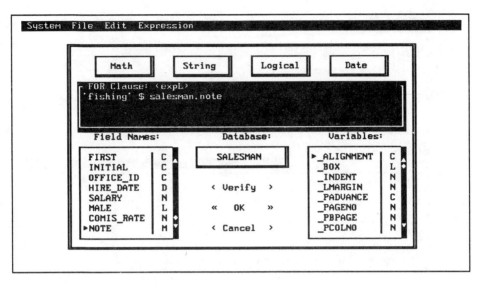

**Figure 9.58    Searching Memo Fields**

salespeople who enjoy fishing, for example, use the following search conditions with the Locate option:

```
FOR 'fishing' $ SALESMAN.NOTE
```

The dollar sign can be interpreted as the "is contained in" operator. FoxPro will search the contents of the memo field SALESMAN.NOTE, which contains all the information about the hobbies of the sales staff. As a result, the condition will be met if the search string 'fishing' is found in any record of the memo field.

Records may be searched in this way by using the menu interface or by issuing the appropriate FoxPro commands. If you select the Locate option from the Record menu popup, define the search condition in the FOR Clause text box (see Figure 9.58). When Locate is executed, FoxPro locates the first record containing a memo field with the search string 'fishing' in it (see Figure 9.59).

The Locate operation also can be invoked by issuing the LOCATE command:

```
CLEAR
USE SALESMAN
LOCATE FOR 'fishing' $ NOTE
```

Once the record is found, it can be displayed in a Browse window for viewing or editing.

It is important to remember that the Locate operation finds only the first record that satisfies the search condition. It does not show any other records that also satisfy the condition. To list *all* the records satisfying the search condition, use the DISPLAY command accompanied by the condition for locating a given string in

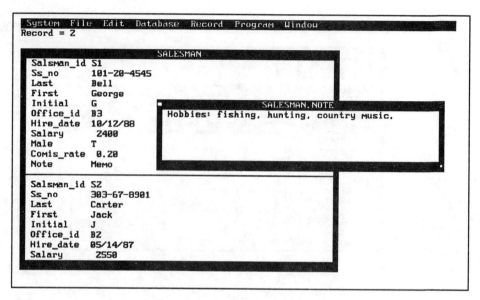

**Figure 9.59   Record Containing Search String**

the memo field. For example, the following DISPLAY command will show the names of all salespeople who list fishing as their hobby:

```
DISPLAY FIRST, LAST, MLINE(NOTE,1) FOR 'fishing' $ NOTE
```

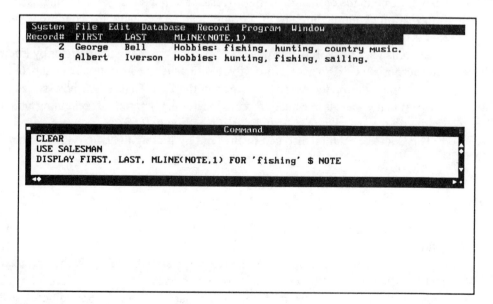

**Figure 9.60   Displaying Contents of Memo Fields**

Remember that MLINE(NOTE,1) is used to display the first line of the memo field, NOTE. When this command is executed, it lists all the records that satisfy the search condition specified in the FOR clause (see Figure 9.60).

# Chapter Summary

This chapter explored the ways in which it is possible to extract useful information from databases. The Locate and Seek operations can be used to find a record that meets certain search conditions. But while Locate allows you to find a record from any database file, to search for a record with the Seek operation, the database file must be indexed on the search expression.

This chapter also detailed how to query data with the powerful RQBE tool. With a RQBE query, you can find a set of records that satisfy a selection criterion that you specify. Your selection criterion can be defined by using data fields which are from one or more database files. In the next chapter you will discover how query results can be displayed on screen, saved to a database file, or used to produce custom reports and labels.

# 10

# Using Memory Variables and Built-in Functions

## An Overview

So far, this book has shown you how to design database files and to access the data that they contain. Frequently, however, your database may not contain the precise information that you need. In some cases, the necessary information must be derived from data stored in the database. Let's assume, for example, that you are interested in the total annual payroll of your sales force. The only information that is available to you in SALESMAN.DBF, however, consists of the monthly salary of each salesperson. In order to obtain the information you need, you must sum the monthly salaries of all salespeople, and multiple that figure by 12.

In other cases, data may not be in the precise format that is needed or desirable. Let's assume that you have decided to store all names in a contact database in uppercase. You now want to create some "personalized" letters, but do not want the letters to look anything like the following:

```
Dear MICHAEL:

     We appreciate your taking the time to call us with your
inquiry. We hope that our customer service department was
```

To create an attractive, personalized form letter, you must convert the contact's first name to a combination of upper- and lowercase letters.

In this chapter, we will examine two features of FoxPro—memory variables and built-in functions—that you can use to extract precisely the kind of information that you want from your database. Although their utility will only become fully

361

apparent to you in later chapters, they enormously increase your flexibility in working with FoxPro databases.

Memory variables are individual data elements that are temporarily stored in the computer's memory rather than in a database file. This makes them ideal for a number of uses, including:

- Temporarily storing intermediate results generated in the course of an application. It might be useful, for example, to sum the total monthly salary of all our salespeople to a memory variable before we multiply it by 12 to derive the total annual salary.
- Retaining summary statistics about your data.
- Passing information from one part of your application to another.

Built-in functions are provided by FoxPro as tools to manipulate data in a wide variety of ways. A function generally takes a particular value—such as the contents of the LAST field in SALESMAN.DBF—and converts it to (or returns) a different value—like an uppercase string. You have already been exposed to several built-in functions, including AVG( ), SUM( ), MAX( ), and MIN( ), that are included in the Expression Builder for defining search and filter conditions. However, FoxPro provides a large number of built-in functions that can be used for such purposes as:

- Generating summary statistics.
- Transforming data for subsequent manipulation.
- Displaying data in a format that you select.

## Memory Variables

Memory variables are individual memory locations that are set aside for holding separate data elements. A memory variable is similar to a data field in many ways: it is used to hold a character string, a numeric value, a date or a logical value; and like a data field, each memory variable is assigned a symbolic name that describes its contents.

There are, however, three major differences between a data field and a memory variable. First, a data field, because it is stored as part of a larger database file, has a definite structure that is defined when the database is created. In contrast, a memory variable, because it is simply stored at a location in memory, does not have a predefined structure. As a result, whereas you must access the correct database and record in order to access the correct element in a data field, memory variables can be accessed independently of one another and of the contents of database files. Second, whereas a data field takes on a different value for each record in the database, a memory variable can take on only a single value at any given time. And finally, a data field is a permanent part of a database file; its contents are stored in a permanent disk file when you close its database or exit from FoxPro. A memory variable, on the other hand, is a temporary location in memory; unless you decide to save a memory variable to a permanent disk file, its contents are erased when you exit from FoxPro.

The contents of a memory variable can be changed. In fact, any time you enter a new data value to the memory variable, its existing contents will be replaced with the new value. Therefore, the same memory variable may be used repeatedly.

Memory variables have many uses. Often they are used to retain intermediate results of data manipulation for later processing. In addition, they are used to pass data values among different data manipulation operations. You may also include memory variables in expressions to define search conditions and selection criteria for data manipulation operations. For example, a character string that you locate in a data field can be stored in a memory variable and used in the FOR clause for defining a search condition.

Another important use of memory variables is to pass values to custom reports. Summary statistics that are computed and held in memory variables enable you to produce more versatile reports. You could, for example, produce a salary summary report that shows the salaries of individual salespeople as percentages of the total salary. To do so, however, requires a two-pass process. First, you must compute the total salary by adding up all the individual salaries; then you must compute the percentages by dividing the salary values by the total. This is where the value of using a memory variable becomes obvious. Because the report generator allows only a single-pass process, you can pass the salary total as a memory variable to the report before the process begins. The salary total can be computed from the database and saved in a memory variable prior to bringing up the report generator. Once you are in the report generator, you can access the memory variable accordingly.

## TYPES OF MEMORY VARIABLES

There are different types of memory variables available for use in FoxPro. The commonly used ones are character, numeric, date, and logical. A character memory variable holds character strings, a numeric memory variable saves values that can be integers or decimal numbers, date memory variables store dates, and logical memory variables hold logical values in the form of .T. or .F. Be aware, however, when building expressions in FoxPro, you cannot mix different types of memory variables and data fields in the same expression.

As already stated, every memory variable is identified by a symbolic name. The variable type is determined only by the type of data element you store in it. For example, once you have stored a character string to a memory variable, it becomes a character memory variable. The memory variable remains of that type until you replace its contents with a different type of data element.

## NAMING MEMORY VARIABLES

Like a data field name, a memory variable name can have up to ten characters, which may be a combination of letters, digits, and underscores (_), but the first character of a memory variable *must* be a letter. Although it it not mandatory, for quick reference purposes you are advised to assign descriptive names to your memory variables that will help you identify their contents.

Case is irrelevant in memory variable names, because FoxPro stores them all in uppercase. You may decide, however, to incorporate lowercase letters when naming memory variables to help differentiate them from from data field names that also appear in uppercase. Here are examples of acceptable memory names:

unit_cost
total_wage
avg_salary
net_profit
tax_withld
fullname
invoice_no

When you assign names to memory variables, avoid using words that have been reserved by FoxPro for its commands, functions, and system variables. Do not use such command words as DISPLAY, LIST, TOTAL, MODIFY, etc., to name your variables. You can, however, alter the command names to clarify the difference, calling them NAME_LIST and TOTAL_PAY, for instance. And, instead of using function names such as SUM, AVG, MAX, MIN, change them to read as SUM_VALUE, AVERAGE, MAX_SALARY, or MIN_COST. Also avoid beginning your memory variable names with an underscore (_), because FoxPro names its system variables that way—_PAGENO is a FoxPro system variable that keeps track of the report pages, for example.

Although FoxPro does not prevent you from doing so, you should not name a memory variable with an existing field name. Besides being confusing, only the data field will be recognized if the database file containing the data field is currently selected. When the data field is active, the contents of the memory variable will be ignored. For certain data manipulation operations, however, it is often useful to store in a memory variable the value that is currently in a data field. If this is the case, assign the memory variable a name that is related to the corresponding data field by adding a letter, such as "m" in front of the name. Then **msalary**, for example, would represent the memory variable holding the value in the SALARY data field.

## STORING DATA IN MEMORY VARIABLES

There are two ways to assign a data element to a memory variable, and both require that you issue a FoxPro command; *a memory variable cannot be created by using FoxPro's menu interface.*

### Using the STORE Command

STORE is one of the two commands that can be invoked to assign a data element to a memory variable. Its format is:

```
STORE <data element TO <memory variable name>
```

The data element can be a character string, a numeric value, a date, or a logical value. The command instructs FoxPro to save the data element in the memory variable specified, which can be a new or an existing one. If it is a new variable name, FoxPro creates a new memory variable and then saves the data element to it accordingly. Otherwise, the data specified in the command element will replace the current contents of the memory variable.

Let's say that you would like to save the string "Hello" in the memory variable named *greeting*. You would issue the following command:

```
STORE 'Hello,' TO greeting
```

Because 'Hello,' is a character string, it must be enclosed in quotation marks. And because a character string is stored to **greeting**, the memory variable becomes a character variable, as defined earlier. Once this command is executed, a memory location is set aside to hold the character string. When this is done, its contents are displayed on the screen for verification.

After you have stored a data element to a memory variable, the contents of the variable is displayed on the screen. This is because, by default, the system setting for TALK is set to ON. If you do not see the value of the memory variable displayed, issue the following command:

```
SET TALK ON
```

On the other hand, if you do not want to see the value of the memory variable displayed after assigning a value to it (and if you do not want the results of a number of other commands displayed on the screen), turn off the TALK setting with the following command:

```
SET TALK OFF
```

In general, you must use a separate command to store each value that you would like to assign to a memory variable. This is illustrated in Figure 10.1 where we have issued a series of commands to fill memory variables with data elements.

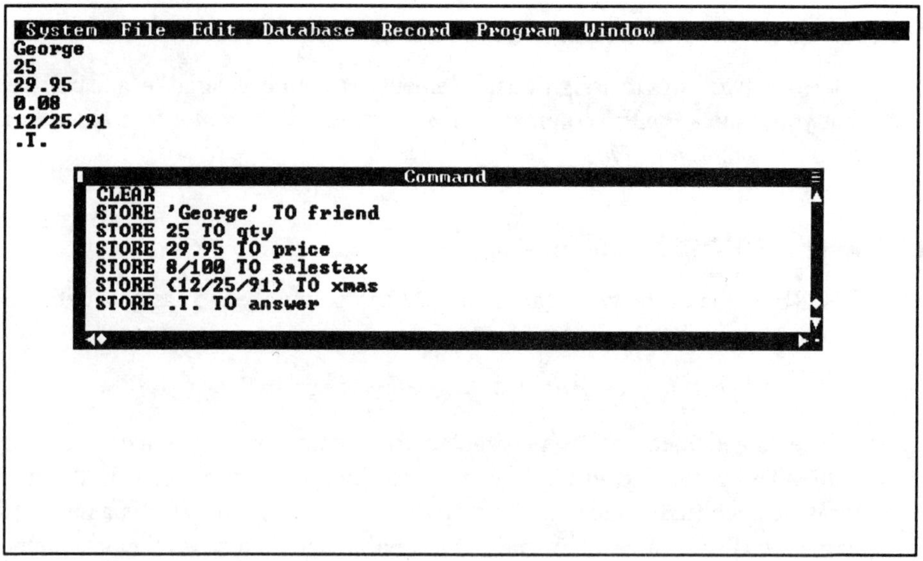

**Figure 10.1  Examples of STORE Commands**

In this figure, the first STORE command stores the character string 'George' to the memory variable named **friend**. The next three commands store values to numeric memory variables. You may assign a value (e.g., 25 or 29.95) to a memory variable (e.g., qty or price). You also may store the result of a formula or numeric expression (e.g., 8/100) to a numeric memory variable.

The fifth command saves the date, December 25, 1991, to the date memory variable named **xmas**. Note that the date must be enclosed in braces (e.g., {12/25/91}); without them, the date would be evaluated erroneously as a numeric expression (e.g., 12/25/91). As a result, the variable **xmas** would equal .01, the result of dividing the answer of (12/25) by 91.

The last command stores a logical value .T. to the logical memory variable named **answer**.

You can, in addition, store the same value to several variables using only a single command by separating the variable names with commas. For example:

```
store 25 to qty, oldqty
store 'George' to friend, newfriend
```

## Using the = Command

Another way to assign a data element to a memory variable is to issue the = command in the following format:

```
<memory variable name = <data element>
```

```
 System  File  Edit  Database  Record  Program  Window
George
25
29.95
0.08
12/25/91
.T.




                              Command
 CLEAR
 friend = 'George'
 qty = 25
 price = 29.95
 salestax = 8/100
 xmas = {12/25/91}
 answer = .T.
```

**Figure 10.2  Using the = Command**

Examples:

```
greeting = 'Hello'
friend = 'George'
qty = 25
price = 29.95
salestax = 8/100
xmas = {12/25/91}
answer = .T.
```

The = command will produce the same result as that of the STORE command (see Figure 10.2); therefore, the two may be used interchangeably. Some programmers adapt a convention whereby they use STORE commands to initialize the values in memory variables and then use = commands to change their values. As a result, when they return to the commands issued, it is possible to tell when the memory variables were first set up.

## ASSIGNING DATA FIELDS TO MEMORY VARIABLES

Previous examples illustrated how to assign a character string, a number, a date and a logical value to a memory variable. This can also be done with the value in a current data field, using either a STORE or an = command in the following format:

```
STORE <data field name> TO <memory variable name>
<memory variable name> = <data field name>
```

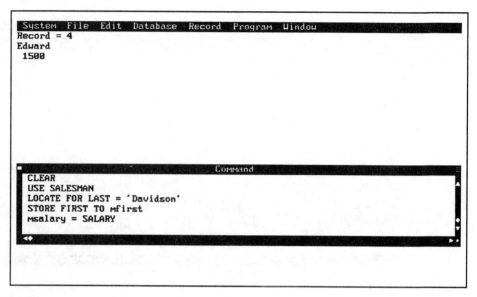

**Figure 10.3   Assign Data Fields to Memory Variables**

You can store for later data manipulation purposes, for example, salesman Davidson's first name and salary in memory variables **mfirst** and **msalary**. To do that, first locate from SALESMAN.DBF the record belonging to Davidson. When the Locate operation returns the record, issue the command to assign the field values to the appropriate memory variables (see Figure 10.3).

In Figure 10.3, the Locate operation found Davidson's record (Record=4). Then the contents of the database FIELD were stored to a memory variable named **mfirst**, while a memory variable named **msalary** was created to hold the contents of the SALARY field. Notice that, in each case, we avoided naming the memory variable after the field simply by adding an "m" to the field name. Although by no means obligatory, this convention has several advantages. First, it "documents" the memory variable; we can easily tell that the value of a memory variable beginning with an "m" has been assigned from a database field. But this convention also avoids confusing FoxPro. If a memory variable and a database field have the same name and you refer to it, FoxPro will only be able to access the value of the current data field. If, for example, you had instead named the memory variable **msalary** as SALARY (the same as the data field), when you try to view the value in the memory variable, it will show only the value of the SALARY data field.

## DISPLAYING MEMORY VARIABLES

When you enter data elements to memory variables, they are stored temporarily in the computer's memory. The contents of these memory variables can be viewed in two ways. You may list some or all of the current memory variables by using the DISPLAY MEMORY command. Or you may display the value of an individual memory variable with a ? command.

## Using the DISPLAY MEMORY Command

Use the DISPLAY MEMORY (or DISP MEMO in short) to show the names of all the current memory variables and their values. If, for example, you issue the DISPLAY MEMORY command now, you would be able to view the values of all the memory variables you have created (see Figure 10.4).

You can see in this figure the list of current memory variables returned by the DISPLAY MEMORY command. In addition to listing their names and the values, FoxPro also shows what type of variables they are. For example, all character variables are indicated by a letter "C." Numeric, date, and logical variables are indicated by letters "N," "D," and "L," respectively.

Memory variables are also classified as either public or private. A public variable is one that is accessible anywhere while you are in FoxPro, whereas private variables are accessible in certain applications or programs only. When memory variables are created in the Command window, they are classified as public, and indicated as "Pub" in the variable list. You don't have to worry about private variables at this point.

Notice the list of system memory variables in Figure 10.4. These variables are used by FoxPro to hold data values for its internal use. For example, FoxPro keeps

```
GREETING    Pub    C    "Hello"
FRIEND      Pub    C    "George"          ┌──────────────────────────────┐
QTY         Pub    N         25  (      Z │ Press any key to continue ... │ █
PRICE       Pub    N      29.95  (        └──────────────────────────────┘
SALESTAX    Pub    N       0.80  (          0.80000000)
XMAS        Pub    D    12/25/91
ANSWER      Pub    L    .T.
MFIRST      Pub    C    "Edward   "
MSALARY     Pub    N       1500  (       1500.00000000)
        9 variables defined,     40 bytes used
      247 variables available

Print System Memory Variables

_ALIGNMENT   Pub    C    "LEFT"
_BOX         Pub    L    .T.
_INDENT      Pub    N         0  (          0.00000000)
_LMARGIN     Pub    N         0  (          0.00000000)
_PADVANCE    Pub    C    "FORMFEED"
_PAGENO      Pub    N         6  (          6.00000000)
_PBPAGE      Pub    N         1  (          1.00000000)
_PCOLNO      Pub    N        55  (         55.00000000)
_PCOPIES     Pub    N         1  (          1.00000000)
_PDRIVER     Pub    C    ""
```

**Figure 10.4  Displaying Current Memory Variables**

track of the page number in the system variable _PAGENO. Although most of these system variables are of no direct interest to you, you can use some of them in your applications and reports, as you will learn in next chapter. There is a large set of system variables requiring several screens to show them all. After viewing one screen, press any key to continue until you have viewed them all.

To display only selected memory variables, use the LIKE operator in the DISPLAY MEMORY command. For example, to display all the memory variables whose names begin with the letter m, issue the following command:

```
DISPLAY MEMORY LIKE m*
```

As a result, the command will display the memory variables such as **mfirst**, **msalary**, etc. The asterisk is a wildcard that accepts any string of characters in its place.

## Using the ? Command

To display the value of a memory variable, invoke the ? command in the following format:

```
? <memory variable list>
```

To view the contents of the memory variable named **greeting**, for example, issue the following command:

```
?greeting
```

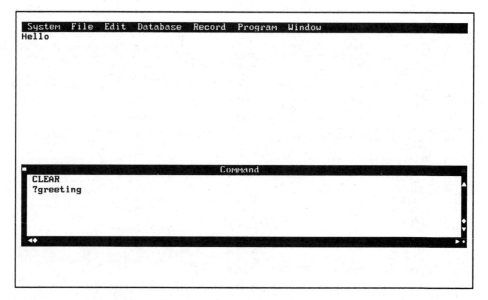

**Figure 10.5  Displaying Contents of a Memory Variable**

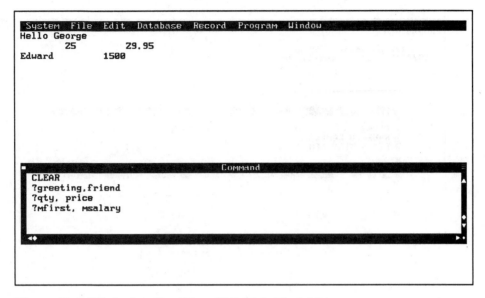

**Figure 10.6  Displaying Contents of Multiple Variables**

Upon execution of the command, the value of the memory variable is displayed, as shown in Figure 10.5. The contents of more than one memory variable may be displayed in the same command. To do that, specify the memory variables and separate them by commas (see Figure 10.6).

## SAVING MEMORY VARIABLES TO MEMORY FILES

Memory variables are temporary storage locations that have been set aside in the computer's RAM. As soon as you exit from FoxPro, the memory variables you have created will be erased and their memory spaces released. You may, however, save memory variables to a permanent file if you intend to use them again later. If they are not saved, obviously they will have to be re-created later. The command for saving memory variables to a memory file is:

```
SAVE TO <memory filename>
```

This command saves all the current memory variables (excluding system variables) to a memory file with a .MEM file extension. For example, if you would like to save the memory variables that you have created to the SAMPLE.MEM memory file, issue the following command:

```
SAVE TO SAMPLE
```

Upon execution, the command creates the memory file named SAMPLE.MEM to hold the current memory variables. To verify the existence of such a memory file, issue the DIR command (see Figure 10.7).

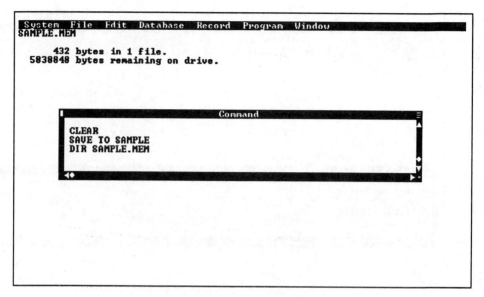

**Figure 10.7  Saving Memory Variables to a File**

The SAVE TO command saves every memory variable to the specified memory file. If you need to save memory variables selectively, use the LIKE qualifier in the SAVE command. For example, to save all the variables whose names begin with a letter "m," issue the following command:

```
SAVE ALL LIKE m* TO MEMFILE
```

The wildcard character (*) stands for any series of characters in the variable names. As a result, the command will save memory variables such as **mfirst, msalary** to the MEMFILE.MEM file.

You may also use another wildcard character, ?, to select the variables to be saved. Each ? represents a single character in the memory name. For example, if you would like to save a series of memory variables that all have seven-character names and contain the string "rate" as the second through fifth characters of their name (for example, **yrate01, yrate02, mrate01, drate01**), issue the following command:

```
SAVE ALL LIKE ?rate?? TO TESTFILE
```

This command will save only those memory variables with names of seven characters and with rate occupying the second through fifth positions, regardless of what characters occupy other positions.

You may also use the EXCEPT qualifier to exclude a set of memory variables to be saved to a file. To save, for example, all memory variables whose names do *not* begin with the letter "m," issue the following command:

```
SAVE ALL EXCEPT m* TO TESTFILE
```

## DELETING MEMORY VARIABLES

Although an individual memory variable does not take up much memory space, it is a good practice to delete those variables that are no longer needed for the current session. When you do this, it frees the computer's valuable memory space to be used for other operations. After you no longer need your memory variables or you have saved them to a disk file, some or all of them can be erased from the computer memory with the RELEASE command. To erase one or more memory variables from memory, specify the name(s) of the memory variable(s) as follows:

```
RELEASE <memory variable list>
```

For example:

```
RELEASE mfirst
```

If you are erasing more than one variable, they must be separated with commas in the RELEASE command, as in the following:

```
RELEASE greeting, friend, qty
```

To erase all the memory variables from memory, use the following command:

```
RELEASE ALL
```

In executing this command, all the current memory variables will be erased and their memory locations released for other use. The LIKE or EXCEPT clauses also may be used to selectively erase certain memory variables. Examples:

```
RELEASE LIKE m*
RELEASE LIKE *cost
RELEASE LIKE ?rate??
RELEASE ALL EXCEPT m*
RELEASE ALL *cost
```

It is important to know that the RELEASE command deletes only the memory variables from the computer memory, not the contents of any memory files.

## RESTORING MEMORY VARIABLES

You may retrieve any memory variables that have been saved in a memory file and then place them into memory with the RESTORE FROM command:

```
RESTORE FROM <memory filename>
```

When the command is issued, any memory variables in memory are erased and replaced with those retrieved from the memory file. Here is an example:

```
RESTORE FROM MEMFILE
```

When the preceding command is issued, all the current memory variables will be released and the contents of the MEMFILE.MEM memory file will be placed into the current memory. As a result, the memory will contain only two memory variables: **mfirst** and **msalary** (those saved with the SAVE ALL LIKE m* TO MEMFILE command).

To add the memory variables from a memory file to the current memory without erasing the existing memory variables, attach the ADDITIVE clause at the end of the command, as in this example:

```
RESTORE FROM SAMPLE ADDITIVE
```

This command will retrieve all the memory variables from SAMPLE.MEM and then add them to memory. The contents of the existing memory variables will not be disturbed unless the entering variables share the same name as any of the existing variables. If that occurs, the values of the existing variables will be replaced with the values retrieved from the memory file.

## DELETING MEMORY VARIABLES FROM MEMORY FILE

The RELEASE command may be invoked to delete memory variables from memory only. It cannot be used to remove any memory variables that are saved in a memory file. To delete some or all of the memory variables that have been saved to a memory file, they must first be retrieved from the file by using the RESTORE command; then they can be deleted with RELEASE command. When that action is complete, again save the remaining memory variables to the memory file. As an exercise, use the following commands to remove the memory variable **mfirst** from the memory file named MEMFILE:

```
RELEASE ALL
RESTORE FROM MEMFILE
RELEASE mfirst
SAVE TO MEMFILE
```

or (better):

```
RESTORE from MEMFILE
RELEASE mfirst
SAVE TO MEMFILE ALL LIKE M*
```

# Built-in Functions

Functions in FoxPro provide a "built-in" way of performing mathematical and string manipulation on different types of data elements. A function takes values that are passed to it and performs a predefined operation on them. The function then returns the result of the operation. For example, ABS(- 123.45) returns the absolute value (i.e., 123.45) of the value that is passed to it in the argument (the value in the parentheses, e.g., -123.45). Similarly, the function RTRIM(FIRST) takes the character string in the FIRST (first name) data field and trims off all the trailing blank spaces and returns the trimmed string.

Functions are divided into groups according to the types of data they return and the kinds of operations they perform. Character and string functions select parts of a character string for use in searching, sorting, and indexing operations. Other string functions can insert blank spaces in a character string or trim off unwanted blank spaces. Date manipulation functions display dates in a number of formats that are used in business data processing applications. Numeric functions can round a decimal number to the integer, compute the square root of a value, and perform many other mathematical operations on the values. Statistical functions can be used to produce summary statistics by using the values in data records.

A built-in function is identified by a symbolic name followed by a pair of parentheses:

```
<function name>([<argument>])
```

The name indicates the type of data manipulation the function performs. The object of the function, which is enclosed in the parentheses, is called an argument. The argument is used to pass the value to the function. With few exceptions, most functions require an argument. Here is an example of a built-in function:

```
SUM(SALARY)
```

It instructs FoxPro to add up the values in the data field SALARY and return the sum. The argument in this case is represented by a data field name. Recall from previous chapters that functions may be used in expressions, and the value of a function may be assigned to a memory variable. Here is an example:

```
STORE 1234.567 TO x
STORE INT(x) TO y
```

The function INT(x) will convert the value in the argument to an integer by eliminating the digits to the right of the decimal point. As a result, the value assigned to variable y will be 1234 (see Figure 10.8).

Although most functions require an argument, some do not. TIME( ) is one that does not. When executed, it returns the current system time. Similarly, DATE( ) returns the current system date (see Figure 10.9).

There are many types of functions. Many, like SUM( ), perform mathematical operations. Others manipulate character strings. The TRIM( ) function, for instance, trims off any trailing blanks in a character string specified in the argument. Still other types of functions process dates. DTOC( ), for example, converts a date to a character string.

```
System  File  Edit  Database  Record  Program  Window
1234.567
          1234
       1234.567        1234




                                    Command
 CLEAR
 STORE 1234.567 TO x
 STORE INT(x) TO y
 ?x,y
```

**Figure 10.8  Assigning a Function to a Memory Variable**

Because of the different operations they perform, the argument or arguments that must be supplied to the functions are different. In addition, different types of functions return different types of data values. For example, a date is supplied in the argument for the DTOC( ) function and it returns a character string, while the CTOD( ) function takes a character string as an argument and returns a date.

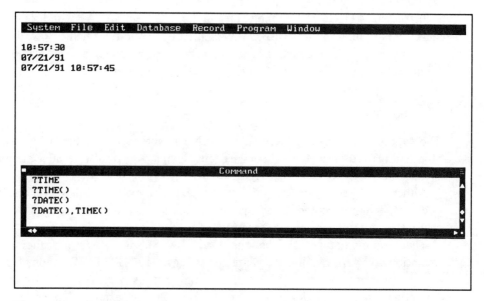

```
System  File  Edit  Database  Record  Program  Window
10:57:30
07/21/91
07/21/91 10:57:45




                                    Command
 ?TIME
 ?TIME( )
 ?DATE( )
 ?DATE( ),TIME( )
```

**Figure 10.9  TIME( ) Function**

FoxPro provides a wealth of built-in functions that enable you to manipulate data. This chapter covers only some of the most commonly used ones, but once you have mastered these, you should have no trouble learning the others.

## CHARACTER STRING FUNCTIONS

A large set of built-in functions are provided that enable you to manipulate a character string that is specified in a function argument. There is a function to remove unwanted blank spaces in the string, another to include a string of blank spaces. There is a function to convert letters from lowercase to uppercase, and vice versa, and still another that converts a string of digits into a value. It is also possible to find and return a subset of a character string with one of these functions.

Most functions require one or more character strings as an argument. In general, each argument can also be supplied to the function as a character expression. A character expression is a combination of character strings, character data fields, and character memory variables joined by one or more operators (such as the plus sign). You can also include a character string returned by another built-in function in the function argument. A simple character expression, on the other hand, can *only* be a character string, a character data field, or a character memory variable.

## RTRIM(), TRIM()

The RTRIM( ) (or TRIM( )) function allows you to trim off the trailing blank spaces in a character string. The format of RTRIM( ) and TRIM( ) is:

```
RTRIM(<character string>)
TRIM(<character string>)
```

The character string to be trimmed can be specified in the function argument as a character expression. The function returns a character string without the trailing blanks.

The TRIM( ) or RTRIM( ) function is most commonly used to eliminate trailing spaces from the character values stored in database fields. When a character string is stored in a data field, FoxPro adds blank spaces to the end of the string to fill out the field width. As a result, when you display the content of the data field, it will include the blank spaces. For example, in SALESMAN.DBF, every first and last name stored in the FIRST and LAST data fields contains 8 characters because both of their field widths are set to 8 characters. If a salesperson's first name has fewer than 8 characters, FoxPro will fill the remainder of the field width with blank spaces. It will do the same for a last name that is shorter than the field width. As a result, when the string in that field is displayed, it will occupy 8 spaces. To trim off those trailing blank spaces, use the TRIM( ) function as detailed in Figure 10.10.

```
 System  File  Edit  Database  Record  Program  Window
Record = 2
George  Bell
GeorgeBell
George Bell
Bell    , George
Bell, George




                        ┌──────────── Command ────────────┐
                        │ LOCATE FOR LAST = 'Bell'         │
                        │ ?FIRST+LAST                      │
                        │ ?TRIM(FIRST)+LAST                │
                        │ ?TRIM(FIRST)+' '+LAST            │
                        │ ?LAST+', '+FIRST                 │
                        │ ?RTRIM(LAST)+', '+FIRST          │
                        │                                  │
                        │ ◄►                         ►•    │
                        └──────────────────────────────────┘
```

**Figure 10.10  TRIM( ) Function**

You can see in this figure that the ?FIRST+LAST command displays the first
and last names of George Bell as 8 characters each, with two trailing blanks added
to the first name. You can also see that the TRIM(FIRST) function is used to remove
the blank spaces between the first and last names. You could also use the
RTRIM(LAST) function, to display last name, comma, and first name.

## LTRIM()

The LTRIM( ) function is similar to TRIM( ) and RTRIM( ). It is used to remove
leading blanking spaces in a character string. The format of the function is:

```
LTRIM(<character string>)
```

The function returns a character string without the leading blank spaces, as shown
in this example:

```
STORE '    Johnson' TO lastname
STORE ' Mary'       TO firstname
STORE ' K. ' TO initial
LTRIM(firstname)+initial+LTRIM(lastname)
```

This function could be used to remove the leading blank spaces in the **firstname**
and **lastname** memory variables (see Figure 10.11).

It is important to remember that a blank space is considered a valid character.
And, when searching for or comparing character strings, leading blanks are

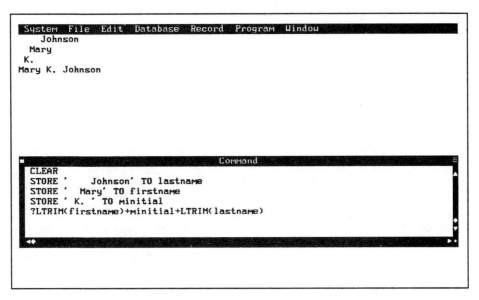

**Figure 10.11  Using LTRIM( )**

important. If, for example, you store ' Johnson' in the LAST data field, you would not be able to find the record by using 'Johnson' as the search string with the following command:

```
LOCATE FOR LAST = 'Johnson'
```

Instead, to find ' Johnson', you must remove the leading blanks from the LAST data field before comparing it with the search string 'Johnson':

```
LOCATE FOR LTRIM(LAST) = 'Johnson'
```

## ALLTRIM()

ALLTRIM( ) removes all the leading and trailing blank spaces from a character string. The format of the function is:

```
ALLTRIM(<character string>)
```

An example of ALLTRIM( ) is shown in Figure 10.12. ALLTRIM(fullname) removes all the blanks before and after a character string stored in the memory variable **fullname**.

The ALLTRIM( ) function is very useful when you do not remember whether a character string was stored with any leading or trailing blanks. For example, the

```
┌─────────────────────────────────────────────────────────────────┐
│ System  File  Edit  Database  Record  Program  Window            │
│    Mary K. Johnson                                                │
│ ×××Mary K. Johnson×××                                            │
│                                                                   │
│                                                                   │
│                                                                   │
│                                                                   │
│                                                                   │
│ ▪                        Command                            ≡     │
│ CLEAR                                                             │
│ STORE '   Mary K. Johnson   ' TO fullname                   ▲    │
│ ?' ×××'+ALLTRIM(fullname)+'×××'                                  │
│                                                                   │
│                                                             ◆     │
│                                                             ▼     │
│ ◂◆                                                          ▸ ▪   │
└─────────────────────────────────────────────────────────────────┘
```

**Figure 10.12  Using ALLTRIM( )**

following LOCATE command will be able to find all the records belonging to Doris regardless of whether there are leading or trailing blanks stored in the FIRST data field:

```
LOCATE FOR ALLTRIM(FIRST) = 'Doris'
```

## UPPER()

The UPPER( ) function converts to uppercase all characters in the expression specified as an argument. Its syntax is:

```
UPPER(<character expression>)
```

The following command, then, converts the character string in memory variable **string_a** to uppercase and stores it to another variable named **string_b**:

```
STORE 'abcXYZ0123$*' TO string_a
string_b = UPPER(string_a)
```

After executing the commands, all the lowercase letters in the memory variable string_a will be converted to uppercase (see Figure 10.13). Notice that UPPER( ) has no effect on uppercase letters or symbols such as $ and *.

Similarly, you may convert all the last names in the LAST data field to uppercase letters in a database file by using the following command:

```
REPLACE ALL LAST WITH UPPER(LAST)
```

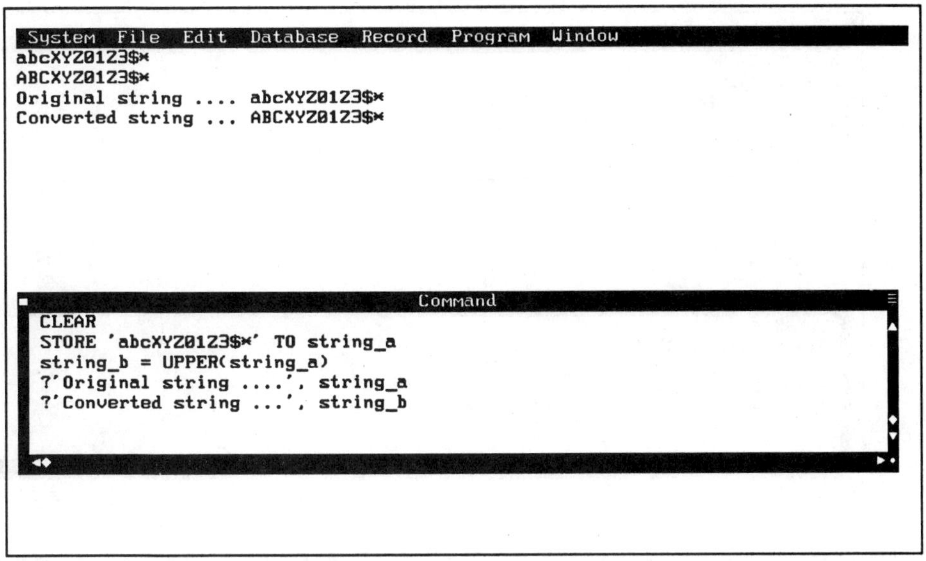

```
 System  File  Edit  Database  Record  Program  Window
abcXYZ0123$×
ABCXYZ0123$×
Original string .... abcXYZ0123$×
Converted string ... ABCXYZ0123$×




                                 Command
 ■
   CLEAR
   STORE 'abcXYZ0123$×' TO string_a
   string_b = UPPER(string_a)
   ?'Original string ....', string_a
   ?'Converted string ...', string_b

   ◄►                                                    ► .
```

**Figure 10.13  Using UPPER( )**

You may also use the UPPER( ) function to find character strings by ignoring case. For example, if you are unsure of how a salesperson's first name was saved in the FIRST data field, you would use the following command to list all salespeople whose first name is 'Doris':

```
LIST FIRST, LAST FOR UPPER(FIRST) = 'DORIS'
```

This command will list all first names in the forms of 'doris', 'Doris', or 'DORIS', etc.

## LOWER()

LOWER( ) is the opposite of UPPER( ). It converts uppercase letters in a character string to lowercase letters. The format of the function is:

```
LOWER(<character string>)
```

The function returns a character string after converting all the uppercase letters in the string represented by the character expression. Here is an example:

```
STORE 'abcXYZ0123$*' TO string_a
string_b = LOWER(string_a)
```

After executing the commands, the memory variable **string_b** contains only lowercase letters, in addition to the numeric digits and special symbols (see Figure 10.14).

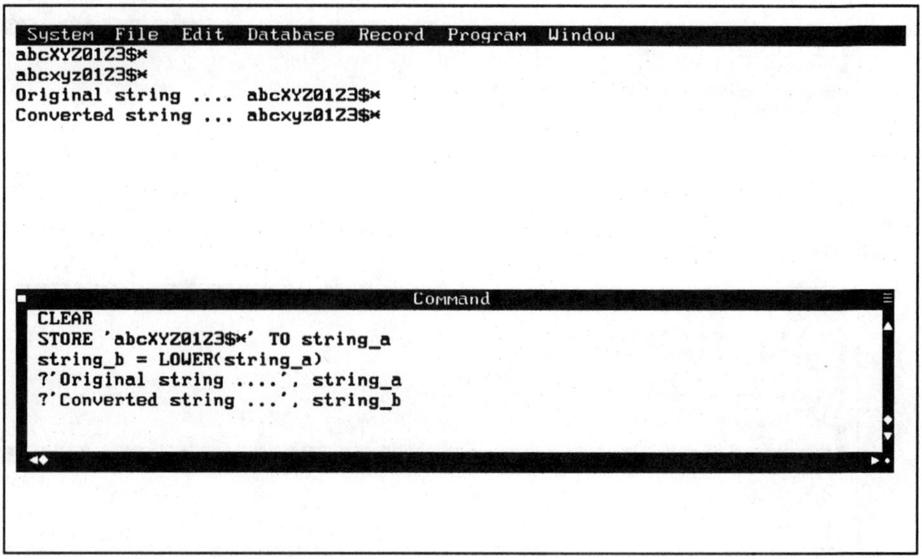

```
 System  File  Edit  Database  Record  Program  Window
abcXYZ0123$×
abcxyz0123$×
Original string .... abcXYZ0123$×
Converted string ... abcxyz0123$×




                             Command
 CLEAR
 STORE 'abcXYZ0123$×' TO string_a
 string_b = LOWER(string_a)
 ?'Original string ....', string_a
 ?'Converted string ...', string_b
```

**Figure 10.14  Using LOWER( )**

Like UPPER( ), you may use LOWER( ) in the REPLACE command to convert all existing character strings in a data field to lowercase. The following command, for example, will convert all the first names in the FIRST data field to lowercase:

```
REPLACE ALL FIRST WITH LOWER(FIRST)
```

More practically, LOWER( ) may be used for searching character strings by disregarding case entirely. It converts a character string to lowercase before comparing it with a search string in lowercase. Here is an example:

```
LOCATE FOR LOWER(LAST) = 'davidson'
```

This command will find last names 'Davidson', 'DAVIDSON', or 'davidson'.

## SPACE()

A string of blank characters may be created in one of two ways. One is to enclose the blanks in quotation marks for the string such as:

```
STORE '     ' TO fivespaces
```

or

```
fivespaces = '     '
```

Another way is to use the SPACE( ) function, which allows you to create a string composed of a specified number of blank spaces. The number of blank spaces is specified in the function argument:

```
SPACE(<number of spaces>)
```

Use SPACE(5) to create a string of five blank spaces, and then use it to assign a character string to a memory variable as in this example:

```
STORE SPACE(5) TO fivespaces
```

or

```
fivespaces = SPACE(5)
```

SPACE( ) can also be used to space output on the screen. SPACE(5) in the following command will insert five blank spaces between the first and last names:

```
LIST OFF FIRST + SPACE(5) + LAST
```

In the SALESMAN database file, then, this command can be used to display the sales staff's first and last names. The keyword OFF is used to suppress the display of the record number (see Figure 10.15). Notice that issuing the SET HEADING OFF command precluded the display of the field names. The ? commands enable you to display your own column headings.

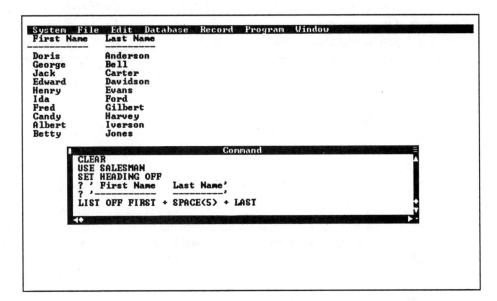

**Figure 10.15  Spacing Output Items**

```
┌──────────────────────────────────────────────────────────────────┐
│ System  File  Edit  Database  Record  Program  Window             │
│ John J. Smith                                                      │
│ John K. Smith                                                      │
│ Content of old_user ...... John J. Smith                          │
│ Content of new_user ...... John K. Smith                          │
│                                                                    │
│                                                                    │
│                                                                    │
│          ┌──────────────────── Command ─────────────────────┐     │
│          │ STORE 'John J. Smith' TO old_user              ▲ │     │
│          │ new_user = STUFF(old_user, 6, 2, 'K.')           │     │
│          │                                                  │     │
│          │ ? 'Content of old_user ......', old_user         │     │
│          │ ? 'Content of new_user ......', new_user         │     │
│          │                                                ◆ │     │
│          │ ◄◆                                          ►  ▼ │     │
│          └──────────────────────────────────────────────────┘     │
│                                                                    │
└──────────────────────────────────────────────────────────────────┘
```

**Figure 10.16  Using STUFF( ) to Replace Character Strings**

## STUFF()

The STUFF( ) function allows you to replace a portion of a character string with another character string. The portion to be replaced is identified by two parameters: the beginning character position and the number of characters to be replaced. The portion of the character string that is to be replaced is specified as the first string in the function argument, followed by the parameters that will replace it. The replacement character string is specified as the last item in the function argument:

```
STUFF(<first character string>, <beginning position>,
      <number of characters to be replaced>,
      <replacing character string>)
```

Here is an example:

```
STORE 'John J. Smith' TO old_user
new_user = STUFF(old_user, 6,2, 'K.')
```

The STUFF( ) function will return a new character string after replacing two characters in the **old_user** string, beginning from the sixth character with the string '**K.**'. As a result, the **new_user** memory variable will hold the string '**John K. Smith**' after executing the second command (see Figure 10.16).

## SOUNDEX()

Often, when comparing strings or searching for a database value, you may know how a string sounds without knowing how it is spelled. In such cases, a useful

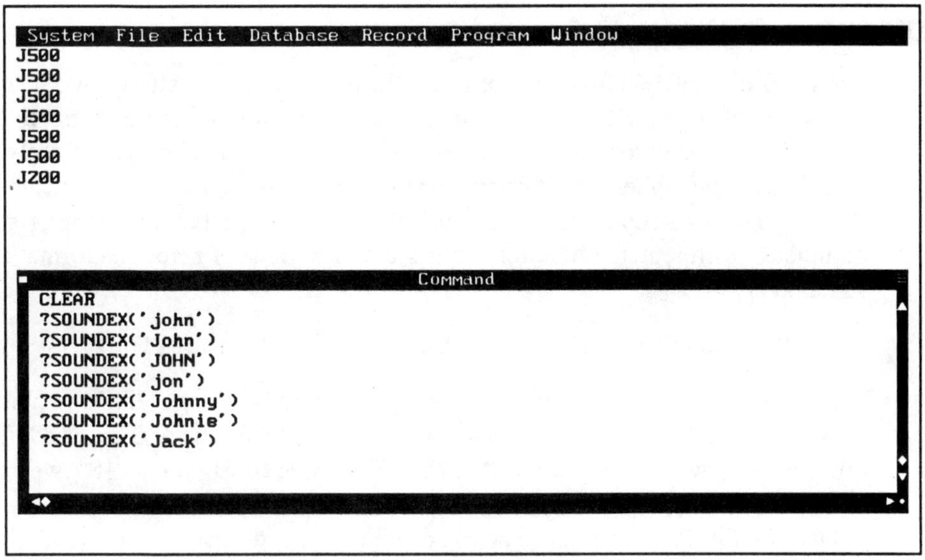

```
 System   File   Edit   Database   Record   Program   Window
J500
J500
J500
J500
J500
J500
J200


                                    Command
 CLEAR
 ?SOUNDEX('john')
 ?SOUNDEX('John')
 ?SOUNDEX('JOHN')
 ?SOUNDEX('jon')
 ?SOUNDEX('Johnny')
 ?SOUNDEX('Johnie')
 ?SOUNDEX('Jack')
```

**Figure 10.17  Examples of Phonetic Index Codes**

function is SOUNDEX( ), which returns a phonetic representation of a character string. Its syntax is:

```
SOUNDEX(<character string>)
```

Here is an example:

```
?SOUNDEX('John')
```

The function will return a phonetic index code (e.g., J500) representing the sound of the character string. Strings that sound alike will have the same phonetic code (see Figure 10.17).

SOUNDEX( ) lets you determine whether two strings sound alike by comparing their phonetic codes. Figure 10.17 shows that the strings 'john', 'John', 'JOHN', 'jon', 'Johnny', and 'Johnie' resulted in the same phonetic index code (J500) while the string 'Jack' produced a different code.

The SOUNDEX( ) function is very useful for locating character strings whose spelling you do not remember. The following commands will list all the first names saved in the FIRST data field as JOHN, John, Johnny, etc.:

```
LIST FIRST FOR SOUNDEX(FIRST) = SOUNDEX('john')
```

or

```
LIST FIRST FOR LIKE(SOUNDEX(FIRST), SOUNDEX('john')
```

## DIFFERENCE()

The DIFFERENCE( ) function compares the SOUNDEX( ) value of two specified character strings and returns a numeric index indicating how much they sound alike. The index value returned ranges from 0 to 4. The more closely they sound alike, the higher the returned index value. An index value of 4 indicates that the two strings sound very much or exactly alike. If the two strings sound completely different, the function returns an index value of zero. The format of the function is:

```
DIFFERENCE(<character string>,<character string>)
```

As examples, the SOUNDEX difference between the strings 'Jim' and 'Jimmy' is 4, whereas the difference between 'Jim' and 'Tim' is 3. The SOUNDEX difference between 'Jim' and 'Albert' obviously is 0. Figure 10.18 gives more examples of these values.

DIFFERENCE( ) also can be invoked to find character strings that sound similar. The following would be used, for example, to find those first names in the FIRST database field that sound like 'Jim':

```
LIST FIRST FOR DIFFERENCE(FIRST,'Jim') >= 3
```

This command will return all first names such as Jim, Tim, and Jimmy.

```
 System  File  Edit  Database  Record  Program  Window
The soundex of James is J520
The soundex of Jim is J500
The soundex of Jimmy is J500
The soundex of Tim is T500
The soundex of Albert is A416
The soundex difference between Jim and Jimmy is          4
The soundex difference between James and Jim is          3
The soundex difference between Jim and Tim is         3
The soundex difference between Jim and Albert is          0
                              Command
 CLEAR
 ?'The soundex of James is',SOUNDEX('James')
 ?'The soundex of Jim is',SOUNDEX('Jim')
 ?'The soundex of Jimmy is',SOUNDEX('Jimmy')
 ?'The soundex of Tim is',SOUNDEX('Tim')
 ?'The soundex of Albert is',SOUNDEX('Albert')
 ?'The soundex difference between Jim and Jimmy is', DIFFERENCE('Jim','Jimmy'
 ?'The soundex difference between James and Jim is', DIFFERENCE('James','Jim'
 ?'The soundex difference between Jim and Tim is', DIFFERENCE('Jim','Tim')
 ?'The soundex difference between Jim and Albert is', DIFFERENCE('Jim','Alber
```

**Figure 10.18  SOUNDEX Differences between Strings**

## LEFT(), RIGHT()

The LEFT( ) and RIGHT( ) functions enable you to find and view the first or last few characters of a character string. They return a number of characters from the left or right respectively, and have the same argument format:

```
LEFT(<character string>, <number of characters from the left>)
RIGHT(<character string>, <number of characters from the right>)
```

The following LEFT( ) function will return the character string 'John', the first four characters from the left of the specified string 'John J. Smith':

```
?LEFT('John J. Smith', 4)
```

Similarly, the last four digits (e.g., 7890) of a phone number (e.g., 123-456-7890) are displayed by using the RIGHT( ) function:

```
?RIGHT('123-456-7890',4)
```

LEFT( ) and RIGHT( ) are most commonly used to find a substring of characters in a character data field; to list, for example, those social security numbers in the SS_NO data field that begin with '111' or that end with '3333' (see Figure 10.19).

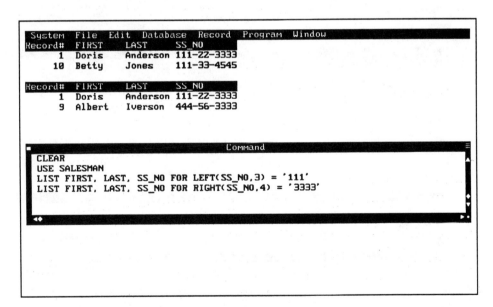

**Figure 10.19  Locating Records with LEFT( ) and RIGHT( )**

## SUBSTR()

SUBSTR( ) is used to extract a portion of a specified character string. The character string, the beginning character position of the portion to be extracted, and the number of characters to be extracted are specified in the function argument:

```
SUBSTR(<character string>, <begin character position>,
       <number of characters to be extracted>)
```

The following command, for example, will extract from the string '123-45-6789' two characters beginning from the fifth character position:

```
?SUBSTR('123-45-6789',5,2)
```

The characters from the character string by the SUBSTR( ) function will be '45'.

Like LEFT( ) and RIGHT( ), SUBSTR( ) can be used to locate a substring within a character field. For example, to find all those salespeople in the SALESMAN database whose middle two digits of their social security numbers are '56' or '33', issue the following LIST command:

```
LIST LAST FOR SUBSTR(SS_NO,5,2)='56' OR
              SUBSTR(SS_NO,5,2)='33'
```

A list of social security numbers satisfying the search condition is shown in Figure 10.20.

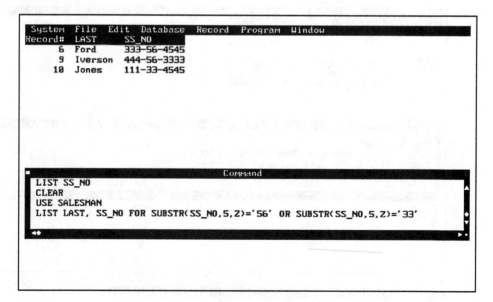

**Figure 10.20  Locating Substring with SUBSTR( )**

## PROPER()

The PROPER( ) function returns a character string with the first letter in each word capitalized and the remainder in lowercase. The format of the function is:

```
PROPER(<character string>)
```

The function may be used to represent a proper name regardless of the case in which the name is stored. The following commands correctly display the country name by using the PROPER( ) function whether the name is stored in lowercase or uppercase letters:

```
?PROPER('united states of america')
?PROPER('UNITED STATES OF AMERICA')
```

Thus, when these two commands are executed, they will all display the country name as United States Of America.

The PROPER( ) function is useful for ensuring that the names of people, cities, countries, etc. are displayed in a proper form. This function would come in handy to correctly display the names of salespeople in a report and and on mailing labels. Regardless of how the names are stored in the FIRST and LAST data fields, use of the PROPER( ) function guarantees that they will be properly output (see Figure 10.21).

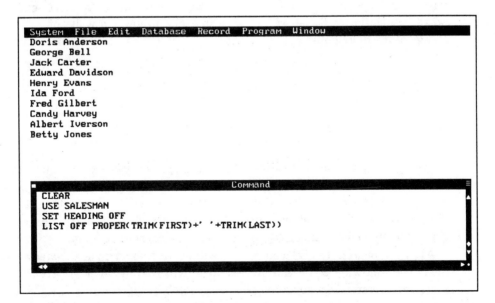

**Figure 10.21  Using the PROPER( ) Function**

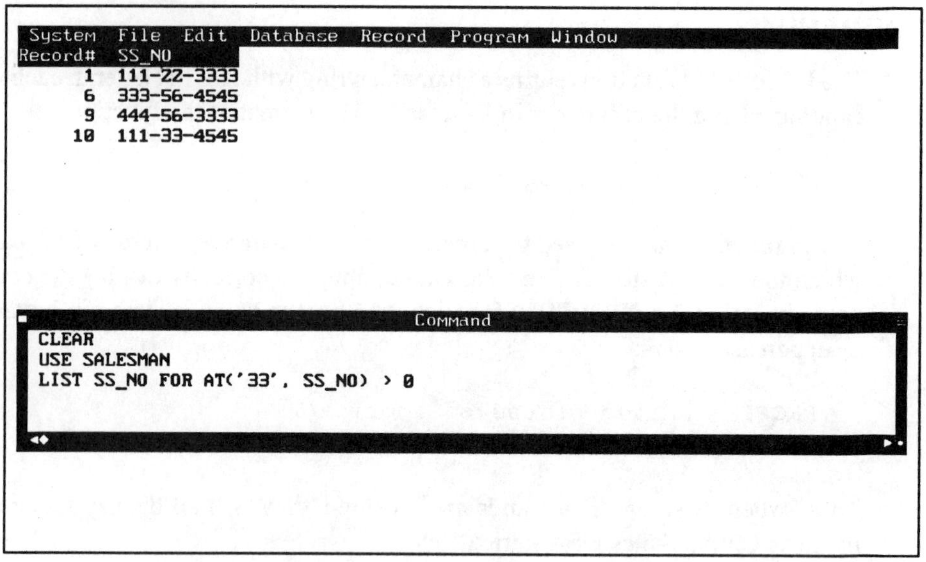

```
 System   File  Edit  Database  Record  Program  Window
 Record#   SS_NO
       1   111-22-3333
       6   333-56-4545
       9   444-56-3333
      10   111-33-4545




                                    Command
  CLEAR
  USE SALESMAN
  LIST SS_NO FOR AT('33', SS_NO) > 0
```

**Figure 10.22  Finding Substrings with the AT( ) Function**

## AT()

The AT( ) function searches a character string for a specified substring. If the substring is contained in the string being searched, the function returns a number indicating the beginning character position of the substring in the larger string. If no such substring is found within the string, AT( ) returns a value of zero. The format of the function is:

```
AT(<substring>, <string to be searched>)
```

Here are two examples:

```
?AT('45', '123-45-6789')
?AT('56', '123-45-6789')
```

When the first command is executed it will return a value of 5 indicating the substring '45' is found beginning from the fifth character position in the '123-45-6789' searched. Because the string '123-45-6789' does not contain the substring '56', the second command will return a value of zero. The substring must appear consecutively in the searched string in order to be considered found.

AT( ) can be used to find a string of consecutive characters in a character data field. The following command, for example, will find in SALESMAN.DBF all social security numbers containing the consecutive string of characters '33'):

```
USE SALESMAN
LIST SS_NO FOR AT('33', SS_NO) > 0
```

When the LIST command is executed, it shows all social security numbers containing the substring '33' regardless of where the substring is found in the SS_NO data field (see Figure 10.22).

## ASC()

As explained in Chapter 6, when character strings are sorted, their order is determined by their ASCII values. Each character is assigned a value that indicates its sequence number in the ASCII table. For example, in the ASCII table (see Appendix A), the letter 'A' has an ASCII value of 65; the letter 'a' has a value of 97.

The ASC( ) function returns the ASCII value of the first character of the string specified in the argument:

```
ASC(<character string>)
```

Here are some examples:

```
?ASC('A')
?ASC('Albert')
?ASC('a')
?ASC('always')
```

The first two commands will return an ASCII value of 65 and the last two commands will return an ASCII value of 97 (see Figure 10.23).

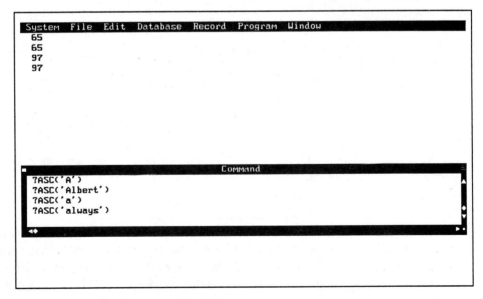

**Figure 10.23  Displaying ASCII Values**

ASC( ) also can be used to retrieve information about the ASCII value of a character. As with sorting, when indexing or sorting characters strings, the order of a character is determined by its ASCII value. Although it is not necessary to know ASCII values for the Index and Sort operations, the information can be useful for understanding the results of the operations.

## CHR()

CHR( ) is the opposite of ASC( ). Where ASC( ) returns an ASCII value of a character, CHR( ) returns the character that has the specified ASCII value in the argument. The format of the function is:

```
CHR(<an ASCII value>)
```

Here are two examples:

```
?CHR(65)
?CHR(97)
```

The first command will display the letter 'A' and the second command will display the letter 'a'.

CHR( ) is useful for issuing printer control commands. You can control various aspects of printing with most printers by issuing an escape sequence before sending the output to the printer. If you are using an HP LaserJet II printer, for example, and want to print your report in Landscape mode (horizontally on the paper), you would issue the following command:

```
??? CHR(27)+'&110'
```

where the ASCII value for the Esc key is 27. On some printers, you can issue CHR(13)+CHR(10), for example, to advance a page when the EJECT command does not work.

## LEN()

The LEN( ) function returns the number of characters in the specified character string. The format of the function is:

```
LEN(<character string>)
```

The character string can also be represented by a character memory variable, a character field, or a memo field. If it is represented by a memory variable, the function counts all the characters including all the blanks stored in the variable. If it is a character field, the function will return the field width. When you specify a

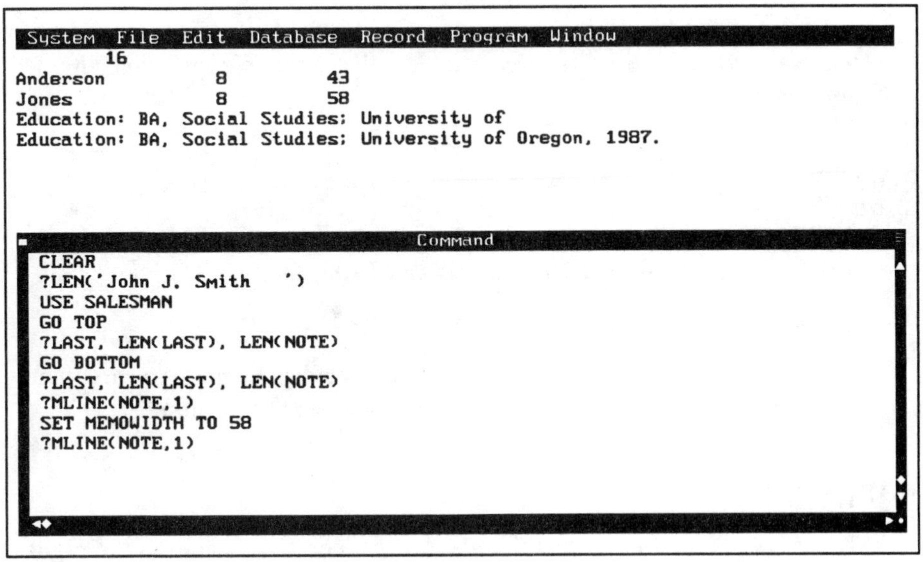

```
 System  File  Edit  Database  Record  Program  Window
       16
Anderson          8          43
Jones             8          58
Education: BA, Social Studies; University of
Education: BA, Social Studies; University of Oregon, 1987.




                                      Command
CLEAR
?LEN('John J. Smith      ')
USE SALESMAN
GO TOP
?LAST, LEN(LAST), LEN(NOTE)
GO BOTTOM
?LAST, LEN(LAST), LEN(NOTE)
?MLINE(NOTE,1)
SET MEMOWIDTH TO 58
?MLINE(NOTE,1)
```

**Figure 10.24  Determining String Length with LEN( )**

memo field in the function argument, the function will return the number of characters in the text, not including trailing blanks (see Figure 10.24).

You can see in this figure that the length of the string 'John J. Smith    ' is 16, including trailing blanks. The length of the string in the LAST data field is always equal to the field width—8—regardless of the actual length of the string. The length of the contents of the memo field NOTE, however, varies. The memo field of the first record contains 43 characters, whereas the memo field of the last record shows a length of 58.

Because the default width of a displayed memo field is 50 characters, the SET MEMOWIDTH command must be used to change the width in order to display a longer memo. The LEN( ) function allows you to determine what width is necessary to accommodate the memo text.

## NUMERIC FUNCTIONS

FoxPro provides a set of numeric functions that enable you to perform various mathematical operations on numeric values. These operations include calculating the square root of a number (SQRT( )), taking the absolute value of a number (ABS( )), converting a decimal value by truncating or by rounding (INT( ), ROUND( )), and others such as LOG( ) and LOG10( ). Most of these functions, except for ROUND( ), follow this format:

```
<function name>(<numeric expression>)
```

Each of these functions returns a numeric value after performing the mathematical operation on the value represented by the numeric expression supplied as an argument.

## SQRT()

SQRT( ) finds the square root of a value; so, if you execute the following command, it will return the value of 10 (square root of 100):

```
?SQRT(100)
```

Of course, a negative value cannot be specified as the function argument—you cannot take the square root of a negative number as a real number.

## ABS()

The ABS( ) function returns the absolute value of the value in the argument. It ignores the sign of the value; therefore, both of these commands will return the value of 123.45:

```
?ABS(123.45)
?ABS(-123.45)
```

## INT()

The INT( ) function returns the integer portion of a decimal value. The integer value of 123 is returned when the following command is executed:

```
?INT(123.89)
```

It is important to note that the INT( ) function does not round the value to its nearest integer. It simply truncates the digits beyond the decimal point.

## ROUND()

To round a decimal value to an integer, use the ROUND( ) function, which allows you to round a decimal value to a specified number of decimal places. The format of the function is:

```
ROUND(<numeric expression>, <number of decimal places>)
```

For example, to round the value of 123.6789 to its nearest integer, issue the following command:

```
?ROUND(123.6789,0)
```

The function will return the integer 124. Issue the next command, and it will return a value of 123.68:

```
?ROUND(123.6789,2)
```

The function rounded the value to two places beyond the decimal point.

## LOG10()

The LOG10( ) function returns the common (base-10) logarithm value of the specified value. The following command, for example, returns the value of 2 as the common logarithm value of 100:

```
?LOG10(100)
```

## LOG()

LOG( ) returns the natural (base-e) logarithm of the specified value. When the following command is executed, the LOG( ) function returns the value of 2.30259 as the natural logarithm value of 10:

```
?LOG(10)
```

## STATISTICAL FUNCTIONS

FoxPro provides a set of statistical functions that you may use to calculate summary statistics such as average, variance, and standard deviation from values in a data field. With these functions, you can find, for example, the maximum and minimum value from a data field; or, count number of records that satisfy certain filter conditions.

The summary statistics returned by these functions may be incorporated directly into a report or to memory variables for later use. To do that, use the CALCULATE command in the following format:

```
CALCULATE <statistical function
         TO <memory variable>
         [FOR <filter condition>]
```

Statistical functions that may be calculated include: CNT( ), SUM( ), AVG( ), STD( ), MAX( ) and MIN( ). Except for CNT( ) that needs no argument, every one of these functions requires a numeric expression as the function argument. The numeric expression must include one or more data fields.

The CALCULATE command offers the convenience of returning multiple summary statistics from a single CALCULATE statement. This ensures that all statistics returned by CALCULATE will be based on the same filter conditions. To have CALCULATE compute multiple summary statistics, you need only provide the command with the list of functions, each separated by a comma. In addition, if you intend to store the values returned by the functions to memory variables, you must create a parallel memory variable list, with each variable name separated from the others by a comma. The syntax of this extended CALCULATE command is:

```
CALCULATE <statistical function list,...>
TO <memory variable list,...>
FOR <filter condition>
```

## CNT()

Use CNT( ) to count selected records and save the result to a memory variable. CNT( ) could, for example, be used to determine the number of female salespeople and number of salespeople earning a salary of $2,600 or more. The functions would be included in CALCULATE commands and the results saved to memory variables as shown in Figure 10.25.

You can see that CNT( ) determined the number of records that satisfied the search conditions. The results were saved in the memory variables **females** and **highpaid**.

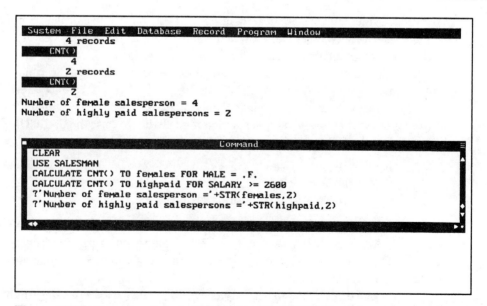

**Figure 10.25  Counting Selected Records with CNT( ) Functions**

## SUM()

The SUM( ) function is incorporated into a CALCULATE command to total the values in a numeric expression that includes one or more data fields. The sum is then saved to a memory variable. For example, the following CALCULATE command sums up the values in the SALARY data field:

```
USE SALESMAN
CALCULATE SUM(SALARY) TO totalpay
```

The SUM( ) function adds up all the values in the SALARY data field and saves the total to the memory variable named **totalpay**.

Instead of a single data field, you may also use a numeric expression in the function argument. Examples:

```
CALCULATE SUM(SALARY*.20) TO total_tax
CALCULATE SUM(QTY_SOLD*UNIT_PRICE) TO total_sale
```

The first command calculates the amount of withholding tax as 20 percent of the value in the SALARY data field. The second command calculates **total sale** by multiplying the values in the QTY_SOLD data field by that in the UNIT_PRICE data field.

You may also add filter conditions to the CALCULATE command to sum up values in selected records (see Figure 10.26).

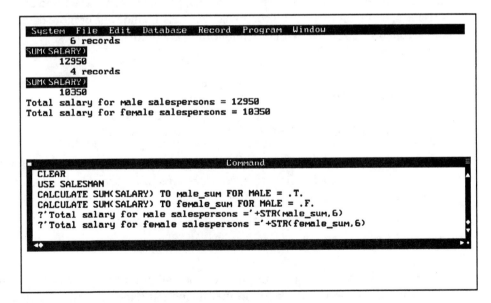

**Figure 10.26  Summing Up Values in Records**

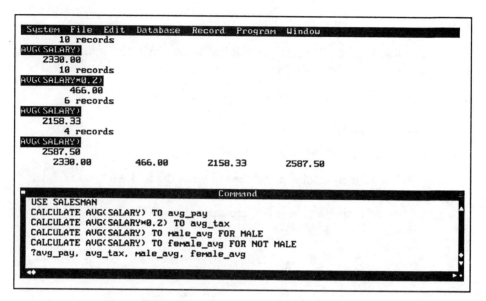

**Figure 10.27  Calculating Average Values**

## AVG()

Similar to SUM( ) is AVG( ), which enables you to calculate averages in a CALCULATE command. The calculated averages are saved to specified memory variables. In the CALCULATE command, you may include one or more data fields in the function argument, with or without filter conditions. Examples:

```
USE SALESMAN
CALCULATE AVG(SALARY) TO avg_pay
CALCULATE AVG(SALARY*0.20) TO avg_tax
CALCULATE AVG(SALARY) TO male_avg FOR MALE
CALCULATE AVG(SALARY) TO female_avg FOR NOT MALE
```

When you execute these commands, they will calculate the averages with the values in the specified data fields for the selected records. The calculated averages are then saved to the memory variables (see Figure 10.27).

## STD()

The STD( ) function calculates the standard deviation for the set of values represented by the numeric expression in the function argument. Standard deviation measures the average amount of deviation from the average value. As with the

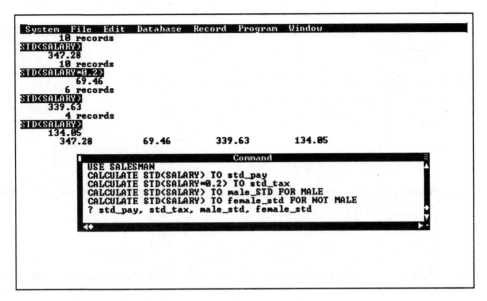

**Figure 10.28  Calculating Standard Deviations**

other mathematical functions, STD( ) is included in the CALCULATE command and the result is stored to a memory variable as shown in Figure 10.28. Examples:

```
USE SALESMAN
CALCULATE STD(SALARY) TO std_pay
CALCULATE STD(SALARY*0.20) TO std_tax
CALCULATE STD(SALARY) TO male_std FOR MALE
CALCULATE STD(SALARY) TO female_std FOR NOT MALE
```

## MAX(), MIN()

MAX( ) and MIN( ) allow you to find the maximum and minimum value in a set of values represented by the numeric expression in the function argument. The functions are incorporated into the CALCULATE command. To find the highest and lowest paid salesperson in the SALESMAN.DBf, the following two commands would be issued:

```
USE SALESMAN
CALCULATE MAX(SALARY) TO max_pay
CALCULATE MIN(SALARY) TO min_pay
```

After executing the two commands, the memory variables **max_pay** and **min_pay** will contain the largest and smallest values in the SALARY data field.

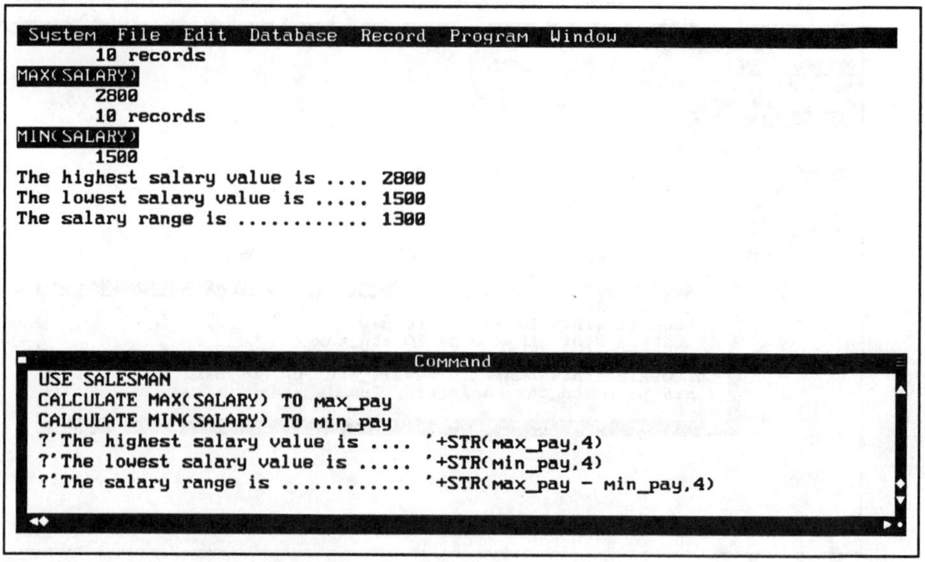

```
 System  File  Edit  Database  Record  Program  Window
       10 records
MAX(SALARY)
       2800
       10 records
MIN(SALARY)
       1500
The highest salary value is .... 2800
The lowest salary value is ..... 1500
The salary range is ........... 1300




                              Command
 USE SALESMAN
 CALCULATE MAX(SALARY) TO max_pay
 CALCULATE MIN(SALARY) TO min_pay
 ?'The highest salary value is .... '+STR(max_pay,4)
 ?'The lowest salary value is ..... '+STR(min_pay,4)
 ?'The salary range is ........... '+STR(max_pay - min_pay,4)
```

**Figure 10.29   Finding Maximum and Minimum Values**

You can also find the salary range by taking the difference between the two memory variables (see Figure 10.29).

## FINANCIAL FUNCTIONS

Two financial functions that may be of use to you are PAYMENT( ) and FV( ).

## PAYMENT()

PAYMENT( ) computes the amount of payment to make on a fixed-rate loan over a period of time. The format of the function is:

```
PAYMENT(<loan amount>, <interest rate>,
        <number of payments>)
```

Let's say that you intend to borrow $100,000 and would like to repay the loan in 360 monthly payments at an interest rate of 12 percent per year (or 1 percent per month). To determine the monthly payment, use the following command:

```
?PAYMENT(100000, 0.01, 360)
```

When the command is executed, it will return a value of $1,028.61, representing the monthly payment necessary to pay off the loan in 360 months (30 years) at the prevailing interest rate of 1 percent (0.01) per month. If the annual interest were 9 percent (.09/12 per month) and you wanted to pay the loan off in 15 years (180 months), you would revise the command to read:

```
?PAYMENT(100000, 0.09/12, 180)
```

resulting in the amount of $1,014.27.

## FV()

FV( ) calculates the future value of a series of equal periodic payments earning a fixed compounded interest. The format of the function is:

```
FV(<payment amount>, <interest rate>, <number of
payments>)
```

Using this format, the following command will return the total investment value if you have made two payments at $100 each, earning 10 percent per year:

```
?FV(100, 0.10, 2)
```

The function returns the value of $210, representing the total value of the investment after you have made two payments of $100 each. The first payment earned $10 (10 percent of $100) and became $110 at the time the second payment was made. As a result, the total value is:

|  | Value At Beginning of | |
| --- | --- | --- |
|  | Period 1 | Period 2 |
| Payment #1 | $100 | $110 |
| Payment #2 |  | $100 |
| Total Value |  | $210 |

Similarly, after making three payments of $100, the total value is $330:

|  | Value At Beginning of | | |
| --- | --- | --- | --- |
|  | Period 1 | Period 2 | Period 3 |
| Payment #1 | $100 | $110 | $121 |
| Payment #2 |  | $100 | $110 |
| Payment #3 |  |  | $100 |
| Total Value |  |  | $331 |

To calculate the future value, use the following FV( ) function:

```
?FV(100, 0.10, 3)
```

## DATA CONVERSION FUNCTIONS

In preceding chapters we used expressions in a number of applications. Expressions were built as conditions for locating records, as selection criteria in query operations, etc. Expressions may include data fields and memory variables, which *must* be of the same data type. You cannot, for example, mix a character data field with a date field in an expression. Therefore, to include data fields or memory variables of different types in the same expression, they must be converted to the same data type.

For this purpose, there is a set of built-in functions that convert data from one type to another.

## CTOD()

The CTOD( ) function converts a character string to a date:

```
CTOD(<character string>)
```

For example, the CTOD( ) function will convert the character string '12/25/91' to a date and save it in the memory variable named **xmas**. As a result, the memory variable becomes a date variable:

```
STORE '12/25/91' TO string_a
xmas = CTOD('12/25/91')
```

The CTOD( ) function is necessary to store a date in a date variable. You cannot use the following command to assign a date into the date variable **xmas**:

```
xmas = '12/25/91'
```

As a result, the character string is stored to the variable **xmas**, and **xmas** becomes a character variable after the command is executed.

## DTOC()

The DTOC( ) function converts a date to a character string:

```
DTOC(<date>)
```

Here is an example:

```
USE SALESMAN
LOCATE FOR LAST = 'Davidson'
?'Mr. '+TRIM(LAST)+' was hired on '+DTOC(HIRE_DATE)
```

After executing the commands, the output will be:

```
Record = 4
Mr. Davidson was hired on 06/04/90
```

## DTOS()

There is another function that converts a date to a character string—DTOS( ), used in the following format:

```
DTOS(<date>)
```

The function returns a string containing eight characters, indicating year (YYYY), month(MM) and day (DD) in the 'YYYYMMDD' format.

For example, the following DTOS( ) function will return a character string of '19911225' after you have executed the following command:

```
STORE {12/25/91} TO xmas
?DTOS(xmas)
```

You may also write the function as DTOS({12/25/91}). Remember, you must enclose the date in braces; otherwise, DTOS(12/25/91) will be considered illegal.

DTOS( ) comes in handy if you need to include a date in a character expression as an index key, because you cannot combine a date with a character string as an index key since all the data elements must be of the same type in an expression.

## VAL()

A character string composed of digits can be converted to a numeric value with the VAL( ) function. The format of the function is:

```
VAL(<character string>)
```

The character string must contain only digits, with or without a leading positive or negative sign, and with or with a decimal point. Here are examples:

```
?VAL('123')
?VAL('123.45')
?VAL('-67.89')
```

After executing these commands, the output will be:

```
123.00
  123.45
  -123.45
```

The character string in the function argument must be enclosed in quotes; otherwise, no value will be returned. For example, if you execute the following command,

```
?VAL(123.45)
```

the error message of "Invalid function argument, type, or count" will result.

Commas or dollar signs may not be included in the character string that is to be converted to a value. For example, the following function argument will not return a correct value.

```
VAL('$12,345.67')
```

The function will return the value of zero when the character string in the argument contains illegal symbols such as a dollar sign and commas.

VAL( ) is useful for converting the contents of a character field to a set of numbers. For example, to store your account numbers (such as 101, 102, 103, etc.) as character strings in the character field ACCT_NO, you can convert the character strings to numeric values and use them for sorting operations. It is faster to sort a list of numeric values than a list of character strings.

## STR()

The STR( ) function enables you to convert a numeric value into a character string. If the argument is an integer, STR( ) will return a string of digits corresponding to the integer. If the value is a decimal number, by default, it will convert the integer portion to a character string. But, as an option, you may specify the number of places after the decimal point that you would like to include in the return string. You may also choose the length of the returned character string. The format of the function is:

```
STR(<numeric value [,<length>, <decimal places>])
```

For example, the following two commands will return '-123' as a character string:

```
?STR(-123)
?STR(-123.45)
```

It will return the character string of '-123.45' if you specify the length of the character string as 6 and the number of decimal places as 2:

```
?STR(-123.45,6,2)
```

The STR( ) function is necessary for converting values in a numeric field so that it can be combined in a character expression as a key for the Index or Sort operations. For example, if you store your account identifications in a numeric field, the STR( ) function must be used if you want to include them in a character expression to be used as an index key. You cannot combine a numeric field and other character strings as an index key.

## DATE MANIPULATION FUNCTIONS

FoxPro's default format for representing dates is MM/DD/YY. But dates can be displayed in other formats. For example, the date {12/25/19}, once stored in a date variable named **xmas**, can also be displayed as December 25, '91 or December 25, 1991 by using one of the date manipulation functions. Other date manipulation functions allow you to extract the year, month, or day portion of a date for use as numeric values or character strings.

In addition, as we will see in a practical example at the end of this section, date manipulation functions are indispensable in using and incorporating dates into reports and labels. Most of these date manipulation functions (except for GOMONTH( )) follow the same format:

```
<name of the function>(<date>)
```

The date value returned by the function may be a number or a character string depending on the type of function you use.

## MDY()

The MDY( ) function converts a date to a character string in the Month DD, YY or the Month DD YYYY format. The result will be Month DD, YY if the CENTURY system parameter is set to OFF (its default value). If SET CENTURY ON has been issued, the character string will be in the Month DD, YYYY format. For example, assuming the CENTURY setting is OFF, the following MDY( ) function returns the character string of 'December 25, 91':

```
?MDY({12/25/91})
```

On the other hand, the function will return the character string of 'December 25, 1991' after you have SET CENTURY ON:

```
SET CENTURY ON
?MDY({12/25/91})
```

## YEAR(), MONTH(), DAY()

To extract the year, month, or day of a date and return it as a number or a character string, use one of the YEAR( ), MONTH( ), or DAY( ) functions. Here are some examples:

```
STORE '07/04/92' TO holiday
?YEAR(holiday)
?MONTH(holiday)
?DAY(holiday)
```

?YEAR(holiday) will return a numeric value of 1991 regardless of whether the CENTURY setting is ON or OFF. ?MONTH(holiday) and DAY(holiday) return the values of 7 and 4 respectively.

## CMONTH()

CMONTH( ) enables you to extract the month of a date, and returns a character string such as January, February, March, etc. The character string 'July' is the result of the following command:

```
?CMONTH({07/04/92})
```

## CDOW()

The day of a week can be determined by using the CDOW( ) function. It returns a character string such as 'Monday', 'Tuesday', 'Wednesday', etc. for the date specified in the function argument. The CDOW( ) function will return 'Saturday' when the following command is executed:

```
?CDOW({07/04/91})
```

## DOW()

DOW( ) also finds the day of week for a date, but while CDOW( ) returns a character string, DOW( ) returns a numeric value representing the day. The range of value is between 1 and 7, representing Sunday through Saturday. Because July 4, 1992 is on Saturday, the following function will return a numeric value of 7:

```
?DOW({07/04/92})
```

## GOMONTH()

The GOMONTH( ) returns a date that is a specified number of months before or after a given date. The format of the function is:

```
GOMONTH(<date>, <number of months>)
```

If a positive number is specified, the function will return a future date; if you specify a negative number, it will return a past date. Examples:

```
?GOMONTH({12/25/91},3)
?GOMONTH({12/25/91},-6)
```

When these commands execute, they will return {03/25/92} and {06/25/91} which are, respectively, three months later and six months before the given date of {12/25/91}.

# Chapter Summary

This chapter introduced the usefulness of memory variables and built-in functions in data manipulation. Memory variables make it possible to store intermediate results for later use. In addition, memory variables provide efficient means for passing data elements between databases and reports.

Built-in functions are shortcuts for manipulating data elements. This chapter explained how to use character strings to manipulate the contents of character variables and character data fields. Similarly, the mathematical functions illustrated the methods for manipulating the numeric values in memory variables and data fields.

In preceding chapters, where expressions were used to specify search conditions and query selection criteria, all the data elements in them had to be of the same data type. This chapter described how to employ data conversion functions so that it is possible to include different types of data variables and data fields in the same expression.

The next chapter describes the procedures for creating custom reports and mailing labels, and some of the built-in functions discussed in this chapter will be used. In addition, you will learn how to pass summary statistics that are created and saved in memory variables to reports.

# 11

# Producing Reports and Mailing Labels

## An Overview

Perhaps the most important function of a database management system is to produce reports based on information extracted from the databases. This chapter details the procedures for designing and producing professional reports in a columnar or free form format with FoxPro's Report Writer.

By the conclusion of this chapter, you will be able to create a quick report in the Report Layout window using FoxPro's default form, or create a custom report based on a format of your own design. You also will be introduced to the procedure for generating mailing labels with FoxPro's Label Designer. Finally, you will learn how to output all these elements both to the printer and the screen.

## FoxPro Reports

After you have gone to all the trouble of storing your data in database files, it is natural that you would want to extract useful information from them. A logical way to present this information is in professional reports that allow you to organize the extracted data elements in a consistent layout that shows precisely the kind of information you wish to see.

The FoxPro Report Writer can be used to produce reports by using information that is taken from one or more database files. Depending on your application, you can choose either column or form reports. A column report obviously presents information in a column format, while a form report allows you to place information anywhere in the report. Most financial or accounting statistics are good candidates for column reports; computer-generated form letters are typical examples of form report output.

As a shortcut, you may choose to produce one of the two basic quick reports provided by FoxPro that present information in a default format. These quick reports label all data fields with their field names and place them in the report at a location determined by FoxPro. Alternatively, you may design a custom report over which you have full control of all the report objects and their placement on the page or screen.

The first step in creating a report is to determine its design in FoxPro's Report Layout window. This involves laying out all the necessary objects, which may include data fields taken from the database files, summary statistics computed from these field values, and text or graphics objects for describing or drawing attention to the information in the report. Once you have finished designing the report form, you can preview it on the screen before directing it to the printer.

# Types of Reports

As mentioned, there are two types of report formats to choose from: column and form. Although they may contain the same data elements, information taken from the database is presented differently in each type of report. The report format you choose usually depends on the type of information that will be presented.

## COLUMN REPORTS

A column report presents information in several columns, each of which contains data elements from one or more data fields. These data fields can be any of the valid data types supported by FoxPro: character strings, dates, logical values, and numeric values. A column report also gives you the capability to calculate summary statistics from the values in the columns and place them at the bottom of the columns. Data elements can be grouped in sections and group statistics can be displayed at the end of each section. An example of a column report is shown in Figure 11.1.

This sample report presents information about the salaries of the sales staff from the SALESMAN database. Social security numbers are presented in the column labeled "Soc. Sec. #." The Last Name and First Name columns display the last and first names of each member of the sales personnel. Monthly salaries are shown in the Monthly Salary column, and the Annual Salary column is calculated from the values in the Monthly Salary column.

Data elements in this report are divided into two groups: male and female sales personnel. Summary statistics, such as the monthly and annual salaries for each gender group, as well as the grand total of the monthly and annual salaries, are calculated and placed at the end of the data section.

```
                    ┌─────────────────────────┐
                    │  SALARY  SUMMARY  REPORT │          Page   1
                    └─────────────────────────┘          09/07/91

     Soc. Sec. #     Last       First      Monthly    Annual
                     Name       Name       Salary     Salary

                         Male Salespersons
     444-56-3333     Iverson    Albert      $2,200     $26,400
     909-78-3434     Gilbert    Fred        $2,300     $27,600
     701-31-8723     Evans      Henry       $2,000     $24,000
     222-55-1000     Davidson   Edward      $1,500     $18,000
     303-67-8901     Carter     Jack        $2,550     $30,600
     101-20-4545     Bell       George      $2,400     $28,800
                                           ────────   ────────
                                Total       $12,950    $155,400
                        Female Salespersons
     111-33-4545     Jones      Betty       $2,500     $30,000
     333-56-4545     Ford       Ida         $2,600     $31,200
     111-22-3333     Anderson   Doris       $2,800     $33,600
                                           ────────   ────────
                                Total       $10,350    $124,200

                         GRAND  TOTAL       $23,300    $279,600
     ×Data updated 12/31/90
```

**Figure 11.1  A Column Report**

Three types of objects may be included in a column report—data fields, text, and graphic objects. Data fields are placed in the report to display information extracted from the selected database files. Text objects are used to describe information contained in the reports; they take the form of report titles, column or group headings, footers, etc. Graphics objects include boxes and vertical and horizontal lines that highlight the information in the report.

## FORM REPORTS

If you decide to present the information extracted from the databases in a form report, you can include the same types of data objects as in a column report—data fields, text, and graphics objects. But be aware, there are significant differences between the two types of reports. Unlike a column report that displays information in a fixed format, a form report shows its information in a free form layout, which means that data fields may be placed anywhere on the report page. And a column report displays the data taken from an individual data record in a row in the detail section of the report, whereas a form report displays the data from a single data record in a separate section or page. An example of a form report is shown in Figure 11.2.

This figure shows a portion of a form report that is produced by using the information taken from the SALESMAN database. You can see that data fields are laid out in a free form. For example, the name of each salesperson is displayed as a character string taken from the FIRST, INITIAL, and LAST data fields of the record belonging to that salesperson. Similarly, values from other data fields are

```
INFORMATION ABOUT OUR SALESPERSONS              Page    1
                                                09/17/91

                     Doris B. Anderson

 Id. No.: S0    Social Security #: 111-22-3333    Male? [N]
 ─────────────────────────────────────────────────────────
 Employment Date: 07/01/86        Office: B1
 Monthly Salary:  $2,800          Commission Rate:  0%
 Hobbies: classical music, painting, travel.


                     George G. Bell

 Id. No.: S1    Social Security #: 101-20-4545    Male? [Y]
 ─────────────────────────────────────────────────────────
 Employment Date: 10/12/88        Office: B3
 Monthly Salary:  $2,400          Commission Rate: 20%
 Hobbies: fishing, hunting, country music.

 ......
 ......
 ......
```

**Figure 11.2   A Example of Form Report**

scattered throughout the report. Descriptive text replaces field names in the report to describe information contained in the data fields. A page heading, including a page number and a report date, is added to the top of a report page for reference purposes.

A popular layout of a form report is a computer form letter, which mixes data fields taken from selected databases with other report objects. An example of such a form letter is shown in Figure 11.3.

```
                     OFFICE MEMORANDUM



     Date:    09/12/91

     To:      Doris B. Anderson

     From:    Personnel Department

     Subject: Personal Data

              Please take a moment to verify the following personal
              data about yourself and report any discrepancies to
              us as soon as possible:

                   Date of Employment:   07/01/86
                   Current Monthly Salary:   $2,800
                        Commission Rate:   0%


     GTC:  tjm
```

**Figure 11.3   Sample Form Letter**

An office memorandum such as this can be produced by mixing the information taken from the SALESMAN database and other report objects. In the memorandum, the name of the salesperson (Doris B. Anderson) is taken from the FIRST, INITIAL, and LAST data fields of her database record. Similarly, information about her employment date, monthly salary, and commission rate is extracted from the HIRE_DATE, SALARY, and COMIS_RATE data fields in the same record. These data field values are merged with the text necessary to convey the memorandum's message. In addition, a report date is inserted into the memorandum.

# Report Components

A report consists of a set of components, some of which are found in all reports, while others may be included for special applications. These components tend to be laid out in sections, and each serves to convey a specific kind of information. These report elements are as follows:

- A **report title** describes the information contained in the report. The report title should appear at the beginning of the report. If the report consists of several pages, subsequent pages may also include a **page heading** that describes the information on each page. In addition, a **footer** may also be displayed at the bottom of each report page. Report titles are included on almost all column reports and on many form reports.

- In a column report, a **detail section** displays the contents of database records. Information taken from data fields of selected database files is presented in various columns, each of which is identified with a column heading. Each data record is presented as a row in the detail section of a column report.

- In a column report, **Summary statistics** are frequently placed at the end of data columns and summarize the data elements. If the data elements are divided into groups, **group statistics** are usually displayed at the end of each data group, and an overall statistical summary is placed at the end of the report. To describe the information in each group, reports also make use of a **group heading**. In a form report, on the other hand, the summary section may appear anywhere in the report.

- A sequential **page number** is usually included in multi-page reports. The **report date** also is often displayed in the report. These two elements are incorporated both in column and form reports.

- Finally, a report may make use of various **graphics objects**, such as boxes and lines, that serve to highlight or to separate certain objects in the report. For example, a rectangular box can be drawn around the report title to highlight it, and horizontal lines can be used to separate the column headings from the body of the details of the report.

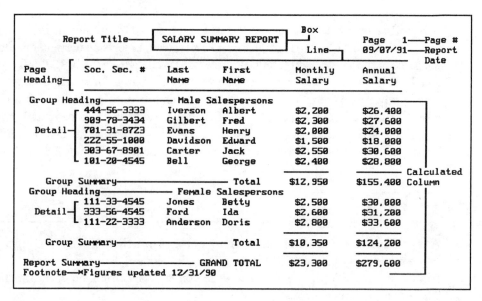

**Figure 11.4  Components of a Typical Column Report**


These components are depicted in the column report shown in Figure 11.4. The report title, SALARY SUMMARY REPORT, appears on top of the first page of the report with a box drawn around it as a highlighting device. Character strings taken from the SS_NO, LAST, and FIRST data fields of the SALESMAN database are displayed in the first three report columns. These are identified with the column headings "Soc. Sec. #," "Last Name," and "First Name," respectively. Values from the numeric field SALARY are shown in the column labeled as Monthly Salary. The column with the Annual Salary heading displays values calculated from the SALARY data field. Two horizontal lines are used to separate the column headings from the field values.

Each row of the detail section in the report shows data elements taken from a data record of the selected database file. Records are grouped in two sections—one that lists data from salesmen and a second that lists data from saleswomen. Each group is identified with a label in the group heading.

Summary statistics, in the form of group totals, are computed and displayed at the end of each group of data records. Grand totals that are calculated from all the individual values listed in the Monthly Salary and Annual Salary columns are shown at the bottom of the two columns. Lines are drawn to separate the report detail and the totals. To complete the report, a footnote is included at the bottom of the report page.

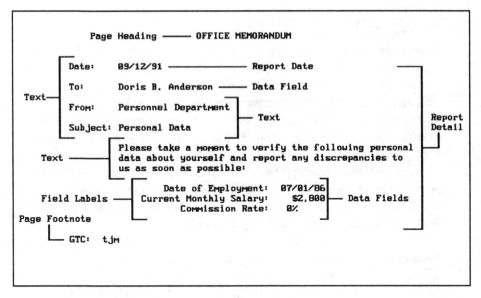

**Figure 11.5   Components of a Typical Form Letter**

Although FoxPro allows you to include in a form report the same types of components as in a column report, usually different elements are chosen for a form report. In a form letter, generally field labels are used in place of column headings, and a page heading is used instead of a report tile to describe the information in each form letter. And, because each form report is generated with data from an individual record, it does not usually include any summary statistics.

Figure 11.5 shows an example of a form report. At the top of the report is the page heading. The report details include the data fields taken from the SALESMAN database and the accompanying labels that describe the field values. In addition to textual information, the report includes a report date and page footnote.

## Creating Reports

To create a column or form report, use the FoxPro Report Writer. The process begins with designing the report form by laying out the report objects in the Report Writer's layout window and extracting selected fields from your database files and placing them in the report. After designing the report form, you may verify its contents by displaying it on the screen. If the report is satisfactory to you, the report can then be sent to the printer. If you choose to make additional changes, simply return to the layout window to make the necessary adjustments before printing the report.

## CREATING COLUMN REPORTS

Before designing a report, it is best to first select the database file or files that the report will incorporate. Data elements from one or more database files may be used in the same report. To simplify the explanation of the design process, however, let's assume that here you will use only one database file, SALESMAN.DBF, to create a report. To do that, select the database as the current database file in work area A. If you have not done this, FoxPro will prompt you to do so before you can begin designing your report.

To create a new column report, select the New menu option from the File menu popup. When the New dialog appears, select the Report radio button, followed by selecting the <<OK>> push button. In return, a report layout form is displayed in the Report Layout window (see Figure 11.6).

This figure shows the layout form that can be used to design either a column or form report. At this point, you may start placing the report objects in the form. Choose the data fields from the selected database and place them in the report form; or choose a FoxPro default layout that places the data fields in the report by using the quick report format. Although we will begin by creating a quick column report, we first will take a closer look at the layout of the FoxPro Report Writer.

## REPORT BANDS

The FoxPro Report Writer divides a report into sections called report bands. Each band is used to hold certain kinds of report objects. In its default layout, as

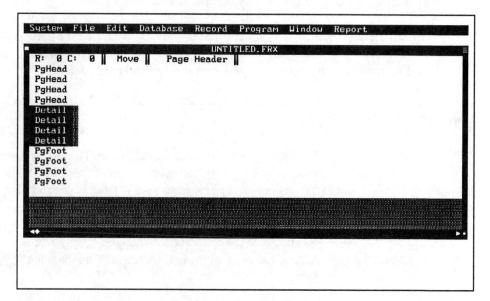

**Figure 11.6   The Report Layout Form**

Figure 11.6 shows, the Report Writer displays three report bands: the Page Header (PgHead) band, the Detail band, and the Page Footer (PgFoot) band. In addition, however, other bands are available for placing different objects in a report. They include the Title band, the Group Header band, the Group Footer band, and the Summary band. Each report band, if it is present, occupies one or more rows in the column report.

At the top of the Report Layout window, there is a status line that shows the location of the cursor and the Report Writer's operating mode. The first pair of values in the status line (in Figure 11.6, R: 0 C: 0) indicates the location of the cursor (row zero and column zero). The second item on the status line is the operating mode. For example, the Move indicator shown in Figure 11.6 indicates that you can move any report object on the report form. The remaining operating modes include:

- *Text.* Allows you to modify a text object (such as field labels) in the Report Writer.

- *Field.* Allows you to define or modify a field or expression or to resize an existing field.

- *Box.* Allows you to draw a sizable box figure in the Report Writer.

The last item on the status line tells you in which band or section of the report the cursor is positioned. For example, "Page Header" indicates that the cursor is positioned in the PgHead band. The seven bands discussed below are all found in the Report Writer.

## Title Band

Typically, the Title band contains the report heading—the name of the report and any other descriptive text that applies to the entire report. The contents of the title band are displayed only once, at the beginning of the report.

## Page Header Band

The Report Writer's Page Header band is used to hold the information that you intend to display at the top of each report page. In a column report, the Page Header band normally contains the column headings. It may also contain the page number or the report date, because the contents of the band will be repeated on each page of the report. In the quick report layout shown in Figure 11.8, for example, FoxPro places the names of the data fields in the Page Header band; these field names become the default column headings in a quick report.

In the Report Writer's default layout, as shown in Figure 11.6, there are four rows or lines used to represent the Page Header band. In a quick column report, as shown in Figure 11.8, column headings occupy only the first row. Empty rows will be displayed as blank lines in the report; therefore, you would use empty lines to create space between the page heading and the body of the report that are represented by the data elements in the Detail band. If the empty lines create too much space between the sections of a report, they can be deleted.

## Detail Band

The Detail band in a column report displays the contents of selected data fields from the records in the database or databases. Because the Detail band displays information taken from one data record, the band will be repeated as many times as the number of records in the database. For example, in the quick report shown in Figure 11.8, data fields from the SALESMAN database are placed in the Detail band. Each data field is identified by the field name that you specified in the database structure. When you display the report, field values from each selected record will be extracted from the database and placed in the designated location.

## Page Footer Band

The Page Footer is the last section of a report page. The information in this element will be displayed at the bottom of every page of the report. Usually, this consists of a footnote or a report date. In the quick report layout of Figure 11.8, for example, FoxPro places the report date (represented by the current system date, DATE( )) on the left-hand side of the last row of the Page Footer band. Similarly, if you scroll to the right-hand side of the quick report layout, you can see that the page number of the report is also placed in the Page Footer band. The report page number is identified by the label "Page," followed by a system variable, _PAG, that contains a sequential page number.

## Group Header Band

If you divide records into groups and present them in different sections in a report, the group heading is placed in the Group Header band. Information placed in this band will be displayed at the beginning of the group.

## Group Footer Band

Like the Group Header, the Group Footer band is used when data records are grouped for a report, and it is displayed at the end of each data group. Typically, the Group Footer band consists of text that describes the information in the group or summary statistics that relate to the group.

## Summary Band

The Summary band is provided for placing summary statistics in the report. Because the summary statistics are calculated by using all the selected records, they will appear only once at the end of the entire report.

## CREATING QUICK REPORTS

To create a quick report using the Report Writer's default layout, choose the Quick Report option from the Report menu popup. In return, FoxPro displays the Quick Report dialog shown in Figure 11.7.

The Quick Report dialog shows two radio buttons and three check boxes. The radio buttons are used to select the type of report layout: column or form; Column Layout is FoxPro's default layout, as displayed in this figure.

The Titles check box, which is selected by default, causes the names of selected data fields be used as column headings. The Add Alias check box is also selected by default; it is used to include the database filename along with the name of the field. For example, when the check box is selected, the data field FIRST will be identified as SALESMAN.FIRST in the report. The Fields check box allows you to select only those data fields from the selected database that you would like to include in the report. Because the SALESMAN database has too many fields to be displayed on a single line of a column, let's select only certain fields from the database to be included in the report.

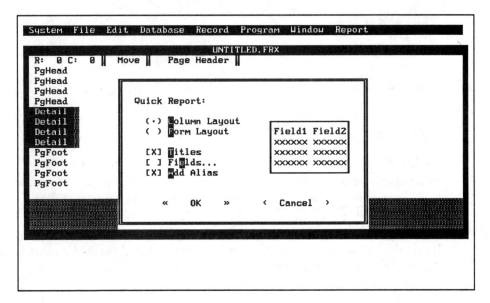

**Figure 11.7  The Quick Report Dialog**

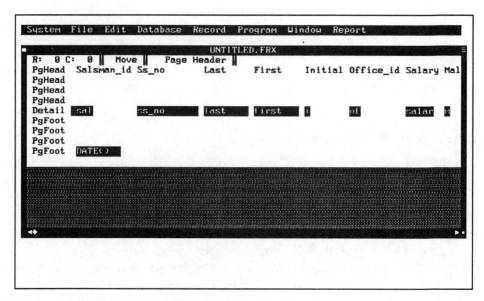

**Figure 11.8  Layout of the Quick Report**

## Selecting Data Fields

To select data fields to be included in the quick report, select the Fields check box. When the Field Picker dialog appears, select the following eight data fields in the order in which they are shown:

```
SALSMAN_ID
SS_NO
LAST
FIRST
INITIAL
OFFICE_ID
SALARY
MALE
```

When this is done, return to the Quick Report dialog and select the <<OK>> push button to return to the Report Layout window. At this point you can see that all the selected data fields are placed in the report, together with the column headings (see Figure 11.8).

This figure shows the layout of the quick report and its report objects, along with all the selected data fields and text in the form of column headings for identifying these fields. It also displays other objects such as the report date.

```
 System   File   Edit   Database   Record   Program   Window   Report
                             Preview
┌─
 Salsman_id Ss_no        Last     First     Initial Office_id Salary Male


 S0           111-22-3333 Anderson Doris      B        B1        2800  N
 S1           101-20-4545 Bell     George     G        B3        2400  Y
 S2           303-67-8901 Carter   Jack       J        B2        2550  Y
 S3           222-55-1000 Davidson Edward     D        B1        1500  Y
 S4           701-31-8723 Evans    Henry      H        B3        2000  Y
 S5           333-56-4545 Ford     Ida        F        B2        2600  N
 S6           909-78-3434 Gilbert  Fred       C        B3        2300  Y
 S7           355-23-7777 Harvey   Candy      E        B3        2450  N
 S8           444-56-3333 Iverson  Albert     I        B2        2200  Y
 S9           111-33-4545 Jones    Betty      A        B1        2500  N




 « Done »  ‹ More ›   Column:    0
```

**Figure 11.9  Viewing the Quick Report**

## Viewing Quick Reports

To view a quick report on the screen, select the Page Preview option from the Report menu popup, and the contents of the report will be displayed (see Figure 11.9). The quick report in this figure displays the column headings in the Page Header band on top of the report. The report body is represented by the information presented in the Detail band. Each line shows information taken from the fields in one record of the SALESMAN database.

At the bottom of the report screen are two push buttons: <Done> and <More>. Choose <Done> to return to the Report Layout window. For a multi-page report, choose the <More> button or press the PgDn key to view the next report page. Note that you can only page forward, not backward, through the report. To view previous pages, you must return to the Layout window and redisplay the report.

## Producing Quick Reports

After viewing the quick report, it can be printed. But, before printing the report, the parameters that determine how the printed report page should look must be specified. These parameters set the length and margins of the report page. In addition, the printer driver to be used by FoxPro must be selected and any printing options must be specified. Printing options determine whether FoxPro will issue page eject before or after it prints a page, whether blank lines will be suppressed, and whether FoxPro will omit the report detail and provide only summary statistics.

### Specifying Page Layout

To specify the page layout for the report, select the <Done> push button to return to the Report Layout window. Then select the Page Layout option from the Report menu popup. As a result, the Report Writer displays the Page Layout dialog shown in Figure 11.10.

You can see in the Page Layout dialog the set of default values chosen by FoxPro for determining the page length and top and bottom margins. These values are displayed in text boxes in the dialog and represent the number of rows in the report. In a quick report, the report page is set to 66 lines without top and bottom margins. The printer indent and the right margin for the printed text also can be specified. They are represented by number of columns or characters from the left edge of the printed page. By default, the right margin is set to 80 and the printer indent is set to 0. You may change any of these parameter values simply by positioning the cursor in the text box and entering the new value. For our example, though, let's accept all the default values specified by the Report Writer.

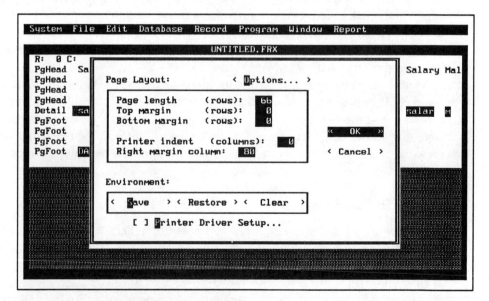

**Figure 11.10  The Page Layout Dialog**

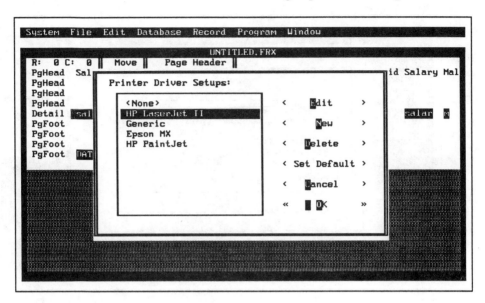

**Figure 11.11  Selecting Report Printer**

### Selecting Printers

The next step is to select the printer. To do that, select the Printer Driver Setup check box. When the Printer Driver Setups dialog appears you should see a list of printer drivers that you previously installed (see Figure 11.11). If the list is empty, select the <New> push button to install a new printer driver (refer to Chapter 3 if you need to review this information). Next highlight the printer you want and select the <<OK>> button to accept it and return to the Page Layout window.

### Setting Printing Options

Before printing a report, be aware that you can control several more options that affect the content and format of your report. These are available by selecting the Options check box in the Page Layout dialog. When the Options dialog appears you will see that it has six check boxes (see Figure 11.12).

When the Page eject before printing check box is selected (the default), the printer will issue a page eject before printing begins; this ensures that it will begin printing at the top of a new page. Similarly, selecting the Page eject after printing option causes the printer to advance to a new page once it has finished printing the entire report.

If you select the Plain page check box, the information in the Page Header band will be printed only on the first page of the report, not on subsequent pages.

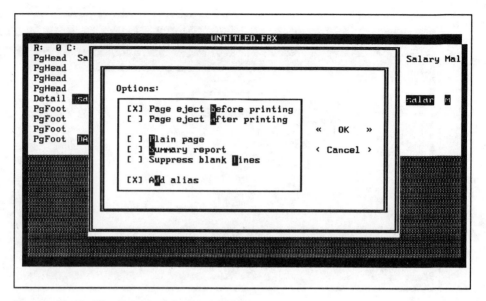

**Figure 11.12  The Printing Options Dialog**

Checking this box does not affect how the information in the Page Footer is printed, however.

When you don't want to print information that is included in the Detail band, select the Summary report check box. In doing so, only information in other bands will be printed.

If you want any blank lines that are included in the report bands for spacing purposes to be ignored, select the Suppress blank lines check box. And to have all the data fields defined in the report identified with the database filename, select the Add alias check box (this is useful only when more than one database file is used in the same report).

To continue with our exercise, let's accept all the default settings for the printing options by selecting the <<OK>> push button, which returns us to the Report Layout dialog.

## Saving the Report Environment

At the bottom of the Page Layout dialog are three push buttons within the Environment group box. These options control the information about the FoxPro environment that is to be passed to the report when it is executing. This environmental information includes the names of all the databases that are open and any relations that have been established among them, the currently selected work area, and the names of all the indexes currently open, as well as the name of the current master index.

The <Save> push button saves the current report environment; the <Restore> push button returns the report environment to its state *prior* to any changes made to it since the last time it was saved; <Clear> cancels all report environments previously saved. Normally, you would select <Save> to retain the current report environment for future use. This will allow you to modify or print the report in the future without first having to open the necessary databases and index files and define the necessary relations.

Next select the <<OK>> push button to return to the Report Layout window. At this point, you may choose to output the report to the printer or save it to a file. A good habit to develop is to save the report layout to a file before printing it in order to avoid the risk of damage in case the printing process is interrupted for any reason. If the printer is improperly connected or configured, for example, FoxPro may "freeze" the action and you will have to abort the printing process before continuing once again. If you have not saved your report form, it may be necessary to set it up again. If, however, you intend to use the report layout once and are certain the printer is properly installed and connected, it is probably safe to print the report without saving the layout to a file.

### Saving Reports

To save the layout that appears in the Report Layout window as a report form, select the Save as option from the File menu popup. When the Save Report As: dialog appears, enter the name of the report; for example, type in QKREPORT, if that's the file you want to save. The report layout will be saved in a report form file with an .FRX extension (e.g., QKREPORT.FRX). When you return to the Report Layout window, the name of the report will appear in the Title Bar of the window.

## Printing Reports

When you are in the Report Layout window, the report can be printed by choosing the Report option from the Database menu popup, which causes the Report dialog to appear (see Figure 11.13).

Information in the Report dialog is displayed in four groups, each of which contains a number of check boxes, push buttons and radio buttons. The first group contains the <Form> check box for identifying the report form (e.g., QKREPORT.FRX) to be used. While the Report Writer is the active window, the report form in it will be selected as the default report form. In addition, this group contains three check boxes: Environment, Quick Report, and Set Printer Driver. If the Environment check box is selected, FoxPro will restore any environment information that had been previously saved. The Quick Report check box is disabled because the Report Writer is open and contains a custom report form, which will be used instead of FoxPro's default quick reports. The Set Printer Driver

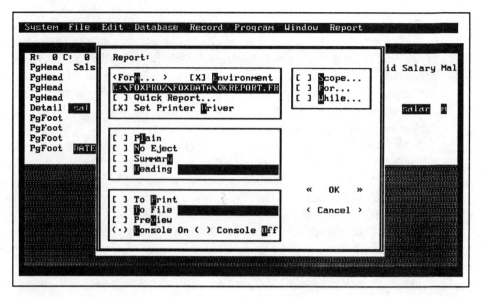

**Figure 11.13  The Report Dialog**

should be checked in order to allow you to print the report with the printer that you selected previously. *Note: You cannot change the printer driver here. To select a different printer, you must go back to the Page Layout dialog and bring up the Printer Driver Setup dialog.*

The second group box contains four check boxes: Plain, No Eject, Summary, and Heading. If you choose the Plain check box, the report will print the information in the Page Header on the first report page only, not on subsequent pages. Choosing the No Eject check box causes the printer to begin printing at the current print position without first advancing to a new page. The Summary check box allows you to print only the information in the Summary band and to suppress the printing of all detail information. An additional line may be added to the page heading on each report page and can be entered as text or an expression by selecting the Heading check box. This text will appear on a line below the information in the Page Header band.

The third group box in the Report dialog contains three check boxes—To Print, To File, and Preview—that are used to direct the report to the printer, a disk file, or the screen. If you are sending the report to a disk file, enter the name of the output file in the text box provided. There are two additional radio buttons in this group: Console On and Console Off. If the report is going either to a printer or a file, you can monitor the output by selecting the Console On radio button; turning on the Console Off radio button sends the report to the printer or a file without being displayed on the screen.

| SALSMAN_ID | Ss_no | LAST | FIRST | INITIAL | Office_id | Salary | MALE |
|---|---|---|---|---|---|---|---|
| S0 | 111-22-3333 | Anderson | Doris | B | B1 | 2800 | N |
| S1 | 101-20-4545 | Bell | George | G | B3 | 2400 | Y |
| S2 | 303-67-8901 | Carter | Jack | J | B2 | 2550 | Y |
| S3 | 222-55-1000 | Davidson | Edward | D | B1 | 1500 | Y |
| S4 | 701-31-8723 | Evans | Henry | H | B3 | 2000 | Y |
| S5 | 333-56-4545 | Ford | Ida | F | B2 | 2600 | N |
| S6 | 909-78-3434 | Gilbert | Fred | C | B3 | 2300 | Y |
| S7 | 355-23-7777 | Harvey | Candy | E | B3 | 2450 | N |
| S8 | 444-56-3333 | Iverson | Albert | I | B2 | 2200 | Y |
| S9 | 111-33-4545 | Jones | Betty | A | B1 | 2500 | N |

**Figure 11.14   The Printed Quick Report**

Finally, three check boxes appear in the upper right-hand corner of the Report dialog: Scope, For, and While. They are used to select the records and fields in the same way as discussed previously.

As an exercise, print the quick report using the report form in the Report Layout window. Select the To Print check box while leaving the Console On radio button on, and the report will be output on the designated printer. A copy of the printed report is shown in Figure 11.14.

When you inspect your quick report, you may want to modify the report form to produce a custom report. The custom report could, for example, incorporate descriptive text as column headings to describe the values in the report columns. You can add new data fields to the report or remove existing ones; you also can rearrange the order of the columns, change the column widths, and format the data values. You can add a report title to the beginning of the report that describes the information in the report, place the report date and page number in different places on the report, or add graphics objects such as boxes and lines to highlight the most important information in the report.

## CREATING CUSTOM REPORTS

There are two ways to create a custom report. One is to design the report form from scratch by individually defining and positioning all the report objects. Or you can modify an existing quick report that was generated by FoxPro, as in the example above. The latter approach often is a time-saver because the quick report provides a basic skeleton on which to build. Because the quick report allows you to select the data fields that you would like to appear in the report, you can quickly rearrange them in a custom report without placing each of them individually.

## Modifying Existing Reports

To create a custom report (using our example) by modifying the report form, open QKREPORT.FRX so that it is displayed in the Report Layout window. If you have exited from the Report Writer, select the Open option from the File menu popup. When the Open dialog appears, select Report from the Type popup and then select the name of the report form file from the list. If you want to modify the report form, QKREPORT.FRX, that you have saved, select it from the file list in the Open dialog. The Open dialog also contains a Restore Environment check box. Check this box to load the environment information that was stored with the report. By choosing this check box, the database file selected for the report will be opened automatically in the currently selected work area even if you have not done so. Now, select QKREPORT.FRX. In return, the report form that was previously saved as QKREPORT.FRX is displayed in the Report Layout window. You can now begin to modify the report form.

### Selecting Report Objects

During the report modification process, you may want to delete unwanted report objects or move report objects from current to new locations. To do that, select the objects you plan to delete or move (you may select one or more objects at a time with the mouse or by using the keyboard).

To select a report object, click your mouse on the object or press the Spacebar after positioning the cursor at the object. If you need to select several objects, click the mouse on each of the objects while holding down the Shift key. On the keyboard, hold down the Shift key and use the arrow key to position the cursor on each object field to be selected and press the Spacebar. When the default color scheme is used with a color monitor, the selected objects will be highlighted in red. If you make a mistake, press Esc to deselect the object.

All the objects also may be selected by using a selection marquee; a selection marquee allows you to define a rectangular area and select all objects within it. To draw the marquee, position the mouse pointer at any corner of a rectangular area that includes all the objects you wish to select and drag it to form the rectangle. As you do this, the selection marquee will appear as a rectangle with dotted lines. When you release the button, all the objects inside the marquee will be selected. To define a selection marquee with the keyboard, position the cursor at one corner of a rectangular area that includes the objects you wish to select and press the Spacebar to anchor the marquee. A dot will appear at the cursor position. Use the arrow keys to draw the marquee around the block.

### Deleting Report Objects

Once you have selected one or more report objects, they can be removed from the report by pressing the Del key. Text, data fields, and graphics objects may be removed in this way; note, however, that data fields that have been removed from the report are not also deleted from the database.

To delete the column heading "Salsman_id," as an example, click the mouse on the heading and then press the Del key. Or use the keyboard to delete the SALSMAN_ID field. The width of the data field is three characters and it is identified as a small rectangular block that is labeled with the three characters "sal" (the remaining part of the field name is hidden from view). To remove the data field from the report, position the cursor on the field and then press the Del key.

To delete the field MALE (labeled "m") and the column heading "Male" as a group, hold down the Shift key, then click the mouse on the field and the column heading in sequence, followed by pressing the Del key. It is also possible to delete a set of data fields and column headings by using the selection marquee. For example, to remove the INITIAL and OFFICE_ID fields (labeled as "i" and "of") and their column headings ("Initial" and "Office_id"), first use the selection marquee to select the fields and column headings. To do that, click the mouse just to the left of the column heading "Initial" and then drag the mouse just to the right of the data field labeled "of." As you do so, a dotted rectangular marquee appears, and all the objects within the marquee will be selected when you release the mouse button. In this case, the selected objects will be the two data fields and the column headings. To delete them, press the Del key.

After removing all the data fields and column headings, the report form will look like that shown in Figure 11.15.

### Restoring Deleted Report Objects

Should you accidentally remove an object from your report, it is easy to restore it, provided that you notice and attempt to correct your mistake before making any further deletions. When a report object is removed from the Report Writer, it is not physically deleted immediately. Instead, FoxPro removes it from the screen and stores it in a temporary holding area called the Clipboard. As long as the contents of the Clipboard have not changed since you deleted the last report object or objects, you can restore them. To do this, use the keyboard or the mouse to place the cursor where the object or objects were positioned and select the Paste command from the Edit menu pad. FoxPro will copy the contents of its Clipboard back to the Report Writer's layout window.

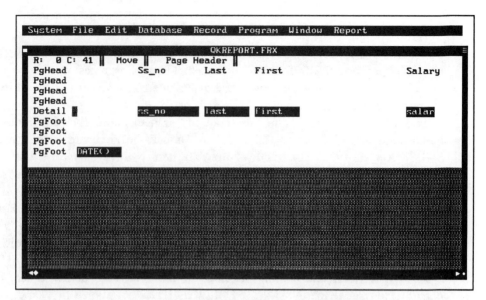

**Figure 11.15   After Removing Data Fields and Column Headings**

It is worthwhile stressing, however, that deleted report objects can be restored only as long as they remain intact on the Clipboard. Once they are removed from the Clipboard—which happens when some other object is deleted or copied to the Clipboard, or when you exit FoxPro—they can no longer be recovered.

## Moving Report Objects

Notice in Figure 11.15 that the space remains blank after the report objects are removed. Remaining objects will not be rearranged to fill the space. You may, however, move the remaining objects around yourself.

Any selected report objects may be repositioned in a report. To move a selected object with the mouse, point the mouse cursor at the object and then drag it to a new location. If more selected objects are to be moved, point the mouse cursor at any one of them and then drag them as a group to the new location. With the keyboard, use the arrow keys to move the selected objects to the new location.

Let's say for example, that you want to move the first column to the left: First select the SS_NO data field (labeled "ss_no") and the column heading "Ss_no" either with the mouse or the keyboard. Then use the mouse to drag it left to the desired location. Use the same method to move the FIRST data field and its column heading closer to the LAST data field. Finally, move the SALARY field and its column heading closer to the LAST data field and its column heading. After moving the data fields and column headings, your report form should look like that shown in Figure 11.16.

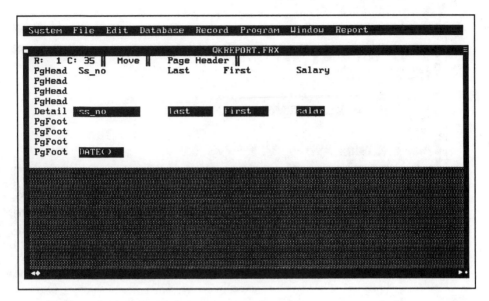

System   File   Edit   Database   Record   Program   Window   Report

QKREPORT.FRX

R:  1 C:  35 ‖  Move ‖    Page Header ‖
PgHead   Ss_no              Last       First           Salary
PgHead
PgHead
PgHead
Detail   ss_no              last       first           salar
PgFoot
PgFoot
PgFoot
PgFoot   DATE()

**Figure 11.16  Rearranging Report Columns**

Note that the column headings contain the names of their corresponding data fields. Because they do not fully describe the information contained in the columns, you may want to use more descriptive text to describe the data fields, which requires that you edit the text of each column heading that now appears in the Page Header band.

### Editing Text

Any text in a report can be edited by using the arrow keys or the mouse to position the cursor on the character to be modified. In doing so, however, be sure that you are not selecting an object; otherwise, when you press an arrow key, the selected object will move in the direction of the arrow key. For example, if you decide to change the heading of the first column from "SS_no" to "Soc. Sec. #," use the arrow keys to move the cursor to the current heading and then enter the new column heading. As a shortcut, use the Home and End keys to move the cursor directly to the beginning and the end of the line in a Report band. After entering the new heading, press Enter. Your report form will now look like that in Figure 11.17.

### Inserting Text

You can place text in the Report band by first positioning the cursor at the initial position of the text. Then simply type in the text from that position. Try this to enter the word "Name" below the current column headings of "First" and "Last."

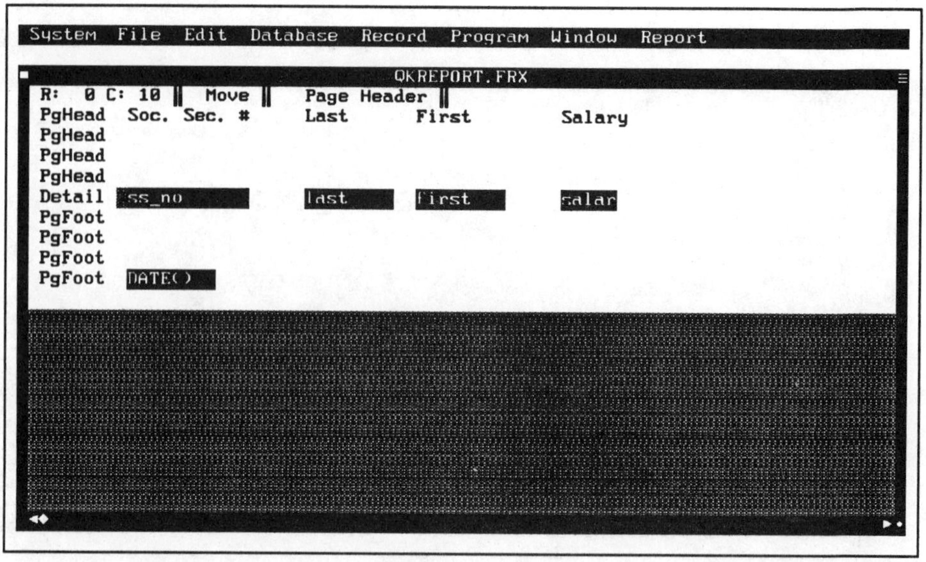

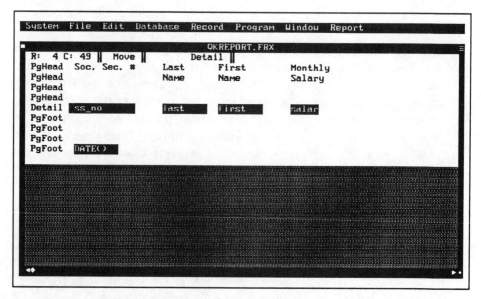

**Figure 11.17  Editing Column Headings**

Similarly, move the current column heading, "Salary" down one row and insert the text "Monthly" above. See if your screen looks like Figure 11.18.

When you place text in the report, press the Enter key after typing in each text string. Each Enter keystroke will be treated as one unit, and each can then be selected independently later to move or delete. If, for example, you type an entire line before pressing the Enter key, that whole line must be selected as a unit; you

**Figure 11.18  Inserting Texts to Column Headings**

cannot select only a portion of it. Conversely, if you press the Enter key after entering each word in the line, the individual words then can be selected to move or delete.

### Placing Data Fields

A new column can be created by using an existing data field from the selected database or by defining an expression with values derived from one or more existing fields. To do that, select the Field option from the Report menu popup or press the Ctrl+F key combination after you have positioned the cursor at the location in the report where you want to place the field.

For example, you might like to add a column showing the annual salaries for the sales staff, which will be computed from the monthly salary values in the SALARY field of the SALESMAN database. To place the annual salary as a computed field in the report, first position the cursor to the right of the Monthly Salary column in the Detail band and then press the Ctrl+F key combination. In return, the Report Expression dialog appears (see Figure 11.19).

In the Report Expression dialog are two check boxes—<Expr> and <Format>—that are used to specify the expression and the format of the data field to be placed. A text box for entering the field width also is included in the dialog, along with six check boxes for specifying other settings related to the field: Style, Calculate, Comment, Suppress, Stretch Vertically, and Float as Band Stretches.

Select the Style check box to bring up the Style dialog (Figure 11.20) and specify the font's style attributes (bold, italic, underlined, superscript, or subscript) in

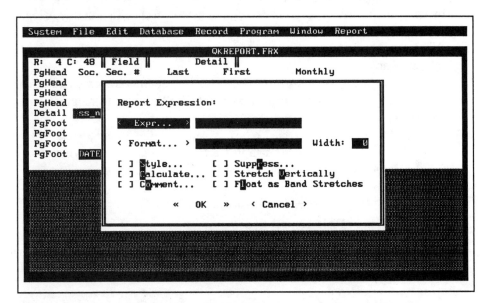

**Figure 11.19  The Report Expression Dialog**

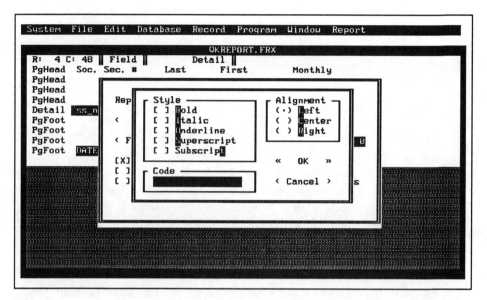

**Figure 11.20  The Style Dialog**

which to print the data field. In the same dialog, determine whether the value is to be left justified, center aligned, or right justified. You can also enter a printer control code for printing the value.

By selecting the Calculate check box in the Report Expression dialog you can determine summary statistics such as sum, average, and standard deviation. When the Calculate dialog appears, select the type of summary statistics to be calculated by using the values in the field expression you have specified in the dialog.

The Comment check box is used to record a note for describing the data field. When this box is selected, the Comment dialog appears, in which you enter the reference note.

Select the Suppress check box to bring up the Suppress Repeated Values dialog. In this dialog, you can select either the On or Off radio button to suppress displaying duplicated values in that data field.

If the Stretch Vertically check box is selected, the Report band will stretch vertically to accommodate all data in the field. Use this option when data in the field varies in size. Memo field is a good candidate for this option.

## Defining Report Field Expressions

To continue with our example, the column that we add will contain values that are computed from the SALARY field by using the following expression:

```
SALARY*12
```

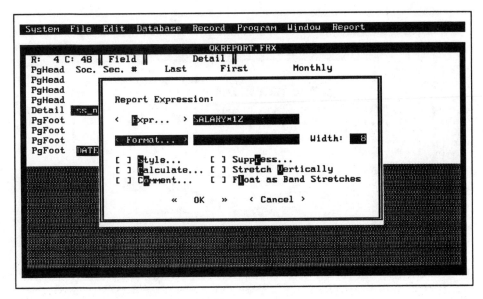

**Figure 11.21   Defining Report Field Expression**

Because the values in the SALARY field represent monthly salaries for the sales staff, multiplying it by 12 produces the annual salary. After selecting the <Expr> push button, enter the expression in the Report Expression Builder; or type the expression directly in the text box next to the push button. After the field expression has been entered, FoxPro automatically sets the field width to 8 characters to accommodate the computed values (see Figure 11.21).

## Formatting Report Fields

FoxPro enables you to specify the format for a set of data values that are displayed in a report column. A monetary value, for example, can be displayed in the conventional format that includes the dollar sign and commas for grouping the digits (e.g., $1,234.45). A character string can be displayed in upper- or lowercase, right justified, and so on. Similarly, you can specify the format in which to display dates in the report.

To define the format for the annual salary column that we are adding to the report, select the <Format> push button to bring up the Format dialog. In the Format dialog select one the four radio buttons—Character, Numeric, Date, or Logical—to identify the type of data. In addition, select one of the Editing Options check boxes to specify the display format for the field. Select the Currency check box to display values in a currency format, for instance (see Figure 11.22).

When you select the <<OK>> push button and return to the Report Expression dialog, you will see the format string "@$" inserted in the Format text box. The

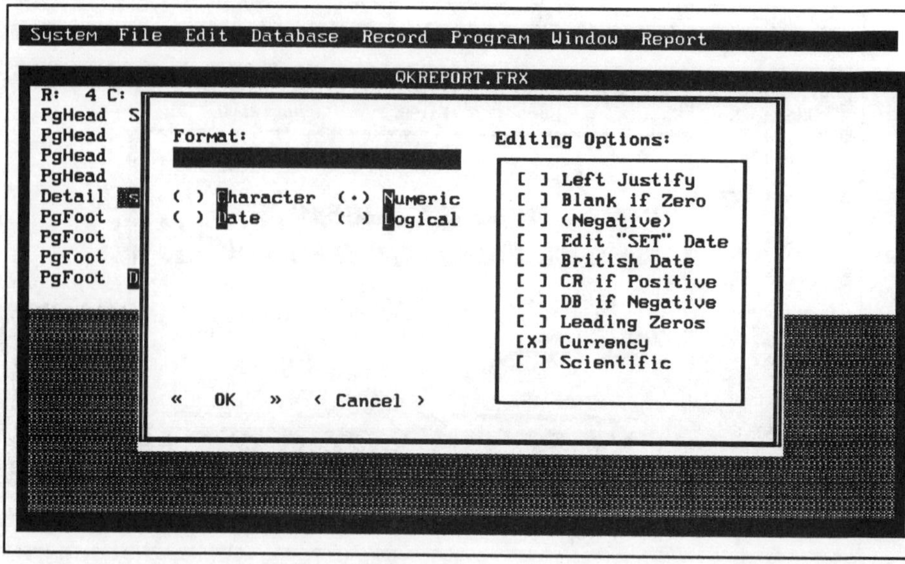

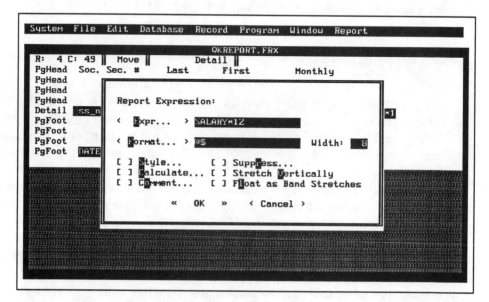

**Figure 11.22  Selecting Editing Options**

string contains control characters that direct how the values are to be displayed (see Figure 11.23).

Select the <<OK>> push button again to accept the report expression and you will return to Report Layout window. At this point, you can add the text, "Annual Salary," to the column heading for describing the new column. Now view the report

**Figure 11.23  Formatting a Currency Field**

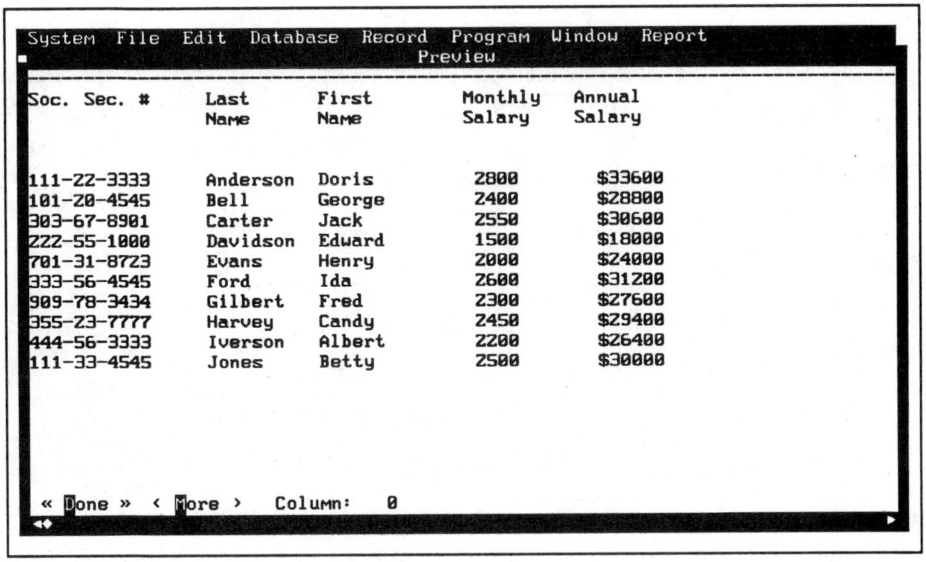

```
System  File  Edit  Database  Record  Program  Window  Report
                              Preview
─────────────────────────────────────────────────────────────
Soc. Sec. #      Last      First      Monthly    Annual
                 Name      Name       Salary     Salary

111-22-3333      Anderson  Doris      2800       $33600
101-20-4545      Bell      George     2400       $28800
303-67-8901      Carter    Jack       2550       $30600
222-55-1000      Davidson  Edward     1500       $18000
701-31-8723      Evans     Henry      2000       $24000
333-56-4545      Ford      Ida        2600       $31200
909-78-3434      Gilbert   Fred       2300       $27600
355-23-7777      Harvey    Candy      2450       $29400
444-56-3333      Iverson   Albert     2200       $26400
111-33-4545      Jones     Betty      2500       $30000




 « Done »  < More >   Column:   0
```

**Figure 11.24   Viewing the Annual Salary Column**

on the screen by choosing the Page Preview option from the Report menu popup or by pressing the Ctrl+I key combination. Note that the annual salaries are displayed with leading dollar signs but without commas (see Figure 11.24). If you would like to add commas to values displayed in a currency format, you can define a field template in the field format.

## Defining Field Templates

A field template is used to specify how particular values are to be displayed. A field template consists of a series of symbols that indicate the type of character that may be displayed in each position of a field value. In displaying a character field, the following are valid symbols in a field template:

X   displays a character of any type

A   displays a letter in lower- or uppercase (a-z, A-Z)

#   displays a numeric digit (0-9)

N   displays a letter, a digit, or an underscore (_)

!   converts a letter to uppercase

Any other character used in the template that is not listed above is treated as a literal character; it will be displayed unchanged at the corresponding character position of the field.

For example, !AAAAAAA might be the template for defining the format for a first name field of 8 characters. As a result, all the first letters of all the first names will be in uppercase. Similarly, if you use !!!!!!!! as a field template to format the last name field of 8 characters, all the last names will be displayed in capital letters.

Valid symbols in a numeric field template are:

9      displays a digit (0–9) or a sign (+ or -)

#      displays a digit

*      displays leading zeros as asterisks

$      displays a dollar sign in front of the value

$$    displays a floating dollar sign in front of the value

,      displays a comma

.      displays a period

In our example, you would use $999,999 or $$999,999 to display the values in the annual salary field in a conventional monetary format. As a result, monetary values will be displayed as:

| Field Template Used: | $999,999 | $$999,999 |
|---|---|---|
| | $  12,345 | $12,345 |
| | $   6,789 | $6,789 |

Note the difference between the two field templates: the left displays the dollar sign in a fixed location while the right displays the dollar sign always next to the leading digit. To display the monetary values in dollars-and-cents format, use $$999,999.99 as the field template. To display a percentage value with the percent sign, use the field template: 999% or 999.9%.

## Reformatting Report Fields

Although we have just defined the format for a field we were adding to our report, it is also possible to view and modify the format for any fields that have been placed in the report form. Either double click the mouse on the field or press Enter after positioning the cursor on the field. To modify the format of the salary field, for example, return to the Report Layout window by choosing the <Done> push button after viewing the report. Then double click the mouse on that SALARY field. When the Report Expression dialog appears, select the <Format> push button to bring up the Format dialog. Finally, enter $$99,999 in the format text box and change the field width to 8 (see Figure 11.25). Similarly, modify the annual salary field by using $$999,999 as the field template and change the field width to 10.

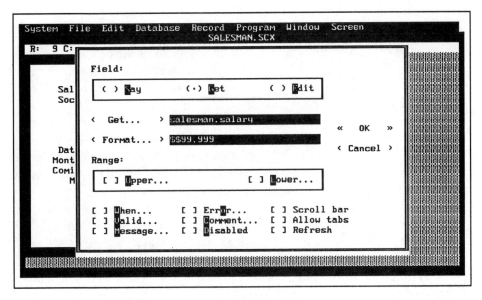

**Figure 11.25   Formatting the Monthly Salary Field**

After you have made these changes in the field formats, the report should look like that shown in Figure 11.26. All the salary values are displayed in a conventional monetary format with dollar signs and commas in their proper places.

```
 System  File  Edit  Database  Record  Program  Window  Report
                                Preview

Soc. Sec. #      Last      First      Monthly   Annual
                 Name      Name       Salary    Salary

111-22-3333      Anderson  Doris      $2,800    $33,600
101-20-4545      Bell      George     $2,400    $28,800
303-67-8901      Carter    Jack       $2,550    $30,600
222-55-1000      Davidson  Edward     $1,500    $18,000
701-31-8723      Evans     Henry      $2,000    $24,000
333-56-4545      Ford      Ida        $2,600    $31,200
909-78-3434      Gilbert   Fred       $2,300    $27,600
355-23-7777      Harvey    Candy      $2,450    $29,400
444-56-3333      Iverson   Albert     $2,200    $26,400
111-33-4545      Jones     Betty      $2,500    $30,000




 « Done »  < More >   Column:    0
```

**Figure 11.26   Showing the Reformatted Report Columns**

## Changing Report Column Widths

A report column width is determined by the width of the column heading or the width of the data field placed in that column, whichever is wider. For example, because the width of the SALARY data was set to 8 characters and the column heading is 7 characters, the column width is set to 8.

There are two ways to widen a report column: Either specify a different width in the Report Expression dialog, or stretch the field directly in the report form. For example, to widen the SALARY field width to 12, bring up the Report Expression dialog for that field and then change the field size accordingly. Alternatively, you can change the size of the data field directly in the report form.

To size a field with the mouse, point to the field, then hold down the Ctrl key and click the mouse. While holding down the Ctrl key, drag left or right until the field is the desired size before releasing the mouse button. With the keyboard, place the cursor anywhere in the field and press the Ctrl+Space key combination once. When the field name blinks, use the left or right arrow keys to shrink or stretch the field until it reaches the desired width.

To widen the SALARY field, point the mouse on the field, hold down the Ctrl key and click the mouse. Then, drag the mouse to the right while holding down the Ctrl key until the field is approximately 12 characters wide (see Figure 11.27).

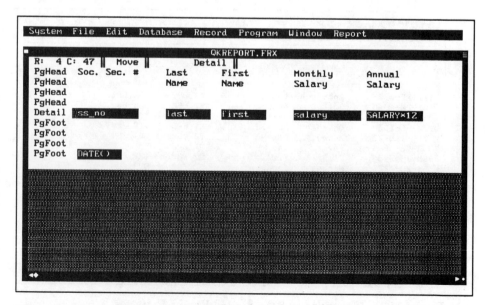

**Figure 11.27   Resizing a Report Field**

### Changing Report Band Widths

Each band of a report form may occupy one or more lines in the report layout. Each line in the report form is displayed as a line in the report. You may add blank lines to any report band so that report objects can be placed in them. It is also possible to delete any existing lines from any report band in this way. If, however, the line you attempt to delete contains one or more report objects, you will be asked to confirm your action.

### Deleting Report Lines

To delete a report line, place the cursor anywhere in that line and select the Remove Line option from the Report menu popup or press the Ctrl+O key combination. For example, to remove the bottom line in the PgHead band from the report form, place the cursor anywhere in that line and then press the Ctrl+O key combination. As a result, the line is removed and all bands beneath it are moved up one line.

### Inserting Report Lines

To add a line to any report band, move the cursor to the position at which you would like to insert the line and then choose the Add Line option from the Report menu popup or press the Ctrl+N key combination. As an example, place the cursor anywhere in the first line of the PgFoot band and then press Ctrl+N. In return, a new PgFoot line will be inserted at that location.

### Sizing Report Bands

Although you can also use the mouse to change the size of a report band, this involves a somewhat different technique than using the keyboard or menu options. With the mouse, you add new lines to a report band or remove existing lines from it by stretching or shrinking the report vertically. To do this, point the mouse at a line in the band you want to size; then drag up to shrink the band or down to stretch it. To shrink the PgFoot band, for example, point the mouse at the last line in the band and drag it up until all the other lines of the PgFoot band have been removed from the screen (see Figure 11.28).

There are two limitations to using the mouse to shrink a report band in this manner. First, FoxPro will not allow you to remove any line that contains a report object or to drag the line in which the mouse pointer is anchored over a line that contains a report object. Second, FoxPro will not allow you to remove all of the lines of a single report band. Therefore, you may sometimes find that there are unwanted blank lines or bands in your report. You can, however, delete them by positioning the cursor on each line and pressing the Ctrl+O key combination.

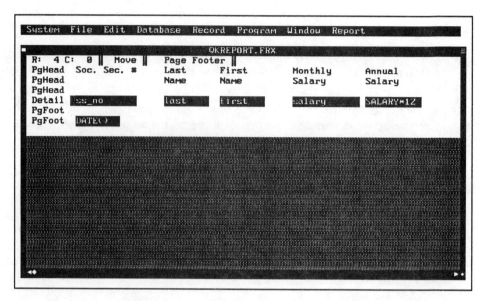

**Figure 11.28   Resizing Report Bands**

### Adding a Report Title

To add a report title to a report, choose the Title/Summary option from the Report menu popup. When the Report Title dialog appears, select the Title Band check box to add a Title band in the report layout and then select <<OK>> to return to the Report Layout window. As a result, a Title band will be inserted at the top of the report form. Then enter the text for the report title. For our example, let's add the title "Salary Summary Report." In addition, to improve the report's appearance, we should add two blank lines each to the Title and Page Header bands to allow some space between the report title and the column headings. (see Figure 11.29).

### Adding Graphics Objects

Boxing selected elements in a report, or incorporating vertical and horizontal lines to separate other elements often helps to make the information more easily understandable to the viewer.

### Drawing Boxes

To draw a box, select the Box option from the Report menu popup or press the Ctrl+B key combination after you have positioned the cursor on the location at which you intend to begin drawing the box. A rectangle will appear at the cursor location, which can be enlarged to the size you want either by using the mouse or the keyboard.

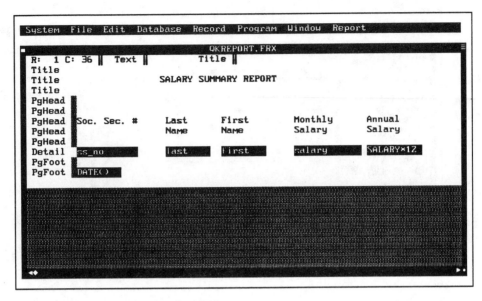

**Figure 11.29    Adding a Report Title**

To draw a box around the report title as an exercise, point and click the mouse on the position that represents the upper left-hand corner of the box (a couple of characters to the left and above the report title) and then press the Ctrl+B key combination. When the small rectangle appears, drag the mouse right and down until the box reaches the desired size and encloses the report title (see Figure 11.30).

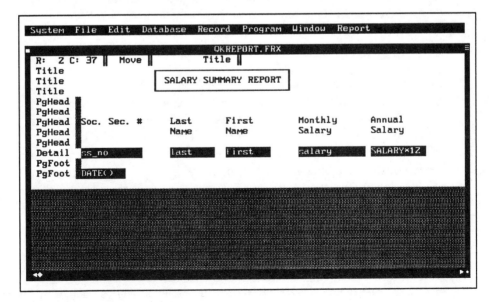

**Figure 11.30    Drawing a Box**

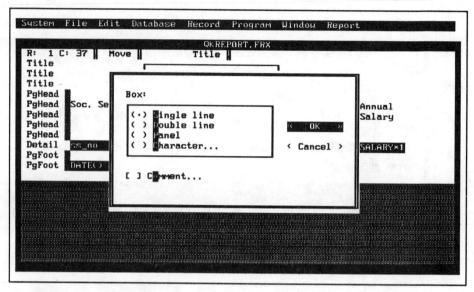

**Figure 11.31   The Box Dialog**

Although this box is drawn with a single line, you may use double lines or other graphics symbols to form the box. To do that, select the box as a report object (click the mouse anywhere on the line of the box, or position the cursor on the line and then press Enter). In return, the Box dialog shown in Figure 11.31 appears.

The Box dialog contains four radio buttons for selecting box type: single-line, double-line, panel (thick borders), or character (a box composed of special graphics symbols that you define).

### Drawing Lines

To draw a line, select the same Box option from the Report menu popup or press the Ctrl+B key combination. When the small rectangle appears at the current cursor location this time, however, use the mouse or the arrow key to stretch the rectangle horizontally or vertically to form a horizontal or vertical line.

To place a line above the report heading, for example, point and click the mouse above the first character in the first column heading and press the Ctrl+B key combination. When the small rectangle appears, drag the mouse up a bit and continue to the right to form the line covering the column headings. Use the same method to draw a line below the column heading (see Figure 11.32).

### Numbering Report Pages

In a multi-page report, the Report Writer automatically keeps track of the current page number when the report is displayed or printed. This sequential page number is stored in a system variable named _PAGENO. In a quick report, the Report

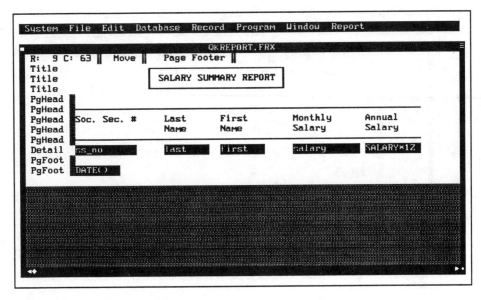

**Figure 11.32    Drawing Lines**

Writer displays the page number on the right-hand side of the Page Footer band by default. Like a field, however, it can be moved anywhere on the report form and its display attributes can be modified.

The page number can be displayed in a format of your choice simply by modifying the format specification in the Report Expression dialog shown in Figure 11.33. To view it, double click the mouse on the _PAGENO variable or

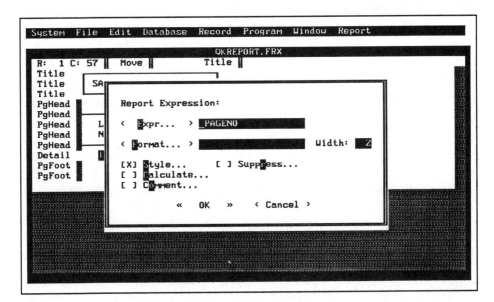

**Figure 11.33    Showing the Page Number Expression**

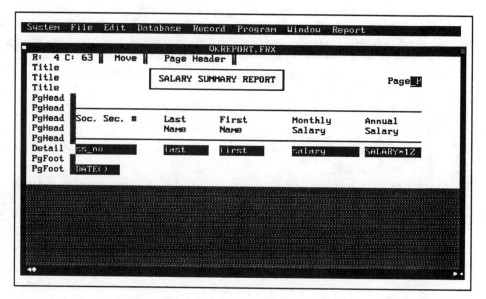

**Figure 11.34   Placing the Report Page Number**

press Enter after positioning the cursor on it. As you can see, the default width is set to 4 digits. As an exercise, let's change it to 2 digits.

If you do not like FoxPro's default positioning of the page number, it can be moved in the same way that you move any report object. For example, to display the page number on top of each page, simply select both the _PAGENO variable and the "Page" text and drag them to the Page Header band. But, because our sample report contains only one page, let's move the page number to the Title band, to the right of the report title (see Figure 11.34).

### Placing Report Dates

In a quick report, the Report Writer will also display the date the report was run on the left-hand side of the Page Footer band. To derive the current date, FoxPro uses the DATE( ) function, which returns the current system date. Like all objects in the FoxPro Report Writer, the date display can be moved anywhere on the report form and its display attributes can be modified.

To view the format specification, double click your mouse on the variable or press the Enter key after positioning the cursor on the variable. When the Report Expression dialog shown in Figure 11.35 appears, specify the expression and format for the date display.

If you prefer that the date be displayed somewhere other than at the bottom of the report, you can move it to the Page Header, where it will be displayed at the

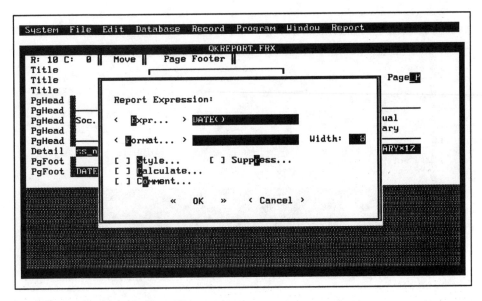

**Figure 11.35   Report Date Expression**

beginning of each page; or to the Title band, where it will be displayed once at the beginning of the report. To continue our example, let's place it in the Title band, directly below the page number (see Figure 11.36).

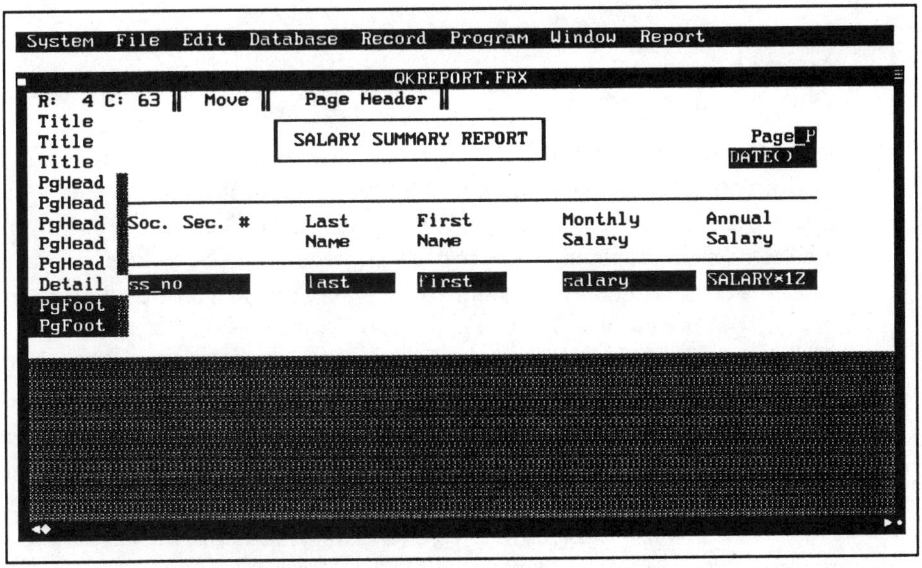

**Figure 11.36   Placing the Report Date**

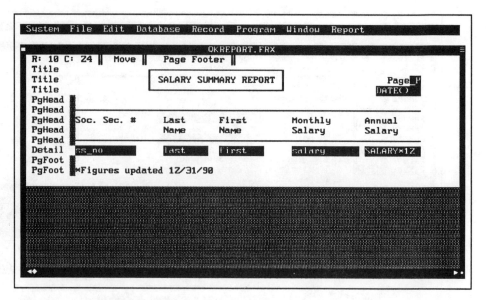

**Figure 11.37    Placing a Footer**

### Placing Footers

To position text used as a footer at the bottom of a page, place the text in the Page Footer band. An example is shown in Figure 11.37. The footer will be displayed at the end of every report page.

### Adding a Report Summary

The FoxPro Report Writer allows you to add descriptive statistics that summarize the information in an entire column of a report. Regardless of the data type, you can count the number of data items in the column and display the total amount at the bottom of the column. If the column contains numeric values, you can also calculate statistics such as the sum, the average, the standard deviation, and the minimum or maximum value, and place them in the report.

Because these statistics are computed using the values in the entire report, they are placed in a Summary band that is inserted at the end of the report. To add the Summary band to the report form, choose the Title/Summary option from the Report menu popup. When the Report Title dialog appears, select the Summary Band check box, then the <<OK>> push button to return to the Report Layout window. The Report Writer will insert a Summary Band at the end of the report form after the Page Footer band.

To insert a summary statistic in the Summary band, position the cursor on the location at which you want the statistic to appear and then choose the Field option

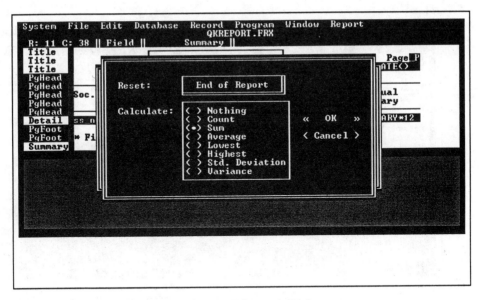

**Figure 11.38    Calculating the Sum of Numeric Values**

from the Report menu popup or press the Ctrl+F key combination. When the Report Expression dialog appears, select the Calculate check box to bring up the Calculate dialog box. At this point, you can choose the type of summary statistic you would like to display.

To show, for example, the total of the Monthly Salary column, position the cursor in the Summary band at the bottom of the column and press Ctrl+F. When the Report Expression appears, select the Calculate check box to bring up the Calculate dialog and check the Sum radio button before selecting the <<OK>> push button to return to the Report Expression dialog (see Figure 11.38).

When you return to the Report Expression dialog, enter the name of the data field in the Expression text box for which you want a summary statistic computed (in our case, SALARY). In the Format text box, enter the field template ($$99,999) that will be used to display the statistic. Set the field width to 12 to accommodate the summary statistics (see Figure 11.39). When you return to the Report Layout dialog, the summary field will be placed on the report form.

We should also add a summary field for the Annual Salary column. This is very much like adding the summary field for monthly salary, although of course the annual salary is a computed value. Begin by positioning the cursor on the position at which you would like to place the field and bring up the Report Expression dialog by pressing CTRL+F. The summary statistic that we want the report to display is the sum of each employee's annual salary. To define it, enter SALARY*12 in the Expression text box (and supply the format ($$99,999) and field width information (12) in the appropriate text boxes. Next, select the Calculate check box to bring up

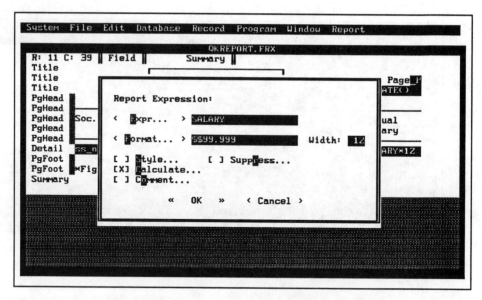

**Figure 11.39    Defining the Expression and Format for the Sum**

the Calculate Fields dialog and select the Sum check box. At this point, take note of the Reset list box. It determines when FoxPro internally reinitializes the value of the statistic and begins to calculate it again. In this case, because we want a single total that applies to all the records displayed in the report, select the default choice, End of Report.

Having finished positioning and defining the summary statistics, you can now insert a line in the Summary band and draw a line above each of the summary statistics. In addition, you can add text ("Grand Total") to describe the statistics. After placing the summary statistics, move the column headings to align with the column values. To determine the exact locations for the column heading, try to view it on screen and then make the necessary adjustments. The final layout of the report should look like that shown in Figure 11.40. Then, when you print the final report on the printer, it will look like the professional report shown in Figure 11.41.

Save the modified report form to disk by choosing the Save option from the File menu popup and the revised report form will be saved in the file QKREPORT.FRX, replacing the form previously held in the file.

### Grouping Data

The salary report in Figure 11.41 shows the salaries for all sales personnel, listed in alphabetical order. This report might be of interest if we are concerned with examining how much each salesperson makes, or with knowing how much the total monthly or annual payroll is. Reports, however, also are used often to separate

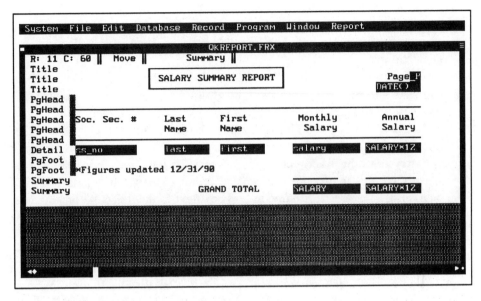

**Figure 11.40   Summary Statistics**

records into individual groups in order to compare them with each another or to gather summary statistics about individual groupings. For example, we might want to produce a salary report in a format similar to the one shown in Figure 11.41 that groups employees based on gender and shows the total monthly and annual salary

| | SALARY SUMMARY REPORT | | Page 1 09/16/91 | |
|---|---|---|---|---|
| Soc. Sec. # | Last Name | First Name | Monthly Salary | Annual Salary |
| 111-22-3333 | Anderson | Doris | $2,800 | $33,600 |
| 101-20-4545 | Bell | George | $2,400 | $28,800 |
| 303-67-8901 | Carter | Jack | $2,550 | $30,600 |
| 222-55-1000 | Davidson | Edward | $1,500 | $18,000 |
| 701-31-8723 | Evans | Henry | $2,000 | $24,000 |
| 333-56-4545 | Ford | Ida | $2,600 | $31,200 |
| 909-78-3434 | Gilbert | Fred | $2,300 | $27,600 |
| 355-23-7777 | Harvey | Candy | $2,450 | $29,400 |
| 444-56-3333 | Iverson | Albert | $2,200 | $26,400 |
| 111-33-4545 | Jones | Betty | $2,500 | $30,000 |
| | GRAND TOTAL | | $23,300 | $30,000 |

**Figure 11.41   A Printed Report**

paid to each group. Similarly, we might want a report that lists the level of salaries in each of the three regional offices; this is the report that we will develop in our next example.

With FoxPro, such a report can be created by adding a Group band to the report form. As a result, data records will be grouped together based on their value in a group field, and different groups will be broken out in the report.

To insert a Group band into the report shown in Figure 11.41, choose the Data Grouping option from the Report menu popup. When the Data Grouping dialog appears, select the <Add> check box to bring up the Group Info dialog to specify the group field. To group the records according to their values in the OFFICE_ID data field, enter the field name in text box next to the <Group> push button (see Figure 11.42). (Alternatively, you may bring up the Expression Builder by selecting the <Group> push button.)

When you return to the Report Layout window after selecting the <<OK>> push button in both the Group Info dialog and the Data Grouping dialog, a Group band labeled 1-OFFIC is inserted both before and after the Detail band in the report. This Group band identifies the level of grouping (FoxPro allows you to further divide each group into subgroups) and contains the partial name of the group field.

Although we have now prepared a report that divides the detail records into groups based on their value in the OFFICE_ID field, the report will not actually show us the value of the OFFICE_ID for any particular group. We could, of course, simply add the OFFICE_ID field to the Detail band, which means that its value will be displayed for each record listed in our report. This, however, is redundant,

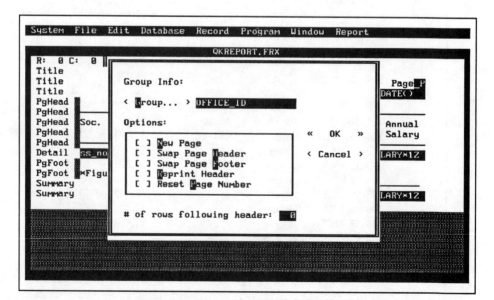

**Figure 11.42   Defining Grouping Information**

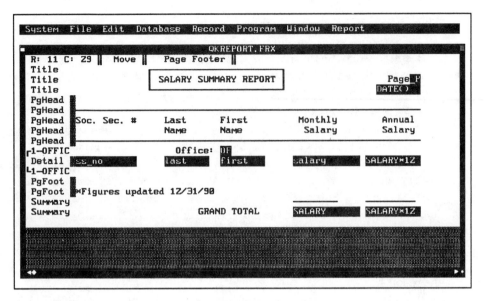

**Figure 11.43    Showing the Group Heading**

because each record in a group will have the same value. Instead, the best method is to identify the group by placing the value of the group field (in our case, OFFICE_ID) and any other descriptive text (like "Office:") in the beginning of the Group band, as we have done in Figure 11.43. In this way, the value of the group field will be displayed only when it changes.

If we preview our report now, however, we will find that the results are somewhat unexpected. Records continue to be listed in alphabetical order and are not grouped according to common values in the OFFICE_ID field. This is because reports that use data groups expect records in the database to be arranged according to their values in the group field. Therefore, you must index the records on the group field (or fields, if subgroups are used in the report) before displaying or printing the report.

In our example, the database must be indexed on the OFFICE_ID field. Recall that we created an index tag named OFFICE_ID in the structural compound index file SALESMAN.CDX. In order to generate our report, we need only set this index tag as the master index. To do this, select the Setup option from the database menu popup to bring up the Setup dialog. Then select SALESMAN:OFFICE_ID from the Indexes list box and select the <Set Order> push button to designate it as the master index. Then return to the Report Layout window by selecting the <<OK>> push button. To avoid the trouble of selecting the proper index whenever you run the report, you may want to store information about the database environment along with the report form. This information includes the name of the controlling master index file. To do this, select the <Save> push button in the Page Layout dialog.

Then, whenever you use the report form in the future, FoxPro will automatically set the appropriate master index.

Besides displaying the individual records based on a common group value, you can also display summary statistics for all of the records that belong to each group. This is very similar to adding summary statistics to the report, except that here the summary statistics are placed on any line of the Group band that is below the Detail band. To continue embellishing our report, we now will add up the monthly and annual salaries in each office and display them at the end of each group.

The method to place these group statistics on the form is identical to the one used previously to create the summary statistics for the report as a whole. The only difference is that in the Reset list box of the Calculate Field dialog, the default option (which is the name of the group field, OFFICE_ID) should now be selected. Of course, you may also add text and boxes to the group lines to highlight the group totals as well. An example of such an enhanced group report form is shown in Figure 11.44. Figure 11.45 shows the printed report that was produced by using the report form.

Now save the revised report form to a file named BYOFFICE.FRX by choosing the Save As option from the File menu popup and then entering the name of the file.

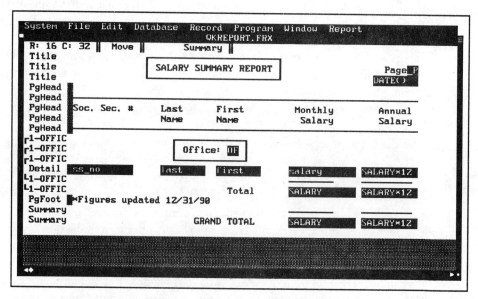

**Figure 11.44   The Layout of an Enhanced Group Report**

| SALARY SUMMARY REPORT | | | Page 1 09/16/91 | |
|---|---|---|---|---|
| Soc. Sec. # | Last Name | First Name | Monthly Salary | Annual Salary |
| **Office: B1** | | | | |
| 111-22-3333 | Anderson | Doris | $2,800 | $33,600 |
| 222-55-1000 | Davidson | Edward | $1,500 | $18,000 |
| 111-33-4545 | Jones | Betty | $2,500 | $30,000 |
| | | Total | $2,500 | $30,000 |
| **Office: B2** | | | | |
| 303-67-8901 | Carter | Jack | $2,550 | $30,600 |
| 333-56-4545 | Ford | Ida | $2,600 | $31,200 |
| 444-56-3333 | Iverson | Albert | $2,200 | $26,400 |
| | | Total | $2,200 | $26,4000 |
| **Office: B3** | | | | |
| 101-20-4545 | Bell | George | $2,400 | $28,800 |
| 701-31-8723 | Evans | Henry | $2,000 | $24,000 |
| 909-78-3434 | Gilbert | Fred | $2,300 | $27,600 |
| 355-23-7777 | Harvey | Candy | $2,450 | $29,400 |
| | | Total | $2,450 | $29,400 |
| | GRAND TOTAL | | $23,300 | $29,400 |

**Figure 11.45    The Printed Group Report**

### Grouping Data by Logical Values

Data records can be grouped in a report according to the values in any database or calculated field, regardless of its data type. In the previous example, data records were grouped according to their value in the character field OFFICE_ID. In that case, the value of the OFFICE.ID field was displayed as a group heading, but you may also group data records based on the values in a numeric or date field. In both cases, the value of the numeric or date field provides sufficient information to describe the group.

This is not the case if data is grouped according to the values in a logical field where you only can display either "T" or "F" as the group heading. There is a way, however, to include more descriptive text for describing group information in a logical field—let's say to produce a salary report showing the sales staff's salaries grouped by sex. To describe the groups with more than the logical values of "T" or "F," use the IIF( ) function to display descriptive text instead of the logical values in the data field. The syntax of the IIF( ) function is as follows:

```
IIF(<logical field name>, <1st string>, <2nd string>)
```

The IIF( ) function displays the first character string when the value of the specified logical field is true; otherwise, it displays the second character string. For example, you may use the following IIF( ) function to display the group headings for salary values that are grouped by the sex of the salesperson:

```
IIF(MALE, 'Male Salespersons', 'Female Salespersons')
```

You can then place a field expression in the Group band that uses this IIF( ) function. The layout of such a group report is shown in Figure 11.46.

For this report to produce the desired results, you must, of course, index the database on the MALE field. Once you do this, you can preview the report, which should look like Figure 11.47. Note that the first group of records is labeled as "Male Salesperson" when the value in the MALE data field is "T." The second group of records with "F" in the logical field is identified as "Females Salespersons."

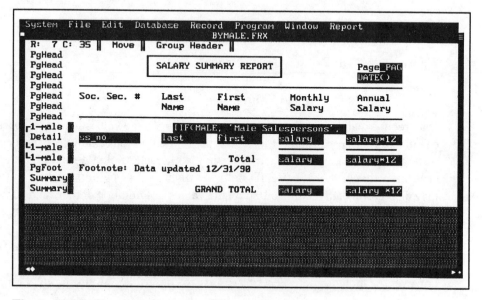

**Figure 11.46   Grouping Data According to Logical Values**

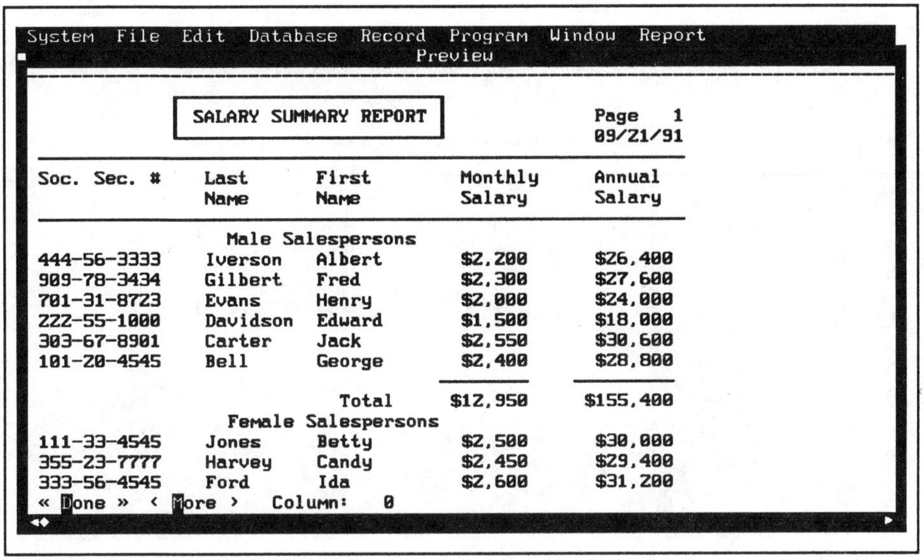

```
System  File  Edit  Database  Record  Program  Window  Report
                             Preview
```

```
       ┌─────────────────────────────┐           Page   1
       │  SALARY SUMMARY REPORT       │           09/21/91
       └─────────────────────────────┘

  Soc. Sec. #    Last      First     Monthly    Annual
                 Name      Name      Salary     Salary
  ─────────────────────────────────────────────────────
                    Male Salespersons
  444-56-3333    Iverson   Albert    $2,200     $26,400
  909-78-3434    Gilbert   Fred      $2,300     $27,600
  701-31-8723    Evans     Henry     $2,000     $24,000
  ZZZ-55-1000    Davidson  Edward    $1,500     $18,000
  303-67-8901    Carter    Jack      $2,550     $30,600
  101-20-4545    Bell      George    $2,400     $28,800
                            _____    _____
                     Total  $12,950    $155,400
                   Female Salespersons
  111-33-4545    Jones     Betty     $2,500     $30,000
  355-23-7777    Harvey    Candy     $2,450     $29,400
  333-56-4545    Ford      Ida       $2,600     $31,200
  « Done »  ‹ More ›   Column:    0
```

Figure 11.47   Viewing Data Grouped by Logical Values

## CREATING FORM REPORTS

The procedure for producing a form report is almost identical to that for generating a column report. The steps for placing the objects in the report are the same, except that a form report allows you to place the fields anywhere in the form without lining them up in a column format. You may insert any additional text in the report to describe the information, or incorporate graphics objects, such as boxes and lines, to outline or highlight various sections of the report.

### Using Quick Report Layouts

The Report Writer provides a quick report format that you can use as the basis for your form report design. Simply select the Report radio button from the New dialog after you have selected the New option from the File menu popup. When the Report Layout window appears, select the Quick Report option from the Report menu popup. From the Quick Report dialog, choose the Form Layout radio button (see Figure 11.48).

Selecting this option means that all fields will be displayed in the default form layout in which data fields are placed sequentially according their order in the data structure and labeled with the field names. The default layout of a quick report using all the data fields in the SALESMAN database is shown in Figure 11.49.

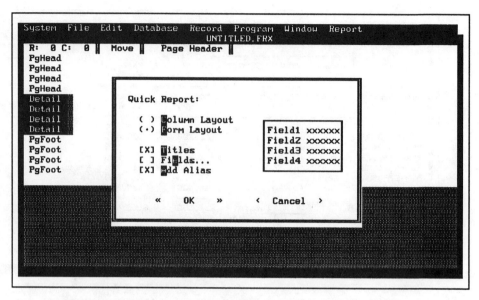

**Figure 11.48　Selecting Form Layout for the Quick Report**

## Creating a Custom Form Report

To modify the default quick report provided by the Report Writer in order to create a form report of your own design, delete the data fields you don't need and create any calculated fields, then add the necessary descriptive text and graphics objects to the report. An example of such a custom report is shown in Figure 11.50.

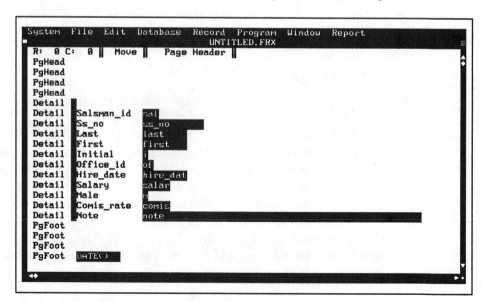

**Figure 11.49　Default Form Layout of a Quick Report**

```
┌─────────────────────────────────────────────────────────────┐
│                                                               │
│    INFORMATION ABOUT OUR SALESPERSONS            Page   1     │
│                                                  09/17/91     │
│                                                               │
│                   Doris B. Anderson                           │
│                                                               │
│   Id. No.: S0    Social Security #: 111-22-3333    Male? [N]  │
│                                                               │
│   Employment Date: 07/01/86         Office: B1                │
│   Monthly Salary:  $2,800           Commission Rate:  0%      │
│   Hobbies: classical music, painting, travel.                 │
│                                                               │
│                                                               │
│                   George G. Bell                              │
│                                                               │
│   Id. No.: S1    Social Security #: 101-20-4545    Male? [Y]  │
│                                                               │
│   Employment Date: 10/12/88         Office: B3                │
│   Monthly Salary:  $2,400           Commission Rate: 20%      │
│   Hobbies: fishing, hunting, country music.                   │
│                                                               │
│   ......                                                       │
│   ......                                                       │
│   ......                                                       │
│                                                               │
│                                                               │
└─────────────────────────────────────────────────────────────┘
```

**Figure 11.50   Sample Custom Form Report**

In the report layout (SLSMINFO.FRX) of Figure 11.50, you can see that the report title, report page number, and report date are placed in the Page Header band. In the Detail band, all the data fields appear in a free form and are placed in various sections of the report, where they are mixed with descriptive texts.

Incidentally, notice that, in rearranging and modifying FoxPro's quick report to produce the report form shown in Figure 11.50, we have made liberal use of calculated expressions and have changed the formatting of the salary and commission fields to enhance the appearance of our report. It is possible, for example, to leave the first and last names and middle initial of each salesperson as separate fields. This, however, leaves blank space between the first name and middle initial of salespeople who have short first names. The solution is to delete the three fields and replace them with a single calculated field that uses the TRIM( ) function to remove trailing spaces from the first name. The following field expression will accomplish this:

```
TRIM(FIRST)+' '+INITIAL+'. '+LAST
```

The following table shows the other changes that have been made to the quick report to produce the report form shown in Figure 11.50:

| FIELD | ATTRIBUTE | TO |
|---|---|---|
| Name | Width | 20 |
| SALARY | Format | $$99,999 |
|  | Width | 11 |

| FIELD | ATTRIBUTE | TO |
|---|---|---|
| Commission Rate | Expression | SALESMAN.COMIS_RATE*100 |
| | Format | 99% |
| | Width | 3 |
| Male | Expression | IIF(MALE,"[Y]","[N]") |
| | Width | 3 |

As in a column report, all the data fields placed in the Detail band of a form report are repeated for each data record in the selected database. There is a major difference between the two report forms, however, as Figure 11.51 shows. In a column report, field values of each record are displayed as a row in the report while in a form report they are displayed in an individual section.

The layout of a form report is ideal for producing computer form letters which mix text with information taken from selected database fields. You can, for example, create a letter in the form of an office memorandum addressed to each member of the sales staff as illustrated in Figure 11.52.

Then you may insert information taken from the data fields in the SALESMAN database into the text of the memorandum, as shown in Figure 11.53. Note that data elements from a number of data fields are taken from the SALESMAN database and inserted into the office memorandum: the name of the salesperson is displayed by using the values from the FIRST, INITIAL, and LAST data fields; information from the HIRE_DATE, SALARY, and COMIS_RATE is displayed at

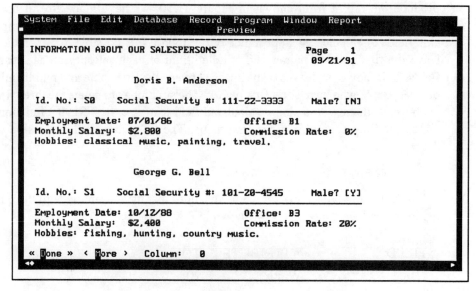

**Figure 11.51   Viewing the Form Report**

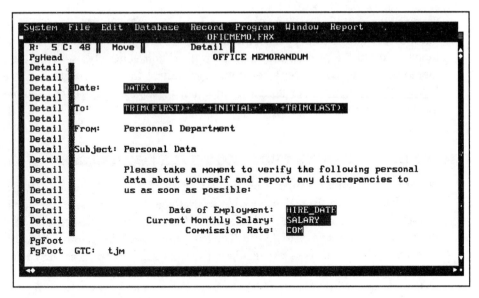

**Figure 11.52  Sample Form Letter**

the end of the memorandum. In addition, the system date function, DATE( ), is used to display the memorandum date.

Figure 11.53 displays the office memorandum to be sent to Doris B. Anderson. You can see that information about her taken from the data record is displayed with

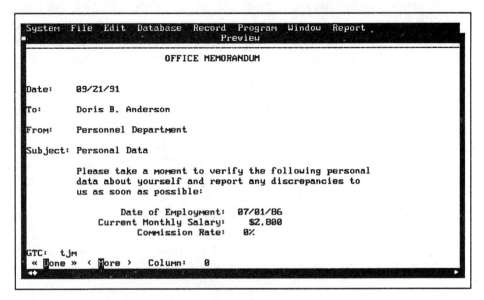

**Figure 11.53  Form Letter Incorporating Data**

the text placed in the Detail band in the report layout. To view the next memorandum, select the <More> push button. Note that if you choose to print all the memoranda to the printer, they will be printed consecutively. In order for each memorandum to output on a separate page, adjust the page length in the Page Layout dialog. To print our sample memoranda on separate pages, for example, set the page length to 20 rows.

## PRODUCING REPORTS FROM MULTIPLE DATABASES

So far in this chapter, we have created a variety of reports by using data from a single database file. It is also possible to produce column and form reports that extract information from multiple database files that are related to one another. There are two major ways to do this. The first, which we will examine only briefly, involves opening the necessary database files and defining the necessary relations before beginning to use the Report Writer to design the report form. The second technique, which takes a bit longer to execute but makes it easier to design the report form, involves creating an RQBE query to extract the necessary information from the linked databases to a temporary database. The data records in this temporary database are then used to design the report form in the Report Layout window and to produce the report itself.

### Creating Relational Reports Directly

To create a report that uses data in multiple linked databases without relying on RQBE, you must first open all of the database files needed for the report, define the master indexes for each database file, and establish all database relations. You can then open the Report Writer and create your report either by modifying a quick report or by building it from scratch.

If you elect to define and modify a quick report, the Field Picker dialog, which you can access by selecting the Fields check box in the Quick Report dialog, allows you select fields from all open database files. In building your report from scratch, the same Field Picker dialog is available when you select the Expr push button from the Report Expression dialog after you position each field. In either case, the Database popup control allows you to select fields from multiple database files for your report.

Aside from selecting the fields to appear in the report from multiple database files rather than a single database, the process of creating a report that uses multiple files is basically identical to that outlined above for single-file reports. It is important to remember, however, to save the environment along with the report; this allows FoxPro to open all the necessary database files, set the appropriate index orders, and link database files automatically the next time you run the report.

## Extracting Data with RQBE Queries

The second method of producing reports with multiple database files involves using both Relational Query by Example queries and the Report Writer. As we will see later, this is a two-stage process which ultimately results in RQBE directly feeding the data that you have requested into the Report Writer, which in turn sends it to the output device you have selected.

The first step, then, is to obtain all data needed for the report by creating an RQBE query. In the process of defining the query, you must identify the database files that will be used and specify how they are linked. In addition, you can specify the data fields that will be used in the report, and determine the order of the query results and how the records are to be grouped.

Let's assume, for instance, that you must produce a report showing the name of each salesperson and information about his or her sales office. Before designing the report form, the first step is to collect the information from the SALESMAN and OFFICE database files by using RQBE to create a query like the one shown in Figure 11.54.

To set up the query, first link the two database files by using the OFFICE_ID field as the link key. Then select the following data fields that are needed for the report:

```
From SALESMAN.DBF: FIRST, INITIAL, LAST
From OFFICE.DBF: OFFICE_ID, ADDRESS, CITY, STATE, ZIP
```

The query results can be ordered according to the value in OFFICE_ID.

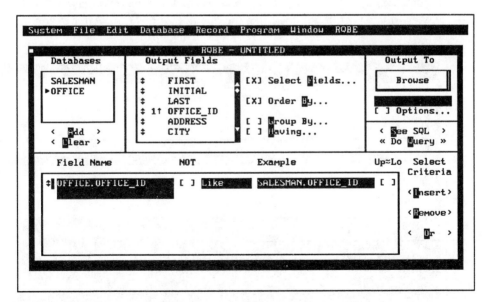

**Figure 11.54  Using a RQBE Query To Extract Data**

To prepare the data for the report, specify Browse as the destination for the query output and select the <Do Query> push button. Besides opening a Browse window that displays the fields and records that you have requested, FoxPro also places the results in a temporary database file (named QUERY), which it selects as the current work area. (If you open the View window, you can see the temporary database file in the current work area. In addition, after you execute the query for the first time, the word QUERY appears in the text box below the Output To popup in the RQBE window.)

## Producing Reports

Because the fields and records that are needed to produce the report now reside in a single temporary database file, the Report Layout window can be brought up to design the report. Select the New option from the File menu popup and then select the Report radio button to open the Report Writer window. Then lay out your report form either by creating a quick report or by designing a custom report like the one shown in Figure 11.55.

In this layout, the sales staff's names are derived from the FIRST, INITIAL, and LAST data fields, as defined in the following expression:

```
TRIM(FIRST)+' '+INITIAL+'. '+TRIM(LAST)
```

Similarly, the office address is composed of the ADDRESS, CITY, STATE, and ZIP data fields, as defined by the expression shown in the report layout. When you preview this report, it will look like the one in Figure 11.56. After examining the

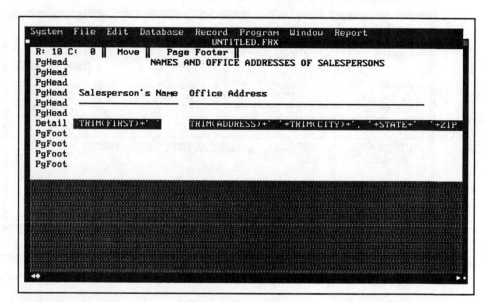

**Figure 11.55   Custom Column Report Layout**

```
 System  File  Edit  Database  Record  Program  Window  Report
                                    Preview
───────────────────────────────────────────────────────────────
            NAMES AND OFFICE ADDRESSES OF SALESPERSONS


Salesperson's Name  Office Address
                    ─────────────────────────────────────────

Doris B.            100 Park Avenue New York, NY   10016
Edward D.           100 Park Avenue New York, NY   10016
Betty A. Jones      100 Park Avenue New York, NY   10016
Jack J. Carter      200 Lake Drive Chicago, IL   60607
Ida F. Ford         200 Lake Drive Chicago, IL   60607
Albert I.           200 Lake Drive Chicago, IL   60607
George G. Bell      500 Century Blvd. Los Angeles, CA   94005
Henry H. Evans      500 Century Blvd. Los Angeles, CA   94005
Fred C. Gilbert     500 Century Blvd. Los Angeles, CA   94005
Candy E. Harvey     500 Century Blvd. Los Angeles, CA   94005



   « Done »  < More >   Column:   0
```

**Figure 11.56   Viewing the Custom Column Report**

report it can be sent to the printer by choosing the Report option from the Database menu popup and selecting the To Print check box.

If you plan to produce the same report again in the future, save the report form to a disk file. But before doing this, you must save the report form's environment by selecting the Save push button in the Report Writer's Page Layout dialog. Then the report form can be saved by choosing the Save As option from the File menu popup and assigning the report form file a name (e.g., ADDRESS.FRX). Finally, you must also save the query to a query file so that you can use it later to generate the results that will be passed to the report. To do that, select the RQBE window, choose the Save As option from the File menu popup, and assign a name (e.g., ADDRESS.QPR) to the query file. Then close both the RQBE and the Report Writer windows.

This completes the first stage in our endeavor to use RQBE and the Report Writer to generate a multi-file report. We have defined a query, ADDRESS.QPR, to generate the information we need for the report, and we have designed a report, ADDRESS.FRX, to display that information. The query and the report work together by means of an intermediate database file, QUERY.DBF. When we execute the query and the report form next, we will integrate them more closely, so that the output from the query goes directly and automatically to the report.

## Producing Reports in Queries

Begin by recalling the ADDRESS.QPR query file that you saved in the section above. When the query appears in the RQBE window, select Report/Label from

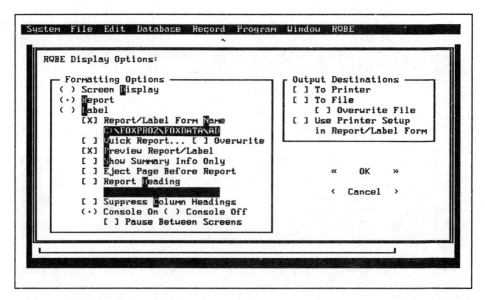

**Figure 11.57   The RQBE Display Options Dialog**

the Output to popup as the destination for the query output and select the Options check box to bring up the RQBE Display Options dialog. In the Formatting Options box in the dialog, select the Report radio button. Then enter the name of the report form file, ADDRESS.FRX, in the text box after you select the Report/Label Form Name check box (see Figure 11.57).

The Preview Report/Label check box is selected by FoxPro as the default display option. To automatically send the report to the printer, turn the Preview Report/Label check box off and select the To Printer check box instead. After specifying other display options, select the <<OK>> push button to return to the RQBE window.

To produce the report, perform the query by selecting the <Do Query> push button. As a result, FoxPro will carry out the query and send the results directly to the report form that you have specified. After viewing or printing the report, you should again save the query, because it now contains new information regarding handling the query results. You can then exit the query by closing the RQBE window.

# Creating Mailing Labels

The process of creating mailing labels is very similar to that for generating reports. It begins with laying out the data fields and any associated text in the Label Designer window. While you are in the Label Designer, you can view the mailing labels on the screen to determine if any modifications are necessary. Once you are

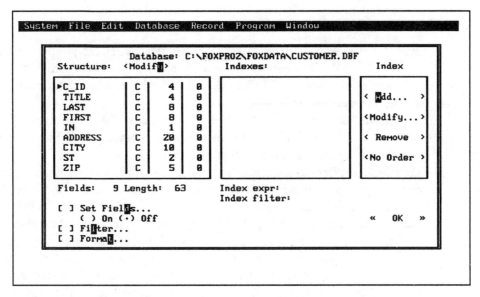

**Figure 11.58   The Data Structure of CUSTOMER.DBF**

satisfied with the label design, you can then output them on the printer. If you plan to use the same label layout again, save it to a label file.

As an example, we will be using the CUSTOMER database to illustrate the process of producing a mailing label. The data structure and the contents of CUSTOMER.DBF are shown in Figures 11.58 and 11.59 respectively.

```
System  File  Edit  Database  Record  Program  Window  Browse

                               CUSTOMER
C_id Title Last      First   In Address             City      St Zip

1004 Mr.   Hanson    Chris   F  500 Broadway        Vancouver WA 98665
1005 Mr.   Knight    Robert  K  100 Wall Street     New York  NY 11014
1006 Mr.   Prutsman  James   L  1010 Ocean Drive    Oakland   CA 94618
1007 Mr.   Chien     Mike    S  900 Michigan Avenue Dearborn  MI 48124
1008 Mrs.  Larson    Amy     H  2020 Parkview       Milwaukee WI 53226
1009 Dr.   Morrow    Tom     J  1000 Mountain Drive Bellevue  WA 98007
1010 Miss  Austin    Carrol  A  2900 Huntland Drive Austin    TX 78752
1011 Miss  Baker     Linda   D  3000 N. 50th Avenue Phoenix   AZ 85031
1012 Ms.   Nelson    Sandy   F  2015 Washington Ave.Evanston  IL 60204
1013 Mr.   Jackson   Peter   W  100 Oceanview Drive Miami     FL 33152
1014 Mr.   Wilson    Larry   S  200 Jackson Street  Portland  OR 97204
1015 Dr.   Swanson   John    R  7070 Mission Avenue Hayward   CA 94541
```

**Figure 11.59   The Contents of the CUSTOMER.DBF**

## DESIGNING MAILING LABELS

Because it is necessary to extract data from the database file to produce mailing labels, the CUSTOMER database file must be opened before designing the label form. In addition, if you would like the labels to print in a particular order, you must index the database as well.

To design the label form, select the New option from the File menu popup. When the New dialog appears, choose the Label radio button and select <<OK>> to bring up the Label Designer window (see Figure 11.60).

When the Label Designer window first opens, as Figure 11.60 shows, it contains the default layout of a label form. The Remarks text box on the top of the window shows the label dimensions. In the default layout, for example, FoxPro uses one-across labels that are 3 1/2" × 15/16". The width of the label also is specified by the number of characters across while the height is measured by number of lines. The left margin and the vertical space between labels (when there is more than one column of labels) is measured by number of characters. The space between rows of labels is specified by number of lines. For example, the default label format uses labels that are 35 characters wide and 5 lines high, with 0 as the left margin. Because the form uses only one column of labels, the space between columns of labels is set to 0. One line is set between rows of labels in the default layout.

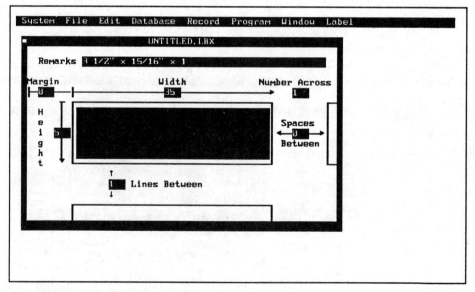

**Figure 11.60   The Label Designer Window**

## Modifying Label Layouts

If the default layout is not what you want, it is a simple matter to modify it. To define a different label size, select the Layout option from the Label menu popup. When the layout popup appears, select a different label size from the list. As an example, let's select the second option, 3 1/2" x 15/16" x 2, from the list (see Figure 11.61).

When you return to the Label Designer window, note that the Number Across text box shows the value of 2, indicating that you will be displaying mailing labels in two columns.

When you select a different label size, FoxPro automatically adjusts the default width and height according to the label size. You can change the height and width of the label simply by editing the values in the associated text boxes. As a result, the values in the text boxes determine the actual size of the label, and because the values in the Remarks text box are not updated automatically, they cease to reflect the label size.

For example, if you set the label width to 50 characters, it may be printed in a label that is wider than 3 1/2". Likewise, if you set the label height to 3 lines high, the actual label may be less than 15/16" high.

Similarly, you can change the space settings between horizontal and vertical labels by editing the values in their associated text boxes (see Figure 11.62). Be

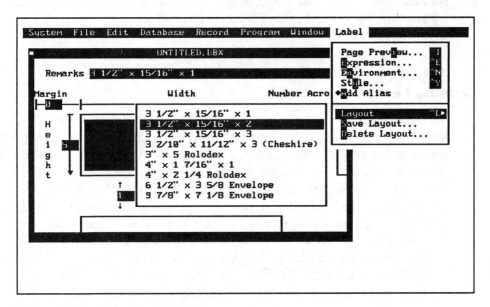

**Figure 11.61   Selecting Label Sizes**

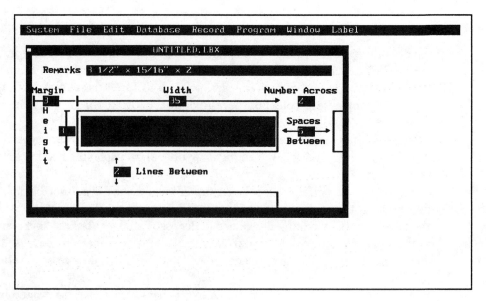

**Figure 11.62    A Modified Label Form**

aware, though, that when you add these numbers together, their dimensions must not exceed the size of your labels, or the capabilities of your printer. You cannot, for example, fit three columns of labels, each of which is 34 characters wide, on an 80-column page.

## Defining Label Contents

After the label size and the spacing between labels is defined, the contents of the labels can be defined by placing the data fields in the label. To do that, position the cursor on the first line on which you want data to appear and then select the Expression option from the Label menu popup or press the Ctrl+E key combination. For example, to place the TITLE, FIRST, INITIAL, and LAST data fields on the first line of the label, position the cursor at the top of the label and press the Ctrl+E key combination. In return, the Label Expression Builder dialog appears. Then enter the expression for the data fields (see Figure 11.63).

When you return to the Label Designer window, the expression will be displayed as the first line of the label. Repeat this process to enter the expressions for the second and third lines in the label. The label form should look like that shown in Figure 11.64.

Although our database contains only a single address field, ADDRESS, it is very common for mailing list databases to contain two address fields (ADDRESS1 and

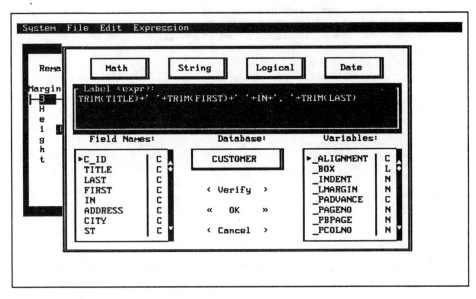

**Figure 11.63   Specifying a Label Expression**

ADDRESS2, for example) or a company name field as well as an address field. Frequently, one of these fields is blank in a fairly large number of records in the database. When you create a label that displays information from these fields, you want to be able to display the contents of the field when it is *not* empty and prevent

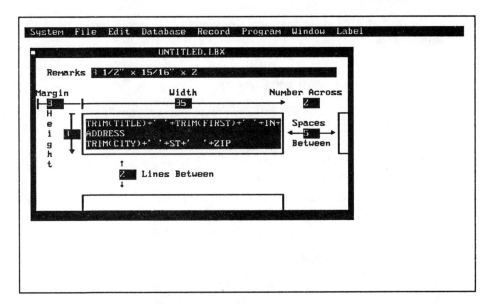

**Figure 11.64   Showing the Label Expressions**

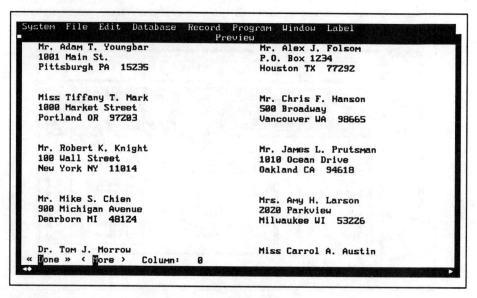

**Figure 11.65   Viewing Mailing Labels on Screen**

it from appearing at all when it *is* empty. Do that by defining the label expressions for these fields as:

```
ADDRESS1;
ADDRESS2;
```

The trailing semi-colon instructs the printer not to print the data field when it is empty.

## Viewing Mailing Labels on Screen

To view mailing labels, select the Page Preview option from the Label menu popup or press the Ctrl+I key combination, and the labels will be displayed on screen in sections (see Figure 11.65).

This figure shows the first section of the mailing labels created by the label form. Once you are satisfied with how the labels look, you can send them to the printer. As a safety measure, to avoid losing the layout, it is a good idea save the label form to a disk file first.

## SAVING LABEL FORMS

To save the current label form to a disk file, select the Save As option from the File menu popup. When the Save As: dialog appears, assign a name to the label file (e.g., CUSTOMER.LBX). In addition, save the selected database as a part of the environment information by choosing the <Yes> push button in response to the

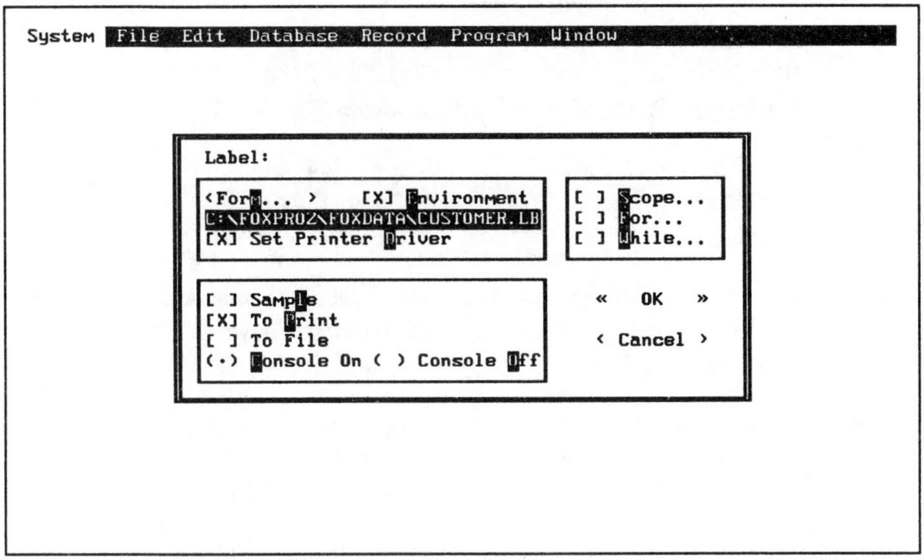

```
System  File  Edit  Database  Record  Program  Window

        Label:
        <Form... >    [X] Environment      [ ] Scope...
        C:\FOXPRO2\FOXDATA\CUSTOMER.LB     [ ] For...
        [X] Set Printer Driver             [ ] While...

        [ ] Sample                         «   OK   »
        [X] To Print
        [ ] To File                        < Cancel >
        (·) Console On ( ) Console Off
```

**Figure 11.66   Printing Mailing Labels**

"Save environment information?" prompt. This allows you to print or display the labels again without first having to open the necessary database and define a master index.

After saving the label form to the CUSTOMER.LBX, you may choose to print the mailing labels, or close the window and run the labels at a later time. Let's exit the Label Designer window by closing the window after saving the label form.

## PRINTING MAILING LABELS

To print mailing labels, select the Label option from the Database menu popup. When the Label dialog appears, select the <Form> check box to retrieve the label form, CUSTOMER.LBL. Then select the To Print check box, followed by selecting the <<OK>> push button (see Figure 11.66). The printed mailing labels are shown in Figure 11.67.

## PRODUCING MAILING LABELS FROM MULTIPLE DATABASES

Earlier in this chapter you learned how to produce a report using data elements that were extracted from two linked database files. Labels can be produced in the same way. To do that, use RQBE to link the data records and generate a temporary database containing the data we requested. Earlier, we used ADDRESS.QPR to

Mr. Adam T. Youngbar
1001 Main St.
Pittsburgh PA 15235

Mr. Alex J. Folsom
P.O. Box 1234
Houston TX 77292

Miss Tiffany T. Mark
1000 Market Street
Portland OR 97203

Mr. Chris F. Hanson
500 Broadway
Vancouver WA 98665

Mr. Rober K. Knight
100 Wall Street
New York NY 11014

Mr. James L. Prutsman
1010 Ocean Drive
Oakland CA 94618

Mr. Mike S. Chien
900 Michigan Avenue
Dearborn MI 48124

Mrs. Amy H. Larson
2020 Parkview
Milwaukee WI 53226

Dr. Tom J. Morrow
1000 Mountain Drive
Bellevue WA 98007

Miss Carrol A. Austin
2900 Huntland Drive
Austin TX 78752

Miss Linda D. Baker
3000 N. 50th Avenue
Phoenix AZ 85031

Ms. Sandy F. Nelson
2015 Washington Ave.
Evanston IL 60204

Mr. Peter W. Jackson
100 Oceanview Drive
Miami FL 33152

Mr. Larry S. Wilson
200 Jackson Street
Portland OR 97204

Dr. John R. Swanson
7070 Mission Avenue
Hayward CA 94541

**Figure 11.67   Printed Mailing Labels**

extract data for a report on sales personnel addresses. We can use the same query to generate the data for our mailing labels. To do that, bring up the ADDRESS query by selecting the Open option from the File menu popup. When the Open dialog appears, set the file type to Query and select ADDRESS.QPR.

When the RQBE window appears, select Browse as the destination for the query output. Then perform the query by selecting the <Do Query> push button. You can now create the label form using the query results. Select the New option from the File menu popup and the Label radio button from the New dialog. When the Label

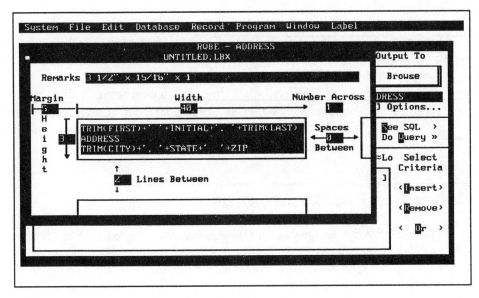

**Figure 11.68    Another Example of Label Form**

Designer window appears, design the label form you want. An example is shown in Figure 11.68.

To view the mailing labels, select the Page Preview option from the Label menu popup. The results will look like that shown in Figure 11.69.

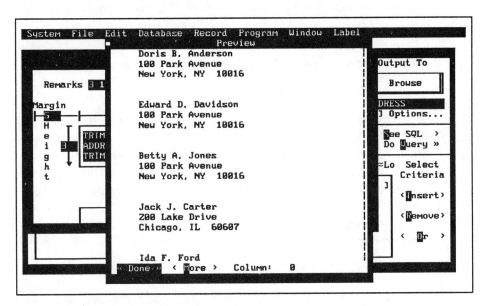

**Figure 11.69    Viewing Sales Staff Mailing Labels**

If you plan to produce the labels later, save the label form to a label form file (named SALESMAN.LBX). When FoxPro prompts you to save the environment information, be sure to answer Yes so that you will continue to be able to link the query and the label form.

To print the mailing labels, select the Label option from the Database menu popup. When the Label dialog appears, specify the name of label form to use and select the To Print check box before selecting the <<OK>> push button to begin printing.

# Using FoxPro Commands

The Report Writer and the Label Designer are powerful tools for creating custom reports and mailing labels. As already explained in this chapter, they can be invoked by selecting appropriate menu options. Reports and mailing labels also can be produced by issuing the appropriate FoxPro commands. In addition, you can create memory variables with the necessary commands and then pass their values into the Report Writer and Label Designer so that you can include them in the reports and mailing labels.

## CREATING AND MODIFYING REPORTS

To create a new report, issue the CREATE REPORT command:

```
CREATE REPORT <name of report form>
```

To create a report to be named SALESRPT.FRX, issue the following command:

```
CREATE REPORT SALESRPT
```

Note that the database to be used for the report must be selected before issuing the CREATE REPORT command. Otherwise, you will be prompted to do so later.

When the command is executed, the Report Writer will be invoked and a blank report form will be displayed in the report Layout window. After that you can place all the report objects in the report form by using the procedures described earlier in this chapter.

To make changes to an existing report form, issue the MODIFY REPORT command:

```
MODIFY REPORT <name of report form>
```

When this command is executed, FoxPro will locate and display the specified report form in the Report Layout window. If the specified report form does not exist, it will create a new report form with that name and display it in the Report

Layout window. Therefore, you may use the MODIFY REPORT command to create a new report form as well.

To modify the report form named SALESRPT, issue the following command:

```
MODIFY REPORT SALESRPT
```

As a result, the report form SALESRPT.FRX will be displayed in the Report Layout window so that you can make the necessary changes to it.

## PRODUCING REPORTS

After you have created the report form, produce the report by issuing the REPORT FORM command:

```
REPORT FORM <name of report form> [TO PRINT/PREVIEW]
```

To produce the report using the report form BYMALE.FRX that was created earlier, issue the following command:

```
REPORT FORM BYMALE
```

Remember though, you will be prompted to select the database file to be used for the report if the database file is not selected in the current work area. Of course, you can do this before issuing the REPORT FORM command in this form:

```
USE SALESMAN
REPORT FORM BYMALE
```

If you need to rearrange the records in the database before producing the report, you must issue the SET ORDER command to index the database file. For example, to arrange the records by sex in the database file, issue the following command to index the file by using the MALE index tag:

```
SET ORDER TO MALE
```

If, however, the indexing information is already an element of the report environment, you may skip this command.

To preview the report on the screen, add the keyword PREVIEW to the command as shown:

```
REPORT FORM BYMALE PREVIEW
```

This command is the equivalent to selecting the Page Preview option from the Report menu popup in the Report Layout window. After viewing the report on the screen, you can issue the command to print it by adding the TO PRINT clause at the end of the command:

```
REPORT FORM BYMALE TO PRINT
```

It is necessary to add either the PREVIEW or TO PRINT clause to the end of the command to view your report, because FoxPro's default screen preview scrolls by too rapidly to be of any viewing use.

## USING MEMORY VARIABLES

Recall from the previous chapter that summary statistics can be created and saved to memory variables so that their values can be passed to a report. The sample report shown in Figure 11.70 uses summary statistics that were saved in a memory variable.

The report displays the compensation of the sales staff as monthly salary values and as percentages of the total salary of the group. The percentages can be calculated only after the total salary value is computed. Due to the limitations of the Report Writer, however, it is not possible to compute the total salary and then calculate the percentages. The use of a memory variable is required. This means, in our example, that you must calculate the total salary and save it to a memory variable before incorporating it in the report.

Thus, to calculate the total salary and save it in a memory variable named **total_pay**, issue the following command:

```
USE SALESMAN
CALCULATE SUM(SALARY) TO total_pay
```

```
                                              Page 1
           COMPENSATION SUMMARY REPORT        11/29/91


    Name of Salesperson    Date Hired    Salary    Percent

    Doris B. Anderson       07/01/86     $2,800     12.02%
    Edward D. Davidson      06/04/90     $1,500      6.44%
    Betty A. Jones          09/26/89     $2,500     10.73%
    Jack J. Carter          05/14/87     $2,550     10.94%
    Ida F. Ford             11/22/87     $2,600     11.16%
    Albert I. Iverson       10/25/88     $2,200      9.44%
    George G. Bell          10/12/88     $2,400     10.30%
    Henry H. Evans          03/08/88     $2,000      8.58%
    Fred C. Gilbert         04/15/87     $2,300      9.87%
    Candy E. Harvey         12/01/89     $2,450     10.52%

                            Total        $23,300   100.00%
```

**Figure 11.70    Percentage Summary Report**

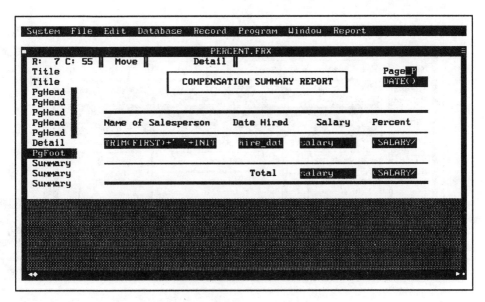

**Figure 11.71 The PERCENT.FRX Report Form**

After that, bring up the Report Writer to create the report form you need. Figure 11.71 shows the report form (PERCENT.FRX) that was used to produce the percentage report shown in Figure 11.70.

When you are designing the report form, you can include the memory variable **total_pay** in the expression for defining a report field. Figure 11.72 shows the expression that was used to define the values for the report column named Percent.

When you are using memory variables in your reports, it is important to remember to create the variables *before* entering the Report Writer. You may use memory variables that have been saved in a disk file, but you need to first recall them by using the RESTORE command.

## CREATING AND MODIFYING MAILING LABELS

To invoke the Label Designer so that you can create a new mailing label form, issue the following command:

```
CREATE LABEL <name of label form>
```

Then, to create the label form named CUSTOMER.LBX after selecting the database needed, issue the following command:

```
CREATE LABEL CUSTOMER
```

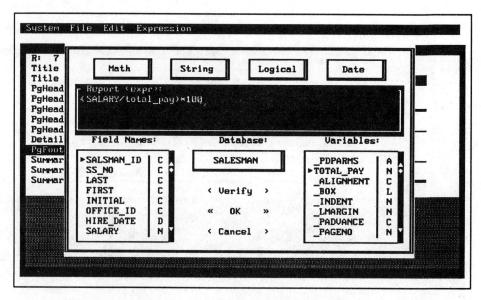

**Figure 11.72   Using Memory Variables in Report Expressions**

In response to the command, the Label Designer will display a new label form with the specified form name. After that, you can follow the same procedure outlined in this chapter to create your mailing labels.

To modify an existing label form, use the MODIFY LABEL command:

```
MODIFY LABEL <name of label form>
```

To make changes to the existing CUSTOMER.LBX label form, issue the following command:

```
MODIFY LABEL CUSTOMER
```

## PRODUCING MAILING LABELS

The command to produce mailing labels by using an existing label form is LABEL FORM:

```
LABEL FORM <name of label form> [TO PRINT/PREVIEW]
```

Add the PREVIEW keyword to the command to view the mailing labels on the screen before sending them to the printer. To print the mailing labels, add the TO PRINT clause to the LABEL FORM command. Examples:

```
LABEL FORM CUSTOMER PREVIEW
LABEL FORM CUSTOMER TO PRINT
```

Again, in this case, the database to be used for the mailing labels must be selected before issuing the LABEL FORM command. In addition, if you would like to rearrange the records in the database file before producing the mailing labels, remember to issue the commands to index the database file.

# Chapter Summary

This chapter detailed the procedures for producing reports and mailing labels. To review: A report form is designed in the Report Layout window; a FoxPro report layout is divided into bands for organizing the information contained in the report, and various report objects can be placed in the report bands.

Information is displayed in a column format in a column report and data from an individual record is shown in a report line. All the information in a form report is displayed in a free form and data from a record is displayed in a report section. Reports can be viewed on screen before being sent to the printer.

This chapter also defined the processes by which to produce mailing labels. A label form is laid out in the Label Designer window; once the label's contents and form are defined, labels incorporating data from selected databases can be produced.

Information from multiple database files may be extracted to produce both reports and mailing labels by creating a RQBE query to link the database files and produce the data records to be used in the reports and mailing labels.

You should now be aware of the capabilities of the FoxPro Report Writer and Label Designer. In the next chapter, you will learn how to use the Screen Builder, another powerful FoxPro tool, to design custom data entry forms.

# 12

# Using Custom Data Screens

## An Overview

In previous chapters, the Browse window was used to view and edit data in Browse or Change mode. In either mode, the default screen provided by FoxPro was used to display data. There may be times, however, when the default screen layout in Browse or Change mode is simply not convenient to use. If you are using the Browse window primarily to view data, for example, it may present too much information in too compact an area. Or the layout of data on the screen may not harmonize well with the needs of data entry. Despite the flexibility that FoxPro does offer in organizing data in the Browse window, you may find yourself wishing that you could replace FoxPro's default layout with one of your own creation.

In fact, FoxPro allows you to do just that. It even allows you to add your own handy controls, like check boxes, popups, radio buttons, and push buttons. In this chapter, you will learn how to use the Screen Builder to create such custom screens, which can then be used either for entering or viewing data.

We will approach designing custom screens very much like we approached designing custom reports and labels in the previous chapter. The chapter begins by illustrating how to design a custom data screen with the quick screen layout feature that the Screen Builder offers. Then you'll learn how to modify the quick screen layout to create custom data screens that display data fields in an aesthetically pleasing layout.

### CREATING CUSTOM DATA SCREENS

As you already learned, in FoxPro, data records can be viewed in a database by bringing up the Browse window, where they are then displayed in Browse or

Change mode. In either of these modes, it is also possible to modify data. Further, by choosing the Append option from the Record menu popup, you can also add new records to the database in the Browse window.

But data can be displayed in the Browse window only on a default screen where fields are identified by their names as defined in the database structure. No text may be added to the screen for describing the displayed data. In addition, all data fields are laid out on the default screen in a predetermined format that cannot be changed. These limitations often render the screen inadequate for satisfying the requirements of your data display and data entry operations.

Greater flexibility in laying out screens for viewing and entering data is provided by FoxPro's powerful Screen Builder, a tool that enables you to design custom screens. These custom screens can then be used for viewing and editing data in one or more databases, as well as for adding new data to an existing database.

The process of creating a data screen begins with laying out the screen objects in the Screen Design window provided by the Screen Builder. Like the Report Builder, the Screen Builder has all the tools needed to lay out screen objects. Data fields, text, graphics objects, as well as control panels, may be added to the screen to facilitate data viewing and data entry operations. The control panel may consist of a number of push buttons that you can use to select the data records to be displayed and edited. Furthermore, check boxes, radio buttons, and scrollable lists may be incorporated in a custom screen to display data field values.

After designing the data screen, the screen layout information is saved in a screen file that uses .SCX as its file extension; this actually is a special kind of database file that FoxPro uses to store screen information. The information is generated into a set of FoxPro commands and saved as a screen program with an .SPR file extension. When you want to use the screen layout to display data, you simply execute the screen program file. At that point, FoxPro compiles the FoxPro commands into computer machine codes and then executes them to produce the data screen. The compiled program then is saved as another disk file with .SPX as its file extension.

## TYPES OF DATA SCREENS

There are two kinds of screens on which to display data: a desktop screen and a window screen.

### Desktop Screens

A desktop screen displays data in the desktop area of the screen, which is that area that underlies all system and user-defined windows. It is the screen that you see when you begin a FoxPro session. It is also the area in which FoxPro displays the

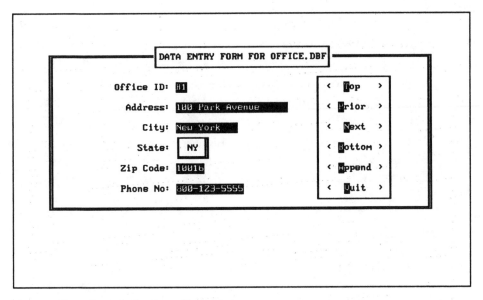

**Figure 12.1  Sample Desktop Data Screen**

results when it executes commands. For example, when you select the Clear option
e Window menu popup or enter the command "Clear" in the Command
FoxPro clears the desktop screen.

12.1 shows an example of a desktop screen that displays all the data fields
rent record of the OFFICE database. In addition to the data fields and
the screen includes a popup for showing the state codes. It also has a
controlling the record sequence; check boxes, radio buttons
used in a data screen. Note that graphics objects
) can be used to frame the data screen and control

ata in a window similar to the Browse window. FoxPro
among four types of windows when creating window
stem windows, dialogs, and alerts. Each of these types
etail below, but regardless of its type, a window can be
attributes it possesses. These attributes in turn determine
e manipulated. FoxPro windows can be characterized by
e of the following attributes:

dow that possesses the float attribute is movable; otherwise, it
ary.

- *Close.* A window that possesses the close attribute can be closed by selecting a menu option, clicking the mouse, or using the keyboard. A window without the close attribute generally is closed by selecting a designated push button.

- *Shadow.* A window defined with a shadow attribute has a darkened area behind it that resembles a shadow. A window without this attribute has no shadow.

- *Minimize.* A window with the minimize attribute can be shrunk to a size of one row by 16 columns that can be placed anywhere on the screen. A window without this attribute cannot be shrunk or iconized in this way.

The Screen Builder allows you to create the four types of windows shown in the table below. The attributes of three of them—System, Dialog, and Alert—are fixed and cannot be changed. For example, the Dialog and Alert windows, which are primarily special-purpose windows used to display dialog boxes and alerts, are displayed with a double-line border (described below) and a shadow. In addition, they can be moved, but they cannot be minimized or closed. The attributes of the User window, on the other hand, are user-definable; although by default the user window's shadow attribute is selected, all four attributes may be either set on or off.

| Window Type | Attributes | Default Settings |
|---|---|---|
| User | Close | Shadow |
| | Float | |
| | Shadow | |
| | Minimize | |
| System | Close | Close |
| | Float | Float |
| | Shadow | Shadow |
| | Minimize | Minimize |
| Dialog | Float | Float |
| | Shadow | Shadow |
| Alert | Float | Float |
| | Shadow | Shadow |

In addition to possessing these four attributes, each window also can be framed by a particular type of border. FoxPro user four different border patterns to frame a window: Single, Double, Panel, and System; or None may be specified. A Single border frames the window with a single line, a Double border with a double-line box; both the Panel and System borders display a wide window border, but any

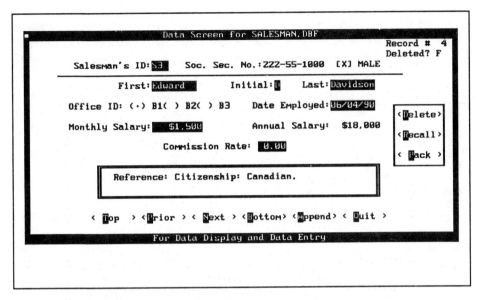

**Figure 12.2  A Data Screen in a System Window**

controls are hidden in a window with a Panel border while they are visible in a window with a System border.

Similar to their window attributes, the border types of three kinds of windows (System, Dialog, and Alert) are predefined and cannot be changed. A System window has a System border, and the Dialog and Alert windows have a Double border. The border type of a User window, on the other hand, is user-definable; by default the User window has a Single border, but any of the five border types can be selected instead.

Because you are already familiar with a System window and the controls needed to manipulate it, we will use it to illustrate the operation of the Screen Builder in this chapter. Figure 12.2 shows such a System window that might be created to display the records in the SALESMAN database. The window has the normal control button to close it; it can be minimized and maximized in the regular manner, as well as moved anywhere on the screen.

The data window displays the values of all the data fields in the current record of the SALESMAN database. The values of some data fields are shown by using check boxes and radio buttons. In addition to graphics objects (boxes and lines), the data window has two sets of push buttons.

## SCREEN LAYOUTS

The Screen Builder is used to create a data screen on which to lay out the objects in the screen form. As a shortcut you can use the quick screen layout provided by the Screen Builder, where data fields are displayed in a column or row layout and are described by using their field names as defined in the database structure. Or you can decide to create a custom screen so that you can place the screen objects in any format. Then, in addition to descriptive texts and data fields, you can add graphics objects (boxes and lines) and controls (popups, radio buttons, push buttons, etc.) to the screen. A custom screen also can be created either by placing each object individually on the screen or by starting with the quick screen and then customizing it.

## Creating Window Screens

The most useful screen type is a System window screen because it can be easily manipulated. And, because the procedure for producing other types of screens is very similar to that for producing a System window screen, we will focus our discussion on that type.

Before designing the screen layout, the necessary databases must be opened. If the screen will display only one database file, open it in the current work area and set the appropriate indexes accordingly. If you intend to display data from more than one database file, you must establish their relations in the View window before invoking the Screen Builder. In our example, to create a screen for displaying data in the SALESMAN database, open SALESMAN.DBF in work area A.

### The Screen Builder Window

To create a new screen, select the New option from the File menu popup. When the New dialog appears, select the Screen radio button and then the <<OK>> push button. As a result, the Screen Builder window shown in Figure 12.3 appears. The screen being designed in the Screen Builder window is labeled UNTITLED.SCX. In addition, the system menu bar now includes a Screen menu pad that contains a variety of options for designing your screen layout.

### Screen Layout Dialog

The first step in creating a custom data screen is to select the screen type. To do this, choose the Screen Layout option from the Screen menu popup, and the Screen Layout dialog shown in Figure 12.4 will appear.

Information in the Screen Layout dialog is divided into five sections. On the top of the dialog are two radio buttons (DeskTop and Window) for selecting the screen type. The second section (below the radio buttons) contains three text boxes (Name, Title, and Footer) for identifying a window screen. The <Type> push button obviously is for selecting the types of window screens. Note: if you choose a Desktop screen, the second section is disabled.

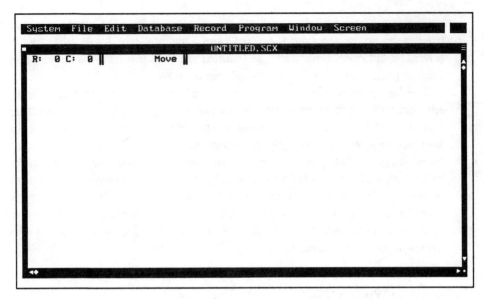

**Figure 12.3   The Screen Builder Window**

The third section contains the Size and Position boxes. The height and width of the screen are defined in the Size box; the coordinates of the upper-left hand corner of the screen are specified in the Position box. Selecting the Center check box centers the screen.

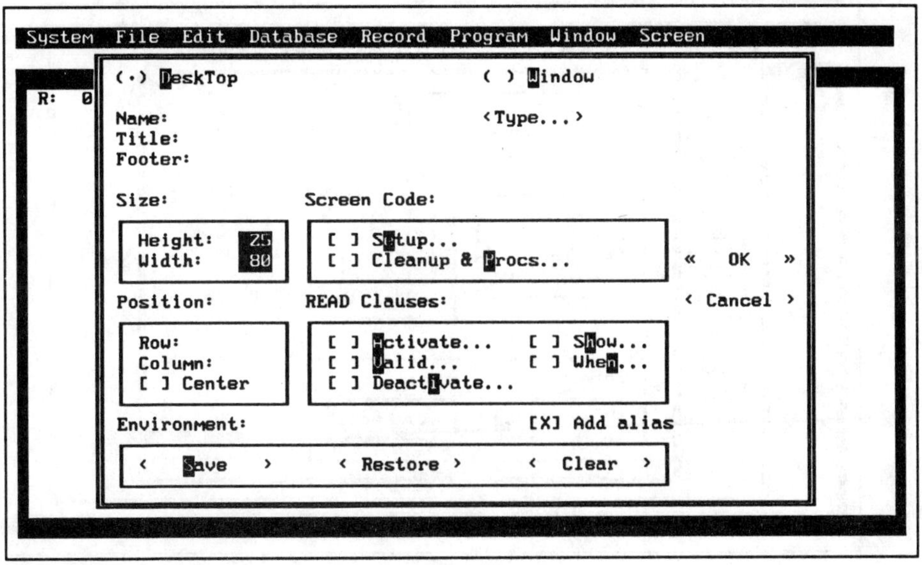

**Figure 12.4   The Screen Layout Dialog**

The fourth section includes the Screen Code and READ Clauses boxes and is used to define the procedures or expressions that are to be included as part of the screen layout code. Because these features are used primarily by more advanced FoxPro programmers, they can be ignored for now.

The last section of the Screen Layout dialog is for determining the type of environment information that is saved along with the screen. By selecting the <Save> push button, for example, the database that was opened in the current work area will be saved as part of the environment information with the screen layout. Later, when you bring up the screen layout again, the database automatically will be opened and selected for you. Selecting <Restore> reinstates the environment information that was previously saved. Selecting the <Clear> push button, on the other hand, erases all the current environment information. If you select the Add Alias check box, the name of the database file will be added to the front of the field names in the field expressions.

### Selecting Window Type

To use the Screen Builder to create a data screen that will appear in a window, select the Window radio button. Then check the <Type> push button to choose the type of window you need. As a result, the Type dialog appears (see Figure 12.5).

The Type dialog contains the Type popup, which allows you to select one of the four types of windows (User, System, Dialog, and Alert) that the Screen Builder can create. Below the Type popup are four check boxes for defining the window

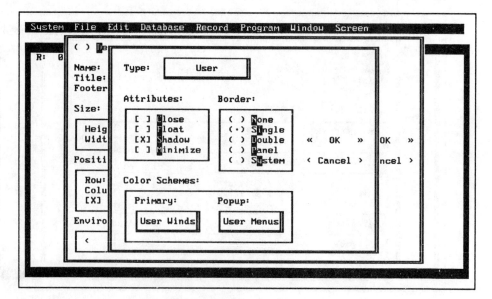

**Figure 12.5  The Window Type Dialog**

attributes and five radio buttons for specifying the window border. Most window types have default selections that you cannot change. For example, if you select a Dialog window from the Type popup, the Float and Shadow check boxes and the Double radio button will be selected, indicating that the window you create will have a double line as a border, will cast a shadow, and will be movable. Both the attribute and border options are grayed, indicating that they cannot be modified; those options that are selected will form the fixed attributes and border of the window. In the case of a User window, although the Shadow attribute and the Single border are selected by default, they can be changed by selecting one or all of the attributes or a different border type.

To select a System window, select System from the Type popup before choosing the <<OK>> push button. Once you return to the Screen Layout dialog, use the screen shown in Figure 12.6 to enter the settings that we will use in building our System window screen.

The first setting, Name, is used by the Screen Builder for identifying the window; it is optional. Unless you need to call the window by name in other FoxPro programs, do not assign a name to the window; FoxPro will automatically assign a unique name to the window upon creating the screen layout. In our example, we have left the window name blank.

In the Title text box you can enter a description that is to appear in the title bar of the window; this too is optional. The text will be centered in the window's title bar, and if it is too long to fit there entirely, it will be truncated. In this example, we have entered "Data Screen for SALESMAN.DBF" as the title of the window.

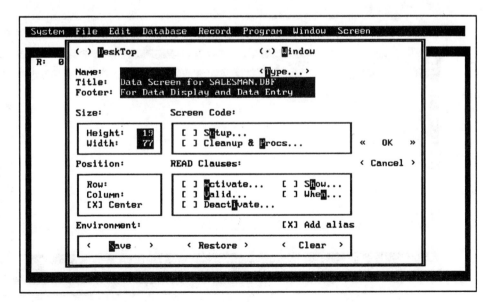

**Figure 12.6  Identifying the Screen Window**

In the same way (this is also optional) you can enter a footer in the dialog's Footer text box. The window footer will be centered in the bottom border of the window. Like the window title, if the length of the footer exceeds the window length, it will be truncated. As Figure 12.6 shows, we have chosen "For Data Display and Data Entry" as the text of our footer.

As the Size group box in Figure 12.6 shows, the System window that we are designing will be 19 rows high and 77 characters wide, the default dimensions that Screen Builder assigns to a window. If you would like a different size window, edit the values in the Height and Width text boxes in the Size group box. It is possible to define a data window screen that is larger than the Screen Builder window. The hidden area of the window screen can be viewed by scrolling the window.

The System window too has a default setting; it is centered on the screen. If you would like to place the window in a different location, deselect the Center check box and then enter the row and column coordinates as you would like them to be positioned. These coordinates are relative to the upper left-hand corner of the desktop screen.

Finally, select the <Save> push button to save the environment information. This allows the screen to automatically open and use the correct database and index files whenever it is displayed. Select the <<OK>> button to exit from the Screen Layout dialog. When you return to the Screen Builder window, the System window that we defined should look like the one in Figure 12.7.

As Figure 12.7 shows, the System window lies inside the Screen Builder window. Each window also has its own Close, Size, and Maximize controls, all of

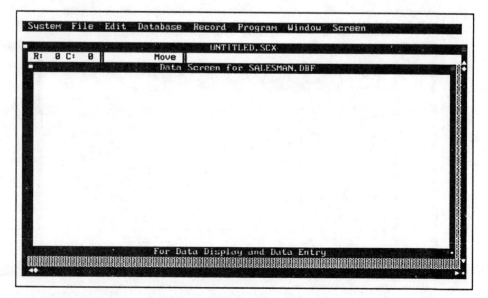

**Figure 12.7  System Window in the Screen Builder Window**

which are fully functional. However, only the Size control is operative within the Screen Builder; Close and Maximize only will work after you execute the completed System window screen *outside* of the Screen Builder. The screen can be sized independently of the Screen Builder window, except that you cannot use the Size control to make the screen larger than the Screen Builder window; to do this, you can use only the Size group box in the Screen Layout dialog, as we discussed earlier.

### Using Quick Screen Layout

Having created the basic framework of the System window, you can begin placing the screen objects on the screen panel. These screen objects can be placed individually or by using a quick screen layout as a shortcut, as mentioned before. To create a quick screen layout, select the Quick Screen option from the Screen menu popup to retrieve the Quick Screen dialog (see Figure 12.8).

The Quick Screen dialog is very similar to the Report Writer's Quick Report dialog that was discussed in the previous chapter. In the Quick Screen dialog, the layout types (column or row layout) are selected by choosing the appropriate radio buttons. To select data fields to be placed on the screen layout, choose the Fields check box. If the Titles check box is selected (the default), data field names will be used as field titles; otherwise, no field titles will be placed on the screen layout. Select the Add Alias check box, and all field names will include the names of their

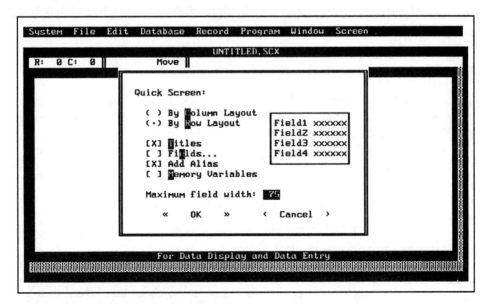

**Figure 12.8  The Quick Screen Dialog**

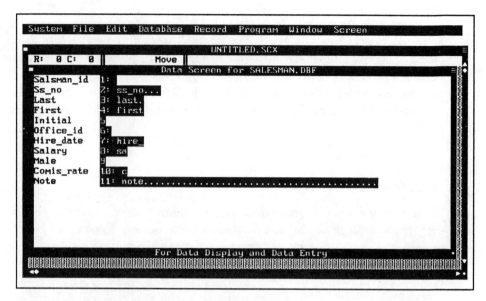

**Figure 12.9  Showing the Quick Screen Panel**

associated database files. The maximum field width, by default, is set to two characters fewer than the window's width (for the window border). You may change the maximum field width, but it cannot exceed the default value.

After defining the Quick Screen settings, you can select the <<OK>> push button to return to the Screen Builder window, and all the data fields (or, if you had chosen the Fields option earlier, all the fields that you had selected) will be displayed in the screen panel as illustrated in Figure 12.9.

## Saving the Screen Layout

The screen panel can now be saved to a disk file with .SCX as its file extension. Select the Save option from the File menu popup, and then assign a name (e.g., SALESMAN.SCX) to the screen file. Be aware that if you did not select the Save push button in the Screen Layout dialog, you should now save the screen environment information by selecting the <Yes> push button in response to the "Save environment information?" prompt. This will allow you to execute the screen without having to prepare the FoxPro environment each time.

### Generating a Screen Program File

After you have finished designing the screen layout, the final step in creating an executable screen is converting the information about that layout into a set of FoxPro commands that are stored in a screen program file (a file with an .SPR file

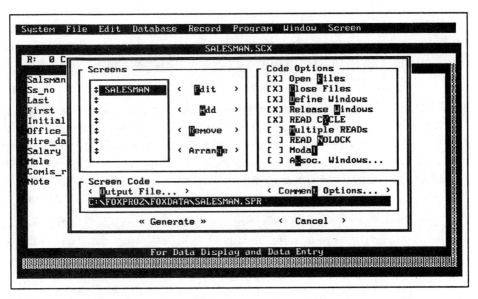

**Figure 12.10  Generating Screen Program File**

extension). This screen program file will then be used to display the custom data screen.

To generate the screen program file, select the Generate option from the Program menu popup when the Screen Builder is the active window; the Generate Screen dialog shown in Figure 12.10 will appear.

Actually, FoxPro allows you to create screen programs that consist of one or multiple screen panels (each panel is a single .SCX file). This capability is reflected in the Screens group box shown in Figure 12.10. The list box, which now contains SALESMAN (the name of the screen that we have just created) by default displays the name or names of all screen panels that are currently open in Screen Builder windows on the FoxPro desktop. The push buttons to the right of the Screens group box allow you to change the screen panels that will be used to create the screen program file. These four push buttons are:

- < Edit > Allows you to open a Screen Builder window to edit screen panels that are not currently open on the FoxPro desktop. This means that you can make last minute changes to all your screens before generating the screen program file.

- < Add > Allows you to add additional screen files that are not currently active in Screen Builder windows.

- < Remove > Allows you to remove screen files that are visible in the Screens list box and will otherwise be included in the screen program file.

- < Arrange > The screen program file will display screens in the order in which their names appear in the list box. The arrange option allows you to change the order of the screen panels when you are generating a screen program file that uses multiple screens.

The Code Options group box in the upper right-hand corner of the Generate Screen dialog contains a number of check boxes that determine how the screen program will behave when it is executed. As you can see in Figure 12.10, the first five options are selected by default. Most of these are advanced options that are of interest only to programmers who are designing screens as portions of a larger program. Two of these options, however, can be used by nonprogrammers:

- Open Files. If environment information is saved with the .SCX file, this option instructs FoxPro to automatically open the necessary databases and indexes and establish any relations that existed among database files when the screen is executed. Because this option saves you from having to perform the same operations yourself, we recommend that you leave it selected, except in those rare instances where multiple databases have identical formats and you are using the same screen for each of them.
- Close Files. This option automatically closes all files when you exit your custom screen. Again, we recommend that you leave this option selected.

The Screen Code group box in the lower portion of the Generate Screen dialog shows the name of the screen program file (in our example, SALESMAN.SPR) in the Output File text box. By default, the root name of this file is the same as the root name of the screen file (SALESMAN.SCX).

Once you have specified the screens, code options, and output file, you can select the <<Generate>> push button to produce the screen program file. After the screen program file is generated, you can then close the Screen Design window and exit from the Screen Builder.

## Using the Data Screen

To use a screen file program that was generated from the Screen Builder, select the Do option from the program menu popup. Next select the screen program file that you would like to execute from the Do Program File list box. The screen program file will then execute and, if the Open Files option was selected when the it was created, will automatically open the necessary database files. For example, after selecting SALESMAN.SPR from the list box, your screen should look something like Figure 12.11. The record pointer is positioned at the beginning of the database, and the first record of SALESMAN.DBF is displayed in the window that you have created. If you need to view the contents of the memo field, position the cursor on

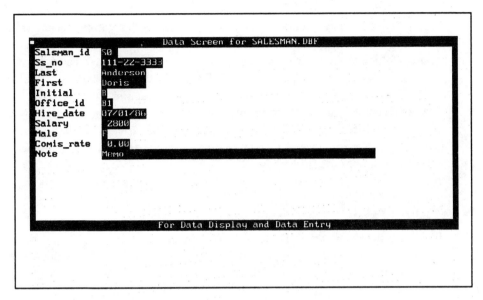

**Figure 12.11  Displaying Data with the Quick Data Screen**

the memo field and double click the mouse, or press the Ctrl+Home key combination. You can move the cursor among the data fields by using the mouse or the arrow keys, and modify the contents of any field in this record.

The window can be minimized and floated in the usual manner; it can be hidden by clicking the mouse on the Close control. To redisplay the window, double click the right-hand mouse button to bring up the System menu bar and then select the window from the Window menu popup. Pressing the Esc key or the Ctrl+End key combination closes the window, causing the System menu bar to reappear. If you selected the Close Files check box in the Generate dialog before creating the screen code, the SALESMAN database will be closed as well.

You should be aware that there are two peculiar features of simple quick screens that are created in this way. First, the value of the screen for data entry or even for browsing the database is strictly limited by the fact that you cannot move beyond the current record to display another data record. The screen is capable of displaying *only* the current record. To display data in another record, it must first be made the current record. To do that, exit the window; because the database is closed as soon as you exit the window, you must first reopen the database before selecting the next record to be displayed and rerunning the screen program file. As an exercise, use this procedure to display the record belonging to salesperson Jack Carter. Select the Locate option from the Record menu popup and define the search condition (e.g., LAST = 'Carter') in the For Clause. After the record is found, display the record by choosing the Do option from the Program menu popup and selecting the SALESMAN screen program file.

The second peculiar feature of simple quick screens is that you cannot exit from the data screen by clicking your mouse on the Close control; this action merely hides the window, which continues to remain open. Instead, to exit the data screen window after viewing the data, you must press either the Esc key or the Ctrl+End key combination.

These limitations can all be overcome by adding custom controls to the screen. The controls then may be used to: move among the data records in the database, more easily close the screen window, and control the process of adding or editing information in the database. To add the control buttons, return to the Screen Builder window to modify the screen layout.

## Modifying Existing Data Screens

To modify an existing screen layout, select the Open option from the File menu popup. When the File Open dialog appears, select the screen file (e.g., SALESMAN.SCX) that you want to modify. As a result, the screen layout will be shown in the Screen Builder window and you can begin making the necessary changes to it.

The procedures for selecting and manipulating screen objects are the same as those you learned in the previous chapter for selecting and manipulating report objects. Follow those procedures to rearrange the data fields on the screen, edit the field titles, and add graphics symbols to highlight certain objects on the screen. To edit an existing text, use the arrow keys to move the cursor to the text to be edited and press the Ins key before making the necessary changes to the text. After you have finished making the changes, press the Enter key to make the changes permanent. As an exercise, modify the screen layout to look like that shown in Figure 12.12.

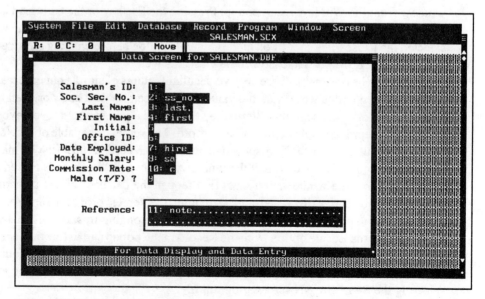

**Figure 12.12  Modified Screen Layout**

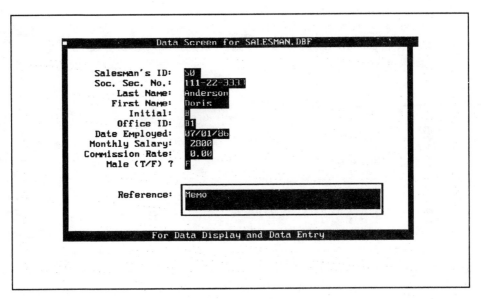

**Figure 12.13  Displaying Data with the Modified Screen**

The modified screen layout has been resized, the data fields have been rearranged, and field titles have been edited. In addition, a box has been placed around the contents of the memo field (NOTE) that is now titled "Reference:." If you were use the modified screen to display a data record, it would look like the one in Figure 12.13.

You can see in this figure that field values are taken from the data record and displayed in the same format as that in the database. The monthly salary, for example, is displayed as 2800 without the dollar sign and commas. The contents of the memo field (NOTE) remain hidden until you double click on the field or press the Ctrl+Home key combination while the field is selected. If you would like to display a data field in a special format and show the contents of the memo fields on the data screen, you can use the Screen Builder to change the fields' default format. You also can make it impossible for viewers of the data to change the field value by specifying how the field value may be handled.

**Formatting Fields**

To format a data field in the screen layout, position the cursor in the field and then choose the Field option from the Screen menu popup by pressing the Ctrl+F key combination or double clicking the mouse. When the Screen Field dialog appears, begin specifying the field template in the text box next to the <Format> push button (see Figure 12.14). To format the SALARY field, for example, position the cursor in the field and press the Ctrl+F key combination. Then enter "$$99,999" in the Format text box.

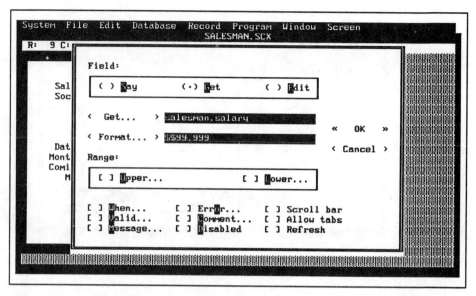

**Figure 12.14  Formatting the SALARY Data Field**

When you return to the screen layout, it is apparent that it is necessary to widen the field to accommodate the added dollar sign and commas. To do this, hold down the Ctrl key and simultaneously point and click the mouse at the end of the field and drag it to the right until the desired field width is achieved. If you are working from the keyboard, press the Ctrl+Spacebar combination, which causes the field to blink. Then use the right arrow key to widen the field to the desired width.

A character field can be formatted in the same way. If, for instance, you would like to make sure that the first letter of all first names are in uppercase, format the FIRST field by using !AAAAAA as the field template. As a result, all first names will be displayed with their first letter capitalized. In addition, when you use the screen for data entry, the first letter you enter in that data field automatically will be converted to uppercase. Similarly, by using ! as the template to format the INITIAL field, all the middle initials will be displayed and entered as capital letters.

### Using Display-Only Fields

When data is displayed on a custom screen, it is also possible, by default, to view and edit the field values on the screen, a useful capability if you intend to modify the field values. But, if you intend to use the data screen only for viewing data, it is a good idea to ensure that users do not accidentally change the values. This "ounce of prevention" requires that you choose the Say radio button in the Screen Field dialog. Whereas the Get radio button, which is selected by default, both displays a record and records any changes made to it by the user, the Say radio

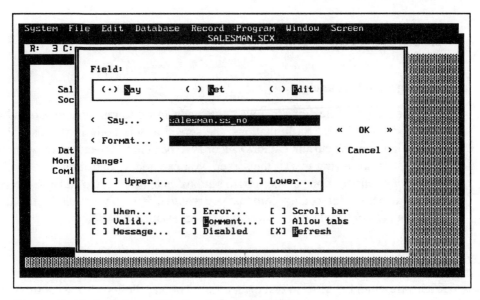

**Figure 12.15 Defining a Display-Only Data Field**

button only displays it. Therefore, to keep a viewer from changing a social security number in the SS_NO data field, select the Say radio button when you bring up the Screen Field dialog. In addition, select the Refresh check box. This insures that the record whose contents are displayed by the custom screen will always be the current one. After making these changes, the Screen Field dialog should look like Figure 12.15.

It is important, however, to recognize the implications of defining a field for display only. First, as you will later see graphically when you create and execute the screen program file, display-only fields are shown in normal text, while other input fields are displayed in reverse video. Second, in addition to being unable to modify the values of existing records, you also cannot enter values into the display-only fields of new records.

### Displaying Memo Fields

When a memo field is displayed on the data screen, its contents will be shown in a default format as "Memo" or "memo" depending on whether or not the field is empty. The actual contents of the memo field will be hidden. If you would like to display the actual contents, you must define the memo field as an Edit region (instead of the default Get region) by selecting the Edit radio button in the Screen Field dialog. For example, to display the contents of the NOTE field on the data screen, double click in the memo field to bring up the Screen Field dialog and select the Edit radio button, followed by selecting the <<OK>> push button to return to the Screen Builder window.

### Adding Control Panels

Although the modifications that we have made so far to our custom screen have removed a number of its limitations, the screen at this point is still capable of displaying only the current database record. To be able to select and view another record without having to exit the screen, you can add a control panel. A control panel may consist of one or more push buttons that allow you to add a new record to the database or select the record that you would like to view or edit. Figure 12.16 shows a control panel that is placed next to an existing data screen.

### Combining Screen Panels

There are a number of ways that to create a set of push buttons in the control panel. A shortcut is to borrow a control panel that has already been created by FoxPro and add it to the data screen.

To combine ready-made control panels with existing data screens in order to generate a single screen program file, select the Generate option from the Program menu popup. When the Generate dialog appears, select all the screen panels to be combined with the current screen by using the <Add> push button. For example, the control panel shown in Figure 12.16 is a screen file named CONTROL3.SCX

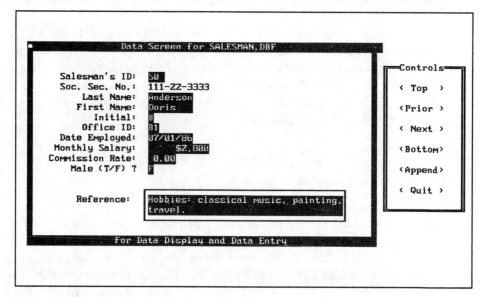

**Figure 12.16  Control Panel**

in the FoxPro TUTORIAL subdirectory. To add it to the screen program file that will be created by the Generate Screen dialog, press the <Add> push button. When the FoxPro Add Screen dialog appears, change the directory to the subdirectory containing the CONTROL3 screen file. Then select the file by double clicking the mouse on the file or by selecting the <Add> push button after highlighting the file. When you return to the Generate dialog, the CONTROL3 screen file should be added to the Screens list box.

Now the control panel can be arranged with the existing screen layout on the same screen by selecting the <Arrange> push button. As a result, the control panel will be displayed as a double-line box behind the existing data screen window. To arrange them together on the screen, use the mouse to point and click in the box or the window border and then drag them to different locations. If you are using the keyboard, you can move the window that is shown in the foreground by first pressing the Ctrl+F7 key combination to cause the window border to blink. While the border is blinking, use the arrow keys to move it to the desired location and press the Enter key to anchor it. To move the control panel that appears behind the window border, press the Ctrl+F1 key combination to bring the control panel to the foreground. When it appears there, move it to a new location by repeating the same method used to move the screen window. As an exercise, place the control panel to the right of the screen window as shown in Figure 12.17.

After you have placed the data screen window and the control panel on the screen, select the Save option from the Arrange menu popup or press the Ctrl+S key combination. When you return to the Generate dialog, select the <<Generate>>

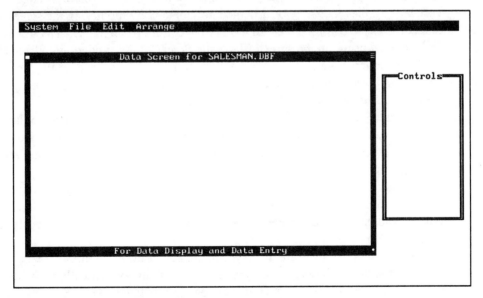

**Figure 12.17  Screen Layout and Control Panel Arrangement**

push button to generate the screen code that combines the existing data screen layout with the control panel on the same screen. The new screen program file will replace the existing SALESMAN.SPR file.

After generating the screen program file, exit from the Screen Builder and execute the SALESMAN.SPR program. (You must return to the FOXDATA subdirectory to find the SALESMAN.SPR program.) The data screen in Figure 12.16 was produced by executing the SALESMAN.SPR program file.

As you can see in Figure 12.16, the first record of the SALESMAN database is shown in the data screen window. To view the next record, select the <Next> push button; to view the previous record, select the <Prior> push button; select the <Top> and <Bottom> push buttons to view the first and last records in the database respectively; press <Append> to display a blank data form for entering data to a new record. To exit from the data screen, select the <Quit> push button.

The <Quit> push button has the same effect as pressing the Ctrl+End key combination. When you select the <Quit> push button, all the changes made to the database will be saved before exiting the data screen. To cancel the changes made to the current data field and exit the data screen, press the Esc key. (Note: This last action is true only if you have chosen the Get operation for editing the current data field. If you have chosen the Edit operation, you cannot cancel the changes by pressing the Esc key.)

### Modifying Control Panels

Although the push buttons in the control panel in Figure 12.16 are arranged in a vertical box, they also may be arranged horizontally by modifying the screen file that contains the control panel. To modify the control panel in CONTROL3.SCX, for example, bring up the screen file in the Screen Builder window by selecting the Open option from the File menu popup and selecting the screen file from the TUTORIAL subdirectory according. As a result, the control panel is displayed in the Screen Builder window as shown in Figure 12.18.

The control panel in this figure is laid out as a double-line dialog box containing a set of push buttons. You can see this by bringing up the Type dialog from the Screen Layout dialog after choosing the Screen Layout option from the Screen menu popup.

To understand how the push buttons are created, double click your mouse on any of them. If you are using the keyboard, position the cursor on any of the push buttons and press the Enter key. As a result, the Push Button dialog appears (see Figure 12.19).

The push button names are displayed in the Push Button Prompts list box in the Push Button dialog. They may be arranged horizontally or vertically in the dialog box by choosing the respective radio buttons in the dialog. The <Spacing> push button is used to define the space between any two push buttons.

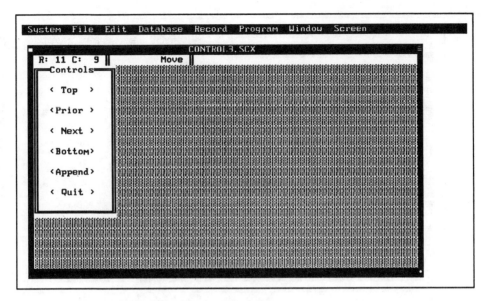

**Figure 12.18 Modifying the Control Panel**

The function of a push button is defined by a series of FoxPro commands known as a procedure. Although the coverage of FoxPro programming techniques is beyond the scope of this book, you can look at an example of a push button procedure by selecting the Valid check box in the Options section of the dialog or by pressing the letter V. When the Valid dialog appears, select the <Edit> push

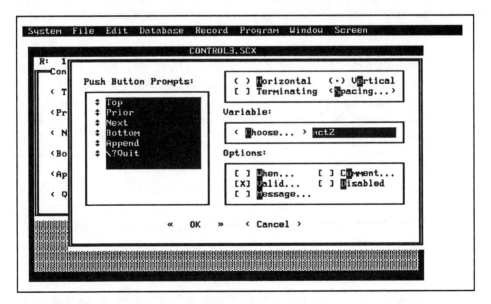

**Figure 12.19 The Push Button Dialog**

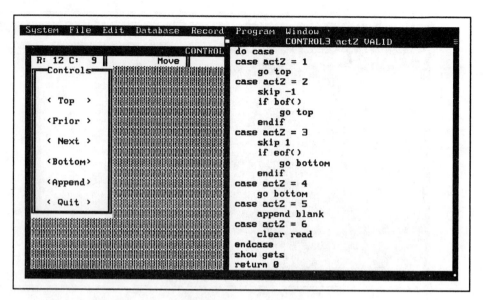

**Figure 12.20  Showing the Push Button Procedure**

button to display the procedure in the Text Editor window. A Text Editor window opens behind the Push Button dialog that contains the program statements making up the procedure. Figure 12.20, for example, shows the Text editor window with the procedure code for the push buttons shown on the left side of the screen.

The procedure consists of a set of FoxPro commands that control the functions of the push buttons and is represented by a set of conditional statements specified between the "do case" and "endcase" statements. One of these will be executed, depending on the value of the variable named "act2" that is specified in the Choose text box of the Push Button dialog. This means that, when you select the first push button (i.e., <Top>), the value of 1 will be assigned to the variable act2. As a result, the command "go top" will be executed and the record pointer will be placed at the first record of the database. Similarly, the value of the variable becomes 5 when you select the fifth push button (i.e., <Append>); the "append blank" command will be executed, causing a blank data form to be displayed for adding a new record to the database.

Modifying these commands means that the functions of the push buttons can be changed. If you decide to create a push button with a procedure, however, you must know more about how to use the FoxPro commands to define how it functions.

### Rearranging Push Buttons

To practice the procedure described above for rearranging push buttons from a vertical layout to a horizontal one, return to the Push Button dialog (by closing the

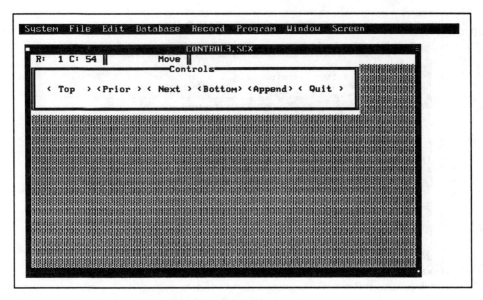

**Figure 12.21   Control Buttons Aligned Horizontally**

Text Editor window, and, if necessary double clicking on one of the push buttons in the dialog box) and select the Horizontal radio button. As a result, the push buttons will be aligned horizontally. Because some the push buttons are hidden from the dialog box, it is necessary to enlarge the dialog box to reveal them. This can be accomplished by modifying the Size parameters in the Screen Layout dialog to a height of 5 and a width of 6. Your screen should then look something like Figure 12.21.

It is also possible to rearrange the order of the push buttons by changing the sequence of the push button prompts in the Push Button dialog's list box.

### Defining Hotkeys for Push Buttons

When using a mouse to select a push button, all you have to do is point at the one you would like to select and click on it. Using the keyboard to perform this same action, on the other hand, can be a much more cumbersome process. It requires that you tab through the available choices until the push button you want is highlighted. Only then can you press the Enter key to select it. FoxPro, in order to facilitate navigating with a keyboard, makes it possible to designate one letter of a push button's label as a hotkey that activates that push button. Pressing the designated hotkey then directly selects that push button. In our example, you might designate the letter "T" for the <Top> push button. Then pressing that letter on the keyboard when any of the push buttons are selected activates the <Top> push button and positions the record pointer at the top of the database file.

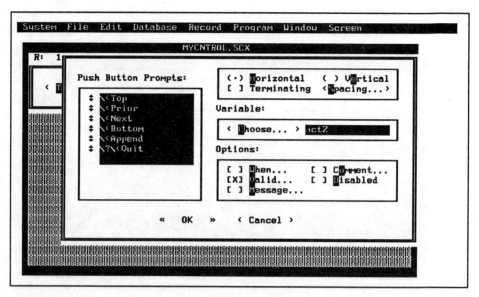

**Figure 12.22  Defining Hotkeys for Push Buttons**

To define a hotkey for a push button, place \< in front of the letter that you want to activate the push button. To continue with the example above, then, "T" as the hotkey for <Top> would be defined as \<Top. Hotkeys for all the push buttons can be defined as we have done in Figure 12.22. Note that the hotkey symbols must immediately precede the key to which they apply.

While looking at Figure 12.22, also pay attention to the fact that the <Quit> push button prompt is defined as \?\<Quit. The symbols \? are used to define an escape push button—a push button that is automatically activated when the Escape key is pressed.

If you would like to see how these push buttons will be displayed on the screen, return to the Screen Builder window by pressing the <<OK>> push button. You should then save the modified control panel as a separate file with a different name, such as MYCNTROL.SCR. This allows you to leave the original CON-TROL3.SCX intact.

### Adding Push Buttons to Data Screens

On the screen shown in Figure 12.16 the set of push buttons is displayed as a separate control panel and not as part of the data screen layout. As a result, each time you modify the data screen layout, it is necessary to combine the control panels when generating the screen program file. There is, however, a way to incorporate the control buttons into an existing data screen layout—use the Copy and Paste operations provided by the Edit menu pad. Specifically, copy the section that contains the push buttons from the control panel and then paste it on the data screen layout at the location you choose.

Let's say, for example, that you would like to incorporate the push buttons in MYCNTROL.SCX into the screen layout that has been saved in the SALES-MAN.CDX screen file. To do that, select the set of push buttons by clicking the mouse on any of the push buttons. If you are using the keyboard, position the cursor on any of the push buttons and press the Spacebar to select it; the push buttons will be highlighted. Then select the Copy option from the Edit menu popup or press the Ctrl+C key combination. This action saves a duplicate copy of the push buttons in a temporary memory location. At this point, close the screen file containing the control panel.

To then incorporate the push buttons in an existing data screen layout, open the screen file containing the screen layout in the Screen Builder window. Next position the cursor on the location at which you would like the push buttons to appear and select the Paste option from the Edit menu popup or press the Ctrl+V key combination. This transfers the set of push buttons that has been saved in the temporary memory location to the existing screen layout. Be aware, however, that you may have to make room for the push buttons by rearranging and editing the screen objects before pasting the push buttons to the layout. A sample modified screen layout is shown in Figure 12.23.

If you were to use the modified screen to display data in the SALESMAN database, the data screen will look like that in Figure 12.24. This figure shows that all the push buttons have been added to the data screen, and every push button has

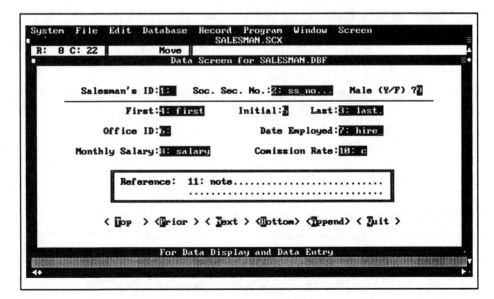

**Figure 12.23  Adding Control Buttons to Data Screen**

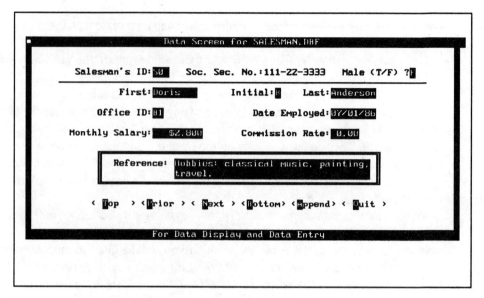

**Figure 12.24  Showing Data on the Modified Screen**

a designated hotkey. Once any of the push buttons are selected, you can press the letter "T" to go to the first record, or the letter "B" to go to the last record in the database file; pressing the letter "Q" activates the <Quit> push button.

### Ordering Data Fields

You can move freely from one data field to another on the data screen with the mouse. But, if you are using the Tab key to move around the data fields, the sequence in which you can move from field to field is determined by a sequence number that the Screen Builder assigns to each field. This sequence number is displayed in front of the input field name in the Screen Builder window (see, for example, the input fields in Figure 12.23).

When you use the Quick Screen option to generate your screen layout, the input sequence is determined by the order of the data fields as defined in the database structure. If you then modify the position of input fields in the screen layout, or if you define your own custom layout from scratch, you will often find that the input order of individual fields is no longer sequential. You can, however, modify the input order of fields on your screen. You can change the order of any one field displayed on the screen or the order of all fields simultaneously. The first step, whether you are reordering one or all the fields displayed on the screen, is to open the SALESMAN.DBF screen file in the Screen Builder window.

Then, to change the order of a specific field, select the data field by clicking the mouse on the field and select the Reorder Fields option from the Screen menu popup. As a result, the selected field becomes numerically the last field in the input order sequence. In addition, the sequential input number of all fields whose input order was greater than the selected field will be decreased by one. To reorder all the fields, first select all the fields and then select the Reorder Fields option from the Screen menu popup. As the result, all the data fields will numbered sequentially from left to right and top to bottom.

As an exercise, reorder all the data fields in the SALESMAN.SCX screen layout. First, select all the screen objects (not just the data fields to be reordered). The simplest way to do that is to use a marquee to select all the screen objects by pointing the mouse on the upper left-hand corner of the screen and then dragging the marquee to cover all the objects. When you release the mouse button, all the screen objects will be selected and highlighted. Next select the Reorder Fields option from the Screen menu popup. If you are using the keyboard to select the fields, place the cursor on the upper left-hand corner of the screen and anchor it by pressing the Spacebar. Then use the arrow keys to create the marquee to cover all the screen objects, followed by pressing the Enter key to select the objects. After you have reordered the data fields selected, your data screen layout should look like that shown in Figure 12.25.

When you use the data screen to display or edit data fields, the data fields will be accessed from left to right, top to bottom as shown in the screen layout.

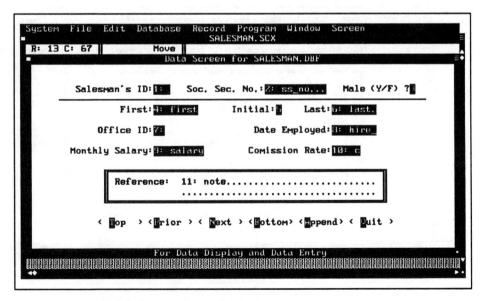

**Figure 12.25 Reordering All Data Fields**

### Adding Check Boxes

Check boxes in a data screen make it possible to display values in a logical data field. For example, instead of showing the value in the MALE field as .T. or .F., you can create a MALE check box and select it to indicate when a salesperson is a man.

To create such a check box, position the cursor on the location where the check box is to appear and select the Check Box option from the Screen menu popup or press the Ctrl+K key combination.

To replace the MALE field on the current screen layout with a check box, for instance, delete the field and its field title by selecting them both and pressing the Del key. After placing the cursor on the desired location for the check box, press the Ctrl+K key combination, and the Check Box dialog will appear. In the Check Box Prompt text box, enter the label (e.g., MALE) that describes the check box. Next define the data field that you intend to use for the check box—in our example, the MALE logical data field. Do this either by entering the field name directly in the Choose text box, or by defining the data field after selecting the <Choose> push button (see Figure 12.26).

When you return to the Screen Builder window after pressing the <<OK>> push button in the Check Box dialog, you will see the MALE check box displayed on the screen layout (see Figure 12.27). Note that you will need to reorder the fields after you have placed the check box on the screen layout.

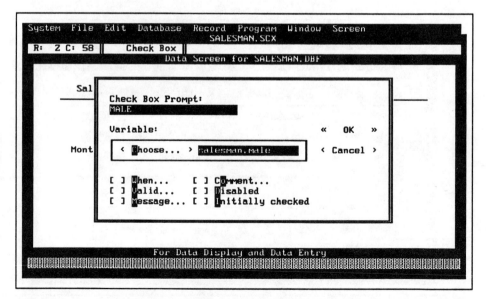

**Figure 12.26  Defining a Check Box**

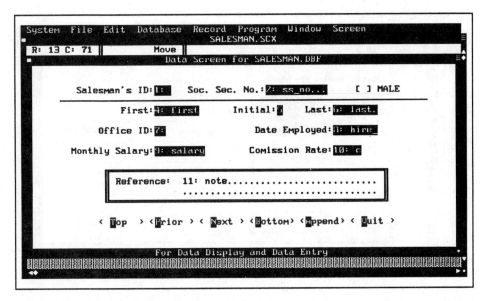

**Figure 12.27  A Check Box in a Screen Layout**

### Adding Radio Buttons

Radio buttons can be very useful for displaying a field that takes on a small set of predetermined values. For example, the OFFICE_ID field in the SALESMAN database can assume one of three values: B1, B2, and B3; and three radio buttons can be created to indicate those values in that field.

To place a set of radio buttons in the screen layout, select the Radio Button option from the Screen menu popup or press the Ctrl+N key combination after you have positioned the cursor on the location at which the radio buttons are to appear.

To replace the OFFICE_ID field in the current screen layout, for example, remove the existing field from the screen layout. Next place the cursor on the *previous* location of the field and press the Ctrl+N key combination. When the Radio Button dialog appears, choose the Horizontal radio button from the dialog to lay the radio buttons to be created horizontally in the screen layout. Then enter the name of the data field (e.g., salesman.office_id) in the Choose text box. Finally, enter the possible values (e.g., B1, B2, B3) for the data field in the Radio Button Prompts list box. In return, the first value you entered will appear as the default initial value in the Initial popup window in the dialog (a different default value may be chosen from the popup window). When you are adding new data records to the database with this data screen, the default value will be used to fill the data field (see Figure 12.28).

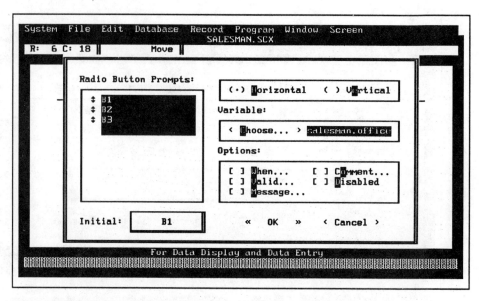

**Figure 12.28  Defining Radio Buttons**

When you return to the Screen Builder window, you will see that the three radio buttons are display horizontally on the screen layout next to the field title "Office ID:." Again, reorder the data fields after you have placed the radio buttons in the layout (see Figure 12.29).

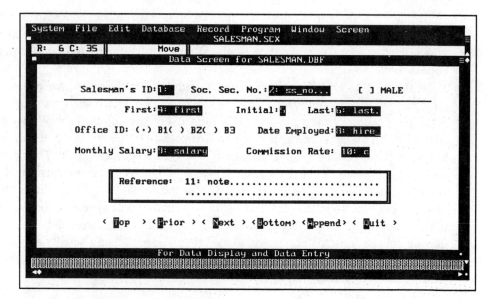

**Figure 12.29  Creating Radio Buttons**

## Adding Calculated Fields

When you are using a custom data screen to display data in a record, it is possible to create data fields that are computed from values in the existing data fields. The SALARY data field in the SALESMAN database, for example, contains monthly salaries for the sales staff. It is possible to use the values in the SALARY data field to create a calculated field that displays *annual* salaries on the screen layout. The calculated field can be used only for display; it cannot be edited.

To create a calculated field, select the Field option from the Screen menu popup or press the Ctrl+F key combination after you have positioned the cursor on the intended location for the field. When the Field dialog appears, select the Say radio button to specify the field for display only. Then enter the expression for the calculated field in the Say text box and enter the field template in the Format text box. For example, to place the annual salary field on the existing screen layout, enter salesman.salary*12 and $$999,999 as the field expression and field template respectively. In addition, select the Refresh check box so that the calculated field will be updated to display a different value when you move to another record (see Figure 12.30).

When you return to the Screen Builder window, you can add the appropriate label (e.g., "Annual Salary:") to the calculated field. After moving the Commission Rate popup to a different location and reordering the data fields, the modified screen layout might look like that shown in Figure 12.31.

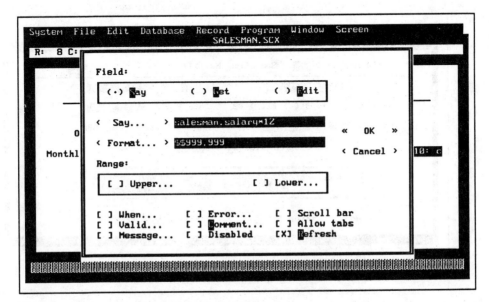

**Figure 12.30  Defining the Calculated Field**

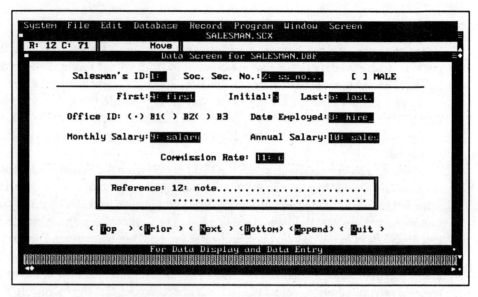

**Figure 12.31  A Calculated Field**

Now when you display data records with the modified data screen, the annual salary for each salesperson will be calculated by using the value in the SALARY data field in the record, as illustrated in Figure 12.32.

This figure shows the calculated field as a display-only field (in normal text instead of in a highlighted text box.) When you move to a different record, the

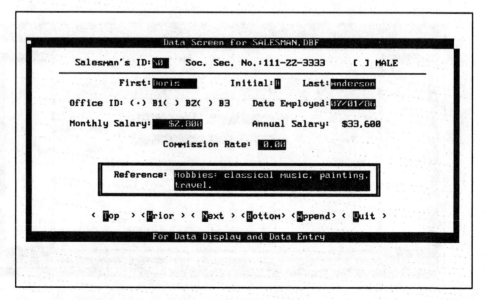

**Figure 12.32  Displaying a Calculated Field Value**

calculated field will be updated automatically using the value in the SALARY field for that record. However, when you are appending a new record to the database with the data screen, the calculated field will not be updated while you are still in the appended record. You will be able to see the calculated value only when you return to the record after you have first moved to a different record.

### Defining Field Value Range

In designing a data entry screen, it is possible to specify a range for the set of values to be entered in a given data field. For example, you may stipulate that all the values to be input in the COMIS_RATE data field must lie between 0.00 and 0.35, thereby excluding any commission rates outside that range.

To specify a range for a character, date, or numeric data field, bring up the Field dialog for the field whose values you want to limit. To set the valid range for the commission rate, for example, double click the mouse on that field or press the Ctrl+F key combination after you have positioned the cursor on that field. When the Field dialog appears, select the check boxes in the Range box to define the upper and lower limits for the range. Note that the check boxes are enabled only when the Get radio button is selected.

To define the upper limit for the range, select the Upper check box. When the Code Snippet dialog appears, select the Expression radio button and enter the maximum value (e.g., 0.35) allowed for that field in the text region (see Figure 12.33).

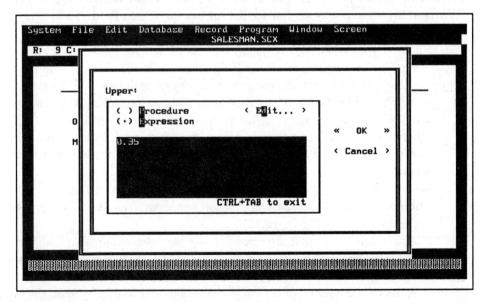

**Figure 12.33  Defining the Upper Limit for a Value Range**

Set the lower limit (e.g., 0.0) for the range in the same way, except enter the minimum value after selecting the Lower check box. It is not necessary, however, to set both the upper and lower limits. Any undefined limits will be ignored.

Once a range for a field value is defined, any value entered in that field that is beyond the valid value will result in an error message reminding you of the range set. Until you change the value to that within the range, you will not be allowed to move to another data field. Therefore, when you enter a new commission rate to the COMIS_RATE data field, it must be between 0.0 and 0.35; any value outside that range will be rejected.

When a range is defined, it should be set wide enough to cover all the possible values for that field; however, if a value outside the valid range was entered in that field *before* you set the value range, it will be displayed. But you cannot change the existing value to a different one that is outside the valid range.

### Displaying Record Numbers

When viewing or editing database records in a Browse window you may want to know which is the current record. This can be determined if the number of the current record is displayed on the data screen. In addition, you can determine the number of records in that database by looking at the record number for the last record in the database.

You can display the number of the current record on a data screen by placing the FoxPro RECNO( ) function in the screen layout. The function is placed in the screen layout in a way similar to that for placing a data field in a Display-only mode. That is, you must choose the Say radio button in the Field dialog. For example, if you would like to display the record number in the upper right-hand corner of the data screen, select the Field option from the Screen menu popup or press the Ctrl+F key combination after you have positioned the cursor in that corner. When the Field dialog appears, select the Say radio button. Then you can define the function for showing the record number by entering the RECNO( ) function in the text box that appears next to the <Say> push button. Finally, select the Refresh check box before selecting the <<OK>> push button to exit from the Field dialog (see Figure 12.34).

When you return to the Screen Builder window, and after you have adjusted its position and field width, you can add the necessary text (e.g., "Record #") to describe the field (see Figure 12.35).

Notice in this figure that the screen layout has been enlarged and all the data fields have been moved down to provide space for the record number to appear in the upper right-hand corner. If you were to display data records with this data screen, the record number of the current record would be displayed on the screen as illustrated in Figure 12.36.

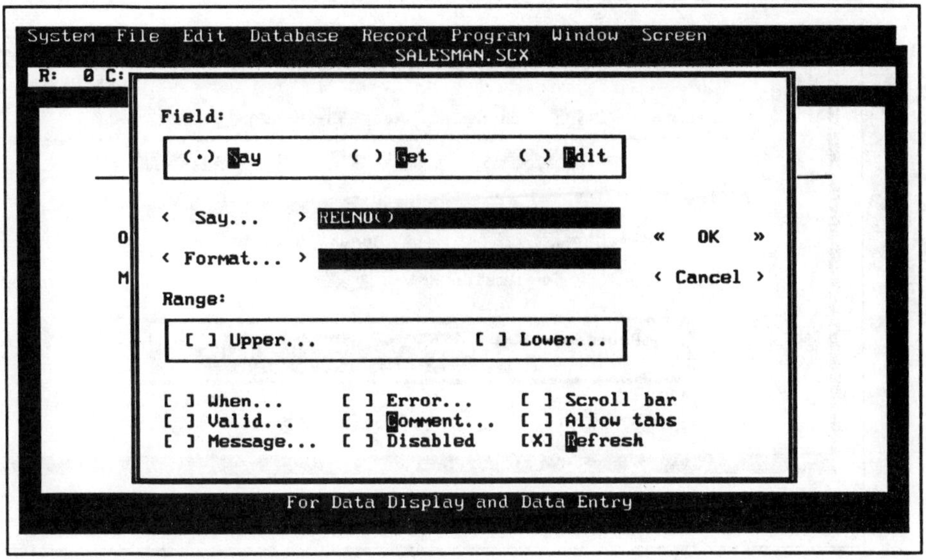

**Figure 12.34  Defining the RECNO( ) Function**

Figure 12.36 shows the sixth record in the SALESMAN database on the screen. To retrieve the number of records in the database, select the <Bottom> push button, which causes the number of the last record in the database to appear; this number, obviously, is also that of the total number of records in the database file.

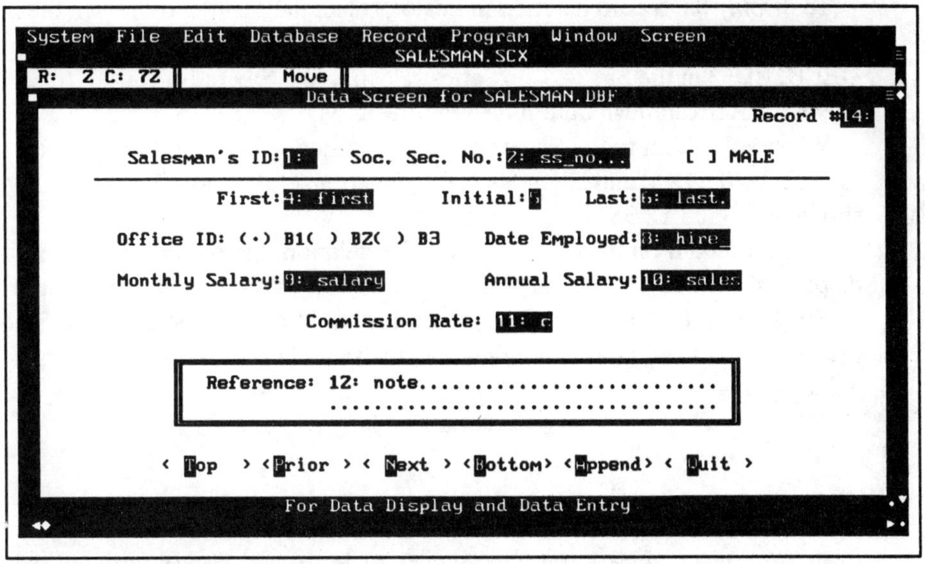

**Figure 12.35  Showing the Record Number Field**

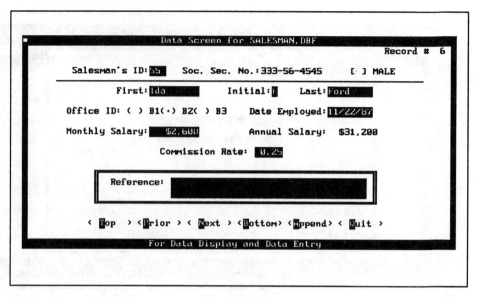

**Figure 12.36  Displaying Current Record Number**

## Displaying Record Deletion Indicators

In the preceding example, we used the RECNO( ) function to display the current record number. Similarly, you may use the DELETED( ) function to indicate whether the current record has been marked for deletion. The DELETED( ) function displays either .T. or .F.

To display the record deletion indicator, select the Field option from the Screen menu option or press the Ctrl+F key combination. Then, enter the function DELETED( ) in the Say text box after selecting the Say radio button. In addition, check the Refresh push button (see Figure 12.37).

When you return to the Screen Builder window, add the text (e.g., "Deleted?") to describe the field and adjust its width, position, etc. A modified screen layout is shown in Figure 12.38.

When a record on display is marked for deletion, the record deletion indicator displays the value of T; otherwise, the value of F is shown. For example, Figure 12.39 shows the data in the third record of the SALESMAN database. Since the record has not been marked for deletion, the record deletion indicator displays the value of F.

### Adding Push Buttons

In an example given earlier in this chapter we borrowed a set of push buttons from the CONTROL3 screen file and added it to the data screen as a control panel.

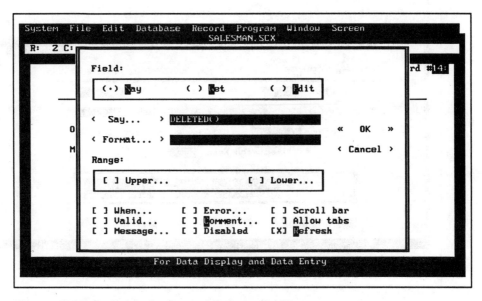

**Figure 12.37  Defining the Record Deletion Indicator**

Adding this set of push buttons allowed us to move around the records in the database and append new records to the database. However, the current data screen layout does not let us delete an existing record. Therefore, another set of push buttons must be added to enable you to delete the current record and to recall the

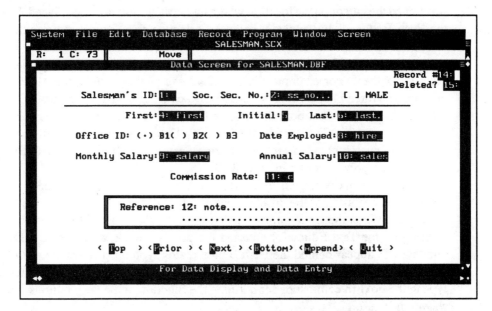

**Figure 12.38  Showing the Record Deletion Indicator**

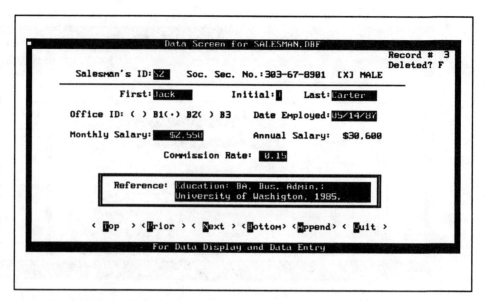

**Figure 12.39  Displaying the Record Deletion Indicator Value**

current record when it has been marked for deletion. Another button is included for packing the databases after marking the records for deletion.

To place a set of push buttons on the screen, choose the Push Button option from the Screen menu popup or press the Ctrl+H key combination after you have positioned the cursor on the location where the push buttons are to be placed. When the Push Button dialog appears, begin by selecting the Vertical radio button to arrange the push buttons in a column.

You can define the prompts for the push buttons as well as the variables for controlling them. For example, Figure 12.40 shows the Push Button dialog for defining the three push buttons <Delete>, <Recall>, and <Pack>. Enter ACT1 in the Variable Choose text box; this will be the variable that controls the operation of the push buttons. Then define the labels (\<Delete, <\Recall, and \<Pack) for each of the push buttons in the Push Button Prompts list box. Your Push Button dialog should now look like Figure 12.40.

The next step in creating customized push buttons is to define the procedure that controls the operation of the push buttons. To do this, begin by selecting the Valid check box. When the Code Snippet dialog appears, select the <Edit> push button to bring up the Text Editor for entering the procedure. Because the Text Editor window will appear behind the Push Button dialog, you must select the <<OK>> push button to exit the dialog and enter the Text Editor window, where you then type in the FoxPro commands for defining the function of the push buttons; this is shown in Figure 12.41.

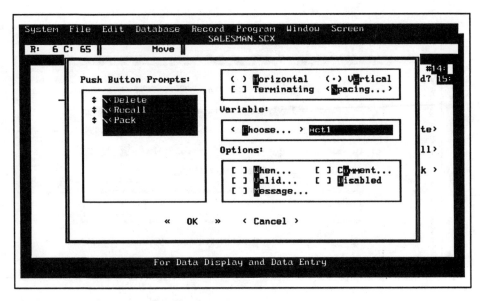

**Figure 12.40  Defining Push Button Prompts**

The set of commands shown in the Text Editor window is called a code snippet. When the first push button is selected (and, as a result, when FoxPro assigns the variable Act1 a value of 1), the DELETE command will be executed. If you select the second push button (i.e., when Act1=2), the RECALL command will be issued.

**Figure 12.41  Defining the Push Button Functions**

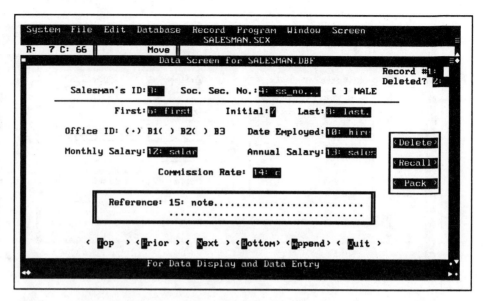

**Figure 12.42  Displaying the Push Buttons**

Finally, the PACK command will be carried out when the third push button is chosen (i.e., when Act1=3).

After defining the procedure for the push buttons, it can be saved by closing the Text Editor window. When you return to the Screen Builder window you should see the set of push buttons displayed in the screen layout as in Figure 12.42.

These push buttons can now be used to delete an existing record or to recall a record that has been marked for deletion. For example, Figure 12.43 shows the data in the fourth record in the database. While the record is displayed in the data screen, you can select the <Delete> push button to mark it for deletion, then change you mind and choose the <Recall> push button to remove the deletion mark. To mark other records for deletion, go through the records and press the <Delete> push button wherever you want. After you have marked all the unwanted records, they can be permanently removed by selecting the <Pack> push button.

## Adding Popups

Radio buttons enable you to display a limited number of predetermined values for a character field on the screen. Similarly, a popup can be created for displaying these character strings. For example, a popup is a convenient way to enter a state code to the STATE data field. Then, during data entry, instead of typing in a state code, you can select one from the list of valid state codes in the popup. There is an another advantage to using a popup for data entry: It ensures the validity of the

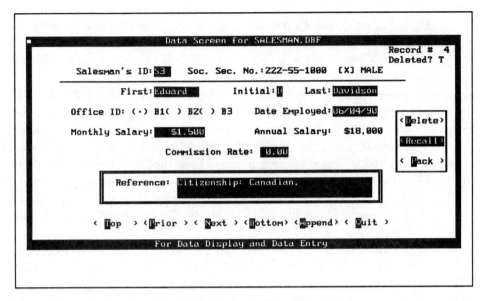

**Figure 12.43  Deleting and Recalling Records**

data input. Because you are limited to choosing a character string from the popup, the possibility of typing errors is precluded.

To practice creating such a popup, first develop the custom data screen layout for OFFICE.DBF as shown in Figure 12.44.

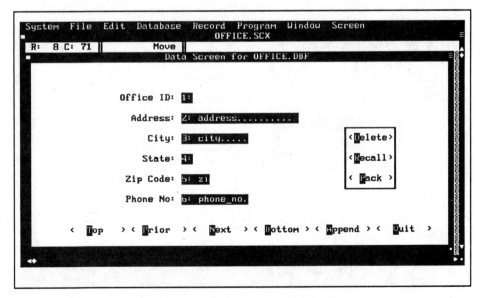

**Figure 12.44  The Custom Data Screen for OFFICE.DBF**

Figure 12.44 shows all the data fields in the OFFICE database on a custom data screen with a set of control push buttons borrowed from the CONTROL3.SCX provided by the FoxPro tutorial. Hotkeys have been added to the push buttons.

In the current screen layout, the character string in the STATE data field will be displayed in a normal text box. To enter a state code into the data field during data entry you would type the state code in the text box. To create a popup for achieving the same result, remove the current STATE field from the screen layout. Then select the Popup option from the Screen popup or press the Ctrl+O key combination after placing the cursor on the location of the removed data field. When the Popup dialog appears, specify the data field involved (e.g., salesman.state) in the Choose text box. Next enter the possible character strings for the specified data field in the dialog (see Figure 12.45).

Figure 12.45 shows a set of valid state codes (IL, NY, and WA) available from the popup for the STATE field in the OFFICE database. When you return to the Screen Builder window you can adjust the position of the popup to fit it in the screen layout. After reordering the data fields and the push buttons, the modified screen layout might look like that shown in Figure 12.46.

When you use the custom data screen to display a record in the OFFICE database, the state code in the STATE data field will be displayed in the popup window. If you need to change the field value, simply open the popup and select another character string (see Figure 12.47).

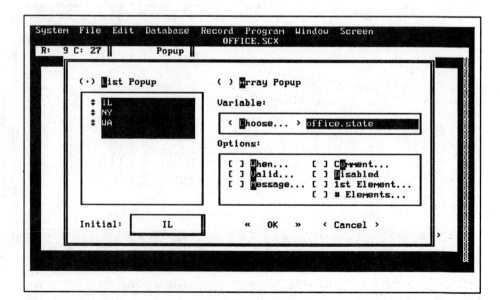

**Figure 12.45  Defining the Popup**

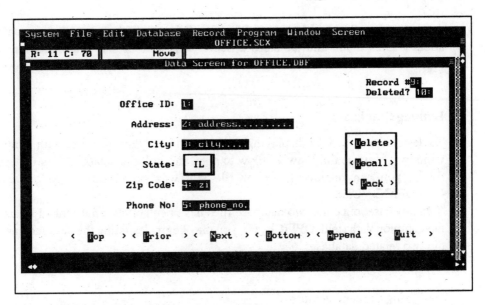

**Figure 12.46  Showing the Popup Created**

## Creating Multi-Window Data Screens

When you design a screen, it is possible to use more than one window to display data from two or more related database files. In our database, for example, information about the sales staff and their sales offices are saved in two separate

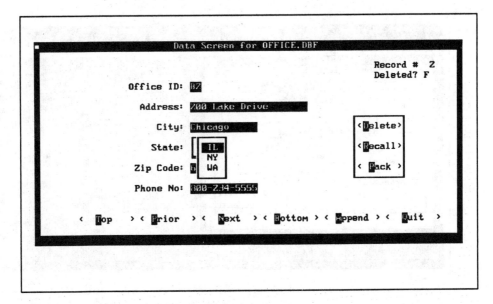

**Figure 12.47  Selecting a Popup Value**

database files, SALESMAN and OFFICE. It is possible to display information about a salesperson and the sales office to which he or she is assigned on two separate windows on the same screen.

### Linking Databases

To design the screen for displaying data from related database files with multiple windows, first use the View window to open and link the database files. Alternatively, you can retrieve the view file that was saved earlier (in our case, LNKOFICE.VUE).

In any case, once the two database files have been opened and linked by using the common data field, OFFICE_ID, you may begin designing the data screens for the two related databases.

### Designing Screen Layouts

When finished, the data screen will contain two separate windows and a control panel. Begin working on it by opening the Screen Builder and laying out a System window for the SALESMAN database. The most efficient way to do this is by first selecting the Quick Screen option. Then you can edit the field titles and adjust the field widths and window size. In addition, choose Edit as the mode for displaying the NOTE memo field and format the SALARY field by using $$99,999 as the

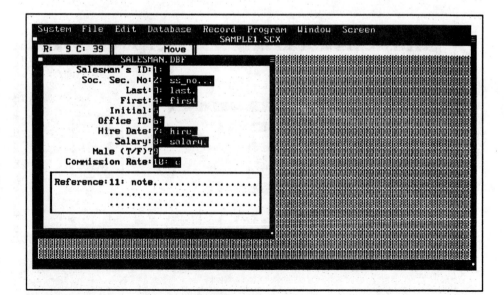

**Figure 12.48  Showing the First Data Window**

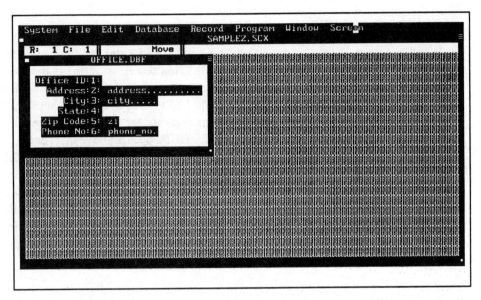

**Figure 12.49 Showing the Second Data Window**

field format template. The screen layout should look something like that shown in Figure 12.48.

After you have finished designing the first data screen, save it to a screen file (named SAMPLE1.SCR) by using the Save as option from the File menu popup.

Now design the screen layout for the second data window by selecting the New option from the File menu popup to bring up a new screen form. However, before actually laying out the second screen, you must make the second database file (i.e., OFFICE.DBF) the current database by using the View window. Once you have done this, you can begin placing fields in the Screen Builder's layout window by again selecting the Quick Screen option and then modifying the layout. Figure 12.49 shows an example of the modified screen layout for the second data window. Now save the screen layout in the second data window to another screen file such as SAMPLE2.SCX.

## Combining Screen Windows

After you have designed these two screens, they can be combined with the control panel to generate the screen program file. To do that, select the Generate option from the Program menu popup to bring up the Generate dialog. When the Generate Screen dialog appears, note that both Screen Builder windows are displayed in the dialog's Screens list box. To add a control panel, add the screen file, MYCONTROL.SCR, that contains the control push buttons to the Screens list box by using the <Add> push button and selecting it from the list box in the Add Screen dialog.

### Ordering Screen Windows

When a screen is created to display data in related database files in multiple windows, the parent database file must be the first screen specified in the Screens list box in the Generate Screen dialog. In our example, SALESMAN.DBF was designated as the parent file when it was linked to OFFICE.DBF; therefore, the screen (SAMPLE1.SCX) for the parent file must appear at the top of the Screens list box. And because the screen for OFFICE.DBF appears above that for SALESMAN.DBF in the Generate Screen dialog, you must switch the order of SAMPLE2.SCX and SAMPLE1.SCX. To do that, point and click the mouse on the double arrow symbol in front of SAMPLE1 and then drag it to the top of the screen list. If you are using the keyboard, first use the arrow key to highlight SAMPLE1 and then use the up arrow to move it up while holding down the Ctrl key. After you have ordered the items in the Screens list box, the Generate Screen dialog should look like that shown in Figure 12.50.

### Arranging Screen Windows

Now is the time to arrange the two data windows and the control panel on the screen. To do that, select the <Arrange> push button from the Generate Screen dialog. Although it is possible to overlap windows on the screen, it is best not to, so as to avoid any data areas being hidden from view. Figure 12.51 shows an example of how to arrange the data windows (SAMPLE1 and SAMPLE2) and the control panel (MYCNTROL) on the same screen.

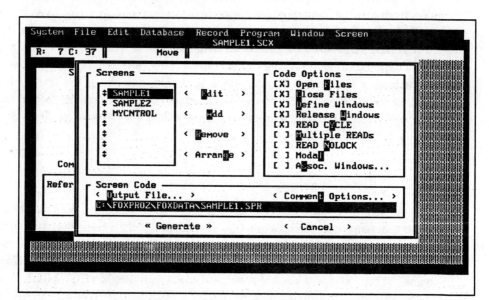

**Figure 12.50  Showing all Screen Files to be Combined**

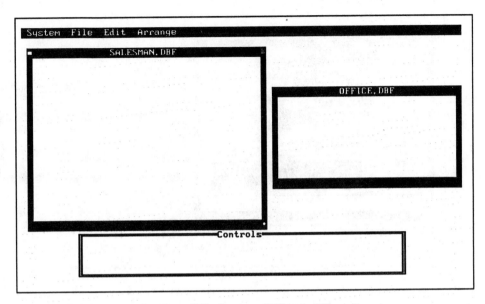

**Figure 12.51  Arranging Data Windows and Control Panel**

### Generating Screen Program File

After you have arranged the data windows and the control panel on the same screen, select the Save option from the Arrange menu popup or press the Ctrl+S key combination, and you will be returned to the Generate Screen dialog; there specify the name of the screen program file, such as SAMPLE.SPR, in the text box below the <Output File> push button. Finally, select the <<Generate>> push button to begin generating the file.

## Displaying Data on a Multi-Window Screen

When you bring up the screen we have just created to display the data in the SALESMAN and OFFICE databases, it will look like that shown in Figure 12.52.

This figure illustrates that data in the current record of the SALESMAN database is shown in the SALESMAN.DBF data window. The OFFICE.DBF data window displays the data in the record that is currently linked to that of the SALESMAN database. If you move to another record in the SALESMAN database, its associated record in the OFFICE database will be displayed accordingly.

While the screen shown in Figure 12.52 is useful for viewing information about a salesperson and the sales office to which he or she is assigned, it is less than desirable for editing all the records in both the SALESMAN and OFFICE databases simultaneously.

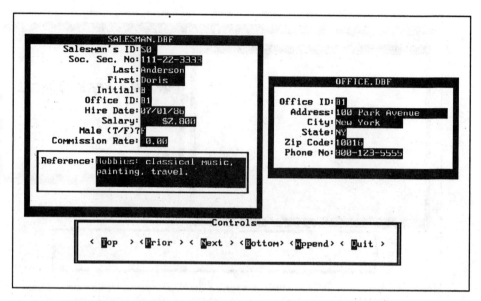

**Figure 12.52  Showing Data from Multiple Databases**

It is important to note that the push buttons in the control panel manipulate the records in the parent database only. That is, you only can move around the records in the SALESMAN database with these push buttons; they cannot be used to independently control the record sequence in the OFFICE database.

Although you can edit the data in both databases on the screen, it can be used to add new records to the parent database file only. If you need to add data records to the child file, a separate screen must be used. For example, when you choose the <Append> push button to add a new record to a database file, you can add it only to the SALESMAN database. The blank screen provided by the Append operation will provide you with space for entering data to the data fields of the SALESMAN database. The data fields in the OFFICE.DBF data window are disabled (see Figure 12.53).

After a new record is entered to the SALESMAN database, it will be linked to the OFFICE database.

# Using FoxPro Commands

The FoxPro command for invoking the Screen Builder is CREATE SCREEN or MODIFY SCREEN. To create a new screen layout, issue the CREATE SCREEN command in the following format:

```
CREATE SCREEN <screen filename>
```

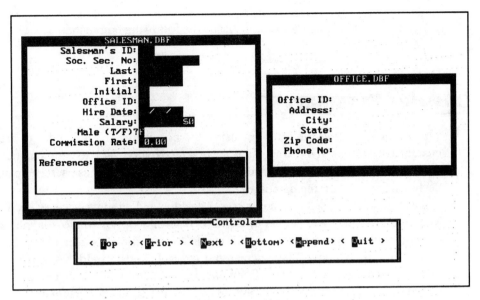

**Figure 12.53  Appending Data in Multiple Windows**

In response to the command, a blank screen is displayed in the Screen Builder window. But before you issue the command, remember that it is necessary to open the database in the current work area. If you forget to take this step, you will be prompted to open the database when you attempt to place any data fields in the screen layout. For example, to create a new screen named TEST.SCX for the SALESMAN database with the Screen Builder, issue the following commands:

```
USE SALESMAN
CREATE SCREEN TEST
```

If you are creating a screen and using more than one database, the databases must be linked before issuing the CREATE SCREEN command.

To modify an existing screen file, issue the MODIFY SCREEN command in the following format:

```
MODIFY SCREEN <screen filename>
```

To make changes to the screen file created earlier, for example, issue the following command:

```
MODIFY SCREEN TEST.SCX
```

After you have generated the screen program file that contains the screen code for the screen layout, execute the program by issuing the DO command:

```
DO <name of screen program file>
```

To execute TEST.SPR, for example, issue the following command:

```
DO TEST.SPR
```

## Chapter Summary

This chapter detailed the steps for using the powerful Screen Builder to create custom data screens. It illustrated how these screens can be used to view and modify data, as well as to add new records to existing databases. These screens can be designed for one or more databases.

The two kinds of data screen layouts—desktop and window—were described. The type of screen you decide to create is determined in a window layout. But regardless of the type you choose, it is created by placing the screen objects in the Screen Builder window. These screen objects include data fields taken from one or more databases, text for describing the data, graphics objects (boxes and lines) and buttons (push buttons, radio buttons), check boxes and scrollable lists.

The chapter also explained how to save a screen layout in an .SCX file. A screen program (.SPR) file is then generated from the screen file. To use the data screen, the screen program file is executed.

The preceding chapters specified all the components of a relational database system. The next chapter explains how to tie them together with a custom menu system.

# 13

# Putting It All Together

## An Overview

The early chapters of this book defined and described the principles for designing and developing a relational database system. Subsequent chapters detailed the procedures for creating and modifying databases with FoxPro. In addition, you learned how to use:

- the powerful RQBE Builder to extract meaningful information from databases.
- the Report Builder to produce professional reports
- the Label Designer to design and output mailing labels
- the Screen Builder to design custom data screens that enable you to view and modify data in existing databases, as well to aid in the data entry process.

This final chapter describes how to design and create a custom menu that integrates all the above information.

## A Custom Menu System

The only menu system that we have used up to this point is the System menu provided by FoxPro. The System menu bar contains a standard set of menu pads, each of which includes the standard set of menu options in the menu popup. Although many of these menu options are useful for certain applications, you may not need all of them in every database application. As a result, you may find it useful to create a customized menu system that includes only those menu

535

options that are tailored for a specific application. This means not only that you can create a menu system that is more compact, but also that you can define a customized menu system that has options for specific operations you commonly perform.

For example, you ordinarily use the Open option in the System menu's File menu popup to open a file. This menu option has been deliberately designed to be so general that you can use it to open any type of file. Consequently, once you have selected this option, you must still specify a file type and a filename before you can actually open a file. A custom menu, on the other hand, allows you to create a menu option that is specifically designed to carry out a particular predefined operation. For example, you can define a menu option for opening a specific file. When you select that menu option, that file will be opened without FoxPro requiring any further information.

With a custom menu system you can execute database management functions by selecting the menu options that are specifically defined for your application. You can, for instance, include a menu pad for viewing each of the existing databases on custom data screens. You also can use the menu options in another menu pad to make changes to your existing databases. And when producing custom reports, you may choose another set of menu options from the custom menu.

Besides custom menu options that you create, you also can include some standard options provided by the FoxPro System menu. You may, for example, want to include the Help, Filer, Calculator, and Calendar/Diary menu options that are provided in the

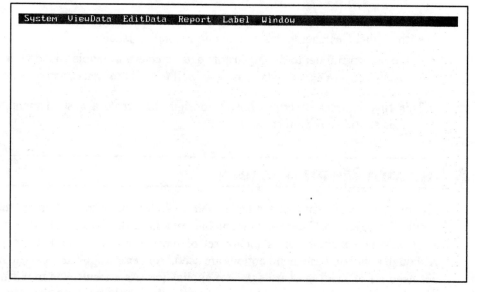

**Figure 13.1  A Custom Menu Bar**

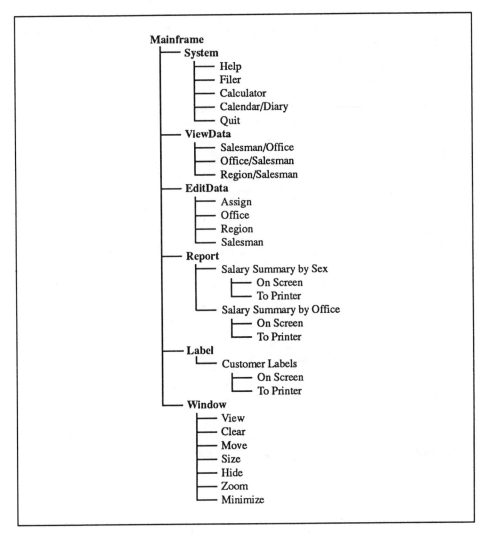

**Figure 13.2  Structure of the Customized Menu System**

FoxPro System menu popup. Similarly, you can include the View option from the Window menu popup of the System menu so that you can use it to open any existing databases. Or you may decide to include those menu options from the Window menu popup that clear the screen desktop area or manipulate the active window. Figure 13.1 shows an example of such a custom menu bar.

This menu bar has six menu pads in the custom menu bar: System, ViewData, EditData, Report, Label, and Window. The structure of the custom menu is depicted in Figure 13.2.

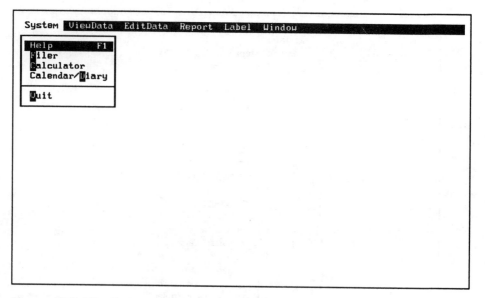

**Figure 13.3  The Custom System Menu Options**

## THE SYSTEM MENU PAD

The custom system menu pad contains five menu options in its menu popup (see Figure 13.3).

The first four options (Help, Filer, Calculator, and Calendar/Diary) execute the same functions as those found in the FoxPro System menu pad. The Quit option, when selected, exits your application and returns you to the FoxPro System menu.

## THE VIEWDATA MENU PAD

The second menu pad in the custom menu bar is for displaying data in various databases. The ViewData menu pad contains three menu options in its menu popup (see Figure 13.4).

You can use these options to view data in the SALESMAN, OFFICE, and REGION databases in different combinations.

### Viewing SALESMAN and OFFICE Databases

The Salesman/Office option allows you to view information about a salesperson and the sales office to which he or she is assigned. When this option is selected,

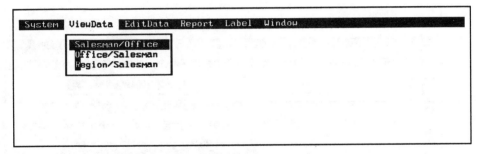

**Figure 13.4   The ViewData Menu Options**

data from the SALESMAN and OFFICE databases is presented on a custom data screen as shown in Figure 13.5.

This figure shows all the data in the SALESMAN and OFFICE databases for Doris B. Anderson. All the data fields in the SALESMAN database are displayed in the upper portion of the screen; the lower portion contains its related record from the OFFICE database. Note that all the field values are not displayed in text boxes (or in reversed video). They are shown in the display-only mode and their contents cannot be edited.

The two databases are linked according to the values in the OFFICE_ID data field. The SALESMAN database was designated as the parent while the OFFICE

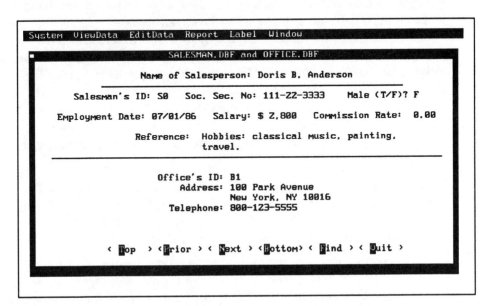

**Figure 13.5   Viewing Data in SALESMAN and OFFICE Databases**

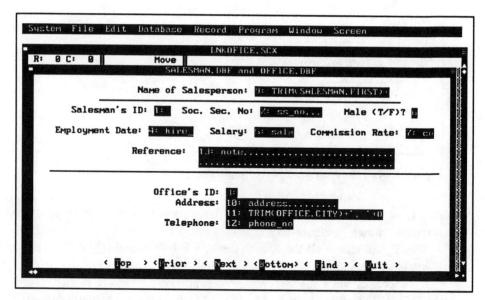

**Figure 13.6  Screen Layout for Viewing SALESMAN and OFFICE Databases**

database was designated as the child. As a result, you can scan the data records in the SALESMAN database by using the <Top>, <Prior>, <Next>, and <Bottom> push buttons provided in the custom data screen. When you do so, its related record in the OFFICE database is displayed on the screen as well.

In designing the menu option that displays this custom screen directly, we have had to do some preliminary work. First, we used the View window to open and link the two database files; in addition, we designated the last index tag as the master index for the SALESMAN database. Next, we used the Screen Builder to design the screen layout shown in Figure 13.6, which we have saved as a screen file named LNKOFICE.SCX. While for the most part you should be able to design this screen after reading the previous chapter, several features are either new or noteworthy:

- Because this screen is used only for viewing data, all the data fields are displayed using the Say (display-only) option. In addition, to insure that the display is updated to reflect fields from the current record, be sure to select the Refresh check box in the Screen Field dialog.

- The control panel at the bottom of the screen contains a set of six push buttons. You can define the operation for five of the six push buttons by using the existing code examples that accompany FoxPro, as we did in Chapter 12.

- In addition, however, there is a <Find> push button that allows you to find a given record based on the salesperson's last name. The fragment of code needed to define the operation of the <Find> push button can be seen in

```
 System  File  Edit  Database  Record  Program  Window
                        LNKOFICE actZ VALID
 do case
 case actZ = 1
     go top
 case actZ = 2
     skip -1
     if bof()
         go top
     endif
 case actZ = 3
     skip 1
     if eof()
         go bottom
     endif
 case actZ = 4
     go bottom
 case actZ = 5
     STORE SPACE(8) TO LASTNAME
     @16,20 SAY "Salesperson's Last Name: " GET LASTNAME
     READ
     LOCATE FOR SALESMAN.LAST = LASTNAME
     @16,20 SAY SPACE(35)
 case actZ= 6
```

**Figure 13.7   Code for Defining the <Find> Push Button**

Figure 13.7. Notice that the activation of a particular push button is governed by the value of the control variable named act2; since <Find> is the fifth push button in the set, its code is executed when act2 has a value of 5 (case act2 = 5).

Because the section of code dealing with the operation of the <Find> push button is somewhat more complicated than the code we've encountered previously, some explanation is in order. The first command uses the SPACE(8) function to store eight blank spaces to the temporary memory variable named LASTNAME; this initializes the space needed to hold up to eight characters of the last name of the salesperson for whom you would like to search in the database. The second command displays a prompt at row 16 and column 20 on the screen and places a text box at the end of the prompt. The READ command takes the character string that you type in the text box and stores it to the LASTNAME memory variable. The LOCATE command searches the SALESMAN database to find the first record whose value in the LAST data field matches the character string in the LASTNAME memory variable. When the record is found, the record pointer will be placed on that record and it will be displayed on the screen; if no record is found, all the data fields will appear blank. The last command displays a string of 35 spaces to blank out the input prompt and the text box after the record search.

- This custom menu system allows only one data window to be open at a single time, so you must select the <Quit> push button when you have finished viewing the data. When you do this, all work areas will be closed and the custom menu will again be displayed.

## Viewing OFFICE and SALESMAN Databases

Data viewed after selecting the second option (Office/Salesman) in the ViewData menu popup appears similar to that of first menu option (Salesman/Office). When you select this option, however, the OFFICE and SALESMAN databases are linked by using the OFFICE database as the parent and SALESMAN as the child. Therefore, data fields of the OFFICE database are shown on the top of the screen and the lower portion of the screen shows the data fields of the SALESMAN database (see Figure 13.8).

Since there is a one-to-many relationship between the OFFICE and SALES-MAN databases, we ordinarily would want to show all the salespeople who are assigned to a given sales office. For example, Figure 13.8 shows the information about sales office B1 and the first salesperson—Doris B. Anderson—who is assigned to it. To see the next salesperson assigned to the same office, if there is one, simply select the <Next> push button.

If, however, we simply create a custom screen modeled after our previous screen, LNKOFICE.SCX, and continue to directly read the records in the two database files, our application will not work as we expect. Because OFFICE is the parent database, selecting the <Top>, <Prior>, <Next>, and <Bottom> push buttons will move the record pointer in the OFFICE database. Whenever the record pointer moves, our screen will display only the first record in the SALESMAN database for that particular office. Because moving the record pointer in the child database is automatically handled by FoxPro whenever the record pointer in the parent

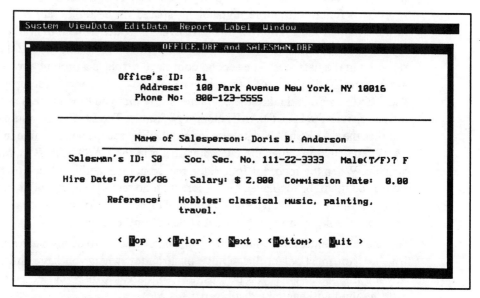

**Figure 13.8 Viewing Data in OFFICE and SALESMAN Databases**

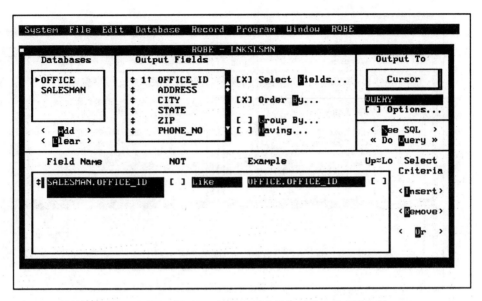

**Figure 13.9  Linking OFFICE and SALESMAN with a RQBE Query**

database moves, we cannot view information on other salespeople assigned to a particular sales office.

There are a number off ways to create the kind of data screen that we want. Perhaps the easiest, since it does not require a knowledge of programming or of FoxPro command syntax, is to create a query that generates a set of records that relate each sales office to all the salespeople who are assigned to it. Such an RQBE query (saved as LNKSLSMN.QPR) is shown in Figure 13.9.

The RQBE query shown in this figure links the two databases according to their values in each database's OFFICE_ID data field. All the data fields in both databases are selected to be included in the query's output, with the exception of the SALES-MAN.OFFICE_ID field (since it is identical to the OFFICE.OFFICE_ID field). The resulting records are to be ordered by their values in the OFFICE_ID field. Because we have chosen Cursor as the output destination, output from the query will be stored in a temporary query table.

The records output by the query are shown in a Browse window in Figure 13.10. Notice that the query table has, in effect, joined the two databases together. Each record in the SALESMAN database has been matched with its corresponding information in the OFFICE database. As a result, we can use this table to easily view all the salespeople who are assigned to a given sales office.

Once you have created and executed the query, you can create the screen shown in Figure 13.11 by using the temporary database created by the query. This screen displays all the data fields from the temporary output database in display-only (SAY) mode, and contains a set of push buttons that allows you to navigate through the database.

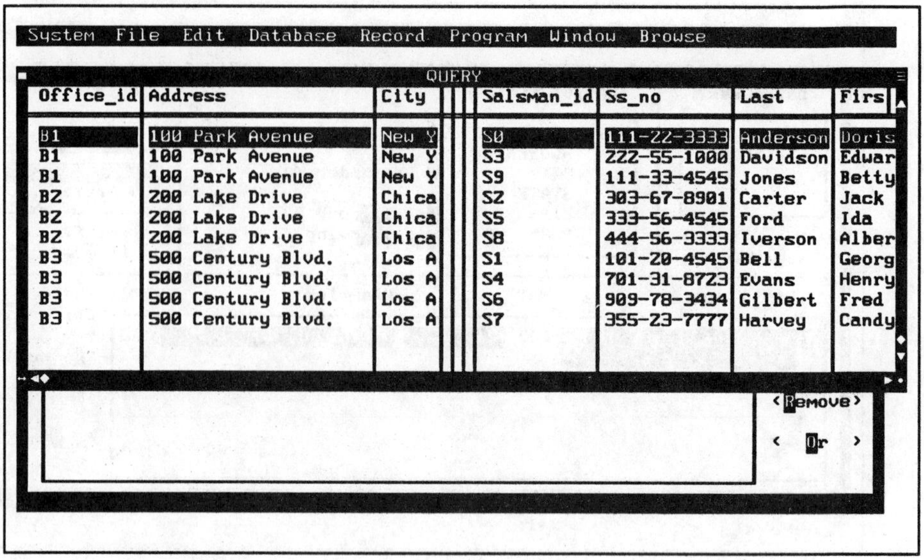

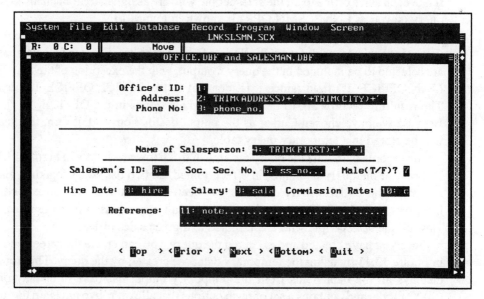

**Figure 13.10   Records Resulting from the RQBE**

## Viewing REGION and SALESMAN Databases

To view information about the sales regions and the salespeople assigned to them, select the Region/Salesman option from the ViewData menu popup and that information is displayed in the custom data screen as shown in Figure 13.12.

**Figure 13.11   Screen Layout for Viewing OFFICE and SALESMAN Databases**

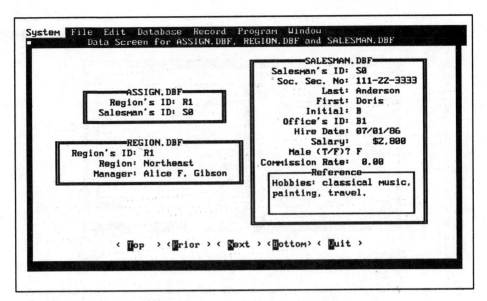

**Figure 13.12  Viewing Data in REGION and SALESMAN Databases**

Data records in the REGION database are linked to those in SALESMAN by the information in the ASSIGN database. Many-to-many relations exist between the REGION and SALESMAN databases, which, if you recall, means that each sales region may have more than one salesperson assigned to it and each salesperson may be assigned to more than one sales region. These relations are defined by using the records in the ASSIGN database, whereby each record in the ASSIGN database file relates a sales region and a salesperson.

Information about the salesperson and sales region is shown on the screen in separate sections as are the contents of the ASSIGN database that links the two files. Since ASSIGN.DBF is the parent in the database link, you can use the push buttons to move between its records. And because we have defined both the SALESMAN and REGION databases as children of ASSIGN, we can access all information from each relevant record in the child databases. For example, if you select the <Next> push button from the control panel on the data screen, the next record in ASSIGN.DBF will be displayed. At the same time, information on the corresponding region and the salesperson will be displayed in their respective windows.

The data screen shown in Figure 13.12 was created by first linking the three databases in the View window. ASSIGN.DBF was linked with REGION.DBF according to values in the REGION_ID data field. ASSIGN.DBF also was linked with SALESMAN.DBF via the SALESMAN_ID data field (see Figure 13.13).

After linking the three database files, the custom screen (named LNKREGIN.SCX) was created with the Screen Builder by placing their data fields

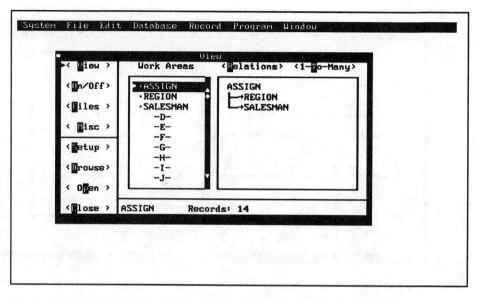

**Figure 13.13   Linking ASSIGN, REGION, and SALESMAN Databases**

in the screen layout (see Figure 13.14). All the data fields are specified as display-only fields by using Say mode. The set of control push buttons was created in the same manner as discussed in Chapter 12.

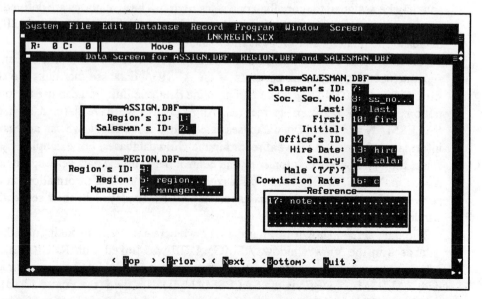

**Figure 13.14   Screen Layout for Viewing REGION and SALESMAN Databases**

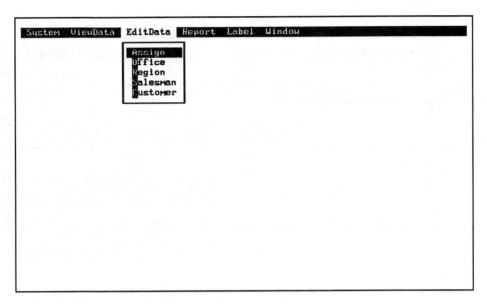

**Figure 13.15  The EditData Menu Options**

## THE EDITDATA MENU PAD

The EditData menu pad on the custom menu bar is for editing data in each of the databases. It contains five options in its menu popup: Assign, Office, Region, Salesman, and Customer (see Figure 13.15).

These menu options can be used to modify the contents of existing database files or to add new records to the databases. Select, for instance, the Assign option from the EditData menu popup to edit the data records in the ASSIGN database; or choose the Office option to add new records to the OFFICE database.

### Editing the ASSIGN Database

When the Assign option is chosen from the EditData menu popup, data in the ASSIGN database is displayed on a custom screen as illustrated in Figure 13.16. The layout of the custom data screen (saved as ASSIGN.SCX) is shown in Figure 13.17.

Because the contents of the data fields are shown in Edit mode (in text boxes), you can edit the field values. This is not true, however, of the record number and the deletion flag in the upper right-hand corner of the screen; these are status indicators that show the number of the current record and whether or not it is tagged for deletion. The record number is defined as a display-only field that uses the RECNO( ) function. Similarly, the DELETED( ) function is used in a display-only field to indicate whether the record has been marked for deletion.

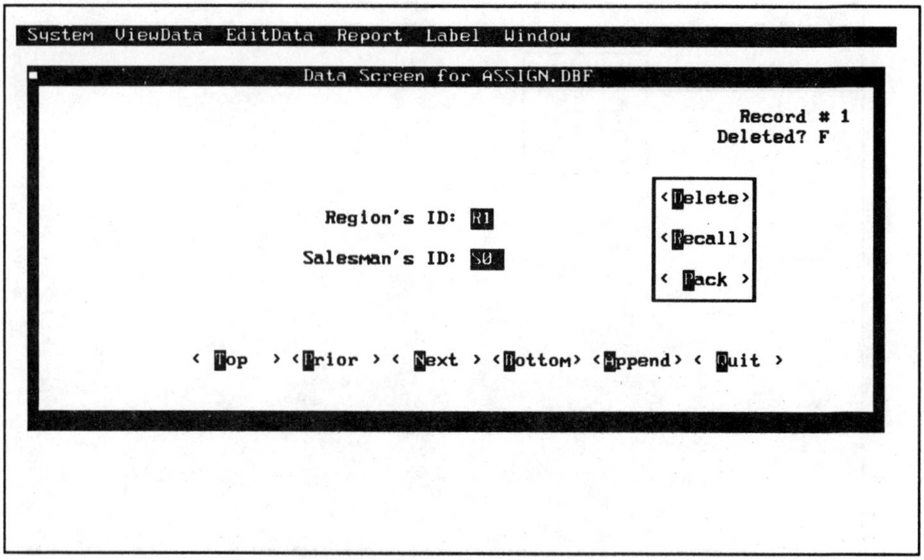

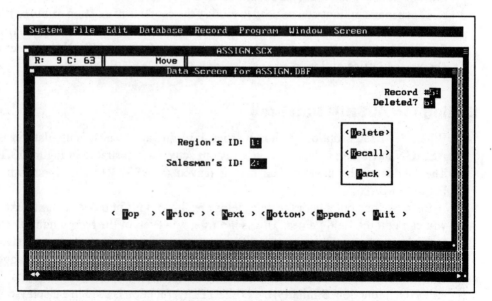

**Figure 13.16  Editing Contents of the ASSIGN Database**

There are two sets of push buttons on the data screen. The set on the bottom of the screen allows you to navigate the database and to add new records to the database file. The second set includes three push buttons: <Delete>, <Recall>, and <Pack>. When you select the <Delete> push button, the current record is marked

**Figure 13.17  Screen Layout for Editing the ASSIGN Database**

for deletion and the value of the DELETED( ) variable, displayed in the upper right portion of the screen, is set to T. To remove the deletion tag, select the <Recall> push button. After you have finished marking records for deletion, select the <Pack> push button to permanently remove them from the database file. The <Delete>, <Recall>, and <Pack> push buttons are defined by using the following valid procedure:

```
do case
    case act1 = 1
        DELETE
    case act1 = 2
        RECALL
    case act1 = 3
        PACK
endcase
show gets
```

The variable act1 is used as a control variable for defining the functions of the push buttons whose prompts are specified in the Push Button dialog shown in Figure 13.18.

The same set of push buttons and the underlying code, incidentally, will be added to all the remaining data screens that allow our database records to be edited.

**Figure 13.18  Defining the Push Buttons**

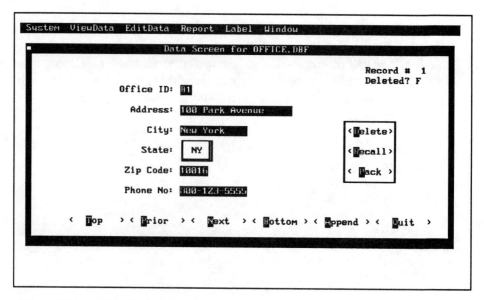

**Figure 13.19  Editing the OFFICE Database**

## Editing the OFFICE Database

The Office option in the EditData menu popup works like the Assign menu option. When it is selected, the contents of the current record in the OFFICE database are displayed for editing on a custom data screen, as shown in Figure 13.19.

This custom screen, which was saved as OFFICE.SCX, is very similar to the screen for editing the ASSIGN database. Like the latter, it permits each field of the OFFICE database to be edited, contains the same two sets of push buttons, and displays the record number and deletion status. Its only distinguishing feature is a popup that is used for defining the state code in the data record.

## Editing the REGION Database

The Region option in the EditData menu popup enables you to edit data in the REGION database. When this option is selected, the custom screen shown in Figure 13.20 appears. The design and layout of this screen is very similar to the previous editing screens that we have built.

## Editing the SALESMAN Database

The Salesman option in the EditData menu popup allows for modification of the contents of the SALESMAN database. When it is selected, a custom data screen displays, in Edit mode, all the data fields in the current record of that database.

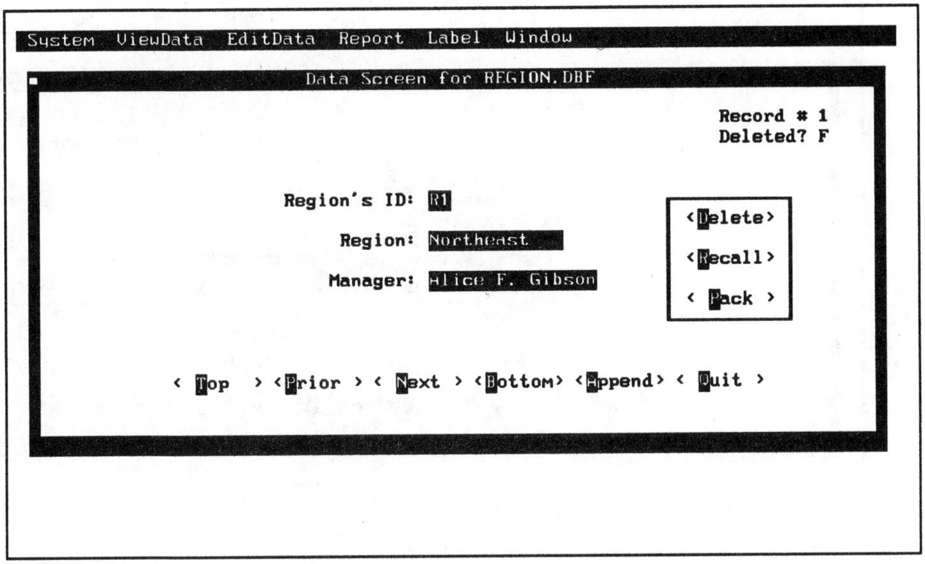

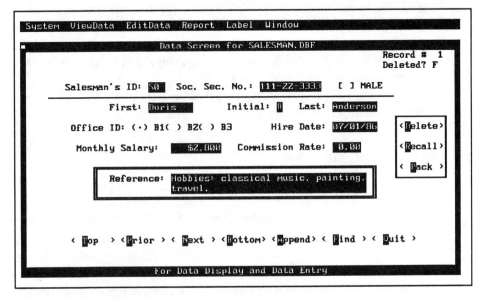

**Figure 13.20  Editing Data in the REGION Database**

Note in Figure 13.21 that some field values are displayed in text boxes while others are shown in popups and as radio buttons.

The screen layout (saved as SALESKAN.SCX) is the same as that created in Chapter 12 except that the <Find> push button has been added to the set of control buttons. This push button is used to locate the record for a salesperson by his or

**Figure 13.21  Editing Data in the SALESMAN Database**

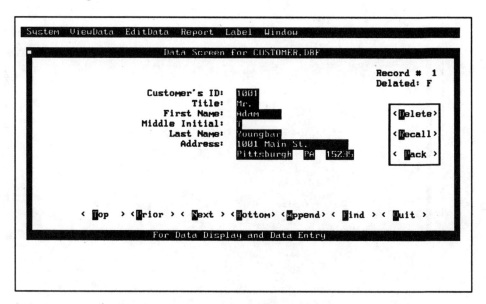

**Figure 13.22  Editing Data in the CUSTOMER Database**

her last name. An example of how to use the <Find> push button, along with the code needed to implement it, was provided earlier in this chapter.

## Editing the CUSTOMER Database

Like all the other screens for editing data, a custom data screen is created for making changes to the data in the records of the CUSTOMER database. To edit in this database, select the Customer option from the EditData menu popup for all the data fields in the CUSTOMER database to be displayed in Edit mode together with the control push buttons (see Figure 13.22).

The screen layout was created and saved as CUSTOMER.SCX in the usual manner with the Screen Builder.

## THE REPORT MENU PAD

The Report menu pad is designed for producing custom reports that were created at an earlier time. In Chapter 11, we created two summary reports using the salary values in the SALESMAN database. One of the reports, which we saved as BYMALE.FRX, summarized the salaries of the sales staff delineated by sex; the other report, which we saved as BYOFFICE.FRX, listed the total salaries by sales office.

Figure 13.23 shows the two menu options that enable you to produce the salary summary reports. Further, each of these options has a set of two menu options. One

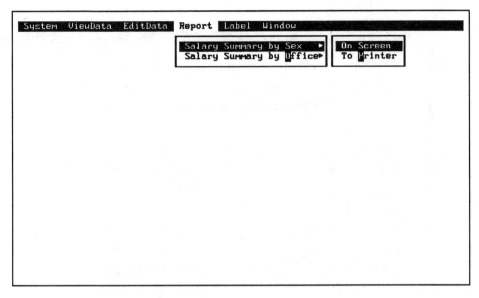

**Figure 13.23  Report Menu Options**

is for displaying the report on the screen for preview purposes and the other is for printing the report. Choose, for instance, the Salary Summary by Sex option from the Report menu popups, and another menu popup will appear. If you then select the On Screen option from the popup, the summary report will be displayed on screen as displayed in Figure 13.24.

| System | ViewData | EditData | Report | Label | Window |
| --- | --- | --- | --- | --- | --- |

|  | SALARY SUMMARY REPORT |  |  | Page   1 11/05/91 |
| --- | --- | --- | --- | --- |

| Soc. Sec. # | Last Name | First Name | Monthly Salary | Annual Salary |
| --- | --- | --- | --- | --- |
|  | Male Salespersons |  |  |  |
| 444-56-3333 | Iverson | Albert | $2,200 | $26,400 |
| 909-78-3434 | Gilbert | Fred | $2,300 | $27,600 |
| 701-31-8723 | Evans | Henry | $2,000 | $24,000 |
| 222-55-1000 | Davidson | Edward | $1,500 | $18,000 |
| 303-67-8901 | Carter | Jack | $2,550 | $30,600 |
| 101-20-4545 | Bell | George | $2,400 | $28,800 |
|  |  | Total | $12,950 | $155,400 |
|  | Female Salespersons |  |  |  |
| 111-33-4545 | Jones | Betty | $2,500 | $30,000 |
| 355-23-7777 | Harvey | Candy | $2,450 | $29,400 |
| 333-56-4545 | Ford | Ida | $2,600 | $31,200 |

« Done »  ‹ More ›   Column:    0

**Figure 13.24  Previewing Salary Summary by Sex Report**

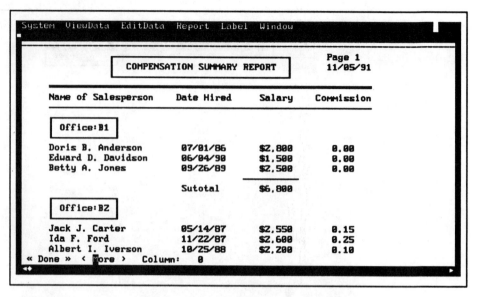

**Figure 13.25  Previewing Salary Summary by Office Report**

To print the report, select the To Printer option from the menu popup of the Salary Summary by Sex option.

Similarly, you can select the Salary Summary by Office option from the Report menu popup to preview and print the report. When you preview the report on the screen, it should look like Figure 13.25.

## THE LABEL MENU PAD

The Label menu pad includes a menu option that enables you to produce mailing labels from data in the CUSTOMER database. The Customer Labels menu popup in turn has two menu options that you can see in Figure 13.26. As with reports described above, labels either can be previewed on screen or printed, and the two menu options provide for these choices. The on-screen option is shown in Figure 13.27. The label design was created in Chapter 12 and saved as CUSTOMER.LBX.

## THE WINDOW MENU PAD

The Window menu pad is included in the custom menu bar to provide the tools that enable you to manipulate the active window. Seven options are included in the Window menu popup and are shown in Figure 13.28.

All of these menu options are borrowed from the Window menu pad in the FoxPro System menu and their functions are identical. Thus, you can use the View option to bring up the View window, select the Clear option to clear the desktop

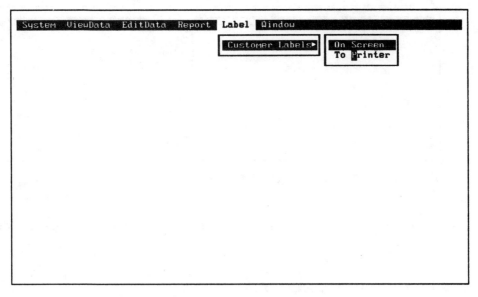

**Figure 13.26  The Label Menu Option**

screen area, or choose Move, Size, Hide, Zoom, and Minimize to manipulate the window.

This completes our preview of the elements of the custom menu system. In the course of it, we also have created all of the procedures—the editing screens, queries, and report and label forms—that our custom menu system will perform.

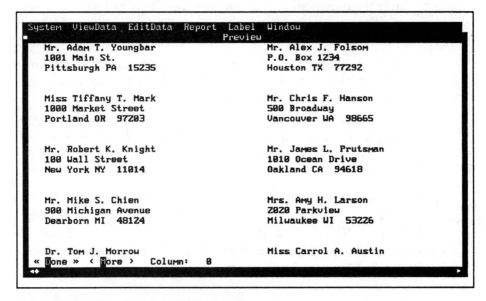

**Figure 13.27  Previewing Mailing Labels**

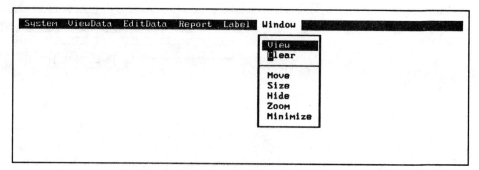

**Figure 13.28  The Window Menu Options**

What remains is to define the actual custom menu that will tie these various elements and procedures together.

## THE FOXPRO MENU BUILDER

FoxPro's Menu Builder is the tool that is used to design and create custom menu systems. It allows for broad flexibility in designing your own menus. With the Menu Builder, for example, you can:

- Define individual menu pads in a menu bar.
- Define a hotkey that allows the menu pad to be activated quickly with the keyboard by pressing Alt along with one other key.
- Define the operation of the menu pad. The menu pad itself can execute a single FoxPro command or a procedure (a set of FoxPro commands), or it can call a submenu (a menu popup) that contains a set of menu options.
- Define the operation of a submenu option. Like a menu pad, the submenu option can execute a single FoxPro command, a procedure (a set of commands), or it can call another submenu.
- Define a shortcut or accelerator key—a single key or key combination that, when pressed, will activate a submenu option. For example, pressing F1 activates the Help submenu option on the System menu pad.

The steps involved in creating a customized menu system are very similar to those described for creating a custom screen in the previous chapter. Once you have finished using the Menu Builder to design a custom menu, you can save it as a file with an .MNX extension; this is actually a special kind of database file that FoxPro uses exclusively for storing menu information. Then, when you select the Generate option from the Program menu pad, FoxPro generates a menu program file with a file extension of .MNX. The menu is executed by selecting this Run command from the Program menu pad and selecting this .MNX file.

# Creating a Quick Menu

The first step in creating a custom menu is, of course, opening the Menu Builder. To do this, select the New option from the File menu popup. When the New dialog appears, select the Menu radio button followed by the <<OK>> push button. FoxPro will open the Menu Builder's Menu Design window, which is shown in Figure 13.29, and add a Menu menu pad to the System menu bar.

Just as it does when you define a custom report or a custom screen, FoxPro allows you to adopt one of two approaches to building a custom menu system. You can design your menus completely from scratch, or you can copy FoxPro's default system menu and modify it until it suits the requirements of your application. We will once again use this latter approach, in part because it will allow us to create our custom menu with far less effort and risk of error, but also because examining the structure of the FoxPro System menu is itself valuable in learning to use the Menu Builder.

To copy FoxPro's default system menu, select the Quick Menu option from the Menu menu popup. The result, which is shown in Figure 13.30, is a menu structure

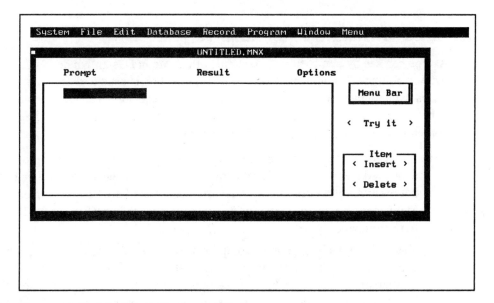

**Figure 13.29  The Menu Designer Window**

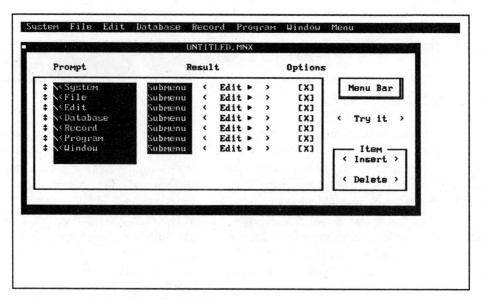

**Figure 13.30  The Quick Menu**

that is identical to the FoxPro System menu. Let's begin by exploring the System menu in the Menu Design window, since from it we can figure out how to build our own custom menu.

## DEFINING THE MENU PAD PROMPTS

As you can see by comparing the contents of the Menu Design window's Prompt list box with the System menu bar, the Prompt list box is used to define the labels for each menu pad. When the menu program file is executed, each menu pad will appear in the order in which it is listed in the Prompt list box. You can change the contents of the Prompt list box in any of several ways:

- You can delete unwanted menu pads by: positioning the cursor on the unwanted menu prompt and pressing the DEL key, selecting the Delete push button in the Item group box, selecting the Delete Item command from the Menu menu popup; or pressing Ctrl+E, which is a shortcut key for the Delete Item command.

- You can insert a blank menu prompt by positioning the cursor on the prompt that you would like to have appear immediately after the new menu pad. Then you can either select the Insert push button in the Item group box, select the Insert Item command from the Menu menu popup; or press Ctrl+I, the shortcut key combination for the Item Delete command. The Menu Builder will insert a new prompt and give it the default label "New Title."

- You can rearrange existing menu prompts by selecting them with the mouse and dragging them to their new location. With the keyboard, simply select the item you would like to move and then press CTRL along with the up or down arrow key to move the item to its new location.

In addition, any single character in a prompt can be designated as a hotkey. A hotkey is defined by placing the \< symbols immediately in front of the letter. For example, the prompt for the first menu pad is:

```
\<System
```

The first letter, 'S,' is designated as a hotkey. The hotkey is normally displayed in a different color or in reverse video in the menu bar. (Note that, due to the limitations of the screen capture program, the menu pad's hotkeys are not visible in the screen shots reproduced in this book.)

## DEFINING THE MENU PAD RESULTS

The result area of the window allows you to determine what happens when a particular menu pad is selected. In Figure 13.30, for example, each of the menu pads in the FoxPro system menu "results" in a submenu—that is, a submenu pops up when the menu pad is selected. So, for example, when you select the System menu pad, the System submenu or System menu popup is displayed. Submenu is the default result when a new menu pad is created; notice also that it is accompanied by the Edit push button to the right of the popup.

However, as Figure 13.31 shows, Submenu is just one option in a popup that contains four choices. The other three possible results are:

- *Command.* If the result of a menu pad is designated as a command, FoxPro will execute a single command when that menu option is selected. When Command is selected from the Result popup, the <Edit> push button that ordinarily appears beside the Submenu option in the result popup is replaced with a text box in which you can enter the command that is to be executed. If a command has already been entered, it will be displayed in the text box.

- *Pad Name.* Selecting this option allows you to incorporate a menu pad from another menu system. This is an advanced feature, however, that requires some programming knowledge.

- *Proc.* Designating the result of a menu pad as a procedure causes FoxPro to execute a set of commands (a procedure) that is stored along with the menu. Selecting the Edit push button will open an editing window where a new procedure can be entered or an existing procedure can be examined or edited.

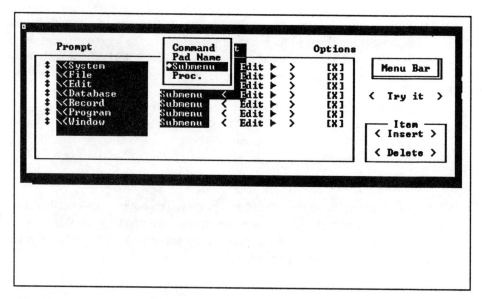

**Figure 13.31 The Result Popup**

## DEFINING PROMPT OPTIONS

In Figure 13.30, note that the Options check boxes for each of the menu pads are all checked. Selecting the Options check box for a particular prompt opens the Prompt Options dialog shown in Figure 13.32. This dialog allows you to add a number of enhancements and fine points to your menu pad, although normally you will probably want to use only the Shortcut option. For example:

- The Comment text box allows you to enter notes to yourself or internal documentation about the menu item. Whatever you enter in the text box has absolutely no effect on the menu pad or on the operation of the menu; it serves only to store comments that might be useful for yourself or for someone else using the Menu Builder to examine your menu system.

- The Shortcut push button, if selected, opens the Key Definition dialog, which allows you to define a shortcut key combination (sometimes called an accelerator key) that provides a quicker method for selecting a particular menu item with the keyboard. If you examine the Key definition dialog for the prompts that appear on the FoxPro System menu bar, note that their shortcut keys are the same as their hotkeys; this is required for menu pads if they are to be activated by the use of the ALT key. Figure 13.33, for example, shows that the shortcut key sequence to select the System menu pad is the Alt+S key combination.

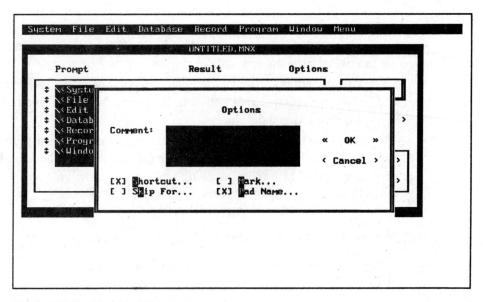

**Figure 13.32  The Options Dialog**

- Selecting the Skip For push button opens the Expression Builder, where you can enter an expression that returns a logical result. The result of this expression then determines whether or not that menu option will be available

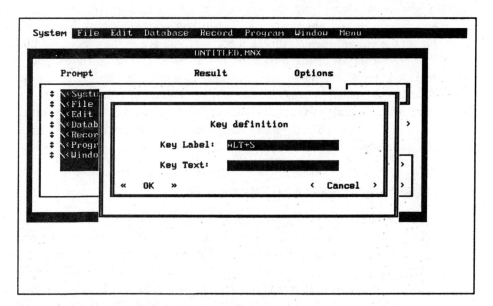

**Figure 13.33  Defining a Shortcut Key Combination**

at any particular time. These options will still appear on a menu, but their text will appear in a light color and they will be disabled. This option is primarily of use to FoxPro programmers and developers.

- The Mark push button allows you to select the kind of checkmark that is placed before the prompt. This option is almost exclusively of interest to FoxPro programmers and developers.

- The Pad Name push button allows you to give the menu pad a name, which in turn allows you both to use it in other menus that you may build and to refer to it by name in FoxPro menuing commands. This, however, is an advanced feature that requires a knowledge of programming.

## OTHER FEATURES OF THE MENU DESIGN WINDOW

The upper right-hand corner of the Menu Design window contains a popup that shows the menu object you are currently defining. As you begin to define your menu, you can move it to navigate between submenus and from a submenu to the menu bar. Right now, however, because we are at the topmost level of our menu—the menu bar—the popup contains only one item. Therefore, it merely reports that you are working with the menu bar; you cannot select any lower-level menus with it. Later, we will see how it can be used to help us maneuver through the menu system that we are building.

Right beneath this popup, the <Try it> push button allows you to preview your menu system as you are creating it. When you select this push button, FoxPro replaces the current menu with the menu that you are in the process of building and opens the Try It dialog shown in Figure 13.34. You can then test your menu by selecting individual menu pads, checking your menu popups, selecting individual menu options, and trying out shortcut key and hotkey combinations. FoxPro will display the name of the menu prompt that is selected in the Prompt text box. Note, however, that while the menu itself will operate normally, the commands or procedures attached to menu options will not execute.

## DEFINING THE SYSTEM MENU POPUP

We have, thus far, used the Menu Builder to explore only the topmost level of the FoxPro system menu. Before we continue our exploration by examining a particular menu popup, let us review menu terminology as it applies to FoxPro menus, in order to avoid ambiguity or confusion. The topmost level of a menu system is known as the **menu bar**; it is located along the top of the FoxPro screen. Each option or label on the menu bar is called a **menu pad**. Ordinarily, although not always, selecting a menu pad opens a second menu, known as a **menu popup**. This menu popup in turn contains additional items, known as **menu options**. Selecting

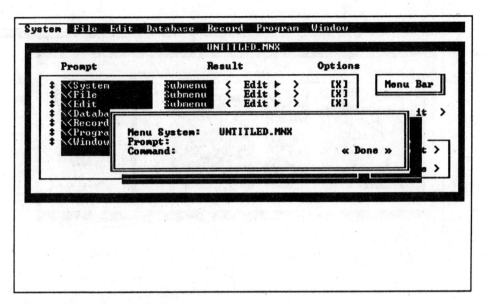

**Figure 13.34  The Try It Dialog**

one of these usually leads to some action (a program executes, a dialog box opens, etc.), although it can also open another menu.

To this point, we have been examining the FoxPro menu bar. Each item in the Prompt list box corresponds to a menu pad. If we select one of these menu pads from the System menu, we open a menu popup. For example, selecting the System menu pad from the menu bar opens the System menu popup, which consists of ten menu options (About FoxPro, Help, Macros, Filer, etc.). In the FoxPro Menu Builder, these menu popups are known as submenus. Note that, in Figure 13.30, Submenu is the result of each of the prompts that represent pads on the FoxPro System menu bar.

To define a submenu or view an existing submenu, select the Edit push button that corresponds to a particular prompt whose result is a Submenu. For example, if we click on the System prompt's Edit push button, the Menu Design window will now look like Figure 13.35, as FoxPro shows the System submenu.

Although the general appearance of the Menu Design window is virtually identical whether a menu bar or a submenu is being displayed, several differences are worth noting. First, along with text to describe particular menu options, FoxPro allows you to include lines that separate groups of options in a menu popup. For example, the FoxPro System menu popup contains one such line to separate the Help and Macros options from the FoxPro desktop accessories (Filer, Calculator, etc.). To include a line in a menu popup instead of text, enter \- in the Prompt text box; when your menu popup is executed, FoxPro will include a line across the width of the popup. Although the Menu Design window in Figure 13.35 shows that

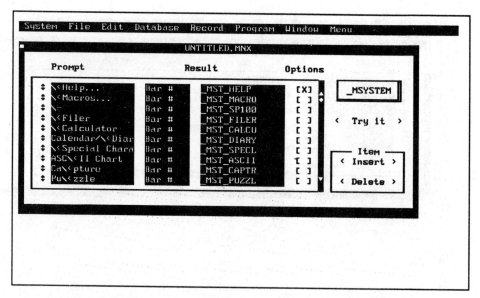

**Figure 13.35  The System Menu Popup**

a result (a Bar # named _MST_SP100) is specified for the line, in fact, lines are not executable menu items; therefore, you can ignore their accompanying results when you define them.

A second notable difference is that the each Result popup now displays Bar # instead of Submenu. This is a new option that did not appear in the Result popup when we were working with the menu bar. And if we examine the options available in the Result popup, we would see that, although three options (Command, Proc., and Submenu) are common to both popups, the Pad Name option in our previous Result popup has been replaced by the Bar # option. Briefly, the Bar # option allows you to execute the same procedures in your own menus that are available from the FoxPro System menu. To do this, you need merely enter the bar name for the proper procedure in the Result text box. For example, a Bar # of _MFI_OPEN will open the File Open dialog, while _MST_HELP will open FoxPro's Help window.

The third notable difference is the popup in the upper right-hand corner of the Menu Design window, which now reads _MSYSTEM instead of Menu Bar. This is the name that FoxPro assigns to the menu popup; usually, it corresponds closely to the menu pad prompt or, if a menu popup is called by another menu popup, to the menu item prompt. If you examine this popup, you will notice that it now contains two elements, _MSYSTEM and Menu Bar. If you select Menu Bar, FoxPro will update the Menu Design window to display the menu pads on the menu bar. So while the Menu Builder provides an Edit push button to allow you to move from a higher- to a lower-level menu, this popup allows you to navigate from lower-level menus back to higher-level menus—from submenus to menu bars, or from submenus to their submenus to their menu bars.

# MODIFYING THE QUICK MENU

With our admittedly hasty exploration of the Menu Builder complete, we hopefully have learned enough about how menus are constructed with the Menu Builder to move from observation to creation. As you may recall, one of our purposes in creating a quick menu was to make a copy of the default FoxPro System menu that we could examine. Our larger goal, however, was to "borrow" the FoxPro System menu so that we could retain some parts of it while modifying it by deleting those parts that we no longer need and adding some other parts required by the custom menu system that was discussed at the very beginning of this chapter. In the remainder of this chapter, we will finally create and implement our customized menu system.

## Deleting Existing Menu Pads

If you have not already done so, return to the menu bar from one of the submenus (make sure that Menu Bar is shown in the popup in the upper right-hand corner of the Menu Design window). Then we can begin by deleting unwanted menu pads. To do this, select the File menu pad and click on the <Delete> push button or press Ctrl+E. When you confirm that you want to delete the submenu, FoxPro will delete the File menu pad and its associated submenu. Since our custom menu will include only the System and Window menu pads, you can also delete the Edit, Database, Record, and Program menu pads. When you are finished, your screen should look something like Figure 13.36.

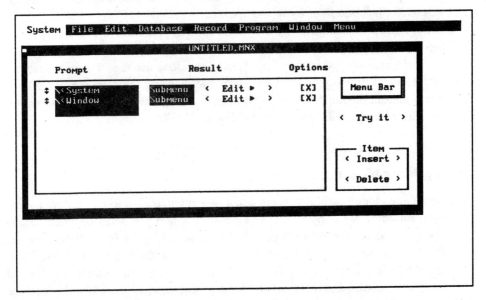

Figure 13.36  The Menu Design Window after Deleting Menu Pads

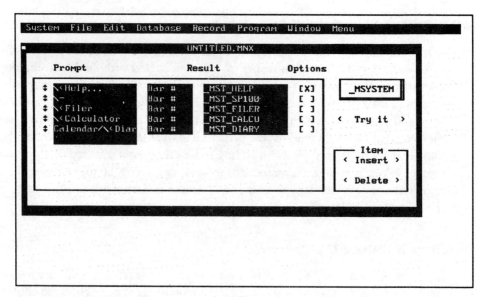

**Figure 13.37  Deleting System Menu Options**

## Deleting Existing Menu Options

The next step is to delete unwanted menu options from the System and Window menu pads. To delete a menu option from the menu pad, its submenu must be displayed in the Menu Design window and the menu option must be selected. The menu option can then be deleted in the manner discussed above, by pressing the <Delete> push button or by typing Ctrl+E.

For example, to delete unwanted menu options from the System menu pad, select the <Edit> push button that corresponds to the System menu pad. When the submenu is displayed in the Menu Design window, use the <Delete> push button or the Delete Item option from the Menu menu popup to delete the first unwanted menu option, About FoxPro.... Continue deleting menu options in this way until the Menu Design window resembles Figure 13.37.

## Adding New Menu Options

As we mentioned earlier, you can add a new menu option to an existing menu pad by positioning the cursor on the location at which you want to insert the menu option and using the <Insert> push button or selecting the Insert Item option from the Menu popup. So to insert a Quit menu option in the System menu pad beneath the Calendar/Diary menu option, position the cursor on the line below the Calendar/Diary prompt and select the <Insert> push button or press Ctrl+I (or select the Insert Item option from the Menu popup). As a result, a new menu option entitled

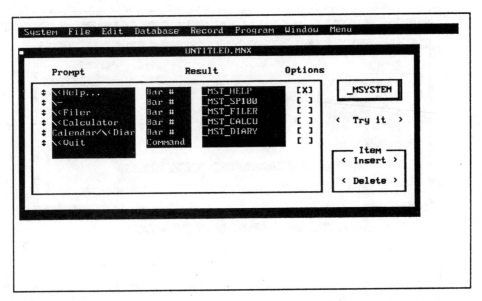

**Figure 13.38  Adding Quit as a New Menu Option**

"New Item" appears in the menu option prompt. At this point, you can rename the prompt to Quit and designate the letter Q as its hotkey so that your screen looks like Figure 13.38. Notice that the result of the menu option is Command, the default.

## Defining the Results of Menu Options

After we have created and named a menu option, the next step is to define its result, which determines what happens when the menu option is selected. The four options available from the result popup are discussed above. In our case, we want the Quit menu option to close our custom menu and return control to the default FoxPro System menu. The following sequence of two commands accomplishes this:

```
CLEAR
SET SYSMENU TO DEFAULT
```

The CLEAR command clears the desktop area of the screen, erasing anything displayed there. The SET SYSMENU command restores the FoxPro System menu bar. Since they are a set of two commands, they form a procedure; you should select Proc. as the result of the Quit prompt. When the result of the Quit menu option changes from Command to Proc., the Menu Builder replaces the Quit prompt's Command text box with a <Create> push button. To define the procedure, select the push button and, when the Text Editor window opens, enter the two commands. Your screen should look like Figure 13.39. Then close the Text Editor window by

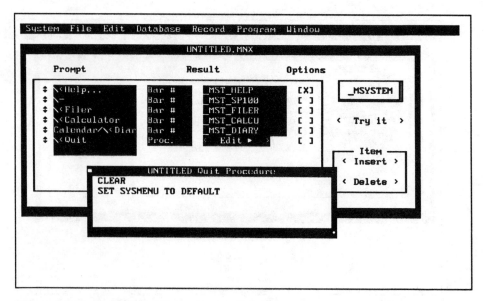

**Figure 13.39  Defining a Menu Option Procedure**

clicking on the Close control or pressing Ctrl+W. When you return to the Menu Design window, note that the Quit prompt's <Create> push button has been replaced by an <Edit> push button.

## Rearranging Menu Options

Menu options can be reordered by moving an existing prompt up or down with the mouse or the keyboard. To change the order of a menu option with the mouse, click on the double-headed arrow and drag the menu option to the desired location. With the keyboard, position the cursor anywhere on the line associated with the prompt to be moved, then press Ctrl+Up (or Ctrl+PgUp) or Ctrl+Down (or Ctrl+PgDn) to move the prompt up or down to the desired location. In our example, we should move the separator line so that it falls between the Calendar/Diary and Quit options. After this is done, the final version of the customized System menu popup is shown in Figure 13.40.

## TESTING THE MENU

While designing the menu system, it is convenient to be able to make sure that the menu looks and is likely to behave in the way you expect. Selecting the <Try it> push button in the Menu Design window allows you to do just that—it causes the menu that you are designing to be temporarily displayed in place of FoxPro's default menu. Since we have just completed our first menu popup, this is a good time to preview our new menu system. When you select the <Try it> push button,

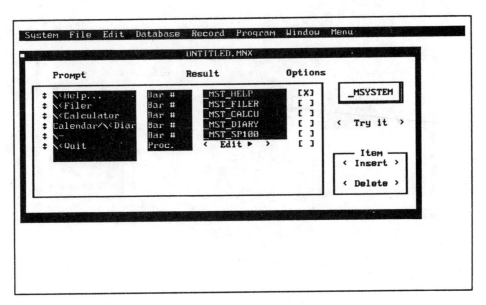

**Figure 13.40  The System Menu Options**

the entire menu that you have created so far is displayed, and individual pads and menu options can be selected, as in Figure 13.41. Note, however, that the menu is display-only; none of the options are actually functional at this point. When you have finished previewing the menu, select the <Done> push button to return to the Menu Design window.

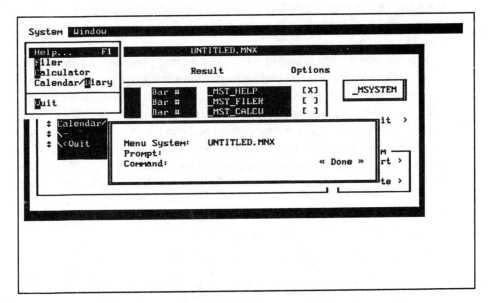

**Figure 13.41  Trying Out the Menu Options**

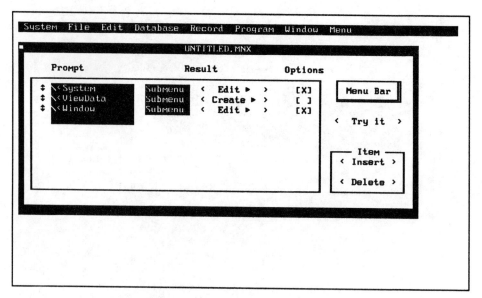

**Figure 13.42  Inserting the ViewData Menu Pad**

## ADDING NEW MENU PADS

So far, we have completed the definition of two menu pads and their associated popups. However, we still must add a number of other new menu pads—ViewData, EditData, Report, and Label—and their associated menu popups before our custom menu is complete. To add these menu pads, the Menu Design screen must display the menu bar. If your Menu Design screen currently shows one of the submenus, select the Menu Bar option from the popup in the upper right-hand corner of the Menu Design window.

You can insert a menu pad in the same way that you insert a menu option. So, to insert the ViewData menu pad between the existing System and Window menu pad, move the cursor to the Window prompt and either select the <Insert> push button, press Ctrl+I, or select the Insert Item option from the Menu popup. The Menu Builder adds a line for a new menu pad and labels it "New Item." Now you can type in the name of the new menu pad, ViewData. Since selecting the ViewData menu pad should open a menu popup with three menu options, you can accept the default result of Submenu. The Menu Design window should now appear like Figure 13.42.

### Creating Menu Popups

To create the individual menu options in the ViewData menu popup, select the ViewData prompt's <Create> push button. When the Menu Builder opens a new

ViewData submenu, you can begin defining its three menu options, which will allow you to view data in linked databases. These three options are:

- *Salesman/Office*. Displays data in the SALESMAN and OFFICE databases on the custom screen named LNKOFICE.SCX. Displaying this screen requires only a single command:

```
DO LNKOFICE.SPR
```

Consequently, select Command from the Result popup and enter the command in its adjacent text box.

- *Office/Salesman*. Displays data from the linked OFFICE and SALESMAN databases. Since the databases were linked by using the LNKSLSMN.QPR RQBE query, we must have our menu system perform the query before it executes the screen program LNKSLSMN.SPR. Therefore, the result of the Office/Salesman prompt is a procedure (Proc.) that contains the following three commands:

```
DO LNKSLSMN.QPR
CLEAR
DO LNKSLSMN.SPR
```

The CLEAR command is needed to erase the message that results from executing the query.

- *Region/Salesman*. Uses the LNKREGIN.SCX screen to display data from the linked REGION, ASSIGN, and SALESMAN databases. Like the Salesman/Office menu option, its result is a single command:

```
DO LNKREGIN.SPR
```

When you finish entering the three menu option prompts and defining the results, your Menu Design window should appear like Figure 13.43.

To complete the custom menu, you can now add the EditData, Report, and Label menu pads to the menu bar. Each of them results in a submenu, and each uses the first letter of its prompt as a hotkey. This enables that key to be used along with the Alt key to select the menu pad. Along with defining the hotkey by including the \< string in the prompt's text box, however, you must also enter this keystroke combination in the Key Definition dialog; otherwise the first letter of the menu pad will be highlighted, but pressing it along with the Alt key will have no effect. To do this, select the Options check box and then select the Shortcut check box. The Menu Builder will then open the Key Definition dialog, which simply records your keystrokes as the shortcut key for that menu item. Simply press Alt+V for the ViewData menu pad, Alt_E for the EditData menu pad, Alt+R for the Report menu pad, and Alt+L for the Label menu pad.

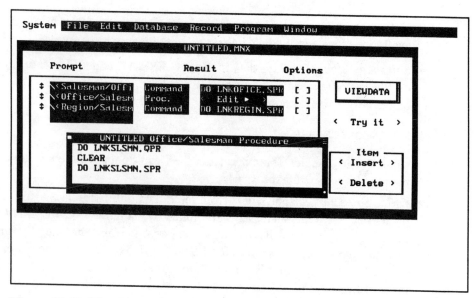

**Figure 13.43  ViewData Menu Options**

Once you have finished defining the additional menu pads for the custom menu, the contents of the Menu Design window should look like Figure 13.44. After defining the menu pads, you can continue to define their associated submenus. Figures 13.45, 13.46, and 13.47 show the submenus of the EditData, Report, and Label menu popups, respectively. Note that the Prompt text box truncates the full menu pad labels as well as the hotkeys in Figure 13.46. The first menu pad should read "Salary Summary by Sex" and be activated by Alt+S, while the second should read "Salary Summary by Office" and be activated by Alt+O.

## USING NESTED SUBMENUS

In designing custom menu systems with the Menu Builder, it is possible to have multiple levels of submenus. For example, on the menu bar, a menu pad can open a submenu that contains a number of menu options. One or more of these menu options, in turn, can have its own submenu with another set of menu options. This use of a submenu to call another submenu, which is referred to as nesting submenus, can continue for any number of levels.

The custom menu system that we have been building in the course of this chapter makes use of nested submenus. As you can see in Figure 13.23, the Report menu pad opens a submenu that contains two options—Salary Summary by Sex, and Salary Summary by Office. Selecting either of these two menu options in turn opens another submenu. So, if you select the Salary Summary by Sex menu option, for example, another menu popup with two options—On Screen and To Printer—opens.

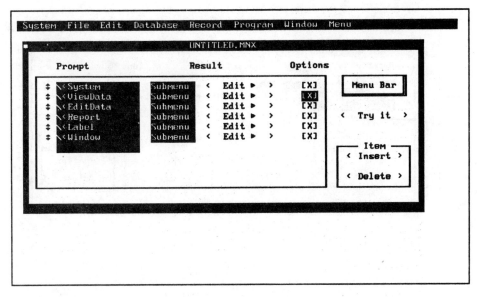

**Figure 13.44  The Complete Set of Menu Pads for the Custom Menu**

Similarly in Figure 13.26, the Label menu pad opens a submenu with a single menu option, and this option in turns opens a submenu with two menu options.

The final step in designing our custom menu system then, is to define these three nested submenus. Let's begin with the submenu that is activated by selecting the Salary Summary by Sex menu option. To create that submenu, navigate through

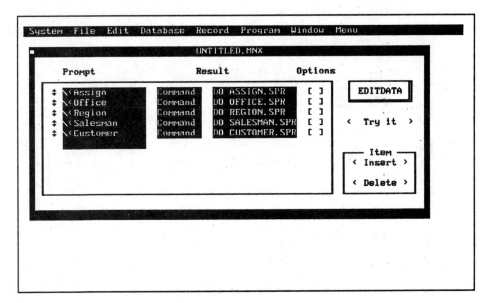

**Figure 13.45  The EditData Submenu**

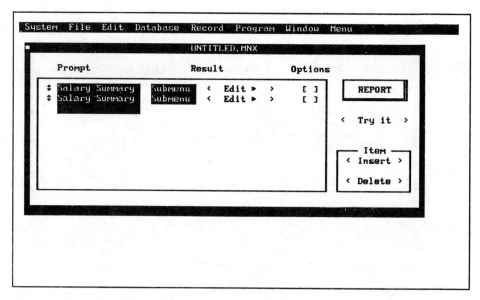

**Figure 13.46  The Report Submenu**

the menu system until you return to the Report submenu, which should be displayed in the Menu Design window. Then select the <Create> push button that corresponds to the first menu option, Salary Summary by Sex. FoxPro will create the new submenu in the Menu Design window. This can be filled in as shown in Figure 13.48.

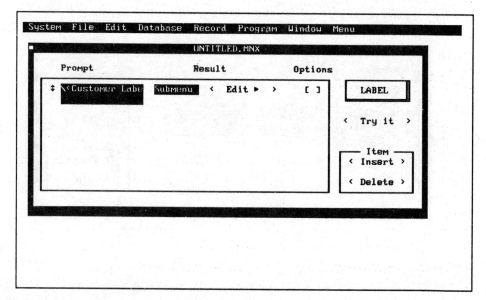

**Figure 13.47  The Label Submenu**

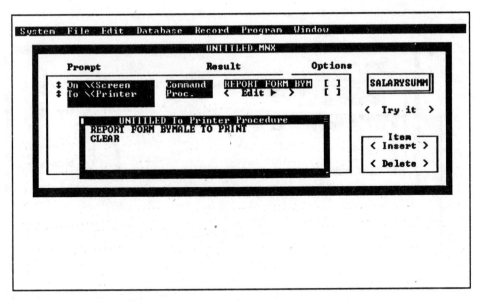

**Figure 13.48   The Salary Summary by Sex Submenu**

Note that this is the final level of submenu. In each case, selecting a menu option will actually cause a report to be run as FoxPro executes either one or a series of commands. Because FoxPro will clear the screen when you finish previewing a report, only a single command is required to view a report on the screen. On the other hand, because FoxPro echoes reports that are being printed on the screen, it is best to clear the screen once a report has finished printing. Consequently, the result of the On Screen menu option is a command, while the result of the To Printer menu option is a procedure (Proc.). Notice that, because we have saved the environment along with our report, we do not have to write program code to take care of such tasks as opening and closing database files and establishing the index order; these are automatically handled for us by FoxPro.

To define the command for the On Screen option, simply type the following in the command text box:

```
REPORT FORM BYMALE PREVIEW
```

This command uses the BYMALE report layout that we designed earlier to display the report on the screen. To define the procedure for the To Printer menu option, first select the <Create> push button and enter the code shown in the Text Editing window in Figure 13.48. The first command is virtually identical to the code that you entered in the On Screen prompt's Command text box, except that the TO PRINT clause sends the report to the printer instead of displaying it on the screen. The second command clears the screen (the FoxPro desktop) once the

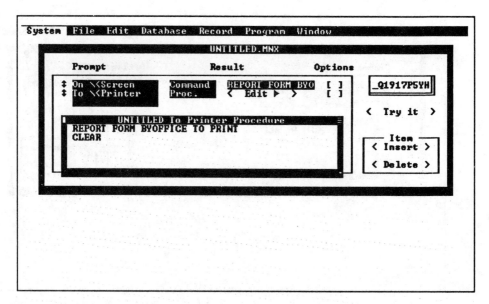

**Figure 13.49  The Salary Summary by Office Submenu**

report has finished printing. Once you finish entering the code for the procedure, close the Text Editor window.

The report menu contains a second report—Salary Summary by Office—that has identical On Screen and To Printer options. To complete this submenu, return to the Report submenu and select the <Create> push button that corresponds to the second menu prompt. Then use Figure 13.49 to define the two menu prompts and to enter the code for the To Printer menu option in the same way that you did for the Salary Summary by Sex submenu. Since the entire command for the On Screen menu option's result is partly obscured, it is:

```
REPORT FORM BYOFFICE PREVIEW
```

In the popup in the upper right-hand corner of Figure 13.49, notice, incidentally, that FoxPro has assigned a rather unusual name (_Q1917P5YH) to the menu popup. This is because FoxPro ordinarily uses or concatenates the popup's menu prompt to form a ten-character menu name. In this case, however, that would result in a duplicate submenu name, since the first ten characters of the two menu options SALARY SUMMARY BY SEX and SALARY SUMMARY BY OFFICE are identical. To avoid confusing itself, FoxPro assigns the name shown in the popup.

The final nested submenu opens when you select the Customer Labels menu option on the Label menu pad. Like the two nested submenus that we have just created, this submenu allows you to preview your labels on the screen or send them to the printer. To complete this submenu, first navigate to the Label submenu and select the <Create> push button that corresponds to the Customer Labels prompt.

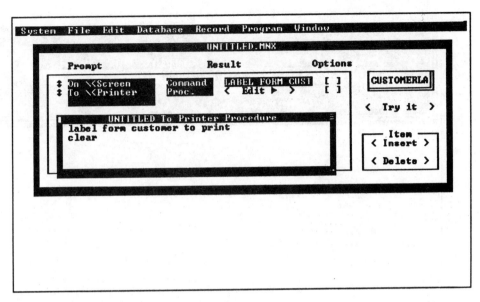

**Figure 13.50   The Customer Labels Submenu**

Then use Figure 13.50 to define the submenu and the To Printer procedure in the Menu Design window.

## SAVING THE CUSTOM MENU FILE

Now that our nested submenus are defined, we have successfully used the Menu Builder to design a complete custom menu system. If you have not already done so, you should now save it as a menu file (a file with an .MNX file extension, which FoxPro assigns automatically) by selecting the Save As... option from the File menu popup and then entering the filename (MAINMENU.MNX).

## GENERATING THE MENU PROGRAM FILE

As we mentioned before, FoxPro actually stores a menu (.MNX) file as a special kind of database file that contains menu information. It cannot be used directly to display a menu. Instead, FoxPro uses the menu file to generate a menu program file (a program file with an extension of .MPR). It is this file that can be executed to display a menu system.

To generate a menu program file from the Menu Design window, select the Generate... option from the Program menu popup. FoxPro first checks to make sure that the menu system in the Menu Design window is identical to the menu system stored on disk. If there is a difference, FoxPro will respond with a prompt asking whether you want to save the changes to your file; selecting either No or Cancel

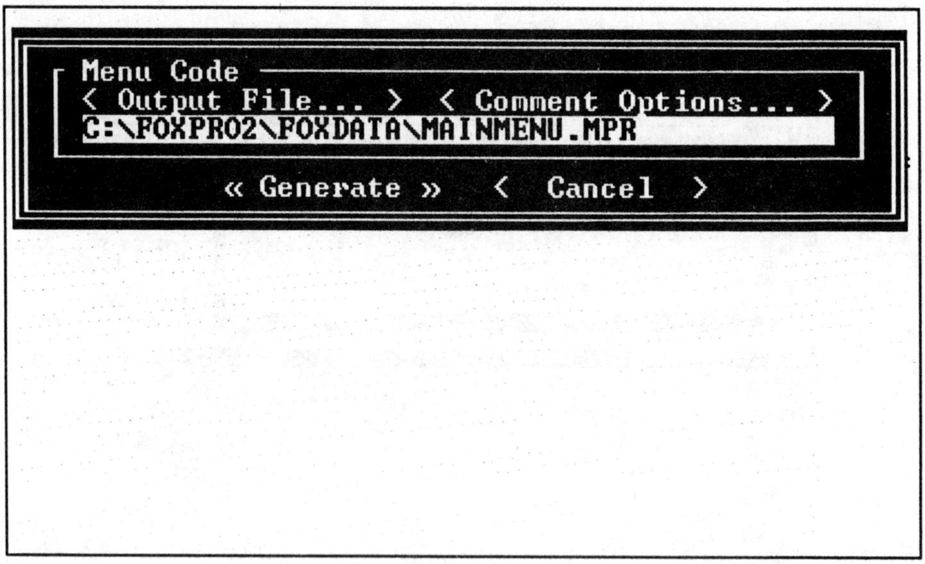

**Figure 13.51  The Generate Menu Dialog**

will return you to the Menu Design window without generating the menu program file. On the other hand, if you select Yes, or if FoxPro can detect no difference between the two versions of the menu system, FoxPro will display the Generate Menu dialog shown in Figure 13.51. Here, FoxPro is simply asking you to confirm the path and filename of the menu program file that it is about to create. By default, the path and root filename are the same as that of the menu file; the only difference is the .MPR file extension that FoxPro automatically uses for menu program files. You can, of course, change the path and filename of the menu program file that FoxPro is about to create, although we suggest that you do not modify FoxPro's default file extension. Once you select the <<Generate>> option, FoxPro will open a dialog box that graphically displays its progress in creating the menu program file. When it is finished and the file has been created, you can close the Menu Design window to exit the Menu Builder and return to the System menu bar.

## Using the Custom Menu

After you have generated the menu program file, you can bring up the custom menu by selecting the Do option from the Program menu popup. When the Do Program File dialog appears, select the menu program filename. For example, to use the custom menu that you have created in the course of this chapter, select MAINMENU.MPR. As a result, the custom menu bar shown earlier in Figure 13.1 should replace FoxPro's default System menu bar.

# Using FoxPro Commands

Although it is easiest to open and close the Menu Builder and select the menu files you would like to work with by using FoxPro's menu driven interface, you can also open the Menu Design window by issuing either of the following commands:

```
CREATE MENU <menu filename>
```

or

```
MODIFY MENU <menu filename>
```

Normally, the first command is used to create a new menu, while the second is used to modify an existing menu. In practice, however, the operation of the two commands is virtually identical. As a result, you can issue either of the following commands to create a new custom menu named NEWMENU.MNX:

```
CREATE MENU NEWMENU
```

```
MODIFY MENU NEWMENU
```

In both cases, if FoxPro is unable to find a menu file named NEWMENU.MNX, it opens an empty Menu Design window and assigns the window the name NEWMENU.MNX. On the other hand, if FoxPro finds a menu file named NEWMENU.MNX, both commands will load the Menu Builder and open the file. The only practical difference between the commands occurs when the two commands are issued without any parameters. The command CREATE MENU will open a blank Menu Design window, which will be named UNTITLED.MNX. The command MODIFY MENU with no parameters, on the other hand, will cause FoxPro to prompt you with the File Open dialog.

To execute a menu program file, use the DO command. For example, to execute the MAINMENU.MPR menu program file, issue the following command:

```
DO MAINMENU.MPR
```

Note that it is important to include the .MPR file extension. Otherwise, FoxPro will search for an ordinary program file with an extension of .PRG; if it is unable to find it, FoxPro will respond with a File Not Found error message.

# Chapter Summary

In line with this book's premise that FoxPro places enormous power in the hands of the user without requiring a knowledge of programming, this concluding chapter has focused on showing you how to integrate FoxPro's various components by building a customized menu system that lets you mold FoxPro to reflect the way you work and the projects you are working on.

The default menu system provided by FoxPro, as we saw, has been designed for flexibility so that it can meet the needs of all users, from the most inexperienced to the most advanced. However, if you intend to use FoxPro repeatedly to execute the same basic operations, developing a custom menu can enormously enhance the productivity of your FoxPro sessions.

In this chapter, we have used the Quick Menu option, which opens a copy of the FoxPro default menu, to introduce you to the Menu Builder and to explore how it can be used to design a menu system. We then significantly modified the quick menu provided by FoxPro in order to develop a custom menu system that integrated the various procedures and applications that we developed in the course of this book. Although this menu system is a highly specific one that is geared to our sample applications, you can nevertheless use it as a model or a starting point for your own menu system.

A customized menu system represents the culmination of FoxPro's interactive power, and provides a fitting conclusion to this book. Knowing just a few FoxPro programming commands, you can create an attractive, powerful menu system that is geared to the way that you work with FoxPro, and that can further increase your productivity while using FoxPro.

# Appendix A

# ASCII Table

| | | | | | | | | | | | |
|---|---|---|---|---|---|---|---|---|---|---|---|
| 0 | NUL | 1 | ☺ SOH | 2 | ☻ STX | 3 | ♥ ETX | 4 | ♦ EOT | 5 | ♣ ENQ |
| 6 | ♠ ACK | 7 | • BEL | 8 | ◘ BS | 9 | ○ HT | 10 | ◙ LF | 11 | ♂ VT |
| 12 | ♀ FF | 13 | ♪ CR | 14 | ♫ SO | 15 | ✳ SI | 16 | ► DLE | 17 | ◄ DC1 |
| 18 | ↕ DC2 | 19 | ‼ DC3 | 20 | ¶ DC4 | 21 | § NAK | 22 | ▬ SYN | 23 | ↨ ETB |
| 24 | ↑ CAN | 25 | ↓ EM | 26 | → SUB | 27 | ← ESC | 28 | ∟ FS | 29 | ↔ GS |
| 30 | ▲ RS | 31 | ▼ US | 32 | | 33 | ! | 34 | " | 35 | # |
| 36 | $ | 37 | % | 38 | & | 39 | ' | 40 | ( | 41 | ) |
| 42 | * | 43 | + | 44 | , | 45 | - | 46 | . | 47 | / |
| 48 | 0 | 49 | 1 | 50 | 2 | 51 | 3 | 52 | 4 | 53 | 5 |
| 54 | 6 | 55 | 7 | 56 | 8 | 57 | 9 | 58 | : | 59 | ; |
| 60 | < | 61 | = | 62 | > | 63 | ? | 64 | @ | 65 | A |
| 66 | B | 67 | C | 68 | D | 69 | E | 70 | F | 71 | G |
| 72 | H | 73 | I | 74 | J | 75 | K | 76 | L | 77 | M |
| 78 | N | 79 | O | 80 | P | 81 | Q | 82 | R | 83 | S |
| 84 | T | 85 | U | 86 | V | 87 | W | 88 | X | 89 | Y |
| 90 | Z | 91 | [ | 92 | \ | 93 | ] | 94 | ^ | 95 | _ |
| 96 | à | 97 | a | 98 | b | 99 | c | 100 | d | 101 | e |
| 102 | f | 103 | g | 104 | h | 105 | i | 106 | j | 107 | k |
| 108 | l | 109 | m | 110 | n | 111 | o | 112 | p | 113 | q |
| 114 | r | 115 | s | 116 | t | 117 | u | 118 | v | 119 | w |
| 120 | x | 121 | y | 122 | z | 123 | { | 124 | \| | 125 | } |
| 126 | ~ | 127 | ⌂ | 128 | Ç | 129 | ü | 130 | é | 131 | â |
| 132 | ä | 133 | à | 134 | å | 135 | ç | 136 | ê | 137 | ë |
| 138 | è | 139 | ï | 140 | î | 141 | ì | 142 | Ä | 143 | Å |
| 144 | É | 145 | æ | 146 | Æ | 147 | ô | 148 | ö | 149 | ò |
| 150 | û | 151 | ù | 152 | ÿ | 153 | Ö | 154 | Ü | 155 | ¢ |
| 156 | £ | 157 | ¥ | 158 | ₧ | 159 | $f$ | 160 | á | 161 | í |
| 162 | ó | 163 | ú | 164 | ñ | 165 | Ñ | 166 | ª | 167 | º |
| 168 | ¿ | 169 | ⌐ | 170 | ¬ | 171 | ½ | 172 | ¼ | 173 | ¡ |
| 174 | « | 176 | ░ | 177 | ▒ | 178 | ▓ | 179 | │ | 180 | ┤ |
| 181 | ╡ | 182 | ╢ | 183 | ╖ | 184 | ╕ | 185 | ╣ | 186 | ║ |

(continued)

| | | | | | | | | | | |
|---|---|---|---|---|---|---|---|---|---|---|
| 187 | ╗ | 188 | ╝ | 189 | ╜ | 190 | ╛ | 191 | ┐ | 192 | └ |
| 193 | ┴ | 194 | ┬ | 195 | ├ | 196 | ─ | 197 | ┼ | 198 | ╞ |
| 199 | ╠ | 200 | ╚ | 201 | ╔ | 202 | ╩ | 203 | ╦ | 204 | ╠ |
| 205 | ═ | 206 | ╬ | 207 | ╧ | 208 | ╨ | 209 | ╤ | 210 | ╥ |
| 211 | ╙ | 212 | ╘ | 213 | ╒ | 214 | ╓ | 215 | ╫ | 216 | ╪ |
| 217 | ┘ | 218 | ┌ | 219 | █ | 220 | ▄ | 221 | ▌ | 222 | ▐ |
| 223 | ▀ | 224 | α | 225 | β | 226 | Γ | 227 | π | 228 | Σ |
| 229 | σ | 230 | μ | 231 | | 232 | | 233 | | 234 | Ω |
| 235 | δ | 236 | ∞ | 237 | | 238 | ∈ | 239 | ∩ | 240 | ≡ |
| 241 | ± | 242 | ≥ | 243 | ≤ | 244 | ⌠ | 245 | ⌡ | 246 | ÷ |
| 247 | ≈ | 248 | ° | 249 | · | 250 | • | 251 | √ | 252 | $n$ |
| 253 | $2$ | 254 | ■ | 255 | NULL | | | | | | |

# Appendix B

# FoxPro Menu Option Names (Bar Names)

| Menu Pad Name | Menu Option | Bar Name |
|---|---|---|
| System | About FoxPro . . . | _MST_ABOUT |
| | Help . . . | _MST_HELP |
| | Macros . . . | _MST_MACRO |
| | Filer | _MST_FILER |
| | Calculator | _MST_CALCU |
| | Calendar/Diary | _MST_DIARY |
| | Special Characters | _MST_SPECL |
| | ASCII Chart | _MST_ASCII |
| | Capture | _MST_CAPTR |
| | Puzzle | _MST_PUZZL |
| File | New . . . | _MFI_NEW |
| | Open . . . | _MFI_OPEN |
| | Close | _MFI_CLOSE |
| | Close All | _MFI_CLALL |
| | Save | _MFI_SAVE |
| | Save as . . . | _MFI_SAVAS |
| | Revert | _MFI_REVRT |
| | Printer Setup . . . | _MFI_SETUP |
| | Print . . . | _MFI_PRINT |
| | Quit | _MFI_QUIT |

*(continued)*

| Menu Pad Name | Menu Option | Bar Name |
|---|---|---|
| Edit | Undo | _MED_UNDO |
|  | Redo | _MED_REDO |
|  | Cut | _MED_CUT |
|  | Copy | _MED_COPY |
|  | Paste | _MED_PASTE |
|  | Clear | _MED_CLEAR |
|  | Select All | _MED_SELCTA |
|  | Goto Line . . . | _MED_GOTO |
|  | Find . . . | _MED_FIND |
|  | Find Again | _MED_FINDA |
|  | Replace and Find Again | _MED_REPL |
|  | Replace All | _MED_REPLA |
|  | Preferences | _MED_PREF |
| Database | Setup . . . | _MDA_SETUP |
|  | Browse | _MDA_BROW |
|  | Append From . . . | _MDA_APPND |
|  | Copy To . . . | _MDA_COPY |
|  | Sort . . . | _MDA_SORT |
|  | Total . . . | _MDA_TOTAL |
|  | Average . . . | _MDA_AVG |
|  | Count . . . | _MDA_COUNT |
|  | Sum . . . | _MDA_SUM |
|  | Calculate . . . | _MDA_CALC |
|  | Report . . . | _MDA_REPRT |
|  | Label . . . | _MDA_LABEL |
|  | Pack | _MDA_PACK |
|  | Reindex | _MDA_RINDX |
| Record | Append | _MRC_APPND |
|  | Change | _MRC_CHNGE |
|  | Goto . . . | _MRC_GOTO |
|  | Locate . . . | _MRC_LOCAT |
|  | Continue | _MRC_CONT |
|  | Seek . . . | _MRC_SEEK |
|  | Replace . . . | _MRC_REPL |
|  | Delete . . . | _MRC_DELET |
|  | Recall . . . | _MRC_RECAL |

| Menu Pad Name | Menu Option | Bar Name |
|---|---|---|
| Program | Do . . . | _MPR_DO |
| | Cancel | _MPR_CANCL |
| | Resume | _MPR_RESUM |
| | Compile . . . | _MPR_COMPL |
| | Generate . . . | _MPR_GENER |
| | FoxDoc | _MPR_DOCUM |
| | FoxGraph . . . | _MPR_GRAPH |
| Window | Hide | _MWI_HIDE |
| | Clear | _MWI_CLEAR |
| | Move | _MWI_MOVE |
| | Size | _MWI_SIZE |
| | Zoom (up) | _MWI_ZOOM |
| | Zoom (down), Minimize | _MWI_MIN |
| | Cycle | _MWI_ROTAT |
| | Color . . . | _MWI_COLOR |
| | Command | _MWI_CMD |
| | Debug | _MWI_DEBUG |
| | Trace | _MWI_TRACE |
| | View | _MWI_VIEW |

# Index